SPSS® Introductory Statistics Student Guide

D1311738

Marija J. Norušis/SPSS Inc.

SPSS Inc.
444 N. Michigan Avenue
Chicago, Illinois 60611
Tel: (312) 329 3500
Fax: (312) 329-3668

SPSS International B.V.
P.O. Box 115
4200 AC Gorinchem
The Netherlands
Tel: +31.1830.36711
Fax: +31.1830.35839

For more information about SPSS® software products, please write or call

Marketing Department
SPSS Inc.
444 North Michigan Avenue
Chicago, IL 60611
Tel: (312) 329-3500
Fax: (312) 329-3668

In Europe and the Middle East, please write or call

SPSS International BV
P.O. Box 115
4200 AC Gorinchem
The Netherlands
Tel: +31.1830.36711
Twx: 21019
Fax: +31.1830.35839

SPSS® Introductory Statistics Student Guide
Copyright © 1990 by SPSS Inc.
All rights reserved.
Printed in the United States of America.

1 2 3 4 5 6 7 8 9 0   93 92 91 90

ISBN 0-923967-02-8

Library of Congress Catalog Card Number: 90-060795

Preface _____

Through and through the world is infested with quantity: To talk sense is to talk quantities. It is no use saying the nation is large—How large? It is no use saying that radium is scarce—How scarce? You cannot evade quantity. You may fly to poetry and music, and quantity and number will face you in your rhythms and your octaves.

—Alfred North Whitehead

Quantity is as inescapable today as it was in Whitehead's time. Even those outside technical professions face a plethora of numbers when they look at a newspaper. The purpose of data analysis is to make it easier to deal with quantity—to simplify and summarize data and to illuminate patterns that are not immediately evident.

THE SPSS SYSTEM

SPSS® is a comprehensive tool for managing, analyzing, and displaying data. A broad range of statistical analyses and data modification tasks are accomplished with a simple, English-like language. Results can be easily obtained with minimal understanding of computer intricacies.

This manual is intended for novice users of SPSS Release 4.0 and introduces the basic features and procedures: descriptive statistics, measures of association for two-way tables, tests for equality of means, nonparametric procedures, and bivariate and multiple regression. It also contains an overview of four commonly used multivariate procedures: discriminant analysis, factor analysis, cluster analysis, and multivariate analysis of variance. Detailed discussion of the multivariate procedures is found in the *SPSS Advanced Statistics Student Guide.*

While this text includes instructions for entering and defining data for analysis, for managing data files, and for transforming, selecting, sampling, and weighting data, it does not attempt to cover the full range of data and file management facilities available in SPSS. For those who want to extend their use of the system beyond the scope of this introduction, documentation can be found in the *SPSS Reference Guide.* The computational methods used are described in *SPSS Statistical Algorithms.*

The system and its documentation are continually being extended. Before obtaining other manuals, check with your computation center or with SPSS Inc. for information about the current release of SPSS being used at your site and the documentation for that release.

USING THIS TEXT

This manual is designed to be a supplement in courses that integrate the teaching of statistics and computing. The first two chapters discuss preparation of a data file and the fundamentals of an SPSS job. Each subsequent chapter describes a problem and the SPSS output useful for its solution, followed by information about the SPSS commands needed to obtain the analysis.

Exercises at the end of each chapter reinforce and extend the material in three main areas: syntax, statistical concepts, and data analysis. Answers for selected questions on syntax and statistical concepts are given in Appendix A. The data analysis exercises provide an opportunity to formulate hypotheses, create the SPSS commands needed to carry out the analysis, and run those jobs using one of four data files distributed with the SPSS system. Those data files are described in Appendix B. Consult the SPSS Coordinator at your installation for information about using the files.

ACKNOWLEDGMENTS

Most of the SPSS Inc. staff have participated either in designing and preparing this manual or in creating and maintaining the system it documents. I am grateful for their advice.

I am also grateful to the reviewers and users of the early editions of this book for many helpful comments and suggestions, and to Harry Roberts, Harry Davis, and Richard Shekelle for permission to use and distribute the data files. Finally, I wish to thank Aušra, Vytas, and Daina.

—Marija J. Norušis

Contacting SPSS Inc.

If you would like to be on our mailing list, write to us at one of the addresses below. We will send you a copy of our newsletter and let you know about SPSS Inc. activities in your area.

United States and Canada

SPSS Inc.
444 North Michigan Avenue
Chicago, IL 60611
Tel: (312) 329-3500
Fax: (312) 329-3668

Federal systems

SPSS Federal Systems (U.S.)
12300 Twinbrook Parkway,
Suite 600
Rockville, MD 20852
Tel: (301) 770-1961
Fax: (301) 881-6898

Latin America

SPSS Latin America
444 North Michigan Avenue
Chicago, IL 60611
Tel: (312) 329-3556
Fax: (312) 329-3558

Europe and the Middle East

SPSS International BV
P.O. Box 115
4200 AC Gorinchem
The Netherlands
Tel: +31.1830.36711
Twx: 21019
Fax: +31.1830.35839

*United Kingdom, Scotland,
Ireland, Israel, Africa*

SPSS UK Ltd.
SPSS House
5 London Street
Chertsey, Surrey KT16 8AP
United Kingdom
Tel: +44.932.566262
Fax: +44.932.567020

*Germany, Italy, Austria,
Switzerland, Eastern Europe*

SPSS GmbH Software
Steinsdorfstrasse 19
D-8000 Munich
Federal Republic of Germany
Tel: +49.89.2283008
Twx: 082+ 5218457
Fax: +49.89.2285413

*The Netherlands, Belgium,
Luxembourg*

SPSS Benelux BV
Gebouw Hagestein
Ir. D.S. Tuijnmanweg 2E
P.O. Box 54
4130 EB Vianen
The Netherlands
Tel: +31.3473.75706
Fax: +31.3473.73026

*Sweden, Denmark,
Norway, Finland*

SPSS Scandinavia AB
Sjoangsvagen 7
S-19172 Sollentuna
Sweden
Tel: +46.8.7549450
Fax: +46.8.7548816

Asia Pacific

SPSS Asia Pacific Pte. Ltd.
26-01
78 Shenton Way
Singapore 0207
Singapore
Tel: +65.221.2577
Fax: +65.221.9920

Japan

SPSS Japan Inc.
Gyoen Sky Bldg.
2-1-11, Shinjuku
Tokyo 160
Japan
Tel: +81.3.350.5261
Fax: +81.3.350.5245

Australia, New Zealand

SPSS Australasia
62/65 Market Street
P.O. Box Q183
Sydney, NSW 2000
Australia
Tel: +61.2.2612380
Fax: +61.2.2615063

Contents _____

Chapter 18   **Multiple Linear Regression Analysis: Procedure REGRESSION 243**

Chapter 21   Factor Analysis: Procedure FACTOR   321

Chapter 22   Cluster Analysis: Procedure CLUSTER   345

1 Getting Started: A Few Useful Terms

SPSS is a powerful, comprehensive, and flexible statistical and information analysis system. With SPSS you can perform highly complex data manipulation and analysis with surprisingly simple, straightforward instructions.

SPSS can take data from almost any type of file and use them to generate tabulated reports, plots of distributions and trends, descriptive statistics, and complex statistical analyses. Chapter 2 describes the basic methods for creating data files that can be read by SPSS. Chapter 3 outlines the ways you can transform and manipulate data for analysis, and Chapter 4 demonstrates some of the techniques for transforming and combining different types of data files.

SPSS has many preset values that control settings such as page width and length, upper and lower case for display of labels and messages, and the number of errors allowed before processing ends. Chapter 5 explains how to display these values with the SHOW command and change them with the SET command.

The statistical chapters are arranged in order of complexity—from procedures for producing simple frequency distributions and descriptive statistics to sophisticated multiple regression models. Each chapter contains an overview of the statistical theory behind the procedure and numerous practical examples, including an explanation of subcommands and specifications for the command.

The SPSS "language" consists of descriptive and usually self-explanatory commands. For example, the command to perform regression analysis is REGRESSION. SPSS is designed to be easy to learn and use; the syntax rules are kept to a minimum, and the system will even accept many nonambiguous departures from those rules.

Nevertheless, there are *some* rules—and there are also a few terms that you may find useful since they occur frequently in this book and have a specific meaning in SPSS. This chapter describes basic syntax rules and SPSS terms.

1.1 THE SPSS SESSION

Whenever you execute a sequence of SPSS commands, it is called an SPSS *session*. A typical SPSS session consists of three main parts:

- *Data definition* commands provide information about the variables and their location in the data file.
- *Data transformation* commands are used to create new variables, modify existing ones, and select subsets of cases for analyses.
- *Procedure commands* indicate what statistics, reports, or tables are to be produced.

Data definition and transformation commands are generally not executed until a command that reads the data is specified. This saves extra passes through the data and reduces processing time. Statistical and reporting procedure commands, such as FREQUENCIES and CROSSTABS, and a number of other commands, such as EXECUTE and SAVE, are commands that read the data.

An SPSS session must begin with at least one data definition command that either defines the data to SPSS or specifies an SPSS system file, which already contains data definition. A session can be a complex series of transformations and statistical procedures, or it can be as simple as the following:

```
GET FILE=ELECTRIC.
FREQUENCIES VARIABLES=DBP58.
```

The GET command is a data definition command, telling SPSS the name of the SPSS system file that contains the data. The FREQUENCIES command is a procedure command, instructing SPSS to produce a frequency table for the variable DBP58.

Getting access to SPSS and handling files are very specific to your computer system. Consult the SPSS *Operations Guide* for your system for additional information. You can also use the INFO command to get information about new features and changes to SPSS since publication of this book.

1.2
WAYS TO PROCESS
SPSS COMMANDS

Your SPSS commands can be processed in several different ways, depending on your computer system:

- You can create a file of SPSS commands using a text editor or word processing program. This command file is then submitted for execution through your operating system. This is sometimes called *batch execution,* and the commands within the file are run as a single *job.*
- You can access SPSS and run commands one at time in a prompted (interactive) session.
- In some systems, you can access SPSS and build command files with the help of a command generator. You can run commands within the file during the SPSS session.

For information about the ways your computer system can run SPSS, see the SPSS *Operations Guide* for your system.

1.3
SPSS FILES

Operating SPSS means dealing with files. Depending on the complexity of your session, you may have one or more of the following types of files:

- *Command files* contain SPSS commands. Command files can be created using a text editor or word processor and submitted to SPSS for execution, or on some systems they can be created within an SPSS session. Refer to the SPSS *Operations Guide* for your system for more information.
- *Raw data files* contain your data in almost any form. The raw data can be included within a command file, or they can be in a separate file on disk or tape.
- *SPSS system files* are data files specifically formatted for use by SPSS. An SPSS system file contains both data and the *dictionary* that defines the data. The dictionary contains descriptive information about the data, including variable names and locations, variable and value labels, and formats. SPSS system files speed processing.
- An *active system file* is created whenever you define a raw data file with DATA LIST or MATRIX DATA, or access an SPSS system file or other data file with commands such as GET, IMPORT, and GET TRANSLATE. The active system file will contain any modifications to the data produced by transformation and procedure commands in that session. It exists only for the duration of the SPSS session but can be saved as an SPSS system file or exported as a portable file.
- *Output files* contain data formatted for reading by a computer. Some procedures create output files containing matrix or other materials.
- *Portable files* are system files created by the EXPORT command and formatted for portability to computers other than the one on which they were created.
- *Listing files* contain the tabular output from SPSS procedures and diagnostic information about your session. A listing file is formatted for display on a terminal or printing on a printer.

Information about creating, modifying and accessing files is contained in Chapters 2 and 4. Conventions for naming, printing, deleting, or permanently saving files, and for submitting command files for processing differ considerably from one computer and operating system to another. Use the INFO command, the SPSS *Operations Guide* for your system, and other documentation available for your computer system for information about handling files.

1.4
SPSS SYNTAX

Before learning about individual SPSS commands, you should have some general information about the SPSS language. The rules, or *syntax,* of the SPSS language are easy to learn.

SPSS commands often require more than one line for complete specification. You can indicate command continuation lines in one of two ways, depending on the way your system is processing your SPSS commands.

- Commands entered into an SPSS command file and submitted for execution through your operating system or specified on an INCLUDE command (see Chapter 5) must begin in column 1. Continuation lines are indented at least one column. Anything that appears in the first column is assumed to be the beginning of a new command.
- Commands entered during an SPSS session must end with a command terminator (except the BEGIN DATA command). The default command terminator is a period (.). Anything that appears between the beginning of the command and the command terminator is assumed to be part of the command. Commands can begin in any column, but each command must begin on a new line. This includes commands run during a prompted (interactive) SPSS session.

For more information about the way your system processes commands, see the SPSS *Operations Guide* for your system.

You can add spaces or break lines at almost any point where a single blank is allowed, such as around slashes, parentheses, arithmetic operators, or between variable names. Text included within apostrophes or quotation marks must be contained on a single line.

1.5
Commands and Specifications

All terms in the SPSS language fall into one or more of the following categories:

- *Keyword*: A word already defined by SPSS to identify a command, subcommand, or specification. Most keywords are, or resemble, common English words.
- *Command*: A specific instruction that controls the execution of SPSS.
- *Subcommand*: Additional instructions on SPSS commands. A command can contain more than one subcommand, each with its own specifications.
- *Specifications*: Instructions added to a command or subcommand. Specifications may include subcommands, keywords, numbers, arithmetic operators, variable names, and special delimiters.

These categories are *not* mutually exclusive. Commands are also keywords; subcommands are both keywords and specifications.

Each command begins with a command keyword (which may contain more than one word). The command keyword is followed by at least one blank space and then any specifications required to complete the command, as in

```
LIST VARIABLES=ALL.
```

The command keyword is LIST, and VARIABLES=ALL is a specification.

Many specifications include subcommands. For example, the LIST command above contains a VARIABLES subcommand. Additional subcommands, separated by slashes, can also be specified. For example, the command

```
LIST VARIABLES=ALL /CASES=10.
```

contains a second subcommand, CASES, indicating the number of cases to list.

This command could also be written on two lines.

```
LIST VARIABLES=ALL
 /CASES=10.
```

The blank space at the beginning of the second line indicates continuation and the period at the end indicates the end of the LIST procedure.

Most keywords that make up a command can be truncated to the least number of characters needed for identification. Exceptions are the reserved keyword WITH, the END DATA command, and all specifications to the INFO command. For example, the following is identical to the LIST command above:

```
LIST VAR=ALL /CAS=10.
```

1.6
Variable Names

When you define data and create variables with SPSS, you assign *names* to your variables. You use the assigned name to refer to a variable in an SPSS session. Keep in mind the following rules when naming variables:

- The name must begin with a letter. The remaining characters can be any letter, any digit, a period, or the symbols @, #, _, or $.
- The length of the name cannot exceed eight characters.
- Blanks and special characters such as &, !, ?, ', and * cannot occur in a variable name.
- Each variable must have a unique name. Duplication is not allowed.
- The reserved keywords in Table 1.6 cannot be used as variable names since they have special meaning in SPSS.

Table 1.6   SPSS reserved keywords

ALL	AND	BY	EQ	GE	GT	LE
LT	NE	NOT	OR	TO	WITH	

The following are all valid variable names: LOCATION, LOC#5, X.1, and OVER$500.

It is a good idea to assign variable names that help you identify variables. You could give the names X and Y to variables for age and sex, but the names AGE and SEX give you a much better idea of the nature of the variables.

Special *system variables* can be used in data transformation commands. The names of these variables begin with a dollar sign. The available system variables are:

$CASENUM *Case sequence number.* For each case, $CASENUM is the number of cases read up to and including the case.

$SYSMIS *System-missing value.*

$JDATE *Current date in YRMODA format.* For information on YRMODA format, see the *SPSS Reference Guide*.

$DATE *Current date in dd-mmm-yy format.*

$TIME *Current date and time.*

$LENGTH *Current page length.* See the SET command in Chapter 5 for information on controlling page length.

$WIDTH *Current page width.* See the SET command in Chapter 5 for information on controlling page width.

1.7
The TO Keyword

You can both create and refer to a set of variable names by using the keyword TO. When you are assigning new variable names, ITEM1 TO ITEM4 is the equivalent of four names: ITEM1, ITEM2, ITEM3, and ITEM4. When you are referring to a list of variables for a procedure, ITEM TO SCORE can be used to refer to all variables between ITEM and SCORE on the active system file, or, for some procedures, all variables between ITEM and SCORE on the preceding VARIABLES subcommand.

1.8
Annotated Example

```
DATA LIST FILE=WEATHER
 FREE /TEMP1 TEMP2 TEMP3 NEWTEMP HUMIDITY PRESSURE WINDDIR WINDSPD.
COMPUTE AVTEMP=MEAN(TEMP1, TEMP2, TEMP3).
REGRESSION VARIABLES=NEWTEMP AVTEMP HUMIDITY TO WINDSPD
 /DEPENDENT=NEWTEMP
 /METHOD=ENTER AVTEMP TO WINDSPD
 /ENTER=AVTEMP TO WINDSPD
 /SAVE=PRED(PREDICT).
SAVE OUTFILE=FORECAST.
```

- The DATA LIST command is a *data definition* command that tells SPSS where to find the data. It also defines and names eight variables. The FILE subcommand indicates that the raw data are contained in a file named WEATHER. The FREE subcommand tells SPSS that the data are in freefield format. Following keyword FREE is the list of variables being defined. For more information about DATA LIST, see Chapter 2.

- The COMPUTE command is a *transformation* command that creates a new variable, AVTEMP, which is the mean of three variables defined on DATA LIST. For more information on COMPUTE and other transformation commands, see Chapter 2.

- The REGRESSION command initiates a *procedure*. The VARIABLES subcommand specifies six variables: NEWTEMP, AVTEMP and the four variables from HUMIDITY to WINDSPD on the active system file. The DEPENDENT subcommand specifies NEWTEMP as the dependent variable, and the METHOD subcommand indicates that the five variables from AVTEMP to WINDSPD on the preceding VARIABLES subcommand are the independent variables. The SAVE subcommand saves the predicted values generated by the REGRESSION procedure and assigns the variable name PREDICT to these values. For more information on REGRESSION, see Chapter 18.

- The SAVE command creates a new SPSS system file and names it FORECAST. This system file contains 10 variables: the eight variables defined on the DATA LIST command, plus the two new variables created by the transformation and procedure commands. For more information on the SAVE command, see Chapter 4.

1.9
EXERCISES

1. Which of the following are valid SPSS variable names?
   a. LASTNAME
   b. FIRSTNAME
   c. SS_NO
   d. PHONE#
   e. S&L
   f. $INCOME

2. a. How many variables are specified on the following DATA LIST command?
   b. What are the names assigned to the variables?

   ```
   DATA LIST FREE /VAR1 TO VAR5.
   ```

3. Is the following set of commands a complete SPSS session?

   ```
   COMPUTE NEWVAR=OLDVAR**2.
   FREQUENCIES VARIABLES=NEWVAR.
   ```

Data Definition _____

In this chapter:

Goals:

- To prepare data for entry into computer files.
- To define and read data for analysis with SPSS.
- To create descriptive variable and value labels that define the contents of the file and explain the meaning of coded values.
- To identify missing values.

Examples:

- Use a simple one-digit code to represent yes/no responses and generate "yes" and "no" labels to identify the codes.
- Use separate codes to distinguish between "don't know" and "not applicable" and flag these as missing values not to be used in analysis.
- Obtain a small subset of variables related to education, occupation, and income from a data set containing hundreds of variables ranging from political opinions to hobbies.

2 Preparing and Defining Data for SPSS Analysis

2.1
PREPARING DATA FOR ANALYSIS

Before information can be analyzed with SPSS, it must be entered into a computer file. This entails two steps:

- Arranging the data into a suitable format.
- Entering the data into the computer.

Sometimes the information to be analyzed is already available on a computer disk or magnetic tape. However, often the data are stored in other forms: in file folders in personnel offices, in patient medical charts, on credit card applications that never leave enough space for the requested information, or some other form that a computer can't read. Sections 2.2 through 2.5 examine the steps necessary to prepare data for analysis.

2.2
Cases, Variables, and Values

Consider Table 2.2, which contains data for five cases from a study designed to identify factors associated with coronary heart disease. In this study, 2,017 male employees of Western Electric with no history of coronary heart disease were followed for 20 years, and the occurrence of heart disease was monitored. Table 2.2 contains only a small portion of the data collected for each man. Each name in the table represents a *case,* or observation, for which *values* are available for a set of *variables.*

Table 2.2 Excerpt from uncoded data for Western Electric study

Name	First event	Age	Diastolic BP	Education	Cholesterol	Cigarettes
John Jones	Nonfatal MI	40	70	B.A.	321	0
Clark Roberts	Nonfatal MI	49	87	11th grade	246	60
Paul Buttons	Sudden death	43	89	High school	262	0
James Smith	Nonfatal MI	50	105	8th grade	275	15
Robert Norris	Sudden death	43	110	Unknown	301	25

Height	Weight	Day of week	Vital10	Family history	Incidence of CHD
68.8	190	None	Alive	Yes	Yes
72.2	204	Thursday	Alive	No	Yes
69.0	162	Saturday	Dead	No	Yes
62.5	152	Wednesday	Alive	Yes	Yes
68.0	148	Monday	Dead	— No	Yes

For the first case, employee John Jones, age is a variable with a value of 40. The same variables are recorded for all cases. What differs are the actual values of the variables. Each case has only one value for each variable. "Unknown" and "missing" are acceptable values for a variable, although they require special treatment during analysis.

The case is the basic unit for which values are recorded for variables. In the Western Electric study, the case is an employee. In studies of political opinion or brand preference, the case is usually the individual respondent to a questionnaire. But a case may be a larger unit, such as a school, county, or nation; it may be a time period, such as a year or month, or it may be an event, such as an auto accident.

For any single analysis, all cases must represent the same basic unit of analysis. If you are studying counties, all cases must be counties, and the values for each variable are values for individual counties. If you are studying states, then all cases must be states, and the values for each variable are the values for individual states.

2.3
Identifying Important Variables

A critical step in any study is the selection of variables to be included. The variables that are relevant to the problem under study must be chosen from a vast array of information available. If important data are excluded from the data file, the results will be of limited use. All potentially relevant variables should be included in the study since it is much easier to exclude unnecessary variables from the analysis than to go back and collect additional information.

2.4
Recording the Data

Once the variables have been selected, you must decide how they will be recorded. Do you need the actual date of birth or simply age in years? It is usually a good idea to record data in as much detail as possible. If you record date of birth, cases can be grouped into age categories later. But if you just record each case as under 50 or over 50, you can never analyze your data using any other age categories.

2.5
Coding the Variables

Once you have all your information, the data must be entered into the computer. One way to simplify data entry is to assign numbers or symbols to represent responses. This is known as *coding* the data. For example, instead of typing "Yes" or "No" as the values for the family history variable, the codes *Y* and *N* can be used. If only numbers are used in a coding scheme, it is called *numeric*. If letters or a combination of numbers, letters, and special characters are used, the code is called *alphanumeric* or *string*. By coding, you substantially decrease the number of symbols that you need to type.

Coding schemes are arbitrary by their very nature. The family history variable could also be coded 0 for no and 1 for yes. All that is necessary is that each possible response have a distinct code.

It is usually helpful to have one variable that uniquely identifies each case. For the Western Electric study, it could be the employee's name—but names are not always unique. The best approach is to assign a unique ID number to each case. This identifier can help you easily locate the data for cases with unusual values or missing information.

Consider the coding scheme in Table 2.5 and the data for the first three cases in Figure 2.5a, coded according to this scheme.

Table 2.5   Coding scheme for employee data form

Variable	Coding scheme
ID	no special code
FIRST CHD EVENT	1=No CHD 2=Sudden death 3=Nonfatal myocardial infarction 4=Fatal myocardial infarction 6=Other CHD
AGE	in years
DIASTOLIC BP	in mm of mercury
EDUCATION	in years
CHOLESTEROL	in milligrams per deciliter
CIGARETTES	number per day
HEIGHT	to nearest 0.1 inch
WEIGHT	in pounds
DAY OF WEEK	1=Sunday 2=Monday 3=Tuesday 4=Wednesday 5=Thursday 6=Friday 7=Saturday 9=Unknown
VITAL10	status at 10 years 0=Alive 1=Dead
FAMILY HISTORY OF CHD	N=No Y=Yes
CHD	0=No 1=Yes

Figure 2.5a   Coded data

CASEID	FIRSTCHD	AGE	DBP58	EDUYR	CHOL58	CGT58	HT58	WT58	DAYOFWK	VITAL10	FAMHXCVR	CHD
13	3	40	70	16	321	0	68.8	190	9	0	Y	1
30	3	49	87	11	246	60	72.2	204	5	0	N	1
53	2	43	89	12	262	0	69.0	162	7	1	N	1

Once the data are coded, a format for arranging the data in a computer file must be determined. Each line of type entered into a computer is called a *record*. Each record is composed of columns in which the numbers or characters are stored. Two decisions that must be made are:

• The number of records needed for each case.
• The column locations for each variable.

Figure 2.5b shows a file containing data for the first three cases in which one record is used for each case. The column locations are also indicated. The ID number is in columns 1–4; first coronary event in column 6; age in columns 17-18; and so forth. This is known as *fixed-column format* (see Section 2.9 for a discussion of fixed versus freefield format).

When there are many variables for each case, more than one record may be necessary. In Figure 2.5c, one case occupies two records. Each record contains the case ID number in columns 1-4 and a record identification number in column 50. It is a good idea to enter the case ID and a record number on all records for each case. You can then easily locate out-of-order or missing records.

Figure 2.5b   One-record file

```
0   0   1   1   2   2   3   3   4   4   5
1   5   0   5   0   5   0   5   0   5   0      Columns

    13 3            40  70 16 321  0 68.8 190 9 0 Y 1
    30 3            49  87 11 246 60 72.2 204 5 0 N 1
    53 2            43  89 12 262  0 69.0 162 7 1 N 1
                        . . .
```

Figure 2.5c   Two-record file

```
0   0   1   1   2   2   3   3   4   4   5
1   5   0   5   0   5   0   5   0   5   0      Column

    13 3 40  70 16 321  0                           1
    13 68.8 190 9 0 Y 1                             2
         . . .
```

It is important to allocate a sufficient number of columns for each variable. If only two columns are allocated for the weight variable, only weights less than 100 pounds will fit. Always allocate the maximum number of columns that your data might need. Don't worry if your observed data don't actually require that many columns.

2.6
SPSS DATA DEFINITION

Before you can analyze your data with SPSS, you must first *define* it in SPSS terms. The data definition commands in SPSS answer the following questions:

- Where is the data stored on your computer?
- How many records are there for each case?
- What are the names of the variables, and where are they located in the data file?
- What labels should be attached to variables and values?
- What values are used to represent missing information?

2.7
DATA LIST Command

The most basic component of SPSS data definition is the DATA LIST command. It tells SPSS where the data can be found, indicates how many records there are for each case, defines the variable names, and specifies their column locations.

The DATA LIST command consists of two basic components:

- Subcommands and keywords that indicate where to find the data, the number of records per case, and the basic data format.
- Definition of individual variables and the location of each variable on the case record(s).

Unlike most other SPSS commands, multiple subcommands in DATA LIST are not separated by slashes. A slash in DATA LIST separates the subcommands and keywords from the variable definition section, and each subsequent slash represents the start of a new record. For example, the command

```
DATA LIST FILE=CORONARY RECORDS=2
 /CASEID 1-4 FIRSTCHD 6 AGE 8-9 DBP58 11-13 EDUYR 15-16
  CHOL58 18-20 CGT58 22-23
 /HT58 6-9 WT58 11-13 DAYOFWK 15 VITAL10 17 FAMHXCVR 19 CHD 21.
```

contains two subcommands. The FILE subcommand specifies the name of the file containing the data, and the RECORDS subcommand indicates the number of records per case. Following the two subcommands is a list of variable names and their column locations on two records. (This command reads the data in Figure 2.5c.)

2.8
FILE Subcommand

Use the FILE subcommand to specify the file containing the data described in the DATA LIST command. The specification

```
DATA LIST FILE=CORONARY
```

indicates that the raw data are in a file named CORONARY.

If your data are included in the same file with your data definition commands (*inline* data), you can omit the FILE subcommand. Inline data must be entered between BEGIN DATA and END DATA commands (see Section 2.13).

2.9
FIXED, FREE, and LIST Keywords

Use one of the following keywords on DATA LIST to indicate the format of the data:

FIXED *Fixed-format data.* Each variable is recorded in the same column location on the same record for each case in the data file. FIXED is the default if no format is specified.

FREE *Freefield-format data.* The variables are recorded in the same order for each case, but not necessarily in the same locations. You can enter more than one case on a record. For example, if you define 10 variables, DATA LIST assumes the start of a new case after reading 10 values. Values are separated by blanks or commas.

LIST *Freefield-data with one case on each record.* The variables are recorded in freefield format as described for the keyword FREE, except the variables for each case must be recorded on a separate record, and each case has only one record.

With fixed format, you must specify the exact column locations for each variable, as in:

```
DATA LIST FILE=CORONARY FIXED
 /CASEID 1-4 FIRSTCHD 6 AGE 8-9 . . .
```

With freefield input, you simply provide the variable names, as in:

```
DATA LIST FILE=CORONARY FREE
 /CASEID FIRSTCHD AGE . . .
```

2.10
RECORDS Subcommand

Use the RECORDS subcommand with fixed-format data to specify the number of records per case. The specification

```
DATA LIST FILE=CORONARY RECORDS=2
```

tells SPSS to expect two records per case in file CORONARY.

By default, SPSS assumes one record per case for fixed-format data. You must use the RECORDS subcommand if there is more than one record per case. You should not use the RECORDS subcommand with freefield-format data.

2.11
Variable Definition

Use the variable definition portion of the DATA LIST command to assign names to your variables and provide information about the location and format of each variable.

Specifying Variable Names. The names you assign to your variables on the DATA LIST command are used on subsequent SPSS commands to refer to your variables.

Variable names can be up to eight characters long and begin with either an alphabetic letter or one of the following characters: @, #, or $. (For more information about SPSS rules for variable names, see Chapter 1.) The order in which variables are named on the DATA LIST command determines their order in the active system file.

Indicating Column Locations. For fixed-format data, follow the variable name with the column location. If the variable is two or more columns wide, specify the number of the first column, followed by a dash (-), and then the number of the last column, as in:

```
DATA LIST FILE=CORONARY
 /CASEID 1-4 FIRSTCHD 6 AGE 8-9...
```

For fixed-format data, you do not need to define all the variables in the data file—only those you intend to use. SPSS ignores data in columns and on records that you do not mention. Within a record, you do not need to specify variables in the same order in which they appear in the data file. The specification

```
DATA LIST FILE=CORONARY
 /CASEID 1-4 AGE 8-9 FIRSTCHD 6...
```

reads the variables from the correct locations but places AGE before FIRSTCHD on the active system file.

Specifying Multiple Records. The list of variables for each record should be preceded by a slash. You can specify the sequence number for the record immediately after the slash, although it is not required. For example,

```
DATA LIST FILE=CORONARY RECORDS=2
 /1 CASEID 1-4 FIRSTCHD 6 AGE 8-9...
 /2 HT58 6-9 WT58 11-13 DAYOFWK 15...
```

defines two records with sequence numbers 1 and 2.

You can skip over records simply by skipping sequence numbers or by specifying a slash with no subsequent variables for any records you wish to skip.

Specifying Multiple Variables in the Same Location. You can specify multiple variables in the same columns. For example, the specification

```
DATA LIST /MONTH 1-2 DAY 3-4 YEAR 5-6 DATE 1-6
```

specifies three variables, MONTH, DAY, and YEAR, in separate column locations and then specifies a fourth variable, DATE, starting in the first column of the field allocated for MONTH and ending in the last column allocated for YEAR. The variable DATE encompasses the values for the other three variables.

Shortcuts. If several variables with the same width and format are recorded in adjacent columns in the data file, you can indicate their column locations with a single specification. For example, the specification

```
DATA LIST /VAR1 1-3 VAR2 4-6 VAR3 7-9
```

could also be expressed as

```
DATA LIST /VAR1 VAR2 VAR3 1-9
```

The DATA LIST command divides the total number of columns equally among the three variables.

You can also use the keyword TO to define consecutive variables. For example, the specification

```
DATA LIST /CASEID 1-4 FIRSTCHD 6 AGE 8-9 DBP58 TO DBP60 11-19
```

defines the variables DBP58, DBP59, and DBP60 in columns 11–13, 14–16, and 17–19, respectively.

2.12
Types of Variables

You can define different types of variables with SPSS. The two most common are numeric and string (alphanumeric). Numeric variables contain only numbers. They can be either decimals (such as 12.345) or integers (such as 1234). A string variable can contain a combination of letters, numbers, and special characters.

There are two types of string variables—short strings and long strings. A string of eight characters or less is considered a short string. Short string variables can be used in some data transformations and procedures in which long strings cannot be used.

Specifying String Variables. By default, SPSS assumes that variables are numeric unless specified otherwise. To identify a string variable on the DATA LIST command, specify (A) after the variable name and column location, as in:

```
DATA LIST FILE=CORONARY /NAME 1-20(A)
```

For freefield-format data, you should also indicate the width of the string variable, as in:

```
DATA LIST FILE=CORONARY FREE /NAME(A20)
```

With freefield format, all preceding variables must also have formats explicitly specified, unless they are separated by an an asterisk. For example, the command

```
DATA LIST FILE=CORONARY FREE
 /WT58 HT58 FIRSTCHD * LNAME (A20) FNAME (A20)
```

tells SPSS that WT58, HT58, and FIRSTCHD are numeric variables (the default format), and LNAME and FNAME are both string variables with a width of 20 characters.

Indicating Decimal Places. By default, SPSS assumes that decimal points are explicitly coded in the data file. If there are no decimal points, the numeric variables are assumed to be integers. To indicate noninteger values for data that have not been coded with decimal points, you can specify the *implied* number of decimal places in parentheses after the variable name and column location, as in:

```
DATA LIST FILE=CORONARY /HEIGHT 34-36(1)
```

The variable HEIGHT is in columns 34-36. If a value is recorded as 688, it will be assigned a value of 68.8.

Any decimal points explicitly recorded in the data file will override the implied decimal point. Implied decimals on the DATA LIST command can be used only with fixed-format data.

Date Formats. SPSS also recognizes dates in a variety of formats. The two most common are:

DATE   *International date.* This format reads international dates in the form dd/mmm/yyyy. Dashes, periods, commas, slashes, or blanks can be used as delimiters. Months can be represented in digits, roman numerals, three-character abbreviations, or they can be spelled out fully. If you enter a two-digit year, SPSS assumes a prefix of 19.

For example, 2/12/89, 02-Dec-89, and 2 December 1989 are all acceptable ways to express the date "December 2, 1989."

For DATE format, the width defined on DATA LIST must be at least nine characters. However, dates with fewer characters are correctly evaluated.

ADATE *American date.* This format reads dates of the general format mm/dd/yyyy. ADATE format follows the same syntax rules as DATE format. For example, 10/28/86, Oct.28.86, and October,28,1986 are all acceptable ways to express the date "October 28, 1986."

For ADATE format, the width defined on DATA LIST must be at least eight characters. However, dates with fewer characters are correctly evaluated.

To define a date variable on the DATA LIST command, specify the date format in parentheses after the variable name and column specifications, as in:

```
DATA LIST /BIRTH 1-8 (ADATE).
```

2.13
BEGIN DATA and END DATA Commands

Sometimes, instead of keeping your data in an external file, you may prefer to enter your data along with your SPSS commands. In such cases, omit the FILE subcommand from the DATA LIST command and separate the inline data from the command lines with the BEGIN DATA and END DATA commands. The BEGIN DATA command follows the DATA LIST command, and the END DATA command follows the last line of data. All procedure commands should come after the END DATA command. Transformation commands can be specified before BEGIN DATA.

For example, the Western Electric data could be included in the same file with DATA LIST and other commands, as in:

```
DATA LIST
 /CASEID 1-4 FIRSTCHD 6 AGE 17-18 DBP58 20-22 EDUYR 24-25
 CHOL58 27-29 CGT58 31-32 HT58 34-37 WT58 39-41 DAYOFWK 43
 VITAL10 45 FAMHXCVR 47 (A) CHD 49.
BEGIN DATA
  13 3         40  70 16 321  0 68.8 190 9 0 Y 1
  30 3         49  87 11 246 60 72.2 204 5 0 N 1
  53 2         43  89 12 262  0 69.0 162 7 1 N 1
                        . . .
END DATA.
FREQUENCIES VARIABLES=DAYOFWK.
```

Note that you do not specify a period after the BEGIN DATA command. A command terminator should be specified after END DATA.

2.14
MISSING VALUES Command

Sometimes information for a particular variable is not available for a case. For example, an employee in the Western Electric study might not know how many cigarettes he smokes each day, or he might refuse to answer the question. It is often useful to be able to distinguish why information is missing. You can assign values that identify information missing for various reasons, and you can instruct SPSS to flag these values with the MISSING VALUES command. The SPSS statistical procedures and transformation commands recognize this flag, and those cases with missing values are handled specially.

The specification on the MISSING VALUES command consists of a variable name or variable list and the specified missing value or values in parentheses, as in:

```
MISSING VALUES CGT58 (-1, -2) DAYOFWK (9).
```

You can specify missing values for any previously defined numeric or short string variable on the active system file. You can specify missing values for more than one variable on the same MISSING VALUES command.

You can specify up to three individual missing values for each variable. Two of those variables can be the endpoints of a range using the keyword THRU. You can also assign the same missing values to more than one variable by specifying a variable list before the missing value(s). For example, the command

```
MISSING VALUES Q1 TO Q8 (0, 7 THRU 9).
```

defines 0 and all values from 7 through 9 as missing for all variables from Q1 to Q8 on the active system file.

The MISSING VALUES command defines *user-missing* values, which should be distinguished from *system-missing* values (indicated by a period in output). SPSS assigns a system-missing value whenever it encounters a value other than a number for a variable defined as numeric on the DATA LIST command. For example, a blank in a field for a numeric variable is set to system-missing. Leaving a field blank is an alternative to entering special codes for missing values—but you will probably find that assigning user-defined missing values gives you more control in most SPSS procedures.

System-missing values are also assigned when new variables created with transformation commands have undefined values. For example, if a case is missing a value for a variable used to compute the new variable, the system-missing value is assigned to the new variable for that case. The system-missing value is indicated by a period in output.

2.15
Variable and Value Labels

The optional VARIABLE LABELS and VALUE LABELS commands supply information that is used for labeling SPSS display output. Some variables, such as age and weight, can be assigned self-explanatory variable names (e.g., AGE and WEIGHT) and have a wide range of possible values that are inherently meaningful. Such variables do not need additional variable or value labels. But sometimes it is difficult to fully describe a variable with eight characters, and coded values may have no apparent meaning by themselves.

Variable and value labels are enclosed within apostrophes or quotation marks. To include an apostrophe in a label, use quotation marks to enclose the label, as in:

```
VARIABLE LABELS SALARY82 'EMPLOYEE"S ANNUAL SALARY IN 1982'.
```

To continue a label from one command line to the next, use the plus sign and enclose both parts of the label in apostrophes or quotation marks. For example, the command

```
VARIABLE LABELS CHD 'INCIDENCE OF CORONARY'
 + " HEART DISEASE".
```

produces the label "INCIDENCE OF CORONARY HEART DISEASE." Since a blank space is a valid part of a label, a space must be inserted after CORONARY or before HEART to be included in the label.

2.16
VARIABLE LABELS Command

Use the VARIABLE LABELS command to assign an extended descriptive label to variables. Specify the variable name followed by at least one comma or blank and then the label enclosed in apostrophes or quotation marks, as in:

```
VARIABLE LABELS
 DAYOFWK 'DAY OF DEATH'
 VITAL10 'STATUS AT TEN YEARS'
 FAMHXCVR 'FAMILY HISTORY OF CHD'.
```

This command assigns variable labels to the variables DAYOFWK, VITAL10, and FAMHXCVR.

You can assign multiple variable labels on the same VARIABLE LABELS command, but each label applies to only one variable. Variable labels can include blanks and any other character. Each label can be up to 120 characters long, although most procedures will print fewer than 120 characters for each label.

Use the VALUE LABELS command to provide descriptive labels for values. The VALUE LABELS command is followed by a variable name, or variable list, and a list of the values with their associated labels enclosed in apostrophes or quotation marks, as in:

```
VALUE LABELS
 DAYOFWK 1 'SUNDAY' 2 'MONDAY' 3 'TUESDAY'
 4 'WEDNESDAY' 5 'THURSDAY' 6 'FRIDAY' 7 'SATURDAY'
 /FAMHXCVR 'Y' 'YES' 'N' 'NO'.
```

Value labels can be assigned to any previously defined numeric or short string variable. For short string variables, such as FAMHXCVR above, the actual value must be enclosed in apostrophes. Value labels can contain blanks and any characters. Each value label can be up to 60 characters long, although most procedures will print fewer than 60 characters for each value.

Value labels for multiple variables can be specified on the same value labels command. A slash is required to separate labels for one variable or variable list from the next variable or variable list.

To assign the same labels to the same values of several variables, list all of the variables followed by the values and associated labels, as in:

```
VALUE LABELS DEPT79 TO DEPT82
 0 'NOT REPORTED' 1 'ADMINISTRATIVE' 2 'PROJECT DIRECTORS'
 3 'CHICAGO OPERATIONS' 4 'ST. LOUIS OPERATIONS'.
```

The default print and write formats are determined by several factors:

• For fixed-format data, the default print and write formats are determined by the input field width and implied decimals specified on the DATA LIST command.

• For freefield-format data, the default print and write formats for numeric variables are both F8.2.

• For new numeric variables created with transformation commands (see Chapter 3), the default print and write formats are both F8.2.

A default format of F8.2 specifies a total width of 8 characters, with two decimal places. The decimal point also counts as one character. Numbers greater than 99,999,999 are expressed in scientific notation. For example, the value 235,012,345 appears as 2.4E+08. Values automatically appear with two decimals, provided there is sufficient space in the 8-character width. For example, the number 2,350 appears as 2350.00; the number 235,012 appears as 235012.0; and the number 2,350,123 appears as 2350123.

For fixed-format data, the default print and write formats for decimal places are determined by the number of implied decimals listed in parentheses for the variable on the DATA LIST command. If no implied decimals are specified on DATA LIST, the default print and write formats produce only integers, with no decimals. Explicitly coded decimals are stored in the system file, but they don't appear in the output produced by the default settings.

If a data value exceeds its width specification, SPSS makes an attempt to produce some value nevertheless. It takes out punctuation characters, and then tries scientific notation. If there still is not enough space, it produces asterisks to indicate a value that cannot be printed in the specified width.

SPSS provides a wide variety of formats for numeric variables. Use the PRINT FORMATS, WRITE FORMATS, and FORMATS commands to override the default formats. Table 2.18 shows a few of the more common formats. For a complete list of numeric and string formats, refer to the SPSS *Operations Guide* for your system.

Table 2.18 Common output data formats

Format	Specification	Input	Output
Default*	F8.2*	2350	2350.00
Fw.d	F9.0	2350	2350
COMMAw.d	COMMA9.1	2350	2,350.0
DOLLARw.d	DOLLAR9.2	2350	$2,350.00

*For freefield-format data and transformation commands.

**2.19
PRINT FORMATS Command**

Use the PRINT FORMATS command to change print formats. Specify the variable name or variable list, followed by the new format specification in parentheses, as in:

```
PRINT FORMATS SALARY79 TO SALARY82 (DOLLAR8).
```

This command specifies dollar print format with 8 positions, including the dollar sign and commas when appropriate.

To specify multiple print formats on the same command, separate the format specifications for each variable or variable list with a slash, as in:

```
PRINT FORMATS SALARY79 TO SALARY82 (DOLLAR8)
 /HOURLY82 (DOLLAR7.2).
```

The formats specified on a PRINT FORMATS command are in effect for the duration of the SPSS session.

**2.20
WRITE FORMATS Command**

The WRITE FORMATS command operates exactly like the PRINT FORMATS command, except that it changes only the write formats of the variables specified. Write formats refer to the format of data sent to computer files to be read by SPSS or other software (see Chapters 4 and 6). They do not affect the format of printed output. There are some additional write formats that are not available as print formats. For a complete list of formats, refer to the SPSS *Operations Guide* for your system.

**2.21
FORMATS Command**

The FORMATS command operates exactly like the PRINT FORMATS and WRITE FORMATS commands, except that it changes both print and write formats for the variables specified.

**2.22
COMPLEX DATA
DEFINITION**

Many data files are not organized into the rectangular, case-ordered structure described at the beginning of this chapter. You may have *matrix files,* which contain summary data in matrix form, *mixed files,* which contain several types of records that define different types of cases, hierarchical or *nested files,* which contain several types of records with defined relationships between the record types, *grouped files,* which contain several records for each case with some records missing or duplicated, or files that contain records with *repeating data.*

For a discussion of the many SPSS commands available to read and define complex data files, see the *SPSS Reference Guide.*

2.23
EXERCISES

Correct the syntax errors in the following commands.

1. DATA LIST FIXED
   /1 ID 1-3 AGE 5-7 SEX 8
   /2 EDUC 1-2 JOBCAT 4.

2. DATA LIST FIXED
   /VAR1 TO VAR3 1-8.

3. MISSING VALUES
   JOBCAT (96, 97, 98, 99).

4. VARIABLE LABELS
   DAYOWK DAY OF DEATH
   VITAL10 STATUS AT TEN YEARS
   FAMHX FAMILY HISTORY.

5. VALUE LABELS
   ITEM1 TO ITEM3 1 'YES' 2 'NO'
   SALARY 1 'LESS THAN $20,000'
         2 '$20,000 TO $49,999'
         3 '$50,000 OR MORE'

6. What is wrong with the following DATA LIST command?

   DATA LIST FILE=CORONARY FREE
   /WT58 HT58 DBP58 NAME (A20).

Data Transformation and Selection

In this chapter:

Goals:

- To transform data (if necessary) for statistical analysis.
- To create new variables through numeric transformations and combinations of existing variables.
- To select a subset of cases for analysis.

Examples:

- Collapse categories for 12 months into four seasons.
- Create a dichotomous social security eligibility variable based on the values of age and sex.
- Compute a windchill variable from temperature and wind speed.
- Select a subset of females, aged 18 to 35, who work full-time.

3 Data Transformation and Selection

In an ideal situation, your raw data are perfectly suitable for the type of analysis you want to perform, and any relationships between variables are either conveniently linear or neatly orthogonal. If this is the case, you can proceed directly from basic data definition to complex statistical analysis. However, you will probably find that this is rarely the case. Preliminary analysis may reveal inconvenient coding schemes or coding errors; complex data transformations may be required to coax out the true relationship between variables; or you may find that only a particular subset of cases is relevant to your analysis.

With SPSS you can perform data transformation ranging from simple tasks, such as collapsing categories for analysis, to creating new variables based on complex equations and conditional statements. You can also select cases for analysis based on an equally complex set of conditions or choose a simple random sample.

This chapter provides an overview of the data transformation and selection commands available with SPSS. For a complete discussion of these commands, see the *SPSS Reference Guide.*

3.1 RECODE COMMAND

The RECODE command tells SPSS to change the values for a variable as the data are being read. The command

```
RECODE X (0=9).
```

instructs SPSS to change all 0's found for variable X to 9's.

The variable or variables to be recoded must already exist on the active SPSS system file. You can specify as many value specifications as needed, enclosing each specification within parentheses, as in:

```
RECODE ITEM1 (0=1) (1=0) (2=-1).
```

You can use multiple input values in a single specification but only one output value following the equals sign, as in:

```
RECODE ITEM2 (8,9=1) (4 THRU 7=2) (1,2=3).
```

The RECODE command is evaluated left to right, and the values for a case are recoded only once per RECODE command. For example, if a case has an input value of 0 for variable ITEM1, the command

```
RECODE ITEM1 (0=1) (1=0) (2=-1).
```

recodes ITEM1 to 1 and SPSS then moves on. The value 1 is *not* recoded back to 0 by the second value specification. Input values not mentioned on the RECODE command are left unchanged.

You can name multiple variables for the same value specifications, as in:

`RECODE ITEM1 TO ITEM3 (0=1) (1=0) (2=-1).`

In addition, you can specify different values for different variables on the same RECODE command by separating the specifications with a slash, as in:

`RECODE AGE (0=9)`
`/ITEM1 TO ITEM3 (0=1) (1=0) (2=-1).`

These rules apply to both numeric and string variables. See Section 3.7 for more information on recoding string variables.

3.2
THRU, LOWEST, and HIGHEST Keywords

To recode ranges of values for numeric variables into a single value, use keyword THRU. Use keyword LO (LOWEST) or HI (HIGHEST) to specify the lowest or highest input value for the variable. For example, to recode all individuals below the United States voting age to 0 and leave all other ages unchanged, specify:

`RECODE AGE (LO THRU 17=0).`

Keywords LOWEST and HIGHEST do not include the system-missing value. However, user-missing values are included.

3.3
ELSE Keyword

To recode all values not previously mentioned into a single catchall category, use the keyword ELSE. For example, to recode AGE to a dichotomous (two-valued) variable with 0 representing individuals below the voting age and 1 representing potential voters, specify:

`RECODE AGE (LO THRU 17=0) (ELSE=1).`

ELSE should be the last specification for the variable. Otherwise all subsequent value specifications for that variable are ignored. Keyword ELSE *does* include the system-missing value.

3.4
Recoding Continuous Variables

If a numeric variable has noninteger values, some values may not be recoded unless you make certain they are included in a value range. For example, if AGE had noninteger values, the command

`RECODE AGE (LO THRU 17=0) (18 THRU HI=1).`

would not recode values between 17 and 18, such as 17.5. You can avoid this problem by using overlapping endpoint values, as in:

`RECODE AGE (18 THRU HI=1) (LO THRU 18=0).`

Note that the order of the recode specifications has been reversed. Since a value is recoded only once, any cases with a value of exactly 18 will be recoded to a value of 1.

3.5
INTO Keyword

To recode the values of one variable and store them in another variable, use the keyword INTO, as in:

`RECODE AGE (18 THRU HI=1) (LO THRU 18=0) INTO VOTER.`

The recoded AGE values are stored in the *target variable* VOTER, leaving AGE unchanged.

Target variables can be existing or new variables. If you use an existing variable, cases with values not mentioned in the recode specification are not changed. If you recode a variable into a new variable, cases with values not specified for recoding are assigned the system-missing value.

3.6
COPY Keyword

When you recode a variable into a new variable or use keyword ELSE as a cleanup category, you may want to retain a set of input values. The command

```
RECODE ITEM1 TO ITEM3 (0=1) (1=0) (2=-1) (ELSE=COPY)
    INTO DEFENSE WELFARE HEALTH.
```

creates three new variables. Input values other than 0, 1, or 2 are retained. In other words, if a case has value 9 for variable ITEM1, it will have value 9 for variable DEFENSE, and so forth.

Keyword COPY is an output specification only. Input values to be copied can be a range of values, keywords SYSMIS or MISSING, or keyword ELSE. User-missing values are copied, but their missing-value status is not. The MISSING VALUES command should be used to redeclare missing values for the new variables (see Chapter 2).

3.7
Recoding String Variables

If you are recoding a string variable, enclose each value specification in apostrophes or quotation marks, as in:

```
RECODE STATE ("IO"="IA").
```

The following additional rules apply to recoding string variables:

- The keywords THRU, HIGHEST, LOWEST, MISSING, and SYSMIS cannot be used.
- If a value specification applies to more than one variable, all the named variables must have string values of equal length.
- New string values cannot be longer than the variable length as defined on the DATA LIST or STRING command (see Section 3.20).
- If you specify fewer characters than the defined string variable length, SPSS right-pads the value with blanks to the defined length. For example, if the defined length is A3, and you specify a value of NO on the RECODE command, SPSS reads the value as NO.
- Target variables specified with the INTO keyword must already exist on the active system file. To create a new variable, use the STRING command (see Section 3.20) before the RECODE command to declare new string target variables.

3.8
COMPUTE COMMAND

The COMPUTE command creates new variables through numeric transformations of existing variables. COMPUTE names the variable you want to create (the *target variable*) followed by an *expression* defining the variable. For example, the command

```
COMPUTE TOTSCORE=MIDTERM+FINAL+HOMEWORK.
```

defines the new variable TOTSCORE as the sum of the variables MIDTERM, FINAL, and HOMEWORK.

The target variable can be a variable that already exists or a new variable. If the target variable already exists, its values are replaced with those produced by the specified transformation. If it is a new variable, it is added to the end of the dictionary in your active system file.

The expression on the COMPUTE command can use existing numeric variables, constants, arithmetic operators (such as + and −), and functions such as SQRT (square root) and TRUNC (truncate). For example, the command

```
COMPUTE GRADESCR=.35*MIDTERM+.45*FINAL+.2*HOMEWORK.
```

creates a new variable, GRADESCR, that is the weighted average of the variables MIDTERM, FINAL, and HOMEWORK.

3.9
Arithmetic Operators

The following arithmetic operators are available for transforming numeric variables with COMPUTE:

+   *Addition.*
−   *Subtraction.*
*   *Multiplication.*
/   *Division.*
**   *Exponentiation.*

Arithmetic operators must be explicitly specified. You cannot, for example, write (PROPTAX)(100) instead of (PROPTAX)*100.

You can include blanks in an arithmetic expression to improve readability, as in the command

```
COMPUTE TAXTOTAL = PROPTAX + FICA + STATETAX + FEDTAX.
```

Since fairly complex expressions are possible, it is important to keep in mind the order in which operations are performed. Functions (see Sections 3.10 through 3.12) are evaluated first, then exponentiation, then multiplication and division, and, finally, addition and subtraction. Thus, if you specify

```
COMPUTE NEWRATE=SQRT(RATE1)/SQRT(RATE1)+SQRT(RATE3).
```

the square roots (SQRT) are calculated first, then the division is performed, and then the addition.

You can control the order in which operations are performed by enclosing the operation you want executed first in parentheses. Thus, the command

```
COMPUTE NEWRATE=SQRT(RATE1)/(SQRT(RATE1)+SQRT(RATE3)).
```

produces different results than the previous command, since the added parentheses cause the addition to be performed before division. Operations at the same level, as far as order of execution is concerned, are evaluated from left to right. If you are uncertain about the order of execution, you should use parentheses to make the order you want explicit.

3.10
Numeric Functions

Many numeric functions are available with the COMPUTE command. Numeric functions always return numbers (or the system-missing value).

The expression to be transformed by a function is called the *argument*. Most functions have a variable name or variable list as arguments. In numeric functions with two or more arguments, each argument must be separated by a comma. You cannot use blanks alone to separate the variable names, expressions, or constants used as arguments.

For example, to generate the square root of variable X, specify variable X as the argument to the SQRT function, as in SQRT(X). Enclose arguments in parentheses, as in

```
COMPUTE INCOME=TRUNC(INCOME).
```

where the TRUNC function returns the integer portion of variable INCOME. Separate multiple arguments with commas, as in

```
COMPUTE SCALE=MEAN(Q1,Q2,Q3).
```

where the MEAN function returns the mean of variables Q1, Q2, and Q3.

Sections 3.11 through 3.13 discuss arithmetic, statistical, and other functions for the COMPUTE command. These functions can also be used with the IF, SELECT IF, DO IF, and ELSE IF commands, which are discussed later in this chapter.

3.11
Arithmetic Functions

The following arithmetic functions are available:

ABS(arg) — *Absolute value.* ABS(SCALE) is 4.7 when SCALE equals 4.7 or -4.7.

RND(arg) — *Round the absolute value to an integer and reaffix the sign.* RND(SCALE) is -5 when SCALE equals -4.7.

TRUNC(arg) — *Truncate to an integer.* TRUNC(SCALE) is -4 when SCALE equals -4.7.

MOD(arg,arg) — *Remainder (modulo) of the first argument divided by the second.* MOD(YEAR,100) is 83 when YEAR equals 1983.

SQRT(arg) — *Square root.* SQRT(SIBS) is 1.41 when SIBS equals 2.

EXP(arg) — *Exponential. e is raised to the power of the argument.* EXP(VARA) is 7.39 when VARA equals 2.

LG10(arg) — *Base 10 logarithm.* LG10(VARB) is .48 when VARB equals 3.

LN(arg) — *Natural or Naperian logarithm (base e).* LN(VARC) is 2.30 when VARC equals 10.

ARSIN(arg) — *Arcsine. The result is given in radians (alias ASIN).* ARSIN(ANG) is 1.57 when ANG equals 1.

ARTAN(arg) — *Arctangent. The result is given in radians (alias ATAN).* ARTAN(ANG2) is .79 when ANG2 equals 1.

SIN(arg) — *Sine. The argument must be specified in radians.* SINE(VARC) is .84 when VARC equals 1.

COS(arg) — *Cosine. The argument must be specified in radians.* COS(VARD) is .54 when VARD equals 1.

All arithmetic functions except MOD have single arguments; MOD has two. The arguments to MOD must be separated by a comma. Arguments can be numeric expressions, as in RND(A**2/B).

3.12
Statistical Functions

Each argument to a statistical function (expression, variable name, or constant) must be separated by a comma. The available statistical functions are:

SUM(arg list) — *Sum of the values across the argument list.*

MEAN(arg list) — *Mean of the values across the argument list.*

SD(arg list) — *Standard deviation of the values across the argument list.*

VARIANCE(arg list) — *Variance of the values across the argument list.*

CFVAR(arg list) — *Coefficient of variation of the values across the argument list. The coefficient of variation is the standard deviation divided by the mean.*

MIN(arg list) — *Minimum value across the argument list.*

MAX(arg list) — *Maximum value across the argument list.*

3.13
Other Functions

Other available functions include:

RANGE(arg,arg list) — *Return 1 (true) if the value of the first argument is in the inclusive range(s). Otherwise, return 0 (false). The arguments must be separated by commas. The first argument is usually a variable, and the list usually contains pairs of values. For example, NONWORK =RANGE(AGE,1,17,62,99) returns a value of 1 for ages 1 through 17 and ages 62 through 99. The value of NONWORK is 0 for any other value of AGE.*

ANY(arg,arg list) — *Return 1 (true) if the value of the first argument matches one of the arguments in the list. Otherwise, return 0 (false). The arguments must be separated by commas. The first argument is usually a variable. For example, PARTIC=ANY(PROJECT, 3, 4, 7, 9) returns a value of 1 if the value of PROJECT is 3, 4, 7, or 9. If PROJECT is any other value, PARTIC has a value of 0.*

UNIFORM(arg)	*A uniform pseudo-random number.* The random number is uniformly distributed with values varying between 0 and the value of the argument. For example, SAMP1=UNIFORM(150) assigns random values between 1 and 150 to the variable SAMP1 for each case in the active system file.
NORMAL(arg)	*A normal pseudo-random number.* The random number is normally distributed, with a mean of approximately 0 and a standard deviation equal to the value of the argument.
VALUE(arg)	*Ignore user-missing values.* User-missing values are treated as valid observations and included in any specified calculations.
MISSING(arg)	*Return 1 (true) if the value of the argument is missing. Otherwise, return 0 (false).* The argument is a variable name, and the missing values include both user- and system-missing values.
SYSMIS(arg)	*Return 1 (true) if the value of the argument is system-missing. Otherwise, return 0 (false).*

There are also numerous functions that enable you to convert and extract dates and times. For example, you can calculate the number of days between two date variables (see Chapter 2) with the command:

```
COMPUTE DAYDIFF=CTIME.DAYS(VISIT2-VISIT1).
```

SPSS stores all dates as the number of seconds since October 14, 1582. The function CTIME.DAYS converts dates into the number of days. The argument (VISIT2 − VISIT1) calculates the difference, in days, between the date variables VISIT2 and VISIT1.

For a complete list of functions, including date and time functions, see the *SPSS Reference Guide.*

3.14
Missing Values

If a case has missing values for any of the variables used in a COMPUTE arithmetic expression, the case is assigned the system-missing value for the computed variable. For example, if the command

```
COMPUTE AGECUBE=AGE**3.
```

is used, the AGECUBE variable will be system-missing for any case with a missing value for AGE.

A case is also assigned the system-missing value for a computed variable when the specified operation is not defined for that case. For example, if the command

```
COMPUTE PCTTAXES=(TAXES/INCOME)*100.
```

is used, a case with the value 0 for INCOME is assigned the system-missing value for PCTTAXES because division by 0 is not defined. If the result of an expression cannot be represented on the computer (even when valid values are used in the expression itself), the system-missing value is assigned to the new variable.

The assignment of missing values is treated differently for numeric functions. For example, the command

```
COMPUTE MEANSCOR=(SCORE1+SCORE2+SCORE3)/3.
```

will return a missing value for MEANSCOR if a case has a missing value for any one of the variables SCORE1, SCORE2, or SCORE3. However, the command

```
COMPUTE MEANSCOR=MEAN(SCORE1, SCORE2, SCORE3).
```

will return a numeric value unless a case has missing values for all three specified variables.

For a complete discussion of the treatment of missing values with numeric functions, see the *SPSS Reference Guide.*

3.15
Computing String Variables

You can also use the COMPUTE command to compute string variables. With strings, the expression on the right of the equals sign must return a string, and the target variable must already exist on the active system file. To declare a new string variable, use the STRING command (see Section 3.20) before the COMPUTE command, as in:

```
STRING NEWVAR(A2).
COMPUTE NEWVAR="NA".
```

which declares a new string variable NEWVAR with a length of two characters and assigns a value of NA to NEWVAR for every case.

There are also numerous string functions, including functions for concatenating string values, converting from upper case to lower case (and from lower to upper), and converting strings to numeric values. For a complete list of string functions, see the *SPSS Reference Guide*.

3.16
COUNT COMMAND

The COUNT command is a special data transformation utility used to create a numeric variable that, for each case, counts the occurrences of the same value (or list of values) across a list of numeric or string variables. For example,

```
COUNT  READER=NEWSWEEK,TIME,USNEWS (2).
```

creates a simple index READER that indicates the number of times the value 2 (those who read each magazine) is recorded for the three variables for a case. Thus, the value of READER will be either 0, 1, 2, or 3. You can enter more than one criterion variable list and more than one criterion value enclosed in parentheses, as in

```
COUNT  READER=NEWSWEEK,TIME,USNEWS (2)
 NYTIMES,WPOST,CHIGTRIB,LATIMES (3,4).
```

which adds four more news sources to the previous index. This time, SPSS increases the count for a case by 1 whenever it encounters either value 3 (Sunday only) or 4 (daily plus Sunday) for each newspaper variable.

You can specify a variable more than once in the variable list to increase the count by more than 1 for that variable, thus giving it more weight. You can also use the TO keyword in the variable list and the THRU, LO (LOWEST), and HI (HIGHEST) keywords in the value list. You can also create more than one variable on a COUNT command by separating the specifications with a slash, as in:

```
COUNT LOWCOUNT=Q1 TO Q10 (LO THRU 5)
 /HICOUNT=Q1 TO Q10 (11 THRU HI).
```

3.17
Initialization and Missing Values

The COUNT command ignores the missing-value status of user-missing values. In other words, the COUNT command counts a value even if that value has been previously declared as missing. In the command

```
COUNT LOWCOUNT=Q1 TO Q10 (LO THRU 5).
```

target variable LOWCOUNT is increased for a case with value 0 for variables Q1, Q2, and so forth, even if 0 was declared user-missing for the Q variables.

COUNT will not propagate missing values automatically. In other words, the target variable will never be system-missing. However, you can use the MISSING VALUES command to declare missing values for the target variable.

3.18
WEIGHT COMMAND

The WEIGHT command is used to weight cases differentially for analysis. For example, if you have a sample from a population for which some subgroup has been over- or undersampled, you can apply weights to obtain population estimates. You can also use the WEIGHT command to replicate an example from a table or other aggregated data as shown for the CROSSTABS procedure in Chapter 10.

The variable named after the keyword BY on the WEIGHT command is used to weight cases, as in:

```
WEIGHT BY WTFACTOR.
```

This command tells SPSS to use the value of variable WTFACTOR to weight cases.

Only one variable can be specified on the WEIGHT command, and it must already exist on the active system file. The weight variable must be numeric, and it cannot be a scratch or system variable.

Cases with missing values, negative values, or a value of 0 for the weight variable are not included in statistical procedures.

The weighting variable can be an existing variable or one created through transformation commands. For example, assume your file contains a sample of households in which rural households were oversampled by a factor of 2. To compensate for oversampling, you can weight the rural households by one half, as in:

```
COMPUTE WT=1.
IF (LOCATE EQ 'RURAL') WT=.5.
WEIGHT BY WT.
```

Variable WT is initialized to 1 with the COMPUTE command and then changed to .5 with the IF command (see Section 3.22) for cases where the value of LOCATE equals RURAL. Be sure to initialize the weighting variable to 1 when creating it with IF commands. Otherwise, cases not covered by IF commands will be missing and will have a zero weight.

3.19
NUMERIC COMMAND

Use the NUMERIC command to declare new numeric variables. While you can also create new numeric variables directly with COMPUTE, IF, RECODE, and COUNT, you may need to refer to a numeric variable in the transformation language before it is created. For example, you might want to add a series of variables to your active system file in a fixed order so you can use the TO keyword to refer to variables on procedure commands. The specification

```
NUMERIC SCALE79 IMPACT79 SCALE80 IMPACT80 SCALE81 IMPACT81.
```

declares variables SCALE79 through IMPACT81. Then, regardless of the order in which you determine values for them, the variables remain in that order on the active system file. You can also use the TO keyword to generate consecutive new variable names.

3.20
STRING COMMAND

A string variable must be declared before it can be used as a target variable in data transformations. If a string variable does not already exist on the active system file, use the STRING command to declare it. The STRING command is followed by the name of the new variable and its simple format in parentheses, as in:

```
STRING SSNUMBER (A11).
```

Multiple string variables can be declared on the same STRING command, and the keyword TO can be used to generate consecutive new variable names. Each format specification applies to the variable or variable list that precedes it. The command

```
STRING ALPHA1 TO ALPHA3(A8)
       BETA1 BETA2(A12).
```

assigns a format of A8 for the new string variables ALPHA1, ALPHA2, and ALPHA3, and a format of A12 for the new string variables BETA1 and BETA2.

The order of the new string variables on the active system file is determined by their order on the STRING command.

3.21
CONDITIONAL TRANSFORMATIONS

You can specify data transformations for selected subsets of cases with conditional transformation commands. The logical expressions used in conditional transformations can include variable names, constants, arithmetic operators, numeric and other functions, logical variables, and relational operators.

3.22
IF Command

The IF command makes COMPUTE-like transformations contingent upon logical conditions found in the data. The IF command is followed by a *logical expression* (see Sections 3.26 through 3.30) followed by an *assignment expression*, which has the same syntax as the COMPUTE command (see Section 3.8). For example, the command

```
IF (X EQ 0) Y=1.
```

assigns a value of 1 to variable Y only for cases with a value of 0 for variable X. The logical expression is X EQ 0 and the assignment expression is Y=1. The target variable (Y) can be either an existing variable or a new variable. The parentheses enclosing the logical expression are optional.

The assignment expression follows all the rules and possibilities described for the COMPUTE command, but the assignment is executed only if the logical expression is true. The command

```
IF (DEPT82 EQ 2) BONUS=.14*SALARY82.
```

creates the new variable BONUS equal to 0.14 times SALARY82 only for cases with a value of 2 for variable DEPT82.

If a logical expression is false or indeterminate becasue of missing values, the target variable remains unchanged from its original value. If the target variable is a new variable being created by the IF command, it is set to the system-missing value.

3.23
DO IF and END IF Commands

You can perform multiple conditional transformations on the same subset of cases using the DO IF—END IF structure. The DO IF—END IF structure must begin with the DO IF command and end with the END IF command. The DO IF command must be followed by a logical expression. For example, the structure

```
DO IF (X EQ 1).
RECODE Y (1=2) (2=1).
RECODE Z (3=4) (4=3).
END IF.
```

recodes variables Y and Z for cases with a value of 1 for variable X.

The structure can be further defined with the ELSE and ELSE IF commands (see Sections 3.24 and 3.25). You can also nest DO IF—END IF structures as long as each DO IF command has a corresponding END IF command. Conditional data definition can be performed within the DO IF—END IF structure using commands such as DATA LIST, END CASE, END FILE, and REREAD (see Chapter 2).

For a complete discussion of the DO IF—END IF structure, see the *SPSS Reference Guide.*

3.24
ELSE Command

Use the ELSE command to perform transformations when the logical expression on the DO IF command is *not* true, as in:

```
DO IF (X EQ 0).
COMPUTE Y=1.
ELSE.
COMPUTE Y=2.
END IF.
```

In this structure, Y is set to 1 for all cases with a value of 0 for X, and Y is set to 2 for cases with any other valid (nonmissing) value for X. For cases with user-missing or system-missing values for X, Y is set to the system-missing value.

You can only use the ELSE command once within the DO IF—END IF structure.

3.25
ELSE IF Command

You can further define subsets within the DO IF—END IF structure by using the ELSE IF command. The ELSE IF command must be followed by a logical expression, as in:

```
DO IF (X EQ 0).
COMPUTE Y=1.
ELSE IF (X LE 9).
COMPUTE (Y=2).
ELSE.
COMPUTE Y=3.
END IF.
```

If X is 0, Y is set to 1; if X is less than or equal to 9, Y is set to 2; and if X is any other valid (nonmissing) value, Y is set to 3.

You can use multiple ELSE IF commands within a DO IF—END IF structure. If you also include an ELSE command, all ELSE IF commands must precede it.

3.26
Logical Expressions

The IF, DO IF, and ELSE IF commands evaluate logical expressions as true, false, or indeterminate. Thus, logical expressions can be any expressions that yield this three-valued logic. The logical expression

```
DO IF (X GE 5).
```

is true if X is 5 or greater, false if X is less than 5, and indeterminate if X is missing.

Logical expressions can be simple logical variables or relations, or they can be complex logical tests involving variables, constants, functions, relational operators, and logical operators.

In addition to the IF, DO IF, and ELSE IF commands, logical expressions can also be used on the LOOP, END LOOP, and SELECT IF commands. For a complete discussion of logical expressions, see the *SPSS Reference Guide.*

3.27
Logical Variables

The simplest logical expression is a logical variable. A logical variable is any variable that has values of 1, 0, or system-missing. For example, the expression

```
DO IF PROMO81.
```

is true if PROMO81 is 1, false if it is 0, and missing if PROMO81 is missing. Any other values will produce a warning message, and SPSS evaluates the expression for that case as 0 and false.

3.28
Relational Operators

A relation is a logical expression that compares two values using a *relational operator*. In the command

```
IF (X EQ 0) Y=1.
```

variable X and 0 are expressions that yield the values to be compared by the EQ relational operator. Relational operators are:

EQ *Equal to.* Returns true if the expression on the left is exactly equal to the expression on the right.

NE *Not equal to.* Returns true if the expression on the left does not equal the expression on the right.

LT *Less than.* Returns true if the expression on the left is less than the expression on the right.

LE *Less than or equal to.* Returns true if the expression on the left is less than or equal to the expression on the right.

GT *Greater than.* Returns true if the expression on the left is greater than the expression on the right.

GE *Greater than or equal to.* Returns true if the expression on the left is greater than or equal to the expression on the right.

You can specify either the relational operators above or their symbolic equivalents: = (EQ), $-=$ or $<>$ (NE), $<$ (LT), $>$ (GT), $<=$ (LE), and $>=$ (GE).

The expressions in a relation can be variables, constants, or more complicated arithmetic expressions, as in:

```
IF (W+Y GT X+Z) NEWX=1.
```

which assigns the value 1 to NEWX if the sum of W and Y is greater than the sum of X and Z. Or you can use one or more of the functions described for the COMPUTE command, as in:

```
IF (MEAN(Q1 TO Q5) LE 5) INDEX=1.
```

which assigns the value 1 to INDEX if the mean of variables Q1 through Q5 is less than or equal to 5.

You must use blanks (not commas) to separate the relational operator from the expressions, but you are free to introduce more blanks and parentheses in order to make the command more readable.

3.29
AND and OR Logical Operators

You can join two or more relations logically using the *logical operators* AND and OR, as in:

```
IF (X EQ 0 AND Z LT 2) Y=2.
```

This command assigns value 2 to variable Y only for cases with X equal to 0 and Z less than 2. The AND logical operator means that both relations must be true. Logical operators combine relations according to the following rules:

AND *Both relations must be true.*

OR *Either relation can be true.*

3.30
NOT Logical Operator

The NOT logical operator reverses the true/false outcome of the expression that immediately follows. For example,

```
IF NOT(X EQ 0) Y=3.
```

assigns value 3 to Y for all cases with values other than 0 for variable X.

The NOT operator affects only the expression that immediately follows, unless more than one expression is enclosed in parentheses. The expression

```
DO IF (NOT X EQ 0 AND Z LT 2).
```

is true for cases where X *is not* 0 and Z *is* less than 2. The expression

```
DO IF  NOT(X EQ 0 OR Z EQ 2).
```

is equivalent to

```
DO IF (X NE 0 AND Z NE 2).
```

because the only way the first logical expression can be true is for the parenthetical expression to be false.

The ¬ symbol is a valid substitute for the NOT keyword.

3.31
DATA SELECTION

You can select subgroups of cases for analysis, take a random sample from the data file, and restrict your analysis to a specified number of cases using SPSS data selection commands. You can also split your data file into subgroups and perform separate, simultaneous analyses on each of the subgroups.

3.32
SELECT IF Command

The SELECT IF command selects cases based on logical criteria. The SELECT IF command is followed by a logical expression that can be evaluated as true, false, or missing. For example, the command

```
SELECT IF (SEX EQ 'M').
```

selects cases for which variable SEX has the value M. The syntax of the logical expression for the SELECT IF command is the same as for the IF and DO IF commands (see Sections 3.22 through 3.30). The parentheses around the logical expression are optional. The specification can be as simple as a logical variable (see Section 3.27), as in:

```
SELECT IF (INVAR).
```

This command selects cases for which INVAR is equal to 1.

The expression can also be a complex combination of relational and logical operators, numeric functions, and arithmetic operations, as in:

```
SELECT IF (SEX EQ "M")
         AND ((MEAN(INC87, INC88, INC89)/FAMSIZE) GT 10000).
```

This command selects males with an average income during a three-year period of over \$10,000 per family member. If the logical expression is true, the case is selected; if it is false or missing, the case is not selected.

3.33
Multiple SELECT IF Commands

Once specified, a SELECT IF command remains in effect for the remainder of the SPSS session. If you use multiple SELECT IF commands in your session, they must all be true for a case to be selected. For example, the commands

```
SELECT IF (SEX EQ 'M').
SELECT IF (AGE GE 18) AND (AGE LE 65).
```

select all males between the ages of 18 and 65.

If you want to select one subset of cases for one analysis and a different subset of cases for another analysis, you can precede the SELECT IF command with the TEMPORARY command (see Section 3.38).

3.34
SAMPLE Command

The SAMPLE command selects a random sample of cases. To select an approximate percentage of cases, specify a decimal value between 0 and 1, as in:

```
SAMPLE .25.
```

This command samples approximately 25% of the cases in the active system file. When you specify a proportional sample, you usually won't obtain the exact proportion specified. If you know exactly how many cases are in the active file, you can obtain an exact-sized random sample by specifying the number of cases to be sampled from the size of the active file, as in:

```
SAMPLE 60 FROM 200.
```

In this example, the active system file must have exactly 200 cases to obtain a random sample of 60 cases. If the file has fewer than 200 cases, proportionally fewer cases are sampled. If the file has more, the sample is drawn from only the first 200 cases. Note that any SELECT IF commands occurring prior to the SAMPLE command will affect the size of the active system file.

3.35
N OF CASES Command

You can use the N OF CASES command to select the first *n* cases from a file. For example, if you have a data file containing 1,000 cases but want to use only the first 100 cases to test your SPSS commands, specify:

```
N OF CASES  100.
```

If you specify N OF CASES before the first PROCEDURE command, before BEGIN DATA, or in conjunction with any transformation commands, it remains in effect for the remainder of the session. Subsequent N OF CASES commands should specify a smaller number, or they will be ignored.

If you specify N OF CASES between two procedures (with no intervening transformation commands), it acts like a temporary SELECT IF, as in

```
DESCRIPTIVES VARIABLES=SALARY79.
N OF CASES 50.
DESCRIPTIVES VARIABLES=SALARY82.
```

3.36
SPLIT FILE Command

You can use the SPLIT FILE command to split the active system file into subgroups that can be analyzed separately by SPSS.

For example, in analyzing attitudes toward abortion, you may want to perform separate analyses for men and women because you suspect the dimensions are very different for each group. Use the SPLIT FILE command to split the active system file into subgroups of men and women.

Since the active system file should be sorted into the appropriate groups before you specify the SPLIT FILE command, you should precede the SPLIT FILE command with the SORT CASES command (see Chapter 4). For both commands, follow the command with the keyword BY and the name of the grouping variable, as in:

```
SORT CASES BY SEX.
SPLIT FILE BY SEX.
```

This command splits the file according to the values for each case for the variable SEX. SPLIT FILE creates a new subgroup each time it reads a case with a different value for SEX than on the previous case. Thus, if SEX is coded 1 for males and 2 for females, SPLIT FILE creates two subgroups for your analyses, assuming that your cases are sorted by SEX.

You can specify or imply up to eight variables on a SPLIT FILE command. You can use both numeric and string variables (including long string variables). Scratch variables and system variables cannot be used with SPLIT FILE.

For a complete discussion of SPLIT FILE, see the *SPSS Reference Guide*.

3.37
TEMPORARY DATA TRANSFORMATION AND SELECTION

Once specified, most data transformation and selection commands affect all subsequent procedure commands in the SPSS session. You can use the TEMPORARY command to confine the effect of data transformation, data selection, and data definition commands to one procedure, leaving all subsequent procedures unaffected.

3.38
TEMPORARY Command

Use the TEMPORARY command before commands that you want to be in effect only for the next procedure. There are no additional specifications on TEMPORARY. For example, the commands

```
TEMPORARY.
RECODE AGE (18 THRU HI=2) (LO THRU 18=1).
FREQUENCIES VARIABLES=AGE.
DESCRIPTIVES VARIABLES=AGE.
```

temporarily recode AGE into two categories for the FREQUENCIES procedure. The subsequent DESCRIPTIVES procedure is not affected by the temporary RECODE and produces descriptive statistics based on the original AGE values.

The following commands can be specified on a temporary basis following the TEMPORARY command:

- Data transformation commands RECODE, COMPUTE, COUNT, WEIGHT, IF, NUMERIC, and STRING.
- Utility commands DO REPEAT, DO IF, LOOP, and VECTOR.
- Data selection commands SELECT IF, SAMPLE, N OF CASES, and SPLIT FILE.
- Data definition commands VARIABLE LABELS, VALUE LABELS, MISSING VALUES, PRINT FORMATS, WRITE FORMATS, and FORMATS.
- Print and write commands PRINT, PRINT EJECT, PRINT SPACE, and WRITE.

Any combination of the above commands can appear between the TEMPORARY command and a procedure command.

Once you specify a TEMPORARY command, you cannot refer to previously existing scratch variables, and you cannot use the TEMPORARY command inside a DO IF or LOOP structure.

3.39
EXERCISES

1. a. If HOURWAGE is a continuous variable, what is wrong with the following RECODE command:

   ```
   RECODE HOURWAGE
       (LO THRU 5=1) (6 THRU 9=2) (10 THRU 14=3) (15 THRU HI=4).
   ```

   b. How would you correct the problem?

2. If a case has variables VAR2=2, VAR3=3, and VAR4=4, what are the values of variables YA through YE for in each of the following?

   a. `COMPUTE YA = VAR2 + VAR3 * VAR4 - 1.`

   b. `COMPUTE YB = (VAR2 + VAR3) * VAR4 -1.`

   c. `COMPUTE YC = (VAR2 + VAR3) * (VAR4 -1).`

   d. `COMPUTE YD = VAR2 + VAR3 * (VAR4 - 1).`

   e. `COMPUTE YE = VAR2 + (VAR3 * VAR4) -1.`

3. If a case has variables VAR2=2, VAR3=3, and VAR4=4, what are the values for variables YF through YI for each of the following?

   a. `COMPUTE YF = SQRT(VAR4).`

   b. `COMPUTE YG = SUM(VAR2,VAR3,VAR4).`

   c. `COMPUTE YH = MEAN(VAR2,VAR3,VAR4).`

   d. `COMPUTE YI = SQRT(SUM(VAR2,VAR3,VAR4)+7).`

4. Will the following two COMPUTE commands always yield the same result?

```
COMPUTE AVERAGE=MEAN(X1, X2, X3).
```

```
COMPUTE AVERAGE=(X1+X2+X3)/3.
```

5. Correct the syntax errors in the following IF commands:

   a. `IF   (JOBCAT EQ 2,4, OR 6) TRAINEE=1.`

   b. `IF   EDLEVEL LE 12 AND SALNOW LE 10000 THEN LOW=1.`

   c. `IF   (AGE LE 20 OR GE 55) OLDYOUNG=1.`

6. The following set of data transformation commands create variables TRAINEE, ACHIEVER, and LOW. Fill in the values for these variables for the five cases listed in the table.

```
COMPUTE TRAINEE=0.
COMPUTE LOW=0.
IF ANY(JOBCAT,2,4,6) TRAINEE=1.
IF (AGE LE 30 AND SALNOW GE 15000) ACHIEVER=1.
IF (AGE LE 30 AND SALNOW LT 15000) ACHIEVER=0.
IF (AGE GT 30 AND SALNOW GE 25000) ACHIEVER=1.
IF (AGE GT 30 AND SALNOW LT 25000) ACHIEVER=0.
IF RANGE(EDLEVEL,1,12) AND RANGE(SALNOW,1,10000) LOW=1.
```

JOBCAT	AGE	SALNOW	EDLEVEL	TRAINEE	ACHIEVER	LOW
6	28.50	16080	16			
5	40.33	41400	16			
1	54.33	8880	12			
2	32.33	22000	17			
3	30.92	19020	19			

7. a. What is wrong with the following set of commands?

```
SELECT IF SEX EQ 'M'.
FREQUENCIES VARIABLES=SALARY.
SELECT IF SEX EQ 'F'.
FREQUENCIES VARIABLES=SALARY.
```

   b. How would you correct the problem?

SPSS
System Files and
File Management

In this chapter:

Goals:

- To create permanent SPSS system files containing all necessary data definition information.
- To transform system files—reorder cases, group cases together, transpose cases and variables—for different types of analysis.
- To combine two or more SPSS system files.

Examples:

- From a large data file containing information ranging from political opinions to hobbies, select only data related to income, occupation, and income for employed females, aged 18 to 35, and save these data in a new SPSS system file.
- From a file in which each case represents a county, group counties together by state and create a new SPSS system file in which each case is a state.
- Transform spreadsheet-like data by transposing rows and columns.
- Combine pre- and post-test files into one SPSS system file.
- Add additional cases to an existing SPSS system file.

4 SPSS System Files and File Management

4.1
SPSS SYSTEM FILES

Once you have defined your data file in SPSS, you do not need to repeat the data definition process. You can save the data definition information along with the data in an SPSS *system file*. An SPSS system file is a self-documented file containing data and descriptive information. The descriptive information is called the *dictionary*. It contains variable names and locations, variable and value labels, print and write formats, and missing-value indicators.

You can access an SPSS system file in subsequent SPSS sessions or later in the same session without respecifying any of the data definition commands, such as DATA LIST, VARIABLE LABELS, VALUE LABELS, and MISSING VALUES. You can update the system file, altering the descriptive information or modifying the data, and you can save the updated version in a new system file. You can also combine data from two or more files into a single SPSS system file.

4.2
GET Command

The GET command reads a previously created SPSS system file. The only specification required is the FILE subcommand, which identifies the name of the system file you want to use. Additional subcommands RENAME, DROP, and KEEP allow you to tailor the file, and the MAP subcommand displays the results of these subcommands.

When you access an SPSS system file with the GET command, SPSS creates an *active system file*. This file will contain any modifications to the data produced by transformation and procedure commands issued during that session. The active system file exists only for the duration of the SPSS session, unless you save it with the SAVE or XSAVE command (see Section 4.9).

4.3
FILE Subcommand

The FILE subcommand is required and must be the first specification on the GET command. The FILE subcommand is followed by the name of the SPSS system file. For example, the Western Electric data on coronary heart disease (see Chapter 2) are saved in an SPSS system file named ELECTRIC. The command

```
GET FILE=ELECTRIC.
```

retrieves all the variables and descriptive information from the SPSS system file containing the data for the Western Electric study.

4.4
RENAME Subcommand

You can use the RENAME subcommand to change the names of variables in the active system file. The RENAME subcommand is followed by a variable name or variable list followed by an equals sign and a new variable name or variable list enclosed in parentheses, as in:

```
GET FILE=ELECTRIC
 /RENAME (AGE=AGE58) (FAMHXCVR=HISTORY).
```

This could also be specified as:

```
GET FILE=ELECTRIC
 /RENAME (AGE FAMHXCVR=AGE58 HISTORY).
```

The variable lists on both sides of the equals sign must name or imply the same number of variables. You can use the TO keyword to imply consecutive variables on the active system file and to create consecutive new variable names.

4.5
DROP Subcommand

If the SPSS system file contains variables you don't need, you can use the DROP subcommand to omit them from the active system file. For example, the command

```
GET FILE=ELECTRIC
 /DROP=EDUYR DAYOFWK.
```

does not include the two variables EDUYR and DAYOFWK in the active system file.

You can name variables on the DROP subcommand in any order, and you can use the TO keyword to imply consecutive variables on the SPSS system file.

4.6
KEEP Subcommand

If the SPSS system file contains many variables and you only want to use a few, you can use the KEEP subcommand to select a subset of variables, as in:

```
GET FILE=ELECTRIC
 /KEEP=FIRSTCHD DBP58 CHOL58 VITAL10.
```

4.7
MAP Subcommand

You can use the MAP subcommand to keep track of changes you have made in the active system file with the RENAME, DROP, and KEEP subcommands. Figure 4.7 shows the MAP output display after a RENAME subcommand.

Figure 4.7   Output display of MAP after RENAME

```
GET FILE=ELECTRIC
 /RENAME (AGE FAMHXCVR=AGE58 HISTORY)
 /MAP.
```

Result	Input1	Result	Input1
CASEID	CASEID	HT58	HT58
FIRSTCHD	FIRSTCHD	WT58	WT58
AGE58	AGE	DAYOFWK	DAYOFWK
DBP58	DBP58	VITAL10	VITAL10
EDUYR	EDUYR	HISTORY	FAMHXCVR
CHOL58	CHOL58	CHD	CHD
CGT58	CGT58		

4.8
Multiple Subcommands

You can use only one FILE subcommand on the GET command, and it must be the first subcommand specified. You can use multiple RENAME, DROP, KEEP, and MAP subcommands. Each subcommand refers to the results of the previous subcommand. If you rename variables on one subcommand, they must be referred to by their new names on any subsequent subcommands. If you drop variables on one subcommand, they cannot be specified on subsequent subcommands.

4.9
SAVE and XSAVE Commands

The SAVE and XSAVE commands save the active system file as a permanent SPSS system file. The SAVE command is a procedure and reads the data. The XSAVE command is a transformation command and must be followed by a command that reads the data for the system file to actually be created and saved.

The placement of SAVE or XSAVE relative to other commands determines what is saved on the SPSS system file. Variables created or altered by transformations and procedures prior to the SAVE or XSAVE command are saved in their modified form. Results of temporary transformations are also saved if there are no intervening procedure commands.

The only required specification on the SAVE and XSAVE commands is the OUTFILE subcommand identifying the name of the new SPSS system file. Additional subcommands are RENAME, DROP, KEEP, and MAP. The syntax and operation of these subcommands is the same as for the GET command (see Sections 4.4 through 4.7).

4.10
OUTFILE Subcommand

The OUTFILE subcommand must be the first specification following the SAVE or XSAVE command. The OUTFILE subcommand is followed by the name of the new SPSS system file, as in:

```
SAVE OUTFILE=ELECTRIC.
```

If you use the XSAVE command, it must be followed by a procedure for the new SPSS system file to actually be created and saved. If you don't want to use a statistical procedure, you can follow the XSAVE command with the EXECUTE command (see Chapter 5).

4.11
SAVE and XSAVE Compared

Since SAVE is a procedure, the data are read every time a SAVE command is encountered. Since XSAVE is a transformation, the data are not read until a procedure command is encountered. For large files, reading the data can be time-consuming and costly. Whenever SAVE does not need to be the last command in the SPSS session, you can probably save time by using XSAVE instead.

4.12
FILE LABEL Command

Use the FILE LABEL command to provide a descriptive label for your data file. The FILE LABEL is printed on the first line of each page of output and is included in the SPSS system file dictionary. For example, the commands

```
FILE LABEL 'WESTERN ELECTRIC CORONARY HEART DISEASE DATA'.
SAVE OUTFILE=ELECTRIC.
```

save the SPSS system file ELECTRIC with a file label describing the contents of the file.

A file label can be up to 60 characters long. If it is longer, it will be truncated to 60 characters.

4.13
DOCUMENT Command

Use the DOCUMENT command to save a block of text of any length on your SPSS system file, as in:

```
FILE LABEL 'WESTERN ELECTRIC CORONARY HEART DISEASE DATA'.
DOCUMENT THIS FILE CONTAINS DATA ON THE INCIDENCE OF CORONARY
 HEART DISEASE AMONG WESTERN ELECTRIC EMPLOYEES, INCLUDING
 A TEN-YEAR FOLLOW-UP.
SAVE OUTFILE=ELECTRIC.
```

The block of text specified on the DOCUMENT command is saved on the SPSS system file and is available via the DISPLAY command whenever you need a detailed description of the system file.

4.14
DISPLAY Command

The dictionary of an SPSS system file is available at any time via the DISPLAY command for exploring an unfamiliar or forgotten system file or for producing a printed archive document. The DISPLAY command can be used during any SPSS session to display the data definitions in the active system file.

By default, DISPLAY prints an unsorted list of the variables on the active system file. For example, the commands

```
GET FILE=ELECTRIC.
DISPLAY.
```

produce the output shown in Figure 4.14.

Figure 4.14 Display of variable names

```
Currently Defined Variables

CASEID    AGE       EDUYR     CGT58     WT58      VITAL10   FAMHXCVR  CHD
FIRSTCHD  DBP58     CHOL58    HT58      DAYOFWK
```

The following keywords can be specified on the DISPLAY command:

NAMES *Display variable names.* A list of the variables on the active file is displayed. The names are displayed in a compressed format, about eight names across the page, in the order in which they appear on the active system file. This is the default.

DOCUMENTS *Display the text provided by the DOCUMENT command.* No error message is issued if there is no documentary information on the system file.

DICTIONARY *Display complete dictionary information for variables.* Information includes the variable names, labels, sequential position of each variable in the file, print and write formats, missing values, and value labels. Up to 60 characters can be displayed for variable and value labels.

INDEX *Display the variable names and positions.*

VARIABLES *Display the variable names, positions, print and write formats, and missing values.*

LABELS *Display the variable names, positions, and variable labels.*

MACROS *Display a list of the currently defined macros.*

Only one of the above keywords can be specified per DISPLAY command, but you can use as many DISPLAY commands as necessary to obtain the desired information.

4.15
FILE TRANSFORMATION COMMANDS

With SPSS, you can transform your active system file in several ways. You can

• Reorder cases in a file with the SORT CASES command.

• Group cases together and create a new file containing one case for each group with the AGGREGATE command.

• Transpose file rows and columns to correctly read spreadsheet-like data with the FLIP command.

• Automatically recode numeric and string variables to consecutive integer variables with the AUTORECODE command.

4.16
SORT CASES Command

Use the SORT CASES command to reorder the sequence of cases on the active system file. The ability to sort cases based on the value of a specified variable is useful in conjunction with commands such as MATCH FILES and ADD FILES (see Sections 4.27 through 4.34), and SPLIT FILE (see Chapter 3).

The SORT CASES command is followed by the optional keyword BY and the name of the variable to be used to determine the sort order, as in:

```
SORT CASES BY AGE.
```

By default, cases are sorted in ascending order based on the value of the sort variable. In this example, cases with the lowest value for variable AGE will be sorted to the front of the file.

You can specify the default sort order by specifying (A) or (UP) after the variable name, or you can override the default by specifying (D) or (DOWN) for descending order, as in:

```
SORT CASES BY AGE(D).
```

You can also specify multiple sort variables, as in:

```
SORT CASES BY AGE WEIGHT.
```

In this example, cases are sorted by AGE and by WEIGHT within categories of AGE, both in ascending order.

4.17
AGGREGATE Command

Use the AGGREGATE command to group cases together based on the value of a grouping variable and create a new SPSS system file containing one case for each group. The minimum specifications on the AGGREGATE command are the OUTFILE subcommand, which identifies the name of the new SPSS system file to which the aggregated data are written, the BREAK subcommand, which specifies the grouping variable(s), and the definition of at least one new variable based on an aggregate function.

Sections 4.18 through 4.20 give an overview of the AGGREGATE command. For a complete discussion of AGGREGATE, see the *SPSS Reference Guide*.

4.18
OUTFILE Subcommand

The OUTFILE subcommand must be the first specification after the AGGRE-GATE command. OUTFILE is followed by either a filename or an asterisk. To create and save a new system file, specify a filename after OUTFILE, as in:

```
GET FILE=ELECTRIC.
RECODE FIRSTCHD (1=0) (2 THRU 6=1).
AGGREGATE OUTFILE=AGGELEC
 /BREAK=AGE
 /AVWGT=MEAN(WT58) /AVCHOL=MEAN(CHOL58) /AVDBP=MEAN(DBP58)
 /TOTALCHD=SUM(FIRSTCHD).
```

To replace the active system file with the aggregated file, specify an asterisk after OUTFILE, as in:

```
GET FILE=ELECTRIC.
RECODE FIRSTCHD (1=0) (2 THRU 6=1).
AGGREGATE OUTFILE=*
 /BREAK=AGE
 /AVWGT=MEAN(WT58) /AVCHOL=MEAN(CHOL58) /AVDBP=MEAN(DBP58)
 /TOTALCHD=SUM(FIRSTCHD).
```

4.19
BREAK Subcommand

The BREAK subcommand follows the OUTFILE subcommand and specifies the grouping variable(s), as in:

```
GET FILE=ELECTRIC.
RECODE FIRSTCHD (1=0) (2 thru 6=1).
AGGREGATE OUTFILE=AGGELEC
 /BREAK=AGE
 /AVWGT=MEAN(WT58) /AVCHOL=MEAN(CHOL58) /AVDBP=MEAN(DBP58)
 /TOTALCHD=SUM(FIRSTCHD).
```

In this example, AGE is the grouping variable, and all cases with the same value for AGE will be grouped together in one case. You can specify multiple BREAK variables. Each unique combination of values defines a group and generates one case in the aggregated file. Optionally, you can specify (A) or (UP) for ascending order or (D) or (DOWN) for descending order after each BREAK variable. The default is ascending order.

All BREAK variables are saved on the aggregated system file with their existing names and dictionary information.

4.20
Creating AGGREGATE Variables

New variables on the aggregate file are created by applying aggregate functions to existing variables on the active system file. The specification of each new variable is separated by a slash, as in:

```
GET FILE=ELECTRIC.
RECODE FIRSTCHD (1=0) (2 thru 6=1).
AGGREGATE OUTFILE=AGGELEC
 /BREAK=AGE
 /AVWGT=MEAN(WT58) /AVCHOL=MEAN(CHOL58) /AVDBP=MEAN(DBP58)
 /TOTALCHD=SUM(FIRSTCHD).
```

In this example, four new variables are created and saved on the aggregated system file AGGLEC: AVWGT, the mean weight for each age group; AVCHOL, the mean cholesterol count; AVDBP, the mean diastolic blood pressure; and TOTALCHD, the total number of cases of coronary heart disease in each age group.

You must specify at least one new variable based on an aggregate function. The following aggregate functions are available:

SUM(varlist)	*Sum across cases.* Dictionary formats are F8.2.
MEAN(varlist)	*Mean across cases.* Dictionary formats are F8.2.
SD(varlist)	*Standard deviation across cases.* Dictionary formats are F8.2.
MAX(varlist)	*Maximum value across cases.* Complete dictionary information is copied from the source variables to the target variables.
MIN(varlist)	*Minimum value across cases.* Complete dictionary information is copied from the source variables to the target variables.

For a complete list of aggregate functions, see the *SPSS Reference Guide*.

4.21
FLIP Command

SPSS assumes a file structure in which the variables are the columns and the cases are the rows. This is the file structure required to correctly read and analyze your data with SPSS. Sometimes, however, data are recorded in just the opposite fashion: the cases are the columns and each variable is a row. You might find this to be the case with spreadsheet data.

Use the FLIP command to get this kind of file into a structure that can be read correctly by SPSS. FLIP switches the columns and rows of your data. For example, if you have two products, each with quarterly sales, and the data are structured like this:

```
         Q1      Q2      Q3      Q4

PROD1     24      36      78      48
PROD2     39      82      31      49
```

The transposed file after FLIP looks like this:

```
          PROD1     PROD2
Q1         24        39
Q2         36        82
Q3         78        31
Q4         48        49
```

The only required specification on the FLIP command is the command keyword FLIP. By default, SPSS transposes all data in the active system file. The optional VARIABLES subcommand names a subset of variables to be transposed. The optional NEWNAMES subcommand specifies a single variable whose values are used to generate new variable names.

Sections 4.22 and 4.23 give a brief overview of these optional subcommands. For a complete discussion of FLIP, see the *SPSS Reference Guide*.

4.22
VARIABLES Subcommand

By default, FLIP transposes all the data in the file. Use the VARIABLES subcommand to name a specific subset of variables (columns) to be transposed. The specified variables become cases (rows) in the new active system file. If you use the VARIABLES subcommand, any variables not named or implied with the TO keyword are not included in the new active system file. For example, the command

```
FLIP VARIABLES=VAR1 TO VAR4.
```

includes only the variables VAR1 through VAR4 as cases on the transposed system file.

4.23
NEWNAMES Subcommand

By default, SPSS assigns new variable names VAR001 to VARn to the transposed data. Use the NEWNAMES subcommand to specify a single variable on the untransposed file whose values will be used as the new variable names. You can only name one variable on the NEWNAMES subcommand, as in:

```
FLIP NEWNAMES=PRODNO.
```

If the variable specified on NEWNAMES is numeric, its values become character strings beginning with the prefix *V*.

4.24
AUTORECODE Command

When category codes are not sequential, the resulting empty cells reduce performance and increase memory requirements for many procedures. For example, if your data only have values of 1, 3, and 14 for a variable, specifying ANOVA with minimum and maximum values of 1 and 14 uses a lot more memory than specifying minimum and maximum values of 1 and 3. For some procedures, such as MANOVA (see the *SPSS Advanced Statistics User's Guide*), consecutive integer values for factor levels are required.

There are also some procedures that cannot use long string variables. For example, the TABLES procedure (see *SPSS Tables*) cannot tabulate long string variables, and you have to create new short string or numeric variables to take the place of long string variables.

Use the AUTORECODE command to recode values of both string and numeric variables to consecutive integers and assign the modified values to new variables. AUTORECODE is similar to RECODE, except that it *automatically* assigns new values. In addition, AUTORECODE automatically uses the original values as value labels.

4.25
VARIABLES and INTO Subcommands

The minimum specifications on the AUTORECODE command are the subcommands VARIABLES, which specifies the variables to be recoded, and INTO, which names the target variables for the new values, as in:

```
AUTORECODE VARIABLES=VAR1 VAR2 VAR4 TO VAR6
  /INTO NEWVAR1 NEWVAR2 NEWVAR4 TO NEWVAR6.
```

You can use the TO keyword to imply consecutive variables on the active system file on the VARIABLES subcommand and to create new variable names on the INTO subcommand. The number of variables named or implied on the VARIABLES subcommand must equal the number of new variables named or implied on the INTO subcommand.

AUTORECODE stores the new values from variables named on the VARIABLES subcommand in target variables listed on the INTO subcommand. The original variables retain their original values. Variable labels are automatically generated for each new variable. If the original value has a label, that label is used for the new value. If the original value doesn't have a label, the original value is used as the label.

4.26
COMBINING SYSTEM FILES

With SPSS, you can combine information from two or more files into a single active system file. The MATCH FILES command combines files with the same cases but different variables. The ADD FILES command combines files with the same variables but different cases.

4.27
MATCH FILES Command

Use the MATCH FILES command to combine files with the same cases but different variables. In the simplest match, you can combine two or more *parallel files*—files with the same cases in the same order but different variables. For parallel files, the only required specification is the FILE subcommand, which identifies the files to be combined.

Nonparallel files have overlapping sets of cases, with some cases appearing in some files but not in others. For nonparallel files, the required specifications on MATCH FILES are the FILE and BY subcommands.

Optionally, you can specify the subcommands RENAME, DROP, KEEP, and MAP with all three types of files. The syntax and function of these subcommands is the same as for the GET command (see Sections 4.4 through 4.7).

Sections 4.28 through 4.31 give an overview of the MATCH FILES command. For a complete discussion of MATCH FILES, see the *SPSS Reference Guide*.

4.28
FILE Subcommand

FILE is the only required subcommand for parallel matching files. Parallel files contain the same cases in the same order but different variables. For example, you might have pre-test and post-test data for the same group of subjects in different files. You can combine these files with the MATCH FILES command and the FILE subcommand. Each file should be specified on a separate FILE subcommand, separated by a slash, as in:

```
MATCH FILES FILE=BEFORE /FILE=AFTER.
```

You can combine up to 50 SPSS system files. If cases do not appear in the same order on all files to be combined, you can use the SORT CASES command (see Section 4.16) before MATCH FILES, provided each case has a distinctive value for the sort variable, such as a case ID variable.

The variables in the files to be combined do not have to be similar in number or nature. New cases are built by matching cases and simply appending the variables from each file for that case. For example, if file X contains variables A, B, and C, and file Y contains variables D, E, F and G, the command

```
MATCH FILES FILE=X /FILE=Y.
```

creates a new active system file containing the variables A, B, C, D, E, F, and G for each case.

You can specify the active system file on a FILE subcommand with an asterisk, as in:

```
MATCH FILES FILE=X /FILE=Y /FILE=*.
```

4.29
BY Subcommand

For nonparallel files, there are two required subcommands: FILE, which identifies the files to be combined; and BY, which specifies a key variable or variable list for matching cases.

There are two reasons why files may not have a parallel, one-to-one case structure: cases in one file may be missing in another file, or cases may be duplicated in a file. As long as each case can be identified by a key variable or set of variables, you can still use MATCH FILES to combine the files.

Use the BY subcommand to list the key variable(s) that are used to match cases, as in:

```
MATCH FILES FILE=FIRST /FILE=SECOND /BY ID.
```

All files must be sorted in ascending order on the key variables and the key variables must have the same name on each file. If your files are not already sorted, use the SORT CASES command (see Section 4.16) before MATCH FILES.

4.30
IN Subcommand

With nonparallel matching files, if a case is missing from one of the files, all of the variables from that input file will be set to system-missing for that case on the combined resulting file. Use the optional IN subcommand to create a new variable on the resulting file that indicates whether a case was contained on the associated input file. Each IN subcommand applies to the previously named input file on the FILE subcommand. The only specification on the IN subcommand is the name of the new indicator variable, as in:

```
MATCH FILES FILE=FIRST /IN=INFIRST /FILE=SECOND /IN=INSECOND
 /BY ID.
```

The indicator variable named on the IN subcommand has a value of 1 in the combined resulting file for all cases contained in the input file and a value of 0 for any cases not found in the input file.

4.31
RENAME Subcommand

When files are matched, the only variable names that should appear in more than one file are the key variable names used to match cases with the BY subcommand. Other variable names should not appear in more than one file.

Use the optional RENAME subcommand to:

• Change key variable names so they are consistent across all files.

• Change nonunique names for variables not used as keys.

Each RENAME subcommand should follow the FILE subcommand that specifies the file containing the variable(s) to be renamed, as in:

```
MATCH FILES FILE=FIRST /RENAME (GPA=GPA87)
 /FILE=SECOND /RENAME (GPA=GPA88) (IDVAR=CASEID)
 /BY CASEID.
```

In this example, variable GPA from file FIRST is renamed GPA87, and variables GPA and IDVAR from file SECOND are renamed GPA88 and CASEID, respectively.

The syntax for the RENAME subcommand is the same as for the GET command (see Section 4.4).

4.32
ADD FILES Command

Use the ADD FILES command to combine files with the same variables but different cases. For example, you might record the same information for students attending three different schools and maintain the data for each school in a separate file. You can combine these files for analysis with the ADD FILES command.

With ADD FILES, you can either *concatenate* or *interleave* files. Concatenating files simply appends cases from each input file to the combined file. The only required subcommand for concatenating files is the FILE subcommand, which identifies the files to be combined. Interleaving files creates a file sorted by the value of a key variable. Interleaving files requires two subcommands: the FILE subcommand and the BY subcommand, which specifies the key variable(s).

Optional subcommands available with the ADD FILES command include: RENAME, DROP, KEEP and MAP, which have the same syntax and function as for the GET command (see Sections 4.4 through 4.7), and IN, which has the same syntax and function as for the MATCH FILES subcommand (see Section 4.30).

Sections 4.33 and 4.34 give a brief overview of ADD FILES. For a complete discussion of the ADD FILES command, see the *SPSS Reference Guide*.

4.33
FILE Subcommand

To concatenate files—to add cases from one file to the end of another—you need to specify only the FILE subcommand, which identifies the input files to be combined in the resulting file. Each input file requires a separate FILE subcommand, separated by a slash, as in:

```
ADD FILES FILE=SCHOOL1 /FILE=SCHOOL2 /FILE=SCHOOL3.
```

You can specify up to 50 SPSS system files on one ADD FILES command. You can specify the active system file with an asterisk, as in:

```
ADD FILES FILE=SCHOOL1 /FILE=SCHOOL2 /FILE=*.
```

4.34
BY Subcommand

To interleave files—to create a file sorted by the value of a key variable or variables—you need to specify two subcommands: FILE, which identifies the files to be combined; and BY, which specifies the key variable(s). For example, to interleave the data from the three school files by grade, specify:

```
ADD FILES FILE=SCHOOL1 /FILE=SCHOOL2 /FILE=SCHOOL3
/BY GRADE.
```

The key variables must have the same names on each input file, and the files must already be sorted in ascending order by the key variables.

If the input files are not sorted, you can either specify a SORT CASES command before ADD FILES (see Section 4.16) for each unsorted input file—or simply omit the BY subcommand, concatenate the unsorted input files, and specify a SORT CASES command after the ADD FILES command to sort the resulting file into the desired order.

The BY subcommand follows all FILE subcommands and any associated RENAME and IN subcommands.

4.35
SPSS FILE INTERFACES

With SPSS, you can read and write *portable files*, as well as read files created with other statistical software.

Portable files are used to transport SPSS files between computers using different conversions of SPSS and to transport files between SPSS and SPSS/PC+ or other software that uses the same portable file format. Use the EXPORT command to write portable files and the IMPORT command to read portable files.

4.36
EXPORT Command

Use the EXPORT command to create a portable file. The EXPORT command is similar to the SAVE command. It can be specified at the same point in the SPSS session, and it saves the current active system file. As with SAVE, the only required specification on the EXPORT command is the OUTFILE subcommand, which names the portable file, as in:

```
EXPORT OUTFILE=PORTFILE.
```

Optional subcommands include RENAME, DROP, KEEP, and MAP, which have the same syntax and function as for the GET command (see Sections 4.4 through 4.7), and the TYPE and DIGITS subcommands described below.

4.37
TYPE Subcommand

By default, SPSS creates a portable file suitable for transmission via a communications program (TYPE=COMM) and removes all control characters and replaces them with the character 0. If you want to transport portable files via magnetic tape, specify TAPE on the optional TYPE subcommand, as in:

```
EXPORT /TYPE=TAPE /OUTFILE=PORTFILE.
```

4.38
DIGITS Subcommand

You can save space on portable files by using the optional DIGITS subcommand to limit the number of decimals used to represent fractional values. The only specification on the DIGITS subcommand is an integer representing the number of digits of precision. For example, the command

```
EXPORT OUTFILE=PORTFILE /DIGITS=6.
```

will round the number 1.23456789 to 1.234568.

The DIGITS subcommand affects all numbers for which no exact representation is possible with the specified number of digits, so it should be set according to the requirements of the variable that needs the greatest precision.

4.39
IMPORT Command

Use the IMPORT command to read SPSS portable files created with the EXPORT command. The IMPORT command is similar to the GET command. The only required specification is the FILE subcommand which identifies the portable file to be read, as in:

```
IMPORT FILE=PORTFILE.
```

Optional subcommands for the IMPORT subcommand are RENAME, DROP, KEEP, and MAP, which have the same syntax and function as for the GET command (see Sections 4.4 through 4.7), and the TYPE subcommand, which has the same syntax and function as for the EXPORT command.

4.40
Interfacing SPSS with Other Statistical Software

With SPSS, you can also read files created with SCSS, SAS, OSIRIS, and BMDP. See the *SPSS Reference Guide* for information on the GET SCSS, GET SAS, GET OSIRIS, and GET BMDP commands.

4.41
EXERCISES

1. Correct the syntax errors in the following commands:
   a. GET FILE=CARDIAC
      /RENAME (HT58 WT58 AGE58 = HEIGHT WEIGHT).
   b. SAVE FILE=NEWFILE.
   c. AUTORECODE VARIABLES=AGE SEX.

2. What is wrong with the following AGGREGATE command?

```
AGGREGATE OUTFILE=CNTYFILE
 /BREAK=COUNTY.
```

3. Fill in the values for the variable NEWSCALE, based on the following commands:

```
DATA LIST FREE /NAME (A5) SCALE (A6).
BEGIN DATA
Moe High
Larry Medium
Curly Low
END DATA.
AUTORECODE VARIABLES=SCALE /INTO NEWSCALE.
```

```
NAME    SCALE    NEWSCALE
Moe     High        ?
Larry   Medium      ?
Curly   Low         ?
```

4. Write the commands to combine two nonparallel files (files with overlapping cases and different variables) named PRETEST and POSTTEST, using the key variable CASENO. Assume that cases are *not* sorted in the same order on both files.

SPSS
Session Control

In this chapter:

Goals:

- To modify the appearance of SPSS output.
- To override SPSS default settings.
- To document command files and incorporate pre-existing command files in an SPSS session.

Examples:

- Insert your own titles and subtitles on the top of each page of output.
- Modify page width and length settings.
- Change the number of errors allowed before a session is terminated.
- Annotate commands with explanatory comments.
- Create a file of commands you use frequently and include these commands in your SPSS session simply by specifying the name of the command file.

5 SPSS Session Control

SPSS has a wide variety of commands, giving you a great deal of flexibility and control in both your SPSS session and output display. You can specify your own output titles with the TITLE and SUBTITLE commands. You can use the SET command to override many of the SPSS default settings with your own specifications. You can summarize or document command files with the COMMENT command, and you can use the INCLUDE command to incorporate an existing command file into the current session.

5.1
TITLE AND SUBTITLE COMMANDS

SPSS places a heading at the top of each page in a display file. The heading includes the date, a title, and the page number. By default, SPSS assigns a title that indicates the version of the system being used. To specify your own title, use the TITLE command. The title should be enclosed in apostrophes or quotation marks, as in:

```
TITLE 'Western Electric Coronary Heart Disease Study'.
```

If the title includes an apostrophe, enclose the title in quotation marks, as in:

```
TITLE "Western Electric's Coronary Heart Disease Study".
```

Titles can be up to 60 characters long.

The SUBTITLE command specifies a subtitle, which prints beneath the title. The subtitle should be enclosed in parentheses or quotation marks, as in:

```
TITLE 'Western Electric Coronary Heart Disease Study'.
SUBTITLE "Crosstabular Analysis".
```

TITLE and SUBTITLE are independent. You can specify SUBTITLE without specifying TITLE, which will change the subtitle and leave the title unaffected.

5.2
COMMENT COMMAND

Use the COMMENT command to insert comments concerning your SPSS commands. Comments can be a useful tool for summarizing the purpose of your commands. The COMMENT command is followed by any message you want, as in:

```
COMMENT  Create uniform distribution for testing computations.
```

You can substitute an asterisk for the command keyword COMMENT, as in:

```
* Create uniform distribution for testing computations.
```

The comment can be continued for as many lines as necessary.

You can place comments at the end of individual command or subcommand lines by separating the comment from the command with a slash followed by an asterisk, as in:

```
FREQUENCIES VARIABLES=DAYOFWK /* Day of week heart attack occurred.
 /MISSING=INCLUDE /* Include user-defined missing values.
```

5.3
FINISH COMMAND

The FINISH command terminates an SPSS session. The only specification is the command keyword FINISH, as in:

```
FINISH.
```

The FINISH command causes SPSS to stop reading commands and unconditionally ends the session. Placing it within a DO IF structure will not end the session conditionally. Any commands following FINISH are ignored.

5.4
EXECUTE COMMAND

Some SPSS commands are not executed unless they are followed by a procedure that reads the data. Commands that are not executed immediately include PRINT, WRITE, data transformation commands such as COMPUTE and RECODE, and data selection commands such as SELECT IF.

If your command file doesn't include a data-reading procedure or if you want SPSS to read the data and execute commands before the first data-reading procedure, you can instruct SPSS to do so with the EXECUTE command. The only specification on the EXECUTE command is the command keyword EXECUTE. For example, the commands

```
SELECT IF (LNAME EQ 'SMITH').
WRITE OUTFILE=SMITHS /LNAME FNAME.
EXECUTE.
```

select all people with the last name of Smith and writes their last and first names to a file named SMITHS. The EXECUTE command tells SPSS to read the data and execute the preceding SELECT IF and WRITE commands.

5.5
INCLUDE COMMAND

The INCLUDE command enables you to include an SPSS command file in your SPSS session (see Chapter 1). If there is a particular set of commands you use frequently, such as a lengthy set of data transformations, you can put them in a command file and then use the INCLUDE command to incorporate that command file into the command sequence.

The required FILE subcommand indicates the name of the command file to be included in the current session, as in:

```
INCLUDE FILE=TRANSCOM.
```

Commands in an included file must begin in column 1, and continuation lines must be indented at least one column.

You can use multiple INCLUDE commands within a command sequence. You can also create nested INCLUDE commands by specifying additional INCLUDE commands within included files.

5.6
SET AND SHOW
COMMANDS

The SET command allows you to control a variety of SPSS settings, overriding the default specifications. The SHOW command displays the current settings, as well as additional information.

The SET command is followed by a subcommand or list of subcommands indicating the settings to be changed. Each subcommand is followed by an equals sign and a user-specified value, as in:

```
SET BLANKS=0 UNDEFINED=NOWARN MXWARNS=200.
```

The SHOW command is followed by a subcommand or list of subcommands for which you want to know the current settings, as in:

```
SHOW BLANKS UNDEFINED NOWARN.
```

If you specify SHOW without any subcommands, all current settings are displayed.

The subcommands listed below are available with both SET and SHOW. For a complete list of SET and SHOW subcommands, see the *SPSS Reference Guide*. For additional system-specific subcommands, see the SPSS *Operations Guide* for your system.

ENDCMD *Command terminator.* The specification can be any single character.

FORMAT *Default print and write formats for numeric variables created by transformations.* The specification can be any F format.

JOURNAL *Journal file for commands entered during an SPSS session.* The specification is either ON or OFF (alias YES or NO). This determines whether the journal file keeps a log of commands entered during the SPSS session. In addition to ON or OFF, you can also specify the name of the file.

LENGTH *Page length for output.* The specification can be any integer in the range 40 through 999,999 inclusive or NONE to suppress page ejects altogether.

MXERRS *Maximum number of errors permitted before session is terminated.* This setting applies only to command files submitted for execution through the operating system.

MXWARNS *Maximum number of warnings and errors permitted, collectively, before session is terminated.* This setting applies only to command files submitted for execution through the operating system.

PRINTBACK *Printback of SPSS commands in the display file.* The specification is either YES or NO (alias ON or OFF).

SYSMIS *The system-missing value.* SYSMIS can be specified on SHOW only.

UNDEFINED *Warning message for undefined data.* Specifications are WARN and NOWARN. NOWARN suppresses messages but does not alter the count of warnings toward the MXWARNS total.

WEIGHT *The name of the variable used to weight cases.* WEIGHT can be specified on SHOW only.

WIDTH *Maximum page width for the display file.* The specification can be any integer from 80 through 132.

ALL *Display all settings.* Can be specified for SHOW only.

The default specifications for these settings vary between operating systems. Use the SHOW command to display the default settings for your computer system.

5.7
EXERCISES

What is wrong with the following commands?

1. TITLE 'The 1989 Study of Very Important Things'
   +'That Everybody Should Know'.

2. COMPUTE AVERAGE=MEAN(SCORE1, SCORE2, SCORE3) /* THIS COMMAND
   COMPUTES THE MEAN VALUE.

3. SET WIDTH=70.

4. DO IF (CASENUM GT 50).
   FINISH.
   END IF.
   FREQUENCIES VARIABLES=A TO Z.

List

Goals:

- To examine data values in an SPSS system file.
- To review the results of transformation and selection commands.
- To look at data values for individual cases or variables.

Examples

- List the values of all variables in a large data set for the first five cases to verify that the data have been defined and read correctly.
- List all the values for the variables HEIGHT and WEIGHT to see if there are any anomalous values — such as a height of 72 inches and a weight of 90 pounds — that may be the result of coding errors.
- Compute the average bowling score for each player in a league and list the result for every fifth case to make sure the average is being calculated correctly.

6 Listing Cases: Procedure LIST

It is sometimes necessary or useful to review the actual contents of your data. You may want to see that a DATA LIST command is defining your data as you intend, or you may want to verify results of transformations or examine cases you suspect have coding errors. The LIST command allows you to display the values of variables for each case in your data file.

6.1 LIST COMMAND

The LIST procedure displays the values of variables for each case in the active system file in a standard format. It can also display a subset of variables or cases.

The minimum specification on the LIST command is the command keyword LIST. By default, LIST displays all variables on the active system file, using the dictionary print format, as shown in Figure 6.1.

Figure 6.1 Default LIST results

```
DATA LIST FILE=HUBDATA RECORDS=3
  /1 MOHIRED YRHIRED 12-15 DEPT82 19
  /2 SALARY79 TO SALARY82 6-25
  /3 NAME 25-48 (A).
LIST.
```

MOHIRED	YRHIRED	DEPT82	SALARY79	SALARY80	SALARY81	SALARY82	NAME
8	69	3	11180	13000	14300	15600	CONNIE E. JANNSEN
3	80	4	0	8190	8840	10050	MARY CHAFEE
2	74	1	13715	14495	16250	18850	HOLLY C. BRADSHAW
10	78	3	6370	7410	0	8872	JACKIE HAMILTON
7	79	2	0	10140	14300	16250	KARIN HEGEL
6	79	1	0	8450	9750	10920	C. M. BROWN
4	80	4	0	13520	16900	18083	VERA D. LOGGINS
9	79	3	0	8060	8866	9840	LUCINDA JACKSON
4	79	3	7605	8255	9750	12328	ANITA PULASKI
1	74	1	14397	15275	16575	19240	REUBEN D. CROSS

Values for each case are always displayed with a blank space between the variables. If a long string variable cannot be listed within the entire page width, it is truncated.

If all the variables fit on a single line, SPSS displays a heading using the variable name. If the variable name is longer than the variable print format width, SPSS centers numeric variables in the column.

When all variables fit on a line, LIST first tries to reserve columns according to the length of the variable name or the print format width, whichever requires more space. If this format is too wide, LIST reduces column widths by displaying variable names vertically.

6.2 VARIABLES Subcommand

By default, all variables are listed. You can limit the listing to specific variables by naming the variables on the VARIABLES subcommand, as in:

```
LIST VARIABLES=MOHIRED YRHIRED DEPT82 NAME.
```

The specified variables must already exist on the active system file. You cannot specify scratch or system variables. You can use the TO keyword to imply consecutive variables on the active system file, as in:

```
LIST VARIABLES=MOHIRED YRHIRED SALARY79 TO SALARY82 NAME.
```

6.3
CASES Subcommand

Use the CASES subcommand to limit the number and pattern of cases listed. Subcommand CASES must be followed by at least one of the following keywords:

FROM n *The case number of the first case to be listed.* The specification CASES FROM 100 starts listing cases at the 100th sequential case. If LIST is preceded by SAMPLE or SELECT IF, it is the 100th case selected. The default is 1, which means the listing begins with the first selected case.

TO n *Upper limit on the cases to be listed.* The specification CASES TO 1000 limits the listing to the 1000th selected case or the end of the file, whichever comes first. The default is to list cases through the end of the file.

BY n *Increment used to choose cases for listing.* The specification CASES BY 5 lists every fifth selected case. The default is 1, which means every case is listed.

You can specify one, two, or all three of these keywords, as in:

```
LIST VARIABLES=MOHIRED YRHIRED DEPT82 SALARY79 TO SALARY82 NAME
/CASES FROM 50 TO 100 BY 5.
```

6.4
FORMAT Subcommand

Use the following keywords on the FORMAT subcommand to control wrapping and numbering of the case listing:

WRAP *Multiple-line format.* If there is not enough room on the line to display the entire variable list, keyword WRAP wraps the listing in multiple lines per case. SPSS then generates a table indicating which variables appear on each line, and the name of the first variable on each line is displayed in the LIST results to identify the line. WRAP is the default.

SINGLE *Single-line format.* If there is not enough room within the line width, SPSS issues an error message and does not execute the listing. Therefore, use SINGLE only if you want one line per case or nothing.

NUMBERED *Number cases.* If you want LIST to number the cases listed, specify keyword NUMBERED (see Figure 6.4).

UNNUMBERED *Do not number cases.* This is the default.

Figure 6.4   List results with numbered format

```
LIST VARIABLES=MOHIRED YRHIRED DEPT82 SALARY79 TO SALARY82 NAME
/CASES FROM 50 TO 100 BY 5
/FORMAT=SINGLE NUMBERED.
```

```
      MOHIRED YRHIRED DEPT82 SALARY79 SALARY80 SALARY81 SALARY82 NAME

   50     2      70      3     11830    12545    13799    18083  FANNIE SMITH
   55    11      72      1      8222     8742     9509    10239  JOHN C. CAMPBELL
   60     6      81      1     10530    12220    13910    13910  CHARLES P. BLACK
   65    11      77      3     10400    11050    12155    15275  PAULINE LATHAN
   70     4      80      4         0     9750    10790    15608  MAUREEN J. WAYNE
   75     2      80      4         0     8190     9750    11240  POLLY E. CHAN
   80    11      73      2      9750    13000    14430    19500  CAROL BEST
   85    10      78      3      9750    11050    12090    15600  JO C. HOAWINSKI
   90     7      78      1      8112     8619     9379    10241  CLIFFORD KOLB
   95     1      76      1     11050    11050    12350    14300  LINDA YOUNG
  100     9      81      3         0     7020        0     8239  PENNY D. STARK

Number of cases read:  100    Number of cases listed:   11
```

6.5
EXERCISES

1. Find the syntax errors in the following commands:
   a. LIST CASES=10 BY 2.
   b. LIST VARIABLES=$CASENUM LNAME AGE SEX HEIGHT WEIGHT
      /FORMAT=NUMBERED.
   c. LIST VARIABLES=THING1 TO THING5
      /CASES FROM 20 TO 10.

2. Write the SPSS command to list the values for all variables in a file, listing every third case from the first 100 cases. Additionally, instruct SPSS to execute this command only if the entire variable list fits on a single line.

Frequencies

In this chapter:

Goals:

- To summarize how often different values of a variable occur in the data.
- To look for cases with values that have been incorrectly entered or coded.
- To identify values that are far removed from the rest.

Examples:

- Determine how satisfied patrons are with the quality of food at a restaurant.
- Look at the distribution of ages of children enrolled in a recreation program.
- Check for any cases with values that are impossible—for example an adult height of two inches or a satisfaction code of 23 when the valid range is from 1 to 10.
- Identify the lone millionnaire in your sample of social workers, so that you can choose appropriate statistics, which are not unduly affected by outlying values, to describe your data.

How it's done:

A frequency table shows the number of cases with each of the different values of a variable. Besides the actual count for each value, it also contains the percentage of the total number of cases and the percentage of cases with known (non-missing) values. For each value, cumulative percentages, which tell you the percent of cases with smaller or equal values, are also calculated.

The frequency distribution can be graphically displayed with a bar chart or a histogram. The length of the bar indicates the number of cases for each data value (bar chart) or range of values (histogram). Empty spaces in a histogram show value ranges that do not occur in the data.

Data considerations:

Frequency tables and bar charts are useful for variables with a limited number of distinct values. If a variable can have many values, such as weight in pounds, a frequency table or bar chart for each different observed weight may be a poor summary. Instead you may want to use a histogram, which represents ranges of values. A histogram should not be used for variables with no underlying order to the values.

7 Data Tabulation: Procedure FREQUENCIES

Few people would dispute the effects of "rainy days and Mondays" on the body and spirit. It has long been known that more suicides occur on Mondays than other days of the week. Recently an excess of cardiac deaths on Mondays has also been noted (Rabkin et al., 1980). In this chapter we will examine the day of the week on which deaths occurred in the Western Electric Study (see Chapter 4) to see if an excess of deaths occurred on Mondays.

7.1 A FREQUENCY TABLE

A first step in analyzing data on day of death might be to count the number of deaths occurring on each day of the week. Figure 7.1a contains this information.

Figure 7.1a Frequency of death by day of week

```
GET FILE=ELECTRIC.
FREQUENCIES VARIABLES=DAYOFWK.
```

```
DAYOFWK     DAY OF DEATH


                                                      Valid      Cum
       Value Label          Value   Frequency  Percent  Percent  Percent
SUNDAY                        1         19       7.9     17.3     17.3
MONDAY                        2         11       4.6     10.0     27.3
TUESDAY                       3         19       7.9     17.3     44.5
WEDNSDAY                      4         17       7.1     15.5     60.0
THURSDAY                      5         15       6.3     13.6     73.6
FRIDAY                        6         13       5.4     11.8     85.5
SATURDAY                      7         16       6.7     14.5    100.0
MISSING                       9        130      54.2    Missing

                           Total      240     100.0    100.0

Valid cases    110     Missing cases    130
```

Each row of the frequency table describes a particular day of the week. The last row represents cases for which the day of death is not known or that have not died. For the table in Figure 7.1a, there are 110 cases for which day of death is known. The first column *(value label)* gives the name of the day, while the second column contains the *value,* which is the symbol given to the computer to represent the day.

The number of people dying on each day is in the third column *(frequency).* Monday is the least-frequent death day with 11 deaths. These 11 deaths are 4.6% (11/240) of all cases. This *percentage* is in the fourth column. However, of the 240 people, 130 had no day of death. The 11 deaths on Monday are 10.0% of the total deaths for which death days are known (11/110). This *valid percentage* is in the fifth column.

The last column of the table contains the *cumulative percentage.* For a particular day, this percentage is the sum of the valid percentages of that day and all other days that precede it in the table. For example, the cumulative percentage for Tuesday is 44.5, which is the sum of the percentage of deaths that occurred on Sunday, Monday, and Tuesday. It is calculated as

$$\frac{19}{110} + \frac{11}{110} + \frac{19}{110} = \frac{49}{110} = 44.5\%$$

59

Sometimes it is helpful to look at frequencies for a selected subset of cases. Figure 7.1b is a frequency table of day of death for cases who experienced sudden coronary death (FIRSTCHD=2). This is a particularly interesting category since it is thought that sudden death may be related to stressful events such as return to the work environment. In Figure 7.1b there does not appear to be a clustering of deaths on any particular day. Sunday has 22.2% of the deaths, while Thursday has 8.3%. Since the number of sudden deaths in the table is small, the magnitude of the observed fluctuations is not very impressive.

Figure 7.1b   Frequency of sudden cardiac death by day of the week

```
GET FILE=ELECTRIC.
SELECT IF (FIRSTCHD EQ 2).
FREQUENCIES VARIABLES=DAYOFWK.
```

```
DAYOFWK    DAY OF DEATH


                                                          Valid      Cum
     Value Label                Value   Frequency  Percent  Percent   Percent

SUNDAY                            1          8      22.2     22.2     22.2
MONDAY                            2          4      11.1     11.1     33.3
TUESDAY                           3          4      11.1     11.1     44.4
WEDNSDAY                          4          7      19.4     19.4     63.9
THURSDAY                          5          3       8.3      8.3     72.2
FRIDAY                            6          6      16.7     16.7     88.9
SATURDAY                          7          4      11.1     11.1    100.0
                                         -------   ------   ------
                         Total             36     100.0    100.0

Valid cases       36     Missing cases      0
```

7.2
Visual Displays

While the numbers in the frequency table can be studied and compared, it is often useful to present results in a visually interpretable form. Figure 7.2a is a pie chart of the data displayed in Figure 7.1a. Each slice represents a day of the week. The size of the slice depends on the frequency of death for that day. Monday is represented by 10.0% of the pie chart since 10.0% of the deaths for which the day is known occurred on Monday.

Figure 7.2a   Frequency of death by day of the week
(Pie chart from SPSS Graphics)

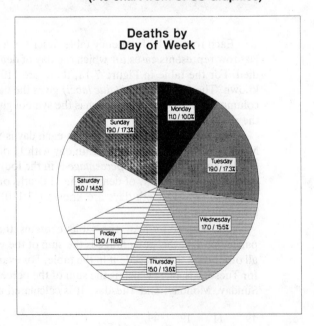

Another way to represent the data is with a bar chart, as shown in Figure 7.2b. There is a bar for each day, and the length of the bar is proportional to the number of deaths observed on that day. At the end of each bar is the number of cases occurring on that day.

Figure 7.2b   Frequency of death by day of the week

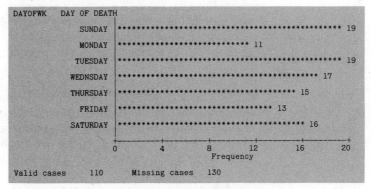

```
GET FILE=ELECTRIC.
FREQUENCIES VARIABLES=DAYOFWK /BARCHART.
```

Only values that actually occur in the data are represented in the bar chart from procedure FREQUENCIES. For example, if no deaths took place on Thursday, no space would be left for Thursday and the bar for Wednesday would be followed by the one for Friday. If you chart the number of cars per family, the bar describing 6 cars may be next to the one for 25 cars if no family has 7 to 24 cars. Therefore, you should pay attention to where categories with no cases may occur.

Although the basic information presented by frequency tables, pie charts, and bar charts is the same, the visual displays enliven the data. Differences among the days of the week are apparent at a glance, eliminating the need to pore over columns of numbers.

7.3
What Day?

Although the number of sudden cardiac deaths is small in this study, the data in Figure 7.1b indicate that the number of deaths on Mondays is not particularly large. In fact, Sunday has the most deaths, slightly over 22%. A recent study of over a thousand sudden cardiac deaths in Rochester, Minnesota, also found a slightly increased incidence of death on weekends for men (Beard et al., 1982). The authors speculate that for men, this might mean "the home environment is more stressful than the work environment." But you should be wary of explanations that are not directly supported by data. It is only too easy to find a clever explanation for any statistical finding. (See Chapter 17 for further analysis of these data.)

7.4
Histograms

A frequency table or bar chart of all values for a variable is a convenient way of summarizing a variable that has a relatively small number of distinct values. Variables such as sex, country, and astrological sign are necessarily limited in the number of values they can have. For variables that can take on many different values, such as income to the penny or weight in ounces, a tally of the cases with each observed value may not be very informative. In the worst situation, when all cases have different values, a frequency table is little more than an ordered list of those values.

Variables that have many values can be summarized by grouping the values of the variables into intervals and counting the number of cases with values within each interval. For example, income can be grouped into $5,000 intervals such as 0–4999, 5000–9999, 10000–14999, and so forth, and the number of observations in each group can be tabulated. Such grouping should be done using SPSS during the actual analysis of the data. As indicated in Chapter 2, the values for variables should be entered into the data file in their original, ungrouped form.

A histogram is a convenient way to display the distribution of such grouped values. Consider Figure 7.4, which is a histogram for body weight in pounds of the sample of 240 men from the Western Electric Study. The first column indicates the number of cases with values within the interval, while the second column gives the midpoint, or middle value, for the interval. Each row of asterisks represents the number of cases with values in the interval. For example, the second row of the histogram has 10 asterisks, which represent 10 men who weighed between 130 and 140 pounds in 1958. The number of cases represented by each asterisk depends on the size of the sample and the maximum number of cases falling into an interval. For each histogram, the number of cases represented by an asterisk is printed on the top of the figure. Intervals that have no observations are included in the histogram but no asterisks are printed. This differs from a bar chart, which does not leave space for the empty categories.

A histogram can be used in any situation in which it is reasonable to group adjacent values. Histograms should not be used to display variables in which there is no underlying order to the values. For example, if 100 different religions are arbitrarily assigned codes of 1 to 100, grouping values into intervals is meaningless. Either a bar chart or a histogram in which each interval corresponds to a single value should be used to display such data.

Figure 7.4   A histogram of body weight

```
GET FILE=ELECTRIC.
FREQUENCIES VARIABLES=WT58
 /HISTOGRAM MIN(120) MAX(280) INCREMENT(10).
```

```
WT58        BODY WEIGHT, 1958 -- LBS

    Count    Midpoint    One symbol equals approximately  1.00 occurrence

        5     125.00   *****
       10     135.00   **********
       20     145.00   ********************
       36     155.00   ************************************
       43     165.00   *******************************************
       39     175.00   ***************************************
       31     185.00   *******************************
       19     195.00   *******************
       15     205.00   ***************
        9     215.00   *********
       10     225.00   **********
        1     235.00   *
        0     245.00
        1     255.00   *
        0     265.00
        1     275.00   *
                       I....+....I....+....I....+....I....+....I....+....I
                       0        10       20       30       40       50
                                     Histogram frequency

Valid cases    240    Missing cases    0
```

Frequency tables, bar charts, and histograms can serve purposes other than summarizing data. Unexpected codes in the tables may indicate errors in data entry or coding. Cases with death days coded as 0 or 8 are in error if the numbers 1 through 7 represent the days of the week and 9 stands for unknown. Since errors in the data should be eliminated as soon as possible, it is a good idea to run frequency tables as the first step in analyzing data.

Frequency tables and visual displays can also help you identify cases with values that are unusual but possibly correct. For example, a tally of the number of cars in families may show a family with 25 cars. Although such a value is possible, especially if the survey did not specify cars in working condition, it raises suspicion and should be examined to ensure that it is really correct.

Incorrect data values distort the results of statistical analyses, and correct but unusual values may require special treatment. In either case, early identification is valuable.

7.6
RUNNING PROCEDURE FREQUENCIES

Procedure FREQUENCIES produces frequency tables, histograms, and bar charts for numeric variables and frequency tables and bar charts for string variables. Additionally, you can obtain percentiles and univariate summary statistics. (See Chapter 8 for examples of percentiles and summary statistics produced with FREQUENCIES.) The EXAMINE procedure (see Chapter 9) provides additional facilities for describing and displaying variables.

The only required subcommand on FREQUENCIES is the VARIABLES subcommand, which specifies the variables to be analyzed. Subcommands can be named in any order and are separated from each other by a slash. With the exception of PERCENTILES and NTILES, each subcommand can be used only once per FREQUENCIES command.

7.7
VARIABLES Subcommand

The VARIABLES subcommand names the variables to be analyzed. FREQUENCIES sets up one cell for each unique value encountered in the data. For example, the following command produced the output in Figure 7.1a:

```
FREQUENCIES  VARIABLES=DAYOFWK.
```

The variable and value labels are printed, followed by the value and the number of cases that have the value. The percentage is based on all the observations, and the valid and cumulative percentages are based on those cases that have valid values. The number of valid and missing observations is also provided. FREQUENCIES tabulates any type of variable, including numeric variables with decimal positions and string variables.

You can use the keyword ALL to name all the variables on the active system file or the keyword TO to refer to a set of consecutive variables on the file.

Optionally, you can specify a range of values in parentheses after each variable or variable list. The command

```
FREQUENCIES VARIABLES=DAYOFWK(2,6).
```

only includes cases with values of 2 through 6 in the frequency table for DAYOFWK. If you specify a range, you must do so for every variable listed on the VARIABLES subcommand. The command

```
FREQUENCIES VARIABLES=THING1 THING2 (1,4).
```

uses the value range 1 through 4 for both THING1 and THING2. The command

```
FREQUENCIES VARIABLES=THING1(1,4) THING2.
```

generates an error message and the command is not executed.

7.8
FORMAT Subcommand

The FORMAT subcommand allows you to control the formatting of tables and the order in which values are sorted within the table, suppress tables, produce an index of tables, and write the FREQUENCIES display to another file. FORMAT applies to all variables named on the VARIABLES subcommand.

Specify as many formatting options as desired on the FORMAT subcommand. For example,

```
FREQUENCIES  VARIABLES=POLVIEWS PRESTIGE
/FORMAT=ONEPAGE DVALUE LIMIT(25).
```

specifies conditional condensed formatting of the tables (keyword ONEPAGE) with values sorted in descending order (keyword DVALUE) and will not display frequency tables for variables with more than 25 categories (keyword LIMIT).

7.9
Table Formats

The following keywords on the FORMAT subcommand control the formatting of tables:

NOLABELS *Suppress variable and value labels.* By default, FREQUENCIES displays variable and value labels defined by the VARIABLE LABELS and VALUE LABELS commands.

DOUBLE *Double-space frequency tables.*

NEWPAGE *Begin each table on a new page.* By default, FREQUENCIES displays as many tables on a page as fit.

CONDENSE *Use condensed format.* This format displays frequency counts in three columns. It does not display value labels and percentages for all cases, and it rounds valid and cumulative percentages to integers.

ONEPAGE *Use conditional condensed format.* Keyword ONEPAGE uses the condensed format for tables that would require more than one page with the default format. All other tables are displayed in default format. If you specify both CONDENSE and ONEPAGE, all tables are displayed in condensed format.

7.10
Order of Values

By default, frequency tables are displayed in ascending order of values. You can override this order with one of three sorting options on the FORMAT subcommand:

AFREQ *Sort categories in ascending order of frequency.*

DFREQ *Sort categories in descending order of frequency.*

DVALUE *Sort categories in descending order of values.*

7.11
Suppressing Tables

You might use FREQUENCIES to obtain univariate statistics not available in other procedures or to display histograms or bar charts, and thus may not be interested in the frequency tables themselves. Or you might want to suppress tables for variables with a large number of values. Two options are available for suppressing tables:

LIMIT(n) *Do not display tables with more categories than the specified value.*

NOTABLE *Suppress all frequency tables.*

If you specify both NOTABLE and LIMIT, NOTABLE overrides LIMIT and no tables are displayed.

7.12
Index of Tables

To obtain both a positional index of frequency tables and an index arranged alphabetically by variable name, use the INDEX keyword on the FORMAT subcommand.

INDEX *Index of tables.*

7.13
Bar Charts and Histograms

You can request bar charts or histograms with the FREQUENCIES command. Use the BARCHART subcommand to produce bar charts (Section 7.2) for all variables named on the VARIABLES subcommand and the HISTOGRAM subcommand to produce histograms (Section 7.4) for all variables. Use the HBAR subcommand to produce bar charts for variables that will fit on one page and histograms for other variables. You can specify only one of these three subcommands on each FREQUENCIES command. If you specify more than one, FREQUENCIES assumes HBAR.

7.14
BARCHART Subcommand

No specifications are required on the BARCHART subcommand. In the default bar chart format, all tabulated values are plotted, and the horizontal axis is scaled in frequencies. The scale is determined by the frequency count of the largest single category plotted. For example, the following commands produced Figure 7.2b:

```
FREQUENCIES VARIABLES=DAYOFWK
 /BARCHART.
```

Available formatting options are:

MIN(n)   *Lower bound.* Values below the specified minimum are not plotted.

MAX(n)   *Upper bound.* Values above the specified maximum are not plotted.

PERCENT(n)   *Horizontal axis scaled in percentages.* The *n* specifies the preferred maximum and is not required. If you do not specify an *n* or your *n* is too small, FREQUENCIES chooses 5, 10, 25, 50 or 100, depending on the percentage for the largest category.

FREQ(n)   *Horizontal axis scaled in frequencies.* While FREQ is the default scaling method, you can use this keyword to specify a maximum frequency *(n)* for the scale. If you do not specify an *n* or your *n* is too small, FREQUENCIES chooses 10, 20, 50, 100, 200, 500, 1000, 2000, and so forth, depending on the frequency count for the largest category.

You can enter optional specifications in any order, as in

```
FREQUENCIES  VARIABLES=SIBS
 /BARCHART=PERCENT MAX(10).
```

which requests a bar chart for SIBS with values through 10 plotted and the horizontal axis scaled in percentages.

7.15
HISTOGRAM Subcommand

No specifications are required on the HISTOGRAM subcommand. In the default histogram format, all tabulated values are included, and the horizontal axis is scaled in frequencies. The scale is determined by the frequency count of the largest category plotted. The number of intervals plotted is 21 (or fewer if the range of values is less than 21).

You can use all of the formatting options available with BARCHART (MIN, MAX, PERCENT, and FREQ) on the HISTOGRAM subcommand. In addition, you can specify the interval width and superimpose a normal curve on the histogram:

INCREMENT(n)   *Interval width.* By default, values are collected into 21 intervals for plotting. You can override the default by specifying the actual interval width. For example, if a variable ranges from 1 to 100 and you specify INCREMENT(2), the width of each interval is 2, producing 50 intervals.

NORMAL   *Superimpose the normal curve.* The normal curve is based on all valid values for the variable and includes values excluded by MIN and MAX. The default is NONORMAL.

You can enter the optional specifications in any order. For example, the following commands produced Figure 7.4:

```
FREQUENCIES VARIABLES=WT58
 /HISTOGRAM MIN(120) MAX(280) INCREMENT(10).
```

7.16
HBAR Subcommand

The HBAR subcommand produces either bar charts or histograms, depending upon the number of values encountered in the data. If a bar chart for a variable fits on a page, HBAR produces a bar chart; otherwise, it produces a histogram. All specifications for HISTOGRAM and BARCHART also work with HBAR.

7.17
Percentiles and Ntiles

You can use either the PERCENTILES or NTILES subcommands to display percentiles for all variables specified on the VARIABLES subcommand. If two or more PERCENTILES and NTILES subcommands are specified, FREQUENCIES displays one table with the values for all requested percentiles.

If a requested percentile cannot be calculated, SPSS displays a period (.) as the value associated with that percentile.

7.18
PERCENTILES Subcommand

Percentiles are the values below which a given percentage of cases fall. Use the PERCENTILES subcommand followed by a list of percentiles between 0 and 100 to display the values for each percentile. For example, to request the values for percentiles 10, 25, 33.3, 66.7, and 75 for variable PRESTIGE, specify:

```
FREQUENCIES  VARIABLES=PRESTIGE
 /PERCENTILES=10 25 33.3 66.7 75.
```

7.19
NTILES Subcommand

*N*tiles are the values that divide the sample into groups of equal numbers of cases. To display the values for each *n*tile, use the NTILES subcommand followed by an integer value specifying the number of subgroups. For example, to request quartiles for PRESTIGE, specify:

```
FREQUENCIES VARIABLES=PRESTIGE /NTILES=4.
```

SPSS displays one less percentile than the number specified on the NTILES subcommand, since, for example, you only need two values to divide a group into three parts.

7.20
STATISTICS Subcommand

The STATISTICS subcommand specifies univariate statistics for all variables named on the VARIABLES subcommand.

MEAN   *Mean.* The arithmetic average.

SEMEAN   *Standard error of the mean.* A measure of variability of the sample mean.

MEDIAN   *Median.* The median is defined as the value below which half the cases fall. If there is an even number of cases, the median is the average of the (nth/2) and (nth/2+1) cases when the cases are sorted in ascending order. The median is not available if you specify AFREQ or DFREQ on the FORMAT subcommand.

MODE   *Mode.* The most frequently occurring value. If several values are tied for the highest frequency, only the smallest value is displayed.

STDDEV   *Standard deviation.* A measure of how much observations vary from the mean, expressed in the same units as the data.

VARIANCE	*Variance.* The same as standard deviation, but expressed in squared units.
SKEWNESS	*Skewness.* (See Chapter 8.)
SESKEW	*Standard error of the skewness statistic.*
KURTOSIS	*Kurtosis.* (See Chapter 8.)
SEKURT	*Standard error of the kurtosis statistic.*
RANGE	*Range.* The difference between the largest and smallest values.
MINIMUM	*Minimum.*
MAXIMUM	*Maximum.*
SUM	*Sum.*
DEFAULT	*Mean, standard deviation, minimum, and maximum.* You can use DE-FAULT jointly with other statistics.
ALL	*All available statistics.*
NONE	*No statistics.*

You can specify as many keywords as you wish on the STATISTICS subcommand. For example,

```
FREQUENCIES  VARIABLES=PRESTIGE POLVIEWS
 /STATISTICS=MEDIAN DEFAULT.
```

displays the median and the default statistics (the mean, standard deviation, minimum, and maximum). If you use the STATISTICS subcommand with no specifications, the default statistics are displayed.

7.21
MISSING Subcommand

FREQUENCIES recognizes three types of missing values: user-missing, system-missing, and, if you specify a value range for variables on the VARIABLES subcommand, out-of-range values. Both user- and system-missing values are included in frequency tables. They are labeled as missing and are not included in the valid and cumulative percentages. Missing values are not used in the calculation of descriptive statistics, nor do they appear in bar charts and histograms.

To treat user-missing values as valid values, use the MISSING subcommand, which has one specification, INCLUDE. For example,

```
MISSING VALUES  SATFAM TO HAPPY(8,9)
FREQUENCIES  VARIABLES=SATFAM HAPPY (0,9)
 /BARCHART
 /MISSING=INCLUDE.
```

includes values 8 and 9 (which were previously defined as missing with the MISSING VALUES command) in the bar charts.

7.22
Annotated Example

The following commands produce the output in Figure 7.4:

```
GET FILE=ELECTRIC.
FREQUENCIES VARIABLES=WT58
 /FORMAT=NOTABLE
 /HISTOGRAM MIN(120) MAX(280) INCREMENT(10).
```

- The GET command specifies the SPSS file (ELECTRIC) to be read.
- The FREQUENCIES command requests frequencies for the variable WT58.
- The FORMAT subcommand suppresses the frequency table.
- The HISTOGRAM subcommand requests a histogram with a lower boundary value of 120 and an upper boundary value of 280, grouped in interval widths of 10.

7.23
EXERCISES

Syntax

1. Given the following command, which of the statements below are true?

```
FREQUENCIES
  FORMAT=NO TABLE
  /VARIABLES=FIRSTCHD DAYOFWK
  /BARCHART.
```

   a. The slashes are misplaced.
   b. Blanks must be inserted around the equals signs.
   c. The keyword specifying no frequency table is misspelled.
   d. The subcommands must begin on the same command line as the FREQUEN-CIES command.
   e. Variables FIRSTCHD and DAYOFWK must be separated by a comma.
   f. Variables FIRSTCHD and DAYOFWK are specified in the wrong order.
   g. Two frequency tables are requested by this command.
   h. Two bar charts are requested by this command.

2. Which command below created the following bar chart:

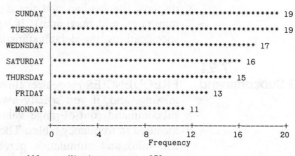

```
   SUNDAY |************************************************* 19
  TUESDAY |************************************************* 19
 WEDNSDAY |******************************************* 17
 SATURDAY |***************************************** 16
 THURSDAY |************************************** 15
   FRIDAY |********************************* 13
   MONDAY |**************************** 11
          +---------+---------+---------+---------+---------+
          0         4         8        12        16        20
                                    Frequency
Valid cases     110      Missing cases     130
```

   a. FREQUENCIES VARIABLES=DAYOFWK/FORMAT=DFREQ/MISSING=INCLUDE.
   b. FREQUENCIES VARIABLES=DAYOFWK/FORMAT=DFREQ/BARCHART/MISSING=INCLUDE.
   c. FREQUENCIES VARIABLES=DAYOFWK/FORMAT=DFREQ/BARCHART.

3. Consider the following section of SPSS output:

```
   2  0          GET FILE=CARDIAC.

FILE CALLED CARDIAC :
  LABEL:
  CREATED 21 JAN 83 10:33:47      14 VARIABLES

   3  0          FREQUENCIES VARIABLES=WEEKDAY.

>ERROR    701 LINE   3, COLUMN 25, TEXT: WEEKDAY
>Undefined variable name, or a scratch or system variable was specified in a
>variable list which accepts only standard variables.  Check spelling, verify
>the existence of this variable.
>THIS COMMAND NOT EXECUTED.
```

   Which of the following problems could have caused the error message?
   a. The syntax of the FREQUENCIES command is in error and SPSS cannot recognize the variable named.
   b. The file specified on the GET command does not exist.
   c. The file found is not an SPSS system file.
   d. The variable named does not exist on the system file.

4. Correct the following commands:
   a. FREQUENCIES BARCHART VARIABLES=DAYOFWK.
   b. FREQUENCIES VARIABLES=DAYOFWK /FIRSTCHD /BARCHART.
   c. FREQUENCIES VARIABLES=FIRSTCHD,DAYOFWK /NOTABLE /HISTOGRAM.
   d. FREQUENCIES MISSING=INCLUDE /HISTOGRAM=FIRSTCHD.

5. Write a FREQUENCIES command that produces histograms for HT58 and WT58. Suppress the frequency tables.

6. Given variables NAME, AGE, and SEX from a random sample of the people who attended a film about Vietnam during its opening week:
   a. Can you test the hypothesis that men are more interested in films about Vietnam than are women?
   b. Can you test the hypothesis that most people interested in films about Vietnam are between the ages of 30 and 50?
   c. Can you represent the hypothesis in (b) with a bar chart?

Statistical Concepts

1. For each of the following variables, which is more appropriate: a histogram or a bar chart?
   a. Race.
   b. Sex.
   c. Age.
   d. Weight.
   e. Political party membership.
   f. Yearly income.
   g. Number of children in family.

2. Which of these statements are true for frequency tables?
   a. Valid percentages must sum to 100.
   b. Percentages must sum to 100.
   c. Valid percentages are never greater than total percentages.
   d. The values for cumulative percentage can decrease.
   e. Cumulative percentages must sum to the total sample size.
   f. Missing values are excluded from the computation of valid percentages.

3. Below is a frequency table for a hypothetical variable. Fill in the missing frequencies and percentages.

VALUE LABEL	VALUE	FREQUENCY	PERCENT	VALID PERCENT	CUM PERCENT
	1	23		47.9	
	2		24.0	25.0	
	3	10	20.0		93.8
	4	3	6.0	6.3	
MISSING	9	2		MISSING	
TOTAL		50	100.0	100.0	

4. Below are three histograms for diastolic blood pressure. Which do you think provides the best summary of the data and why?

a.

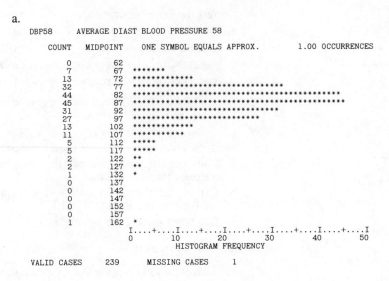

```
DBP58      AVERAGE DIAST BLOOD PRESSURE 58

   COUNT   MIDPOINT   ONE SYMBOL EQUALS APPROX.        1.00 OCCURRENCES

     0       62
     7       67    *******
    13       72    *************
    32       77    ********************************
    44       82    ********************************************
    45       87    *********************************************
    31       92    *******************************
    27       97    ***************************
    13      102    *************
    11      107    ***********
     5      112    *****
     5      117    *****
     2      122    **
     2      127    **
     1      132    *
     0      137
     0      142
     0      147
     0      152
     0      157
     1      162    *
                   I....+....I....+....I....+....I....+....I....+....I
                   0        10        20        30        40        50
                              HISTOGRAM FREQUENCY

   VALID CASES    239    MISSING CASES    1
```

b.

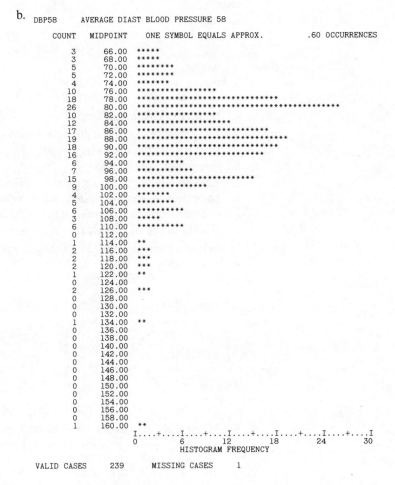

```
DBP58      AVERAGE DIAST BLOOD PRESSURE 58

   COUNT   MIDPOINT   ONE SYMBOL EQUALS APPROX.         .60 OCCURRENCES

     3      66.00   *****
     3      68.00   *****
     5      70.00   ********
     5      72.00   ********
     4      74.00   *******
    10      76.00   *****************
    18      78.00   *******************************
    26      80.00   *********************************************
    10      82.00   ****************
    12      84.00   ********************
    17      86.00   ****************************
    19      88.00   ********************************
    18      90.00   ******************************
    16      92.00   ***************************
     6      94.00   **********
     7      96.00   ***********
    15      98.00   *************************
     9     100.00   ***************
     4     102.00   *******
     5     104.00   ********
     6     106.00   **********
     3     108.00   *****
     6     110.00   **********
     0     112.00
     1     114.00   **
     2     116.00   ***
     2     118.00   ***
     2     120.00   ***
     1     122.00   **
     0     124.00
     2     126.00   ***
     0     128.00
     0     130.00
     0     132.00
     1     134.00   **
     0     136.00
     0     138.00
     0     140.00
     0     142.00
     0     144.00
     0     146.00
     0     148.00
     0     150.00
     0     152.00
     0     154.00
     0     156.00
     0     158.00
     1     160.00   **
                   I....+....I....+....I....+....I....+....I....+....I
                   0        6        12        18        24        30
                              HISTOGRAM FREQUENCY

   VALID CASES    239    MISSING CASES    1
```

c.
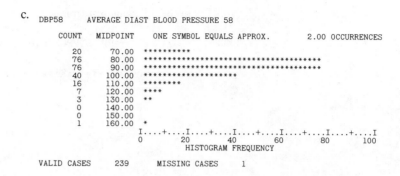

```
DBP58        AVERAGE DIAST BLOOD PRESSURE 58

     COUNT    MIDPOINT    ONE SYMBOL EQUALS APPROX.        2.00 OCCURRENCES
       20      70.00   **********
       76      80.00   **************************************
       76      90.00   **************************************
       40     100.00   ********************
       16     110.00   ********
        7     120.00   ****
        3     130.00   **
        0     140.00
        0     150.00
        1     160.00   *
                       I....+....I....+....I....+....I....+....I....+....I
                       0        20       40       60       80      100
                                     HISTOGRAM FREQUENCY

     VALID CASES    239      MISSING CASES    1
```

5. Fill in the missing counts and midpoints in following histogram:

```
HT58        STATURE, 1958 -- TO NEAREST 0.1 INCH

     COUNT    MIDPOINT    ONE SYMBOL EQUALS APPROX.  1.00  OCCURRENCES


        0        59
                 60
        1        61    *
        0
                 63    ***
        8        64    ********
                 65    ************
                 66    *************************
       32        67    *******************************
                 68    *******************************************************
       29        69    ******************************
                       ***************************
                 71    *********************
                 72    **************
        8        73    ********
                 74    ******
        3        75    ***
        1        76    *
        1              *
        0        78
        0        79

                 I....+....I....+....I....+....I....+....I....+....I....+....I
                 0        10       20       30       40       50

                             HISTOGRAM FREQUENCY

     VALID CASES     240      MISSING CASES      0
```

6. The following data represent the number of periodicals read by 25 college students:
   1, 1, 1, 1, 1, 1, 2, 2, 2, 3, 3, 3, 3, 3, 3, 4, 4, 5, 5, 5, 5, 8, 9, 9, 10.
   a. Fill in the following frequency table:

VALUE LABEL	VALUE	FREQUENCY	PERCENT	VALID PERCENT	CUM PERCENT
	1.00				
	2.00				
	3.00				
	4.00				
	5.00				
	8.00				
	9.00				
	10.00				
		-------	-------	-------	
	TOTAL	25	100.0	100.0	

b. Fill in the following histogram:

```
COUNT      VALUE    ONE SYMBOL EQUALS APPROX.      .20  OCCURRENCES

  6        1.00    ******************************


           4.00
           5.00


           8.00
  1       10.00    *****
                   I.........I.........I.........I.........I.........I
                   0         2         6                            10
```

                                          HISTOGRAM FREQUENCY

c. Fill in the following bar chart:

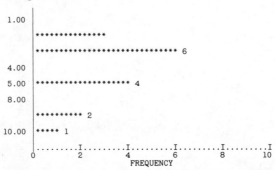

```
          1.00 |
               |***************
               |********************************** 6
          4.00 |
          5.00 |******************** 4
          8.00 |
               |********** 2
         10.00 |***** 1
               |.........I.........I.........I.........I.........I
               0         2         4         6         8        10
                                      FREQUENCY
```

d. Which is more appropriate for summarizing the data: the histogram or the bar chart?

e. Run an SPSS job to produce the frequency table, histogram, and bar chart.

7. Which of the following statements about SPSS histograms and bar charts are correct?

a. For variables like AGE in years, a bar chart is preferable to a histogram since it has a bar for each value.

b. A bar chart includes bars for values that have not been observed in the data.

c. A histogram is useful for variables like place of birth, religious preference, and astrological sign since adjacent values (codes) may be grouped together.

d. A bar chart of weights may take up many pages of output.

8. A manufacturer of automobiles recorded the zip codes of people who bought cars during a particular sale. He asked a marketing-research specialist to analyze the information for him. The analyst returned with a histogram of zip codes. Explain to the manufacturer how these results should be interpreted.

9. For which of the following variables would cumulative percents be readily interpretable?

a. Years of education completed

b. Attitude toward federal spending

c. Number of days of work missed in a year

d. Favorite color

e. Breed of dog owned

10. Describe five variables for which you would not construct a frequency table.

11. Describe five variables for which you would not make a histogram.

Data Analysis

1. Choose one of the files from Appendix B. For which variables on the file are frequency tables and bar charts appropriate?

2. a. For three variables of your choice, obtain bar charts and frequency tables. On the output, indicate how the entries of the frequency tables are calculated.

   b. For one of the variables selected in Question 2.a, obtain a histogram. Use the NOTABLE option to suppress printing of the frequency table. (Note that both histograms and bar charts cannot be obtained for the same variable on one FREQUENCIES command.) Describe the differences between the bar charts and histograms.

   c. Rerun one of the bar charts for a variable with missing values with the MISSING=INCLUDE subcommand. Compare the two bar charts and indicate under what circumstances you might want to include missing values in a bar chart.

3. Using the BANK system file, prepare frequency tables and bar charts for the distributions of the sex, race, education, and job category variables. Write a paragraph describing these characteristics of the sample.

4. Using the BANK system file, do the following:

   a. Obtain a histogram for the age variable.

   b. Explain why you would not want to obtain a bar chart for age.

   c. Rerun the histogram in (a) using specifications which will result in midpoints of 25, 35, 45, and so forth.

5. Using the Western Electric data file:

   a. Obtain a frequency table, bar chart, and histogram for the number of cigarettes smoked per day in 1958 (CGT58). Discuss the advantages and disadvantages of the different summaries.

   b. Obtain a frequency table for the type of first CHD event (FIRSTCHD). Discuss the meaning of the cumulative percent column for the table.

   c. Obtain histograms for the years of education (EDUYR) and the serum cholesterol (CHOL58) variables. Make sure to suppress the frequency tables for these two variables.

Descriptive Statistics

In this chapter:

Goals:

- To summarize the distribution of a variable by computing measures of central tendency and dispersion.
- To position a case in a distribution by calculating a percentile or standard score value.
- To compare an observed distribution to the normal distribution.

Examples:

- Determine the average number of cans of soda consumed by a teenager in a week.
- Look at the variability in the number of hours of television viewed by third graders.
- Determine the income levels that divide the cases into four equal groups.
- Determine how well a student scored on an exam by calculating how many standard deviation units above or below the mean his score is.

How it's done:

Commonly used measures of central tendency are the mode (the most frequently occurring value), the median (the value above which and below which half of the cases fall), the arithmetic mean, or average (the sum of the values for all of the cases divided by the number of cases).

Variability of the data values can be measured using the range (the difference between the largest and smallest values), the variance (the sum of the squared differences from the mean, divided by the number of cases minus one), and the standard deviation (the square root of the variance).

Percentiles are values below which a certain percentage of cases fall. A standard score for a case is calculated by subtracting the mean from the observed value and dividing by the standard deviation.

Data considerations:

The mode is an appropriate measure of central tendency for variables measured on a nominal scale. The median can be used for data measured on ordinal, interval and ratio scales. The mean is most useful for data measured on interval and ratio scales, unless there are extreme data values. Variances, percentiles and standard scores cannot be used for nominal data.

8 Descriptive Statistics: Procedure DESCRIPTIVES

Survey data that rely on voluntary information are subject to many sources of error. People deliberately distort the truth, inadvertently fail to recall events correctly, or refuse to participate. Refusals influence survey results by failing to provide information about a particular type of person—one who refuses to answer surveys at all or avoids certain types of questions. For example, if college graduates tend to be unwilling to answer polls, results of surveys will be biased.

One possible way to examine the veracity of responses is to compare them to official records. Systematic differences between the two sources jeopardize the usefulness of the survey. Unfortunately, for many sensitive questions such as illicit drug use, abortion history, or even income, official records are usually unavailable.

Wyner (1980) examined the differences between the true and self-reported numbers of arrests obtained from 79 former heroin addicts enrolled in the Vera Institute of Justice Supported Employment Experiment. As part of their regular quarterly interviews, participants were asked about their arrest histories in New York City. The self-reported value was compared to arrest record data coded from New York City Police Department arrest sheets. The goal of the study was not only to quantify the extent of error but also to identify factors related to inaccurate responses.

8.1
EXAMINING THE DATA

Figure 8.1a shows histograms for the three variables—true number of arrests, reported arrests, and the discrepancy between the two. From a histogram it is possible to see the *shape* of the distribution, that is, how likely the different values are, how much spread or *variability* there is among the values, and where typical values are concentrated. Such characteristics are important because of the direct insight they provide into the data and because many statistical procedures are based on assumptions about the underlying distributions of variables.

Figure 8.1a   Reported and true arrests

```
FREQUENCIES VARIABLES=ACTUAL SELF
 /FORMAT=NOTABLE /HISTOGRAM MIN(0) INCREMENT(2).
FREQUENCIES VARIABLES=ERRORS
 /FORMAT=NOTABLE /HISTOGRAM INCREMENT(2).
```

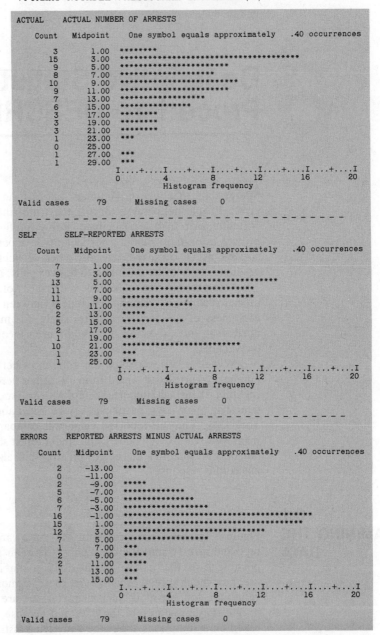

The distributions of the reported and true number of arrests have a somewhat similar shape. Neither distribution has an obvious central value, although the self-reported values have the tallest peak at 4 to 5 arrests, while the actual number of arrests has its peak at 2 to 3 arrests. The distribution of self-reported arrests also has a peak at 20 to 21 arrests. The peaks corresponding to intervals which contain 5, 15, and 20 arrests arouse the suspicion that people may be more likely to report their arrest records as round numbers. Examination of the true number of arrests shows no corresponding peaks at multiples of five.

The distribution of the differences between reported and true number of arrests is not as irregularly shaped as the two distributions from which it is derived. It has two adjacent peaks with midpoint values of -1 and $+1$. Most cases cluster around the peak values, and cases far from these values are infrequent. Figure 8.1b is a condensed frequency table for the response errors (the adjusted and cumulative percentages are rounded to the nearest integer). Almost 47% of the sample (37 cases) reported their arrest record to within two arrests of the true value. Only 22% (17 cases) misrepresented their records by more than 5 arrests. Underreporting is somewhat more likely than exaggeration, with 39% of the cases overestimating and 48% of the cases underestimating.

Figure 8.1b   Error in reported arrests

FREQUENCIES VARIABLES=ERRORS /FORMAT=CONDENSE.

```
ERRORS     REPORTED ARRESTS MINUS ACTUAL ARRESTS


                       Cum                        Cum                       Cum
       Value Freq Pct  Pct    Value Freq Pct Pct    Value Freq Pct Pct
        -14    2    3    3      -2    6    8   35      7    1    1   92
         -9    2    3    5      -1   10   13   48      8    1    1   94
         -8    3    4    9       0   10   13   61      9    1    1   95
         -7    2    3   11       1    5    6   67     10    1    1   96
         -6    1    1   13       2    6    8   75     11    1    1   97
         -5    5    6   19       3    6    8   82     12    1    1   99
         -4    3    4   23       4    4    5   87     15    1    1  100
         -3    4    5   28       5    3    4   91

Valid cases      79      Missing cases      0
```

8.2
Percentile Values

Percentiles are values above and below which certain percentages of the cases fall. For example, 95% of the cases have values less than or equal to the 95th percentile. From the cumulative percentage column in the frequency table in Figure 8.1b, the value for the 95th percentile is 9.

Figure 8.2 contains some commonly used percentiles for the distributions in Figure 8.1a. The three percentiles (25%, 50%, and 75%) divide the observed distributions into approximately four equal parts. The actual and self-reported number of arrests have the same 25th percentile, the value 4. This means that about 75% of the values are greater than or equal to 4, and 25% less than 4.

Figure 8.2   Percentiles for reported and actual arrests and errors

FREQUENCIES VARIABLES=ACTUAL SELF ERRORS
 /FORMAT=NOTABLE /PERCENTILE=25 50 75.

```
ACTUAL     ACTUAL NUMBER OF ARRESTS

 Percentile    Value      Percentile    Value      Percentile    Value
   25.00       4.000        50.00       8.000        75.00       13.000

Valid cases      79      Missing cases      0

- - - - - - - - - - - - - - - - - - - - - - - - - - - - - - - - -

SELF       SELF-REPORTED ARRESTS

 Percentile    Value      Percentile    Value      Percentile    Value
   25.00       4.000        50.00       7.000        75.00       14.000

Valid cases      79      Missing cases      0

- - - - - - - - - - - - - - - - - - - - - - - - - - - - - - - - -

ERRORS     REPORTED ARRESTS MINUS ACTUAL ARRESTS

 Percentile    Value      Percentile    Value      Percentile    Value
   25.00      -3.000        50.00        .000        75.00        3.000

Valid cases      79      Missing cases      0
```

8.3
SUMMARIZING THE DATA

Although frequency tables and bar charts are useful for summarizing and displaying data (see Chapter 7), further condensation and description is often desirable. A variety of summary measures that convey information about the data in single numbers can be computed. The choice of summary measure, or *statistic*, as it is often called, depends upon characteristics of the data as well as of the statistic. One important characteristic of the data that must be considered is the *level of measurement* of each variable being studied.

8.4
Levels of Measurement

Measurement is the assignment of numbers or codes to observations. Levels of measurement are distinguished by ordering and distance properties. A computer does not know what measurement underlies the values it is given. You must determine the level of measurement of your data and apply appropriate statistical techniques.

The traditional classification of levels of measurement into nominal, ordinal, interval, and ratio scales was developed by S. S. Stevens (1946). This remains the basic typology and is the one used throughout this manual. Variations exist, however, and issues concerning the statistical effect of ignoring levels of measurement have been debated (see, for example, Borgatta & Bohrnstedt, 1980).

8.5
Nominal Measurement

The nominal level of measurement is the "lowest" in the typology because no assumptions are made about relations between values. Each value defines a distinct category and serves merely as a label or name (hence, "nominal" level) for the category. For instance, the birthplace of an individual is a nominal variable. For most purposes, there is no inherent ordering among cities or towns. Although cities can be ordered according to size, density, or air pollution, a city thought of as "place of birth" is a concept that is normally not tied to any order. When numeric values are attached to nominal categories, they are merely identifiers. None of the properties of numbers such as relative size, addition, or multiplication, can be applied to these numerically coded categories. Therefore, statistics that assume ordering or meaningful numerical distances between the values do not ordinarily give useful information about nominal variables.

8.6
Ordinal Measurement

When it is possible to rank or order all categories according to some criterion, the ordinal level of measurement is achieved. For instance, classifying employees into clerical, supervisory, and managerial categories is an ordering according to responsibilities or skills. Each category has a position lower or higher than another category. Furthermore, knowing that supervisory is higher than clerical and that managerial is higher than supervisory automatically means that managerial is higher than clerical. However, nothing is known about how much higher; no distance is measured. Ordering is the sole mathematical property applicable to ordinal measurements, and the use of numeric values does not imply that any other property of numbers is applicable.

8.7
Interval Measurement

In addition to order, interval measurements have the property of meaningful distance between values. A thermometer, for example, measures temperature in degrees which are the same size at any point on the scale. The difference between 20°C and 21°C is the same as the difference between 5°C and 6°C. However, an interval scale does not have an inherently determined zero point. In the familiar Celsius and Fahrenheit systems, 0° is determined by an agreed-upon definition, not by the absence of heat. Consequently, interval-level measurement allows us to study differences between items but not their proportionate magnitudes. For example, it is incorrect to say that 80°F is twice as hot as 40°F.

8.8
Ratio Measurement

Ratio measurements have all the ordering and distance properties of an interval scale. In addition, a zero point can be meaningfully designated. In measuring physical distances between objects using feet or meters, a zero distance is naturally defined as the absence of any distance. The existence of a zero point means that ratio comparisons can be made. For example, it is quite meaningful to say that a 6-foot-tall adult is twice as tall as a 3-foot-tall child or that a 500-meter race is five times as long as a 100-meter race.

Because ratio measurements satisfy all the properties of the real number system, any mathematical manipulations appropriate for real numbers can be applied to ratio measures. However, the existence of a zero point is seldom critical for statistical analyses.

8.9
Summary Statistics

Figure 8.9 contains a variety of summary statistics that are useful in describing the distributions of reported arrests, true number of arrests, and the discrepancy. The statistics can be grouped into three categories according to what they quantify: central tendency, dispersion, and shape.

Figure 8.9 Statistics describing arrest data

```
FREQUENCIES VARIABLES=ACTUAL SELF ERRORS
  /FORMAT=NOTABLE  /STATISTICS=ALL.
```

```
ACTUAL      ACTUAL NUMBER OF ARRESTS


Mean          9.253      Std err        .703      Median      8.000
Mode          3.000      Std dev       6.248      Variance   39.038
Kurtosis       .597      S E Kurt       .535      Skewness     .908
S E Skew       .271      Range       28.000      Minimum     1.000
Maximum      29.000      Sum        731.000


Valid cases      79      Missing cases      0

- - - - - - - - - - - - - - - - - - - - - - - - - - - - - - - -

SELF        SELF-REPORTED ARRESTS


Mean          8.962      Std err        .727      Median      7.000
Mode          5.000      Std dev       6.458      Variance   41.704
Kurtosis      -.485      S E Kurt       .535      Skewness     .750
S E Skew       .271      Range       25.000      Minimum      .000
Maximum      25.000      Sum        708.000


Valid cases      79      Missing cases      0

- - - - - - - - - - - - - - - - - - - - - - - - - - - - - - - -

ERRORS      REPORTED ARRESTS MINUS ACTUAL ARRESTS


Mean          -.291      Std err        .587      Median       .000
Mode         -1.000      Std dev       5.216      Variance   27.209
Kurtosis      1.102      S E Kurt       .535      Skewness     .125
S E Skew       .271      Range       29.000      Minimum   -14.000
Maximum      15.000      Sum        -23.000


Valid cases      79      Missing cases      0
```

8.10
Measures of Central Tendency

The mean, median, and mode are frequently used to describe the location of a distribution. The *mode* is the most frequently occurring value (or values). For the true number of arrests, the mode is 3 (see Figure 8.9); for the self-reported values, it is 5. The distribution of the difference between the true and self-reported values is multimodal. That is, it has more than one mode since the values −1 and 0 occur with equal frequency. SPSS, however, displays only one of the modes, as shown in Figure 8.9. The mode can be used for data measured at any level. It is usually not the preferred measure for interval and ordinal data since it ignores much of the available information.

The *median* is the value above and below which one half of the observations fall. For example, if there are 79 observations the median is the 40th largest observation. When there is an even number of observations, no unique center value exists, so the mean of the two middle observations is usually taken as the median value. For the arrest data, the median is 0 for the differences, 8 for the true arrests, and 7 for reported arrests. For ordinal data the median is usually a good measure of central tendency since it uses the ranking information. The median should not be used for nominal data since ranking of the observations is not possible.

The *mean*, also called the arithmetic average, is the sum of the values of all observations divided by the number of observations. Thus

$$\bar{X} = \sum_{i=1}^{N} \frac{X_i}{N}$$

Equation 8.10

where N is the number of cases and X_i is the value of the variable for the ith case. Since the mean utilizes the distance between observations, the measurements should be interval or ratio. Mean race, religion, and auto color are meaningless. For dichotomous variables coded as 0 and 1, the mean has a special interpretation: it is the proportion of cases coded 1 in the data.

The three measures of central tendency need not be the same. For example, the mean number of true arrests is 9.25, the median is 8, and the mode is 3 (see Figure 8.9). The arithmetic mean is greatly influenced by outlying observations, while the median is not. Adding a single case with 400 arrests would increase the mean from 9.25 to 14.1, but it would not affect the median. Therefore, if there are values far removed from the rest of the observations, the median may be a better measure of central tendency than the mean.

For symmetric distributions, the observed mean, median, and mode are usually close in value. For example, the mean of the differences between reported and true arrest values is -0.291, the median is 0, and the modes are -1 and 0. All three measures give similar estimates of central tendency in this case.

8.11
Measures of Dispersion

Two distributions can have the same values for measures of central tendency and yet be very dissimilar in other respects. For example, if the true number of arrests for five cases in two methadone clinics is

CLINIC A: 0, 1, 10, 14, 20
CLINIC B: 8, 8, 9, 10, 10

the mean number of arrests (9) is the same in both. However, even a cursory examination of the data indicates that the two clinics are different. In the second clinic, all cases have fairly comparable arrest records while in the first the records are quite disparate. A quick and useful index of dissimilarity, or dispersion, is the *range*. It is the difference between the *maximum* and *minimum* observed values. For Clinic B the range is 2, while for Clinic A it is 20. Since the range is computed only from the minimum and maximum values, it is sensitive to extremes.

Although the range is a useful index of dispersion, especially for ordinal data, it does not take into account the distribution of observations between the maximum and minimum. A commonly used measure of variation that is based on all observations is the *variance*. For a sample, the variance is computed by summing the squared differences from the mean for all observations and then dividing by one less than the number of observations. In mathematical notation this is

$$S^2 = \sum_{i=1}^{N} \frac{(X_i - \bar{X})^2}{N - 1}$$

Equation 8.11

If all observations are identical—that is, if there is no variation—the variance is 0. The more spread out they are, the greater the variance. For the methadone clinic example above, the sample variance for Clinic A is 73, while for Clinic B it is 1.

The square root of the variance is termed the *standard deviation*. The standard deviation is expressed in the same units of measurement as the observations, while the variance is in units squared. This is an appealing property since it is much clearer to think of variability in terms of the number of arrests instead of the number of arrests squared.

8.12
The Normal Distribution

For many variables, most observations are concentrated near the middle of the distribution. As distance from the central concentration increases, the frequency of observation decreases. Such distributions are often described as "bell-shaped." An example is the *normal* distribution (see Figure 8.12a). A broad range of observed phenomena in nature and in society are approximately normally distributed. For example, the distributions of variables such as height, weight, and blood pressure are approximately normal. The normal distribution is by far the most important theoretical distribution in statistics and serves as a reference point for describing the form of many distributions of sample data.

Figure 8.12a   A normal curve

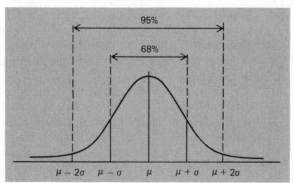

The normal distribution is symmetric: when it is folded in the center, the two sides are identical. Three measures of central tendency—the mean, median, and mode—coincide exactly (see Section 8.10). As shown in Figure 8.12a, 95% of all observations fall within two standard deviations (σ) of the mean (μ), and 68% within one standard deviation. The exact theoretical proportion of cases falling into various regions of the normal curve can be found in tables given in most introductory statistics textbooks.

In SPSS, you can superimpose a normal distribution on a histogram. Consider Figure 8.12b, which contains a histogram of the differences in arrest records. The colons and periods indicate what the distribution of cases would be if the variable had a normal distribution with the same mean and variance. Tests for normality are available in the EXAMINE procedure (see Chapter 9).

Figure 8.12b   Histogram of errors with the normal curve superimposed

```
FREQUENCIES VARIABLES=ERRORS
 /FORMAT=NOTABLE /HISTOGRAM=NORMAL.
```

```
ERRORS      REPORTED ARRESTS MINUS ACTUAL ARRESTS

   Count    Midpoint      One symbol equals approximately    .40 occurrences

      2      -14.5     :****
      0      -13.0     .
      0      -11.5         .
      0      -10.0         .
      5       -8.5     ******:******
      2       -7.0     *****     .
      6       -5.5     **************:*
      3       -4.0     ********
     10       -2.5     ********************:****
     10       -1.0     *********************:**
     15        .5      ***********************:****************
      6       2.0      ***************
     10       3.5      *****************:********
      3       5.0      ********    .
      1       6.5      ***       .
      1       8.0      *** .
      2       9.5      ***.*
      1      11.0      *:*
      1      12.5      :**
      0      14.0      .
      1      15.5      ***
                       I....+....I....+....I....+....I....+....I....+....I
                       0        4        8       12       16       20
                                        Histogram frequency

Valid cases    79    Missing cases    0
```

8.13
Measures of Shape

A distribution that is not symmetric but has more cases, or more of a "tail," toward one end of the distribution than the other is called *skewed*. If the tail is toward larger values, the distribution is positively skewed or skewed to the right. If the tail is toward smaller values, the distribution is negatively skewed or skewed to the left.

Another characteristic of the form of a distribution is called *kurtosis*, the extent to which, for a given standard deviation, observations cluster around a central point. If cases within a distribution cluster more than those in the normal distribution (that is, the distribution is more peaked), the distribution is called *leptokurtic*. A leptokurtic distribution also tends to have more observations straggling into the extreme tails than does a normal distribution. If cases cluster less than in the normal distribution (that is, it is flatter), the distribution is termed *platykurtic*.

Although examination of a histogram provides some indication of possible skewness and kurtosis, it is often desirable to compute formal indexes that measure these properties. Values for skewness and kurtosis are 0 if the observed distribution is exactly normal. Positive values for skewness indicate a positive skew, while positive values for kurtosis indicate a distribution that is more peaked than normal. For samples from a normal distribution, measures of skewness and kurtosis typically will not be exactly zero but will fluctuate about zero because of sampling variation.

8.14
Standard Scores

It is often desirable to describe the relative position of an observation within a distribution. Knowing that a person achieved a score of 80 in a competitive examination conveys little information about performance. Judgment of performance would depend on whether 80 is the lowest, the median, or the highest score.

One way of describing the location of a case in a distribution is to calculate its *standard score*. This score, sometimes called the Z score, indicates how many standard deviations above or below the mean an observation falls. It is calculated by finding the difference between the value of a particular observation X_i and the mean of the distribution, and then dividing this difference by the standard deviation:

$$Z_i = \frac{X_i - \overline{X}}{S}$$

Equation 8.14

The mean of Z scores is 0, and the standard deviation is 1.

For example, a participant with 5 actual arrests would have a Z score of $(5-9.25)/6.25$, or -0.68. Since the score is negative, the case had fewer arrests than the average for the individuals studied.

Standardization permits comparison of scores from different distributions. For example, an individual with Z scores of -0.68 for actual arrests and 1.01 for the difference between reported and actual arrests had fewer arrests than the average but exaggerated more than the average.

When the distribution of a variable is approximately normal and the mean and variance are known or are estimated from large samples, the Z score of an observation provides more specific information about its location. For example, if actual arrests and response error were normally distributed, 75% of cases would have more arrests than the example individual but only 16% would have exaggerated as much (75% of a standard normal curve lies above a Z score of -0.68, and 16% lies above a score of 1.01).

8.15
Who Lies?

The distribution of the difference between reported and actual arrests indicates that response error exists. Although observing a mean close to zero is comforting, misrepresentation is obvious. What then are the characteristics that influence willingness to be truthful?

Wyner identifies three factors that are related to inaccuracies: the number of arrests before 1960, the number of multiple-charge arrests, and the perceived desirability of being arrested. The first factor is related to a frequently encountered difficulty—the more distant an event in time, the less likely it is to be correctly recalled. The second factor, underreporting of multiple-charge arrests, is probably caused by the general social undesirability of serious arrests. Finally, persons who view arrest records as laudatory are likely to inflate their accomplishments.

8.16
RUNNING PROCEDURE DESCRIPTIVES

Procedure DESCRIPTIVES computes univariate summary statistics and standardized variables that are saved on the active system file. Although it computes statistics also available in procedure FREQUENCIES (see Chapter 7), DESCRIPTIVES computes descriptive statistics for continuous variables more efficiently because it does not sort values into a frequencies table.

By default, DESCRIPTIVES calculates the mean, standard deviation, minimum, and maximum. You can request optional statistics and Z-score transformations.

The only required subcommand on DESCRIPTIVES is the VARIABLES subcommand, which specifies the variable list to be analyzed.

8.17
VARIABLES Subcommand

The VARIABLES subcommand names the variable list. You can use keyword TO in the list to refer to consecutive variables in the active system file. The variables must be numeric.

To request the default summary statistics, specify the VARIABLES subcommand and a simple list of variables, as in:

```
DESCRIPTIVES VARIABLES=NTCPRI FOOD RENT.
```

You can also use the keyword ALL to specify all variables in the active system file.

You can specify only one variable list with DESCRIPTIVES, but there is no limit to the number of variables named or implied on one command. Variables named more than once will appear in the output more than once. If there is insufficient space to process all the requested variables, DESCRIPTIVES truncates the variable list.

8.18
Z Scores

The Z-score variable transformation standardizes variables with different observed scales to the same scale. DESCRIPTIVES generates new variables, each with a mean of 0 and a standard deviation of 1, and stores them on the active system file. Z scores can be created by using the SAVE subcommand (Section 8.19) or by naming Z-score variable names on the VARIABLES subcommand (Section 8.20).

8.19
SAVE Subcommand

Use the SAVE subcommand to obtain one Z-score variable for each variable specified on the DESCRIPTIVES variable list. The SAVE subcommand calculates standardized variables and stores them on the active system file. The command

```
DESCRIPTIVES VARIABLES=ALL
 /SAVE.
```

produces new Z-score variables for all the variables on the active system file.

DESCRIPTIVES automatically supplies variable names and labels for the new variables. The new variable name is created by prefixing the letter Z to the first seven characters of the variable name. For example, ZFOOD is the Z-score variable for FOOD. When DESCRIPTIVES creates new Z-score variables, it displays a table containing the original variable name, the new variable name and its label, and the number of cases for which the Z score is computed.

If DESCRIPTIVES cannot use the default naming convention because it would produce duplicate names, it uses an alternative naming convention: first

ZSC001 through ZSC099, then STDZ01 through STDZ09, then ZZZZ01 through ZZZZ09, then ZQZQ01 through ZQZQ09.

DESCRIPTIVES automatically supplies variable labels for the new variables by prefixing *ZSCORE:* to the first 31 characters of the original variable's label. If it uses a name like ZSC001, it prefixes *ZSCORE(varname)* to the first 31 characters of the original variable's label. If the original variable has no label, it uses *ZSCORE(varname)* for the label.

8.20
Creating Z Scores on the VARIABLES Subcommand

If you want *Z* scores for a subset of the variables listed on DESCRIPTIVES, specify the name of the new variable in parentheses following the original variable on the VARIABLES subcommand, and *do not use the SAVE subcommand.* For example,

```
DESCRIPTIVES VARIABLES=NTCSAL NTCPUR (PURCHZ) NTCPRI (PRICEZ).
```

creates *Z*-score variables for NTCPUR and NTCPRI.

If you specify new names on the VARIABLES subcommand *and* use the SAVE subcommand, DESCRIPTIVES creates one new variable for each variable on the VARIABLES subcommand, using the default names for variables that are not explicitly assigned names. For example,

```
DESCRIPTIVES VARIABLES=NTCSAL NTCPUR (PURCHZ) NTCPRI (PRICEZ)
  /SAVE.
```

creates PURCHZ and PRICEZ and assigns a default name to the *Z*-score variable for NTCSAL. When you specify the name of the new variable, you can use any acceptable eight-character variable name, including any default variable name, that is not already part of the active system file.

8.21
STATISTICS Subcommand

By default, DESCRIPTIVES displays the mean, standard deviation, minimum, and maximum values. If you use the STATISTICS subcommand and any of its keywords, you can specify alternative statistics. When you specify statistics, DESCRIPTIVES displays *only* those statistics you request.

You can use the keyword ALL to obtain all statistics. When requesting the default statistics plus additional statistics, you can specify DEFAULT to obtain the default statistics without having to name MEAN, STDDEV, MIN, and MAX.

The following keywords can be specified on the STATISTICS subcommand:

MEAN	*Mean.*
SEMEAN	*Standard error of the mean.*
STDDEV	*Standard deviation.*
VARIANCE	*Variance.*
KURTOSIS	*Kurtosis.* Also displays standard error.
SKEWNESS	*Skewness.* Also displays standard error.
RANGE	*Range.*
MIN	*Minimum.*
MAX	*Maximum.*
SUM	*Sum.*
DEFAULT	*Mean, standard deviation, minimum, and maximum.* These are the default statistics if you omit the STATISTICS subcommand.
ALL	*All the statistics available on DESCRIPTIVES.*

8.22
MISSING Subcommand

By default, DESCRIPTIVES deletes cases with missing values on a variable-by-variable basis. A case missing on a variable will not be included in the summary statistics for that variable, but the case *will* be included for variables where it is not missing.

The MISSING subcommand controls missing values, and three keywords are available:

VARIABLE *Exclude missing values on a variable-by-variable basis.* A case is excluded from the computation of statistics for a variable if it has a missing value for that variable. This is the default if you omit the MISSING subcommand.

LISTWISE *Exclude missing values listwise.* Cases missing on any variable named on the VARIABLES subcommand are excluded from the computation of summary statistics for all variables.

INCLUDE *Include user-defined missing values.*

The VARIABLE and LISTWISE keywords cannot be specified together. However, each can be specified with INCLUDE. For example, to include user-missing values in an analysis that excludes missing values listwise, specify

```
DESCRIPTIVES VARIABLES=ALL
  /MISSING=INCLUDE LISTWISE.
```

When you use the keyword VARIABLE or the default missing-value treatment, DESCRIPTIVES reports the number of valid cases for each variable. It always displays the number of cases that would be available if listwise deletion of missing values had been selected.

8.23
FORMAT Subcommand

The FORMAT subcommand controls the formatting options available in DESCRIPTIVES. The following keywords can be specified on it:

LABELS *Display variable labels.* This is the default if you omit the FORMAT subcommand.

NOLABELS *Suppress variable labels.*

INDEX *Display reference indexes.* INDEX displays a positional and an alphabetic reference index following the statistical display. The index shows the page location in the output of the statistics for each variable. The variables are listed by their position in the active file and alphabetically.

NOINDEX *Suppress reference indexes.* This is the default if you omit the FORMAT subcommand.

LINE *Display statistics in line format.* LINE displays statistics on the same line as the variable name. It is the default if you omit the FORMAT subcommand.

SERIAL *Display statistics in serial format.* SERIAL displays statistics below the variable name, permitting greater field widths and more decimal digits for very large or very small numbers. DESCRIPTIVES automatically forces this format if the number of statistics requested does not fit in the column format.

8.24
SORT Subcommand

By default, DESCRIPTIVES lists variables in the order in which they appear on the VARIABLES subcommand. You can use the SORT subcommand to list variables in ascending or descending alphabetical order or by numerical value of any of the statistics available with DESCRIPTIVES.

The following keywords can be specified on the SORT subcommand:

MEAN *Sort by mean.* This is the default.

SEMEAN *Sort by standard error of the mean.*

STDDEV *Sort by standard deviation.*

VARIANCE	*Sort by variance.*
KURTOSIS	*Sort by kurtosis.*
SKEWNESS	*Sort by skewness.*
RANGE	*Sort by range.*
MIN	*Sort by minimum observed value.*
MAX	*Sort by maximum observed value.*
SUM	*Sort by sum.*
NAME	*Sort by variable name.*
(A)	*Sort in ascending order.* This is the default.
(D)	*Sort in descending order.*

If you specify SORT without any of the optional keywords, variables are listed by mean in ascending order.

The SORT subcommand sorts variables by the value of any of the statistics available with DESCRIPTIVES, but only those statistics specified on the STATISTICS subcommand are displayed. If you specify SORT without STATISTICS, the default statistics are displayed. The command

```
DESCRIPTIVES VARIABLES=A B C
 /STATISTICS=DEFAULT RANGE
 /SORT=RANGE (D).
```

sorts variables A, B, and C by range in descending order and displays the mean, standard deviation, minimum and maximum values, number of cases, value labels, and the range.

8.25
Annotated Example

Figures 8.25a and 8.25b show the statistics for original variables and new *Z*-score variables produced by the following DESCRIPTIVES commands:

```
DESCRIPTIVES VARIABLES=ACTUAL SELF ERRORS
 /SAVE.
DESCRIPTIVES VARIABLES=ZACTUAL, ZSELF, ZERRORS
 /STATISTICS=DEFAULT RANGE /FORMAT=NOLABELS.
```

- The first DESCRIPTIVES command produces the default statistics for all three variables.
- The SAVE subcommand saves three new *Z*-score variables and assigns them the names ZACTUAL, ZSELF, and ZERRORS.
- The second DESCRIPTIVES command requests statistics for the three new *Z*-score variables.
- The STATISTICS subcommand produces the default statistics plus the range.
- The FORMAT subcommand suppresses the value labels for the new *Z*-score variables.

Figure 8.25a   Default statistics available with DESCRIPTIVES

```
Number of valid observations (listwise) =          79.00

                                                  Valid
Variable     Mean    Std Dev   Minimum   Maximum     N  Label

ACTUAL       9.25     6.25          1        29      79  ACTUAL NUMBER OF ARRESTS
SELF         8.96     6.46          0        25      79  SELF-REPORTED ARRESTS
ERRORS       -.29     5.22     -14.00        15      79  REPORTED ARRESTS MINUS ACTUAL ARRESTS
```

Figure 8.25b   Statistics for new Z-score variables

```
                                                     Valid
Variable     Mean    Std Dev   Range   Minimum   Maximum    N

ZACTUAL       .00      1.00     4.48  -1.32093   3.16050    79
ZSELF         .00      1.00     3.87  -1.38777   2.48349    79
ZERRORS       .00      1.00     5.56  -2.62812   2.93146    79
```

8.26
EXERCISES

Syntax

1. Five students boast scores of 90, 93, 87, 96, and 89 on a Statistics exam, when their actual scores are 79, 81, 77, 89, and 72. Write the complete SPSS job, including data definition, to compute descriptive statistics and a frequency table for the discrepancy between the two scores.

2. Modify your previous job to get descriptive statistics and a histogram, without the frequency table.

3. Modify the job again to get a compact table of descriptive statistics for the actual, boasted, and discrepancy scores.

Statistical Concepts

1. A sample consists of 21 patients with a mild case of a disease (coded 1), 10 patients with a moderately severe case (coded 2), and 12 patients with an extremely severe case (coded 3). Does it make sense to determine the following statistics? If so, compute them.
   a. Modal severity
   b. Median severity
   c. Mean severity

2. A sample consists of 11 blacks (coded 1), 10 Asians (coded 2), and 5 whites (coded 3). Does it make sense to determine the the following statistics? If so, compute them.
   a. Modal race
   b. Median race
   c. Mean race

3. Indicate the level of measurement for each of the following variables:
   a. Race
   b. Age
   c. The ranking of 100 judges by an independent lawyers' group.
   d. Diastolic blood pressure
   e. IQ score
   f. Eye color

4. If a sample has 155 observations ranked so that the first observation is the largest, the second is next largest, and so on, which observation is the median?

5. A certain variable is known to be normally distributed with a mean of 0.267 and a standard deviation of 0.112. Given this information, can you determine the following statistics? If so, what are they?
   a. The median
   b. The mode
   c. The variance
   d. The kurtosis

6. A researcher transformed data into standardized scores and obtained a mean standardized score of 1.438. Does this constitute grounds for rechecking the calculations? Why or why not?

7. The "average sex" for a sample where sex is coded as female=1 and male=0 is 0.72. What (if anything) does this average mean?

8. Which of the following statements are true?
   a. Unlike the variance, the range is not greatly affected by extreme values.
   b. Distributions with similar means, medians, and modes also tend to have similar variances.
   c. The variance measures how spread out observations are, with a larger variance indicating greater spread.

9. In a certain corporation, a very small group of employees has extremely high salaries, while the majority of employees receive much lower salaries. If you were the bargaining agent for the union, what statistic would you calculate to illustrate the low pay level and why? If you were the employer, what statistic would you use to demonstrate a higher pay level and why?

10. The numbers of cars owned by 10 families are as follows: 0, 1, 1, 1, 2, 2, 2, 2, 2, 4. Fill in the following table based on these values:

```
MEAN                    MEDIAN                  MODE
STD DEV       1.059     VARIANCE                RANGE
MINIMUM                 MAXIMUM
```

11. The following Z (standard) scores are printed from procedure DESCRIPTIVES: Calculate the original scores using the following descriptive statistics: mean=10; standard deviation=2.

Case	Standard score	Original score
1	1	
2	0	
3	−2	

12. The mean and standard deviation on a history test are mean=70, s=12. Calculate the Z (standard) scores for the following students:

Student	Score	Standardized score
1	70	
2	58	
3	94	

13. Compute the missing entries in the following table:

a.
VARIABLE	STD DEV	VARIANCE	VALID N
VARA	6.529		10

b.
VARIABLE	RANGE	MINIMUM	MAXIMUM	VALID N
VARB		.000	19.000	10

c.
VARIABLE	MEAN	SUM	VALID N
VARC		85.000	10

14. An absent-minded instructor calculated the following statistics for an examination: mean=50; range=50; N=99; minimum=20; and maximum=70. He then found an additional examination with a score of 50. Recalculate the statistics, including the additional exam score.

15. The numbers of pairs of shoes owned by seven college freshmen are 1, 2, 2, 3, 4, 4, and 5.
   a. Compute the mean, median, mode, range and standard deviation.
   b. An eighth student, the heir to a shoe empire, is added to the sample. This student owns 50 pairs of shoes. Recompute the statistics in (a).
   c. Which of the statistics are not much affected by the inclusion of an observation that is far removed from the rest?

Data Analysis

Use the BANK system file for Questions 1–3.

1. Variables of possible interest in describing the sample are ages of the employees, work experience, job seniority, beginning salary, and current salary. Calculate summary statistics for these variables. Summarize your findings.

2. a. Obtain separate histograms for beginning salaries for males and females using the SELECT command described in 3. Which, if any, look normal? What deviations from normality are evident?

   b. For the female and male beginning salaries, obtain all summary statistics concerned with the shape of the distribution. Examine the values of these statistics. Are they consistent with your observations in Question 2.a?

   c. For male and female beginning salaries, obtain the mean, median, mode, maximum, minimum, range, and standard deviation. How do these statistics differ for the two groups? In what ways would you expect them to differ if the bank discriminates against women?

3. Repeat Question 2 using nonwhite and white beginning salaries.

4. Choose one of the data sets in Appendix B.

   a. Determine the level of measurement for the variables on the data file.

   b. Choose four variables and obtain the appropriate summary statistics for them. Discuss the reasons for your selection.

   c. Obtain a frequency table, histogram, and percentiles for one variable. Indicate how you would calculate percentiles from the frequency table.

   d. Rerun the histogram, selecting your own interval widths and plotting percentages.

5. Write a brief description of the characteristics of the men included in the Western Electric study. Run whatever analysis you need to prepare your report.

6. Calculate the mean and median for the number of cigarettes smoked (CGT58). Explain why these two numbers are not the same. Based on a histogram of the variable, which of the measures of central tendency provides the best description of the smoking habits of the sample?

Examine _____

In this chapter:

Goals:

- To look at the distribution of the values of a variable.
- To identify unusual observations.
- To test for equality of group variances.
- To test for normality.

Examples:

- Look at the distribution of maze learning times for rats under four different reinforcement schedules.
- Test the hypothesis that the variances in heart rates are the same for patients with five types of diagnoses.
- Test the hypothesis that scores on a test are normally distributed.

How it's done:

Stem and leaf plots and box and whiskers plots are used to examine the distribution of a variable, either for all cases or for subgroups of cases. The Levene test is used to test for equality of variances across subgroups. Normal probability plots, detrended normal plots, and the Shapiro-Wilks and Lilliefors tests are used for testing whether the sample comes from a normal population.

Data considerations:

Any variable with a limited number of distinct values can be used to form the subgroups. The variable being described cannot be nominal.

9 Looking First: Procedure EXAMINE

The first step of data analysis should always be a detailed examination of the data. It doesn't matter whether the problem you're solving is simple or complex, whether you're planning to do a t-test or a multivariate repeated measures analysis of variance. First you should take a careful look at the data.

9.1 REASONS FOR EXAMINING DATA

There are several important reasons for examining your data carefully before you begin your analysis. Let's start with the simplest.

9.2 Identifying Mistakes

Data must make a hazardous journey before they find final rest in a computer file. First a measurement is made or a response elicited, sometimes with a faulty instrument or by a sleepy experimenter. The result is then recorded, often barely legibly, in a lab notebook, medical chart, or personnel record. Often this information is not actually coded and entered onto a data form until much later. From this form the numbers must yet find their way into their designated slot in the computer file. Then they must be properly introduced to a computer program. Their correct location and missing values must be specified.

Errors can be introduced at any step. Some errors are easy to spot. For example, forgetting to declare a value as missing, using an invalid code, or entering the value 701 for age will be apparent from a frequency table. Other errors, like entering an age of 54 instead of 45, may be difficult, if not impossible, to spot. Unless your first step is to carefully check your data for mistakes, errors may contaminate all of your analyses.

9.3 Exploring the Data

After the commotion of data acquisition, entry, and checking, it's time to actually look at the data—not to search frantically for statistical significance, but to examine the data carefully using simple exploratory techniques. Why bother? you might ask. Why not just begin your analysis?

Data analysis has often been compared to detective work. Before the actual trial of a hypothesis there is much evidence to be gathered and sifted. Based on the clues, the hypothesis itself may be altered, or the methods for testing it may have to be changed. For example, if a display of the distribution of data values reveals a "gap," that is, a range where no values occur, we must ask why. If there are some values far removed from the others, we must also ask why. If the pattern of numbers is strange—for example, if all values are even—we must determine why. If we see unexpected variability in the data, we must look for possible explanations. Perhaps there are additional variables that might explain some of the variability.

9.4
Preparing for Hypothesis Testing

Looking at the distribution of the values is also important for evaluating the appropriateness of the statistical techniques we are planning to use for hypothesis testing or model building. Perhaps the data must be transformed so that the distribution is approximately normal, or so that the variances in the groups are similar. Or perhaps a nonparametric technique is needed.

9.5
WAYS OF DISPLAYING DATA

Now that we've established why it's important to look at data, we'll consider some of the techniques that are available for exploring data. To illustrate the methods, we'll use the Western Electric data (see Chapter 2) and the bank salary data (see Chapter 11).

9.6
The Histogram

The histogram is a commonly used display. The range of observed values is subdivided into equal intervals and then the number of cases in each interval is obtained. Each row of symbols in a histogram represents the number of cases with values within the interval.

Figure 9.6 is a histogram of diastolic blood pressure for a sample of 239 men from the Western Electric study. The first column, labeled **Frequency,** is the number of cases with values in the intervals. The second column, **Bin Center,** is the midpoint of each of the bins. For example, the midpoint of the first bin is 65. The text underneath the histogram shows that the length of each bin is 10. Thus, the first interval contains cases with diastolic blood pressures in the 60's. Cases with diastolic blood pressures in the 70's go into the next interval. The last bin center is labeled **125** and includes cases with values in the 120's.

Figure 9.6   Histogram of diastolic blood pressure

```
GET FILE=ELECTRIC.
EXAMINE VARIABLES=DBP58 /PLOT=HISTOGRAM.
```

```
Frequency   Bin Center

    7.00         65    ***
   45.00         75    ***********************
   89.00         85    ********************************************
   58.00         95    *****************************
   24.00        105    ************
   10.00        115    *****
    2.00        125    *
    4.00    Extremes    **

Bin width :    10
Each star:       2 case(s)
```

The last row of this histogram is for cases whose values are much larger than the rest. These are labeled **Extremes.** The reason the histogram is not extended to accommodate these cases is to avoid having too many intervals or intervals that are very wide. For example, if there is a person with a diastolic blood pressure of 200, the histogram would have a lot of empty bins between the bin centers of 125 and 205. Of course, we could have fewer bins and make them wider, but this would obscure potentially interesting information. That's why the histogram contains special bins for very large and very small values.

9.7
The Stem-and-Leaf Plot

A display closely related to the histogram is the stem-and-leaf plot. The stem-and-leaf plot provides more information about the actual values than does a histogram. Consider Figure 9.7a, which is a stem-and-leaf plot of the diastolic blood pressures. As in a histogram, the length of each row corresponds to the number of cases that fall into a particular interval. However, instead of representing all cases with the same symbol (say, a star), the stem-and-leaf plot represents each case with a symbol that corresponds to the actual observed value. This is done by dividing observed values into two components—the leading digit or digits, called the stem, and a trailing digit, called the leaf. For example, the value 75 has a stem of 7 and a leaf of 5. In the plot, each row represents a stem and each case is represented by its leaf value.

Figure 9.7a   Stem-and-leaf plot of diastolic blood pressure

EXAMINE VARIABLES=DBP58 /**PLOT=STEMLEAF**.

```
Frequency     Stem &  Leaf

     .00       6  *
    7.00       6  .  5558889
   13.00       7  *  0000111223344
   32.00       7  .  55555555667777777777788888889999
   44.00       8  *  00000000000000000000001111122222333333334444
   45.00       8  .  555555555566666667777777777777788888999999999
   31.00       9  *  0000000001111111122222222333334
   27.00       9  .  556666667777778888888888899999
   13.00      10  *  0000122233333
   11.00      10  .  55555577899
    5.00      11  *  00003
    5.00      11  .  55789
    2.00      12  *  01
    4.00  Extremes     (125), (133), (160)

Stem width:     10
Each leaf:         1 case(s)
```

In this example, each stem is subdivided into two rows. The first row of each pair has cases with leaves of 0 through 4, while the second row has cases with leaves of 5 through 9. Consider the two rows that correspond to the stem of 11. From the first of these rows, we can see that there are four cases with diastolic blood pressures of 110, and one case with a pressure of 113. Similarly, there are two cases with values of 115, and one each with a value of 117, 118, and 119.

The last row of the stem-and-leaf plot is for cases with values far removed from the rest. In this row, the actual values are displayed in parentheses. From the frequency column, we see that there are four extreme cases. Their values are 125, 133, and 160. Only distinct values are listed.

To identify cases with extreme values, you can display a table containing identifying information for cases with the largest and smallest values. Figure 9.7b shows the five cases with the largest and smallest values for diastolic blood pressure. When the data file contains names or other information that can be used to identify cases, this information can be listed. Otherwise, the sequence of the case in the data file is reported.

Figure 9.7b   Extreme cases

EXAMINE VARIABLES=DBP58 /STATISTICS=EXTREME.

```
                                Extreme Values
                                ───────  ──────

  5   Highest      Case #              5   Lowest      Case #

        160         CASE120                  65         CASE73
        133         CASE56                   65         CASE157
        125         CASE163                  65         CASE156
        125         CASE42                   68         CASE34
        121         CASE26                   68         CASE175
```

9.8
Other Stems

In Figure 9.7a, each stem was subdivided into two parts—one for leaves of 0 thru 4, the other for leaves of 5 thru 9. When there are few stems, it is sometimes useful to subdivide each stem even further. Consider Figure 9.8, which is a stem-and-leaf plot of cholesterol levels for the men in the Western Electric study. In this figure, stems are divided into five parts—each is used to represent two leaf values. The first, designated by an asterisk, is for leaves of 0 and 1; the next, designated by **t**, is for leaves of 2's and 3's; the **f** is for leaves of 4's and 5's; the **s** for 6's and 7's; and a period for 8's and 9's.

This stem-and-leaf plot differs from the previous in yet another way. Since cholesterol values have a wide range, in this example from 106 to 515, using the first two digits for the stem would result in an unnecessarily detailed plot. To avoid this, we will use only the hundreds digit as the stem instead of the first two digits. The line after the stem-and-leaf plot tells us that the stems are in hundreds. The leaf is then the tens digit. The last digit is ignored. Thus, from this stem-and-leaf plot, it is not possible to determine the exact cholesterol level for a case. Instead, each case is classified by its first two digits only.

Figure 9.8   Stem-and-leaf plot of cholesterol levels

EXAMINE VARIABLES=CHOL58 /PLOT=STEMLEAF.

```
 Frequency    Stem &  Leaf

     1.00  Extremes    (106)
     2.00      1   f   55
     6.00      1   s   677777
    12.00      1   .   888889999999
    23.00      2   *   00000000000001111111111
    36.00      2   t   222222222222222233333333333333333333
    35.00      2   f   44444444444444444455555555555555555
    42.00      2   s   666666666666666666666677777777777777777777
    28.00      2   .   8888888888888899999999999999
    18.00      3   *   000000011111111111
    17.00      3   t   22222222222233333
     9.00      3   f   444445555
     6.00      3   s   666777
     1.00      3   .   8
     3.00  Extremes    (393), (425), (515)

 Stem width:     100
 Each leaf:        1 case(s)
```

9.9
The Boxplot

Both the histogram and the stem-and-leaf plot provide useful information about the distribution of observed values. We can see how tightly cases cluster together. We can see if there is a single peak or several peaks. We can determine if there are extreme values.

A display that further summarizes information about the distribution of the values is the boxplot. Instead of plotting the actual values, a boxplot displays summary statistics for the distribution. It plots the median, the 25th percentile, the 75th percentile, and values that are far removed from the rest.

Figure 9.9a shows an annotated sketch of a boxplot. The lower boundary of the box is the 25th percentile, and the upper boundary is the 75th percentile. (These percentiles are sometimes called Tukey's hinges and are calculated a little differently from ordinary percentiles.) The asterisk in the box represents the median. Fifty percent of the cases have values within the box. The length of the box corresponds to the interquartile range, which is the difference between the 75th and 25th percentiles.

Figure 9.9a   Annotated sketch of a boxplot

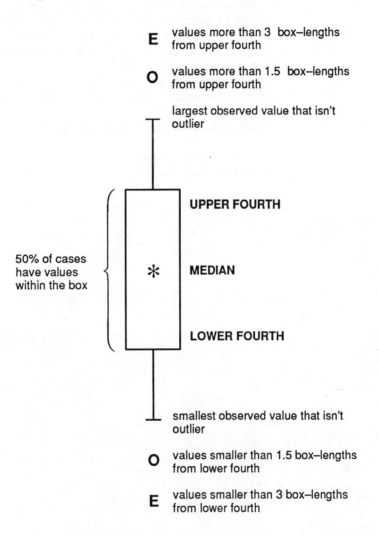

The boxplot includes two categories of cases with outlying values. Cases with values more than 3 box-lengths from the upper or lower edge of the box are called *extreme values.* On the boxplot these are designated with the letter E. Cases with values between 1.5 and 3 box-lengths from the edge of the box are called *outliers* and are designated with the letter O. The largest and smallest observed values that aren't outliers are also shown. Lines are drawn from the ends of the box to these values. (These lines are sometimes called whiskers and the plot is called a box-and-whiskers plot.)

What can you tell about your data from a boxplot? From the median you can determine the central tendency, or location. From the length of the box you can see the spread, or variability, of your observations. If the median is not in the center of the box you know that the observed values are skewed. If the median is closer to the bottom of the box than the top, the data are positively skewed. There is a tail with large values. If the median is closer to the top of the box than the bottom, the opposite is true. The distribution is negatively skewed. The length of the tail is shown by the whiskers and the outlying and extreme points.

Boxplots are particularly useful for comparing the distribution of values in several groups. For example, suppose you want to compare the distribution of beginning salaries for people employed in several different positions at a bank. Figure 9.9b contains boxplots of the bank salary data. From this plot you can see that the first two job categories have similar distributions for salary, although the first has several extreme values. The third job category has little variability. All 27 people in this category earn similar amounts of money. The last two groups have much higher median salaries than the other groups, and larger spread as well.

Figure 9.9b   Boxplots for bank salary data

```
GET FILE=BANK.
SELECT IF (JOBCAT LE 5).
EXAMINE VARIABLES=SALBEG BY JOBCAT /PLOT=BOXPLOT.
```

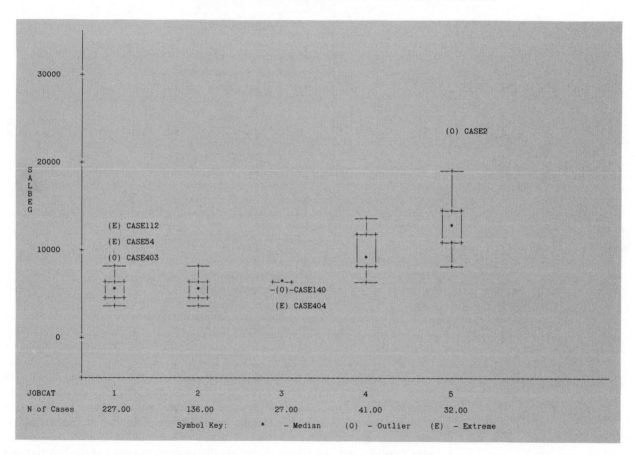

9.10
EVALUATING ASSUMPTIONS

Many statistical procedures, such as analysis of variance, require that all groups come from normal populations with the same variance. Therefore, before using them, we often wish to test the hypothesis that all the group variances are equal or that the samples are from normal populations. If it appears that the assumptions are violated, we may want to determine appropriate transformations.

9.11
The Levene Test

There is a wide variety of tests available for evaluating the assumption that all groups come from populations with equal variances. Many of these tests, however, are heavily dependent on the data being samples from normal populations. Analysis-of-variance procedures, on the other hand, are reasonably robust to departures from normality. The Levene test is a homogeneity-of-variance test that is less dependent on the assumption of normality than most tests and thus is particularly useful with analysis of variance. It is obtained by computing for each case the absolute difference from its cell mean and then performing a one-way analysis of variance on these differences.

From Figure 9.11 you can see that, for the salary data, the null hypothesis that all group variances are equal is rejected. We should consider transforming the data if we plan to use a statistical procedure which requires equality of variance. Next we'll consider how to select a transformation.

Figure 9.11   The Levene test

Test of homogeneity of variance		df1	df2	Significance
Levene Statistic	28.9200	4	458	.0000

9.12
Spread-and-Level Plots

Often there is a relationship between the average value, or level, of a variable, and the variability or spread associated with it. For example, we can see in Figure 9.9b that as salaries increase, so does the variability.

One way of studying the relationship between spread and level is to plot the values of spread and level for each group. If there is no relationship, the points should cluster around a horizontal line. If this is not the case, we can use the observed relationship between the two variables to choose an appropriate transformation.

9.13
Determining the Transformation

A power transformation is frequently used to stabilize variances. All a power transformation does is raise each data value to a specified power. For example, a power transformation of 2 squares all of the data values. A transformation of 1/2 indicates that the square root of all the values be taken. If the power is 0, the log of the numbers is used.

To determine an appropriate power for transforming the data, we can plot for each group the log of the median against the log of the interquartile range. Figure 9.13 shows such a plot for the salary data shown in Figure 9.9b. You see that there is a fairly strong linear relationship between spread and level. From the slope of the line, we can estimate the power value that will eliminate or lessen this relationship. The power is obtained by subtracting the slope from 1. That is,

Power $= 1 -$ slope

Equation 9.13

Although this formula can result in all sorts of powers, for simplicity and interpretability we usually choose the closest powers that are multiples of 1/2. Table 9.13 shows the most commonly used transformations.

Figure 9.13 Spread-and-level plot of bank data

EXAMINE VARIABLES=SALBEG BY JOBCAT /**PLOT=SPREADLEVEL**.

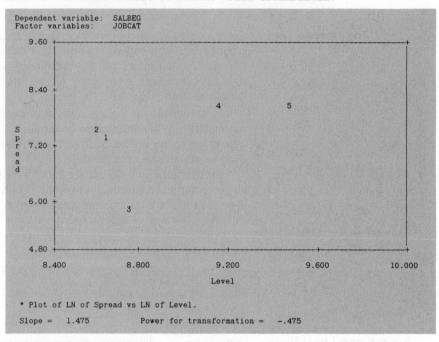

Table 9.13 Commonly used transformations

Power	Transformation
3	Cube
2	Square
1	No change
1/2	Square root
0	Logarithm
−1/2	Reciprocal of the square root
−1	Reciprocal

As shown in Figure 9.13, the slope of the least-squares line for the bank data is 1.475, so the power for the transformation is −.475. Rounding to the nearest multiple of a half, we will use the reciprocal of the square root.

After applying the power transformation, it is wise to obtain a spread-and-level plot for the transformed data. From this plot you can judge the success of the transformation.

9.14
Tests of Normality

Since the normal distribution is very important to statistical inference, we often want to examine the assumption that our data come from a normal distribution. One way to do this is with a normal probability plot. In a normal probability plot each observed value is paired with its expected value from the normal distribution. (The expected value from the normal distribution is based on the number of cases in the sample and the rank order of the case in the sample.) If the sample is from a normal distribution, we expect that the points will fall, more or less, on a straight line.

Figure 9.14a is a normal probability plot of a sample of 200 points from a normal distribution. Note how the points cluster about a straight line. You can also plot the actual deviations of the points from a straight line. This is called a detrended normal plot and is shown in Figure 9.14b. If the sample is from a normal population, the points should cluster around a horizontal line through 0 and there should be no pattern. A striking pattern suggests departure from normality.

Figure 9.14a   Normal probability plot   Figure 9.14b   Detrended normal plot

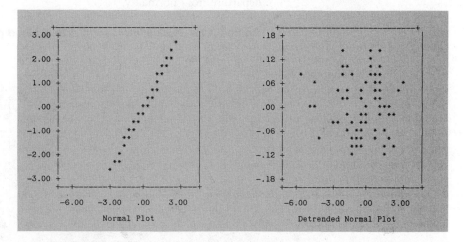

Figure 9.14c shows a normal probability plot and a detrended plot for data from a uniform distribution. The points do not cluster around a straight line, and the deviations from a straight line are not randomly distributed about 0.

Figure 9.14c   Normal plots for a uniform distribution

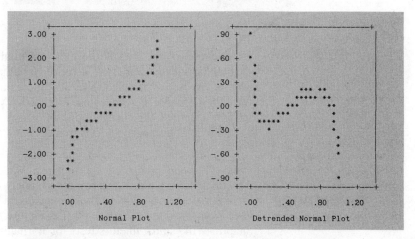

Although normal probability plots provide a visual basis for checking normality, it is often desirable to compute a statistical test of the hypothesis that the data are from a normal distribution. Two commonly used tests are the Shapiro-Wilks and the Lilliefors. The Lilliefors test is based on a modification of the Kolmogorov-Smirnov test for the situation when means and variances are not known but must be estimated from the data. The Shapiro-Wilks test has been found to have good power in many situations when compared to other tests of normality (Conover, 1980).

Figure 9.14d contains normal probability plots and tests of normality for the diastolic blood pressure data. From the small observed significance levels, you see that the hypothesis of normality can be rejected. However, it is important to remember that whenever the sample size is large, almost any goodness-of-fit test will result in rejection of the null hypothesis. It is almost impossible to find data that are *exactly* normally distributed. For most statistical tests, it is sufficient that the data are approximately normally distributed. Thus, for large data sets, you should look not only at the observed significance level but also at the actual departure from normality.

Figure 9.14d   Normal plots for diastolic blood pressure

```
SET WIDTH=90.
EXAMINE VARIABLES=DBP58 /PLOT=NPPLOT.
```

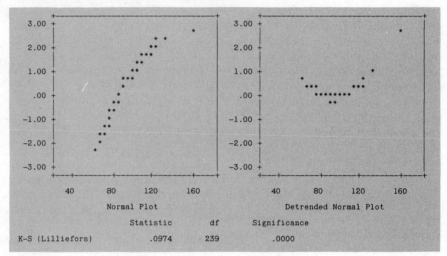

9.15
SUMMARY

Examination of the data is the most essential step in good data analysis. This chapter has shown a variety of descriptive statistics and displays that is useful as a preliminary step in data analysis. All of these statistics and displays are available in the SPSS EXAMINE procedure. With EXAMINE, you can screen your data, visually examine the distributions of values for various groups, and test for normality and homogeneity of variance.

9.16
RUNNING PROCEDURE EXAMINE

The EXAMINE procedure provides a variety of descriptive plots and statistics, including stem-and-leaf plots, boxplots, normal probability plots, and spread-and-level plots. Also available are the Levene test for homogeneity of variance, the Shapiro-Wilks and Lilliefors tests for normality, and several robust maximum-likelihood estimators of location. Cases can be subdivided into groups, and statistics can be obtained for each group.

9.17
VARIABLES Subcommand

The only required specification is the VARIABLES subcommand and a list of variables for which descriptive statistics are to be calculated. For example, to obtain descriptive statistics for the variables SALBEG and EDUC, specify

EXAMINE **VARIABLES=SALBEG EDUC**.

The VARIABLES subcommand can be specified only once.

9.18
Specifying Cells

To subdivide cases into cells based on their values for grouping (factor) variables, specify the factor variables after keyword BY. String variables can be used as factors, but only the first eight characters are used.

For example, to obtain summary statistics for SALBEG and EDUC when cases are subdivided into employment categories (JOBCAT), specify

```
EXAMINE VARIABLES=SALBEG EDUC BY JOBCAT.
```

If several variables are listed after keyword BY, separate analyses are obtained for each factor variable. For example, the command

```
EXAMINE VARIABLES=SALBEG EDUC BY JOBCAT SEX.
```

will produce summary statistics for salary and education for categories of JOBCAT and for categories of SEX. To obtain summary statistics for cells based on the combination of values of JOBCAT and SEX, use the keyword BY to separate the factor names. The command

```
EXAMINE VARIABLES=SALBEG EDUC BY JOBCAT BY SEX.
```

will produce descriptive statistics for cells formed by the combination of values of sex and job category. That is, there will be cells for males and females within each job category. If there are five job categories, you will obtain 11 analyses: one for all cases combined, and one for each of the ten cells formed by the combinations of JOBCAT and SEX. Note that you will not obtain analyses for each individual job category and for each sex. To obtain this additional output, specify

```
EXAMINE VARIABLES=SALBEG EDUC BY SEX JOBCAT JOBCAT BY SEX.
```

Note that specifying many cells will generate a large amount of output. Be sure to request only the analyses that you need.

9.19
ID Subcommand

Individual cases can be identified in the output according to their values for a selected variable specified on the ID subcommand. For example, to identify cases by their values for EMPLNO, specify:

```
EXAMINE VARIABLES=SALBEG BY JOBCAT /ID=EMPLNO.
```

If the ID subcommand is not specified, the SPSS system variable $CASENUM is used.

9.20
STATISTICS Subcommand

Use the STATISTICS subcommand to control the output of basic descriptive statistics. The following keywords can be specified:

DESCRIPTIVE *Basic descriptive statistics only.* This includes the mean, median, mode, 5% trimmed mean, standard error, variance, standard deviation, minimum, maximum, range, interquartile range and skewness and kurtosis, and their standard errors. Interquartile range computations are based on the method specified with the PERCENTILES subcommand.

EXTREMES (n) *The cases with the* n *largest and* n *smallest values.* If *n* is omitted, the cases with the five largest and five smallest values are displayed. Cases are identified by their values for the variable specified on the ID subcommand. If the ID subcommand is not used, cases are identified by their values for the SPSS system variable $CASENUM.

ALL *Basic descriptive statistics and extreme values.* All statistics available with DESCRIPTIVE and EXTREMES are displayed. The default *n* of 5 is used for EXTREMES.

NONE *Neither basic descriptive statistics nor extreme values.*

9.21
MESTIMATORS Subcommand

Use the MESTIMATORS subcommand to obtain robust maximum-likelihood estimators of location. If the MESTIMATORS subcommand is specified without keywords, all four M-estimators are calculated. Individual estimators and constants at which the weighting scheme changes can be selected with the following keywords:

HUBER(c)   *Huber's M-estimator with constant* c. By default, $c=1.339$.

ANDREWS(c)   *Andrews' wave estimator with constant* c. The constant is multiplied by pi. By default, $c=1.34$.

HAMPEL(a,b,c)   *Hampel's redescending M-estimator with constants* a, b, *and* c. By default, $a=1.7$, $b=3.4$, and $c=8.5$.

TUKEY(c)   *Tukey's biweight estimator with constant* c. By default, $c=4.685$.

ALL   *All four M-estimators.* This is the default when MESTIMATORS is specified without a keyword.

NONE   *No M-estimators.* This is the default if MESTIMATORS is omitted.

For example, to calculate all four M-estimators for the variable DBP58, specify:

```
EXAMINE VARIABLES=DBP58 /MESTIMATORS.
```

To obtain only the Andrew's estimator with a constant of 2 pi, specify:

```
EXAMINE VARIABLES=DBP58 /MESTIMATORS ANDREWS(2).
```

9.22
FREQUENCIES Subcommand

Use the FREQUENCIES subcommand to obtain frequency tables. You can specify starting values and increment sizes. For example, to obtain a frequency table for DBP58 using increments of 5 and starting at 70, specify

```
EXAMINE VARIABLES=DBP58 /FREQUENCIES FROM (70) BY (5).
```

If you do not specify a starting value or increment, EXAMINE will select a value based on the data. If you specify an increment of 0, a frequency table for each distinct value is produced.

9.23
PERCENTILES Subcommand

Use the PERCENTILES subcommand to obtain percentiles. You can also select the method of estimation. For example, to calculate the 25th, 50th, and 75th percentiles using the default method of estimation, specify

```
EXAMINE VARIABLES=DBP58 /PERCENTILES(25,50,75).
```

If you specify the PERCENTILES subcommand without percentile values in parentheses, the default percentiles are 5, 10, 25, 50, 75, 90, and 95.

The following methods are available for calculating the percentiles, where W is the sum of weights for all nonmissing cases, p is the percentile divided by 100, i is the rank of the case when cases are sorted in ascending order, and X_i is the value for the ith case.

HAVERAGE   *Weighted average at* $X_{(W+1)p}$. The percentile value is the weighted average of X_i and X_{i+1} using the formula $(1-f)X_i + fX_{i+1}$, where $(W+1)p$ is decomposed into an integer part i and fractional part f. This is the default if PERCENTILES is specified without a keyword.

WAVERAGE   *Weighted average at* X_{Wp}. The percentile value is the weighted average of X_i and X_{i+1} using the formula $(1-f)X_i + fX_{i+1}$, where i is the integer part of Wp.

ROUND   *Observation closest to* Wp. The percentile value is X_i, where i is the integer part of $(Wp + 0.5)$.

EMPIRICAL   *Empirical distribution function.* The percentile value is X_i when the fractional Wp is equal to 0 and i is the integer part. The percentile value is X_{i+1} when the fractional part of Wp is greater than 0.

AEMPIRICAL   *Empirical distribution with averaging.* The percentile value is $(X_i + X_{i+1})/2$ when the fractional part of Wp equals 0. The percentile value is X_{i+1} when the fractional part of Wp is greater than 0.

NONE   *No percentile output.* This is the default if PERCENTILES is omitted.

The keyword for the method to be used for calculating the percentiles follows the list of percentile values, as in:

```
EXAMINE  VARIABLES=DBP58 /PERCENTILES(25 50 75)=WAVERAGE.
```

To obtain default percentiles for a specified method, specify the method keyword in parentheses after the PERCENTILES subcommand, as in:

```
EXAMINE VARIABLES=DBP58 /PERCENTILES=EMPIRICAL.
```

9.24
PLOT Subcommand

EXAMINE produces boxplots, stem-and-leaf plots, histograms, normal probability plots, and spread-and-level plots. If the PLOT subcommand is specified without any keywords or if the subcommand is omitted, stem-and-leaf plots and boxplots are produced. If any plots are specified on PLOT, only the requested plots are displayed.

The following keywords can be used with the PLOT subcommand:

BOXPLOT   *Boxplot.* The boundaries of the box are Tukey's hinges. The median is identified by an asterisk. The length of the box is the interquartile range (IQR) based on Tukey's hinges. Values more than 3 IQR's from the end of the box are labeled as extreme (E). Values more than 1.5 IQR's from the end of the box but less than 3 IQR's are labeled as outliers (O). This is produced by default.

STEMLEAF   *Stem-and-leaf plot.* Plot in which each observed value is divided into two components—the leading digits (stem) and trailing digits (leaf). This is produced by default.

HISTOGRAM   *Histogram.*

SPREADLEVEL(p)   *Spread-and-level plot.* If the keyword appears alone, for each cell, the natural log of the interquartile range is plotted against the log of the median. If the power for transforming the data (p) is supplied, the power transformation is performed and the IQR and median of the transformed data are plotted. If p=0 is specified, a natural log transformation of the data is done. The slope of the regression line and Levene's test for homogeneity of variance are also displayed. Levene's test is based on the original data if no transformation is specified and on the transformed data if a transformation is done.

NPPLOT   *Normal probability and detrended probability plots.* The Shapiro-Wilks statistic and the Kolmogorov-Smirnov statistic with a Lilliefors significance level for testing normality are calculated. The Shapiro-Wilks statistic is not calculated when the sample size exceeds 50.

ALL   *All available plots.*

NONE   *No plots.*

For example, to request stem-and-leaf plots and normal probability plots, specify:

```
EXAMINE VARIABLES=DBP58 /PLOT=STEMLEAF NPPLOT.
```

To determine an appropriate transformation of the data based on a plot of the logs of the interquartile ranges against the logs of the medians, specify:

```
EXAMINE VARIABLES=DBP58 /PLOT=SPREADLEVEL.
```

To obtain a plot of interquartile ranges against medians when the data values are squared, specify:

```
EXAMINE VARIABLES=DBP58 /PLOT=SPREADLEVEL(2).
```

To obtain a plot of the interquartile ranges against the medians after the data have been log transformed, specify:

```
EXAMINE VARIABLES=DBP58 /PLOT=SPREADLEVEL(0).
```

The following commands produced Figures 9.9b, 9.11, and 9.13:

```
SELECT IF (JOBCAT LE 5).
EXAMINE VARIABLES=SALBEG BY JOBCAT
 /PLOT=BOXPLOT SPREADLEVEL.
```

9.25
COMPARE Subcommand

Use the COMPARE subcommand to control how boxplots are displayed. Two methods are available. For each variable, you can display the boxplots for all cells side by side, or you can display all of the boxplots for a cell together. (You will have several boxplots for a single cell only if you specify more than one dependent variable.)

The method you use depends on the comparisons of interest. If you display the boxplots for all cells together, you can see how the distribution of a particular variable differs for the cells. For example, suppose you have variables SAL1, SAL2, SAL3, and SAL4, containing yearly salaries for the first four years of employment. If you specify

```
EXAMINE VARIABLES=SAL1 SAL2 SAL3 SAL4 BY JOBCAT BY SEX
 /COMPARE GROUPS.
```

you could easily compare each of the yearly salaries for the JOBCAT/SEX groups, since the distribution of SAL1 would be shown for all groups, followed by the distribution of SAL2 for all groups, and so forth. However, if you specify

```
EXAMINE VARIABLES=SAL1 SAL2 SAL3 SAL4 BY JOBCAT BY SEX
 /COMPARE VARIABLES.
```

for each group, the boxplots for the four salaries will be displayed together. This allows you to examine salary changes over time for each group.

9.26
SCALE Subcommand

By default, the histogram and stem-and-leaf scale are based on the values of the cases in a particular plot. You can, however, use the same scale for all plots for each dependent variable by specifying the SCALE subcommand. The following keywords are available:

PLOTWISE   *Scales are based on the values of cases in each plot.* This is the default.
UNIFORM   *All plots for each dependent variable use the same scale.*

For example, if you specify

```
EXAMINE VARIABLES=SAL1 BY JOCBCAT /SCALE=UNIFORM.
```

the same scale is used for all stem-and-leaf plots. If histograms are requested, they will also be on the same scale.

9.27
MISSING Subcommand

By default, cases with either system- or user-missing values for any variable specified on the VARIABLES subcommand are excluded from the analysis. You can specify other missing-value treatments using the MISSING subcommand. The following keywords are available:

LISTWISE   *Cases with any missing values are deleted.* This is the default.
PAIRWISE   *Cases with nonmissing values for a cell are included in the analysis of that cell.* The case may have missing values for variables used in other cells.

REPORT   *Missing values for factor variables are treated as a separate category.* All output is produced for this additional category. Frequency tables include categories for missing values.

INCLUDE   *Cases with user-missing values are included.* Only cases with system-missing values are excluded from the analysis. This keyword can be used together with LISTWISE, PAIRWISE, or REPORT.

For example, the command

```
EXAMINE VARIABLES=SALBEG EDUC BY JOBCAT /MISSING PAIRWISE.
```

excludes cases from the analysis of SALBEG only if they have missing values for SALBEG or JOBCAT. It doesn't matter whether the value of EDUC is missing or not. Only cases with missing values for EDUC or JOBCAT will be excluded from the analysis of EDUC.

9.28
Annotated Example

```
GET FILE=ELECTRIC.
SET WIDTH=90.
EXAMINE VARIABLES=DBP58
 /PLOT=STEMLEAF NPPLOT
 /STATISTICS=ALL.
```

- The GET command specifies the SPSS system file (ELECTRIC) to be read.
- The SET command sets the page width to 90 characters (allowing enough space for the plots in Figure 9.14d to be displayed side by side) in the output.
- The EXAMINE command and VARIABLES subcommand name the variable to be examined.
- The PLOT subcommand produces the stem-and-leaf plot in Figure 9.7a and the side-by-side normal probability and detrended normal plots in Figure 9.14d.
- The STATISTICS subcommand displays the default five lowest and five highest extreme values in Figure 9.7b and descriptive statistics.

9.29
EXERCISES

Syntax

Find the syntax errors in the following EXAMINE commands:

1.  ```
    EXAMINE VARIABLES=INCOME IQ
       /PLOT=HISTOGRAM
       /PLOT=STEMLEAF.
    ```

2.  ```
    EXAMINE VARIABLES=ATTNSPAN BY TVHOURS
       /STATISTICS=MEAN
       /PLOT=SPREADLEVEL.
    ```

3.  ```
    EXAMINE VARIABLES=GPA BY MAJOR BY SEX
       /PLOT=NONE /STATISTICS=EXTREME(3)
       /PERCENTILES=25, 50, 75.
    ```

4. Write the EXAMINE command to produce boxplots—with no additional plots or statistics—for INCOME within categories of RELIGION and for INCOME broken down by both RELIGION and belief in an afterlife (POSTLIFE).

5. Modify the above command to include the Levene test for homogeneity of variance.

Statistical Concepts

1. Consider the following twenty ages:

   21 22 22 22 25 28 30 31 32 34 35 35 35 35 38 39 40 40 41 80

   Complete the following stem-and-leaf plots for them:

   a.
   ```
      Frequency    Stem & Leaf

          ?          2  .  ?
          ?          3  .  ?
          ?          4  .  ?
          ?        Extremes   ?
   ```
   ```

```
b.   Frequency     Stem & Leaf
         ?            2  *    ?
         ?            2  .    ?
         ?            3  *    ?
         ?            3  .    ?
         ?            4  *    ?
         ?         Extremes   ?

c.   Frequency     Stem & Leaf
         ?            2  *    ?
         ?            2  t    ?
         ?            2  f    ?
         ?            2  s    ?
         ?            2  .    ?
         ?            3  *    ?
         ?            3  t    ?
         ?            3  f    ?
         ?            3  s    ?
         ?            3  .    ?
         ?            4  *    ?
         ?         Extremes   ?
```

2. Complete the following historgram for the data in problem 1:

```
Frequency    Bin Center

    ?          25.00    ?
    ?          35.00    ?
    ?          45.00    ?
    ?         Extremes  ?

Bin width :    10.00
Each star:      1 case(s)
```

3. Compared to a histogram, what are the advantages of a stem-and-leaf plot?

4. Answer the following questions based on the accompanying box-and-whisker plot. The box-and-whisker plots represent the time it took to ship products from three warehouses.

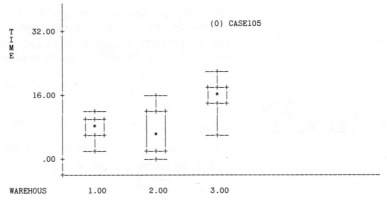

   a. Estimate the median for warehouse 1.

   b. Estimate the interquartile range for warehouse 2.

   c. For warehouse 3, what is the largest value that is not an outlier?

   d. Which warehouse has the most variability?

   e. If you were to choose one of the warehouses to ship your product, which warehouse would you select and why?

5. Based on the following stem-and-leaf plot, complete the frequency table below.

```
Frequency    Stem & Leaf

   5.00       15  .  03469
   8.00       16  .  11235788
   4.00       17  .  0022
   2.00       18  .  08
   1.00       19  .  0
   1.00       20  .  4
   1.00       21  .  5
   3.00       22  .  228

Stem width:    10.0C
Each leaf:      1 case(s)
```

                    Frequency Table
                    ───────── ─────

Bin Center	Freq	Pct	Cum Pct
<150.0	?	?	?
162.5	?	?	?
187.5	?	?	?
212.5	?	?	?
237.5	?	?	?

6. The following is a stem-and-leaf plot for the starting salaries of 25 men.

```
Frequency    Stem &  Leaf

    2.00        21  .  56
    3.00        22  .  344
    4.00        23  .  0168
    4.00        24  .  2355
    5.00        25  .  04789
    1.00        26  .  7
    2.00        27  .  07
    1.00        28  .  5
     .00        29  .
    2.00        30  .  05
    1.00     Extremes      (35150)

Stem width:      1000
Each leaf:       1 case(s)
```

a. From the plot can you tell what the actual salaries for all of the men?

b. List the salaries in an as much detail as you can.

7. What is the null hypothesis being tested by the Levene test? Give an example of a statistical technique for which the test may be useful.

8. Based on the following table what would you conclude about the results of the Levene test?

Test of homogeneity of variance		dfl	df2	Significance
Levene Statistic	1.5667	11	1449	.1025

9. Select the normal probability plot that corresponds to each of the following stem-and-leaf plots.

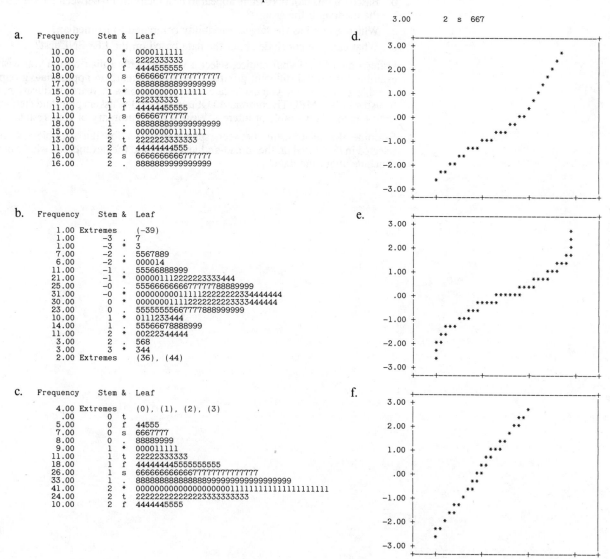

a.
```
Frequency    Stem &  Leaf

    10.00       0  *   0000111111
    10.00       0  t   2222333333
    10.00       0  f   4444555555
    18.00       0  s   666666777777777777
    17.00       0  .   88888888899999999
    15.00       1  *   000000000111111
     9.00       1  t   222333333
    11.00       1  f   44444455555
    11.00       1  s   66666777777
    18.00       1  .   888888899999999999
    15.00       2  *   000000001111111
    13.00       2  t   2222223333333
    11.00       2  f   44444444555
    16.00       2  s   6666666666777777
    16.00       2  .   8888889999999999
```

b.
```
Frequency    Stem &  Leaf

     1.00    Extremes      (-39)
     1.00      -3  .   7
     1.00      -3  *   3
     7.00      -2  .   5567889
     6.00      -2  *   000014
    11.00      -1  .   55566888999
    21.00      -1  *   000001112222223333444
    25.00      -0  .   5556666666677777788889999
    31.00      -0  *   0000000001111122222222334444444
    30.00       0  *   000000111122222222223333444444
    23.00       0  .   55555555667777888999999
    10.00       1  *   0111233444
    14.00       1  .   55566678888999
    11.00       2  *   00222344444
     3.00       2  .   568
     3.00       3  *   344
     2.00    Extremes      (36), (44)
```

c.
```
Frequency    Stem &  Leaf

     4.00    Extremes      (0), (1), (2), (3)
      .00       0  t
     5.00       0  f   44555
     7.00       0  s   6667777
     8.00       0  .   88889999
     9.00       1  *   000011111
    11.00       1  t   22222333333
    18.00       1  f   444444445555555555
    26.00       1  s   66666666666677777777777777
    33.00       1  .   888888888888889999999999999999999
    41.00       2  *   00000000000000000000111111111111111111111
    24.00       2  t   222222222222223333333333
    10.00       2  f   4444445555
```

10. Based on the summary statistics shown in the table below, sketch a box-and-whiskers plot.

Mean	44.0048	Std Err	.4650	Min	18.0000	Skewness	.5317
Median	40.0000	Variance	317.2203	Max	89.0000	S E Skew	.0639
5% Trim	43.2546	Std Dev	17.8107	Range	71.0000	Kurtosis	-.8026
				IQR	29.0000	S E Kurt	.1277

Percentiles

Percentiles	10.0000	25.0000	50.0000	75.0000	90.0000
HAVERAGE	23.0000	29.0000	40.0000	58.0000	70.0000
TUKEY'S HINGES		29.0000	40.0000	58.0000	

Data Analysis

Use the BANK system file for Questions 1-2.

1. a. Obtain a box-and-whiskers plot showing the age distributions in each of the four sex-race groups.
    b. Which group has the highest median age?
    c. Which group has the smallest variability?
    d. Below which value do 25% of the ages fall in the last group? In the first group?
    e. Estimate the interquartile range for the third group.
    f. Write a brief summary comparing the age distributions in the four groups.

2. a. Obtain a spread-and-level plot for age for the four sex-race groups.
    b. Based on this plot does there appear to be a relationship between the spread and the median of the groups?
    c. Which group has the largest variability compared to its median?
    d. What can you conclude about the data based on the LEVENE test?

3. Using a data file of your choice, select a variable with a distribution you wish to examine for several different groups. If necessary create an appropriate grouping variable. (For example you can create groups based on age, years of education, etc. by using the COMPUTE command.) Obtain box-and-whiskers plots and stem-and-leaf plots for the variable of interest. Write a brief summary of your results.

4. Examine the relationship between spread-and-level for the variable you have selected in (3). Based on the spread-and-level plot and the Levene test, what can you conclude about the data?

Crosstabulation

In this chapter:

Goals:

- To determine the number of cases for each possible combination of values of two or more variables.
- To statistically test whether two variables are independent.
- To quantify the strength of the association between two variables.

Examples:

- Look at satisfaction with educational curricula for students in three different majors.
- Establish whether brand preference for soap is independent of socioeconomic status.
- Measure how strong the relationship between husbands' and wives' attitudes is towards the importance of religion in family life.

How it's done:

The number of cases in each cell of a crosstabulation table can be expressed as a percentage of the row total, column total and table total. These percentages are useful for describing the table and for looking at relationships between the two variables.

The chi-square statistic can be used to test whether the two variables in a crosstabulation are independent. Expected frequencies for each cell, based on the assumption of independence, are compared to the observed frequencies. If the observed significance level for the chi-square statistic is small, the hypothesis of independence can be rejected.

Numerous measures of association, which attempt to quantify the strength and nature of the relationship of the two variables, are available. They differ in the way they define association.

Data considerations:

The variables used for constructing the rows and columns of the table must have a limited number of distinct values, though they may represent an underlying continuum. For example, salary may be grouped into four categories. To use the chi-square statistic, none of the expected values should be less than 1, and no more than 20 percent of the expected values should be less than five. When selecting a measure of association, the level of measurement of the variables must be considered.

Crosstabulation and Measures of Association: Procedure CROSSTABS

Newspapers headline murders in subway stations, robberies on crowded main streets, suicides cheered by onlookers. All are indications of the social irresponsibility and apathy said to characterize city residents. Since overcrowding, decreased sense of community, and other urban problems are usually blamed, you might ask whether small town residents are more responsible and less apathetic than their urban counterparts.

Hansson and Slade (1977) used the "lost letter technique" to test the hypothesis that altruism is higher in small towns than in cities, unless the person needing assistance is a social deviant. In this technique, stamped and addressed letters are "lost," and the rate at which they are returned is examined. A total of 216 letters were lost in Hansson and Slade's experiment. Half were dropped within the city limits of Tulsa, Oklahoma, the others in 51 small towns within a 50-mile radius of Tulsa. The letters were addressed to three fictitious people at a post-office box in Tulsa: M. J. Davis; Dandee Davis, c/o Pink Panther Lounge; and M. J. Davis, c/o Friends of the Communist Party. The first person is considered a normal "control," the second a person whose occupation is questionable, and the third a subversive or political deviant.

10.1 CROSSTABULATION

To see whether the return rate is similar for the three addresses, the letters found and mailed and those not mailed must be tallied separately for each address. Figure 10.1 is a *crosstabulation* of address type and response. The number of cases (letters) for each combination of values of the two variables is displayed in a *cell* in the table, together with various percentages. These cell entries provide information about relationships between the variables.

Figure 10.1 Crosstabulation of status of letter by address

```
CROSSTABS TABLES=RETURNED BY ADDRESS
  /CELLS.
```

RETURNED FOUND AND MAILED by ADDRESS ADDRESS ON LETTER				
	ADDRESS			Page 1 of 1
Count Row Pct Col Pct Tot Pct	CONTROL 1	DANDEE 2	COMMUNIS T 3	Row Total
RETURNED				
YES 1	35 45.5 48.6 16.2	32 41.6 44.4 14.8	10 13.0 13.9 4.6	77 35.6
NO 2	37 26.6 51.4 17.1	40 28.8 55.6 18.5	62 44.6 86.1 28.7	139 64.4
Column Total	72 33.3	72 33.3	72 33.3	216 100.0
Number of Missing Observations: 0				

113

In Figure 10.1, the address is called the *column* variable since each address is displayed in a column of the table. Similarly, the status of the letter, whether it was returned or not, is called the *row* variable. With three categories of the column variable and two of the row, there are six cells in the table.

10.2
Cell Contents and Marginals

The first entry in the table is the number of cases, or *frequency*, in that cell. It is labeled as **Count** in the key displayed in the upper-left corner of the table. For example, 35 letters addressed to the control were returned, and 62 letters addressed to the Communist were not returned. The second entry in the table is the *row percentage* (**Row Pct**). It is the percentage of all cases in a row that fall into a particular cell. Of the 77 letters returned, 45.5% were addressed to the control, 41.6% to Dandee, and 13.0% to the Communist.

The *column percentage* (**Col Pct**), the third item in each cell, is the percentage of all cases in a column that occur in a cell. For example, 48.6% of the letters addressed to the control were returned and 51.4% were not. The return rate for Dandee is similar (44.4%), while that for the Communist is markedly lower (13.9%).

The last entry in the table is the *table percentage* (**Tot Pct**). The number of cases in the cell is expressed as a percentage of the total number of cases in the table. For example, the 35 letters returned to the control represent 16.2% of the 216 letters in the experiment.

The numbers to the right and below the table are known as *marginals*. They are the counts and percentages for the row and column variables taken separately. In Figure 10.1, the row marginals show that 77 (35.6%) of the letters were returned, while 139 (64.4%) were not.

10.3
Choosing Percentages

Row, column, and table percentages convey different types of information, so it is important to choose carefully among them.

In this example, the row percentage indicates the distribution of address types for returned and "lost" letters. It conveys no direct information about the return rate. For example, if twice as many letters were addressed to the control, an identical return rate for all letters would give row percentages of 50%, 25%, and 25%. However, this does not indicate that the return rate is higher for the control. In addition, if each category had the same number of returned letters, the row percentages would have been 33.3%, 33.3%, and 33.3%, regardless of whether one or all letters were returned.

The column percentage is the percentage of letters returned and not returned for each address. By looking at column percentages across rows, you can compare return rates for the address types. Interpretation of this comparison would not be affected if unequal numbers of letters had been addressed to each category.

Since it is always possible to interchange the rows and columns of any table, general rules about when to use row and column percentages cannot be given. The percentages to use depend on the nature of the two variables. If one of the two variables is under experimental control, it is termed an *independent variable*. This variable is hypothesized to affect the response, or *dependent variable*. If variables can be classified as dependent and independent, the following guideline may be helpful: If the independent variable is the row variable, select row percentages; if the independent variable is the column variable, select column percentages. In this example the dependent variable is the status of the letter, whether it was mailed or not. The type of address is the independent variable. Since the independent variable is the column variable in Figure 10.1, column percentages should be used for comparisons of return rates.

10.4
Adding a Control Variable

Since Figure 10.1 combines results from both the city and the towns, differences between the locations are obscured. Two separate tables, one for the city and one for the towns, are required. Figure 10.4 shows crosstabulations of response and address for each of the locations. SPSS produces a separate table for each value of the location (control) variable.

Figure 10.4 Crosstabulations of status of letter by address controlled for location

```
CROSSTABS TABLES=RETURNED BY ADDRESS BY LOCATION
 /CELLS=COUNT COLUMN /STATISTICS=CHISQ.
```

```
RETURNED  FOUND AND MAILED  by  ADDRESS  ADDRESS ON LETTER
Controlling for..
LOCATION  LOCATION LOST  Value = 1  CITY

                    ADDRESS                      Page 1 of 1
           Count
           Col Pct  CONTROL  DANDEE  COMMUNIS
                                         T
                                                 Row
                       1  |    2  |    3  | Total
RETURNED   ---------+------+------+------+
           1  |    16 |    14 |     9 |    39
   YES         44.4    38.9    25.0    36.1
           ---------+------+------+------+
           2  |    20 |    22 |    27 |    69
   NO          55.6    61.1    75.0    63.9
           ---------+------+------+------+
           Column    36      36      36     108
           Total   33.3    33.3    33.3   100.0

      Chi-Square             Value        DF        Significance
   --------------------   ---------     ----      ------------

Pearson                    3.13043        2           .20904
Likelihood Ratio           3.21256        2           .20063
Mantel-Haenszel            2.92252        1           .08735

Minimum Expected Frequency -   13.000




RETURNED  FOUND AND MAILED  by  ADDRESS  ADDRESS ON LETTER
Controlling for..
LOCATION  LOCATION LOST  Value = 2  TOWN

                    ADDRESS                      Page 1 of 1
           Count
           Col Pct  CONTROL  DANDEE  COMMUNIS
                                         T
                                                 Row
                       1  |    2  |    3  | Total
RETURNED   ---------+------+------+------+
           1  |    19 |    18 |     1 |    38
   YES         52.8    50.0     2.8    35.2
           ---------+------+------+------+
           2  |    17 |    18 |    35 |    70
   NO          47.2    50.0    97.2    64.8
           ---------+------+------+------+
           Column    36      36      36     108
           Total   33.3    33.3    33.3   100.0

      Chi-Square             Value        DF        Significance
   --------------------   ---------     ----      ------------

Pearson                   24.92932        2           .00000
Likelihood Ratio          31.25342        2           .00000
Mantel-Haenszel           19.54962        1           .00001

Minimum Expected Frequency -   12.667


Number of Missing Observations:  0
```

These tables show interesting differences between cities and towns. Although the overall return rates are close, 36.1% for the city and 35.2% for the towns, there are striking differences between the addresses. Only 2.8% of the Communist letters were returned in towns, while 25.0% of them were returned in Tulsa. (At least two of the Communist letters were forwarded by small-town residents to the FBI for punitive action!) The return rates for both the control (52.8%) and Dandee (50.0%) are higher in towns.

The results support the hypothesis that, in small towns, suspected social deviance influences the response more than in big cities, although it is surprising that Dandee and the Pink Panther Lounge were deemed worthy of as much assistance as they received. If the Communist letter is excluded, inhabitants of small towns are somewhat more helpful than city residents, returning 51% of the other letters, in comparison to the city's 42%.

10.5 GRAPHICAL REPRESENTATION OF CROSSTABULATIONS

As with frequency tables, visual representation of a crosstabulation often simplifies the search for associations. Figure 10.5 is a bar chart of letters returned from the crosstabulations shown in Figure 10.4. In a bar chart, the length of each bar represents the frequencies or percentages for each category of a variable. In Figure 10.5, the percentages plotted are the column percentages shown in Figure 10.4 for the returned letters only. This chart clearly shows that the return rates for the control and Dandee are high compared to the return rate for the Communist. Also, it demonstrates more vividly than the crosstabulation that the town residents' return rates for the control and Dandee are higher than city residents' return rates but that the reverse is true for the Communist.

Figure 10.5 Status of letter by address by location (bar chart from SPSS Graphics)

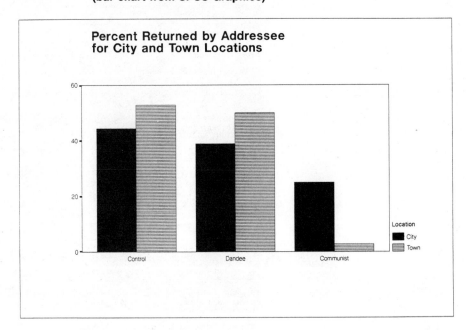

10.6 USING CROSSTABULATION FOR DATA SCREENING

Errors and unusual values in data entry that cannot be spotted with FREQUEN-CIES can sometimes be identified using crosstabulation. For example, a case coded as a male with a history of three pregnancies would not be identified as suspicious in FREQUENCIES tables of sex and number of pregnancies. When considered separately, the code for male is acceptable for variable sex and the value 3 is acceptable for number of pregnancies. Jointly, however, the combination is unexpected.

Whenever possible, crosstabulations of related variables should be obtained so that anomalies can be identified and corrected before further statistical analysis of the data.

10.7
CROSSTABULATION STATISTICS

Although examination of the various row and column percentages in a crosstabulation is a useful first step in studying the relationship between two variables, row and column percentages do not allow for quantification or testing of that relationship. For these purposes, it is useful to consider various indexes that measure the extent of association as well as statistical tests of the hypothesis that there is no association.

10.8
The Chi-Square Test of Independence

The hypothesis that two variables of a crosstabulation are *independent* of each other is often of interest to researchers. Two variables are by definition independent if the probability that a case falls into a given cell is simply the product of the marginal probabilities of the two categories defining the cell.

For example, in Figure 10.1 if returns of the letter and address type are independent, the probability of a letter being returned to a Communist is the product of the probability of a letter being returned and the probability of a letter being addressed to a Communist. From the table, 35.6% of the letters were returned and 33.3% of the letters were addressed to a friend of the Communist party. Thus, if address type and status of the letter are independent, the probability of a letter being returned to the Communist is estimated to be

$$P(\text{return}) \ P(\text{Communist}) = 0.356 \times 0.333 = 0.119$$

The *expected* number of cases in that cell is 25.7, which is 11.9% of the 216 cases in the sample. From the table, the *observed* number of letters returned to the Communist is 10 (4.6%), nearly 16 fewer than expected if the two variables are independent.

To construct a statistical test of the independence hypothesis, you repeat the above calculations for each cell in the table. The probability under independence of an observation falling into cell (ij) is estimated by

$$P(\text{row} = i \text{ and column} = j) = \left(\frac{\text{count in row } i}{N}\right)\left(\frac{\text{count in column } j}{N}\right) \quad \textbf{Equation 10.8a}$$

To obtain the expected number of observations in cell (ij), the probability is multiplied by the total sample size.

$$E_{ij} = N\left(\frac{\text{count in row } i}{N}\right)\left(\frac{\text{count in column } j}{N}\right)$$

$$= \frac{(\text{count in row } i)(\text{count in column } j)}{N}$$

Equation 10.8b

Figure 10.8 contains the observed and expected frequencies and the *residuals*, which are the observed minus the expected frequencies for the data in Figure 10.1.

Figure 10.8 Observed, expected, and residual values

```
CROSSTABS TABLES=RETURNED BY ADDRESS
 /CELLS=COUNT EXPECTED RESID
 /STATISTICS=CHISQ.
```

RETURNED FOUND AND MAILED by ADDRESS ADDRESS ON LETTER				
	ADDRESS			Page 1 of 1
Count Exp Val Residual	CONTROL	DANDEE	COMMUNIST	Row Total
	1	2	3	
RETURNED				
YES 1	35	32	10	77
	25.7	25.7	25.7	35.6%
	9.3	6.3	-15.7	
NO 2	37	40	62	139
	46.3	46.3	46.3	64.4%
	-9.3	-6.3	15.7	
Column Total	72	72	72	216
	33.3%	33.3%	33.3%	100.0%

Chi-Square	Value	DF	Significance
Pearson	22.56265	2	.00001
Likelihood Ratio	24.68680	2	.00000
Mantel-Haenszel	18.83234	1	.00001

```
Minimum Expected Frequency -  25.667


Number of Missing Observations:  0
```

A statistic often used to test the hypothesis that the row and column variables are independent is the *Pearson chi-square*. It is calculated by summing over all cells the squared residuals divided by the expected frequencies.

$$\chi^2 = \sum_i \sum_j \frac{(O_{ij} - E_{ij})^2}{E_{ij}}$$

Equation 10.8c

The calculated chi-square is compared to the critical points of the theoretical chi-square distribution to produce an estimate of how likely (or unlikely) this calculated value is if the two variables are in fact independent. Since the value of the chi-square depends on the number of rows and columns in the table being examined, you must know the *degrees of freedom* for the table. The degrees of freedom can be viewed as the number of cells of a table that can be arbitrarily filled when the row and column totals (marginals) are fixed. For an $r \times c$ table, the degrees of freedom are $(r - 1) \times (c - 1)$, since once $(r-1)$ rows and $(c-1)$ columns are filled, frequencies in the remaining row and column cells must be chosen so that marginal totals are maintained.

In this example, there are two degrees of freedom (1×2), and the Pearson chi-square value is 22.56 (see Figure 10.8). If type of address and return rate are independent, the probability that a random sample would result in a chi-square value of at least that magnitude is less than 0.00001. This probability is also known as the *observed significance level* of the test. If the probability is small enough (usually less than 0.05 or 0.01), the hypothesis that the two variables are independent is rejected.

Since the observed significance level in Figure 10.1 is very small (based on the combined city and town data), the hypothesis that address type and return rate are independent is rejected. When the chi-square test is calculated for the city and town data separately (Figure 10.4), different results are obtained. The observed significance level of the city data is 0.209, so the independence hypothesis is not rejected. For the towns, the observed significance level is less than 0.000005, and the hypothesis that address and return rate are independent is rejected. These results support the theory that city and town residents respond differently.

An alternative to the commonly used Pearson chi-square is the likelihood ratio chi-square (see Figure 10.8). This test is based on maximum likelihood theory and is often used in the analysis of categorical data. For large samples, the Pearson and likelihood ratio chi-square statistics give very similar results. (The test labeled **Mantel-Haenszel** is discussed in section 10.15.)

The chi-square test is a test of independence; it provides little information about the strength or form of the association between two variables. The magnitude of the observed chi-square depends not only on the goodness of fit of the independence model but also on the sample size. If the sample size for a particular table increases n-fold, so does the chi-square value. Thus, large chi-square values can arise in applications where residuals are small relative to expected frequencies but where the sample size is large.

Certain conditions must be met for the chi-square distribution to be a good approximation of the distribution of the statistic in the equation given above. The data must be random samples from multinomial distributions and the expected values must not be too small. While it has been recommended that all expected frequencies be at least 5, recent studies indicate that this is probably too stringent and can be relaxed (Everitt, 1977). CROSSTABS displays the number of cells with expected frequencies less than 5 and the minimum expected cell value.

To improve the approximation for a 2 × 2 table, *Yates' correction for continuity* is sometimes applied. Yates' correction for continuity involves subtracting 0.5 from positive differences between observed and expected frequencies (the residuals) and adding 0.5 to negative differences before squaring. For a discussion of some of the controversy regarding the merits of this correction, see Conover (1974) and Mantel (1974).

An alternative test for the 2 × 2 table is based on the hypergeometric distribution. Exact probabilities of obtaining the observed results if the two variables are independent and the marginals fixed are calculated. This is called *Fisher's exact test*. It is most useful when the total sample size and the expected values are small. SPSS calculates Fisher's exact test if any expected cell value in a 2 × 2 table is less than 5.

10.9
Measures of Association

In many research situations, the strength and nature of the dependence of variables is of central concern. Indexes that attempt to quantify the relationship between variables in a cross-classification are called *measures of association*. No single measure adequately summarizes all possible types of association. Measures vary in their interpretation and in the way they define perfect and intermediate association. These measures also differ in the way they are affected by various factors such as marginals. For example, many measures are "margin sensitive" in that they are influenced by the marginal distributions of the rows and columns. Such measures reflect information about the marginals along with information about association.

A particular measure may have a low value for a given table, not because the two variables are not related but because they are not related in the way to which the measure is sensitive. No single measure is best for all situations. The type of data, the hypothesis of interest, as well as the properties of the various measures must all be considered when selecting an index of association for a given table. It is not, however, reasonable to compute a large number of measures and then to report the most impressive as if it were the only one examined.

The measures of association available in CROSSTABS are computed only from bivariate tables. For example, if three dichotomous variables are specified in the table, two sets of measures are computed, one for each subtable produced by the values of the controlling variable. In general, if relationships among more than two variables are to be studied, examination of bivariate tables is only a first step. For an extensive discussion of various more sophisticated multivariate procedures for the analysis of qualitative data, see Feinberg (1977), Everitt (1977), and Haberman (1978).

10.10
Nominal Measures

Consider measures that assume only that both variables in the table are nominally measured. As such, these measures can only provide some indication of the strength of association between variables; they cannot indicate direction or anything about the nature of the relationship. The measures provided are of two types: those based on the chi-square statistic and those that follow the logic of proportional reduction in error, denoted PRE.

10.11
Chi-Square-Based Measures

As explained above, the chi-square statistic itself is not a good measure of the degree of association between two variables. But its widespread use in tests of independence has encouraged the use of measures of association based upon it. Each of these measures based on the chi-square attempts to modify the chi-square statistic to minimize the influence of sample size and degrees of freedom as well as to restrict the range of values of the measure to those between 0 and 1. Without such adjustments, comparison of chi-square values from tables with varying dimensions and sample sizes is meaningless.

The *phi-coefficient* modifies the Pearson chi-square by dividing it by the sample size and taking the square root of the result:

$$\phi = \sqrt{\frac{\chi^2}{N}}$$

Equation 10.11a

For tables in which one dimension is greater than 2, phi may not lie between 0 and 1 since the chi-square value can be greater than the sample size. To obtain a measure that must lie between 0 and 1, Pearson suggested the use of

$$C = \sqrt{\frac{\chi^2}{\chi^2 + N}}$$

Equation 10.11b

which is called the *coefficient of contingency*. Although the value of this measure is always between 0 and 1, it cannot generally attain the upper limit of 1. The maximum value possible depends upon the number of rows and columns. For example, in a 4 × 4 table, the maximum value of C is 0.87.

Cramér introduced the following variant:

$$V = \sqrt{\frac{\chi^2}{N(k-1)}}$$

Equation 10.11c

where k is the smaller of the number of rows and columns. This statistic, known as *Cramér's V*, can attain the maximum of 1 for tables of any dimension. If one of the table dimensions is 2, V and phi are identical.

Figure 10.11 shows the values of the chi-square based measures for the letter data. The test of the null hypothesis that a measure is 0 is based on the Pearson chi-square probability.

Figure 10.11   Chi-square-based measures

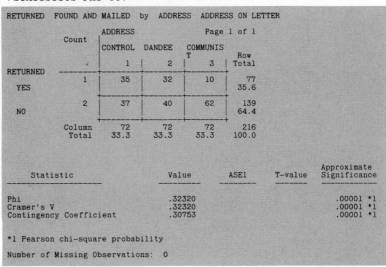

```
CROSSTABS TABLES=RETURNED BY ADDRESS
 /STATISTICS=PHI CC.
```

The chi-square-based measures are hard to interpret. Although when properly standardized they can be used to compare strength of association in several tables, the "strength of association" being compared is not easily related to an intuitive concept of association.

10.12
Proportional Reduction in Error

Common alternatives to chi-square-based measurements are those based on the idea of *proportional reduction in error* (PRE), introduced by Goodman and Kruskal (1954). With PRE measures, the meaning of association is clearer. These measures are all essentially ratios of a measure of error in predicting the values of one variable based on knowledge of that variable alone and the same measure of error applied to predictions based on knowledge of an additional variable.

For example, Figure 10.12 is a crosstabulation of depth of hypnosis and success in treatment of migraine headaches by suggestion (Cedercreutz, 1978). The best guess of the results of treatment when no other information is available is the outcome category with the largest proportion of observations (the modal category). In Figure 10.12, "no change" is the largest outcome category, with 45% of the subjects. The estimate of the probability of incorrect classification is 1 minus the probability of the modal category:

$$P(1) = 1 - 0.45 = 0.55$$

Equation 10.12a

Figure 10.12 Depth of hypnosis and success of treatment

```
CROSSTABS TABLES=HYPNOSIS BY MIGRAINE
 /CELLS=COUNT COLUMN TOTAL
 /STATISTICS=LAMBDA.
```

HYPNOSIS DEPTH OF HYPNOSIS by MIGRAINE OUTCOME

Count Col Pct Tot Pct	MIGRAINE CURED 1.00I	BETTER 2.00I	NO CHANGE 3.00I	Page 1 of 1 Row Total
HYPNOSIS				
1.00 DEEP	13 56.5 13.0	5 15.6 5.0		18 18.0
2.00 MEDIUM	10 43.5 10.0	26 81.3 26.0	17 37.8 17.0	53 53.0
3.00 LIGHT		1 3.1 1.0	28 62.2 28.0	29 29.0
Column Total	23 23.0	32 32.0	45 45.0	100 100.0

Statistic	Value	ASE1	T-value	Approximate Significance
Lambda :				
symmetric	.35294	.11335	2.75267	
with HYPNOSIS dependent	.29787	.14702	1.72276	
with MIGRAINE dependent	.40000	.10539	3.07580	
Goodman & Kruskal Tau :				
with HYPNOSIS dependent	.29435	.06304		.00000 *2
with MIGRAINE dependent	.34508	.04863		.00000 *2

```
*2 Based on chi-square approximation
```

Number of Missing Observations: 0

Information about the depth of hypnosis can be used to improve the classification rule. For each hypnosis category, the outcome category that occurs most frequently for that hypnosis level is predicted. Thus, no change is predicted for participants achieving a light level of hypnosis, better for those achieving a medium level, and cured for those achieving a deep level. The probability of error when depth of hypnosis is used to predict outcome is the sum of the probabilities of all the cells that are not row modes:

$$P(2) = 0.05 + 0.10 + 0.17 + 0.01 = 0.33$$ **Equation 10.12b**

Goodman and Kruskal's *lambda*, with outcome as the predicted (dependent) variable, is calculated as

$$\lambda_{outcome} = \frac{P(1) - P(2)}{P(1)} = \frac{0.55 - 0.33}{0.55} = 0.40$$ **Equation 10.12c**

Thus, a 40% reduction in error is obtained when depth of hypnosis is used to predict outcome.

Lambda always ranges between 0 and 1. A value of 0 means the independent variable is of no help in predicting the dependent variable. A value of 1 means that the independent variable perfectly specifies the categories of the dependent variable (perfection can occur only when each row has at most one nonzero cell). When the two variables are independent, lambda is 0; but a lambda of 0 need not imply statistical independence. As with all measures of association, lambda is constructed to measure association in a very specific way. In particular, lambda reflects the reduction in error when values of one variable are used to predict values of the other. If this particular type of association is absent, lambda is 0. Other measures of association may find association of a different kind even when lambda is 0. A measure of association sensitive to every imaginable type of association does not exist.

For a particular table, two different lambdas can be computed, one using the row variable as the predictor and the other using the column variable. The two do not usually have identical values, so care should be taken to specify which is the dependent variable, that is, the variable whose prediction is of primary interest. In some applications, dependent and independent variables are not clearly distinguished. Then, a symmetric version of lambda, which predicts the row variable and column variable with equal frequency, can be computed. When the lambda statistic is requested, SPSS displays the symmetric lambda as well as the two asymmetric lambdas.

10.13
Goodman and Kruskal's Tau

When lambda is computed, the same prediction is made for all cases in a particular row or column. Another approach is to consider what happens if the prediction is randomly made in the same proportion as the marginal totals. For example, if you're trying to predict migraine outcome without any information about the depth of the hypnosis, you can use the marginal distributions in Figure 10.12 instead of the modal category to guess cured for 23% of the cases, better for 32% of the cases, and no change for 45% of the cases.

Using these marginals, you would expect to correctly classify 23% of the 23 cases in the cured category, 32% of the 32 cases in the better category, and 45% of the 45 cases in the no change category. This results in the correct classification of 35.78 out of 100 cases. When additional information about the depth of hypnosis is incorporated into the prediction rule, the prediction is based on the probability of the different outcomes for each depth of hypnosis. For example, for those who experienced deep hypnosis, you would predict cure 72% of the time (13/18) and better 28% of the time (5/18). Similarly, for those with light hypnosis, you would predict better 3% of the time and no change 97% of the time. This results in correct classification for about 58 of the cases.

Kruskal and Goodman's tau is computed by comparing the probability of error in the two situations. In this example, when predicting only from the column marginal totals, the probability of error is 0.64. When predicting from row information the probability of error is 0.42. Thus:

tau (migraine|hypnosis) = (0.64 − 0.42)/0.64 = 0.34   **Equation 10.13**

By incorporating information about the depth of hypnosis we have reduced our error of prediction by about 34%.

A test of the null hypothesis that tau is 0 can be based on the value of $(N-1)(c-1)$ tau (col|row), which has a chi-square distribution with $(c-1) \times (r-1)$ degrees of freedom. In this example, the observed significance level for tau is very small, and you can reject the null hypothesis that tau is 0. The asymptotic standard error for the statistic is shown in the column labeled **ASE1**. The asymptotic standard error can be used to construct confidence intervals.

10.14
Measuring Agreement

Measures of agreement allow you to compare the ratings of two observers for the same group of objects. For example, consider the data reported in Bishop et al. (1975), shown in Figure 10.14.

Figure 10.14   Student teachers rated by supervisors

```
CROSSTABS TABLES=SUPRVSR1 BY SUPRVSR2
 /CELLS=COUNT TOTAL
 /STATISTICS=KAPPA.
```

```
SUPRVSR1  Supervisor 1  by  SUPRVSR2  Supervisor 2

                    SUPRVSR2                    Page 1 of 1
            Count   Authorit Democrat Permissi
            Tot Pct arian    ic       ve          Row
                      1.00     2.00    3.00      Total
SUPRVSR1    --------+--------+--------+--------+
              1.00  |   17   |    4   |    8   |    29
Authoritarian       |  23.6  |   5.6  |  11.1  |   40.3
                    +--------+--------+--------+
              2.00  |    5   |   12   |        |    17
Democratic          |   6.9  |  16.7  |        |   23.6
                    +--------+--------+--------+
              3.00  |   10   |    3   |   13   |    26
Permissive          |  13.9  |   4.2  |  18.1  |   36.1
                    +--------+--------+--------+
            Column      32       19       21       72
             Total     44.4     26.4     29.2    100.0


                                                    Approximate
     Statistic            Value     ASE1    T-value  Significance
  _____    _____   _____  _____  _____


Kappa                     .36227   .09144  4.32902


Number of Missing Observations:  0
```

Two supervisors rated the classroom style of 72 teachers. You are interested in measuring the agreement between the two raters. The simplest measure that comes to mind is just the proportion of cases for which the raters agree. In this case it is 58.3%. The disadvantage of this measure is that no correction is made for the amount of agreement expected by chance. That is, you would expect the supervisors to agree sometimes even if they were assigning ratings by tossing dice.

To correct for chance agreement you can compute the proportion of cases that you would expect to be in agreement if the ratings are independent. For example, Supervisor 1 rated 40.3% of the teachers as authoritarian, while Supervisor 2 rated 44.4% of the teachers as authoritarian. If their rankings are independent, you would expect that 17.9% (40.3% × 44.4%) of the teachers would be rated as authoritarian by both. Similarly, 6.2% would be rated as democratic (23.6% × 26.4%) and 10.5% (36.1% × 29.2%) as permissive. Thus, 34.6% of all the teachers would be classified the same merely by chance.

The difference between the observed proportion of cases in which the raters agree and that expected by chance is 0.237 (0.583 − 0.346). *Cohen's kappa* (1960) normalizes this difference by dividing it by the maximum difference possible for the marginal totals. In this example, the largest possible "non-chance" agreement is 1 − 0.346 (the chance level). Therefore:

kappa = 0.237/(1 − 0.346) = 0.362   **Equation 10.14**

The test of the null hypothesis that kappa is 0 can be based on the *t* statistic shown in Figure 10.14. (See Benedetti & Brown, 1977, for further discussion of standard errors for measures of association as well as discussion of the degrees of freedom for the *t* statistic.) The *t* value is the ratio of the value of kappa to its asymptotic standard error when the null hypothesis is true. (This asymptotic error is not the one shown on the output. The asymptotic standard error on the output, ASE1, does not assume that the true value is 0.)

Since the kappa statistic measures agreement between two raters, the two variables that contain the ratings must have the same range of values. If this is not true, CROSSTABS will not compute kappa.

10.15
Ordinal Measures

Although relationships among ordinal variables can be examined using nominal measures, other measures reflect the additional information available from ranking. Consideration of the kind of relationships that may exist between two ordered variables leads to the notion of direction of relationship and to the concept of *correlation*. Variables are positively correlated if cases with low values for one variable also tend to have low values for the other and cases with high values on one also tend to be high on the other. Negatively correlated variables show the opposite relationship: the higher the first variable, the lower the second tends to be.

The Spearman correlation coefficient is a commonly used measure of correlation between two ordinal variables. For all of the cases, the values of each of the variables are ranked from smallest to largest and the Pearson correlation coefficient is computed on the ranks. The Mantel-Haenszel chi-square is another measure of linear association between the row and column variables in a crosstabulation. It is computed by multiplying the Pearson correlation coefficient by the number of cases minus 1. The resulting statistic has one degree of freedom (Mantel & Haenszel, 1959). (Although the Mantel-Haenszel statistic is displayed whenever chi-square is requested, it should not be used for nominal data.)

10.16
Ordinal Measures Based On Pairs

For a table of two ordered variables, several measures of association based on a comparison of the values of both variables for all possible *pairs* of cases or observations are available. Cases are first compared to determine if they are *concordant, discordant,* or *tied.* A pair of cases is *concordant* if the values of both variables for one case are higher (or both are lower) than the corresponding values for the other case. The pair is *discordant* if the value of one variable for a case is larger than the corresponding value for the other case, and the direction is reversed for the second variable. When the two cases have identical values on one or on both variables, they are *tied.*

Thus, for any given pair of cases with measurements on variables X and Y, the pair may be concordant or discordant, or tied in one of three ways: they may be tied on X but not on Y, they may be tied on Y but not on X, or they may be tied on both variables. When data are arranged in crosstabulated form, the number of concordant, discordant, and tied pairs can be easily calculated since all possible pairs can be conveniently determined.

If the preponderance of pairs is concordant, the association is said to be positive: as ranks of variable X increase (or decrease), so do ranks of variable Y. If the majority of pairs is discordant, the association is negative: as ranks of one variable increase, those of the other tend to decrease. If concordant and discordant pairs are equally likely, no association is said to exist.

The ordinal measures presented here all have the same numerator: the number of concordant pairs (P) minus the number of discordant pairs (Q) calculated for all distinct pairs of observations. They differ primarily in the way in which $P-Q$ is normalized. The simplest measure involves subtracting Q from P and dividing by the total number of pairs. If there are no pairs with ties, this measure (Kendall's tau-a) is in the range from -1 to $+1$. If there are ties, the range of possible values is narrower; the actual range depends on the number of ties. Since all observations within the same row are tied, so also are those in the same column, and the resulting tau-a measures are difficult to interpret.

A measure that attempts to normalize $P-Q$ by considering ties on each variable in a pair separately but not ties on both variables in a pair is tau-b:

$$\tau_b = \frac{P - Q}{\sqrt{(P + Q + T_X)(P + Q + T_Y)}}$$

Equation 10.16a

where T_X is the number of pairs tied on X but not on Y, and T_Y is the number of pairs tied on Y but not on X. If no marginal frequency is 0, tau-b can attain $+1$ or -1 only for a square table.

A measure that can attain, or nearly attain, $+1$ or -1 for any $r \times c$ table is tau-c

$$\tau_c = \frac{2m(P - Q)}{N^2(m - 1)}$$

Equation 10.16b

where m is the smaller of the number of rows and columns. The coefficients tau-b and tau-c do not differ much in value if each margin contains approximately equal frequencies.

Goodman and Kruskal's *gamma* is closely related to the tau statistics and is calculated as

$$G = \frac{P - Q}{P + Q}$$

Equation 10.16c

Gamma can be thought of as the probability that a random pair of observations is concordant minus the probability that the pair is discordant, assuming the absence of ties. The absolute value of gamma is the proportional reduction in error between guessing concordant and discordant ranking of each pair depending on which occurs more often and guessing ranking according to the outcome of the toss of a fair coin. Gamma is 1 if all observations are concentrated in the upper-left to lower-right diagonal of the table. In the case of independence, gamma is 0. However, the converse (that a gamma of 0 necessarily implies independence) need not be true except in the 2×2 table.

In the computation of gamma, no distinction is made between the independent and dependent variable; the variables are treated symmetrically. Somers (1962) proposed an asymmetric extension of gamma that differs only in the inclusion of the number of pairs not tied on the independent variable (X) in the denominator. Somers' d is

$$d_Y = \frac{P - Q}{P + Q + T_Y}$$

Equation 10.16d

The coefficient d_Y indicates the proportionate excess of concordant pairs over discordant pairs among pairs not tied on the independent variable. The symmetric variant of Somers' *d* uses for the denominator the average value of the denominators of the two asymmetric coefficients.

These ordinal measures for the migraine data are shown in Figure 10.16. All of the measures indicate that there is a fairly strong linear association between the two variables.

Figure 10.16   Ordinal measures

```
CROSSTABS TABLES=HYPNOSIS BY MIGRAINE
  /FORMAT=NOTABLE
  /STATISTICS=CORR BTAU CTAU GAMMA D.
```

HYPNOSIS DEPTH OF HYPNOSIS by MIGRAINE OUTCOME

Number of valid observations = 100

Statistic	Value	ASE1	T-value	Approximate Significance
Kendall's Tau-b	.67901	.04445	11.96486	
Kendall's Tau-c	.63360	.05296	11.96486	
Gamma	.94034	.02720	11.96486	
Somers' D :				
symmetric	.67866	.04443	11.96485	
with HYPNOSIS dependent	.65774	.05440	11.96485	
with MIGRAINE dependent	.70096	.03996	11.96486	
Pearson's R	.71739	.04484	10.19392	.00000
Spearman Correlation	.72442	.04317	10.40311	.00000

Number of Missing Observations: 0

10.17
Measures Involving Interval Data

If the two variables in the table are measured on an interval scale, various coefficients that make use of this additional information can be calculated. A useful symmetric coefficient that measures the strength of the *linear* relationship is the Pearson correlation coefficient, or *r*. It can take on values from -1 to $+1$, indicating negative or positive linear correlation.

The *eta* coefficient is appropriate for data in which the dependent variable is measured on an interval scale and the independent variable on a nominal or ordinal scale. When squared, eta can be interpreted as the proportion of the total variability in the dependent variable that can be accounted for by knowing the values of the independent variable. The measure is asymmetric and does not assume a linear relationship between the variables.

10.18
Estimating Risk in Cohort Studies

Often you want to identify variables that are related to the occurrence of a particular event. For example, you may want to determine if smoking is related to heart disease. A commonly used index that measures the strength of the association between presence of a factor and occurence of an event is the *relative risk ratio*. It is estimated as the ratio of two incidence rates, for example, the incidence rate of heart disease in those who smoke and the incidence rate of heart disease in those who do not smoke.

For example, suppose you observe for five years 1000 smokers without a history of heart disease and 1000 non-smokers without a history of heart disease, and you determine how many of each group develop heart disease during this time period. (Studies in which a group of disease-free people are studied to see who develops the disease are called *cohort* or *prospective* studies.) Figure 10.18 contains hypothetical results from such a cohort study.

Figure 10.18 Hypothetical cohorts

```
CROSSTABS TABLES=SMOKING BY HDISEASE
    /STATISTICS=RISK.
```

```
SMOKING  Smoking  by  HDISEASE  Heart Disease

                    HDISEASE       Page 1 of 1
              Count
                     Yes     No
                                        Row
                     1.00|   2.00| Total
   SMOKING  ---------+-------+-------+
              1.00|   100     900  |  1000
   Yes              |               |  50.0
           +--------+-------+-------+
              2.00|    50     950  |  1000
   No               |               |  50.0
           +--------+-------+-------+
           Column    150    1850     2000
            Total    7.5    92.5    100.0
```

```
    Statistic                       Value         95% Confidence Bounds
-------------------------------------------------------------------------
Relative Risk Estimate (SMOKING 1.0 / SMOKING 2.0) :
    case control                   2.11111         1.48544       3.00032
    cohort (HDISEASE 1.0 Risk)     2.00000         1.44078       2.77628
    cohort (HDISEASE 2.0 Risk)      .94737          .92390        .97143

Number of Missing Observations:  0
```

The five-year incidence rate for smokers is 100/1000, while the incidence rate for nonsmokers is 50/1000. The relative risk ratio is 2 (100/1000 divided by 50/1000). This indicates that, in the sample, smokers are twice as likely to develop heart disease as nonsmokers.

The estimated relative risk and its 95% confidence interval are in the row labeled **cohort (HDISEASE 1.0 Risk)** in Figure 10.18. In CROSSTABS, the ratio is always computed by taking the incidence in the first row and dividing it by the incidence in the second row. Since either column can represent the event, separate estimates are displayed for each column. The 95% confidence intervals do not include the value of 1, so you can reject the null hypothesis that the two incidence rates are the same.

10.19
Estimating Risk in Case-Control Studies

In the cohort study described above, we took a group of disease-free people (the cohort) and watched what happened to them. Another type of study that is commonly used is called a retrospective, or *case-control* study. In this type of study, we take a group of people with the disease of interest (the cases) and a comparable group of people without the disease (the controls) and see how they differ. For example, we could take 100 people with documented coronary heart disease and 100 controls without heart disease and establish how many in each group smoked. The hypothetical results are shown in Figure 10.19.

Figure 10.19 Hypothetical Smoking Control

```
CROSSTABS TABLES=GROUP BY SMOKING
 /CELLS=COUNT ROW
 /STATISTICS=RISK.
```

```
GROUP   by   SMOKING

                    SMOKING        Page 1 of 1
            Count
            Row Pct  Yes      No
                                        Row
                      1.00|    2.00|   Total
GROUP      --------+--------+--------+
             1.00 |    30  |    70  |    100
  Cases           |   30.0 |   70.0 |   50.0
           --------+--------+--------+
             2.00 |    10  |    90  |    100
  Controls        |   10.0 |   90.0 |   50.0
           --------+--------+--------+
            Column     40      160      200
            Total     20.0     80.0    100.0


      Statistic                   Value        95% Confidence Bounds
  --------------------------    ---------     ----------------------
  Relative Risk Estimate (GROUP 1.0 / GROUP 2.0) :
      case control               3.85714       1.76660     8.42156
      cohort (SMOKING 1.0 Risk)  3.00000       1.55083     5.80334
      cohort (SMOKING 2.0 Risk)   .77778        .67348      .89823

  Number of Missing Observations:  0
```

From a case-control study we cannot estimate incidence rates. Thus we cannot compute the relative risk ratio. Instead we estimate relative risk using what is called an *odds ratio*. We compute the odds that a "case" smokes and divide it by the odds that a control smokes.

For example, from Figure 10.19, the odds that a case smokes are 30/70. The odds that a control smokes is 10/90. The odds ratio is then 30/70 divided by 10/90, or 3.85. The odds ratio and its confidence interval are in the row labeled **case control** in Figure 10.19. The CROSSTABS procedure expects the cases to be in the first row and the controls in the second. Similarly, the event of interest of interest must be in the first column. For further discussion of measures of risk, see Kleinbaum et al. (1982).

10.20
RUNNING PROCEDURE CROSSTABS

Procedure CROSSTABS produces two-way to *n*-way crosstabulations and related statistical measures for variables with numeric or string values. In addition to cell counts, you can obtain cell percentages and expected values. You can alter the handling of missing values, reorder rows, request an index of tables, and write cell frequencies to a file.

10.21
TABLES Subcommand

The only required subcommand for CROSSTABS is the TABLES subcommand. The minimum specification for the TABLES subcommand is a list of one or more variables followed by the keyword BY and a second list of one or more variables, as in:

```
CROSSTABS TABLES=RETURNED BY ADDRESS.
```

The first variable list specifies the *row variables*, and the variable list following the first BY keyword specifies the *column variables*.

Optionally, you can specify *control variables* with additional BY keywords and variable lists, as in:

```
CROSSTABS TABLES=RETURNED BY ADDRESS BY LOCATION.
```

A separate subtable is generated for each value of the control variable(s). In this example, the control variable LOCATION has two values, producing two subtables (as in Figure 10.4).

You can specify more than one variable in each dimension. Use the TO keyword to imply consecutive variables on the active system file, as in:

```
CROSSTABS  TABLES=CONFINAN TO CONARMY BY SEX TO REGION.
```

This command will produce CROSSTABS tables for all the variables between and including CONFINAN and CONARMY by all the variables between and including SEX and REGION.

You can specify multiple TABLES subcommands. Each subcommand should be separated by a slash.

10.22
VARIABLES Subcommand

To run CROSSTABS in *integer mode*, use the VARIABLES subcommand. Integer mode builds tables more quickly than general mode but requires more space if the table has many empty cells. You must specify an integer value range enclosed in parentheses for each variable, as in:

```
CROSSTABS VARIABLES=RETURNED(1,2) ADDRESS(1,3)
/TABLES=RETURNED BY ADDRESS.
```

Since only values within the specified range will be included, you can use the VARIABLES subcommand to select subsets of cases for analysis. If multiple variables have the same range, you need to specify the range only once, as in:

```
CROSSTABS VARIABLES=ADDRESS(1,3) RETURNED LOCATION(1,2)
/TABLES=RETURNED BY ADDRESS BY LOCATION.
```

which specifies the same range for variables RETURNED and LOCATION.

If used, the VARIABLES subcommand must be the first subcommand specified, and it must include all variables specified on subsequent TABLES subcommands. The TO keyword on subsequent TABLES subcommands refers to the order of variables on the VARIABLES subcommand, not the order of variables on the active system file.

10.23
CELLS Subcommand

By default, CROSSTABS displays only the number of cases in each cell. Use the CELLS subcommand to display row, column, or total percentages, expected values, residuals. These items are calculated separately for each bivariate table or subtable.

You can specify the CELLS subcommand by itself, or with one or more keywords. If you specify the CELLS subcommand by itself, CROSSTABS displays cell counts plus row, column, and total percentages for each cell. If you specify keywords, CROSSTABS displays only the cell information you request.

The following keywords can be specified on the CELLS subcommand:

COUNT   *Cell counts.* This is the default if you omit the CELLS subcommand.

ROW   *Row percentages.* Row percentages are the number of cases in each cell in a row expressed as a percentage of all cases in that row.

COLUMN   *Column percentages.* Column percentages are the number of cases in each cell in a column expressed as a percentage of all cases in that column.

TOTAL   *Two-way table total percentages.* This is the number of cases in each cell of a subtable expressed as a percentage of all cases in that subtable.

EXPECTED   *Expected frequencies.* Expected frequencies are the number of cases expected in each cell if the two variables in the subtable were statistically independent.

RESID   *Residuals.* The residual is the value of the observed cell count minus the expected value.

SRESID   *Standardized residuals.* (Haberman, 1978).

ASRESID   *Adjusted standardized residuals.* (Haberman, 1978).

ALL   *All cell information.* This includes cell counts, row, column, and total percentages, expected values, residuals, standardized residuals, and adjusted standardized residuals.

NONE   *No cell information.* Use NONE to write tables to a file without displaying any tables. This has the same effect as specifying FORMAT=NOTABLES (see Section 10.26).

For example, the command

```
CROSSTABS TABLES=RETURNED BY ADDRESS
 /CELLS.
```

produces Figure 10.1, and the command

```
CROSSTABS TABLES=RETURNED BY ADDRESS
 /CELLS=COUNT EXPECTED RESID.
 /STATISTICS=CHISQ.
```

produces Figure 10.8.

10.24
STATISTICS Subcommand

CROSSTABS can calculate a number of summary statistics for each subtable. Unless you specify otherwise, it calculates statistical measures of association for the cases with valid values included in the subtable. If you include user-missing values with the MISSING subcommand, cases with user-missing values are included in the tables as well as in the calculation of statistics.

The STATISTICS subcommand requests summary statistics. You can specify the STATISTICS subcommand by itself, or with one or more keywords. If you specify STATISTICS by itself, CROSSTABS calculates CHISQ. If you include a keyword or keywords on the STATISTICS subcommand, CROSSTABS calculates all the statistics you request.

Asymptotic standard errors (ASE1) that are not based on the assumption that the true value is 0 are also calculated. The t statistics displayed are the ratio of the measure to an asymptotic standard error which assumes the true coefficient is 0.

The following keywords can be specified on the STATISTICS subcommand:

CHISQ   *Chi-square.* The output includes the Pearson chi-square, likelihood-ratio chi-square, and Mantel-Haenszel linear association chi-square. For 2×2 tables, Fisher's exact test is computed when a table that does not result from missing rows or columns in a larger table has a cell with an expected frequency less than 5; Yates' corrected chi-square is computed for all other 2×2 tables. This is the default if STATISTICS is specified without keywords.

PHI   *Phi and Cramer's* V.

CC   *Contingency coefficient.*

LAMBDA   *Lambda, symmetric and asymmetric, and Goodman and Kruskal's tau.*

UC   *Uncertainty coefficient, symmetric and asymmetric.*

BTAU   *Kendall's tau-*b.

CTAU   *Kendall's tau-*c.

GAMMA   *Gamma.* Partial and zero-order gammas for 3-way to 8-way tables are available in integer mode only (see Section 10.22). Zero-order gammas are displayed for 2-way tables and conditional gammas are displayed for 3-way to 10-way tables in general mode.

D   *Somers' d, symmetric and asymmetric.*

ETA   *Eta.* Available for numeric data only.

CORR   *Pearson's r, and Spearman's correlation coefficient.* Available for numeric data only.

KAPPA   *Kappa coefficient.* Kappa can only be computed for square tables in which the row and column values are identical. If there is a missing row or column, use integer mode to specify the square table since a missing column or row in general mode would keep the table from being square (see Section 10.22). (Kraemer, 1982.)

RISK   *Relative risk.* Relative risk can be calculated only for 2 × 2 tables. (Kleinbaum et al., 1982).

ALL   *All available statistics.*

NONE   *No summary statistics.* This is the default if STATISTICS is omitted.

For example, the command

```
CROSSTABS TABLES=RETURNED BY ADDRESS
 /STATISTICS=PHI CC.
```

produces Figure 10.11.

10.25
MISSING Subcommand

By default, CROSSTABS deletes cases with missing values on a table-by-table basis. A case missing on any of the variables specified for a table is not used either in the table or in the calculation of the statistics. Missing values are handled separately for each TABLES subcommand. The number of missing cases is displayed at the end of the table, following the last subtable and after any requested statistics.

The MISSING subcommand controls missing values. The following keywords can be specified on the MISSING subcommand:

TABLE   *Delete cases with missing values on a table-by-table basis.* This is the default if you omit the MISSING subcommand.

INCLUDE *Include cases with user-missing values.*

REPORT   *Report missing values in the tables.* This option includes missing values in tables but not in the calculation of percentages or statistics. The letter **M** is used to indicate that cases within a cell are missing. REPORT is available only in integer mode (see Section 10.22).

10.26
FORMAT Subcommand

Use the FORMAT subcommand to modify the default formats. The following keywords can be specified:

LABELS   *Display both variable and value labels for each table.* This is the default. The values for the row variables are displayed in order from lowest to highest. CROSSTABS uses only the first 16 characters of the value labels. Value labels for the columns are displayed on two lines with eight characters per line.

NOLABELS *Suppress variable and value labels.*

NOVALLABS *Suppress value labels but display variable labels.*

AVALUE   *Display row variables ordered from lowest to highest.* This is the default.

DVALUE   *Display row variables ordered from highest to lowest.*

NOINDEX *Suppress a table index.* This is the default.

INDEX   *Display an index of tables.* The index lists all tables produced by the CROSSTABS command and the page number where each table begins. The index follows the last page of tables produced by the tables list.

TABLES	*Display the crosstabulation tables.* This is the default.
NOTABLES	*Suppress table display.* If you use the STATISTICS subcommand (see Section 10.24) and specify NOTABLES, only the statistics are displayed. If you do not use the STATISTICS subcommand and specify NOTABLES, the CROSSTABS command produces no output.
BOX	*Use box drawing characters around every cell.* This is the default.
NOBOX	*Suppress the box drawing characters around each cell.* The banner and stub are still separated from the table by by box drawing characters.

10.27
WRITE Subcommand

The WRITE subcommand writes cell frequencies to a procedure output file (specified on the PROCEDURE OUTPUT command), for subsequent use by SPSS or some other program. The output file contains one record per cell.

NONE	*Do not write the cell counts to the file.* This is the default if you omit the WRITE subcommand.
CELLS	*Write the cell count for nonempty cells to a file.*
ALL	*Write the cell count for all cells to a file.* This is only available in integer mode. (See the VARIABLES subcommand, Section 10.22.)

For more information about the WRITE subcommand, see the *SPSS Reference Guide*.

10.28
Entering Crosstabulated Data

You can use the CROSSTABS procedure to calculate statistics for a pre-existing crosstabulation without entering the individual case data. Each cell of the table is considered a case. The variables for each case are the cell count and the values of the row, column, and control variables.

Define this file as you would any other file. Then use the WEIGHT command (see Chapter 2) to count each "case" as many times as the value of the cell count variable. For example, Figure 10.18 was produced from a table, rather than raw data, using the following commands:

```
DATA LIST FREE /SMOKING HDISEASE COUNT.
BEGIN DATA.
1 1 100
1 2 900
2 1 50
2 2 950
END DATA.
VARIABLE LABELS
 SMOKING 'Smoking'
 HDISEASE 'Heart Disease'.
VALUE LABELS SMOKING HDISEASE l 'Yes' 2 'No'.
WEIGHT BY COUNT.
CROSSTABS TABLES=SMOKING by HDISEASE
 /STATISTICS=RISK.
```

• The DATA LIST command names three variables: SMOKING is the row variable; HDISEASE is the column variable, and COUNT is the cell count.

• The optional VARIABLE LABELS and VALUE LABELS commands identify and the variables in the tables.

• The WEIGHT command weights each case by the cell count.

• The CROSSTABS command re-creates the table, and the STATISTICS subcommand provides summary statistics not provided with the original table.

10.29
EXERCISES Syntax

1. Given the following commands, which of the statements below are true?

```
CROSSTABS TABLES=ADDRESS BY LOCATION
         /CELLS=ROW.
```

   a. Two subtables are produced.
   b. The variable ADDRESS is the row variable.
   c. The variable ADDRESS is the column variable.
   d. The CROSSTABS command will cause an error because the VARIABLES subcommand is missing.
   e. The cells include row percentages and total percentages.
   f. The cells include row percentages only.
   g. The output includes the chi-square statistic.

2. Which of the commands below produced the following crosstabulation?

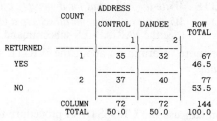

```
                          ADDRESS
                COUNT   ┌─────────┬────────┐
                        │CONTROL  │DANDEE  │   ROW
                        │         │        │  TOTAL
                        │       1 │      2 │
        RETURNED   ─────┼─────────┼────────┤
                     1  │   35    │   32   │    67
          YES           │         │        │   46.5
                   ─────┼─────────┼────────┤
                     2  │   37    │   40   │    77
          NO            │         │        │   53.5
                   ─────┼─────────┼────────┘
                COLUMN      72        72       144
                TOTAL      50.0      50.0    100.0

NUMBER OF MISSING OBSERVATIONS =    72
```

   a. CROSSTABS   VARIABLES = RETURNED ADDRESS
         /TABLES = RETURNED BY ADDRESS
         /CELLS=TOTAL.

   b. CROSSTABS   VARIABLES = RETURNED (1,2) ADDRESS (1,2)
         /TABLES = RETURNED BY ADDRESS.

   c. CROSSTABS   VARIABLES = RETURNED ADDRESS (1,2)
         TABLES = ADDRESS BY RETURNED.

   d. CROSSTABS   TABLES = RETURNED (1,2) BY ADDRESS (1,2).

3. Given the following job, fill in the cells of the CROSSTABS table below.

```
DATA LIST  FIXED /VARA 1-2 VARB 4 VARC 6.
BEGIN DATA
72 1 1
20 2 1
54 1 2
16 2 2
END DATA.
WEIGHT BY VARA.
CROSSTABS  TABLES = VARB BY VARC.
```

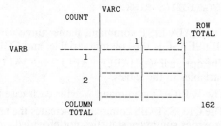

```
                        VARC
              COUNT   ┌─────────┬────────┐
                      │         │        │   ROW
                      │         │        │  TOTAL
                      │       1 │      2 │
       VARB     ──────┼─────────┼────────┤
                   1  │         │        │
                      │         │        │
                ──────┼─────────┼────────┤
                   2  │         │        │
                      │         │        │
                ──────┴─────────┴────────┘
              COLUMN                         162
              TOTAL
```

4. For variables SEX, JOBTITLE, and HAPPY, write the SPSS command to produce:
   a. A crosstabulation with HAPPY in rows and JOBTITLE in columns.
   b. A crosstabulation with JOBTITLE in rows and SEX in columns.
   c. A crosstabulation with JOBTITLE in rows and HAPPY in columns, controlling for SEX.
   d. The table in (a) with column, row, and total percents.
   e. The table in (b) with cell counts, column and row percents, and chi-square and lambda statistics.

Statistical Concepts

1. Which of the following statements are true?
   a. If one of the measures of association provided by CROSSTABS is very low, it is safe to assume that the other measures of association will also be low.
   b. PRE measures of association are easier to interpret than chi-square-based measures of association.
   c. Measures of association for nominal variables indicate the direction as well as the strength of the association.
   d. The eta coefficient measures the strength of the linear relationship between two variables.

2. For each of the following measures of association, indicate whether its value depends on which variable is specified as the row variable.
   a. Goodman and Kruskal's gamma.
   b. Eta.
   c. Somers' d.
   d. Kruskal's lambda.

3. Which of the measures of association calculated by CROSSTABS are sensitive to all types of association?

4. What is the reason for normalizing measures of association, thereby forcing their values to range from -1 to $+1$ or from 0 to 1?

5. A researcher studying the association between two variables obtained all of the appropriate measures of association provided by CROSSTABS. Only one measure was large, so he included only this measure in his summary of results. Was this reasonable? Why or why not?

6. A study to determine the effect of grade-point average on performance on a test resulted in the following table:

	COUNT	PERFORM			
		POOR	FAIR	GOOD	ROW TOTAL
		1	2	3	
GPA	1	56	54	12	122
BELOW AVERAGE					36.2
AVERAGE	2	31	65	43	139
					41.2
ABOVE AVERAGE	3	12	25	39	76
					22.6
COLUMN TOTAL		99	144	94	337
		29.4	42.7	27.9	100.0

   a. What is the independent variable? What is the dependent variable?
   b. Would you look at row percentages or column percentages to see whether the independent variable seems to affect the dependent variable?

7. a. Fill in the missing information in the following table:

	COUNT ROW PCT COL PCT	DEPTH			
		SMALL	MEDIUM	LARGE	ROW TOTAL
		1	2	3	
CURE	1	29		30	69
NO					
YES	2	15	10	20	
COLUMN TOTAL					

8. a. Fill in the missing information in the following table and calculate the chi-square test for independence.

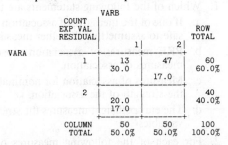

COUNT EXP VAL RESIDUAL	VARB		ROW TOTAL
VARA	1	2	
1	13 30.0	47 17.0	60 60.0%
2	20.0 17.0		40 40.0%
COLUMN TOTAL	50 50.0%	50 50.0%	100 100.0%

9. Suppose a random sample of size 100 resulted in Table 1 below, while another random sample of size 1,000 resulted in Table 2. If you know that the chi-square value for Table 1 is 9.09, can you find the chi-square value for Table 2 without doing any chi-square calculations involving the data in Table 2?

Table 1

COUNT	VARB		
	COUGH	NO COUGH	ROW TOTAL
VARA	1	2	
1 SMOKER	30	20	50 50.0
2 NONSMOKER	15	35	50 50.0
COLUMN TOTAL	45 45.0	55 55.0	100 100.0

Table 2

COUNT	VARB		
	COUGH	NO COUGH	ROW TOTAL
VARA	1	2	
1 SMOKER	300	200	500 50.0
2 NONSMOKER	150	350	500 50.0
COLUMN TOTAL	450 45.0	550 55.0	1000 100.0

10. Consider the following table:

COUNT	VARB		
	SMOKER	NONSMOKER	ROW TOTAL
SEX	1	2	
1 MALE	45	55	100 50.0
2 FEMALE	30	70	100 50.0
COLUMN TOTAL	75 37.5	125 62.5	200 100.0

a. If sex and smoking status are independent, what frequencies would you expect in each cell?
b. What are the degrees of freedom for this table?
c. Calculate the chi-square test for independence.

Data Analysis

Use the BANK system file for Questions 1–4.

1. a. Prepare a table that shows the number of women and men in each of the first four job categories (use the SELECT IF command).
   b. Construct another table crosstabulating the first four job categories with the sex-race variable.
   c. What do you conclude and why? Justify your answer with a statistical analysis.

2. a. Collapse work experience into several categories and crosstabulate this collapsed variable with sex. Do sex and work experience appear to be related? Justify your answer with a statistical analysis. Can your choice of categories affect your answer? Why or why not?

   b. If sex and work experience appear to be related, obtain a measure of the strength of the association. What are the disadvantages of the measure you used?

   c. Repeat the analysis in Question 2.b using race instead of sex.

3. Collapse job seniority into several categories and examine the relationship between job seniority and sex and between job seniority and race, as in Question 2.

4. Collapse education into several categories. Are education and sex related at the bank? Are education and race related? Perform an analysis like the one in Question 2.

5. Choose one of the data files from Appendix B. Describe five possible relationships between variables that can be examined using crosstabulations. For example, the relationship between number of evenings spent at a bar and the sex of the respondent can be studied by tabulating SOCBAR against SEX on the GSS82 system file.

6. Run three of the tables described in Question 5, including at least one table that has a control variable. For example, tabulate husbands' and wives' responses to a particular product, controlling for whether the questionnaire included pictures or not.

   a. Write a brief paragraph summarizing your results. Indicate whether row or column percentages are appropriate for describing the relationships in the tables.

   b. Test the hypothesis that the two variables are independent.

   c. If some of the variables have many categories, the resulting tables may have many cells with few observations in each. Use the RECODE command to group some of the categories and rerun the tables.

7. Take a continuous variable like age or years of education and recode it into quartiles. In other words, assign a code of 1 to the lowest 25%, a code of 2 to the next 25%, and so forth. Obtain a crosstabulation of this variable with one of the other variables in the file. Describe the results.

8. Use the Western Electric data file for the following exercises:

   a. Write a short paragraph describing the relationship between incidence of coronary heart disease (CHD) and family history of CHD (FAMHXCVR).

   b. Describe the relationship between the type of first coronary event (FIRSTCHD) and family history of CHD (FAMHXCVR).

   c. Obtain a frequency table for the number of cigarettes smoked per day (CGT58). Based on the frequency table, recode the number of cigarettes per day into three categories. Make sure that one of the categories is "no cigarettes smoked." Write a paragraph describing the relationship between incidence of coronary heart disease (CHD) and cigarette smoking.

   d. Repeat (c) for serum cholesterol (CHOL58) and diastolic blood pressure (DBP58). (Base your cut-points for these variables on a histogram.)

Means

In this chapter:

Goals:

- To classify cases into several mutually exclusive groups based on the values of one or more grouping variables, and then, for each group, to calculate descriptive statistics for additional variables.

- To look for relationships between a dependent variable which can be summarized by the mean, and a set of independent variables with a limited number of categories.

Examples:

- To look at the average cholesterol levels for three groups of men: those who are disease-free, those who had a recent heart attack, and those who had a non-recent heart attack.

- To examine average starting salaries for four different majors from each of three institutions.

- To see if there is a relationship between the average number of miles driven to work per week, region of the country, and socioeconomic status.

How it's done:

Cases are subdivided into subgroups based on the combinations of values of the grouping variables. For each subgroup, sums, means, standard deviations, and variances of additional variables are computed.

Data considerations:

The grouping variables must have a limited number of values. Since the number of subgroups formed is equal to the product of the number of values for each grouping variable, the number of resulting subgroups will be large if there are many grouping variables, or grouping variables with many values.

The variables that are described in each of the subgroups should not be nominal, since the mean and variance are not appropriate statistics for such variables.

11 Describing Subpopulation Differences: Procedure MEANS

The 1964 Civil Rights Act prohibits discrimination in the workplace based on sex or race. Employers who violate the act by unfair hiring or advancement practices can be prosecuted. Numerous lawsuits have been filed on behalf of women, blacks, and other groups offered equal protection under the law.

The courts have ruled that statistics can be used as *prima facie* evidence of discrimination, and many lawsuits depend heavily on complex statistical analyses, which attempt to demonstrate that similarly qualified individuals are not treated equally. Identifying and measuring all variables that legitimately influence promotion and hiring is difficult, if not impossible, especially for nonroutine jobs. Years of schooling and prior work experience can be quantified, but what about the more intangible attributes such as enthusiasm and creativity? How are they to be objectively measured so as not to become convenient smoke screens for concealing discrimination?

11.1 SEARCHING FOR DISCRIMINATION

In this chapter, employee records for 474 individuals hired between 1969 and 1971 by a bank engaged in Equal Employment Opportunity (EEO) litigation are analyzed. Two types of unfair employment practices are of particular interest: shunting (placing some employees in lower job categories than others with similar qualifications) and salary and promotion inequities.

Although extensive and intricate statistical analyses are usually involved in studies of this kind (see, for example, Roberts, 1980), the discussion here is necessarily limited. The SPSS MEANS procedure is used to calculate average salaries for groups of employees based on race and sex. Additional grouping variables are introduced to help "explain" some of the observed variability in salary.

11.2
Who Does What?

Figure 11.2 is a crosstabulation of job category at the time of hiring with sex and race characteristics. The first three job classifications contain 64% of white males (adding column percents), 94% of both nonwhite males and white females, and 100% of nonwhite females. Among white males, 17% are in the college trainee program, compared to 4% of white females.

Figure 11.2 Crosstabulation of job category by sex-race

```
COMPUTE   SEXRACE=1.
IF (MINORITY EQ 1 AND SEX EQ 0) SEXRACE=2.
IF (MINORITY EQ 0 AND SEX EQ 1) SEXRACE=3.
IF (MINORITY EQ 1 AND SEX EQ 1) SEXRACE=4.
CROSSTABS TABLES=JOBCAT BY SEXRACE /CELLS=COUNT, COLUMN, TOTAL.
```

JOBCAT EMPLOYMENT CATEGORY by SEXRACE SEX & RACE CLASSIFICATION

		WHITE MALES	MINORITY MALES	WHITE FEMALES	MINORITY FEMALES	Row
Count Col Pct Tot Pct		1	2	3	4	Total
JOBCAT						
CLERICAL	1	75 38.7 15.8	35 54.7 7.4	85 48.3 17.9	32 80.0 6.8	227 47.9
OFFICE TRAINEE	2	35 18.0 7.4	12 18.8 2.5	81 46.0 17.1	8 20.0 1.7	136 28.7
SECURITY OFFICER	3	14 7.2 3.0	13 20.3 2.7			27 5.7
COLLEGE TRAINEE	4	33 17.0 7.0	1 1.6 .2	7 4.0 1.5		41 8.6
EXEMPT EMPLOYEE	5	28 14.4 5.9	2 3.1 .4	2 1.1 .4		32 6.8
MBA TRAINEE	6	3 1.5 .6	1 1.6 .2	1 .6 .2		5 1.1
TECHNICAL	7	6 3.1 1.3				6 1.3
Column Total		194 40.9	64 13.5	176 37.1	40 8.4	474 100.0

Number of Missing Observations: 0

Although these observations are interesting, they do not imply discriminatory placement into beginning job categories because the qualifications of the various groups are not necessarily similar. If women and nonwhites are more qualified than white males in the same beginning job categories, discrimination may be suspected.

11.3
Level of Education

One easily measured employment qualification is years of education. Figure 11.3a shows the average years of education for the entire sample (labeled **For Entire Population**) and then for each of the two sexes (labeled **SEX** and **MALES** or **FEMALES**) and then for each of the two race categories within each sex category (labeled **MINORITY** and **WHITE** or **NONWHITE**).

Figure 11.3a   Education broken down by race within sex

```
MEANS  TABLES=EDLEVEL BY SEX BY MINORITY.
```

```
                      - - Description of Subpopulations - -

Summaries of      EDLEVEL      EDUCATIONAL LEVEL
By levels of      SEX          SEX OF EMPLOYEE
                  MINORITY     MINORITY CLASSIFICATION


Variable          Value  Label                  Mean     Std Dev    Cases

For Entire Population                          13.4916    2.8848      474

SEX                 0    MALES                 14.4302    2.9793      258
  MINORITY          0    WHITE                 14.9227    2.8484      194
  MINORITY          1    NONWHITE              12.9375    2.8888       64

SEX                 1    FEMALES               12.3704    2.3192      216
  MINORITY          0    WHITE                 12.3409    2.4066      176
  MINORITY          1    NONWHITE              12.5000    1.9081       40

   Total Cases = 474
```

The entire sample has an average of 13.49 years of education. Males have more years of education than females—an average of 14.43 years compared to 12.37. White males have the highest level of education, almost 15 years, which is 2 years more than nonwhite males and approximately 2.5 years more than either group of females.

Figure 11.3b   Education by sex-race and job category

```
MEANS TABLES=EDLEVEL BY JOBCAT BY SEXRACE.
```

```
                       - - Cross-Breakdown - -

Summaries of       EDLEVEL      EDUCATIONAL LEVEL
By levels of       JOBCAT       EMPLOYMENT CATEGORY
                   SEXRACE      SEX & RACE CLASSIFICATION


                  SEXRACE
         Mean
         Count    WHITE     MINORITY    WHITE      MINORITY
         Std Dev  MALES     MALES       FEMALES    FEMALES     Row
                     1         2           3          4        Total
JOBCAT   ------+---------+-----------+----------+-----------+
         1    |  13.87  |   13.77   |   11.46  |   12.63   |   12.78
CLERICAL |     75  |      35   |      85  |      32   |     227
         |   2.30  |    2.31   |    2.43  |    2.12   |    2.56
         +---------+-----------+----------+-----------+
         2    |  13.89  |   12.58   |   12.81  |   12.00   |   13.02
OFFICE TRAINEE|  35  |      12   |      81  |       8   |     136
         |   1.41  |    2.61   |    1.93  |     .00   |    1.89
         +---------+-----------+----------+-----------+
         3    |  10.29  |   10.08   |          |           |   10.19
SECURITY OFFICER| 14  |      13   |          |           |      27
         |   2.05  |    2.47   |          |           |    2.22
         +---------+-----------+----------+-----------+
         4    |  17.21  |   17.00   |   16.00  |           |   17.00
COLLEGE TRAINEE| 33  |       1   |       7  |           |      41
         |   1.34  |     .     |     .00  |           |    1.28
         +---------+-----------+----------+-----------+
         5    |  17.61  |   14.00   |   16.00  |           |   17.28
EXEMPT EMPLOYEE| 28  |       2   |       2  |           |      32
         |   1.77  |    2.83   |     .00  |           |    1.97
         +---------+-----------+----------+-----------+
         6    |  18.33  |   19.00   |   16.00  |           |   18.00
MBA TRAINEE  |    3  |       1   |       1  |           |       5
         |   1.15  |     .     |     .    |           |    1.41
         +---------+-----------+----------+-----------+
         7    |  18.17  |           |          |           |   18.17
TECHNICAL|       6  |           |          |           |       6
         |   1.47  |           |          |           |    1.47
         +---------+-----------+----------+-----------+
  Column Total |  14.92  |   12.94   |   12.34  |   12.50   |   13.49
              194  |      64   |     176  |      40   |     474
              2.85  |    2.89   |    2.41  |    1.91   |    2.88
```

In Figure 11.3b, the cases are further subdivided by their combined sex-race characteristics and by their initial job category. For each cell in the table, the average years of education, the standard deviation, and number of cases are displayed. White males have the highest average years of education in all job categories except MBA trainees, where the single nonwhite male MBA trainee has nineteen years of education. From this table, it does not appear that females and nonwhites are overeducated when compared to white males in similar job categories. However, it is important to note that group means provide information about a particular class of employees. While discrimination may not exist for a class as a whole, some individuals within that class may be victims (or beneficiaries) of discrimination.

11.4
Beginning Salaries

The average beginning salary for the 474 persons hired between 1969 and 1971 is $6,806. The distribution by the four sex-race categories is shown in Figure 11.4a.

Figure 11.4a   Beginning salary by sex-race

MEANS TABLES=SALBEG BY SEXRACE.

```
                  - - Description of Subpopulations - -

Summaries of        SALBEG      BEGINNING SALARY
By levels of        SEXRACE     SEX & RACE CLASSIFICATION


Variable      Value Label                    Mean     Std Dev    Cases

For Entire Population                      6806.4346  3148.2553    474

SEXRACE          1   WHITE   MALES          8637.5258  3871.1017    194
SEXRACE          2   MINORITY MALES         6553.5000  2228.1436     64
SEXRACE          3   WHITE   FEMALES        5340.4886  1225.9605    176
SEXRACE          4   MINORITY FEMALES       4780.5000   771.4188     40

   Total Cases = 474
```

White males have the highest beginning salaries—an average of $8,638—followed by nonwhite males. Since males are in higher job categories than females, this difference is not surprising.

Figure 11.4b   Beginning salary by sex-race and job category

MEANS VARIABLES=SALBEG(LO,HI) SEXRACE(1,4) JOBCAT(1,7)
  /CROSSBREAK=SALBEG BY JOBCAT BY SEXRACE /CELLS=MEAN.

```
                     - - Cross-Breakdown - -

Summaries of        SALBEG      BEGINNING SALARY
By levels of        JOBCAT      EMPLOYMENT CATEGORY
                    SEXRACE     SEX & RACE CLASSIFICATION
```

	Mean	SEXRACE WHITE MALES 1	MINORITY MALES 2	WHITE FEMALES 3	MINORITY FEMALES 4	Row Total
JOBCAT CLERICAL	1	6553.44	6230.74	5147.32	4828.13	5733.95
OFFICE TRAINEE	2	6262.29	5610.00	5208.89	4590.00	5478.97
SECURITY OFFICER	3	6102.86	5953.85			6031.11
COLLEGE TRAINEE	4	10467.64	11496.00	7326.86		9956.49
EXEMPT EMPLOYEE	5	13255.29	15570.00	10998.00		13258.88
MBA TRAINEE	6	14332.00	13992.00	7200.00		12837.60
TECHNICAL	7	19996.00				19996.00
Column Total		8637.53	6553.50	5340.49	4780.50	6806.43

Figure 11.4b shows beginning salaries subdivided by race, sex, and job category. For most of the job categories, white males have higher beginning salaries than the other groups. There is a $1,400 salary difference between white males and white females in the clerical jobs and a $1,000 difference in the general office trainee classification. In the college trainee program, white males averaged over $3,000 more than white females. However, Figure 11.3b shows that white females in the college trainee program had only an undergraduate degree, while white males had an average of 17.2 years of schooling.

11.5
Introducing More Variables

The differences in mean beginning salaries between males and females are somewhat suspect. It is, however, unwise to conclude that salary discrimination exists since several important variables, such as years of prior experience, have not been considered. It is necessary to control (or to adjust statistically) for other relevant variables. Crossclassifying cases by the variables of interest and comparing salaries across the subgroups is one way of achieving control. However, as the number of variables increases, the number of cases in each cell rapidly diminishes, making statistically meaningful comparisons difficult. To circumvent these problems, regression methods, which achieve control by specifying certain statistical relations that may describe what is happening, are used. Regression methods are described in Chapter 19.

11.6
RUNNING PROCEDURE MEANS

MEANS calculates means and variances for a dependent variable within subgroups defined by control variables. For most applications, you can specify your variables on the TABLES subcommand. If your control variables are discrete, integer values and you want the special crosstabulation-like format, you can use the VARIABLES and CROSSBREAK subcommands.

11.7
TABLES Subcommand

Use the TABLES subcommand followed by one or more dependent variables, the keyword BY, and one or more control variables. For example,

MEANS **TABLES=SALBEG BY SEXRACE.**
describes SALBEG within categories of SEXRACE, as in Figure 11.4a. Additional BY keywords and control variables can subdivide the the sample into further subgroups. For example,

MEANS TABLES=EDLEVEL BY SEX **BY MINORITY.**

calculates statistics for EDLEVEL for each category of SEX and for each category of MINORITY within categories of SEX, producing the output in Figure 11.3a. A maximum of six dimensions can be specified on a TABLES subcommand: one dependent variable followed by up to five BY keywords and control variables.

The first variable is always the dependent variable. The control variables appear in the table in the order in which they are specified. MEANS displays subpopulation statistics for each category of the first control variable. However, for subsequent variables, it displays statistics only for each category of the variable within a category of the preceding control variable.

You can specify more than one dependent variable and more than one control variable in each dimension. Use the keyword TO to name a set of adjacent variables in the active system file, as in:

MEANS TABLES=**RAISE79 TO RAISE81** BY **DEPT TO AGE.**

This command will produce summary tables for each variable from RAISE79 to RAISE81 within categories of each variable from DEPT to AGE. The variables to the right of the last BY change most quickly. Within lists separated with a BY, variables rotate from left to right. For example,

```
MEANS  TABLES=VAR1 TO VAR3 BY VAR4 VAR5 BY VAR6 TO VAR8.
```

produces 18 tables. The first table is VAR1 by VAR4 by VAR6, the second is VAR1 by VAR4 by VAR7, and the third is VAR1 by VAR4 by VAR8. The combinations of VAR1 and VAR5 follow the combinations of VAR1 and VAR4. The last table produced is VAR3 by VAR5 by VAR8.

To specify multiple tables lists, use multiple TABLES subcommands or a slash to separate tables lists on one TABLES subcommand. For example,

```
MEANS  TABLES=RAISE82 BY GRADE/SALARY BY DEPT.
```

specifies two tables: RAISE82 by GRADE, and SALARY by DEPT.

11.8
VARIABLES Subcommand

Use the VARIABLES subcommand to define a list of variables and their value ranges for subsequent TABLES and CROSSBREAK subcommands. Specify the lowest and highest values in parentheses after each variable. For control variables, these must be integer values.

You do not have to specify an explicit range for dependent variables because they are usually continuous and are not assumed to be integers. However, you must provide bounds. You can use the keyword LOWEST (LO) and HIGHEST (HI) for dependent, or criterion, variables. You can also use explicit bounds to eliminate outliers from the calculation of summary statistics. For example, (0,HI) excludes negative values. You cannot use LOWEST, LO, HIGHEST, HI with control variables. For variables with the same range, the lowest and highest values only have to be specified once.

The final variable or set of variables must be followed by a slash and either the TABLES or CROSSBREAK subcommand. The variables may appear in any order. However, the order in which you place them on the VARIABLES subcommand affects their implied order on the TABLES and CROSSBREAK subcommands.

For example,

```
MEANS VARIABLES=DEPT80 DEPT81 DEPT82 (1,3) GRADE81S (1,4)
      SALARY82 (LO,HI)
      /TABLES=SALARY82 BY DEPT80 TO DEPT82 BY GRADE81S.
```

defines 1 as the lowest value and 3 as the highest value for DEPT80, DEPT81, and DEPT82. The TABLES subcommand will produce the following tables:

- SALARY82 by DEPT80 and by GRADE81S within categories of DEPT80.
- SALARY82 by DEPT81 and by GRADE81S within categories of DEPT81.
- SALARY82 by DEPT82 and by GRADE81S within categories of DEPT82.

11.9
CROSSBREAK Subcommand

To display tables in a crosstabular format when the values of all control variables are integers, use the VARIABLES and CROSSBREAK subcommands. Tables displayed in crossbreak format resemble CROSSTABS tables, but their contents are considerably different. The cells contain means, counts, and standard deviations for the dependent variable.

The VARIABLES subcommand specifies the variables to be used and the minimum and maximum values for building tables, and the CROSSBREAK subcommand specifies the tables. CROSSBREAK has exactly the same specification field as the TABLES subcommand.

The CROSSBREAK format is especially suited to breakdowns with two control variables. The first control variable defines the rows and the second control variable defines the columns. For example, Figure 11.3b was produced with the following commands:

```
MEANS VARIABLES=EDLEVEL(LO,HI) SEXRACE(1,4) JOBCAT(1,7)
/CROSSBREAK=EDLEVEL BY JOBCAT BY SEXRACE.
```

The CROSSBREAK subcommand displays separate subtables for each combination of values when you specify three or more dimensions (two or more BY keywords).

11.10
CELLS Subcommand

By default, MEANS displays the means, standard deviations, and cell counts in each cell. Use the CELLS subcommand to modify cell information.

If you specify the CELLS subcommand with no keywords, MEANS displays all cell information (keyword ALL below). If you specify a keyword or keywords, MEANS displays only the information you request.

The following keywords can be specified on the CELLS subcommand:

DEFAULT *Means, standard deviations, and cell counts in each cell.* This is the default if you omit the CELL subcommand.

MEAN *Cell means.*

STDDEV *Cell standard deviations.*

COUNT *Cell frequencies.*

SUM *Cell sums.*

VARIANCE *Variances.*

ALL *Means, counts, standard deviations, sums, and variances in each cell.* This is the default if you specify the CELLS subcommand with no keyword(s).

The following commands produced Figure 11.4b:

```
MEANS  VARIABLES=SALBEG(LO,HI) SEXRACE(1,4) JOBCAT(1,7)
/CROSSBREAK=SALBEG BY JOBCAT BY SEXRACE
/CELLS=MEAN.
```

11.11
STATISTICS Subcommand

MEANS automatically computes means, standard deviations, and counts for subpopulations. Optionally, you can obtain a one-way analysis of variance for each table as well as a test of linearity. The STATISTICS subcommand computes these additional statistics. Statistics you request on the STATISTICS subcommand are computed *in addition to* the default statistics or those you request on the CELLS subcommand.

If you specify the STATISTICS subcommand with no keyword, MEANS computes an analysis of variance for each table (keyword ANOVA below). If you specify a keyword, MEANS computes the additional statistics you request.

The following keywords can be specified on the STATISTICS subcommand:

ANOVA *Analysis of variance.* Displays a standard analysis of variance table and calculates *ETA* and *ETA*^{2}. This is the default if you specify the STATIS-TICS subcommand with no keyword.

LINEARITY *Test of linearity.* Calculates the sums of squares, degrees of freedom, and mean square associated with linear and nonlinear components, as well as the *F* ratio, Pearson's *r*, and *r*^{2}. ANOVA *must* be requested to obtain LINEARITY. LINEARITY is ignored if the control variable is a short string.

ALL *Both ANOVA and LINEARITY.*

NONE *No additional statistics.* This is the default if you omit the STATISTICS subcommand.

If you specify a two-way or higher-order breakdown, the second and subsequent dimensions are ignored in the analysis of variance table. To obtain a two-way and higher analysis of variance, use procedure ANOVA (see Chapter 16).

11.12
MISSING Subcommand

By default, MEANS deletes cases with missing values on a tablewide basis. A case missing on any of the variables specified for a table is not used. Every case contained in a table will have a complete set of nonmissing values for all variables in that table. When you separate tables requests with a slash, missing values are handled separately for each list.

The MISSING subcommand controls missing values, and the following keywords can be specified on it:

TABLE   *Delete cases with missing values on a tablewide basis.* This is the default if you omit the MISSING subcommand.

INCLUDE   *Include user-defined missing values.* User-defined missing values are treated as nonmissing.

DEPENDENT *Exclude cases with missing values for the dependent variable only.* A case is included if it has a valid value for the dependent variable, although it may have missing values for the control variables. Categories of the control variables defined as missing are not included in the tables.

11.13
FORMAT Subcommand

By default, MEANS displays variable and value labels and the names and values of control variables. All tables are in report format.

The FORMAT subcommand controls table formats. The following keywords can be specified:

LABELS   *Display both variable and value labels for each table.* This is the default if you omit the FORMAT subcommand.

NOLABELS   *Suppress variable and value labels.*

NOCATLABS *Suppress value (category) labels.*

NAMES   *Display the names of control variables.* This is the default if you omit the FORMAT subcommand.

NONAMES   *Suppress names of control variables.*

VALUES   *Display the values of control variables.* This is the default if you omit the FORMAT subcommand.

NOVALUES   *Suppress values of control variables.* This is useful when there are category labels.

TABLE   *Display each table in report format.* This is the default if you omit the FORMAT subcommand.

TREE   *Display each table in tree format.*

11.14
Annotated Example

The following SPSS command file produced Figures 11.3a and 11.4b:

```
GET FILE=BANK.
COMPUTE SEXRACE=1.
IF (MINORITY EQ 1 AND SEX EQ 0) SEXRACE=2.
IF (MINORITY EQ 0 AND SEX EQ 1) SEXRACE=3.
IF (MINORITY EQ 1 AND SEX EQ 1) SEXRACE=4.
PRINT FORMATS SEXRACE(F1.0).
MEANS  TABLES=EDLEVEL BY SEX BY MINORITY.
VALUE LABELS  SEXRACE 1 'WHITE  MALES' 2 'MINORITYMALES'
 3 'WHITE  FEMALES' 4 'MINORITYFEMALES'.
MEANS  VARIABLES=SALBEG(LO,HI) SEXRACE(1,4) JOBCAT(1,7)
 /CROSSBREAK=SALBEG BY JOBCAT BY SEXRACE
 /CELLS=MEAN.
```

• The COMPUTE command and the three IF commands create a single four-category variable that combines the sex and race variables already on the file. The COMPUTE command sets the new variable SEXRACE to 1, which will be the white-male category. The IF commands change the value to 2 for nonwhite males, 3 for white females, and 4 for nonwhite females. Refer to Chapter 4 for an additional discussion of the COMPUTE and IF commands.

- The first MEANS command summarizes education for race within each sex category (see Figure 11.3a).
- A set of VALUE LABELS is assigned to the new variable SEXRACE for the second MEANS command. These labels are specially formatted to display well in the CROSSBREAK tables in Figures 11.3b and 11.4b, as described for CROSSTABS in Chapter 10.
- The second MEANS command requests crosstabular format (see Figure 11.4b). The keywords LO and HI specify the minimum and maximum values for variable SALBEG.
- The CELLS subcommand requests only means in each cell.

11.15 EXERCISES

Syntax

1. Write a MEANS command to request a summary of current salary (SALNOW) for job category (JOBCAT) within each sex category (SEX). Include cases with missing values on JOBCAT or SEX in the summary table.

2. The following MEANS command requesting a crosstabulation-like format has a syntax error. What is the error?

```
MEANS  CROSSBREAK=EDLEVEL BY SEX BY MINORITY.
```

3. Which of the MEANS commands below produced the following table?

```
            - - Description of Subpopulations - -

Summaries of     SALNOW      CURRENT SALARY
By levels of     MINORITY    MINORITY CLASSIFICATION
                 SEX         SEX OF EMPLOYEE


Variable        Value  Label                   Mean     Std Dev    Cases

For Entire Population                      13767.8270   6830.2646    474

MINORITY          0    WHITE                14409.3243   7217.6382    370
  SEX             0    MALES                17790.1649   8132.2646    194
  SEX             1    FEMALES              10682.7159   3204.7575    176

MINORITY          1    NONWHITE             11485.5769   4568.6551    104
  SEX             0    MALES                12898.4375   5223.9525     64
  SEX             1    FEMALES               9225.0000   1588.9474     40

  Total Cases = 474
```

   a. MEANS TABLES=SALNOW BY SEX MINORITY.

   b. MEANS TABLES=SALNOW BY MINORITY BY SEX.

   c. MEANS TABLES=MINORITY BY SALNOW BY SEX.

4. Write the command to calculate average ages (variable AGE) for people in various job categories (variable JOBTITLE).

5. Correct the following jobs:

   a. MEANS INCOME BY SEX /STATISTICS=MEAN STDDEV.

   b. MEANS TABLES=INCOME, SEX /MISSING=TABLE /CELLS=TABLE.

   c. MEANS TABLES=INCOME BY JOBTITLE BY SEX
           /VARIABLES=INCOME(LO,HI) BY JOBTITLE(1,4) BY SEX(1,2).

   d. MEANS TABLES=INCOME, AGE BY SEX
           CELLS=COLUMN ROW TOTAL.

   e. MEANS TABLES=INCOME(LO,HI) BY SEX(1,2)/
           CELLS=COUNT COLUMN ROW.

6. Assume that data in file LIFE are defined and labeled. Use variables SEX (coded 1=female, 2=male) and LOOKS (coded 0=unattractive, 1=attractive) to create variable POPULAR and code it for attractive and unattractive women and men. Then write the SPSS command to display in crosstabulation-like format the average income (variable INCOME) of popular and unpopular (variable POPULAR) professionals (variable JOB, coded 1=counselor, 2=professor, 3=doctor, 4=lawyer, 5=politician).

Statistical Concepts

1. Indicate whether you would use procedure FREQUENCIES, CROSSTABS, or MEANS to find the following:

   a. The average years of education for members of different political parties.

   b. The number of men and women in each political party.

   c. The number of members in each political party.

   d. The average years of education for men and women in each political party.

   e. The number of men and women in each religious affiliation within each political party.

2. How are the values in the cells of MEANS tables different from those in CROSSTABS tables?

3. Suppose you are using MEANS to see whether women at a particular company are discriminated against in regard to salary. Indicate whether the following statements are true:

   a. If your MEANS analysis shows no discrimination as far as average salary is concerned, it is safe to assume that no individual women are discriminated against in regard to salary.

   b. If average salaries are the same for men and women, it is safe to assume that there appears to be no salary discrimination against women as a class at this company.

4. Below is a MEANS table of average diastolic blood pressure subdivided by family history of coronary heart disease and by status at 10 years.

   a. Fill in the missing information:

```
                    - - Description of Subpopulations - -

Summaries of        DBP58        AVERAGE DIAST BLOOD PRESSURE 58
By levels of        FAMHXCVR     FAMILY HISTORY OF CHD
                    VITAL10      STATUS AT TEN YEARS


Variable        Value  Label                     Mean     Std Dev   Cases

For Entire Population                           88.7908   13.0499

FAMHXCVR        N      NO                        87.7740              177
   VITAL10         0                             86.6015   11.1137    133
   VITAL10         1   DEAD                                 17.0304

FAMHXCVR        Y      YES                                  13.0039
   VITAL10         0   ALIVE                     90.4000   12.0593     45
   VITAL10         1   DEAD                      95.1176   15.0868     17

   Total Cases = 240
   Missing Cases = 1 or      .4 Pct
```

   b. Based on the table above can you determine mean diastolic blood pressure for all men without a history of heart disease?

   c. Can you determine mean diastolic blood pressure for all men still alive at 10 years?

5. A survey of new-car owners asks the question "What is the body style of your new car?" The following choices are offered: two-door with trunk; two-door with hatchback; convertible; four-door with trunk; four-door with hatchback; station wagon. A research analyst assigns the code 1 through 6 to the above responses and uses procedure MEANS to find average styles controlling for sex and income level. How would you interpret the resulting table?

Data Analysis

Use the BANK system file for Questions 1–3.

1. Describe the distribution of age, educational level, work experience, and beginning salary for the sex-race groups. Summarize your findings.

2. Collapse education into several categories and describe the distribution of beginning salary for sex-race groupings, controlling for education. Do the results indicate that discrimination may be present? What are the weaknesses of this sort of analysis?

3. Collapse beginning salary into several categories and describe the distribution of current salary across the sex-race groups, controlling for beginning salary. Is there evidence of discrimination?

4. Choose one of the data files from Appendix B and formulate several hypotheses that can be examined using procedure MEANS. For example, the hypothesis that men and women of similar educational backgrounds watch comparable amounts of television can be studied by calculating average hours of television viewing for each sex for different education levels. Remember to group years of education into broader categories, such as high-school graduate, college graduate, and so forth. Otherwise, there will be only a few subjects at each education level.

   a. Obtain tables from procedure MEANS for three relationships. If there are only a few cases in any of the categories, RECODE the variables.

   b. Write a paragraph describing your results.

5. Use the Western Electric data file for the following questions:

   a. Calculate the average number of cigarettes smoked, serum cholesterol, diastolic blood pressure, age, and years of education for men who developed and those who did not develop coronary heart disease.

   b. Write a brief paragraph describing the results you found in (a). How do these compare to the results you obtained to Question 8.d. in the previous chapter?

   c. Determine whether there are differences in smoking, cholesterol, blood pressure, age, and years of education for the different types of CHD events (FIRSTCHD). Write a paragraph describing your results.

   d. Repeat (a) for men who have and do not have a family history of heart disease.

T-Test _____

In this chapter:

Goals:

- To test the hypothesis that two independent samples come from populations with the same mean.
- To test the hypothesis that two related samples come from populations with the same mean.

Examples:

- To test whether the average systolic blood pressure is the same for white males and black males.
- To test if the average years of education is the same for married and single women.
- To see if at age 40 the oldest children in families earn more than the youngest.

How it's done:

For each of the two samples, the means, the difference of the means, and the standard error of the difference of the two means are computed. (The standard error of the mean difference is computed differently for independent and related samples.) Based on the ratio of the difference of the means divided by their standard error (the *t*-statistic), the probability of observing a difference in the means, at least as large as the one observed, is computed if the two samples come from the same population. If this observed significance level is small, the hypothesis of no difference can be rejected.

Data considerations:

If you have two independent samples, you must have a grouping variable that indicates into which of the two groups each case falls. If you have two related samples, each case in your file must represent the two members of a pair. The values for a pair are stored in two different variables. The t-test also requires that, if your sample sizes are small, the variable being compared must be approximately normally distributed in the population and that the sample be chosen without bias from the population.

12 Testing Hypotheses about Differences in Means: Procedure T-TEST

Would you buy a disposable raincoat, vegetables in pop-top cans, or investment counseling via closed-circuit television? These products and 17 others were described in questionnaires administered to 100 married couples (Davis & Ragsdale, 1983). Respondents were asked to rate on a scale of 1 (definitely want to buy) to 7 (definitely do not want to buy) their likelihood of buying the product. Of the 100 couples, 50 received questionnaires with pictures of the products and 50 received questionnaires without pictures. In this chapter we will examine whether pictures affect consumer preferences and whether husbands' and wives' responses differ.

12.1 TESTING HYPOTHESES

The first part of the table in Figure 12.1 contains basic descriptive statistics for the buying scores of couples receiving questionnaires with and without pictures. A couple's buying score is simply the sum of all ratings assigned to products by the husband and wife individually. Low scores indicate buyers while high scores indicate reluctance to buy. The 50 couples who received questionnaires without pictures (Group 1) had a mean score of 168 while the 48 couples who received forms with pictures had an average score of 159. (Two couples did not complete the questionnaire and are not included in the analysis.) The standard deviations show that scores for the second group were somewhat more variable than those for the first.

Figure 12.1 Family buying scores by questionnaire type

```
T-TEST GROUPS=VISUAL(0,1) /VARIABLES=FAMSCORE.
```

```
- - - - - - - - - - - - - - - - - - - - - - - - - - T - T E S T - - - - - - - - - - - - - - - - - - - - - - - - - - - - -

GROUP 1 - VISUAL   EQ   0:   NO PICTURES
GROUP 2 - VISUAL   EQ   1:   PICTURES
                                                           *  Pooled Variance estimate * Separate Variance Estimate
                                                           *                            *
Variable            Number                Standard  Standard *   F     2-tail  *    t   Degrees of 2-tail *    t   Degrees of 2-tail
                    of Cases      Mean    Deviation    Error  * Value  Prob.   *  Value   Freedom   Prob.  *  Value   Freedom  Prob.

FAMSCORE  FAMILY BUYING SCORE                               *                  *                           *
      GROUP 1      50      168.0000    21.787    3.081   *                  *                           *
                                                           *  1.60   .106   *  1.78     96      .078   *  1.77    89.43    .080
      GROUP 2      48      159.0833    27.564    3.979   *                  *                           *
                                                           *                  *                           *
```

If you are willing to restrict the conclusions to the 98 couples included in the study, it is safe to say that couples who received forms with pictures indicated a greater willingness to purchase the products than couples who received forms without pictures. However, this statement is not very satisfying. What is needed is some type of statement about the effect of the two questionnaire types for all couples—or at least some larger group of couples—not just those actually studied.

12.2
Samples and Populations

The totality of all cases about which conclusions are desired is called the *population*, while the observations actually included in the study are the *sample*. The couples in this experiment can be considered a sample from the population of couples in the United States.

The field of statistics helps us draw inferences about populations based on observations obtained from *random samples,* or samples in which the characteristics and relationships of interest are independent of the probabilities of being included in the sample. The necessity of a good research design cannot be overemphasized. Unless precautions are taken to ensure that the sample is from the population of interest and that the cases are chosen and observed without bias, the results obtained from statistical analyses may be misleading. For example, if a sample contains only affluent suburban couples, conclusions about all couples may be unwarranted.

If measurements are obtained from an entire population, the population can be characterized by the various measures of central tendency, dispersion, and shape described in Chapter 8. The results describe the population exactly. If, however, you obtain information from a random sample—the usual case—the results serve as *estimates* of the unknown population values. Special notation is used to identify population values, termed *parameters*, and to distinguish them from sample values, termed *statistics*. The mean of a population is denoted by μ, and the variance by σ^2. The symbols $\bar{X}$ and S^2 are reserved for the mean and variance of samples.

12.3
Sampling Distributions

The observations actually included in a study are just one of many random samples that could have been selected from a population. For example, if the population consists of married couples in the United States, the number of different samples that could be chosen for inclusion in a study is mind-boggling. The estimated value of a population parameter depends on the particular sample chosen. Different samples usually produce different estimates.

Figure 12.3 is a histogram of 400 means. Each mean is calculated from a random sample of 25 observations from a population which has a normal distribution with a mean value of 0 and a standard deviation of 1. The estimated means are not all the same. Instead, they have a distribution. Most sample means are fairly close to 0, the population mean. The mean of the 400 means is 0.010 and the standard deviation of these means is 0.205. In fact, the distribution of the means appears approximately normal.

Although Figure 12.3 gives some idea of the appearance of the distribution of sample means of size 25 from a standard normal population, it is only an approximation since all possible samples of size 25 have not been taken. If the number of samples taken is increased to 1000, an even better picture of the distribution could be obtained. As the number of samples of a fixed size increases, the observed (or empirical) distribution of the means approaches the underlying or theoretical distribution.

The theoretical distribution of all possible values of a statistic obtained from a population is called the *sampling distribution* of the statistic. The mean of the sampling distribution is called the *expected value* of the statistic. The standard deviation is termed the *standard error*. The sampling distributions of most commonly used statistics calculated from random samples are tabulated and readily accessible. Knowing the sampling distribution of a statistic is very important for hypothesis testing, since from it you can calculate the probability of obtaining an observed sample value if a particular hypothesis is true. For example, from Figure 12.3, it appears quite unlikely that a sample mean based on a sample of size 25 from a standard normal distribution would be greater than 0.5 if the population mean were 0.

Figure 12.3   Means of 400 samples of size 25 from a normal distribution

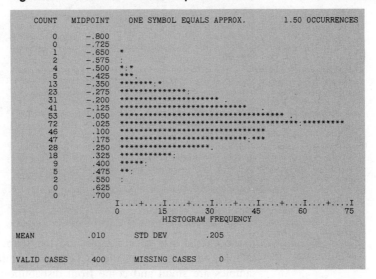

12.4
Sampling Distribution of the Mean

Since hypotheses about population means are often of interest, the sampling distribution of the mean is particularly important. If samples are taken from a normal population, the sampling distribution of the sample mean is also normal. As expected, the observed distribution of the 400 means in Figure 12.3 is approximately normal. The theoretical distribution of the sample mean, based on all possible samples of size 25, is exactly normal.

Even when samples are taken from a nonnormal population, the distribution of the sample means will be approximately normal for sufficiently large samples. This is one reason for the importance of the normal distribution in statistical inference. Consider Figure 12.4a, which shows a sample from a uniform distribution. In a uniform distribution all values of a variable are equally likely, and hence the proportion of cases in each bin of the histogram is roughly the same.

Figure 12.4a   Values from a uniform distribution

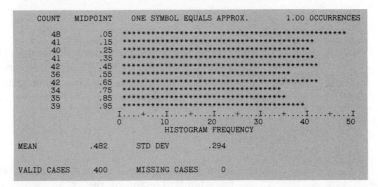

Figure 12.4b is a histogram of 400 means calculated from samples of size 25 from a uniform distribution. Note that the observed distribution is approximately normal even though the distribution from which the samples were taken is markedly nonnormal.

**Figure 12.4b   Distribution of 400 means calculated from samples of size 25
from a uniform distribution**

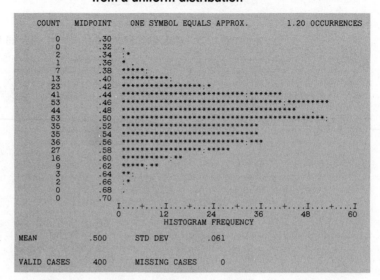

Both the size of a sample and the shape of the distribution from which samples are taken affect the shape of the sampling distribution of the mean. If samples are small and come from distributions that are far from normal, the distribution of the means will not be even approximately normal. As the size of the sample increases, the sampling distribution of the mean will approach normality.

The mean of the theoretical sampling distribution of the means of samples of size n is μ, the population mean. The standard error, which is another name for the standard deviation of the sampling distribution of the mean, is

$$\sigma_{\bar{X}} = \frac{\sigma}{\sqrt{N}}$$ **Equation 12.4a**

where σ is the standard deviation of the population, and N is the sample size.

The standard deviation of the observed sampling distribution of means in Figure 12.3 is 0.205. This is close to the value of the standard error for the theoretical distribution which, from the previous formula, is 1/5, or 0.20.

Usually the value of the standard error is unknown and is estimated from a single sample using

$$S_{\bar{x}} = \frac{S}{\sqrt{N}}$$ **Equation 12.4b**

where S is the *sample* standard deviation. The estimated standard error is displayed in the FREQUENCIES procedure and is also part of the output shown in Figure 12.1. For example, for Group 1 the estimated standard error of the mean is

$$\frac{21.787}{\sqrt{50}} = 3.081$$ **Equation 12.4c**

This value is displayed in the column labeled **Standard Error** in Figure 12.1.

The standard error of the mean depends on both the sample standard deviation and the sample size. As the size of a sample increases, the standard error decreases. This is intuitively clear, since the more data are gathered, the more confident you can be that the sample mean is not too far from the population mean. Also, as the standard deviation of the observations decreases, the standard error decreases as well. Small standard deviations occur when observations are fairly homogeneous. In this case, means based on different samples should also not vary much.

12.5
THE TWO-SAMPLE
T-TEST

Consider again whether there is evidence that the type of form administered influences couples' buying decisions. The question is not whether the two sample means are equal, but whether the two population means are equal.

To test the hypothesis that, in the population, buying scores for the two questionnaire types are the same, the following statistic can be calculated:

$$t = \frac{\overline{X}_1 - \overline{X}_2}{\sqrt{S_1^2/N_1 + S_2^2/N_2}}$$ **Equation 12.5a**

$\overline{X}_1$ is the sample mean of Group 1, S_1^2 is the variance, and N_1 is the sample size.

Based on the sampling distribution of the above statistic, you can calculate the probability that a difference at least as large as the one observed would occur if the two population means (μ_1 and μ_2) are equal. This probability is called the *observed significance level*. If the observed significance level is small enough, usually less than 0.05, or 0.01, the hypothesis that the population means are equal is rejected.

The t value and its associated probability are given in Figure 12.1 in the section labeled **Separate Variance Estimate**. The t value is

$$t = \frac{168.0 - 159.08}{\sqrt{\dfrac{21.787^2}{50} + \dfrac{27.564^2}{48}}} = 1.77$$ **Equation 12.5b**

If $\mu_1 = \mu_2$, the probability of observing a difference at least as large as the one in the sample is estimated to be about 0.08. Since this probability is greater than 0.05, the hypothesis that mean buying scores in the population are equal for the two types of forms is not rejected. The entry under **Degrees of Freedom** in Figure 12.1 is a function of the sample size in the two groups and is used together with the t value in establishing the observed significance level.

Another statistic based on the t distribution can be used to test the equality of means hypothesis. This statistic, known as the *pooled-variance t-test,* is based on the assumption that the population variances in the two groups are equal and is obtained using a pooled estimate of that common variance. The test statistic is identical to the equation for t given previously except that the individual group variances are replaced by a pooled estimate S_p^2. That is,

$$t = \frac{\overline{X}_1 - \overline{X}_2}{\sqrt{S_p^2/N_1 + S_p^2/N_2}}$$ **Equation 12.5c**

where S_p^2, the pooled variance, is a weighted average of the individual variances and is calculated as

$$S_p^2 = \frac{(N_1 - 1)S_1^2 + (N_2 - 1)S_2^2}{N_1 + N_2 - 2}$$ **Equation 12.5d**

From the output in Figure 12.1, the pooled t-test value for the study is 1.78. The degrees of freedom for the pooled t-test are 96, the sum of the sample sizes in both groups minus 2. If the pooled-variance t-test is used when the population variances are not equal, the probability level associated with the statistic may be in error. The amount of error depends on the inequality of the sample sizes and of the variances. However, using the separate-variance t value when the population variances are equal will usually result in an observed significance level somewhat larger than it should be. For large samples, the discrepancy between the two methods is small. In general, it is a good idea to use the separate-variance t-test whenever you suspect that the variances are unequal.

The statistic used to test the hypothesis that the two population variances are equal is the F value, which is the ratio of the larger sample variance to the smaller. In Figure 12.1, this value is $(27.6^2/21.8^2 = 1.6)$. If the observed significance level for the F test is small, the hypothesis that the population variances are equal is rejected, and the separate-variance t-test for means should be used. In this example, the significance level for the F test is large, and thus the pooled-variance t-test is appropriate. The F test for the equality of two variances depends heavily on the data being from normal populations, while the t-test does not. Thus, the F test is not a very good test for the hypothesis.

12.6
Significance Levels

The commonsense interpretation of a small observed significance level is straight-forward: it appears unlikely that the two population means are equal. Of course, there is a possibility that the means are equal and the observed difference is due to chance. The *observed significance level* is the probability that a difference at least as large as the one observed would have arisen if the means were really equal.

When the observed significance level is too large to reject the equality hypothesis, the two population means may indeed be equal, or the means may be unequal but the difference cannot be detected. Failure to detect can be due to a true difference that is very small. For example, if a new cancer drug prolongs survival time by only one day when compared to the standard treatment, it is unlikely that such a difference will be detected, especially if survival times vary substantially and the additional day represents a small increment.

There are other reasons why true differences may not be found. If the sample sizes in the two groups are small or the variability large, even substantial differences may not be detected. Significant t values are obtained when the numerator of the t statistic is large when compared to the denominator. The numerator is the difference between the sample means, and the denominator depends on the standard deviations and sample sizes of the two groups. For a given standard deviation, the larger the sample size, the smaller the denominator. Thus, a difference of a given magnitude may be significant if obtained with a sample size of 100, but not significant with a sample size of 25.

12.7
One-Tailed vs. Two-Tailed Tests

A two-tailed test is used to detect a difference in means between two populations regardless of the direction of the difference. For example, in the study of buying scores presented in this chapter, we are interested in whether buying scores without pictures are larger *or* smaller than buying scores with pictures. In applications where you are interested in detecting a difference in one direction—such as whether a new drug is better than the current treatment—a so-called one-tailed test can be performed. The procedure is the same as for the two-tailed test, but the resulting probability value is divided by 2, adjusting for the fact that the equality hypothesis is rejected only when the difference between the two means is sufficiently large and in the direction of interest. In a two-tailed test, the equality hypothesis is rejected for large positive or negative values of the statistic.

12.8
What's the Difference?

It appears that the questionnaire type has no significant effect on couples' willingness to purchase products. Overall buying scores for the two conditions are similar. Pictures of the products do not appear to enhance their perceived desirability. In fact, the pictures actually appear to make several products somewhat less desirable. However, since the purpose of the questionnaires is to ascertain buying intent, including a picture of the actual product may help gauge true product response. Although the concept of disposable raincoats may be attractive, if they make the owner look like a walking trash bag their appeal may diminish considerably.

12.9
USING PROCEDURE CROSSTABS TO TEST HYPOTHESES

The T-TEST procedure is used to test hypotheses about the equality of two means for variables measured on an interval or ratio scale. Procedure CROSSTABS and the Pearson chi-square statistic can be used to test hypotheses about a dichotomous variable, such as purchase of a particular product.

Figure 12.9 is a crosstabulation showing the number of husbands who would definitely want to buy (value 1) vegetables in pop-top cans when shown a picture and when not shown a picture of the product. The vegetables in pop-top cans were chosen by 6.0% of the husbands who were tempted with pictures and 16.0% of the husbands who were not shown pictures. The chi-square statistic provides a test of the hypothesis that the proportion of husbands selecting the vegetables in pop-top cans is the same for the picture and no-picture forms.

Figure 12.9   Preference of husbands for vegetables in pop-top cans

```
CROSSTABS TABLES=H2S BY VISUAL
 /CELLS=COUNT COLUMN /STATISTICS=CHISQ.
```

```
H2S   POP-TOP CANS HUSB SELF  by  VISUAL  PICTURE ACCOMPANIED QUESTION

                       VISUAL
              Count
              Col Pct NO PICTU PICTURES
                      RES               Row
                         0   |    1   | Total
H2S          ---------+--------+--------+
           1 |      8 |      3 |     11
   DEFINITELY|   16.0 |    6.0 |   11.0
             +--------+--------+
           2 |     42 |     47 |     89
  VERY LIKELY|   84.0 |   94.0 |   89.0
             +--------+--------+
       Column       50       50      100
        Total      50.0     50.0    100.0

     Chi-Square              Value         DF        Significance
   _____

   Pearson                  2.55362          1           .11004
   Continuity Correction    1.63432          1           .20111
   Likelihood Ratio         2.63925          1           .10425
   Mantel-Haenszel          2.52809          1           .11184

   Minimum Expected Frequency -   5.500


   Number of Missing Observations:  0
```

The probability of 0.11 associated with the Pearson chi-square in Figure 12.9 is the probability that a difference at least as large as the one observed would occur in the sample if in the population there were no difference in the selection of the product between the two formats. Since the probability is large, the hypothesis of no difference between the two formats is not rejected.

12.10
INDEPENDENT VS. PAIRED SAMPLES

Several factors contribute to the observed differences in response between two groups. Part of the observed difference in scores between the picture and no-picture formats may be attributable to form type. Another component is due to differences between individuals. Not all couples have the same buying desires, so even if the type of form does not affect buying, differences between the two groups will probably be observed due to differences between the couples within the two groups.

One method of minimizing the influence of individual variation is to choose the two groups so that the couples within them are comparable on characteristics that can influence buying behavior, such as income, education, family size, and so forth.

It is sometimes possible to obtain pairs of subjects, such as twins, and assign one member of each pair to each of the two treatments. Another frequently used experimental design is to expose the same individual to both types of conditions. (In this design, care must be taken to ensure that the sequential administration of treatments does not influence response by providing practice, decreasing attention span, or affecting the second treatment in other ways.) In both designs, subject-to-subject variability has substantially less effect. These designs are called *paired-samples designs,* since for each subject there is a corresponding pair in the other group. In the second design, a person is paired with himself or herself. In an *independent-samples design,* there is no pairing of cases; all observations are independent.

12.11
Analysis of Paired Data

Although the interpretation of the significance of results from paired experiments is the same as those from the two independent samples discussed previously, the actual computations are different. For each pair of cases, the difference in the responses is calculated. The statistic used to test the hypothesis that the mean difference in the population is 0 is

$$t = \frac{\overline{D}}{S_D/\sqrt{N}}$$

Equation 12.11

where $\overline{D}$ is the observed difference between the two means and $S_{\overline{D}}$ is the standard deviation of the differences of the paired observations. The sampling distribution of t, if the differences are normally distributed with a mean of 0, is Student's t with $N-1$ degrees of freedom, where N is the number of pairs. If the pairing is effective, the standard error of the difference will be smaller than the standard error obtained if two independent samples with N subjects each were chosen. However, if the variables chosen for pairing do not affect the responses under study, pairing may result in a test that is less powerful since true differences can be detected less frequently.

For example, to test the hypothesis that there is no difference between husbands' and wives' buying scores, a paired t-test should be calculated. A paired test is appropriate since husbands and wives constitute matched observations. Hopefully, including both members of a couple controls for some nuisance effects like socioeconomic status, age, and so forth. The observed differences are more likely to be attributable to differences in sex.

Figure 12.11 contains output from the paired t-test. The entry under number of cases is the number of pairs of observations. The mean difference is the difference between the mean scores for males and females. The t value is the mean difference divided by the standard error of the difference ($0.55/1.73=0.32$). The two-tailed probability for this test is 0.75, so there is insufficient evidence to reject the null hypothesis that married males and females have similar mean buying scores.

Figure 12.11   Husbands' versus wives' buying scores

T-TEST PAIRS=HSSCALE, WSSCALE.

```
- - - - - - - - - - - - - - - - - - - - - - - - - - - - - T - T E S T - - - - - - - - - - - - - - - - - - - - - - - - - - - - -
```

Variable	Number of Cases	Mean	Standard Deviation	Standard Error	* *	(Difference) Mean	Standard Deviation	Standard Error	* *	2-tail Corr. Prob.	* *	t Value	Degrees of Freedom	2-tail Prob.
HSSCALE	HUSBAND SELF SCALE				*						*			
		82.0918	14.352	1.450	*				*		*			
	98				*	.5510	17.095	1.727	*	.367 .000	*	.32	97	.750
		81.5408	15.942	1.610	*				*		*			
WSSCALE	WIFE SELF SCALE				*						*			

The correlation coefficient between husbands' and wives' scores is 0.367. A positive correlation indicates that pairing has been effective in decreasing the variability of the mean difference. The larger the correlation coefficient, the greater the benefit of pairing.

12.12
HYPOTHESIS TESTING: A REVIEW

The purpose of hypothesis testing is to help draw conclusions about population parameters based on results observed in a random sample. The procedure remains virtually the same for tests of most hypotheses.

• A hypothesis of no difference (called a *null hypothesis*) and its alternative are formulated.

• A test statistic is chosen to evaluate the null hypothesis.

• For the sample, the test statistic is calculated.

• The probability, if the null hypothesis is true, of obtaining a test value at least as extreme as the one observed is determined.

• If the observed significance level is judged small enough, the null hypothesis is rejected.

12.13
The Importance of Assumptions

In order to perform a statistical test of any hypothesis, it is necessary to make certain assumptions about the data. The particular assumptions depend on the statistical test being used. Some procedures require stricter assumptions than others. For *parametric tests,* some knowledge about the distribution from which samples are selected is required.

The assumptions are necessary to define the sampling distribution of the test statistic. Unless the distribution is defined, correct significance levels cannot be calculated. For the pooled t-test, the assumption is that the observations are random samples from normal distributions with the same variance.

For many procedures, not all assumptions are equally important. Moderate violation of some assumptions may not always be serious. Therefore, it is important to know for each procedure not only what assumptions are needed but also how severely their violation may influence results. For example the *F* test for equality of variances is quite sensitive to departures from normality, while the t-test for equality of means is less so.

The responsibility for detecting violations of assumptions rests with the researcher. Unfortunately, unlike the experimenter in chemistry, no explosions or disintegrating terminals threaten the investigator who does not comply with good statistical practice. However, from a research viewpoint, the consequences can be just as severe.

Wherever possible, tests of assumptions—often called diagnostic checks of the model—should be incorporated as part of the hypothesis-testing procedures. Throughout SPSS, attempts have been made to provide facilities for examining assumptions. For example, in the EXAMINE procedure there are several tests for normality. Discussions of other such diagnostics are included with the individual procedures.

12.14
RUNNING
PROCEDURE T-TEST

Procedure T-TEST computes the Student's *t* statistic for testing the significance of a difference in means for independent or paired samples. For independent samples, procedure T-TEST provides both separate- and pooled-variance estimates.

12.15
Independent Samples

An independent-samples test divides the cases into two groups and compares the group means on a single variable (Section 12.5). This test requires the GROUPS and VARIABLES subcommands.

12.16
GROUPS Subcommand

The GROUPS subcommand names the variable and the criterion for dividing the cases into two groups. You can name only one variable. You can use any of three different methods to define the two groups. In the first method, a single value in parentheses groups all cases with a value equal to or greater than the specified value into one group and the remaining cases into the other group. For example, the command

```
T-TEST GROUPS=WORLD(2) /VARIABLES=NTCPUR.
```

groups together all cases with the value of WORLD greater than or equal to 2. The remaining cases go into the other group.

Alternatively, if you specify two values in parentheses, one group includes cases with the first value on the grouping variable, and the other includes cases with the second value. For example, the following command produced Figure 12.1:

```
T-TEST GROUPS=VISUAL(0,1) /VARIABLES=FAMSCORE.
```

In this example, any cases with values other than 0 and 1 for variable VISUAL would not be used. You can also use the RECODE command (see Chapter 3) to collapse or combine categories of the variable named on the GROUPS subcommand.

If the grouping variable has only two values, coded 1 and 2, you do not have to specify a value list. For example, the command

```
T-TEST GROUPS=SEX /VARIABLES=GRADES.
```

groups all cases having the value 1 for SEX into one group and cases having the value 2 for SEX into the other group. All other cases are not used.

12.17
VARIABLES Subcommand

The VARIABLES subcommand names the variables being analyzed. You can use only numeric variables. The command

```
T-TEST GROUPS=WORLD(1,3) /VARIABLES=NTCPRI NTCSAL NTCPUR.
```

compares the means of the two groups defined by WORLD for the variables NTCPRI, NTCSAL, and NTCPUR, while

```
T-TEST GROUPS=WORLD(1,3) /VARIABLES=NTCPRI TO MCLOTHES.
```

compares the means of the groups defined by WORLD for all variables on the active system file between and including NTCPRI and MCLOTHES.

12.18
PAIRS Subcommand

To compute tests for paired samples (Section 12.10) you need two variables that represent values for the two members of the pair for each case, such as pre- and post-test scores for students in a class. Figure 12.11, comparing husbands' and wives' buying scores, was produced with the following command:

```
T-TEST  PAIRS=HSSCALE, WSSCALE.
```

You can name only numeric variables. If you specify a list of variables, each variable is compared with every other variable. For example, the command

```
T-TEST PAIRS=TEACHER CONSTRUC MANAGER.
```

compares TEACHER with CONSTRUC, TEACHER with MANAGER, and CONSTRUC with MANAGER.

You can use the keyword WITH to request a test comparing every variable to the left of the keyword with every variable to the right of the keyword. For example,

```
T-TEST  PAIRS=TEACHER MANAGER WITH CONSTRUC ENGINEER.
```

compares TEACHER with CONSTRUC, TEACHER with ENGINEER, MANAGER with CONSTRUC, and MANAGER with ENGINEER. TEACHER is not compared with MANAGER, and CONSTRUC is not compared with ENGINEER.

You can use the slash to separate lists of variables, as in

```
T-TEST  PAIRS=WCLOTHES MCLOTHES/NTCPRI WITH NTCPUR NTCSAL.
```

which specifies two lists.

You can also use the keyword (PAIRED) to specify multiple paired-sample analyses. Each variable before the keyword WITH is paired with a variable after the WITH keyword, as in:

```
T-TEST  PAIRS=TEACHER MANAGER WITH CONSTRUC ENGINEER (PAIRED).
```

TEACHER is paired with CONSTRUC and MANAGER is paired with ENGINEER. You must name or imply the same number of variables on each side of the keyword WITH. If the number of variables is not equal, SPSS will generate as many t-tests as it can and will then issue a warning indicating that the number of variables is not equal.

12.19
Independent and Paired Designs

You can request both independent- and paired-samples tests on a single T-TEST command, but you must specify the independent-samples test first. Thus, the GROUPS subcommand is first, followed by the VARIABLES subcommand, and finally the PAIRS subcommand, as in the following example:

```
T-TEST GROUPS=VISUAL(0,1) /VARIABLES=FAMSCORE
 /PAIRS=HSSCALE WSSCALE.
```

12.20
One-Tailed Significance Levels

By default, the probability is based on the two-tailed test. This is appropriate when differences in either direction are of interest. When theoretical considerations predict that the difference will be in a given direction (such as the Group 1 mean will be higher than the Group 2 mean), a one-tailed test is appropriate. To calculate the one-tailed probability, divide the two-tailed probability by 2.

12.21
MISSING Subcommand

By default, T-TEST deletes cases with missing values on an analysis-by-analysis basis. For independent-samples tests, cases missing on either the grouping variable or the analysis variable are excluded from the analysis of that variable. For paired-samples tests, a case missing on either of the variables in a given pair is excluded from the analysis of that pair. The following keyword options are available using the MISSING subcommand:

ANALYSIS *Delete cases with missing values on an analysis-by-analysis basis.* This is the default if you omit the MISSING subcommand.

LISTWISE *Exclude missing values listwise.* A case missing for any variable specified on either the GROUPS or the VARIABLES subcommand is excluded from any independent sample analysis. A case missing for any variable specified on the PAIRS subcommand is excluded from any paired sample analysis.

INCLUDE *Include user-missing values.* Cases with user-missing values are included in the analysis. By default, cases with user-missing values are excluded.

The ANALYSIS and LISTWISE keywords are mutually exclusive; however, each can be specified with INCLUDE.

12.22
FORMAT Subcommand

By default, T-TEST displays variable labels. You can suppress variable labels by specifying NOLABELS on the FORMAT subcommand:

LABELS *Display variable labels.* This is the default if you omit the FORMAT subcommand.

NOLABELS *Suppress variable labels.*

12.23
EXERCISES

Syntax

1. In the following T-TEST commands, who is in Group 1? Who is in Group 2?
   a. T-TEST GROUPS=SHOESIZE(8)/VARIABLES=WEIGHT.
   b. T-TEST GROUPS=SHOESIZE(1,9)/VARIABLES=WEIGHT.
   c. T-TEST GROUPS=SHOESIZE/VARIABLES=WEIGHT.

2. Which of the following T-TEST commands contain errors?
   a. T-TEST GROUPS=SEX/VARIABLES=HEIGHT/PAIRS=TEST1 TEST2.
   b. T-TEST PAIRS=TEST1 TEST2/GROUPS=SEX/VARIABLES=WEIGHT.
   c. T-TEST PAIRS=SCORE.
   d. T-TEST PAIRS=SCORE1 SCORE2 SCORE3.
   e. T-TEST GROUPS=SEX(1,2,3)/VARIABLES=WEIGHT.

3. Write the commands that produce the tables in Questions 8.a and 8.b below (Statistical Concepts).

4. You type the following command:

   T-TEST WORLD(2) /VARIABLES=NTCPUR.

   and get the following error message:

   ```
   >Error # 11800 on line 7 in column 9.  Text: WORLD
   >The T-TEST command includes an unrecognized subcommand.  The recognized
   >subcommands are GROUPS, VARIABLES, PAIRS, MISSING, and FORMAT.
   >This command not executed.
   ```

   Fix the command.

5. You want to test the hypothesis that Republicans earn more money than Democrats. Write the T-TEST command to test the hypothesis that there is no difference in income between the two parties. Use variables PARTY and INCOME; code Republicans as 1 and Democrats as 2.

6. You want to test the hypothesis that people who meditate can reduce their heart rates and blood pressures. You have measures for the pulse and blood pressure of a group of meditation practitioners before and after they meditate. Test the hypothesis that meditation has no affect on pulse and blood pressure.

Statistical Concepts

1. Which of the following statements are true?
   a. The observed significance level for a t-test is the probability that the population means are equal. F
   b. If the observed significance level is large, you can be fairly sure that the means are exactly equal. F
   c. The sample size influences, in part, whether a difference in means is detected. T
   d. Small significance levels are associated with t values close to zero. F
   e. The variance of the sample mean is the square of the standard error of the sample mean. T
   f. The larger the sample, the larger the standard error of the sample mean. F
   g. The paired t-test is always more sensitive to true differences in means than is the independent-samples t-test. F
   h. A large positive correlation coefficient for paired variables indicates that pairing is a good strategy. T

2. A researcher wants to determine whether a company is releasing, on the average, higher levels of sulfur into the air than are permitted by federal law.
   a. Should she use a one- or a two-tailed test?
   b. Suppose the company is notorious for violating pollution laws. Would it be in the company's interest for the researcher to use a one- or two-tailed test?
   c. If she uses a one-tailed test and the t-test output lists a 2-tailed probability of .082, what is the observed significance level?

3. If you use a paired t-test to test the hypothesis that two means are equal and you obtain P=0.0002, is it possible that the two means are equal?

4. The F test for equality of variances requires that the two variables being compared be normally distributed.
   a. What SPSS procedure would you use to check this assumption?
   b. What output would you obtain from this procedure to check normality?

5. a. What is the null hypothesis for an independent-samples t-test?
   b. What is the null hypothesis for a paired t-test?

6. For the following experimental designs, indicate whether an independent-samples or paired t-test is appropriate:
   a. Weight is obtained for each subject before and after Dr. Nogani's new treatment. The hypothesis to be tested is that the treatment has no effect on weight loss.
   b. The Jenkins Activity Survey is administered to 20 couples. The hypothesis to be tested is that husbands' and wives' scores do not differ.
   c. Elephants are randomly selected from a jungle and Trunkgro1 is administered to one group of elephants and Trunkgro2 to the other. The hypothesis to be tested is that both agents are equally effective in promoting trunk growth.
   d. Subjects are asked their height and then a measurement of height is obtained. The hypothesis to be tested is that self-reported and actual heights do not differ.
   e. Two sleeping pills (Drugs A and B) are given to a sample of insomniacs. The subjects take Drug A during the first week of the study and Drug B during the second week. The total amount of time before falling asleep is recorded for each subject for each week.

7. a. When is the separate-variance t-test appropriate?

   b. When is the pooled-variance t-test appropriate?

8. a. The following table is the output from an independent-samples t-test. Fill in the missing information and interpret the results.

```
- - - - - - - - - - - - - - - - - - - - - - - - - - - T - T E S T - - - - - - - - - - - - - - - - - - - - - - - - - - - - -

GROUP 1 - TYPE    EQ    1.
GROUP 2 - TYPE    EQ    2.
                                                              * POOLED VARIANCE ESTIMATE * SEPARATE VARIANCE ESTIMATE
                                                          *   *
VARIABLE        NUMBER              STANDARD    STANDARD  *  F   2-TAIL  *   T   DEGREES OF 2-TAIL *  T   DEGREES OF 2-TAIL
                OF CASES    MEAN    DEVIATION   ERROR     * VALUE PROB.  * VALUE  FREEDOM    PROB. * VALUE   FREEDOM  PROB.

RECALL    COMMERCIAL RECALL SCORE                         *             *                         *
      GROUP 1    66     17.1087     2.804                 *             *                         *
                                                          *       0.000 *  2.12             0.036 *  2.02  103.96   0.046
      GROUP 2    82     16.3093                  0.193    *             *                         *
                                                          *             *                         *
```

   b. The following table is the output from a paired-sample t-test. Fill in the missing information and interpret the results.

```
- - - - - - - - - - - - - - - - - - - - - - - - - - T - T E S T - - - - - - - - - - - - - - - - - - - - - - - - - - - - -

VARIABLE     NUMBER             STANDARD   STANDARD   *(DIFFERENCE) STANDARD   STANDARD   *      2-TAIL  *   T   DEGREES OF 2-TAIL
             OF CASES   MEAN    DEVIATION  ERROR      *   MEAN      DEVIATION  ERROR      * CORR. PROB. * VALUE  FREEDOM   PROB.

SELF     SELF-REPORTED ARRESTS                        *                                  *             *
                    8.9620     6.458                  *                                  *             *
               79                                     *             5.216                * 0.654 0.000 *                  0.621
                    9.2532     6.248                  *                                  *             *
ACTUAL   ACTUAL ARRESTS                               *                                  *             *
```

Data Analysis

Use the BANK system file for Questions 2–6.

1. Seven patients each underwent three different methods of kidney dialysis (Daugirdas, 1982). The following values were obtained for weight change in kilograms between dialysis sessions:

Patient	Treatment 1	Treatment 2	Treatment 3
1	2.90	2.97	2.67
2	2.56	2.45	2.62
3	2.88	2.76	1.87
4	2.73	2.20	2.33
5	2.50	2.16	1.27
6	3.18	2.89	2.39
7	2.83	2.87	2.39

   a. Using SPSS, test the null hypothesis that there is no difference in mean weight change between Treatments 1 and 3 and between Treatments 2 and 3.

   b. Compute a new variable which is the difference in weight gain between Treatments 1 and 3. Using procedure FREQUENCIES, calculate the mean, standard deviation, and standard error for the new variable.

   c. Compare the values obtained in 1.a to those obtained in 1.b.

2. a. Evaluate the overall difference between men and women in beginning salary. Repeat this evaluation for each of the first two job categories (use the SELECT IF command). Is there evidence suggesting that women and men are not equally compensated? Which of these tests is the better comparison?

   b. Repeat the analysis above for the race variable.

   c. What statistical assumptions are you making?

3. For the analysis in Question 2.a, what are some arguments in favor of a one-tailed test? What arguments can you state for a two-tailed test? Which test would you use?

4. Repeat the analysis in Question 2.a, using current salary instead of beginning salary.

5. a. Do the educational backgrounds of women and men appear to be the same? Justify your answer with a statistical analysis.

   b. Obtain histograms of female and male educational levels. How appropriate does a t-test seem, given the appearance of these histograms? What does the large sample size have to do with the appropriateness of the t-test?

6. Repeat the analysis in Question 5, comparing the educational backgrounds of nonwhites and whites instead of women and men.

7. Choose one of the data sets from Appendix B and formulate several hypotheses that can be tested using paired- or independent-samples t-tests. For example, using the Western Electric data, you can test the hypothesis that men who develop coronary heart disease have higher diastolic blood pressure or smoke more than those who do not.

   a. Obtain a separate histogram for the variables to be tested for each of the two groups. In each of the groups, do the data appear to be approximately normally distributed?

   b. Perform the appropriate t-tests. Indicate whether you would use pooled- or separate-variance t-test results and why. Write a paragraph summarizing your findings. Be sure to include a statement about the observed significance level and its interpretation.

   c. Use the chi-square test to test the hypothesis that two proportions are equal. Summarize your findings.

8. Test the null hypothesis that the average number of cigarettes smoked does not differ for men who develop heart disease and those who do not.

9. Repeat Question 8 for the following variables: age at entry, average diastolic blood pressure, years of education, serum cholesterol, and body weight.

10. Write a paragraph describing differences between men who develop coronary heart disease and those who do not.

11. Perform the analyses necessary to determine whether there are differences in the previously described variables for men who have a family history of heart disease and those who do not.

Plotting Data

In this chapter:

Goals:

- To display the relationship between two variables measured on at least an ordinal scale.
- To examine the relationship between two variables when points are identified by the values of a third variable.

Examples:

- Look at the relationship between high school GPA and college GPA for males and females.
- Examine the relationship between systolic blood pressure and percent overweight.
- Display for all cases the values of both education and family income.

How it's done:

Each axis on the plot corresponds to one of the variables being displayed. Each symbol on the plot corresponds to the values of the pair of variables for one or more cases. Each point can be identified by value for a third (control) variable.

Data considerations:

Both of the variables being plotted must be at least ordinal. The control variable must have a limited number of distinct values in order to be useful. The control variable can be nominal.

13 Plotting Data: Procedure PLOT

Today the quest for the Fountain of Youth has been replaced by the Search for Slimness. It's almost acceptable to grow old, as long as one remains trim and fit. Programs for weight loss are assuming ever-increasing attention, and behavioral psychologists are studying the effectiveness of many different weight-loss strategies. Black and Sherba (1983) studied the effects of two different types of behavior programs on weight loss. One group of subjects was taught behavioral weight-loss techniques, while the second was taught weight-loss techniques and problem-solving behavior. Their data set is examined in this chapter.

13.1
DESCRIBING WEIGHT LOSS

As discussed in Chapter 9, a stem-and-leaf plot is a convenient method for displaying the distribution of a variable that can have many values. Figure 13.1a shows the percentage of excess weight actually lost during the treatment for each of the twelve cases in the study. From this figure we can see that about one-third of the participants lost 20% or more of the required weight during treatment. To see if weight loss is maintained, consider Figure 13.1b, which shows the percentage of weight loss one year after treatment. It appears that subjects did not gain back the weight but maintained weight loss.

Figure 13.1a   Stem-and-leaf plot of weight loss during treatment

```
EXAMINE VARIABLES=TREATRED
 /PLOT=STEMLEAF /SCALE=UNIFORM.

    Frequency    Stem &  Leaf

         4.00    -2  .   1445
         5.00    -1  .   23449
         2.00    -0  .   05
         1.00     0  .   0

    Stem width:     10.00
    Each leaf:       1 case(s)
```

Figure 13.1b   Stem-and-leaf plot of weight loss after one year

```
EXAMINE VARIABLES=TWELVRED
 /PLOT=STEMLEAF /SCALE=UNIFORM.

    Frequency    Stem &  Leaf

         3.00    -4  .   057
         1.00    -3  .   9
         1.00    -2  .   0
         3.00    -1  .   279
         2.00    -0  .   27
         2.00     0  .   15

    Stem width:     10.00
    Each leaf:       1 case(s)
```

Although the stem-and-leaf plots provide information about the weight loss during treatment and weight loss after twelve months, they reveal nothing about the relationship between the two variables since they each describe single variables. To determine whether lost weight during treatment is maintained or replaced at twelve months, the two variables must be studied together.

Figure 13.1c is a scatterplot of the percentage of weight loss during treatment and at one year for the twelve cases. Each symbol 1 on the plot represents one case, showing the values for that case on two variables: loss during treatment and loss at one year. For example, the circled point represents a case with a treatment loss of 25% and a twelve month value of −18%.

Figure 13.1c   Scatterplot for weight loss during treatment and after one year

PLOT PLOT=TREATRED WITH TWELVRED.

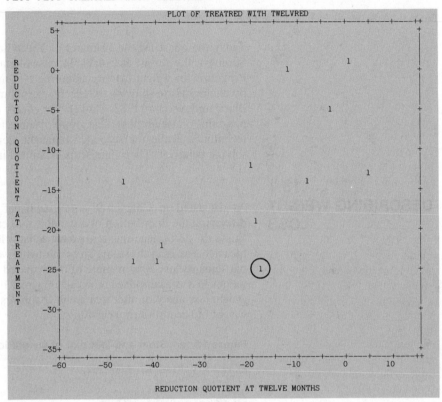

Since plots generated for terminals and printers have a limited number of positions in which to display points, it may not be possible to distinguish cases with similar values for the two variables. When two or more cases with similar values fall on the same point on the scatterplot, a number is displayed indicating how many cases overlap at that point. The scale of the plot depends on the minimum and maximum values for the two variables plotted. If the values for a few cases are far removed from the others, the majority of cases may appear bunched together in order to permit the outlying cases to appear on the same plot.

Figure 13.1d contains the symbols used to represent multiple cases at each point. For example, the symbol **D** is used when there are 13 coincident points.

Figure 13.1d   Scatterplot symbols for multiple cases

Frequencies and symbols used (not applicable for control or overlay plots)

1 − 1	11 − B	21 − L	31 − V
2 − 2	12 − C	22 − M	32 − W
3 − 3	13 − D	23 − N	33 − X
4 − 4	14 − E	24 − O	34 − Y
5 − 5	15 − F	25 − P	35 − Z
6 − 6	16 − G	26 − Q	36 − *
7 − 7	17 − H	27 − R	
8 − 8	18 − I	28 − S	
9 − 9	19 − J	29 − T	
10 − A	20 − K	30 − U	

13.2
Controlled Scatterplots

Often it is informative to identify each point on a scatterplot by its value on a third variable. For example, cases may be designated as males or females, or as originating from the West, Midwest, or East. Figure 13.2 is the same plot as Figure 13.1c except each case is identified as being a participant in the behavior program (value 1) or the problem-solving program (value 2). A dollar sign is displayed if cases from different groups coincide.

Figure 13.2 Scatterplot identifying the two programs

PLOT PLOT=TREATRED WITH TWELVRED **BY TREATMNT.**

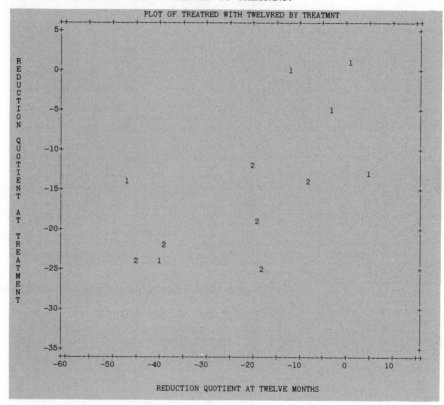

By examining Figure 13.2 you can see if the weight-loss-maintenance relationships are similar for the two groups.

13.3
Plotting Multiple Variables

Weight-loss maintenance may be associated with many variables, including age. Figure 13.3a is a plot of age with weight loss during treatment while Figure 13.3b is a plot of weight loss at twelve months with age. There appears to be a somewhat negative relationship between age and weight loss. Older people appear to have lost a greater percentage of weight than younger ones.

Figure 13.3a   Scatterplot of age with weight loss during treatment

PLOT PLOT=TREATRED WITH AGE.

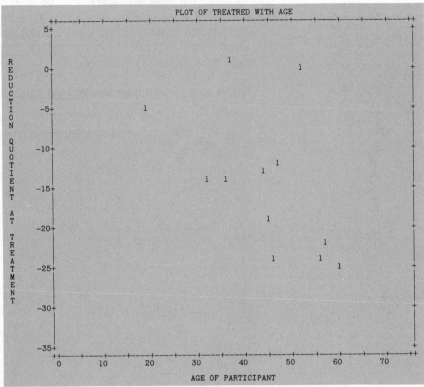

Figure 13.3b   Scatterplot of age with weight loss at twelve months

PLOT PLOT=TWELVRED WITH AGE.

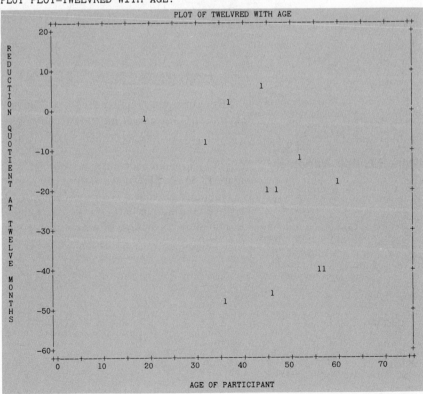

Figures 13.3a and 13.3b can be combined into a single plot, as shown in Figure 13.3c. Each case appears twice on Figure 13.3c, once with treatment weight loss (denoted as **1**) and once with twelve-month loss (denoted as **2**).

Figure 13.3c   Overlay plot of weight loss during treatment and at twelve months

PLOT **FORMAT=OVERLAY**
 /PLOT=TREATRED TWELVRED WITH AGE.

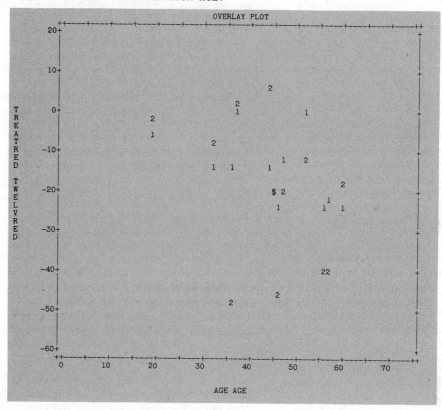

13.4
RUNNING
PROCEDURE PLOT

You can use the PLOT procedure to obtain bivariate scatterplots or regression plots (with or without control variables), contour plots, overlay plots, and some regression statistics. (For complete regression analysis, use procedure REGRESSION, described in Chapter 19.) Formatting options enable you to control axis size and scale, the plotting symbols used, and the frequency they represent. You can also label the plot and axes, request reference lines, and plot standardized variables.

The only required subcommand on PLOT is the PLOT subcommand. There are two types of optional subcommands: global subcommands (HSIZE, VSIZE, CUTPOINT, SYMBOLS, and MISSING) and local subcommands (FORMAT, TITLE, HORIZONTAL, and VERTICAL).

You can specify each of the global subcommands only once, and each must be prior to the first occurrence of the PLOT subcommand. You can use the PLOT subcommand and accompanying local subcommands more than once within a PLOT command. However, local subcommands apply only to the *immediately following* PLOT subcommand. A PLOT subcommand must be the last subcommand you specify.

13.5
PLOT Subcommand

Use the PLOT subcommand to specify the variables to be plotted. Variables to be plotted on the vertical (Y) axis are specified first, followed by the WITH keyword, followed by the variables to be plotted on the horizontal (X) axis.

By default, PLOT produces bivariate scatterplots. For example, the following command produces the output in Figure 13.1c:

```
PLOT PLOT=TREATRED WITH TWELVRED.
```

You can produce multiple plots with one PLOT subcommand. For example, the command

```
PLOT PLOT=IQ GRE WITH GPA SAT.
```

produces four plots: IQ with GPA, IQ with SAT, GRE with GPA, and GRE with SAT.

You can also use semicolons to separate multiple plot lists. For example,

```
PLOT PLOT=BONUS WITH TENURE SALNOW; SALNOW WITH SALBEG.
```

requests three scatterplots. The first request produces plots of BONUS with TENURE and BONUS with SALNOW. The second request produces the plot of SALNOW with SALBEG.

In the output, an information table precedes the plots you request on a PLOT subcommand. This table shows the number of cases used, the size of the plot, and a list of symbols and frequencies.

13.6
Control and Contour Variables

Use the BY keyword on the PLOT subcommand to specify a control variable or a contour variable (see Section 13.2) for a set of plots. You can specify only one such variable on any plot list. To produce a contour plot you must also use a FORMAT subcommand (see Section 13.9).

PLOT uses the first character of the control variable's value label as the plot symbol. If no value labels are supplied, PLOT uses the first character of the actual value. For the numeric value 28, the symbol would be 2; for the string value MALE, the symbol would be M. (PLOT does not check uniqueness of symbols, but you can use the VALUE LABELS command to create appropriate value labels that prevent ambiguity.) When cases with different values for the control value fall in the same position on the plot, they are represented by a single $.

The following command produced Figure 13.2:

```
PLOT PLOT=TREATRED WITH TWELVRED BY TREATMNT.
```

13.7
TITLE Subcommand

You can provide a title for a plot by enclosing the title in apostrophes on the TITLE subcommand. The default plot title uses either the names of the variables for a bivariate plot or the type of plot requested on the FORMAT subcommand (see Section 13.9). The command

```
PLOT TITLE='Plot of Beginning Salary on Current Salary'
 /PLOT=SALNOW WITH SALBEG.
```

requests a title that overrides the default.

A title can contain up to 60 characters. A title longer than the horizontal width specified on the HSIZE subcommand (see Section 13.10) will be truncated.

Procedure PLOT   173

13.8
VERTICAL and HORIZONTAL Subcommands

Use the HORIZONTAL and VERTICAL subcommands to control axis labels, minimum and maximum values plotted, standardization of axes, reference lines, and uniform scales across plots.

Adjusting minimum and maximum values is especially useful when you want to focus on a subset of a larger plot. The minimum and maximum value specifications function like a TEMPORARY SELECT IF transformation (see Chapter 4). PLOT excludes values outside the specified range from the immediately following PLOT subcommand. The axes are scaled to include the specified values, but PLOT may extend the scales slightly beyond the specified minimum and maximum to ensure that integers or simple decimals are on the axes.

The VERTICAL and HORIZONTAL subcommands have the same keyword specifications:

'label'
: *Axis label.* You can specify a label of up to 40 characters. The default is the variable label for the variable on the axis. If there is no variable label, PLOT uses the variable name. If you specify a label longer or wider than the plot frame size (see Section 13.10), the label will be truncated.

MIN(min)
: *Minimum value plotted for that axis.* The default is the minimum observed value. With the MIN option, only data values greater than or equal to *min* are plotted. The axis scale includes this value.

MAX(max)
: *Maximum value plotted for that axis.* The default is the maximum observed value. With the MAX option, only data values less than or equal to *max* are plotted. The axis scale includes this value.

UNIFORM
: *Uniform values on axis.* This option specifies that all plots will have scales with the same values on the vertical or horizontal axis. Uniform scales also result if you specify both MIN and MAX. If you specify UNIFORM but not MIN and MAX, PLOT determines the minimum and maximum across all variables for the axis.

REFERENCE(value list)
: *Reference lines for axis.* The value list specifies values at which to draw reference lines perpendicular to the axis.

STANDARDIZE
: *Standardize variables on axis.* With this option, PLOT standardizes variables to have a mean of 0 and a standard deviation of 1. This option is useful if you want to overlay plots of variables that otherwise would have different scales.

The command

```
PLOT TITLE='Annual Salary by Age, XYZ Corporation  1983'
 /VERTICAL='Annual salary before taxes' MIN (500) MAX (75000)
 REFERENCE (25000,50000)
 /HORIZONTAL='Age of employee' MIN (18) MAX (65)
 REFERENCE (33,48)
 /PLOT=INCOME WITH AGE.
```

produces a bivariate scatterplot with labeled axes that include values of INCOME between 500 and 75,000 and values of AGE between 18 and 65. The keyword REFERENCE requests reference lines at 25,000 and 50,000 on the vertical axis and at 33 and 48 on the horizontal axis.

13.9
FORMAT Subcommand

Use the FORMAT subcommand to specify the type of plot you want to produce. Four types of plots are available: scatterplots, regression plots, contour plots, and overlay plots. If FORMAT is not used, or is specified without keywords, scatterplots are displayed. To specify plot type, use the following keywords:

DEFAULT   *Bivariate scatterplot.* When there are no control variables each symbol represents the case count at that plot position. When a control variable is specified, each symbol represents the first character of the value label of the control variable.

REGRESSION   *Scatterplot plus regression statistics.* The vertical-axis variable is regressed on the horizontal-axis variable, and the regression line intercepts on each axis are indicated with the letter R. In a control plot, regression statistics are pooled over all categories.

CONTOUR(n)   *Contour plot with* n *levels.* Contour plots use a continuous variable as the control variable. The control variable is specified after BY on the PLOT subcommand. The contour variable is recoded into *n* intervals of equal width. Up to 35 contour levels can be specified. If *n* is omitted, the default is 10 levels.

OVERLAY   *Overlay plots.* All plots specified on the next PLOT subcommand are displayed in one plot frame. A unique plotting symbol is used for each overlaid plot. An additional symbol indicates multiple plot points at the same position. Control plots cannot be overlaid.

Specify the FORMAT subcommand before the PLOT subcommand to which it refers. One FORMAT subcommand can be specified before each PLOT subcommand.

For example, the command

```
PLOT FORMAT=OVERLAY
 /PLOT=TREATRED TWELVRED WITH AGE.
```

produces the overlay plot in Figure 13.3c.

Overlay plots are useful when several variables represent the same type of measurement or when the same variable is measured at different times (see Figure 13.11). Contour plots evaluate the effects of a continuous variable as a control variable. If you use symbols (see Section 13.12) with degrees of density, you can produce visual representation of the density of the control variable (see Figure 13.16).

13.10
HSIZE and VSIZE Subcommands

Use the HSIZE and VSIZE subcommands to specify dimensions for your plots. The HSIZE and VSIZE subcommands must precede all PLOT subcommands and can be specified only once. All plots requested on one PLOT command are drawn to the same specified size.

The default size of your plot depends on current page size. With a typical computer page, the default width is 80 positions and the default length is 40 lines. You can override the defaults by using the VSIZE and HSIZE subcommands. The VSIZE subcommand specifies the vertical frame size (length) of the plot, and the HSIZE subcommand specifies the horizontal frame size (width). For example,

```
PLOT VSIZE=30/HSIZE=70
 /PLOT=Y WITH X.
```

requests a length of 30 print lines and a width of 70 print positions. The specified size does *not* include print lines for the plot frames or for auxiliary information such as titles, axis scale numbers, regression statistics, or the symbol table.

**13.11
HSIZE and VSIZE with
HORIZONTAL and VERTICAL**

If you specify both MIN and MAX values on the HORIZONTAL or VERTICAL subcommands, your axes may contain some fractional values, even if your data contain only integer values. You can control the axis values displayed and the interval between values by specifying HSIZE and VSIZE in conjunction with MIN and MAX values on the HORIZONTAL and VERTICAL subcommands.

For the horizontal axis, use the formula

$$\frac{\text{MAX} - \text{MIN}}{\text{interval}} \times 10 = \text{HSIZE}$$

For the vertical axis, use the formula

$$\frac{\text{MAX} - \text{MIN}}{\text{interval}} \times 5 = \text{VSIZE}$$

For example, to display the years from 1880 to 2000 in 20 year increments on the horizontal axis, you would calculate the HSIZE as

$$\frac{2000 - 1880}{20} \times 10 = 60$$

and you would specify

```
/HSIZE=60
/HORIZONTAL MIN(1880) MAX(2000)
```

The results are shown in Figure 13.11.

If the result of (MAX − MIN)/interval is not an integer, some of your axis values will be fractional. You can compensate by adjusting either your MIN, MAX, or interval values.

Figure 13.11 Overlay plot of marriage and divorce rates

```
PLOT SYMBOLS='MD'
 /FORMAT=OVERLAY
 /TITLE='MARRIAGE AND DIVORCE RATES  1900-1981'
 /VSIZE=20 /HSIZE=60
 /VERTICAL='RATES PER 1000 POPULATION' MIN(0) MAX(20)
 /HORIZONTAL='YEAR' REFERENCE (1918,1945) MIN(1880) MAX(2000)
 /PLOT=MARRATE DIVRATE WITH YEAR.
```

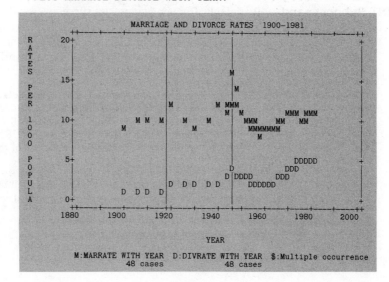

13.12
Controlling Plot Symbols

Two subcommands, CUTPOINT and SYMBOLS, control the frequencies that plotted symbols represent and the characters for the symbols in plots.

Use the CUTPOINT subcommand to adjust the frequencies represented by each plot symbol in bivariate plots (simple scatterplots and regression plots). Use the SYMBOLS subcommand to specify which characters represent a given frequency value in bivariate scatter and regression plots, overlay, and contour plots. Both CUTPOINT and SYMBOLS must precede the first PLOT subcommand and can be specified only once on a PLOT command. All requested plots use the same cutpoint values and symbols.

13.13
SYMBOLS Subcommand

Use the SYMBOLS subcommand to specify the plotting symbols. The SYMBOLS subcommand applies to bivariate, overlay, and contour plots. It does not apply to control plots. You can use only one SYMBOLS subcommand on a PLOT command. The available keywords are:

ALPHANUMERIC *Alphanumeric plotting symbols.* PLOT uses the characters 1–9, A–Z, and * as plot symbols. Thus, * represents 36 or more cases at a print position. This is the default symbol set.

NUMERIC *Numeric plotting symbols.* PLOT uses the characters 1–9 and * as plot symbols. Thus, * represents 10 or more cases at a print position.

'symbols'[,'ovprnt'] *List of plot symbols.* You can provide your own list of symbols enclosed in apostrophes. You can also specify a second list of overprinting symbols, separated from the first list by a comma or space and enclosed in apostrophes or quotation marks. A blank space can be used as an overprint "symbol" if you only want to overprint some symbols (see Figure 13.16). The overprinting symbols can be either hexadecimal representations (preceded by an X) or keyboard characters.

X'hexsym'[,'ovprnt'] *List of hexadecimal plot symbols.* Indicate hexadecimal symbols by specifying X before the hexadecimal representation list enclosed in apostrophes. Optionally, you can specify a second list of overprinting symbols separated from the first list by a comma or space. The overprinting symbols can be either hexadecimal representations or keyboard characters.

13.14
CUTPOINT Subcommand

By default, frequency plots use successive symbols in print positions corresponding to 1, 2, 3... cases, respectively. To define your own set of frequency values for the successive symbols, use the CUTPOINT subcommand. You can specify the desired interval width on the EVERY keyword, or you can use a value list in parentheses to specify cutpoints:

EVERY(n) *Frequency intervals of width* n. The default is an interval size of 1, meaning that each individual frequency up to 35 has a different symbol. The last default frequency interval includes all frequencies greater than 35. If you specify SYMBOLS as well as EVERY, the last symbol specified will represent all frequencies greater than those for the next-to-last symbol.

(value list) *Cutpoints at the values specified.*

You can specify only one CUTPOINT subcommand on a PLOT command, and it applies only to bivariate plots, not to control, overlay, or contour plots. If you specify

```
PLOT   CUTPOINT=EVERY(4)
 /PLOT = Y WITH X.
```

1 will represent 1 to 4 cases at a print position, 2 will represent 5 to 8 cases, and so forth. If you specify

```
PLOT  CUTPOINT=(4, 10, 25)
 /PLOT = Y WITH X.
```

1 will represent 1 to 4 cases at a print position, 2 will represent 5 to 10 cases, 3 will represent 11 to 25 cases, and 4 will represent 26 or more cases.

13.15
MISSING Subcommand

Use the MISSING subcommand to change or make explicit the treatment of cases with missing values. You can use only one MISSING subcommand on a PLOT command. Three specifications are available:

PLOTWISE *Exclude cases with missing values plotwise.* For each plot within a single frame, cases that have missing values on any variable for that plot are excluded. This is the default.

LISTWISE *Exclude cases with missing values listwise.* Cases with missing values on any variable named on any PLOT subcommand are excluded from all plots specified on the PLOT command.

INCLUDE *Include user-defined missing values as valid.*

If you specify

```
PLOT MISSING = LISTWISE
 /FORMAT=REGRESSION
 /PLOT = Y WITH A; Z WITH B.
```

PLOT excludes cases with missing values on any of the variables Y, A, Z, and B.

For overlay plots, plotwise deletion applies to each subplot requested. With the command

```
PLOT FORMAT=OVERLAY
 /PLOT = INCOME82 TAXES82 WITH YEAR82.
```

cases with missing values on INCOME82 or YEAR82 will be deleted from that subplot only, and cases with missing values on TAXES82 or YEAR82 will be deleted from the other subplot. The complete overlay plot may have a different number of cases for each subplot that is overlaid. The number of cases plotted in each subplot is stated below the plot frame.

13.16
Annotated Example

The following commands produce the output in Figure 13.16:

```
PLOT FORMAT=CONTOUR (10)
 /HSIZE=100 /VSIZE=60
 /SYMBOLS='.-=*+OXOXM','        -OW'
 /TITLE='SOLUBILITY OF AMMONIA IN WATER'
 /HORIZONTAL='ATMOSPHERIC PRESSURE'
 /VERTICAL='TEMPERATURE'
 /PLOT=TEMP WITH PRESSURE BY CONCENT.
```

- The FORMAT subcommand requests a contour plot with the control variable divided into 10 equal width intervals, corresponding to 10 plotting symbols.
- The HSIZE and VSIZE subcommands specify a plot width of 100 characters and a length of 60 lines.
- The SYMBOLS subcommand specifies the plotting symbols and overprint symbols to be used.
- The TITLE subcommand names a title to override the default title.

- The HORIZONTAL and VERTICAL subcommands indicate labels for the X and Y axes.
- The PLOT subcommand requests a plot of TEMP on the vertical (Y) axis with PRESSURE on the horizontal (X) axis. The keyword BY specifies CONCENT as the control, or contour, variable.

Figure 13.16   A contour plot

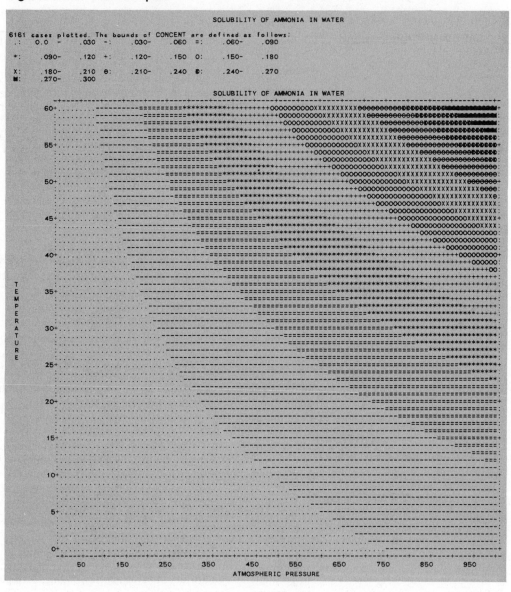

13.17
EXERCISES

Syntax

1. Write the appropriate command to obtain a plot of INCOME and AGE. Put values of INCOME on the vertical axis.

2. How would you change the command in Question 1 so that INCOME is on the horizontal axis?

3. Write the command to identify each of the points on the INCOME and AGE plot as males or females (variable SEX).

4. Correct the errors in the following PLOT commands:

   a. PLOT SBP BY AGE.

   b. PLOT SPB WITH AGE.

   c. PLOT PLOT SBP WITH AGE BY SEX(1,2).

   d. PLOT PLOT AGE BY SEX WITH SBP.

5. You run the PLOT procedure and obtain the following error messages. Explain the error messages and indicate how you would correct the mistake.

```
>ERROR   14104 LINE   4, COLUMN  6, TEXT: EDUC
>An illegal subcommand has been specified.  The valid subcommands are: MISSING,
>HSIZE, VSIZE, CUTPOINT, SYMBOL, TITLE, HORIZONTAL, VERTICAL, FORMAT and PLOT.
>THIS COMMAND NOT EXECUTED.


>ERROR   14102
>'PLOT' must be the last subcommand.
```

Statistical Concepts

1. Indicate whether you would use the CROSSTABS procedure, the MEANS procedure, or the PLOT procedure to display the relationship between the following pairs of variables:

   a. Job satisfaction and income measured in dollars.

   b. Race and marital status.

   c. Systolic blood pressure and age.

   d. Husband's highest degree and wife's highest degree.

   e. Hours studied for an examination and letter grade on the exam.

   f. Miles per gallon that a car gets and its weight in pounds.

2. Describe the relationships between the variables in the following plots:

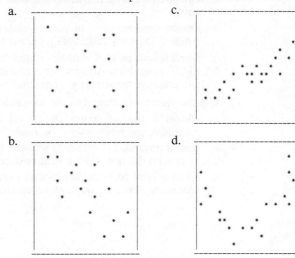

3. The following table contains age at first marriage, years of education, and sex for five people. Plot these values, identifying whether each is for a male or female.

AGEWED	EDUC	SEX
18	12	Male
22	13	Female
30	16	Male
16	10	Male
25	18	Female

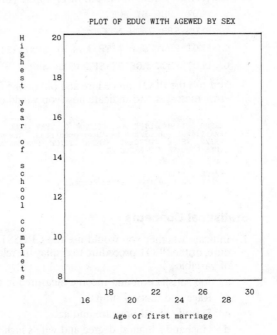

PLOT OF EDUC WITH AGEWED BY SEX

Age of first marriage

Data Analysis

1. Use the BANK data file for the following questions:
   a. Obtain a plot of current salary and educational level. Describe the relationship if any.
   b. Obtain separate plots of current salary and educational level for males and females. Does the relationship appear to be similar?
   c. Select several pairs of variables whose relationship you might examine using the PLOT procedure. Analyze the variables you have selected and write a brief paragraph summarizing your results.

2. Use the Western Electric data file for the following questions:
   a. Obtain a plot of serum cholesterol and weight. Write a brief paragraph describing any relationship you might see.
   b. Repeat question (a) obtaining separate plots for men who developed CHD and those who did not. Do the relationships, if any, appear similar?
   c. Select several pairs of variables and examine their relationship using the plot procedure. Write a paragraph summarizing your results.

Correlation and
Bivariate Regression _____

In this chapter:

Goals:

- To assess the strength of the linear relationship between two variables.
- To test the null hypothesis that, in the population from which the sample was selected, there is no linear relationship between the two variables.
- To estimate the equation for predicting the values of the dependent variable from the values of the independent variable.

Examples:

- To see if there is a linear association between family income and percent of total income saved.
- To see if an infant's birthweight can be predicted based on maternal weight gain.
- To estimate the equation that can be used to predict the actual selling price from the asking price of a home.

How it's done:

A Pearson correlation coefficient can be calculated to quantify the strength of the linear relationship between two variables. The coefficient ranges from -1 to +1. The absolute value of the coefficient indicates the strength of the linear relationship. To test the hypothesis that the population correlation coefficient is zero, the probability of obtaining a sample coefficient at least as large as the one observed, when there is no linear relationship in the population, is calculated.

The coefficients for the straight line which can be used to predict the values of the dependent variable from the values of the independent variable are estimated using the method of least squares. This results in the line that has the smallest possible sum of squared distances from the points to the line.

Data considerations:

Nominal variables cannot be used for correlation or regression analysis. For testing the hypothesis that the population correlation coefficient is zero, the two variables together should have a normal distribution, or for each value of the independent variable there should be a normal distribution of values of the dependent variable.

14 Measuring Linear Association: Procedure CORRELATIONS

Youthful lemonade-stand entrepreneurs as well as balding executives of billion-dollar corporations share a common concern—increasing sales. Hand-lettered signs affixed to neighborhood trees, television campaigns, siblings and friends canvassing local playgrounds, and international sales forces are known to be effective tactics. However, the impact of various intertwined factors on sales can be difficult to isolate, and much effort in the business world is expended on determining exactly what makes a product sell.

Churchill (1979) describes a study undertaken by the manufacturer of Click ball-point pens on the effectiveness of the firm's marketing efforts. A random sample of forty sales territories is selected, and sales, amount of advertising, and number of sales representatives are recorded. This chapter looks at the relationship between sales and these variables.

14.1 EXAMINING RELATIONSHIPS

Figure 14.1a is a scatterplot of the amount of sales and the number of television spots in each of forty territories. A scatterplot can reveal various types of associations between two variables. Figure 14.1b contains some commonly encountered patterns. In the first panel there appears to be no discernible relationship between the two variables. The variables are related exponentially in the second panel. That is, Y increases very rapidly for increasing values of X. In the third panel, the relationship between the two variables is U-shaped. Small and large values of the X variable are associated with large values of the Y variable.

From Figure 14.1a there appears to be a positive association between sales and advertising. That is, as the amount of advertising increases, so does the number of sales. The relationship between sales and advertising may also be termed *linear*, since the observed points cluster more or less around a straight line.

Figure 14.1a   Scatterplot showing a linear relationship

`PLOT PLOT=SALES WITH ADVERTIS.`

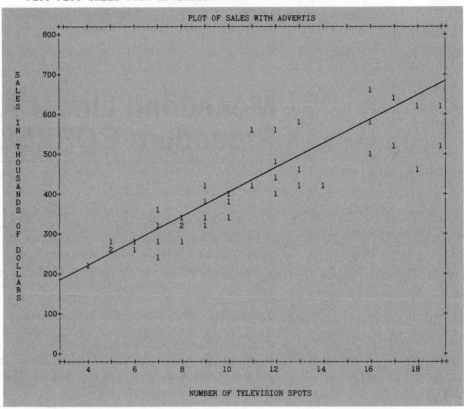

Figure 14.1b   Some common relationships

14.2
THE CORRELATION
COEFFICIENT

Although a scatterplot is an essential first step in studying the association between two variables, it is often useful to quantify the strength of the association by calculating a summary index. One commonly used measure is the Pearson correlation coefficient, denoted by r. It is defined as

$$r = \frac{\sum_{i=1}^{N}(X_i - \bar{X})(Y_i - \bar{Y})}{(N - 1)S_X S_Y}$$

Equation 14.2

where N is the number of cases and S_x and S_y are the standard deviations of the two variables. The absolute value of r indicates the strength of the linear relationship. The largest possible absolute value is 1, which occurs when all points fall exactly on the line. When the line has a positive slope, the value of r is positive, and when the slope of the line is negative, the value of r is negative (see Figure 14.2a).

Figure 14.2a   Scatterplots with correlation coefficients of +1 and −1

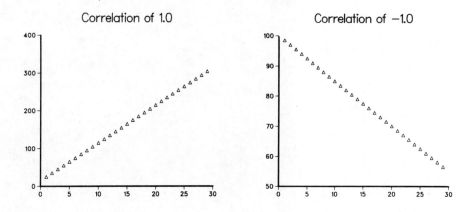

A value of 0 indicates no *linear* relationship. Two variables can have a strong association but a small correlation coefficient if the relationship is not linear. Figure 14.2b shows two plots with correlation coefficients of 0.

Figure 14.2b   Scatterplots with correlation coefficients of 0

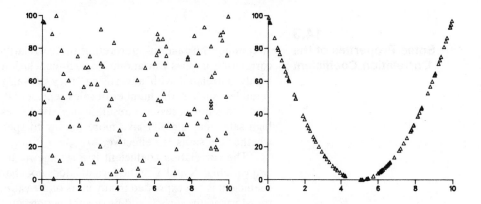

It is important to examine correlation coefficients together with scatterplots since the same coefficient can result from very different underlying relationships. The variables plotted in Figure 14.2c have a correlation coefficient greater than 0.8, as do the variables plotted in Figure 14.1a. But note how different the relationships are between the two sets of variables. In Figure 14.2c there is a strong positive linear association only for part of the graph. The relationship between the two variables is basically nonlinear. The scatterplot in Figure 14.1a is very different. The points cluster more or less around a line. Thus, the correlation coefficient should be used only to summarize the strength of linear association.

Figure 14.2c Scatterplot of percentage no facial hair with year

PLOT PLOT=CLEAN WITH YEAR.

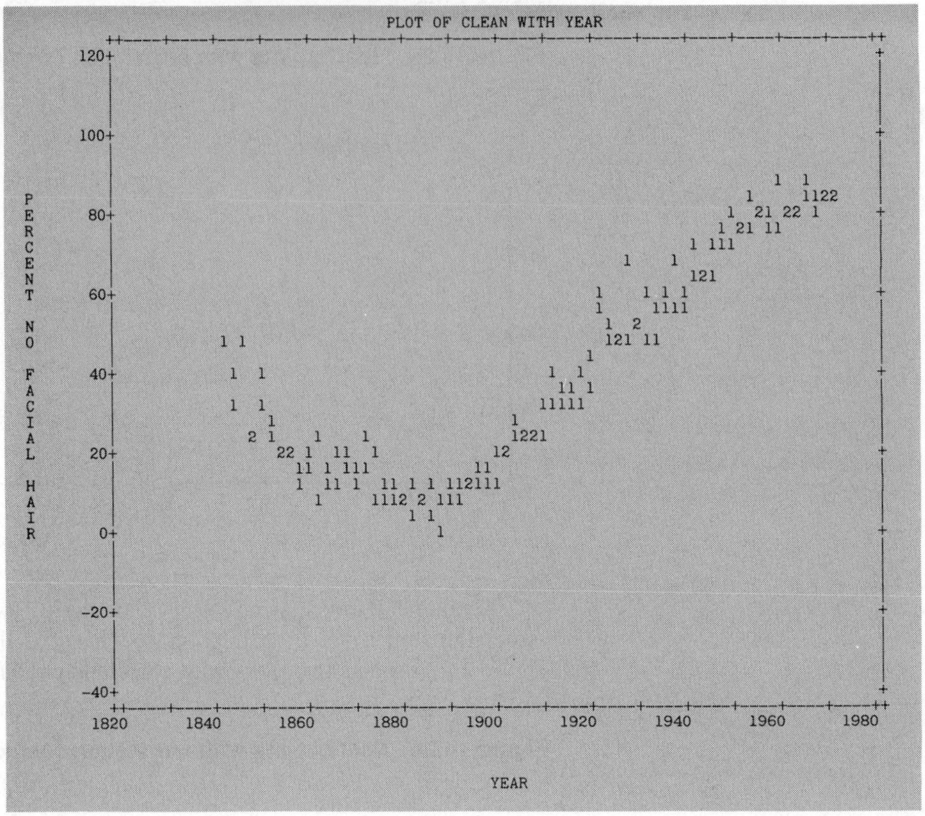

14.3
Some Properties of the
Correlation Coefficient

A common mistake in interpreting the correlation coefficient is to assume that correlation implies causation. No such conclusion is automatic. While sales are highly correlated with advertising, they are also highly correlated with other variables, such as the number of sales representatives in a territory. Advertising alone does not necessarily result in increased sales. For example, territories with high sales may simply have more money to spend on TV spots, regardless of whether the spots are effective.

The correlation coefficient is a symmetric measure since interchanging the two variables X and Y in the formula does not change the results. The correlation coefficient is not expressed in any units of measure, and it is not affected by linear transformations such as adding or subtracting constants or multiplying or dividing all values of a variable by a constant.

14.4
Calculating Correlation
Coefficients

Figure 14.4 is a table of correlation coefficients for the number of television spots, number of sales representatives, and amount of sales. The entry in each cell is the correlation coefficient. For example, the correlation coefficient between advertising and sales is 0.8802. This value indicates that there is a fairly strong linear association between the two variables, as shown in Figure 14.1a. The table is symmetric since the correlation between X and Y is the same as the correlation between Y and X. The values on the diagonal are all 1 since a variable is perfectly related to itself.

Figure 14.4 Correlation coefficients

CORRELATIONS VARIABLES=ADVERTIS REPS SALES.

```
                    - - Correlation Coefficients - -

             ADVERTIS   REPS      SALES

   ADVERTIS  1.0000     .7763**   .8802**
   REPS       .7763**  1.0000     .8818**
   SALES      .8802**   .8818**  1.0000

 * - Signif. LE .05    ** - Signif. LE .01   (2-tailed)      " . " printed if a coefficient cannot be computed
```

14.5
Hypothesis Tests about the Correlation Coefficient

Although the correlation coefficient is sometimes used only as a summary index to describe the observed strength of the association, in some situations description and summary are but a first step. The primary goal may be to test hypotheses about the unknown population correlation coefficient—denoted as ρ—based on its estimate, the sample correlation coefficient r. In order to test such hypotheses, certain assumptions must be made about the underlying joint distribution of the two variables. A common assumption is that independent random samples are taken from a distribution in which the two variables together are distributed normally. If this condition is satisfied, the test that the population coefficient is 0 can be based on the statistic

$$t = r\sqrt{\frac{N - 2}{1 - r^2}}$$

Equation 14.5

which, if $\rho=0$, has a Student's t distribution with $N-2$ degrees of freedom. Either one- or two-tailed tests can be calculated. If nothing is known in advance, a two-tailed test is appropriate. That is, the hypothesis that the coefficient is zero is rejected for both extreme positive and extreme negative values of t. If the direction of the association can be specified in advance, the hypothesis is rejected only for t values that are of sufficient magnitude and in the direction specified.

In SPSS, coefficients with two-tailed observed significance levels less than 0.05 are designated with a single asterisk. Those with two-tailed significance levels less than 0.01 are designated with two asterisks. From Figure 14.4, the probability that a correlation coefficient of at least 0.88 is obtained when there is no linear association in the population between sales and advertising is less than 0.01. Care should be exercised when examining the significance levels for large tables. Even if there is no association between the variables, if many coefficients are computed some would be expected to be statistically significant by chance alone.

Special procedures must be employed to test more general hypotheses of the form $\rho=\rho_0$, where ρ_0 is a constant. If the assumptions of bivariate normality appear unreasonable, a variety of *nonparametric* measures, which make limited assumptions about the underlying distributions of the variables, can be calculated. See Chapter 17 for further discussion.

14.6
Correlation Matrices and Missing Data

For a variety of reasons, data files frequently contain incomplete observations. Respondents in surveys scrawl illegible responses or refuse to answer certain questions. Laboratory animals die before experiments are completed. Patients fail to keep scheduled clinic appointments.

Analysis of data with missing values is troublesome. Before even considering possible strategies, you should determine whether there is evidence that the missing-value pattern is not random. That is, are there reasons to believe that missing values for a variable are related to the values of that variable or other variables? For example, people with low incomes may be less willing to report their financial status than more affluent people. This may be even more pronounced for people who are poor but highly educated.

One simple method of exploring such possibilities is to subdivide the data into two groups—those observations with missing data for a variable and those with complete data—and examine the distributions of the other variables in the file across these two groups. The SPSS procedures CROSSTABS and T-TEST are particularly useful for this. For a discussion of more sophisticated methods for detecting nonrandomness, see Frane (1976).

If it appears that the data are not missing randomly, use great caution in attempting to analyze the data. It may be that no satisfactory analysis is possible, especially if there are only a few cases.

If you are satisfied that the missing data are random, several strategies are available. First, if the same few variables are missing for most cases, exclude those variables from the analysis. Since this luxury is not usually available, you can alternatively keep all variables but eliminate the cases with missing values on any of them. This is termed *listwise* missing-value treatment since a case is eliminated if it has a missing value on any variable in the list.

If many cases have missing data for some variables, listwise missing-value treatment could eliminate too many cases and leave you with a very small sample. One common technique is to calculate the correlation coefficient between a pair of variables based on all cases with complete information for the two variables regardless of whether the cases have missing data on any other variable. For example, if a case has values only for variables 1, 3, and 5, it is used only in computations involving variable pairs 1 and 3, 1 and 5, and 3 and 5. This is *pairwise* missing-value treatment.

14.7
Choosing Pairwise Missing-Value Treatment

Several problems can arise with pairwise matrices, one of which is inconsistency. There are some relationships between coefficients that are clearly impossible but may seem to occur when different cases are used to estimate different coefficients. For example, if age and weight and age and height have a high positive correlation, it is impossible in the same sample for height and weight to have a high negative correlation. However, if the same cases are not used to estimate all three coefficients, such an anomaly can occur.

There is no single sample size that can be associated with a pairwise matrix since each coefficient can be based on a different number of cases. Significance levels obtained from analyses based on pairwise matrices must be viewed with caution since little is known about hypothesis testing in such situations.

It should be emphasized that missing-value problems should not be treated lightly. You should base your decision on careful examination of the data and not leave the choices up to system defaults.

14.8
THE REGRESSION LINE

If there is a linear relationship between two variables, a straight line can be used to summarize the data. When the correlation coefficient is $+1$ or -1, little thought is needed to determine the line that best describes the data: the line passes through all of the observations. When the observations are less highly correlated, many different lines can be drawn to represent the data.

One of the most commonly used procedures for fitting a line to the observations is the method of *least squares*. This method results in a line that minimizes the sum of squared vertical distances from the data points to the line.

The equation for the straight line that relates predicted sales to advertising is

PREDICTED SALES = a + b(ADVERTISING)   **Equation 14.8a**

The intercept, *a*, is the predicted sales when there is no advertising. The slope, *b*, is the change in predicted sales for a unit change in advertising. That is, it is the amount of change in sales per television spot.

The actual values of *a* and *b* calculated with the method of least squares are printed as part of the SPSS PLOT output (see Figure 14.8). The least-squares equation for the line is

PREDICTED SALES = 135.4 + 25.31(ADVERTISING) **Equation 14.8b**

Figure 14.1a shows this regression line.

Figure 14.8 Intercept and slope from PLOT

```
PLOT FORMAT=REGRESSION
 /PLOT=SALES WITH ADVERTIS.
         40 cases plotted. Regression statistics of SALES on ADVERTIS:
      Correlation  .88016 R Squared  .77467  S.E. of Est  59.56023  2-tailed Sig.  .0000
      Intercept(S.E.)  135.43360( 25.90649)  Slope(S.E.)  25.30770(  2.21415)
```

For each pair of variables, two different regression lines can be calculated, since the values of the slope and intercept depend on which variable is dependent (the one being predicted) and which is independent (the one used for prediction). In the SPSS PLOT output, the variable plotted on the vertical axis is considered the dependent variable in the calculation of statistics.

14.9
Prediction

Based on the regression equation, it is possible to predict sales from advertising. For example, a territory with 10 television spots per month is expected to have sales of about $388,400 (135.4 + 25.3(10)). Considerable caution is needed when predictions are made for values of the independent variable which are much larger or much smaller than those used to derive the equation. A relationship which is linear for the observed range of values may not be linear everywhere. For example, estimating *Y* values for the beginning of Figure 14.1b based on a regression line for the latter part of the plot would result in a very poor fit.

The difference between observed sales and sales predicted by the model is called a *residual*. The residual for a territory with 10 television spots and observed sales of 403.6 is 15.2:

RESIDUAL = OBSERVED − PREDICTED = 403.6 − 388.4 **Equation 14.9**
　　　　　= 15.2

Residuals can be calculated for each of the sales territories. Figure 14.9 contains the observed value (SALES), the predicted value (*PRED), and the residual for the first 10 territories (*RESID). The residuals provide an idea of how well the calculated regression line actually fits the data.

Figure 14.9 Residuals from the regression line

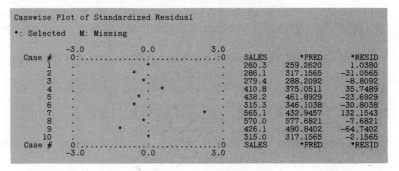

```
Casewise Plot of Standardized Residual
*: Selected   M: Missing

          -3.0          0.0          3.0
 Case #    0:...................:...................:0   SALES     *PRED      *RESID
     1     .         *         .                    .   260.3   259.2620      1.0380
     2     .              *   .                     .   286.1   317.1565    -31.0565
     3     .               *  .                     .   279.4   288.2092     -8.8092
     4     .                  . *                   .   410.8   375.0511     35.7489
     5     .             *    .                     .   438.2   461.8929    -23.6929
     6     .              *   .                     .   315.3   346.1038    -30.8038
     7     .                  .        *            .   565.1   432.9457    132.1543
     8     .                 *.                     .   570.0   577.6821     -7.6821
     9     .           *      .                     .   426.1   490.8402    -64.7402
    10     .               *  .                     .   315.0   317.1565     -2.1565
 Case #    0:...................:...................:0   SALES     *PRED      *RESID
          -3.0          0.0          3.0
```

14.10
Goodness of Fit

Although the regression line is a useful summary of the relationship between two variables, the values of the slope and intercept alone do little to indicate how well the line actually fits the data. A goodness-of-fit index is needed.

The observed variation in the dependent variable can be subdivided into two components: the variation explained by the regression and the residual from the regression, or

TOTAL SS = REGRESSION SS + RESIDUAL SS   **Equation 14.10a**

The *total sum of squares* is a measure of overall variation and is given by

$$\text{TOTAL SUM OF SQUARES} = \sum_{i=1}^{N} (Y_i - \overline{Y})^2$$ **Equation 14.10b**

The total sum of squares for sales is 598,253. (It is N-1 times the variance.)

The *regression sum of squares*, or the sum of squares due to regression, is

$$\text{REGRESSION SUM OF SQUARES} = \sum_{i=1}^{N} (\hat{Y}_i - \overline{Y})^2$$ **Equation 14.10c**

where $\hat{Y}_i$ is the predicted value for the ith case. The regression sum of squares is a measure of how much variability in the dependent variable is attributable to the linear relationship between the two variables. For this example, the regression sum of squares is 463,451.

The *residual sum of squares*, sometimes called the error sum of squares, is obtained by squaring each of the residuals and then summing them.

$$\text{RESIDUAL SUM OF SQUARES} = \sum_{i=1}^{N} (Y_i - \hat{Y}_i)^2$$ **Equation 14.10d**

The residual sum of squares for sales is 134,802. The standard deviation of the residuals, called the standard error of the estimate, is

$$\text{SEE} = \sqrt{\frac{\text{RESIDUAL SUM OF SQUARES}}{N-2}} = \sqrt{\frac{134,802}{38}} = 59.56$$ **Equation 14.10e**

The standard error is displayed in Figure 14.2b.

The proportion of the variation in the dependent variable that is explained by the linear regression is computed by comparing the total sum of squares and the regression sum of squares:

$$r^2 = \frac{\text{REGRESSION SUM OF SQUARES}}{\text{TOTAL SUM OF SQUARES}} = \frac{463,451}{598,253} = 0.775$$ **Equation 14.10f**

If there is no linear association in the sample, the value of r^2 is 0 since the predicted values are just the mean of the dependent variable and the regression sum of squares is 0. If Y and X are perfectly linearly related, the residual sum of squares is 0 and r^2 is 1. The square root of r^2 is r, the Pearson correlation coefficient between the two variables.

14.11
Further Topics in Regression

In this chapter, only the most basic concepts in regression analysis are discussed. Chapter 18 contains detailed descriptions of simple two-variable regression as well as multiple regression analysis.

14.12
RUNNING PROCEDURE CORRELATIONS

Procedure CORRELATIONS produces Pearson product-moment correlations with significance levels and, optionally, univariate statistics, covariances, and cross-product deviations. The only required subcommand on CORRELATIONS is the VARIABLES subcommand, which specifies the variable list to be analyzed. Optional subcommands can be entered in any order after the variable list.

14.13
VARIABLES Subcommand

CORRELATIONS displays either a square (symmetric) or rectangular (asymmetric) matrix, depending on how you specify the variable list. Both forms of the specification allow you to use the keyword TO to refer to consecutive variables on the active system file.

If you provide a simple list of variables, CORRELATIONS displays the correlations of each variable with every other variable in the list in a symmetric, square matrix. The correlation of a variable with itself is always 1.0000 and can be found on the diagonal of the matrix. Each pair of variables appears twice in the matrix (e.g., FOOD with RENT and RENT with FOOD) with identical coefficients, and the upper and lower triangles of the matrix are mirror images.

The square correlation matrix in Figure 14.4 was produced with the following command:

```
CORRELATIONS VARIABLES=ADVERTIS REPS SALES.
```

If you specify two variable lists separated by the keyword WITH, SPSS produces an asymmetric matrix of variables in the first list correlated with variables in the second list. For example,

```
CORRELATIONS VARIABLES=MECHANIC BUS WITH PUBTRANS.
```

produces two correlations, MECHANIC with PUBTRANS and BUS with PUB-TRANS, while

```
CORRELATIONS VARIABLES=FOOD RENT WITH COOK TEACHER MANAGER.
```

produces six correlations. The variables listed before the keyword WITH define the rows of the matrix and those listed after the keyword WITH define the columns. Unless a variable is in both lists, there are no redundant coefficients in the matrix.

You can request more than one matrix on a CORRELATIONS command. Use a slash (/) to separate the specifications for each of the requested matrices. For example,

```
CORRELATIONS VARIABLES=FOOD RENT WITH COOK TEACHER MANAGER
  /FOOD TO MANAGER /PUBTRANS WITH MECHANIC.
```

produces three separate correlation matrices. The first matrix contains six nonredundant coefficients, the second matrix is a square matrix of all the variables from FOOD to MANAGER, and the third matrix consists of one coefficient for PUBTRANS and MECHANIC.

If all cases have a missing value for a given pair of variables or if they all have the same value for a variable, the coefficient cannot be computed. A period is displayed if a coefficient cannot be calculated.

14.14
PRINT Subcommand

By default, CORRELATIONS calculates two-tailed significance levels. A single asterisk appears next to the coefficient if it is significant at the 0.05 level; two asterisks indicate significance at the 0.01 level.

The PRINT subcommand allows you to switch to a one-tailed test and/or display both the number of cases and the significance level. The following keywords can be specified on the PRINT subcommand:

TWOTAIL   *Use two-tailed test of significance.* This test is appropriate when the direction of the relationship cannot be determined in advance, as is often the case in exploratory data analysis. This is the default.

ONETAIL   *Use one-tailed test of significance.* This test is appropriate when the direction of the relationship between a pair of variables can be specified in advance of the analysis.

NOSIG   *Suppress the display of the number of cases and significance level.* This is the default.

SIG   *Display the number of cases and significance level.*

14.15
STATISTICS Subcommand

The STATISTICS subcommand provides the following keywords for obtaining additional statistics:

DESCRIPTIVES   *Mean, standard deviation, and number of nonmissing cases for each variable.* Missing values are handled on a variable-by-variable basis regardless of the missing-value option in effect for the correlations.

XPROD   *Cross-product deviations and covariance for each pair of variables.*

ALL   *All additional statistics available in CORRELATIONS.* Includes the mean, standard deviation, and number of nonmissing cases for each variable. Also includes the cross-product deviations and covariance for each pair of variables.

For example, the following command produces the statistics shown in Figure 14.15:

```
CORRELATIONS VARIABLES=ADVERTIS REP SALES
 /STATISTICS=DESCRIPTIVES.
```

Figure 14.15   Univariate statistics

VARIABLE	CASES	MEAN	STD DEV
ADVERTIS	40	10.9000	4.3074
REPS	40	5.0000	1.6486
SALES	40	411.2875	123.8540

14.16
MISSING Subcommand

By default, CORRELATIONS deletes cases with missing values for one or both of the pair of variables for a correlation coefficient. Since each coefficient is based on all cases that have valid codes on that particular pair of variables, the maximum information available is used in every calculation. This can result in a set of coefficients based on a varying number of cases.

The MISSING subcommand controls missing values. The following keywords can be specified on the MISSING subcommand:

PAIRWISE   *Exclude missing values pairwise.* Cases missing for one or both of a pair of variables for a correlation coefficient are excluded from the analysis. This is the default.

LISTWISE   *Exclude missing values listwise.* Cases missing on any variable named in a list are excluded from all analyses.

INCLUDE   *Include user-missing values.* User-missing values are included in the analysis.

The PAIRWISE and LISTWISE keywords are mutually exclusive; however, each can be specified with INCLUDE.

14.17
FORMAT Subcommand

By default, CORRELATIONS includes redundant coefficients in the correlation and uses matrix format. The FORMAT subcommand has two keywords that control matrix format:

MATRIX *Use matrix format with redundant coefficients.* This is the default.
SERIAL *Use in serial string format with nonredundant coefficients.*

If you specify FORMAT=SERIAL, the number of cases and significance levels will also be displayed, overriding the PRINT=NOSIG default.

14.18
MATRIX Subcommand

Use the MATRIX subcommand to write matrix materials to an SPSS system file. The matrix materials include the mean, standard deviation, number of cases used to compute each coefficient, and Pearson correlation coefficient for each variable.

The OUT keyword on MATRIX specifies the file to which the matrix is written. Specify the matrix file in parentheses. There are two options:

(file) *Write the correlation matrix to an SPSS system file.* Specify the filename in the parentheses. CORRELATIONS creates a system file containing the matrix materials. The system file is stored on disk and can be retrieved at any time.

(*) *Replace the active system file with the correlation matrix system file.* The matrix materials replace the active system file. The correlation matrix is *not* stored on disk unless the active system file is saved.

14.19
Annotated Example

The following commands produced Figure 14.19:

```
CORRELATION VARIABLES=ADVERTIS REPS SALES
  /MISSING=LISTWISE
  /PRINT=ONETAIL SIG
  /MATRIX=OUT(CORRFILE).
```

- The VARIABLES subcommand specifies that correlation coefficients should be computed for all possible pairs of the variables ADVERTIS, REPS, and SALES.
- The MISSING subcommand indicates that if a case has a missing value for any of the three specified variables, the case should be excluded from the computation of all correlation coefficients.
- The PRINT subcommand computes significance levels based on a one-tailed test and displays the significance levels and the number of cases used in the calculation of each coefficient.
- The MATRIX subcommand creates a matrix system file called CORRFILE, which contains the matrix of correlation coefficients.

Figure 14.19 Correlation coefficients with significance levels

```
                 - -  Correlation Coefficients  - -

             ADVERTIS    REPS       SALES

ADVERTIS      1.0000      .7763      .8802
             (    40)    (    40)   (    40)
             P= .       P= .000    P= .000

REPS           .7763    1.0000       .8818
             (    40)    (    40)   (    40)
             P= .000    P= .       P= .000

SALES          .8802      .8818    1.0000
             (    40)    (    40)   (    40)
             P= .000    P= .000    P= .

(Coefficient / (Cases) / 1-tailed Sig)          " . " is printed if a coefficient cannot be computed
```

14.20
EXERCISES

Syntax

1. Write the SPSS command to obtain correlation coefficients and one-tailed significance levels for all pairs of the following variables: MONEY, INVEST, SALARY, and WEALTH.

2. Correct the errors in the following commands:
   a. `CORRELATIONS VARIABLES=A B C D /PRINT=SERIAL.`
   b. `CORRELATIONS VARIABLES=ONE TWO THREE MANY /XPROD.`
   c. `CORRELATIONS VARIABLES=AGE.`

3. Correct the errors in the following commands:
   a. `PLOT PLOT=DEP WITH INDEP /FORMAT=REGRESSION.`
   b. `PLOT FORMAT=REGRESSION /DEP WITH INDEP.`
   c. `PLOT FORMAT=REGRESSION /PLOT=FATIGUE BY HOMEWORK.`

4. Write the SPSS commands to obtain a plot of AGEDEATH and EDUCATION. Obtain the regression statistics, with age at death being the dependent variable and years of education the independent variable.

5. Repeat the previous analysis with education as the dependent variable and age at death as the independent variable.

Statistical Concepts

1. For the following pairs of variables, would you expect the correlation coefficient to be positive, negative, or zero?
   a. A person's total family income and his neighbor's total family income.
   b. Number of registered voters in a district and the number voting on election day.
   c. Number of cigarettes smoked and lung function.
   d. Calories consumed and weight.
   e. Altitude and mean temperature.
   f. Gross national product and infant mortality rate.
   g. Age at first marriage and years of education.
   h. Number of cars in a household and total family income.

2. A medical researcher studying the relationship between two variables finds a correlation coefficient of 0.02. She concludes that there is no relationship between the two variables. Do you agree or disagree with her conclusion? Why?

3. A mail-order house is interested in studying the relationship between income and type of product purchased. They take a random sample of orders, and then they call people to determine family income. They then calculate the correlation coefficient between income and product code. The value is 0.76, and the two-tailed observed significance level is 0.03. Based on this study, what can you conclude about the relationship between income and type of product purchased? Explain.

4. A dental association is studying the relationship between ounces of orange juice consumed per week and yearly family dental bill. They find a large positive coefficient, with an observed significance level of less than .01. What do you think of their conclusion that orange juice causes tooth decay? Discuss other possible explanations for their findings.

5. A friend of yours is analyzing the relationships among large numbers of variables. He's decided that the best strategy is to compute correlation coefficients among all of them and see which relationships appear to be significant. Advise him on issues he must consider when using the correlation coefficient to describe the relationships between variables.

6. The correlation coefficient between variables A and B is 0.62. For variables C and D, it is −0.62. Which of the pairs of variables is more strongly related?

7. An educator wishes to study the relationship between father's and son's educational attainment. Five hundred randomly selected fathers of sons are interviewed and the years of education are recorded for both fathers and sons. Since a fairly high proportion of "Unknown" responses was obtained, the educator divides the education variables into two groups and obtains the following table:

```
PAEDUC  Father's Education  by  EDUCSON  Son's Education

                EDUCSON                      Page 1 of 1
         Count
               |Low      High     Missing
               |                             Row
               |   1.00I    2.00I    3.00|  Total
PAEDUC   ------+--------+--------+--------+
          1.00 |  120   |   120  |   10   |   250
    Low        |        |        |        |   50.0
               +--------+--------+--------+
          2.00 |   40   |   130  |   80   |   250
    High       |        |        |        |   50.0
               +--------+--------+--------+
        Column     160      250       90      500
         Total    32.0     50.0     18.0    100.0

Number of Missing Observations:  0
```

a. Is there reason to suspect that there is a relationship between father's education and nonresponse to son's education level? What may be going on?

b. Is there a satisfactory way to deal with the missing values when estimating the correlation coefficient between father's and son's education?

8. Plot the following two points and write the equation of the straight line that passes through them:

Point 1   age = 20   income = 20,000
Point 2   age = 30   income = 25,000

9. In the previous question, what is the value for the intercept? For the slope? If the line you've calculated predicts income exactly, what would be the income for a 40-year-old?

10. Consider the following plot:

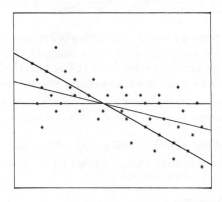

a. Of the three lines drawn on the plot, which one is most likely to be the regression line?

b. Is the correlation between the two variables positive, negative, or can you not tell from the plot? Why?

11. Consider the following plot and statistics obtained from procedure PLOT:

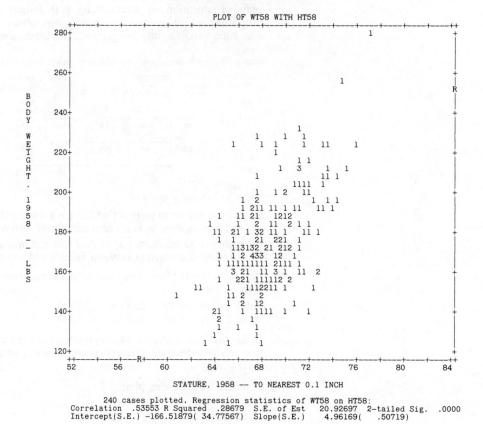

PLOT OF WT58 WITH HT58

STATURE, 1958 -- TO NEAREST 0.1 INCH

240 cases plotted. Regression statistics of WT58 on HT58:
Correlation .53553 R Squared .28679 S.E. of Est 20.92697 2-tailed Sig. .0000
Intercept(S.E.) -166.51879(34.77567) Slope(S.E.) 4.96169(.50719)

a. Write the equation predicting WT58 from HT58 and draw the line on the plot.

b. For a case with an observed value of 68 for HT58 and 200 for WT58, calculate the predicted value for WT58 and the residual.

c. Draw a line that represents the residual on the plot.

12. Here are the equations for two regression lines:

Predicted weight $= 100 + 5 \times$ Adjusted height

Predicted weight $= 105 + 50 \times$ Ring size

Is the correlation coefficient larger for weight and adjusted height, or for weight and ring size? How can you tell?

Data Analysis

1. Use the BANK data file for the following questions:

   a. Obtain correlation coefficients for the variables you analyzed in the previous chapter. Describe the strength of the observed relationships on the basis of the correlation coefficients.

   b. Calculate the regression lines for the variables you examined in (a). For each pair of variables, write the regression equation.

   c. Obtain a regression equation describing the relationship, if any, between years of work experience and current salary. If necessary, try to transform the data to obtain a linear relationship between the variables.

2. Use the Western Electric data for the following questions:
   a. Obtain a correlation matrix for serum cholesterol, weight, age, and number of cigarettes smoked. Write a brief paragraph describing the relationships you see.
   b. Repeat (a) separately for men who experienced an episode of CHD and those who did not. Do the relationships appear to be similar?
   c. Compute a regression equation to try to predict cholesterol levels from weight. Describe how successful your analysis was.

One-way Analysis of Variance

In this chapter:

Goals:

- To test the hypothesis that in the population several groups have the same mean.
- To identify groups that are significantly different from each other while maintaining control over the error rate.

Examples:

- Three weight-loss programs are equally effective.
- The amount of money spent on consumer products by regular viewers of four different channels is the same.
- There are no differences among average starting salaries for graduates of the top ten MBA programs.

How it's done:

Two estimates of variability within the population are derived. One is based on the variability of the observations within each group; the other is based on the variability of the observed sample means for the different groups. If the group means are equal in the population, these two estimates should be comparable.

To determine which groups are significantly different from each other, special multiple comparisons procedures are used. These procedures protect you from finding false "significant" differences when you make many pairwise comparisons.

Data considerations:

The variable used to form the groups can be nominal. The variable whose means are compared should be measured on an interval or ratio scale. In the population, the distribution of the variable being compared should be normal for each group and all of the variances should be the same. Each case can be a member of only one group.

15 One-Way Analysis of Variance: Procedure ONEWAY

Rotund Italians washing down carbohydrate-laden feasts with jugs of chianti, somber Jews ritualistically sipping Sabbath wine, melancholy Irish submerging grief and frustration in a bottle—all are common ethnic stereotypes. Is there any evidence to support these notions? In *Ethnic Drinking Subcultures,* Greeley et al. (1980) examine drinking habits in a sample of five ethnic populations within four major American cities.

A total of 1,107 families completed questionnaires detailing their drinking behavior and ancestral origins. Irish, Italian, Jewish, Swedish, and English families were included. Greeley investigates possible differences in drinking habits and a variety of cultural and psychological explanations for them. In this chapter, only differences in total alcohol consumption are considered.

15.1 DESCRIPTIVE STATISTICS AND CONFIDENCE INTERVALS

Figure 15.2 contains basic descriptive statistics for total yearly alcohol consumption in pints for the adult males in the study. The Italians and Irish are the biggest consumers, drinking an average of 24 pints a year. The Jewish males drink the least, an average of slightly more than 9 pints a year.

The sample mean for a group provides the single best guess for the unknown population value μ_i. It is unlikely that the value of the sample mean is exactly equal to the population parameter. Instead, it is probably not too different. Based on the sample mean, it is possible to calculate a range of values that, with a designated likelihood, include the population value. Such a range is called a *confidence interval*. For example, as shown in Figure 15.2, the 95% confidence interval for μ_{Irish} is the range 19.61 to 28.89 pints. This means that if repeated samples are selected from a population under the same conditions and 95% confidence intervals are calculated, 95% of the intervals will contain the unknown parameter μ_{Irish}. Since the parameter value is unknown, it is not possible to determine whether a particular interval contains it.

15.2 ANALYSIS OF VARIANCE

Looking at the sample means in Figure 15.2, you might wonder whether the observed differences can be reasonably attributed to chance or whether there is reason to suspect true differences between the five groups. One of the statistical procedures commonly used to test the hypothesis that several population means are equal is *analysis of variance,* or ANOVA.

Figure 15.2   Total yearly alcohol consumption for adult males (in pints)

ONEWAY AMOUNT BY ETHNIC(1,5)   /STATISTICS=DESCRIPTIVES.

GROUP	COUNT	MEAN	STANDARD DEVIATION	STANDARD ERROR	MINIMUM	MAXIMUM	95 PCT CONF INT FOR MEAN		
IRISH	119	24.2500	25.5620	2.3433	0.0	145.0	19.6097	TO	28.8903
ITALIAN	84	24.3120	24.1880	2.6391	0.0	128.0	19.0629	TO	29.5611
JEWISH	41	9.2500	21.6250	3.3773	0.0	87.0	2.4243	TO	16.0757
SWEDISH	74	16.5630	26.7500	3.1096	0.0	112.0	10.3655	TO	22.7605
ENGLISH	90	21.8750	21.5630	2.2729	0.0	117.0	17.3587	TO	26.3913
TOTAL	408	20.8373	24.6519	1.2204	0.0	145.0	18.4381	TO	23.2365

Certain assumptions are required for correct application of the ANOVA test. Independent samples from normally distributed populations with the same variance must be selected. In subsequent discussion, it is assumed that the populations sampled constitute the entire set of populations about which conclusions are desired. For example, the five ethnic groups are considered to be the only ones of interest. They are not viewed as a sample from all possible ethnic groups. This is called a *fixed-effects model*.

15.3
Partitioning Variation

In analysis of variance, the observed variability in the sample is subdivided into two components—variability of the observations within a group about the group mean and variability of the group means. If the amount of alcohol consumed doesn't vary much for individuals within the same ethnic group—for example, all the Swedes seem to drink about the same—but the group means differ substantially, there is evidence to suspect that the population means are not all equal.

The *within-groups sum of squares* is a measure of the variability within groups. It is calculated as

$$\text{SSW} = \sum_{i=1}^{k} (N_i - 1)S_i^2$$

Equation 15.3a

where S_i^2 is the variance of group i about its mean, and N_i is the number of cases in group i. For the data shown in Figure 15.2, the within-groups sum of squares is

$$\text{SSW} = 25.56^2(118) + 24.19^2(83) + 21.63^2(40) + 26.75^2(73)$$
$$+ 21.56^2(89) = 237{,}986.20$$

Equation 15.3b

Variability of the group means is measured by the *between-groups sum of squares*, which is

$$\text{SSB} = \sum_{i=1}^{k} N_i (\overline{X}_i - \overline{X})^2$$

Equation 15.3c

The mean of the ith group is denoted $\overline{X}_i$, and the mean of the entire sample is $\overline{X}$. For the drinking study, the between-groups sum of squares is

$$\text{SSB} = (24.25-20.84)^2(119) + (24.31-20.84)^2(84)$$
$$+ (9.25-20.84)^2(41) + (16.56-20.84)^2(74)$$
$$+ (21.88-20.84)^2(90) = 9{,}353.89$$

Equation 15.3d

The sums of squares, and other related statistics, are usually displayed in an analysis of variance table, as shown in Figure 15.3.

Figure 15.3   Analysis of variance table

ONEWAY AMOUNT BY ETHNIC(1,5).

```
- - - - - - - - - - - - - - - - - - - - - O N E W A Y - - - - - - - - - - - - - - - - - - - - - - - -
      VARIABLE   AMOUNT      AMOUNT OF ALCOHOL CONSUMED IN PINTS
      BY VARIABLE ETHNIC     ETHNIC BACKGROUND

                                  ANALYSIS OF VARIANCE

                  SOURCE         D.F.    SUM OF SQUARES    MEAN SQUARES    F RATIO   F PROB.

      BETWEEN GROUPS              4        9353.8877        2338.4717       3.960    0.0036

      WITHIN GROUPS             403      237986.2031         590.5364

      TOTAL                     407      247340.0625
```

The mean squares in Figure 15.3 are obtained by dividing the sums of squares by their degrees of freedom. The between-groups degrees of freedom are $k-1$, where k is the number of groups. The within-groups degrees of freedom are $N-k$, where N is the number of cases in the entire sample.

15.4
Testing the Hypothesis

To test the hypothesis that the five ethnic groups under study consume the same average amount of alcohol—that is, that

$$\mu_{\text{Irish}} = \mu_{\text{Italian}} = \mu_{\text{Jewish}} = \mu_{\text{Swedish}} = \mu_{\text{English}}$$

the following statistic is calculated (see Figure 15.3):

$$F = \frac{\text{BETWEEN GROUPS MEAN SQUARE}}{\text{WITHIN GROUPS MEAN SQUARE}} = \frac{2338.47}{590.54} = 3.96 \qquad \textbf{Equation 15.4}$$

When the assumptions described in Section 15.2 are met, the observed significance level is obtained by comparing the calculated F to values of the F distribution with $k-1$ and $N-k$ degrees of freedom. The observed significance level is the probability of obtaining an F statistic at least as large as the one calculated when all population means are equal. If this probability is small enough, the hypothesis that all population means are equal is rejected. In this example, the observed significance level is approximately 0.0036 (Figure 15.3). Thus, it appears unlikely that men in the five ethnic populations consume the same mean amount of alcohol.

15.5
MULTIPLE COMPARISON PROCEDURES

A significant F statistic indicates only that the population means are probably unequal. It does not pinpoint where the differences are. A variety of special techniques, termed *multiple comparison* procedures, are available for determining which population means are different from each other.

You may question the need for special techniques—why not just calculate the t-test described in Chapter 12 for all possible pairs of means? The problem is that when many comparisons are made, some will appear to be significant even when all population means are equal. With five groups, for example, there are ten possible comparisons between pairs of means. When all population means are equal, the probability that at least one of the ten observed significance levels will be less than 0.05 is about 0.29 (Snedecor & Cochran, 1967).

Multiple comparison procedures protect against calling too many differences significant. These procedures set up more stringent criteria for declaring differences significant than does the usual t-test. That is, the difference between two sample means must be larger to be identified as a true difference.

15.6
The Scheffé Test

Many multiple comparison procedures are available, and they all provide protection in slightly different ways (for further discussion, see Winer, 1971, or Neter & Wasserman, 1985). Figure 15.6a is output from the Scheffé multiple comparison procedure for the ethnic drinking data. The Scheffé method is conservative for pairwise comparisons of means. It requires larger differences between means for significance than most of the other methods.

Figure 15.6a   The Scheffé multiple comparison procedure

```
ONEWAY AMOUNT BY ETHNIC(1,5)
 /RANGES=SCHEFFE /FORMAT=LABELS.
```

```
        VARIABLE  AMOUNT       AMOUNT OF ALCOHOL CONSUMED IN PINTS
      BY VARIABLE  ETHNIC       ETHNIC BACKGROUND


MULTIPLE RANGE TEST


SCHEFFE PROCEDURE
RANGES FOR THE 0.050 LEVEL -

        4.38  4.38  4.38  4.38


THE RANGES ABOVE ARE TABLE RANGES.  THE VALUE ACTUALLY COMPARED WITH MEAN(J)-MEAN(I) IS..
        17.1834 * RANGE * SQRT(1/N(I) + 1/N(J))


    (*) DENOTES PAIRS OF GROUPS SIGNIFICANTLY DIFFERENT AT THE 0.050 LEVEL


                                J S E I I
                                E W N R T
                                W E G I A
                                I D L S L
                                S I I H I
                                H S H   A
                                H   H   N

    MEAN        GROUP

     9.2500     JEWISH
    16.5630     SWEDISH
    21.8750     ENGLISH
    24.2500     IRISH     *
    24.3120     ITALIAN   *
```

The means are ordered and displayed from smallest to largest, as shown in Figure 15.6a. Pairs of means that are significantly different at the 0.05 level in this case are indicated with an asterisk in the lower half of the matrix at the bottom of the output. In this example, the asterisks under the vertical column labeled **JEWISH** mean that Jews are significantly different from the Irish and the Italians. No other pair is found to be significantly different. If no pairs are significantly different, a message is displayed and the matrix is suppressed.

The formula above the matrix indicates how large an observed difference must be to attain significance using the particular multiple comparison procedure. The table ranges are the values for the range variable in the formula.

If the sample sizes in all groups are equal, or an average sample size is used in the computations, a somewhat modified table is also displayed (Figure 15.6b). Instead of indicating which groups are significantly different, means that are not different are grouped. Subset 1 shows that Jews, Swedes, and English are not different. Subset 2 groups Swedes, English, Irish, and Italians. Jews do not appear in the same subset as Irish and Italians since they are significantly different from these two.

Figure 15.6b   Homogeneous subsets

```
          VARIABLE  AMOUNT      AMOUNT OF ALCOHOL CONSUMED IN PINTS
       BY VARIABLE  ETHNIC      ETHNIC BACKGROUND


MULTIPLE RANGE TEST


SUBSET  1

GROUP        JEWISH        SWEDISH        ENGLISH
MEAN         9.2500        16.5630        21.8750
- - - - - - - - - - - - - - - - - - - - - - - - -

SUBSET  2

GROUP       SWEDISH        ENGLISH         IRISH         ITALIAN
MEAN        16.5630        21.8750        24.2500        24.3120
```

15.7 EXPLANATIONS

Both cultural and psychological explanations for differences in drinking habits among ethnic groups have been suggested (Greeley et al., 1980). In Jewish culture, the religious symbolism associated with drinking, as well as strong cultural norms against drunkenness, seem to discourage alcohol consumption. For the Irish, alcohol is a vehicle for promotion of fun and pleasure, as well as a potent tranquilizer for dissipating grief and tension. Such high expectations of alcohol make it a convenient escape and foster dependency. Italians have accepted drinking as a natural part of daily life. Alcohol is treated almost as a food and not singled out for its special pleasures.

15.8 Tests for Equality of Variance

As previously discussed, one of the assumptions needed for applying analysis of variance properly is that of equality of variances. That is, all of the populations from which random samples are taken must not only be normal but must also have the same variance σ^2. Several procedures are available for testing this assumption of *homogeneity of variance*. Unfortunately, many of them are not very useful since they are influenced by characteristics of the data other than the variance. The Levene test, available in the EXAMINE procedure (see Chapter 9) is the best test to use for testing if all variances are equal.

Figure 15.8   Tests for homogeneity of variance

```
ONEWAY AMOUNT BY ETHNIC(1,5)
  /STATISTICS=HOMOGENEITY.
```

```
TESTS FOR HOMOGENEITY OF VARIANCES

    COCHRANS C = MAX. VARIANCE/SUM(VARIANCES) = 0.2479, P = 0.248 (APPROX.)
    BARTLETT-BOX F =                            1.349, P = 0.249
    MAXIMUM VARIANCE / MINIMUM VARIANCE =       1.539
```

Figure 15.8 contains the three tests for homogeneity of variance available in the ONEWAY procedure. If the significance levels are not small, there is no reason to worry. Also, even if the variances appear different but the sample sizes in all groups are similar, there is no cause for alarm since the ANOVA test is not particularly sensitive to violations of equality of variance under such conditions. However, if the sample sizes are quite dissimilar and the variances are unequal, you should consider transforming the data or using a statistical procedure that requires less stringent assumptions (Chapter 17).

15.9
RUNNING PROCEDURE ONEWAY

Procedure ONEWAY produces a one-way analysis of variance for an interval-level variable by one independent variable. You can test for trends across categories, specify contrasts, and use a variety of range tests. Procedure ONEWAY requires a dependent variable list and the independent variable with its range of integer values. All ONEWAY subcommands are optional and may be entered in any order, provided they appear after the variable list.

15.10
Specifying the Design

A ONEWAY analysis list contains a dependent variable list and one independent (grouping) variable with its minimum and maximum values. Use only one analysis list per ONEWAY command. Dependent variables must be numeric. The independent variable follows the keyword BY and must include a value range specifying the highest and lowest values to be used in the analysis. These values are separated by a comma and are enclosed in parentheses. For example, the following command produced Figure 15.3:

```
ONEWAY AMOUNT BY ETHNIC(1,5).
```

While you can specify any number of categories for the independent variable, contrasts and multiple comparison tests are not available for more than 50 groups. ONEWAY deletes empty groups for the analysis of variance and range tests. The independent variable must have integer values. Noninteger values encountered in the independent variable are truncated.

15.11
RANGES Subcommand

The RANGES subcommand specifies any of seven different tests appropriate for multiple comparisons between means (see Section 15.5). Each RANGES subcommand specifies one test. For example,

```
ONEWAY AMOUNT BY ETHNIC(1,5)
  /RANGES=SCHEFFE
  /RANGES=SNK.
```

produces the Scheffé range test in Figure 15.6a and one additional range test. RANGES subcommands cannot be separated by CONTRAST or POLYNOMIAL subcommands. The available tests are:

LSD (alpha)   *Least-significant difference.* Any alpha between 0 and 1 can be specified. The default is 0.05. This is equivalent to doing multiple t-tests between all pairs of groups. No "multiple comparisons" protection is provided.

DUNCAN (alpha)   *Duncan's multiple range test.* Only 0.01, 0.05, and 0.10 are available as the alpha value. The default alpha is 0.05. DUNCAN uses 0.01 if the alpha specified is less than 0.05; 0.05 if the alpha specified is greater than or equal to 0.05 but less than 0.10; and 0.10 if the alpha specified is greater than or equal to 0.10.

SNK   *Student-Newman-Keuls.* Only 0.05 is available as the alpha value.

TUKEYB   *Tukey's alternate procedure.* Only 0.05 is available as the alpha value.

TUKEY   *Honestly significant difference.* Only 0.05 is available as the alpha value.

LSDMOD (alpha)   *Modified LSD.* Any alpha between 0 and 1 can be specified. The default alpha is 0.05. This is the Bonferroni test.

SCHEFFE (alpha)   *Scheffé's test.* Any alpha between 0 and 1 can be specified. The default alpha is 0.05.

Range tests always produce multiple comparisons between all groups. Nonempty group means are sorted in ascending order. Asterisks in the matrix indicate significantly different group means. In addition to this output, homogeneous subsets are calculated for balanced designs and for all designs that use either the Duncan (DUNCAN) or the Student-Newman-Keuls (SNK) procedure to calculate multiple range tests.

15.12
User-Specified Ranges

You can specify any other type of range by coding specific range values. You can specify up to $k - 1$ range values in ascending order, where k is the number of groups and where the range value times the standard error of the combined subset is the critical value. If fewer than $k - 1$ values are specified, the last value specified is used for the remaining ones. You can also specify n repetitions of the same value with the form $n * r$. To use a single critical value for all subsets, specify one range value, as in:

```
ONEWAY  WELL BY EDUC6(1,4)
  /RANGES=5.53.
```

15.13
HARMONIC Subcommand

The HARMONIC subcommand determines the sample size estimate to be used when the sample sizes are not equal in all groups. Either the sample sizes in the two groups being compared are used, or an average sample size of all groups is used.

The default keyword for HARMONIC is NONE, which uses the harmonic mean of the sizes of just the two groups being compared. To use the harmonic mean of *all* group sizes, specify keyword ALL. If ALL is used, ONEWAY calculates homogeneous subsets for SCHEFFE, TUKEY, TUKEYB, and LSDMOD tests on unbalanced designs. Specify only one keyword on the HARMONIC subcommand.

NONE *Harmonic mean of the sizes of the two groups being compared.* This is the default. You can also use keyword PAIR as an alias for NONE.

ALL *Harmonic mean of group sizes as sample sizes for range tests.* If the harmonic mean is used for unbalanced designs, ONEWAY determines homogeneous subsets for all range tests.

15.14
STATISTICS Subcommand

By default ONEWAY calculates the analysis of variance table. It also calculates any statistics specified by the CONTRAST and RANGES subcommands.

Use the STATISTICS subcommand to request additional statistics. The default keyword for STATISTICS is NONE, for no additional statistics. You can specify any one or all of the following statistics:

NONE *No optional statistics.* This is the default if you specify STATISTICS without keywords.

DESCRIPTIVES *Group descriptive statistics.* Displays the number of cases, mean, standard deviation, standard error, minimum, maximum, and 95% confidence interval for each dependent variable for each group.

EFFECTS *Fixed- and random-effects statistics.* Displays the standard deviation, standard error, and 95% confidence interval for the fixed-effects model, and the standard error, 95% confidence interval, and estimate of between-component variance for the random-effects model.

HOMOGENEITY *Homogeneity-of-variance tests.* Displays Cochran's *C*, the Bartlett-Box *F*, and Hartley's *F* max.

ALL   *All statistics available for ONEWAY.*

The following commands produce the output in Figures 15.2 and 15.8:

```
ONEWAY AMOUNT BY ETHNIC(1,5)
 /STATISTICS=DESCRIPTIVES HOMOGENEITY.
```

15.15
MISSING Subcommand

Use the MISSING subcommand to control the treatment of cases with missing values. The following keywords are available:

ANALYSIS *Exclude missing values on a pair-by-pair basis.* A case missing on either the dependent variable or grouping variable for a given analysis is not used for that analysis. Also, a case outside the range specified for the grouping variable is not used. This is the default.

LISTWISE *Exclude missing values listwise.* Cases missing on any variable named are excluded from all analyses.

EXCLUDE *Exclude cases with user-missing values.* This is the default.

INCLUDE *Include cases with user-missing values.* User-defined missing values are included in the analysis.

Keywords ANALYSIS and LISTWISE are mutually exclusive. Each can be used with either INCLUDE or EXCLUDE. The defaults are ANALYSIS and EX-CLUDE.

15.16
FORMAT Subcommand

By default, ONEWAY identifies groups as GRP1, GRP2, GRP3, etc. Use the FORMAT subcommand to identify the groups by their value labels. The FORMAT subcommand has only two keywords, NOLABELS and LABELS. NOLABELS is the default.

NOLABELS *Suppress value labels.* This is the default.

LABELS *Use the first eight characters from value labels for group labels.* The value labels are those defined for the independent variable.

The following commands produced Figure 15.6a:

```
ONEWAY AMOUNT BY ETHNIC
 /RANGES=SCHEFFE /FORMAT=LABELS.
```

15.17
MATRIX Subcommand

ONEWAY writes means, standard deviations, and frequencies to a matrix system file that can be used by subsequent ONEWAY procedures. In addition, it can read a matrix containing means, frequencies, pooled variance, and degrees of freedom for the pooled variance.

The OUT keyword on MATRIX specifies the file to which the matrix is written. The IN keyword specifies the file from which the matrix is read. In both cases, specify the matrix file in parentheses, with one of the following options:

(file) *Write the correlation matrix to, or read it from, the SPSS system file specified in the parentheses.*

(*) *Replace the active system file with the correlation matrix, or read the matrix from the system active file.*

In addition to OUT and IN, ONEWAY allows the keyword NONE to explicitly indicate that the data are not matrix materials.

15.18
POLYNOMIAL Subcommand

The POLYNOMIAL subcommand partitions the between-groups sum of squares into linear, quadratic, cubic, or higher-order trend components. The value specified in the POLYNOMIAL subcommand indicates the highest-degree polynomial to be used. This value must be a positive integer less than or equal to 5 and less than the number of groups. Use only one POLYNOMIAL subcommand per ONEWAY command.

Specify this subcommand after the analysis specification, as in:

```
ONEWAY  WELL BY EDUC6 (1,4)
  /POLYNOMIAL = 2.
```

When you use the POLYNOMIAL subcommand with balanced designs, ONE-WAY computes the sum of squares for each order polynomial from weighted polynomial contrasts, using the group code as the metric. These contrasts are orthogonal; hence the sum of squares for each order polynomial is statistically independent. If the design is unbalanced and there is equal spacing between groups, ONEWAY also computes sums of squares using the unweighted polynomial contrasts. These contrasts are not orthogonal. The deviation sums of squares are always calculated from the weighted sums of squares (Speed, 1976).

15.19
CONTRAST Subcommand

The CONTRAST subcommand specifies a priori contrasts to be tested by the t statistic. The specification for the CONTRAST subcommand is a vector of coefficients, with each coefficient corresponding to a category of the grouping variable. For example, the command

```
ONEWAY  WELL BY EDUC6(1,6)
  /CONTRAST = -1 -1 -1 -1 2 2.
```

contrasts the combination of the first four groups with the combination of the last two groups.

You can also specify fractional weights, as in:

```
/CONTRAST = -1 0 0 0 .5 .5
```

This subcommand contrasts Group 1 and the combination of Groups 5 and 6.

For most applications, the coefficients should sum to 0. Those sets that do not sum to 0 are used, but a warning message is displayed. In addition, you can use the repeat notation $n * c$ to specify the same coefficient for a consecutive set of means. For example,

```
/CONTRAST = 1 4*0 -1
```

specifies a contrast coefficient of 1 for Group 1, 0 for Groups 2 through 5, and -1 for Group 6. You must specify a contrast for every group implied by the range specification in the analysis list, even if a group is empty. However, you do not have to specify trailing zeros. For example,

```
/CONTRAST = -1 0 0 1 0 0
```

```
/CONTRAST = -1 2*0 1 2*0
```

```
/CONTRAST = -1 2*0 1
```

all specify the same set of contrast coefficients for a six-group analysis.

You can specify only one set of contrast coefficients per CONTRAST subcommand and no more than 50 coefficients per set. Output for each contrast list includes the value of the contrast, the standard error of the contrast, the t statistic, the degrees of freedom for t, and the two-tailed probability of t. Both pooled- and separate-variance estimates are displayed.

15.20
Annotated Example

The SPSS commands that produce the output in this chapter are:

```
TITLE 'DRINKING STUDY'.
DATA LIST /1 ETHNIC 1 AMOUNT 2-6 (2).
BEGIN DATA.
[data records]
END DATA.
VARIABLE LABELS
  AMOUNT 'AMOUNT OF ALCOHOL CONSUMED IN PINTS'
  /ETHNIC 'ETHNIC BACKGROUND'.
VALUE LABELS
  ETHNIC 1 'IRISH' 2 'ITALIAN' 3 'JEWISH' 4 'SWEDISH' 5 'ENGLISH'.
ONEWAY AMOUNT BY ETHNIC(1,5)
  /RANGES=SCHEFFE
  /FORMAT=LABELS
  /STATISTICS=DESCRIPTIVES HOMOGENEITY.
```

- The TITLE command puts the text, DRINKING STUDY, at the top of each page of output.
- The DATA LIST, VARIABLE LABELS, and VALUE LABELS commands define the variables used in this analysis. To define the variable AMOUNT with two decimal places, specify the number 2 enclosed in parentheses following the column specification, as shown in the DATA LIST command.
- The ONEWAY command requests a one-way analysis of variance of variable AMOUNT for five ethnic groups (variable ETHNIC). The RANGES subcommand requests Scheffé tests for comparing group means.
- The FORMAT subcommand instructs SPSS to use the first eight characters of the value labels to label output.
- The STATISTICS subcommand requests the group means, standard deviations, standard errors, minimum, maximum, 95% confidence intervals, and homogeneity-of-variance statistics.

15.21
EXERCISES   Syntax

1. The following commands contain syntax errors. Write the correct syntax.
   a. ONEWAY INCOME EDUCATION(1,6)/ RANGES=LSD SCHEFFE.
   b. ONEWAY INCOME BY EDUCATION(6).
   c. INCOME BY EDUCATION(1,6) SEX(1,2)/ RANGES SCHEFFE.

2. Write the command that produces the following table:

```
- - - - - - - - - - - - - - - - - - - - - - O N E W A Y - - - - - - - - - - - - - - - - - - - - - - - - - -
     VARIABLE  WELL      SENSE OF WELL-BEING SCALE
     BY VARIABLE EDUC6    EDUCATION IN 6 CATEGORIES

                              ANALYSIS OF VARIANCE

              SOURCE        D.F.    SUM OF SQUARES    MEAN SQUARES     F RATIO    F PROB.

     BETWEEN GROUPS          5         361.3217          72.2643       11.526     0.0000

     WITHIN GROUPS         494        3097.3463           6.2699

     TOTAL                499        3458.6680
```

3. You type the following command:

   ```
   ONEWAY  WELL BY EDUC6 (1,6) HAPPY(1,3) /MISSING=INCLUDE.
   ```

   and get the following warning:

   ```
   EWarning # 11415 on line 24.  Command name: ONEWAY
   EThe slash is missing following the parenthesized range values on the ONEWAY
   Ecommand.
   ```

   Fix the command.

4. Given data for the sex, age, weight, daily fiber consumption (variable FIBER), and blood iron levels (variable IRON) of a random selection of office workers, write the SPSS transformation commands and ONEWAY analysis for each of the following:

   a. Test the hypothesis that there is no difference in average iron levels between people in three age categories: people under 25, people from 25–45, and people over 45. Perform separate analyses for men and women.

   b. Test the hypothesis that there is no difference in average iron levels between women in four weight categories: women under 80 pounds, women 80–120 pounds, women 120–150 pounds, and women over 150 pounds. Calculate descriptive statistics for the analysis.

   c. Test the hypothesis that there is no difference in average iron levels for people whose daily fiber consumption is: under 2 grams, 2–4 grams, 4–6 grams, 6–8 grams, and over 8 grams. Perform both TUKEY's and DUNCAN's range tests. Perform separate analyses for men and women, and include only men who weigh 100–150 pounds and women who weigh 80–130 pounds.

Statistical Concepts

1. Indicate whether the following statements are true or false.

   a. If you calculate a 95% confidence interval for a population mean and obtain the range 4.89 to 13.23, there is a 95% chance that the population mean is between 4.89 and 13.23.

   b. If group sample sizes are equal, inequality of variances does not cause major problems in the analysis of variance.

2. In an experiment comparing four drugs, each drug was randomly assigned to ten subjects, yielding a total of 40 observations. An analysis of variance produces a pooled estimate of variance of 21.69 and the (incomplete) analysis of variance table below. Fill in the missing entries in this table.

```
                    ANALYSIS OF VARIANCE

SOURCE              D.F.   SUM OF SQUARES   MEAN SQUARES   F RATIO

BETWEEN GROUPS

WITHIN GROUPS

TOTAL                        964.84
```

3. Are the entries in the analysis of variance table shown below correct?

```
SOURCE              D.F.   SUM OF SQUARES   MEAN SQUARES   F-RATIO

BETWEEN GROUPS       3         258            43.00         2.6331

WITHIN GROUPS        6          49            16.33

TOTAL                9         304
```

4. Using the Scheffé output shown below, determine which means are significantly different and which are not.

```
HOMOGENEOUS SUBSETS     (SUBSETS OF GROUPS, WHOSE HIGHEST AND LOWEST MEANS DO NOT DIFFER
                         BY MORE THAN THE SHORTEST SIGNIFICANT RANGE FOR A SUBSET OF
                         THAT SIZE)

SUBSET  1

GROUP        GROUP1      GROUP2
MEAN         9.2500      16.5630
- - - - - - - - - - - - - - - -

SUBSET  2

GROUP        GROUP2      GROUP3      GROUP4      GROUP5
MEAN         16.5630     21.8750     24.2500     24.3120
- - - - - - - - - - - - - - - - - - - - - - - - - - - -
```

5. Using the Scheffé output shown below, determine which pairs of means have differences that are significantly different from zero.

```
                          1  2  3  4  5  6
      MEAN    GROUP
      102.22    1
      118.31    2
      143.62    3          *
      165.89    4          *  *
      177.64    5          *  *
      201.45    6          *  *  *
```

6. What is wrong with the following Scheffé output?

```
                  1  2  3
      MEAN  GROUP
      0.11    1    *
      0.34    2    *
      0.39    3    *
```

7. Suppose you perform an analysis of variance and then make six comparisons between means by using six t-tests. Someone else then uses multiple comparison procedures to make the same comparisons using the same significance level. Is it possible that you will find fewer significant differences than the person using multiple comparisons? Why or why not?

Data Analysis

Use the BANK system file for Exercises 1–4.

1. For job category 1, test the hypothesis that the four race-sex groups are initially equally compensated.

2. a. Although you would not expect people in different job categories to have the same beginning salaries, you might be interested in examining to what degree average salaries differ for the various job categories and how much variation there is in individuals' salaries within job categories. Perform the appropriate analysis of variance for investigating these questions using only the first four job categories.

   b. What assumptions are you making? Obtain histograms of beginning salary for each of the first four job categories. Are these histograms consistent with your assumptions?

   c. Do salaries appear to be more variable between the first four job categories than within these categories? (Hint: Look at the mean squares.)

   d. What comparisons between means might be of interest? Carry out these comparisons using one of the multiple comparison procedures.

3. Collapse education into fewer categories and examine the effect of collapsed education on beginning salary using a one-way analysis of variance. What do your results indicate? Obtain the appropriate histograms for checking your assumptions.

4. Collapse beginning salary into several categories and perform a one-way analysis of variance to investigate the effect of collapsed beginning salary on current salary. Interpret your results. Obtain the histograms appropriate for checking your assumptions.

5. a. Choose three hypotheses that can be tested using a one-way analysis of variance. If necessary, use the COMPUTE command to create new variables, such as a combined minority and sex variable, which can be used to define the groups. State and check your assumptions.

   b. Obtain a separate histogram for each of the groups. Do the observations appear to be normally distributed with constant variance?

   c. Obtain the analysis of variance table for your hypotheses. Summarize your results.

   d. If there are statistically significant differences between the groups, run one of the multiple comparison procedures and interpret the output.

6. Enter the lost-letter data from Chapter 5. Test the hypothesis that overall return rates are the same in cities and towns.

7. Use the Western Electric data for the following exercises:

   a. Test the null hypothesis that the average number of cigarettes smoked does not differ for men who did not develop CHD, those who died of sudden death, those who had nonfatal MIs and those who had other CHD. (FIRSTCHD) If necessary, perform a multiple comparison procedure to determine where the differences are. Write a paragraph describing your results.

   b. Recode the number of years of education into 3 categories: 8 years or fewer, 9–12, and more than 12. Test the null hypothesis that the average number of cigarettes smoked is the same in the three groups. Write a paragraph describing your results.

   c. Repeat (a) and (b) for average diastolic pressures, averages weights, and average cholesterols.

Analysis
of Variance

In this chapter:

Goals:

- To determine whether one or more discrete factors has an effect on the mean of a dependent variable.
- To see whether the effect of one factor depends on the value of another factor.

Examples:

- To see if the average heart rate is the same for men and women and for those who are overweight, normal in weight, and underweight.
- To see if four proposed advertising campaigns in five regions result in the same average purchase volume.
- To determine if five different coaching methods result in the same average GRE scores for students in three different majors.

How it's done:

The total variability in the dependent variable is subdivided into components attributable to each of the factors as well as their interaction. Based on these, you can test whether each factor has an effect on the dependent variable and whether the effect of one factor depends on the levels of another factor.

Data considerations:

The factor variables (the variables used to form the groups) can be nominal. In the population, the values of the dependent variable for each of the factor combinations must be normally distributed with the same variance. Each case can be observed only once. That is, the same case cannot be observed at several different combinations of factors.

16 Analysis of Variance: Procedure ANOVA

Despite constitutional guarantees, any mirror will testify that all citizens are not created equal. The consequences of this inequity are pervasive. Physically attractive persons are perceived as more desirable social partners, more persuasive communicators, and generally more likeable and competent. Even cute children and attractive burglars are disciplined more leniently than their homely counterparts (Sigall & Ostrove, 1975).

Much research on physical attractiveness focuses on its impact on heterosexual relationships and evaluations. Its effect on same-sex evaluations has received less attention. Anderson and Nida (1978) examined the influence of attractiveness on the evaluation of writings by college students. In the study, 144 male and 144 female students were asked to appraise essays purportedly written by college freshmen. A slide of the "author" was projected during the rating as part of supplemental information. Half of the slides were of authors of the same sex as the rater; the other half were of authors of the opposite sex. The slides had previously been determined to be of high, medium, and low attractiveness. Each participant evaluated one essay for creativity, ideas, and style. The three scales were combined to form a composite measure of performance.

16.1 DESCRIPTIVE STATISTICS

Figure 16.1 contains average composite scores for the essays, subdivided by the three categories of physical attractiveness and the two categories of sex similarity. The table is similar to the summary table shown for the one-way analysis of variance in Chapter 15. The difference here is that there are two independent (or grouping) variables, attractiveness and sex similarity. The first mean displayed (25.11) is for the entire sample. The number of cases (288) is shown in parentheses. Then for each of the independent variables, mean scores are displayed for each of the categories. The attractiveness categories are ordered from low (coded 1) to high (coded 3). Evaluations in which the rater and author are of the same sex are coded as 1, while opposite-sex evaluations are coded as 2. Finally, a table of means is displayed for cases classified by both grouping variables. Attractiveness is the row variable, and sex is the column variable. Each mean is based on the responses of 48 subjects.

Figure 16.1   Table of group means

```
ANOVA   VARIABLES=SCORE BY ATTRACT(1,3) SEX(1,2)
  /STATISTICS=MEAN.

                         * * *   C E L L   M E A N S   * * *

                    SCORE      COMPOSITE SCORE
                 BY ATTRACT    ATTRACTIVENESS LEVEL
                    SEX        SEX SIMILARITY


     TOTAL POPULATION

          25.11
        (   288)


     ATTRACT
             1           2           3

          22.98       25.78       26.59
        (   96)     (   96)     (   96)


     SEX
             1           2

          25.52       24.71
        (  144)     (  144)


               SEX
                   1           2
     ATTRACT
          1     22.79       23.17
              (   48)     (   48)

          2     28.63       22.92
              (   48)     (   48)

          3     25.13       28.04
              (   48)     (   48)
```

The overall average score is 25.11. Highly attractive individuals received the highest average score (26.59), while those rated low in physical appeal had the lowest score (22.98). There doesn't appear to be much difference between the average scores assigned to same (25.52) and opposite-sex (24.71) individuals. Highly attractive persons received an average rating of 25.13 when evaluated by individuals of the same sex and 28.04 when evaluated by students of the opposite sex.

16.2
ANALYSIS OF VARIANCE

Three hypotheses are of interest in the study: Does attractiveness relate to the composite scores? Does sex similarity relate to the scores? And is there an interaction between the effects of attractiveness and sex? The statistical technique used to evaluate these hypotheses is an extension of the one-way analysis of variance outlined in Chapter 15. The same assumptions as before are needed for correct application: the observations should be independently selected from normal populations with equal variances. Again, discussion here is limited to the situation in which both grouping variables are considered fixed. That is, they constitute the populations of interest.

The total observed variation in the scores is subdivided into four components: the sums of squares due to attractiveness, sex, their interaction, and the residual. This can be expressed as

TOTAL SS = ATTRACTIVENESS SS + SEX SS   **Equation 16.2**
            + INTERACTION SS + RESIDUAL SS

Figure 16.2 is the analysis of variance table for this study. The first column lists the sources of variation. The sums of squares attributable to each of the components are given in the second column. The sums of squares for each independent variable alone are sometimes termed the "main effect" sums of squares. The "explained" sum of squares is the total sum of squares for the main effect and interaction terms in the model.

The degrees of freedom for sex and attractiveness, listed in the third column, are one fewer than the number of categories. For example, since there are three levels of attractiveness, there are two degrees of freedom. Similarly, sex has one degree of freedom. Two degrees of freedom are associated with the interaction term (the product of the degrees of freedom of each of the individual variables). The degrees of freedom for the residual are $N-1-k$, where k equals the degrees of freedom for the explained sum of squares.

Figure 16.2   Analysis of variance table

```
ANOVA VARIABLES=SCORE BY ATTRACT(1,3) SEX(1,2).
```

```
         * * * A N A L Y S I S   O F   V A R I A N C E * * *

              SCORE       COMPOSITE SCORE
         by   ATTRACT     ATTRACTIVENESS LEVEL
              SEX         SEX SIMILARITY

                               Sum of                 Mean              Sig
Source of Variation            Squares     DF         Square      F     of F

Main Effects                   733.700      3         244.567    3.276  .022
    ATTRACT                    686.850      2         343.425    4.600  .011
    SEX                         46.850      1          46.850    0.628  .429

2-Way Interactions             942.350      2         471.175    6.311  .002
    ATTRACT  SEX               942.350      2         471.175    6.311  .002

Explained                     1676.050      5         335.210    4.490  .000

Residual                     21053.140    282          74.656

Total                        22729.190    287          79.196
```

The mean squares shown in Figure 16.2 are obtained by dividing each sum of squares by its degrees of freedom. Hypothesis tests are based on the ratios of the mean squares of each source of variation to the mean square for the residual. When the assumptions are met and the true means are in fact equal, the distribution of the ratio is an F with the degrees of freedom for the numerator and denominator terms.

16.3
Testing for Interaction

The F value associated with the attractiveness and sex interaction is 6.311. The observed significance level is approximately 0.002. Therefore, it appears that there is an interaction between the two variables. What does this mean?

Figure 16.3a   Cell means
(Plot from SPSS Graphics)

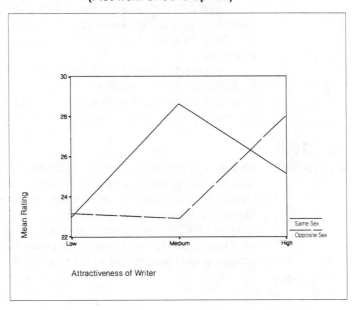

Consider Figure 16.3a, which is a plot of the cell means in Figure 16.1. Notice how the mean scores relate not only to the attractiveness of the individual and to the sex of the rater, but also to the particular combination of the values of the variables. Opposite-sex raters assign the highest scores to highly attractive individuals. Same-sex raters assign the highest scores to individuals of medium attractiveness. Thus, the ratings for each level of attractiveness depend on the sex variable. If there were no interaction between the two variables, a plot like that shown in Figure 16.3b might result, where the difference between the two types of raters is the same for the three levels of attractiveness.

Figure 16.3b   Cell means with no interaction
(Plot from SPSS Graphics)

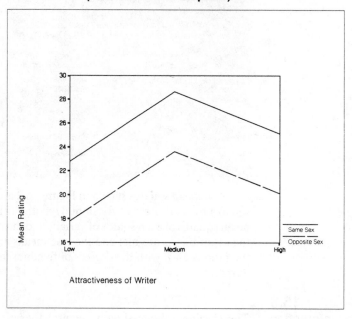

16.4
Tests for Sex and Attractiveness

Once the presence of interaction has been established, it is not particularly useful to continue hypothesis testing since the two variables *jointly* affect the dependent variable. If there is no significant interaction, the grouping variables can be tested individually. The F value associated with attractiveness would provide a test of the hypothesis that attractiveness does not affect the rating. Similarly, the F value associated with sex would test the hypothesis that sex has no main effect on evaluation.

Note that the small F value associated with sex does not indicate that response is unaffected by sex, since sex *is* included in the significant interaction term. Instead, it shows that when response is averaged over attractiveness levels, the two sex category means are not significantly different.

16.5
EXPLANATIONS

Several explanations are consistent with the results of this study. Since most people consider themselves moderately attractive, the highest degree of identification should be with same-sex individuals of moderate attractiveness. The higher empathy may result in the higher scores. An alternative theory is that moderately attractive individuals are generally perceived as more desirable same-sex friends: they have more favorable personality profiles and don't encourage unfavorable comparisons. Their writing scores may benefit from their perceived popularity.

Although we don't want friends who outshine us, handsome (and beautiful) dates provide a favorable reflection and enhance our status. Physical beauty is advantageous for heterosexual relationships, but not same-sex friendships. This prejudice may affect all evaluations of highly attractive members of the opposite sex. Regardless of the explanation, certain practical conclusions are apparent. Students, choose your instructors carefully! Authors, think twice before including your photo on the book jacket!

16.6
EXTENSIONS

Analysis of variance techniques can be used with any number of grouping variables. For example, the data in Table 16.1 originated from a more complicated experiment than described here. There were four factors—essay quality, physical attractiveness, sex of writer, and sex of subject. The original data were analyzed with a $3 \times 3 \times 2 \times 2$ ANOVA table. (The numbers indicate how many categories each grouping variable has.) The conclusions from our simplified analysis are the same as those from the more elaborate analysis.

Each of the cells in our experiment had the same number of subjects. This greatly simplifies the analysis and its interpretation. When unequal sample sizes occur in the cells, the total sum of squares cannot be partitioned into nice components that sum to the total. A variety of techniques are available for calculating sums of squares in such "nonorthogonal" designs. The methods differ in the way they adjust the sums of squares to account for other effects in the model. Each method results in different sums of squares and tests different hypotheses. However, when all cell frequencies are equal, the methods yield the same results. For discussion of various procedures for analyzing designs with unequal cell frequencies, see Kleinbaum and Kupper (1978) and Overall and Klett (1972).

16.7
RUNNING
PROCEDURE ANOVA

Analysis of variance tests the hypothesis that the group means of the dependent variable are equal. The dependent variable must be interval level, and one or more categorical variables define the groups. These categorical variables are termed *factors*. The ANOVA procedure also allows you to include continuous explanatory variables, termed *covariates*. When there are five or fewer factors, the default model is *full factorial,* meaning that all interaction terms are included. If there are more than five factors, only interaction terms up to order five are included.

The only required subcommand on ANOVA is the VARIABLES subcommand, which specifies the variable list to be analyzed.

16.8
VARIABLES Subcommand

The VARIABLES subcommand specifies the name of at least one dependent variable, the keyword **BY**, and one to five independent variables followed by their minimum and maximum values separated by a comma and enclosed in parentheses. To produce the analysis of variance table in Figure 16.2, specify:

```
ANOVA VARIABLES=SCORE BY ATTRACT(1,3) SEX (1,2).
```

By default, the model effects are the ATTRACT and SEX main effects and the ATTRACT by SEX interaction.

If several independent variables have the same value range, you can specify a list of variables followed by the value range in parentheses. Only cases with values within the specified range are included in the analysis. For example, if you specify

```
ANOVA VARIABLES=SCORE BY ATTRACT SEX (1,2).
```

cases with a value of 3 for ATTRACT will be omitted from the analysis.

16.9
Specifying Covariates

The *covariate list* follows the keyword WITH. You do not specify a value range for the covariates. For example, the command

```
ANOVA VARIABLES=PRESTIGE BY REGION(1,9) SEX(1,2) WITH EDUC.
```

names EDUC as the covariate.

16.10
COVARIATES
Subcommand

By default, ANOVA assesses the covariates before it assesses the factor main effects. Use the COVARIATES subcommand to specify a different order for assessing blocks of covariates and factor main effects. The following keywords can be specified on the COVARIATES subcommand:

FIRST   *Process covariates before main effects for factors.* This is the default if you omit the COVARIATES subcommand.

WITH   *Process covariates concurrently with main effects for factors.*

AFTER   *Process covariates after main effects for factors.*

Note that the order of entry is irrelevant when METHOD=UNIQUE (see Section 16.12).

16.11
MAXORDERS
Subcommand

By default, ANOVA examines all the interaction effects up to and including the fifth order. Use the MAXORDERS subcommand to suppress the effects of various orders of interaction. The following keywords can be specified on the MAX-ORDERS subcommand:

ALL   *Examine all the interaction effects up to and including the fifth order.* This is the default if you omit the MAXORDERS subcommand.

n   *Examine all the interaction effects up to and including the n-order effect.* For example, if you specify MAXORDERS=3, ANOVA examines all the interaction effects up to and including the third order. All higher-order interaction sums of squares are pooled into the error term.

NONE   *Delete all interaction terms from the model.* All interaction sums of squares are pooled into the error sum of squares. Only main effects and covariate effects appear in the ANOVA table.

For example, to suppress all interaction effects, specify

```
ANOVA VARIABLES=PRESTIGE BY REGION(1,9) SEX, RACE(1,2)
  /MAXORDERS=NONE.
```

16.12
METHOD Subcommand

By default, ANOVA uses what is termed the *classic experimental approach* for decomposing sums of squares. Optionally, you can request the *regression approach* or the *hierarchical approach* on the METHOD subcommand. The following keywords can be specified on METHOD:

EXPERIMENTAL   *Classic experimental approach.* This is the default if you omit the METHOD subcommand.

UNIQUE   *Regression approach.* UNIQUE overrides any specifications on the COVARIATES subcommand. All effects are assessed simultaneously for their partial contribution, so order is irrelevant. The MCA and MEAN specifications on the STATISTICS subcommand are not available with the regression approach.

HIERARCHICAL   *Hierarchical approach.*

If you select the default classic-experimental approach and the default treatment of covariates (before the main effects), effects are assessed in the following order: covariates, main effects, two-way interactions, three-way interactions, four-way interactions, and five-way interactions. This means that covariates are not adjusted for any other terms in the model except for other covariates, main effects are adjusted only for covariates and other main effects, and interactions are adjusted for all interactions of the same and lower order as well as for all main effects and covariates.

The effects within each type are adjusted for all other effects of that type and also for the effects of all prior types. For example, all two-way interactions are adjusted for other two-way interactions and, as described above, for all main effects and covariates.

In the regression approach all effects are assessed simultaneously. That is, each effect is adjusted for all other effects in the model. The COVARIATE subcommand has no effect if METHOD=UNIQUE.

The hierarchical approach differs from the experimental approach only in the treatment of covariates and main effects. In the hierarchical approach, covariates and main effects are adjusted only for effects that precede them on the VARIABLES subcommand. (By default, covariates are considered to precede all other effects on VARIABLES, even though they are actually specified after the main effects.) For example, if the command is

```
ANOVA VARIABLES=DEP BY F1 F2 F3 (1,4) WITH COV1 COV2 COV3
/METHOD=HIERARCHICAL.
```

COV1 is not adjusted for any other terms, COV2 is adjusted only for COV1, and COV3 is adjusted for both COV1 and COV2. Similarly, F1 is adjusted only for the covariates, F2 is adjusted for the covariates and F1, and F3 is adjusted for F1, F2, and all of the covariates. Note that interactions are not processed hierarchically; they are adjusted for all covariates, factors and other interactions of the same and lower orders, just as in the default classical experimental approach.

The COVARIATES subcommand allows you to change the order in which covariates are entered into the model. For example, if you select the default experimental approach but request COVARIATES=AFTER, main effects are entered first and adjusted only for other main effects, covariates are entered after the main effects and adjusted for other covariates and main effects. If, instead, you select the default experimental approach with COVARIATES=WITH, covariates are entered together with the main effects. This means that all covariates and main effects are adjusted for each other.

16.13
STATISTICS Subcommand

By default, ANOVA calculates only the statistics needed for analysis of variance. Optionally, you can request a means and counts table, unstandardized regression coefficients, and multiple classification analysis on the STATISTICS subcommand.

You can specify the STATISTICS subcommand by itself or with one or more keywords. If you specify the STATISTICS subcommand with no keywords, ANOVA calculates MEAN and REG, if there are covariates. If you include a keyword or keywords on the STATISTICS subcommand, ANOVA calculates only the additional statistics you request.

The following keywords can be specified on the STATISTICS subcommand:

MEAN *Means and counts table.* MEAN requests means and counts for each dependent variable for groups defined by each factor and each combination of factors up to the fifth level. This statistic is not available with METHOD= UNIQUE.

REG *Unstandardized regression coefficients for the covariates.* The coefficients are computed at the point where the covariates are entered into the equation. Thus, their values depend on the type of design you have specified.

MCA *Multiple classification analysis.* The MCA table is not available with METHOD=UNIQUE. In the MCA table, effects are expressed as deviations from the grand mean. The table includes a listing of unadjusted category effects for each factor, category effects adjusted for other factors, category effects adjusted for all factors and covariates, and eta and beta values.

ALL   *Means and counts table, unstandardized regression coefficients, and multiple classification analysis.*

NONE   *No additional statistics.* This is the default if you omit the STATISTICS subcommand.

For example, the following commands produce Figure 16.1:

```
ANOVA VARIABLES=SCORE BY ATTRACT(1,3) SEX(1,2)
 /STATISTICS=MEAN.
```

16.14
MISSING Subcommand

By default, a case that is missing for any variable named in the analysis list is deleted for all analyses specified by that list. Use the MISSING subcommand to ignore missing-data indicators and to include all cases in the computations. Two keywords can be specified on the MISSING subcommand:

EXCLUDE   *Exclude cases with missing data.* This is the default if you omit the MISSING subcommand.

INCLUDE   *Include cases with user-missing data.*

16.15
FORMAT Subcommand

By default, ANOVA displays variable or value labels if they have been defined. Use the FORMAT subcommand to suppress variable and value labels. Two keywords can be specified on the FORMAT subcommand:

LABELS   *Display variable and value labels.* This is the default if you omit the FORMAT subcommand.

NOLABELS *Suppress variable and value labels.*

16.16
Annotated Example

The SPSS commands used to produce the results in Figures 16.1 and 16.2 are:

```
TITLE 'ANALYSIS OF VARIANCE'.
DATA LIST  /1 ATTRACT 1-2 SEX 3 SCORE 4-5.
BEGIN DATA.
data records
END DATA.
RECODE  ATTRACT (1=1) (5=2) (10=3).
VARIABLE LABELS
 ATTRACT 'ATTRACTIVENESS LEVEL'
 SEX 'SEX SIMILARITY'
 SCORE 'COMPOSITE SCORE'.
VALUE LABELS
 ATTRACT  1 'LOW' 2 'MEDIUM' 3 'HIGH'
 /SEX  1 'SAME' 2 'OPPOSITE'.
ANOVA  VARIABLES=SCORE BY ATTRACT (1,3) SEX (1,2)
 /STATISTICS=MEAN.
FINISH.
```

Thess commands assume that the variable ATTRACT is originally coded 1=low, 5=medium, and 10=high.

- The TITLE command displays the title ANALYSIS OF VARIANCE at the top of each page of output.

- The DATA LIST command defines the variables.

- The RECODE command changes the values of ATTRACT to consecutive values of 1, 2, and 3 so that the ANOVA procedure will be more efficient. The recode specification (1=1), although unnecessary, is included to give a complete description of the values of ATTRACT. All values not mentioned on the RECODE command remain unchanged. See Chapter 2 for a discussion of the RECODE command.

- The VARIABLE LABELS and VALUE LABELS commands assign variable and value labels.
- The ANOVA command requests an analysis of variance of variable SCORE by SEX and three categories of attractiveness (variable ATTRACT).
- The STATISTICS command requests the means and counts table.

16.17 EXERCISES

Syntax

1. Write the command to perform a two-way analysis of variance where DIAS is the dependent variable and RACE (coded 1 through 4) and CHD (coded 0 and 1) are the independent variables.

2. The following commands contain errors. Write the correct commands.

   a. `ANOVA VARIABLES=SCORE BY REGION (1,4) SEX.`

   b. `ANOVA VARIABLES=SCORE BY REGION BY SEX.`

   c. `ANOVA VARIABLES=SCORE(1,100) BY RACE(1,3) SEX(1,2).`

   d. `ANOVA VARIABLES=SCORE1 SCORE2 BY RACE(1,3) SEX.`

3. If variable REGION has four categories coded 1 through 4 and ATTRACT has three categories coded 1 through 3, how many cells result from the following specifications?

   a. `ANOVA VARIABLES=SCORE BY REGION(1,4) ATTRACT(1,3).`

   b. `ANOVA VARIABLES=SCORE BY REGION(2,4) ATTRACT(1,3).`

   c. `ANOVA VARIABLES=SCORE BY REGION(2,4) ATTRACT(2,3).`

4. You type the following command:

   `ANOVA VARIABLES=PRESTIGE BY SEX.`

   and get the following error message:

   ```
   >Error # 10713 on line 4 in column 72.  Text: (End of Command)
   >You omitted the parenthesized value range after a list of independent
   >variables in an ANOVA command model specification.
   >This command not executed.
   ```

   Fix the command.

5. Given data for the sex, age, weight, daily fiber consumption (variable FIBER), and blood iron levels (variable IRON) of a random selection of office workers, write the SPSS transformation commands and ANOVA analysis for each of the following:

   a. Perform a two-way analysis of variance to determine whether there is an interaction between the effects of age and sex on an individual's blood iron level. Use the following age categories: people under 25, people 25–45, and people over 45.

   b. Perform a two-way analysis of variance to determine whether there is an interaction between the effects of age and weight on an individual's blood iron level. Use the same age categories as in (a). Use the following weight categories: under 100 pounds, 100–130 pounds, 130–160 pounds, 160–190 pounds, and over 190 pounds.

   c. Perform a two-way analysis of variance to determine whether weight and daily fiber intake affect an individual's blood iron level. Perform separate analyses for men and women. For women, use weight categories from 80 to 160 pounds, in increments of 20 pounds, and account for women under 80 pounds and for women over 160 pounds. For men, use weight categories from 100 to 250 pounds, in increments of 30 pounds, and account for men under 100 pounds and for men over 250 pounds. For both men and women, use the following fiber categories: under 2 grams, 2–4 grams, 4–6 grams, 6–8 grams, and over 8 grams.

Statistical Concepts

1. Are the following statements true or false?

   a. If an interaction effect is evident, it is important to perform individual F tests for the variables in the interaction.

   b. If an interaction term has a significant F value, it is not possible to obtain a nonsignificant F value for one of the variables in the interaction.

2. Complete the following two-way analysis of variance table.

```
        * * *   A N A L Y S I S   O F   V A R I A N C E   * * *

              VAR A
          BY  FACTOR1
              FACTOR2
```

SOURCE OF VARIATION	SUM OF SQUARES	DF	MEAN SQUARE	F-VALUE
MAIN EFFECTS	524.61	5		
FACTOR1	310.11	3		
FACTOR2	214.50	2		
2-WAY INTERACTIONS	104.17	6		
FACTOR1 FACTOR2	104.17	6		
EXPLAINED	628.78	11		
RESIDUAL	4988.02	49		
TOTAL	5616.80	60		

3. Based on the plot of cell means given below, do you think there is an interaction between treatment and smoking status?

Cell means

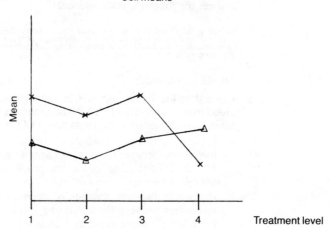

Data Analysis

Use the BANK system file for Questions 1–4.

1. Examine the effects of the first two job categories and the sex-race variable on beginning salary using a two-way analysis of variance. Is there an interaction effect? What do your results suggest?

2. Repeat the analysis in Question 1 looking at current salary instead of beginning salary.

3. Use a two-way analysis of variance to examine the effects of collapsed educational level (up to 16 years) and the first two job categories on beginning salary. What assumptions are you making? Summarize your results.

4. Using a two-way analysis of variance, investigate the effects of collapsed educational level (up to 16 years) and collapsed job seniority on current salary. Summarize your results.

5. Choose one of the data sets from Appendix B.

   a. Formulate four hypotheses that can be tested using two-way analysis of variance techniques. For example, with the Western Electric data file you can use a two-way analysis of variance to test the hypothesis that family history of heart disease and cigarette smoking are related to diastolic blood pressure. Make sure to indicate which variables are the factors and how many levels there are for each factor.

   b. For two of the hypotheses in Question 5.a, use the ANOVA procedure to determine whether there are significant main effects and a significant interaction. Summarize your findings.

   c. Using the cell means obtained from procedure ANOVA, draw a plot like the one in Figure 10.3b.

6. Use the Western Electric data for the following exercises.

   a. Use analysis of variance to examine the relationship between family history of coronary heart disease, incidence of coronary heart disease, and diastolic blood pressure. Write a paragraph describing your results.

   b. Use analysis of variance to examine the relationship between education (8 years or fewer, 9–12, and more than 12), incidence of coronary heart disease, and number of cigarettes smoked. Is there a difference in the average number of cigarettes smoked for men who developed heart disease and those who did not? Is there a difference in the average number of cigarettes smoked for the three categories of education? Is there an interaction between incidence of coronary heart disease and education?

   c. If there is an interaction in (b) does it make sense to look at the main effects? Why or why not?

Nonparametric Tests

In this chapter:

Goals:

- To test hypotheses when the assumptions required for standard parametric statistical techniques cannot be met.
- To test the hypothesis that two or more independent samples come from the same distribution. The shape of the distribution does not have to be known.
- To test the hypothesis that two related samples come from the same population.
- To examine the strength of the linear relationship between two variables when they are not normally distributed.
- To test the hypothesis that a sample is from a population with a particular probability distribution.

Examples:

- To test whether the preference scores for a particular product differ for three age groups.
- To test whether the probability of closing a sale is the same for all months of the year.
- To see whether there is a linear relationship between class rank in high school and class rank in college.

How it's done:

In many nonparametric procedures the observed values are replaced by ranks. It is the ranks that are then analyzed. The Mann-Whitney test can be used to test the hypothesis that two independent samples come from the same population. The sign test or the Wilcoxon signed ranks test can be used to test the hypothesis that two related samples come from the same population. The Kruskal-Wallis test can be used to test the hypothesis that several independent samples come from the same population. The one-sample chi-square test can be used to test the hypothesis that a sample comes from a population with a particular probability distribution. The Spearman rank correlation coefficient can be used to test the hypothesis that there is no linear association between the ranks of two variables.

17 Distribution-Free or Nonparametric Tests: Procedures NONPAR CORR and NPAR TESTS

Coffee and carrots have recently joined saccharin, tobacco, Laetrile, and interferon on the ever-expanding list of rumored causes of and cures for cancer. This list is necessarily tentative and complicated. The two major sources of evidence—experiments on animals and examination of the histories of afflicted persons—are fraught with problems. It is difficult to predict, based on large doses of suspect substances given to small animals, the consequences of small amounts consumed by humans over a long time span.

In studies of people, lifestyle components are difficult to isolate, and it is challenging—if not impossible—to unravel the contribution of a single factor. For example, what is the role of caffeine based on a sample of overweight, sedentary, coffee- and alcohol-drinking, cigarette-smoking, urban dwellers?

Nutrition is also thought to be an important component in cancer development and progression. For example, the per capita consumption of dietary fats is positively correlated with the incidence of mammary and colon cancer in humans (Wynder, 1976). In a recent study, King et al. (1979) examined the relationship between diet and tumor development in rats. Three groups of animals of the same age, species, and physical condition were injected with tumor cells. The rats were divided into three groups and fed diets of either low, saturated, or unsaturated fat.

One hypothesis of interest is whether the length of time until a tumor develops in rats fed saturated diets differs from the length of time in rats fed unsaturated diets. If it is tenable to assume that tumor-free time is normally distributed, the two-sample t-test described in Chapter 12 can be used to test the hypothesis that the population means are equal. However, if the distribution of times does not appear to be normal, and especially if the sample sizes are small, statistical procedures that do not require assumptions about the shapes of the underlying distributions should be considered.

17.1 THE MANN-WHITNEY TEST

The *Mann-Whitney test*, also known as the Wilcoxon test, does not require assumptions about the shape of the underlying distributions. It tests the hypothesis that two independent samples come from populations having the same distribution. The form of the distribution need not be specified. The test does not require that the variable be measured on an interval scale; an ordinal scale is sufficient.

17.2
Ranking the Data

To compute the test, the observations from both samples are first combined and ranked from smallest to largest. Consider Table 17.2, which shows a sample of the King data reported by Lee (1980). Case 4 has the shortest elapsed time to development of a tumor, 68 days. It is assigned a rank of 1. The next shortest time is for Case 3, so it is assigned a rank of 2. Cases 5 and 6 both exhibited tumors on the same day. They are both assigned a rank of 3.5, the average of the ranks (3 and 4) for which they are tied. Case 2, the next largest, is given a rank of 5, and Case 1 is given a rank of 6.

Table 17.2   Ranking the data

	Saturated			Unsaturated	
Case	Time	Rank	Case	Time	Rank
1	199	6	4	68	1
2	126	5	5	112	3.5
3	81	2	6	112	3.5

17.3
Calculating the Test

The statistic for testing the hypothesis that the two distributions are equal is the sum of the ranks for each of the two groups. If the groups have the same distribution, their sample distributions of ranks should be similar. If one of the groups has more than its share of small or large ranks, there is reason to suspect that the two underlying distributions are different.

Figure 17.3 shows the output from the Mann-Whitney test for the complete King data. For each group, the mean rank and number of cases is given. (The mean rank is the sum of the ranks divided by the number of cases.) Note that the saturated-diet group has only 29 cases since one rat died of causes unrelated to the experiment. The entry displayed under W is the sum of the ranks for the group with the smaller number of observations. If both groups have the same number of observations, W is the rank sum for the group named first in the NPAR TESTS command (see Section 17.33). For this example, W is 963, the sum of the ranks for the saturated-diet group.

Figure 17.3   Mann-Whitney output

```
NPAR TESTS M-W=TUMOR BY DIET(0,1).
```

```
- - - - - Mann-Whitney U - Wilcoxon Rank Sum W Test

     TUMOR
 by DIET

   Mean Rank    Cases

      26.90        30   DIET = 0   UNSATURATED
      33.21        29   DIET = 1   SATURATED
                   --
                   59   Total

                                        Corrected for ties
         U              W              Z        2-Tailed P
      342.0          963.0        -1.4112          .1582
```

The number identified on the output as U is the number of times a value in the unsaturated-diet group precedes a value in the saturated-diet group. To understand what this means, consider the data in Table 17.2 again. All three cases in the unsaturated-diet group have smaller ranks than the first case in the saturated-diet group, so they all precede Case 1 in the rankings. Similarly, all three cases in the unsaturated-diet group precede Case 2. Only one unsaturated-diet case (Case 4) is smaller in value than Case 3. Thus, the number of times the value for an unsaturated-diet case precedes the value for a saturated-diet case is

3+3+1=7. The number of times the value of a saturated-diet case precedes the value of an unsaturated-diet case is 2, since Case 3 has a smaller rank than both Cases 5 and 6. The smaller of these two numbers is displayed on the output as U. If the two distributions are equal, values from one group should not consistently precede values in the other.

The significance levels associated with U and W are the same. They can be obtained by transforming the score to a standard normal deviate (Z). If the total sample size is less than 30, an exact probability level based on the distribution of the score is also displayed. From Figure 17.3, the observed significance level for this example is 0.158. Since the significance level is large, the hypothesis that tumor-free time has the same distribution for the two diet groups is not rejected.

17.4
Which Diet?

You should not conclude from these findings that it doesn't matter—as far as tumors are concerned—what kind of fat you (or rats) eat. King et al. found that rats fed the unsaturated diet had a total of 96 tumors at the end of the experiment, while rats fed the saturated diet had only 55 tumors. They also found that large tumors were more common in the unsaturated-diet group than in the saturated-diet group. Thus, unsaturated fats may be more hazardous than saturated fats.

17.5
Assumptions

The Mann-Whitney test requires only that the observations be a random sample and that values can be ordered. These assumptions, especially randomness, are not to be made lightly, but they are less restrictive than those for the two-sample t-test for means. The t-test further requires that the observations be selected from normally distributed populations with equal variances. (An approximate test for the case of unequal variances is presented in Chapter 12).

Since the Mann-Whitney test can always be calculated instead of the t-test, what determines which should be used? If the assumptions needed for the t-test are met, the t-test is more powerful than the Mann-Whitney test. That is, the t-test will detect true differences between the two populations more often than will the Mann-Whitney test since the t-test uses more information from the data. Substitution of ranks for the actual values loses potentially useful information. On the other hand, using the t-test when its assumptions are substantially violated may result in an erroneous observed significance level.

In general, if the assumptions of the t-test appear reasonable, it should be used. When the data are ordinal—or interval but from a markedly nonnormal distribution—the Mann-Whitney test is the procedure of choice.

17.6
NONPARAMETRIC TESTS

Many statistical procedures, like the Mann-Whitney test, require limited distributional assumptions about the data. Collectively these procedures are termed *distribution-free* or *nonparametric tests*. Like the Mann-Whitney test, distribution-free tests are generally less powerful than their parametric counterparts. They are most useful in situations where parametric procedures are not appropriate: when the data are nominal or ordinal, or when interval data are from markedly nonnormal distributions. Significance levels for certain nonparametric tests can be determined regardless of the shape of the population distribution since they are based on ranks.

In the following sections, various nonparametric tests will be used to reanalyze some of the data described in previous chapters. Since the data were chosen to illustrate the parametric procedures, they satisfy assumptions that are more restrictive than those for nonparametric procedures. However, they provide an opportunity for learning new procedures with familiar data and for comparing results from different types of analyses.

17.7
The Sign Test

In Chapter 12, the paired t-test for means is used to test the hypothesis that the mean buying scores for husbands and wives are equal. Remember that the assumption that the differences are normally distributed is required for this test.

The *sign test* is a nonparametric procedure used with two related samples to test the hypothesis that the distributions of two variables are the same. This test makes no assumptions about the shape of these distributions.

To compute the sign test, the difference between the buying scores of husbands and wives is calculated for each case. Next, the numbers of positive and negative differences are obtained. If the distributions of the two variables are the same, the numbers of positive and negative differences should be similar.

Figure 17.7   Sign test output

```
NPAR TESTS SIGN=HSSCALE WITH WSSCALE.

- - - - - Sign Test

      HSSCALE    HUSBAND SELF SCALE
with WSSCALE    WIFE SELF SCALE


        Cases

          56   - Diffs (WSSCALE LT HSSCALE)          Z =      1.6416
          39   + Diffs (WSSCALE GT HSSCALE)
           3     Ties                        2-Tailed P =       .1007
         ___
          98     Total
```

The output in Figure 17.7 shows that the number of negative differences is 56, while the number of positive differences is 39. The total number of cases is 98, including 3 with 0 differences. The observed significance level is 0.1007. Since this value is large, the hypothesis that the distributions are the same is not rejected.

17.8
The Wilcoxon Signed-Ranks Test

The sign test uses only the direction of the differences between the pairs and ignores the magnitude. A discrepancy of 15 between husbands' and wives' buying scores is treated in the same way as a discrepancy of 1. The *Wilcoxon signed-ranks test* incorporates information about the magnitude of the differences and is therefore more powerful than the sign test.

To compute the Wilcoxon signed-ranks test, the differences are ranked ignoring the signs. In the case of ties, average ranks are assigned. The sums of the ranks for positive and negative differences are then calculated.

Figure 17.8   Wilcoxon signed-ranks test output

```
NPAR TESTS WILCOXON=HSSCALE WITH WSSCALE.

- - - - - Wilcoxon Matched-Pairs Signed-Ranks Test

      HSSCALE    HUSBAND SELF SCALE
with WSSCALE    WIFE SELF SCALE

  Mean Rank    Cases

     45.25        56   - Ranks (WSSCALE LT HSSCALE)
     51.95        39   + Ranks (WSSCALE GT HSSCALE)
                   3     Ties  (WSSCALE EQ HSSCALE)
                 ___
                  98     Total

     Z =   -.9428              2-Tailed P =   .3458
```

From Figure 17.8, the average rank of the 56 negative differences is 45.25. The average positive rank is 51.95. There are 3 cases with the same value for both variables. This is the entry under TIES in Figure 17.8. The observed significance level associated with the test is large (0.3458), and again the hypothesis of no difference is not rejected.

17.9
The Kruskal-Wallis Test

The experiment described in the first sections of this chapter investigates the effects of three diets on tumor development. The Mann-Whitney test was calculated to examine possible differences between saturated and unsaturated diets. To test for differences between all three diets, an extension of the Mann-Whitney test can be used. This test is known as the *Kruskal-Wallis one-way analysis of variance*.

The procedure for computing the Kruskal-Wallis test is similar to that used in the Mann-Whitney test. All cases from the groups are combined and ranked. Average ranks are assigned in the case of ties. For each group, the ranks are summed, and the Kruskal-Wallis *H* statistic is computed from these sums. The *H* statistic has approximately a chi-square distribution under the hypothesis that the three groups have the same distribution.

Figure 17.9   Kruskal-Wallis one-way analysis of variance output

```
NPAR TESTS K-W=TUMOR BY DIET(0,2).
```

```
- - - - - Kruskal-Wallis 1-Way Anova

      TUMOR
   by DIET


   Mean Rank    Cases

       34.12      30     DIET = 0    UNSATURATED
       43.50      29     DIET = 1    SATURATED
       56.24      29     DIET = 2    LOW-FAT

                  —

                  88     Total

                                              Corrected for ties
      Cases    Chi-Square   Significance    Chi-Square   Significance
        88      11.1257       .0038           11.2608        .0036
```

The output in Figure 17.9 shows that the third group, the low-fat-diet group, has the largest average rank. The value of the Kruskal-Wallis statistic is 11.1257. When the statistic is adjusted for the presence of ties, the value changes to 11.2608. The small observed significance level suggests that the time until development of a tumor is not the same for all three groups.

17.10
The One-Sample Chi-Square Test

In Chapter 7, frequencies of deaths for the days of the week are examined. The FREQUENCIES output suggests that the days of the week are equally hazardous in regard to death. To test this conclusion, the *one-sample chi-square test* can be used. This nonparametric test requires only that the data be a random sample.

To calculate the one-sample chi-square statistic, the data are first classified into mutually exclusive categories of interest—days of the week in this example—and then expected frequencies for these categories are computed. Expected frequencies are the frequencies that would be expected if a given hypothesis is true. For the death data, the hypothesis to be tested is that the probability of death is the same for each day of the week. The day of death is known for 110 subjects. The hypothesis implies that the expected frequency of deaths for each weekday is 110 divided by 7, or 15.71. Once the expected frequencies are obtained, the chi-square statistic is computed as

$$\chi^2 = \sum_{i=1}^{k} (O_i - E_i)^2 / E_i$$

Equation 17.10

where O_i is the observed frequency for the ith category, E_i is the expected frequency for the ith category, and k is the number of categories.

Figure 17.10   One-sample chi-square output

```
NPAR TESTS CHISQUARE=DAYOFWK.
```

```
- - - - - Chi-Square Test

    DAYOFWK    DAY OF DEATH

                                        Cases
                            Category   Observed   Expected   Residual

        SUNDAY                 1          19        15.71       3.29
        MONDAY                 2          11        15.71      -4.71
        TUESDAY                3          19        15.71       3.29
        WEDNSDAY               4          17        15.71       1.29
        THURSDAY               5          15        15.71       -.71
        FRIDAY                 6          13        15.71      -2.71
        SATURDAY               7          16        15.71        .29
                                        ----
                            Total        110

            Chi-Square            D.F.           Significance
              3.400                6                .757
```

If the hypothesis is true, the chi-square statistic has approximately a chi-square distribution with $k-1$ degrees of freedom. This statistic will be large if the observed and expected frequencies are substantially different. Figure 17.10 is the output from the one-sample chi-square test for the death data. The codes associated with the days of the week are listed in the column labeled **Category.** The observed frequencies are in the next column, labeled **Cases Observed.** The observed significance level is 0.757, so it appears that the day of the week does not affect the chance of death.

17.11
The Rank Correlation
Coefficient

The Pearson product-moment correlation discussed in Chapter 14 is appropriate only for data that attain at least an interval level of measurement, such as the sales and advertising data used as examples in that chapter. Normality is also assumed when testing hypotheses about this correlation coefficient. For ordinal data or interval data that do not satisfy the normality assumption, another measure of the linear relationship between two variables, *Spearman's rank correlation coefficient,* is available.

The rank correlation coefficient is the Pearson correlation coefficient based on the ranks of the data if there are no ties (adjustments are made if some of the data are tied). If the original data for each variable have no ties, the data for each variable are first ranked and then the Pearson correlation coefficient between the ranks for the two variables is computed. Like the Pearson correlation coefficient, the rank correlation ranges between -1 and $+1$, where -1 and $+1$ indicate a perfect linear relationship between the ranks of the two variables. The interpretation is therefore the same except that the relationship between *ranks* and not values is examined.

Figure 17.11   The rank correlation coefficient

```
NONPAR CORR VARIABLES=ADVERTIS REPS SALES.
```

```
- - - - - - - - - - - - - SPEARMAN   CORRELATION   COEFFICIENTS - - - - - - - - - - - - -




REPS          .7733
          N(   40)
          SIG .000


SALES         .9182       .8636
          N(   40)    N(   40)
          SIG .000    SIG .000


          ADVERTIS      REPS

" . " IS PRINTED IF A COEFFICIENT CANNOT BE COMPUTED.
```

Figure 17.11 shows the matrix of rank correlation coefficients for the sales and advertising data. As expected, these coefficients are similar in sign and magnitude to the Pearson coefficients obtained in Chapter 14.

17.12
RUNNING PROCEDURE NONPAR CORR

NONPAR CORR computes two rank-order correlation coefficients, Spearman's rho and Kendall's tau-*b*, with their significance levels. You can obtain either or both coefficients.

The only required subcommand on NONPAR CORR is the VARIABLES subcommand, which specifies the list of variables to be analyzed. VARIABLES must be specified first. You can specify the optional subcommands in any order, separated by slashes.

17.13
VARIABLES Subcommand

The VARIABLES subcommand names the variable list. You can use the keyword TO in the list to refer to consecutive variables in the active system file. The variables must be numeric.

Depending on how you specify the variable list, NONPAR CORR displays either a lower-triangular or a rectangular matrix. If you provide a simple list of variables, NONPAR CORR displays the correlations of each variable with every other variable in the list in a lower-triangular matrix. For example, the triangular matrix in Figure 17.11 was produced with the following command:

```
NONPAR CORR VARIABLES=ADVERTIS REPS SALES.
```

The correlation of a variable with itself (the diagonal) and redundant coefficients are not displayed.

To obtain the rectangular matrix, specify two variable lists separated by the keyword WITH. NONPAR CORR then displays a rectangular matrix of variables in the first list correlated with variables in the second list. For example,

```
NONPAR CORR VARIABLES=PRESTIGE SPPRES PAPRES16
   WITH DEGREE PADEG MADE.
```

produces nine correlations. The variables listed before keyword WITH define the rows of the matrix, and those listed after keyword WITH define the columns. Unless a variable is in both lists, there are no identity coefficients in the matrix.

You can request more than one matrix on a NONPAR CORR command. Use a slash to separate the specifications for each of the requested matrices. For example,

```
NONPAR CORR VARIABLES=SPPRES PAPRES16 PRESTIGE
   /SATCITY WITH SATHOBBY SATFAM.
```

produces two correlation matrices. The first matrix contains three coefficients in triangular form. The second matrix is rectangular and contains two coefficients.

If all cases have a missing value for a given pair of variables, or if they all have the same value for a variable, the coefficient cannot be computed and NONPAR CORR displays a period for the coefficient.

17.14
PRINT Subcommand

By default, NONPAR CORR displays Spearman correlation coefficients. Below each coefficient it displays the number of cases and the significance level. The significance level is based on a one-tailed test.

Use the PRINT subcommand to request the Kendall correlation coefficient or both Spearman and Kendall coefficients. Both coefficients are based on ranks.

You can also use PRINT to switch to a two-tailed test and to suppress the display of the number of cases and significance level.

The following keywords are available on PRINT:

SPEARMAN *Spearman's rho.* Only Spearman coefficients are displayed. This is the default.

KENDALL *Kendall's tau-b.* Only Kendall coefficients are displayed.

BOTH *Kendall and Spearman coefficients.* Both coefficients are displayed.

SIG *Display the number of cases and significance level.* This is the default.

NOSIG *Suppress the display of the number of cases and significance level.*

ONETAIL *One-tailed test of significance.* This is the default.

TWOTAIL *Two-tailed test of significance.*

If you specify both FORMAT=SERIAL (Section 17.17) and PRINT= NOSIG, only FORMAT=SERIAL will be in effect.

17.15
SAMPLE Subcommand

NONPAR CORR must store cases in memory to build matrices. You may not have sufficient computer resources to store all the cases to produce the coefficients requested. The SAMPLE subcommand allows you to select a random sample of cases when there is not enough space to store all the cases. To request a random sample, simply specify the subcommand, as in:

```
NONPAR CORR VARIABLES=PRESTIGE SPPRES PAPRES16
   DEGREE PADEG MADEG
    /SAMPLE.
```

The SAMPLE subcommand has no additional specifications.

17.16
MISSING Subcommand

By default, NONPAR CORR deletes a case from the computation of a coefficient if it is missing on one or both of the pair of variables. Because each coefficient is based on all cases that have valid codes on that particular pair of variables, the maximum information available is used in every calculation. This results in a set of coefficients based on a varying number of cases.

Use the MISSING subcommand to specify alternative missing-value treatments. The following keywords are available:

PAIRWISE *Exclude missing values pairwise.* Cases missing on one or both variables in a pair for a specific correlation coefficient are excluded from the computation of that coefficient. This is the default.

LISTWISE *Exclude missing values listwise.* Cases missing on any variable named in a list are excluded from all analyses. Each variable list on a command is evaluated separately. If you specify multiple variable lists, a case missing for one list might be used in another list. This option decreases the amount of memory required and significantly decreases computational time.

INCLUDE *Include user-missing values.* Cases with user-missing values are included in the analysis.

Only one of these keywords can be specified on MISSING.

17.17
FORMAT Subcommand

The FORMAT subcommand controls the format of the correlation matrix. The following keywords are available:

MATRIX *Print correlations in matrix format.* This is the default.

SERIAL *Print correlations in serial string format.*

17.18
RUNNING
PROCEDURE NPAR
TESTS

Procedure NPAR TESTS is a collection of nonparametric tests that make minimal assumptions about the underlying distributions of data. In addition to the nonparametric tests available in NPAR TESTS, the k-sample chi-square and Fisher's exact test are available in procedure CROSSTABS (see Chapter 10).

Each NPAR TESTS subcommand names a specific test, followed by a variable list. You can use the keyword TO to reference consecutive variables in the active system file. The form of the variable list differs with the data organization required for the test. You can request any or all of the available tests, separated by slashes, on one NPAR TESTS command. Some tests require additional parameters, and the CHISQUARE test has an optional subcommand.

17.19
One-Sample Tests

In a one-sample test, variables being tested are not subdivided into groups (see Section 17.10). Specify the name of the test and one or more variables. The test is repeated for each variable specified.

17.20
CHISQUARE Subcommand

Subcommand CHISQUARE tabulates a variable into categories and computes a chi-square statistic based on the differences between observed and expected frequencies. By default, the CHISQUARE test assumes equal expected frequencies. The following command produced Figure 17.10:

NPAR TESTS **CHISQUARE=DAYOFWK.**

Optionally, you can specify a range after a variable or variable list. If you do not specify a range, each distinct value encountered is defined as a category. If you do specify a range, integer-valued categories are established for each value within the inclusive range. Noninteger values are truncated, and cases with values outside the bounds are excluded. For example,

NPAR TESTS   CHISQUARE=RANK(1,4).

uses only the integer values 1 through 4 for the chi-square test of the variable RANK.

EXPECTED Subcommand. To specify expected frequencies, percentages, or proportions for the chi-square test, use the EXPECTED subcommand and a value list. You must specify a value greater than 0 for each observed category of the data. The values listed after the EXPECTED subcommand are summed. Each value is then divided by this sum to calculate the proportion of cases expected in the corresponding category. For example,

NPAR TESTS   CHISQUARE=RANK(1,4) /**EXPECTED = 3 4 5 4**.

specifies expected proportions of 3/16, 4/16, 5/16, and 4/16 for categories 1, 2, 3, and 4, respectively. You can specify the same expected proportion for two or more consecutive categories with an asterisk (*), as in:

NPAR TESTS   CHISQUARE=A(1,5) /**EXPECTED=12, 3*16, 18**.

This command tests the observed frequencies for variable A against the hypothetical proportions of 12/78 for category 1; 16/78 each for categories 2, 3, and 4; and 18/78 for category 5.

The EXPECTED subcommand applies to all variables named on the preceding CHISQUARE subcommand. If you want to specify different expected proportions for each variable, use multiple combinations of the CHISQUARE and EXPECTED subcommands. If you want to test the same variable against different proportions, you can also use multiple combinations.

17.21
K-S Subcommand
(One-Sample Test)

Subcommand K-S compares the observed cumulative distribution function for a variable with a specified distribution, which may be uniform, normal, or Poisson. The Kolmogorov-Smirnov Z is computed from the largest difference (in absolute value) between the observed and theoretical distribution functions. Each of these distributions has optional parameters:

(UNIFORM,lo,hi)   *Uniform distribution.* The optional parameters are user-specified minimum and maximum values (in that order). If you do not specify them, K-S uses the observed minimum and maximum values.

(NORMAL,m,sd)   *Normal distribution.* The optional parameters are user-specified mean and standard deviation (in that order). If you do not specify them, K-S uses the observed mean and standard deviation.

(POISSON,m)   *Poisson distribution.* The one optional parameter is a user-specified mean. If you do not specify it, K-S uses the observed mean. A word of caution about testing against a Poisson distribution: if the mean of the test distribution is large, evaluating the probabilities is a very time-consuming process. If a mean of 100,000 or larger is used, K-S uses a normal approximation to the Poisson distribution.

For example, the command

```
NPAR TESTS  K-S(UNIFORM)=A.
```

compares the distribution for variable A with a uniform distribution which has the same range as variable A, while the command

```
NPAR TESTS  K-S(NORMAL,0,1)=B.
```

compares the distribution for variable B with a normal distribution that has a mean of 0 and standard deviation of 1.

K-S assumes that the test distribution is entirely specified in advance. When parameters of the test distribution are estimated from the sample, the distribution of the test statistic changes. NPAR TESTS does not provide any correction for this. Tests for normality are also available with the EXAMINE procedure.

The K-S subcommand can also be used for tests of two independent samples (see Section 17.34).

17.22
RUNS Subcommand

Subcommand RUNS performs the runs test to test whether the two values of a dichotomous variable occur randomly. A run is defined as a sequence of one of the values which is preceded and followed by the other data value (or the end of the series). For example, the following sequence

| 1 1 | 0 0 0 | 1 | 0 0 0 0 | 1 | 0 | 1 |

contains seven runs (vertical bars are used to separate the runs).

You must specify a cutpoint (enclosed in parentheses) to dichotomize the variable. Use either the observed mean, median, or mode, or a specified value, as the cutpoint. One category comes from cases with values below the cutpoint and the other category comes from cases with values equal to or greater than the cutpoint. To specify the cutpoint, use either the keywords MEAN, MEDIAN, MODE, or a value. Even if the variable is already dichotomized, you still must specify a cutting point. For example, if the variable has values 0 and 1, you can use 1 as the cutting point. The command

```
NPAR TESTS RUNS(MEDIAN)=RANK.
```

uses the median as the cutpoint, assigning cases with values below the median to one category, and cases with values equal to or above the median to the other category.

17.23
BINOMIAL Subcommand

Subcommand BINOMIAL compares the observed frequency in each category of a dichotomous variable with expected frequencies from the binomial distribution. BINOMIAL tabulates a variable into two categories based on the way you specify a cutpoint. The command

```
NPAR TESTS BINOMIAL=RANK(2).
```

specifies the value 2 as the cutting point for the variable RANK. Cases with values of less than 2 for RANK are assigned to one group, and cases with values of 2 or greater are assigned to the other group. If you specify *two* values in parentheses following the variable list, all cases with the first value will be in the first category, and all cases with the second value will be in the second category. If you specify two values and the variable is not a dichotomy, only cases with the two values specified are included in the analysis.

By default, the null hypothesis is that the data are from a binomial distribution with a probability of 0.5 for both values. You can change the probabilities by specifying a probability for the first value in parentheses after the subcommand BINOMIAL. For example, the command

```
NPAR TESTS BINOMIAL(.25)=RANK(2).
```

tests the null hypothesis that the data are from a binomial distribution with a probability of 0.25 for the first value and a probability of 0.75 for the second value.

17.24
Tests for Two Related Samples

Tests for two related samples compare pairs of variables (see Section 17.7). Specify the name of the test and two or more variables to be tested. If you specify a simple variable list, a test is performed for each variable paired with every other variable on the list. To obtain tests for specific pairs of variables, use two variable lists separated by keyword WITH. Each variable in the first list is tested with each variable in the second list. For example,

```
NPAR TESTS  SIGN=A WITH B C.
```

produces sign tests for A with B and A with C. No test is performed for B with C.

The keyword (PAIRED) used in conjunction with the keyword WITH provides additional control over which variables are paired together. When you specify (PAIRED), the first variable in the first list is paired with the first variable in the second list, the second variable in the first list is paired with the second variable in the second list, and so on. You must name or imply the same number of variables in both lists. For example,

```
NPAR TESTS  MCNEMAR=A B WITH C D (PAIRED).
```

pairs A with C and B with D. You must specify (PAIRED) after the second variable list. You cannot use (PAIRED) if keyword WITH is not specified.

17.25
MCNEMAR Subcommand

McNemar's test looks at the cases with different values for two related variables. The hypothesis that both combinations of different values are equally likely is tested.

Subcommand MCNEMAR produces a 2×2 table for each pair of dichotomous variables. Pairs of variables being tested must be coded with the same two values. A chi-square statistic is computed for cases with different values for the two variables. If fewer than 25 cases have different values for the two variables, the binomial distribution is used to compute the significance level. The command

NPAR TESTS MCNEMAR=A B C D.

produces tests for A with B, A with C, A with D, B with C, B with D, and C with D.

17.26
SIGN Subcommand

The sign test analyzes the signs of the differences between two paired values. Subcommand SIGN counts the positive and negative differences between each pair of variables and ignores 0 differences. Under the null hypothesis for large sample sizes, the test statistic Z is approximately normally distributed with mean 0 and variance 1. The binomial distribution is used to compute an exact significance level if 25 or fewer differences are observed. The following command produced Figure 17.7:

NPAR TESTS SIGN=HSSCALE WITH WSSCALE.

17.27
WILCOXON Subcommand

Subcommand WILCOXON computes differences between pairs of variables, ranks the absolute differences, sums ranks for the positive and negative differences, and computes the test statistic Z from the positive and negative rank sums. Under the null hypothesis, Z is approximately normally distributed with mean 0 and variance 1 for large sample sizes. The following command produced Figure 17.8:

NPAR TESTS WILCOXON=HSSCALE WITH WSSCALE.

17.28
Tests for *k* Related Samples

Tests for k related samples compare sets of variables. Specify the name of the test and two or more variables to be tested. The k variables in the list produce one test for k related samples. The COCHRAN, FRIEDMAN, and KENDALL tests are available for k related samples.

17.29
COCHRAN Subcommand

Cochran's test is used to test the null hypothesis that the proportion of cases in a particular category is the same for several related variables.

Subcommand COCHRAN produces a $k \times 2$ contingency table (variable vs. category) for dichotomous variables and computes the proportions for each variable. If your data are not dichotomous, recode them (see Chapter 3). Cochran's Q statistic has approximately a chi-square distribution. The command

NPAR TESTS COCHRAN=A B C.

produces a 3×2 with three rows for the variables A, B, and C, and two columns for the dichotomous values.

17.30
FRIEDMAN Subcommand

The Friedman test is used to test the hypothesis that k-related variables are from the same distribution. Subcommand FRIEDMAN ranks k variables from 1 to k for each case, calculates the mean rank for each variable over all the cases, and then calculates a test statistic with approximately a chi-square distribution. The command

NPAR TESTS FRIEDMAN=A B C D.

tests whether the four variables are from the same distribution.

17.31
KENDALL Subcommand

Subcommand KENDALL ranks k variables from 1 to k for each case, calculates the mean rank for each variable over all the cases, and then calculates Kendall's W and a corresponding chi-square statistic, correcting for ties. W ranges between 0 and 1, with 0 signifying no agreement and 1 signifying complete agreement. The command

```
NPAR TESTS KENDALL=A B C.
```

produces mean ranks for the three variables listed.

This test assumes that each case is a judge or rater. If you want to perform this test with variables as judges and cases as entities, you must first transpose your data matrix (see Chapter 4).

17.32
Tests for Two Independent Samples

Tests for two independent samples compare two groups of cases on one variable (see Section 17.1). Specify the name of the test and one or more variables to be tested. Each variable in the list produces one test. The variable following the keyword BY splits the file into two groups or samples, based on two values specified in parentheses after the grouping variable. All cases with the first value are in the first group, and all cases with the second value are in the second group. If the grouping variable is not a dichotomy, only cases with the two specified values are included in the analysis.

17.33
M-W Subcommand

Subcommand M-W (Mann-Whitney) ranks all the cases in order of increasing size and computes the test statistic U, the number of times a score from Group 1 precedes a score from Group 2. If the samples are from the same population, the distribution of scores from the two groups in the ranked list should be random; an extreme value of U indicates a nonrandom pattern. For samples with fewer than 30 cases, the exact significance level for U is computed using the algorithm of Dineen and Blakesly (1973). For larger samples, U is transformed into a normally distributed Z statistic. The following command produces Figure 17.3:

```
NPAR TESTS M-W=TUMOR BY DIET(0,1).
```

17.34
K-S Subcommand
(Two-Sample Test)

Subcommand K-S computes the observed cumulative distributions for both groups and the maximum positive, negative, and absolute differences. The Kolmogorov-Smirnov Z is then computed along with the two-tailed probability level based on the Smirnov (1948) formula. The one-tailed test can be used to determine whether the values of one group are generally larger than the values of the other group. For example, the command

```
NPAR TESTS K-S = PCTERR BY GRADE (7,11)
```

analyzes PCTERR by GRADE.

17.35
W-W Subcommand

Subcommand W-W combines observations from both groups and ranks them from lowest to highest. If the samples are from the same population, the two groups should be randomly scattered throughout the ranking. A runs test is performed using group membership as the criterion. If there are ties involving observations from both groups, both the minimum and maximum number of runs possible are calculated. If the total sample size is 30 cases or fewer, the exact one-tailed significance level is calculated. Otherwise, the normal approximation is used. For example, the command

```
NPAR TESTS  W—W = SCORE BY SEX (1,2)
```

tests SCORE by SEX.

17.36
MOSES Subcommand

Subcommand MOSES arranges the scores from the groups in a single ascending sequence. The span of the control group is computed as the number of cases in the sequence containing the lowest and highest control score. The exact significance level can be computed for the span. Chance outliers can easily distort the range of the span. To minimize this problem, you can specify that a certain number of outliers be trimmed from each end of the span. No adjustments are made for tied observations.

The percentage of outliers to be trimmed is specified in parentheses after the MOSES subcommand. If you do not specify the percentage, MOSES automatically trims 5% of the cases from each end. The control group is defined by the first grouping value specified. For example,

```
NPAR TESTS MOSES (10) = SCORE BY SECTION (1,2)
```

trims 10% of the cases from each end. The control group is defined as the group with value 1 for SECTION.

17.37
Tests for *k* Independent Samples

Tests for *k* independent samples compare *k* groups of cases on one variable. Specify the name of the test and one or more variables to be tested. Each variable in the list produces one test. The variable following the keyword BY splits the file into *k* groups. You must specify a minimum and maximum value (enclosed in parentheses) for the grouping variable. If the first value specified is *greater* than the second value, only cases with those two values are included in the analysis.

17.38
MEDIAN Subcommand
(*k*-Sample Test)

Subcommand MEDIAN produces a $2 \times k$ contingency table with counts of the number of cases with values greater than the median and less than or equal to the median for the *k* groups. A chi-square statistic for the table is computed. The command

```
NPAR TESTS MEDIAN=TUMOR BY DIET(0,2).
```

produces a 2×3 table, with categories for values 0, 1, and 2 for the grouping variable DIET. The command

```
NPAR TESTS MEDIAN=TUMOR BY DIET(2,0).
```

produces a 2×2 table and a two-sample test for cases with values of 0 and 2 on the grouping variable DIET.

By default, the observed median is used as the test median, but you can specify any value. For example, the command

```
NPAR TESTS MEDIAN(100)=TUMOR BY DIET(0,2).
```

divides cases into three groups based on the value of DIET and compares the proportion of cases in each group with values less than or equal to 100 and with values greater than 100.

17.39
K-W Subcommand

Subcommand K-W ranks all cases from the k groups in a single series, computes the rank sum for each group, and computes the Kruskal-Wallis H statistic, which has approximately a chi-square distribution. The following command produced Figure 17.9:

```
NPAR TESTS K-W=TUMOR BY DIET(0,2).
```

17.40
STATISTICS Subcommand

In addition to the statistics provided for each test, you can also obtain two types of summary statistics for variables named on each of the subcommands. Use the STATISTICS subcommand to request the following statistics for NPAR TESTS:

DESCRIPTIVES *Univariate statistics.* Displays the mean, maximum, minimum, standard deviation, and number of nonmissing cases for each variable named on the combined subcommands.

QUARTILES *Quartiles and number of cases.* Displays values corresponding to the 25th, 50th, and 75th percentiles for each variable named on the combined subcommands.

ALL *All statistics available on NPAR TESTS.*

17.41
MISSING Subcommand

By default, NPAR TESTS deletes cases with missing values on a test-by-test basis. For subcommands where you can specify several tests, it evaluates each test separately for missing values. For example,

```
NPAR TESTS  MEDIAN=A B BY GROUP (1,5).
```

specifies two tests, A by GROUP and B by GROUP. A case missing for GROUP is excluded from both tests, but a case missing for A is not excluded from the test for B if it is not missing for B.

Use the MISSING subcommand to specify alternative missing-value treatments. The following keywords can be specified:

ANALYSIS *Exclude missing values on a test-by-test basis.* This is the default.

LISTWISE *Exclude missing values listwise.* Cases missing on any variable named on any subcommand are excluded from all analyses.

INCLUDE *Include user-missing values.* User-missing values are treated as if they were not missing.

The ANALYSIS and LISTWISE keywords are mutually exclusive; however, each can be specified with INCLUDE.

17.42
SAMPLE Subcommand

NPAR TESTS must store cases in memory. You may not have sufficient computer resources to store all the cases to produce the tests requested. The SAMPLE subcommand allows you to select a random sample of cases when there is not enough space to store all the cases. The SAMPLE subcommand has no additional specifications.

Because sampling would invalidate a runs test, this option is ignored when you use the RUNS subcommand.

17.43
EXERCISES

Syntax

1. The following commands contain syntax errors. Write the correct syntax.

   a. NPAR TESTS CHI-SQUARE=DAY/EXPECTED=10 9 8 7 0 9 10.

   b. NPAR TESTS K-W TUMOR BY DIET.

   c. NPAR TESTS M-W TUMOR DIET(0,1).

2. Write the NPAR TESTS command that produces the following output:

```
- - - - - MANN-WHITNEY U - WILCOXON RANK SUM W TEST
     TUMOR
  BY DIET

     MEAN RANK    CASES

       26.90        30   DIET = 0   UNSATURATED
       33.21        29   DIET = 1   SATURATED
                    --
                    59   TOTAL

                                 CORRECTED FOR TIES
        U           W             Z        2-TAILED P
      342.0       963.0        -1.4112       0.1582
```

3. You want to test the hypothesis that vitamin C helps cure the common cold. Variable MEDS (coded 1=200mg vitamin C/day, 2=placebo, and 3=no meds) indicates whether an individual took vitamin C, and variable RECOVER indicates for each individual the time it took cold symptoms to subside.

   a. What SPSS command(s) perform a Mann-Whitney test that compares the recovery times of people who took vitamin C with the recovery times of people who did not take medications?

   b. What SPSS command(s) perform a Kruskal-Wallis one-way analysis of variance on the recovery times of all three groups of people?

4. You want to determine whether secondary school experience fosters an interest in sports. You randomly ask 100 students from each of three categories (variable EDUC, coded 1=public school education, 2=private school education, 3=attended both) whether they love sports. You discover that 79 students from public schools, 74 students from private schools, and 68 students who have attended both public and private schools express a love for sports.

   a. Write an SPSS job to test the hypothesis that secondary school experience has no influence on an individual's love of sports.

   b. How would you modify the job in (a) to determine whether secondary school experience fosters a dissatisfaction with sports?

Statistical Concepts

1. For each of the nonparametric procedures below, indicate the lowest level of measurement for which the procedure is appropriate:

   a. Mann-Whitney test.

   b. Sign test.

   c. One-sample chi-square test.

   d. Rank correlation coefficient.

2. Identify the nonparametric analogs of each of the following parametric statistics or procedures.

   a. Pearson correlation coefficient.

   b. Independent-samples t-test.

   c. Analysis of variance.

   d. Paired-samples t-test.

3. State the null hypothesis tested by the following nonparametric procedures:

   a. Mann-Whitney test.

   b. Kruskal-Wallis test.

   c. Sign test.

   d. One-sample chi-square test.

4. If your data satisfy the assumptions for a one-way analysis of variance, is it reasonable to perform a Kruskal-Wallis test instead of a (parametric) one-way analysis of variance? Why or why not?

Data Analysis

Use the BANK system file for Questions 1–3.

1. a. Using the Mann-Whitney procedure, test the hypothesis that work experience has the same distribution for women and men. What do your results indicate?

   b. Repeat the above analysis, comparing nonwhites and whites rather than women and men.

2. a. Use the Kruskal-Wallis procedure to test the hypothesis that the four sex-race groups have the same age distribution. Summarize your results.

   b. What assumptions are you making? Are they satisfied for these data?

3. Compute the Spearman rank correlation coefficients for the education, sex, work experience, race, and age variables. Compute Pearson correlations for the same variables and compare the coefficients from the two procedures.

4. Data for cardiac arrests are given below. Use the WEIGHT command to enter these data and obtain a one-sample chi-square test of the hypothesis that the days of the week are equally hazardous for people with a history of heart disease. Repeat the analysis, this time examining people with *no* history of heart disease. What do the results indicate?

DAY	NO	YES
MONDAY	22	16
TUESDAY	7	10
WEDNESDAY	6	10
THURSDAY	13	16
FRIDAY	5	10
SATURDAY	4	13
SUNDAY	6	14

5. a. Redo some of your analyses from previous chapters using the appropriate nonparametric tests described in this chapter. Identify a situation in which each test is useful.

   b. Compare the results obtained from the nonparametric procedures to those obtained from the parametric tests. Do you obtain similar results?

6. Use the Western Electric data for the following exercises.

   a. Use an appropriate nonparametric procedure to test the hypothesis that smokers and nonsmokers have the same distribution of serum cholesterol.

   b. Calculate a nonparametric correlation coefficient between serum cholesterol and diastolic blood pressure. Compare this value to that obtained from the correlations procedure. Why are the values different?

   c. For the three education groups, use a nonparametric procedure to examine the relationship between educational level and number of cigarettes smoked.

Multiple Linear Regression Analysis

In this chapter:

Goals:

- To develop an equation that summarizes the relationship between a dependent variable and a set of independent variables.
- To identify the subset of independent variables that are most useful for predicting the dependent variable.
- To predict values for a dependent variable from the values of the independent variables.

Examples:

- Determine the relationship between systolic blood pressure and age, weight, height, cigarettes smoked, and level of physical activity.
- Predict a salesperson's total dollar sales for the year based on years of experience, age, sales territory, years of education, and sex.
- Predict a student's score on the Graduate Record Exam based on undergraduate GPA, IQ score, and major.

How it's done:

A linear model of the form

$$\hat{Y} = B_0 + B_1X_1 + B_2X_2 + \ldots + B_nX_n$$

where $\hat{Y}$ is the dependent variable and X_1 to X_n are the independent variables is formulated. The coefficients for the independent variables are chosen so that the sum of the squared differences between the observed and predicted values of the dependent variable based on the model is as small as possible. Various diagnostic plots and statistics are used to identify departures from the model and "unusual" points.

Data considerations:

Each case must have values for the dependent and independent variables. For all combinations of values of the independent variables, the distribution of the dependent variable must be normal with a constant variance. The independent and dependent variables should be measured on an interval scale. (Binary variables satisfy this requirement.) Nominal variables such as religion, major, or region of residence must be recoded to binary (dummy) variables.

General references:

Draper & Smith (1981)
Belsley, Kuh, & Welsch (1980)
Gunst & Mason (1980)

18 Multiple Linear Regression Analysis: Procedure REGRESSION

The 1964 Civil Rights Act prohibits discrimination in the workplace based on sex or race. Employers who violate the act by unfair hiring or advancement are liable to prosecution. Numerous lawsuits have been filed on behalf of women, blacks, and other groups on these grounds.

The courts have ruled that statistics can be used as *prima facie* evidence of discrimination. Many lawsuits depend heavily on complex statistical analyses, which attempt to demonstrate that similarly qualified individuals are not treated equally (Roberts, 1980). In this chapter, employee records for 474 individuals hired between 1969 and 1971 by a bank engaged in Equal Employment Opportunity litigation are analyzed. A mathematical model is developed that relates beginning salary and salary progression to various employee characteristics such as seniority, education, and previous work experience. One objective is to determine whether sex and race are important predictors of salary.

The technique used to build the model is linear regression analysis, one of the most versatile data analysis procedures. Regression can be used to summarize data as well as to study relations among variables.

18.1
LINEAR REGRESSION

Before examining a model that relates beginning salary to several other variables, consider the relationship between beginning salary and current (as of March, 1977) salary. For employees hired during a similar time period, beginning salary should serve as a reasonably good predictor of salary at a later date. Although superstars and underachievers might progress differently from the group as a whole, salary progression should be similar for the others. The scatterplot of beginning salary and current salary produced by the PLOT procedure and shown in Figure 18.1 supports this hypothesis.

A scatterplot may suggest what type of mathematical functions would be appropriate for summarizing the data. A variety of functions are useful in fitting models to data. Parabolas, hyperbolas, polynomials, trigonometric functions, and many more are potential candidates. For the scatterplot in Figure 18.1, current salaries tend to increase linearly with increases in beginning salary. If the plot indicates that a straight line is not a good summary measure of the relationship, you should consider other possibilities, including attempts to transform the data to achieve linearity (see Section 18.25).

Figure 18.1 Scatterplot of beginning and current salaries

```
PLOT VERTICAL=MIN(0) /HORIZONTAL=MIN(0) /VSIZE=30 /HSIZE=90
   /CUTPOINTS=EVERY(3) /SYMBOLS='.+*#@'
   /PLOT=SALNOW WITH SALBEG.
```

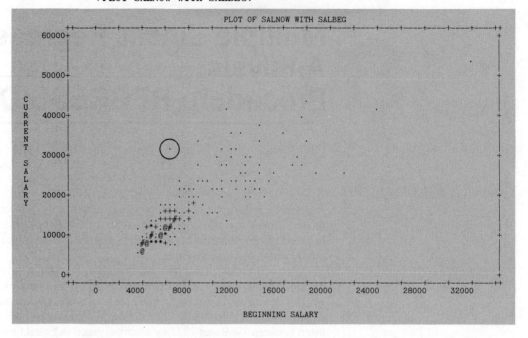

18.2
Outliers

A plot may also indicate the presence of points suspiciously different from the others. Examine such observations, termed *outliers*, carefully to see if they result from errors in gathering, coding, or entering data. The circled point in Figure 18.1 appears to be an outlier. Though neither the value of beginning salary ($6,300) nor the value of current salary ($32,000) is unique, jointly they are unusual.

The treatment of outliers can be difficult. If the point is incorrect due to coding or entry problems, you should correct it and rerun the analysis. If there is no apparent explanation for the outlier, consider interactions with other variables as a possible explanation. For example, the outlier may represent an employee who was hired as a low-paid clerical worker while pursuing an MBA degree. After graduation, a rapid rise in position was possible, making education the variable that explains the unusual salary characteristics of the employee.

18.3
Choosing a Regression Line

Since current salary tends to increase linearly with beginning salary, a straight line can be used to summarize the relationship. The equation for the line is

$$\text{predicted current salary} = B_0 + B_1(\text{beginning salary}) \qquad \textbf{Equation 18.3a}$$

The *slope* (B_1) is the dollar change in the fitted current salary for a dollar change in the beginning salary. The *intercept* (B_0) is the theoretical estimate of current salary if there were a beginning salary of 0.

However, the observed data points do not all fall on a straight line but cluster about it. Many lines can be drawn through the data points; the problem is to select among them. The method of *least squares* results in a line that minimizes the sum of squared vertical distances from the observed data points to the line. Any other line has a larger sum. Figure 18.3a shows the least-squares line superimposed on the salary scatterplot. Several vertical distances from points to the line are also shown.

Figure 18.3a   Regression line for beginning and current salaries

```
PLOT FORMAT=REGRESSION
   /VERTICAL=MIN(0) /HORIZONTAL=MIN(0) /VSIZE=30 /HSIZE=90
   /CUTPOINTS=EVERY(3) /SYMBOLS='.+*#@'
   /PLOT=SALNOW WITH SALBEG.
```

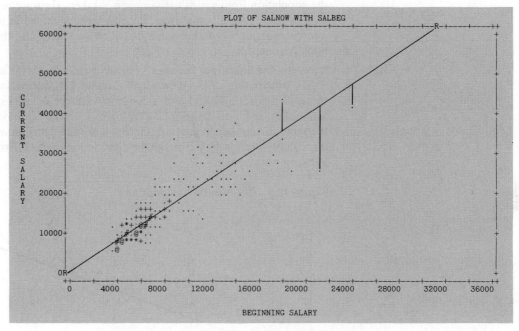

You can use the SPSS REGRESSION procedure to calculate the least-squares line. For the data in Figure 18.1, that line is

predicted current salary = 771.28 + 1.91(beginning salary)   **Equation 18.3b**

The slope and intercept values are shown in the column labeled **B** in the output shown in Figure 18.3b.

Figure 18.3b   Statistics for variables in the equation

```
REGRESSION
  /DEPENDENT=SALNOW
  /METHOD=ENTER SALBEG.
```

```
------------------ Variables in the Equation ------------------

Variable              B        SE B        Beta        T    Sig T

SALBEG         1.909450     .047410     .880117    40.276   .0000
(Constant)   771.282303  355.471941                 2.170   .0305
```

18.4
The Standardized Regression
Coefficient

The *standardized regression coefficient*, labeled **Beta** in Figure 18.3b, is defined as

$$BETA = B_1 \frac{S_X}{S_Y}$$ **Equation 18.4**

Multiplying the regression coefficient (B_1) by the ratio of the standard deviation of the independent variable (S_X) to the standard deviation of the dependent variable (S_Y) results in a dimensionless coefficient. In fact, the beta coefficient is the slope of the least-squares line when both X and Y are expressed as Z scores. The beta coefficient is further discussed in Section 18.36.

18.5
From Samples to Populations

Generally, more is sought in regression analysis than a description of observed data. You usually want to draw inferences about the relationship of the variables in the population from which the sample was taken. How are beginning and current salaries related for all employees, not just those included in the sample? To draw inferences about population values based on sample results, the following assumptions are needed:

Normality and Equality of Variance. For any fixed value of the independent variable X, the distribution of the dependent variable Y is normal, with mean $\mu_{Y/X}$ (the mean of Y for a given X) and a constant variance of σ^2 (see Figure 18.5). This assumption specifies that not all employees with the same beginning salary have the same current salary. Instead, there is a normal distribution of current salaries for each beginning salary. Though the distributions have different means, they have the same variance σ^2.

Figure 18.5   Regression assumptions

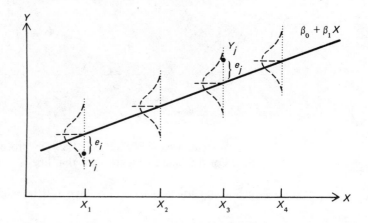

Independence. The Y's are statistically independent of each other. That is, observations are in no way influenced by other observations. For example, observations are *not* independent if they are based on repeated measurements from the same experimental unit. If three observations are taken from each of four families, the twelve observations are not independent.

Linearity. The mean values $\mu_{Y/X}$ all lie on a straight line, which is the population regression line. This line is drawn in Figure 18.5. An alternative way of stating this assumption is that the linear model is correct.

When there is a single independent variable, the model can be summarized by

$$Y_i = \beta_0 + \beta_1 X_i + e_i \qquad \text{Equation 18.5}$$

The population parameters (values) for the slope and intercept are denoted by β_1 and β_0. The term e_i, often called an error or disturbance, is the difference between the observed value of Y_i and the subpopulation mean at the point X_i. The e_i are assumed to be normally distributed, independent, random variables with a mean of 0 and variance of σ^2 (see Figure 18.5).

18.6
Estimating Population Parameters

Since β_0 and β_1 are unknown population parameters, they must be estimated from the sample. The least-squares coefficients B_0 and B_1, discussed in Section 18.3, are used to estimate the population parameters.

However, the slope and intercept estimated from a single sample typically differ from the population values and vary from sample to sample. To use these estimates for inference about the population values, the sampling distributions of the two statistics are needed. When the assumptions of linear regression are met, the sampling distributions of B_0 and B_1 are normal with means of β_0 and β_1.

The standard error of B_0 is

$$\sigma_{B_0} = \sigma \sqrt{\frac{1}{N} + \frac{\overline{X}^2}{(N-1)S_X^2}}$$

Equation 18.6a

where S_X^2 is the sample variance of the independent variable. The standard error of B_1 is

$$\sigma_{B_1} = \frac{\sigma}{\sqrt{(N-1)S_X^2}}$$

Equation 18.6b

Since the population variance of the errors, σ^2, is not known, it must also be estimated. The usual estimate of σ^2 is

$$S^2 = \frac{\sum_{i=1}^{N}(Y_i - B_0 - B_1 X_i)^2}{N-2}$$

Equation 18.6c

The positive square root of σ^2 is termed the *standard error of the estimate,* or the standard deviation of the residuals. (The reason for this name is discussed in Section 18.15.) The estimated standard errors of the slope and intercept are displayed in the third column (labeled **SE B**) in Figure 18.3b.

18.7
Testing Hypotheses

A frequently tested hypothesis is that there is no linear relationship between X and Y—that the slope of the population regression line is 0. The statistic used to test this hypothesis is

$$t = \frac{B_1}{S_{B_1}}$$

Equation 18.7a

The distribution of the statistic, when the assumptions are met and the hypothesis of no linear relationship is true, is Student's t distribution with $N-2$ degrees of freedom. The statistic for testing the hypothesis that the intercept is 0 is

$$t = \frac{B_0}{S_{B_0}}$$

Equation 18.7b

Its distribution is also Student's t with $N-2$ degrees of freedom.

These t statistics and their two-tailed observed significance levels are displayed in the last two columns of Figure 18.3b. The small observed significance level (less than 0.00005) associated with the slope for the salary data supports the hypothesis that beginning and current salary are linearly related.

18.8
Confidence Intervals

A statistic calculated from a sample provides a point estimate of the unknown parameter. A point estimate can be thought of as the single best guess for the population value. While the estimated value from the sample is typically different from the value of the unknown population parameter, the hope is that it isn't too far away. Based on the sample estimate, it is possible to calculate a range of values that, with a designated likelihood, includes the population value. Such a range is called a *confidence interval*. For example, as shown in Figure 18.8, the 95% confidence interval for β_1, the population slope, is 1.816 to 2.003.

Figure 18.8 Confidence intervals

```
REGRESSION
  /STATISTICS=CI
  /DEPENDENT=SALNOW
  /METHOD=ENTER SALBEG.
```

```
Variable        95% Confdnce Intrvl B

SALBEG          1.816290      2.002610
(Constant)     72.779206   1469.785399
```

Ninety-five percent confidence means that, if repeated samples are drawn from a population under the same conditions and 95% confidence intervals are calculated, 95% of the intervals will contain the unknown parameter β_1. Since the parameter value is unknown, it is not possible to determine whether or not a particular interval contains it.

18.9
Goodness of Fit

An important part of any statistical procedure that builds models from data is establishing how well the model actually fits. This topic encompasses the detection of possible violations of the required assumptions in the data being analyzed. Sections 18.10 through 18.16 are limited to the question of how close to the fitted line the observed points fall. Subsequent sections discuss other assumptions and tests for their violation.

18.10
The R^2 Coefficient

A commonly used measure of the goodness of fit of a linear model is R^2, sometimes called the *coefficient of determination*. It can be thought of in a variety of ways. Besides being the square of the correlation coefficient between variables X and Y, it is the square of the correlation coefficient between Y, the observed value of the dependent variable, and $\hat{Y}$, the predicted value of Y from the fitted line. If for each employee you compute (based on the coefficients in the output in Figure 18.3b) the predicted salary

predicted current salary = 771.28 + 1.91(beginning salary)   **Equation 18.10a**

and then calculate the square of the Pearson correlation coefficient between predicted current salary and observed current salary, R^2 is obtained. If all the observations fall on the regression line, R^2 is 1. If there is no linear relationship between the dependent and independent variables, R^2 is 0.

Note that R^2 is a measure of the goodness of fit of a particular model and that an R^2 of 0 does not necessarily mean that there is no association between the variables. Instead, it indicates that there is no *linear relationship*.

In the output in Figure 18.10, R^2 is labeled **R Square.** Its square root is called **Multiple R.** The sample R^2 tends to be an optimistic estimate of how well the model fits the population. The model usually does not fit the population as well as it fits the sample from which it is derived. The statistic *adjusted R^2* attempts to correct R^2 to more closely reflect the goodness of fit of the model in the population.

Adjusted R^2 is given by

$$R_a{}^2 = R^2 - \frac{p(1 - R^2)}{N - p - 1}$$

Equation 18.10b

where p is the number of independent variables in the equation (1 in the salary example).

Figure 18.10   Summary statistics for the equation

```
REGRESSION
  /DEPENDENT=SALNOW
  /METHOD=ENTER SALBEG.
```

```
Multiple R              .88012
R Square                .77461
Adjusted R Square       .77413
Standard Error     3246.14226
```

18.11
Analysis of Variance

To test the hypothesis of no linear relationship between X and Y, several equivalent statistics can be computed. When there is a single independent variable, the hypothesis that the population R^2 is 0 is identical to the hypothesis that the population slope is 0. The test for $R^2_{pop}=0$ is usually obtained from the *analysis of variance* (ANOVA) table (see Figure 18.11a).

Figure 18.11a   Analysis of variance table

```
REGRESSION
  /DEPENDENT=SALNOW
  /METHOD=ENTER SALBEG.
```

```
Analysis of Variance
                    DF     Sum of Squares        Mean Square
Regression           1  17092967800.01931  17092967800.0193
Residual           472   4973671469.79484     10537439.55465

F =    1622.11776      Signif F =  .0000
```

The total observed variability in the dependent variable is subdivided into two components—that which is attributable to the regression (labeled **Regression**) and that which is not (labeled **Residual**). Consider Figure 18.11b. For a particular point, the distance from Y_i to $\overline{Y}$ (the mean of the Y's) can be subdivided into two parts:

$$Y_i - \overline{Y} = (Y_i - \hat{Y}_i) + (\hat{Y}_i - \overline{Y})$$

Equation 18.11a

Figure 18.11b   Components of variability

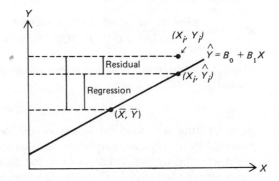

The distance from Y_i, the observed value, to $\hat{Y}_i$, the value predicted by the regression line, or $Y_i - \hat{Y}_i$, is 0 if the regression line passes through the point. It is called the *residual from the regression*. The second component $(\hat{Y}_i - \bar{Y})$ is the distance from the regression line to the mean of the Y's. This distance is explained by the regression in that it represents the improvement in the estimate of the dependent variable achieved by the regression. Without the regression, the mean of the dependent variable $(\bar{Y})$ is used as the estimate. It can be shown that

$$\sum_{i=1}^{N} (Y_i - \bar{Y})^2 = \sum_{i=1}^{N} (Y_i - \hat{Y}_i)^2 + \sum_{i=1}^{N} (\hat{Y}_i - \bar{Y})^2 \qquad \text{Equation 18.11b}$$

The first quantity following the equals sign is called the *residual sum of squares* and the second quantity is the *regression sum of squares*. The sum of these is called the *total sum of squares*.

The analysis of variance table displays these two sums of squares under the heading **Sum of Squares** (Figure 18.11a). The **Mean Square** for each entry is the sum of squares divided by the degrees of freedom (**DF**). If the regression assumptions are met, the ratio of the mean square regression to the mean square residual is distributed as an F statistic with p and $N-p-1$ degrees of freedom. F serves to test how well the regression model fits the data. If the probability associated with the F statistic is small, the hypothesis that $R^2_{pop}=0$ is rejected. For this example, the F statistic is

$$F = \frac{\text{MEAN SQUARE REGRESSION}}{\text{MEAN SQUARE RESIDUAL}} = 1622 \qquad \text{Equation 18.11c}$$

The observed significance level (SIGNIF F) is less than 0.00005.

The square root of the F value (1622) is 40.28, which is the value of the t statistic for the slope in Figure 18.3b. The square of a t value with k degrees of freedom is an F value with 1 and k degrees of freedom. Therefore, either t or F values can be computed to test that $\beta_i=0$.

Another useful summary statistic is the standard error of the estimate, S, which can also be calculated as the square root of the residual mean square (Section 18.15).

18.12
Another Interpretation of R^2

Partitioning the sum of squares of the dependent variable allows another interpretation of R^2. It is the proportion of the variation in the dependent variable explained by the model.

$$R^2 = 1 - \frac{\text{RESIDUAL SUM OF SQUARES}}{\text{TOTAL SUM OF SQUARES}} = 0.775 \qquad \text{Equation 18.12a}$$

Similarly, adjusted R^2 is

$$R^2_a = 1 - \frac{\text{RESIDUAL SUM OF SQUARES}/(N-p-1)}{\text{TOTAL SUM OF SQUARES}/(N-1)} \qquad \text{Equation 18.12b}$$

where p is the number of independent variables in the equation (1 in the salary example).

18.13
Predicted Values and Their Standard Errors

By comparing the observed values of the dependent variable to the values predicted by the regression equation, you can learn a good deal about how well a model and the various assumptions fit the data (see the discussion of residuals beginning with Section 18.17). Predicted values are also of interest when the results are used to predict new data. You may wish to predict the mean Y for all cases with a given value of X, denoted X_0, or to predict the value of Y for a single case. For example, you can predict either the mean salary for all employees with a beginning salary of \$10,000 or the salary for a particular employee with a beginning salary of \$10,000. In both situations, the predicted value

$$\hat{Y}_0 = B_0 + B_1 X_0 = 771 + 1.91 \times 10,000 = 19,871 \qquad \textbf{Equation 18.13}$$

is the same. What differs is the standard error.

18.14
Predicting Mean Response

The estimated standard error for the predicted mean Y at X_0 is

$$S_{\hat{Y}} = S \sqrt{\frac{1}{N} + \frac{(X_0 - \overline{X})^2}{(N-1)S_X{}^2}} \qquad \textbf{Equation 18.14a}$$

The equation for the standard error shows that the smallest value occurs when X_0 is equal to $\overline{X}$, the mean of X. The larger the distance from the mean, the greater the standard error. Thus, the mean of Y for a given X is better estimated for central values of the observed X's than for outlying values. Figure 18.14a is a plot from the PLOT procedure of the standard errors of predicted mean salaries for different values of beginning salary.

Figure 18.14a   Standard errors for predicted mean responses

```
REGRESSION
   /DEPENDENT=SALNOW
   /METHOD=ENTER SALBEG
   /SAVE=SEPRED(SE).
PLOT VERTICAL=MIN(0) /VSIZE=25
   /CUTPOINTS=EVERY(20) /SYMBOLS='*'
   /PLOT=SE WITH SALBEG.
```

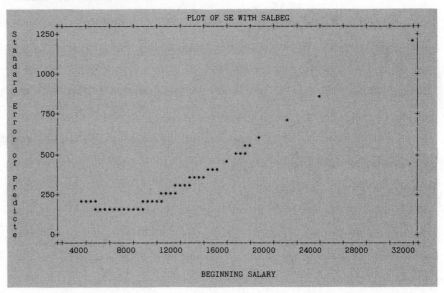

Prediction intervals for the mean predicted salary are calculated in the standard way. The 95% confidence interval at X_0 is

$$\hat{Y} \pm t_{\left(1 - \frac{\alpha}{2}, N-2\right)} S_{\hat{Y}} \qquad \textbf{Equation 18.14b}$$

Figure 18.14b shows a typical 95% confidence band for predicted mean responses. It is narrowest at the mean of X and increases as the distance from the mean $(X_0 - \overline{X})$ increases.

Figure 18.14b   95% confidence band for mean prediction

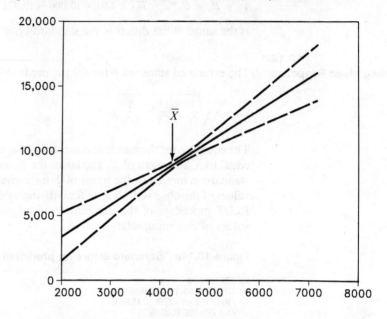

18.15
Predicting a New Value

Although the predicted value for a single new observation at X_0 is the same as the predicted value for the mean at X_0, the standard error is not. The two sources of error when predicting an individual observation are illustrated in Figure 18.15. They are

1   The individual value may differ from the population mean of Y for X_0.
2   The estimate of the population mean at X_0 may differ from the population mean.

Figure 18.15   Sources of error in predicting individual observations

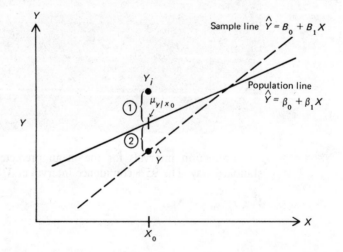

When estimating the mean response, only the second error component is considered. The variance of the individual prediction is the variance of the mean prediction plus the variance of Y_i for a given X. This can be written as

$$S^2_{ind\hat{Y}} = S^2_{\hat{Y}} + S^2 = S^2\left(1 + \frac{1}{N} + \frac{(X_0 - \overline{X})^2}{(N-1)S_X{}^2}\right)$$

Equation 18.15a

Prediction intervals for the new observation are obtained by substituting S_{indY} for S_Y in the equation for the confidence intervals for the mean given in Section 18.14. If the sample size is large, the terms $1/N$ and

$$\frac{(X_0 - \overline{X})^2}{(N-1)S_X{}^2}$$

Equation 18.15b

are negligible. In that case, the standard error is simply S, which explains the name *standard error of the estimate* for S (see Section 18.6).

18.16
Reading the Casewise Plot

Figure 18.16 shows the output from the beginning and end of a plot of the salary data. The sequence number of the case and an optional labeling variable (SEXRACE) are listed first, followed by the plot of standardized residuals, the observed (SALNOW), predicted (PRED), and residual (RESID) values, and, finally, the standard error of the mean prediction (SEPRED). In the REGRESSION procedure you can generate predicted values and confidence intervals for the mean responses (MCIN) and for individual responses (ICIN), and you can display these values for all cases or for a subset of cases along with a casewise plot.

Figure 18.16   Casewise plot with predicted values and standard errors

```
REGRESSION
  /DEPENDENT=SALNOW
  /METHOD=ENTER SALBEG
  /RESIDUALS=ID(SEXRACE)
  /CASEWISE=ALL DEPENDENT PRED RESID SEPRED.
```

```
Casewise Plot of Standardized Residual
*: Selected   M: Missing
              -3.0        0.0        3.0
Case #  SEXRACE  0:........:........:0   SALNOW      *PRED       *RESID      *SEPRED
     1      1       .        *  .      .    16080    16810.6600   -730.6600   167.1489
     2      1       .    *    .        .    41400    46598.0758  -5198.0758   828.6655
     3      1       .        . *       .    21960    20247.6695   1712.3305   219.3531
     4      1       .        . *       .    19200    17383.4949   1816.5051   174.0406
     5      1       .    *   .         .    28350    33995.7076  -5645.7076   523.9021
     6      1       .        .*        .    27250    25586.4910   1663.5090   329.1520
     7      1       .        . *       .    16080    13946.4854   2133.5146   149.1662
     8      1       .        .  *      .    14100    11082.3108   3017.6892   163.3307
     9      1       .        . *       .    12420    10394.9089   2025.0911   171.0096
    10      1       .       *.         .    12300    12800.8156   -500.8156   151.0211
    11      1       .        . *       .    15720    12800.8156   2919.1844   151.0211
    12      1       .     *  .         .     8880    12227.9807  -3347.9807   153.9241
    ...
    ...
    ...
   470      4       .        *         .     9420     9592.9401   -172.9401   181.5927
   471      4       .        .*        .     9780     9134.6721    645.3279   188.3196
   472      4       .       *.         .     7680     9249.2391  -1569.2391   186.5956
   473      4       .      * .         .     7380     8561.8372  -1181.8372   197.3294
   474      4       .     *  .         .     8340    10738.6099  -2398.6099   166.9964
Case #  SEXRACE  0:........:........:0   SALNOW      *PRED       *RESID      *SEPRED
              -3.0        0.0        3.0
```

18.17
Searching for Violations of Assumptions

You usually don't know in advance whether a model such as linear regression is appropriate. Therefore, it is necessary to conduct a search focused on residuals to look for evidence that the necessary assumptions are violated.

18.18
Residuals   In model building, a *residual* is what is left after the model is fit. It is the difference between an observed value and the value predicted by the model.

$$E_i = Y_i - B_0 - B_1X_i = Y_i - \hat{Y}_i$$ **Equation 18.18**

In regression analysis, the true errors e_i are assumed to be independent normal values with a mean of 0 and a constant variance of σ^2. If the model is appropriate for the data, the observed residuals E_i, which are estimates of the true errors e_i, should have similar characteristics.

If the intercept term is included in the equation, the mean of the residuals is always 0, so it provides no information about the true mean of the errors. Since the sum of the residuals is constrained to be 0, they are *not* strictly independent. However, if the number of residuals is large when compared to the number of independent variables, the dependency among the residuals can be ignored for practical purposes.

The relative magnitudes of residuals are easier to judge when they are divided by estimates of their standard deviations. The resulting standardized residuals are expressed in standard deviation units above or below the mean. For example, the fact that a particular residual is -5198.1 provides little information. If you know that its standardized form is -3.1, you know not only that the observed value is less than the predicted value but also that the residual is larger than most in absolute value.

Residuals are sometimes adjusted in one of two ways. The *standardized residual* for case i is the residual divided by the sample standard deviation of the residuals. Standardized residuals have a mean of 0 and a standard deviation of 1. The *Studentized residual* is the residual divided by an estimate of its standard deviation that varies from point to point, depending on the distance of X_i from the mean of X. Usually standardized and Studentized residuals are close in value, but not always. The Studentized residual reflects more precisely differences in the true error variances from point to point.

18.19
Linearity   For the bivariate situation, a scatterplot is a good means for judging how well a straight line fits the data. Another convenient method is to plot the residuals against the predicted values. If the assumptions of linearity and homogeneity of variance are met, there should be no relationship between the predicted and residual values. You should be suspicious of any observable pattern.

For example, fitting a least-squares line to the data in the two left-hand plots in Figure 18.19a yields the residual plots shown on the right. The two residual plots show patterns since straight lines do not fit the data well. Systematic patterns between the predicted values and the residuals suggest possible violations of the linearity assumption. If the assumption was met, the residuals would be randomly distributed in a band about the horizontal straight line through 0, as shown in Figure 18.19b.

Figure 18.19a   Standardized residuals scatterplots

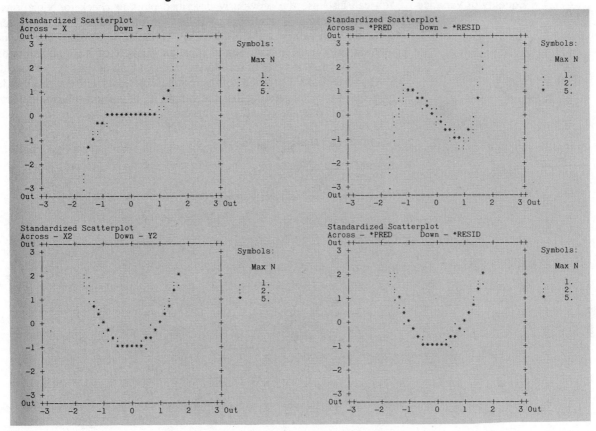

Figure 18.19b   Randomly distributed residuals

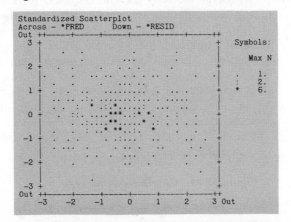

Residuals can also be plotted against individual independent variables. Again, if the assumptions are met, you should see a horizontal band of residuals. Consider plotting the residuals against independent variables not in the equation as well. If the residuals are not randomly distributed, you may want to include the variable in the equation for a multiple regression model (see Sections 18.30 through 18.49).

18.20
Equality of Variance

You can also use the previously described plots to check for violations of the equality of variance assumption. If the spread of the residuals increases or decreases with values of the independent variables or with predicted values, you should question the assumption of constant variance of Y for all values of X.

Figure 18.20 is a plot of the Studentized residuals against the predicted values for the salary data. The spread of the residuals increases with the magnitude of the predicted values, suggesting that the variability of current salaries increases with salary level. Thus, the equality of variance assumption appears to be violated.

Figure 18.20   Unequal variance

```
REGRESSION
  /DEPENDENT=SALNOW
  /METHOD=ENTER SALBEG
  /SCATTERPLOT=(*SRESID,*PRED).
```

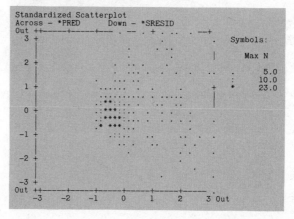

18.21
Independence of Error

Whenever the data are collected and recorded sequentially, you should plot residuals against the sequence variable. Even if time is not considered a variable in the model, it could influence the residuals. For example, suppose you are studying survival time after surgery as a function of complexity of surgery, amount of blood transfused, dosage of medication, and so forth. In addition to these variables, it is also possible that the surgeon's skill increased with each operation and that a patient's survival time is influenced by the number of prior patients treated. The plot of residuals corresponding to the order in which patients received surgery shows a shorter survival time for earlier patients than for later patients (see Figure 18.21). If sequence and the residual are independent, you should not see a discernable pattern.

Figure 18.21   Casewise serial plot

```
Casewise Plot of Studentized Residual

            -3.0      0.0      3.0      LIFE      *PRED     *RESID    *SRESID
  Case #  TIME  0:........:........:0
      1   78012    .  *      .        .      15.0000    19.5624    -4.5624    -2.2598
      2   78055    .  *      .        .      13.5000    17.8974    -4.3974    -2.1856
      3   78122    .   *     .        .       9.9000    13.8390    -3.9390    -1.9871
      4   78134    .    *    .        .      15.5000    18.5218    -3.0218    -1.4997
      5   78233    .    *    .        .      35.0000    38.2933    -3.2933    -1.7466
      6   78298    .    *    .        .      14.7000    16.6487    -1.9487     -.9720
      7   78344    .     *   .        .      34.8000    36.0040    -1.2040     -.6258
      8   79002    .      * . .       .      20.8000    20.8111     -.0111     -.0055
      9   79008    .       . *        .      15.9000    14.8796     1.0204      .5123
     10   79039    .       .*         .      22.0000    21.6436      .3564      .1762
     11   79101    .       . *        .      13.7000    11.7578     1.9422      .9910
     12   79129    .       .  *       .      14.2000    11.4456     2.7544     1.4082
     13   79178    .       .  *       .      33.2000    30.3847     2.8153     1.4144
     14   79188    .       .   *      .      26.2000    22.4761     3.7239     1.8401
     15   79189    .       .    *     .      37.4000    33.2984     4.1016     2.0920
  ...
```

The *Durbin-Watson* statistic, a test for sequential correlation of adjacent error terms, is defined as

$$D = \frac{\sum_{t=2}^{N} (E_t - E_{t-1})^2}{\sum_{t=1}^{N} E_t^2}$$

Equation 18.21

The differences between successive residuals tend to be small when error terms are positively correlated and large when error terms are negatively correlated. Thus, small values of D indicate positive correlation and large values of D indicate negative correlation. Consult tables of the D statistic for bounds upon which significance tests can be based (Neter & Wasserman, 1985).

18.22
Normality

The distribution of residuals may not appear to be normal for reasons other than actual nonnormality: misspecification of the model, nonconstant variance, a small number of residuals actually available for analysis, etc. Therefore, you should pursue several lines of investigation. One of the simplest is to construct a histogram of the residuals such as the one shown in Figure 18.22a for the salary data.

Figure 18.22a   Histogram of Studentized residuals

```
REGRESSION
  /DEPENDENT=SALNOW
  /METHOD=ENTER SALBEG
  /RESIDUALS=HISTOGRAM(SRESID) SIZE(SMALL).
```

```
Histogram - Studentized Residual

    N   Exp N        (* = 2 Cases,   . : = Normal Curve)
    7    .37    Out  ****
    2    .73   3.00  *
    4   1.85   2.67  :*
    2   4.23   2.33  *.
    6   8.65   2.00  ***.
   12  15.85   1.67  ******  .
    7  26.01   1.33  ****        .
   18  38.23   1.00  ********       .
   35  50.34    .67  *****************       .
   63  59.38    .33  *********************************  **
   87  62.74    .00  ********************************:*************
  114  59.38   -.33  *********************************:***********************
   64  50.34   -.67  **************************:*******
   32  38.23  -1.00  ****************  .
    9  26.01  -1.33  *****        .
    6  15.85  -1.67  ***    .
    1   8.65  -2.00  *  .
    1   4.23  -2.33  *.
    2   1.85  -2.67  :
    0    .73  -3.00
    2    .37    Out  *
```

The REGRESSION histogram contains a tally of the observed number of residuals (labeled **N**) in each interval and the number expected in a normal distribution with the same mean and variance as the residuals (**Exp N**). The first and last intervals (**Out**) contain residuals more than 3.16 standard deviations from the mean. Such residuals deserve examination. A histogram of expected N's is superimposed on that of the observed N's. Expected frequencies are indicated by a period. When observed and expected frequencies overlap, a colon is displayed. However, it is unreasonable to expect the observed residuals to be exactly normal—some deviation is expected because of sampling variation. Even if the errors are normally distributed in the population, sample residuals are only approximately normal.

In the histogram in Figure 18.22a, the distribution does not seem normal since there is an exaggerated clustering of residuals toward the center and a straggling tail toward large positive values. Thus, the normality assumption may be violated.

Another way to compare the observed distribution of residuals to that expected under the assumption of normality is to plot the two cumulative distributions against each other for a series of points. If the two distributions are identical, a straight line results. By observing how points scatter about the expected straight line, you can compare the two distributions.

Figure 18.22b is a cumulative probability plot of the salary residuals. Initially, the observed residuals are below the straight line, since there is a smaller number of large negative residuals than expected. Once the greatest concentration of residuals is reached, the observed points are above the line, since the observed cumulative proportion exceeds the expected. Tests for normality are available in the EXAMINE procedure (see Chapter 9).

Figure 18.22b   A normal probability (P-P) plot

```
REGRESSION
  /DEPENDENT=SALNOW
  /METHOD=ENTER SALBEG
  /RESIDUALS=HISTOGRAM(SRESID) NORMPROB.
```

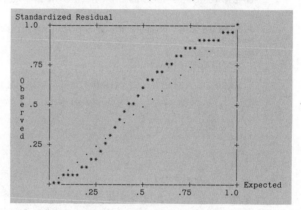

18.23
Locating Outliers

You can spot outliers readily on residual plots since they are cases with very large positive or negative residuals. In the histogram, cases with values greater than $+3.16$ or less than -3.16 appear in the interval labeled **Out**. In the scatterplots, they appear on the borders of the plot, again labeled **Out**. Since you usually want more information about outliers, you can use the casewise plotting facility to display identification numbers and a variety of other statistics for cases having residuals beyond a specified cutoff point.

Figure 18.23 lists information for the nine cases with Studentized residuals greater than 3 in absolute value. Only two of these nine employees have current salaries less than those predicted by the model (Cases 67 and 122), while the others have larger salaries. The second column contains identifier information that indicates that all outliers are white males (SEXRACE=1). They all have large salaries, an average of $33,294, while the average for the sample is only $13,767. Thus, there is some evidence that the model may not fit well for the highly paid cases.

Figure 18.23 Casewise plot of residuals outliers

```
REGRESSION
  /DEPENDENT=SALNOW
  /METHOD=ENTER SALBEG
  /CASEWISE=PLOT(SRESID)
  /RESIDUALS=ID(SEXRACE).
```

```
Casewise Plot of Studentized Residual

Outliers = 3.     *: Selected   M: Missing

                  -6.     -3.  3.     6.
  Case #  SEXRACE  0:.......:  :.......:0    SALNOW      *PRED       *RESID
     24      1     .        ..*     .        28000    17383.4949   10616.5051
     60      1     .        ..      *.       32000    12800.8156   19199.1844
     67      1     .     *  ..      .        26400    37043.1894  -10643.1894
    114      1     .        ..  *   .        38800    27511.2163   11288.7837
    122      1     .  *     ..      .        26700    40869.7266  -14169.7266
    123      1     .        ..  *   .        36250    24639.4039   11610.5961
    129      1     .        ..    * .        33500    17383.4949   16116.5051
    149      1     .        ..      *        41500    21782.8671   19717.1329
    177      1     .        ..  *   .        36500    23295.1513   13204.8487

        9 Outliers found.
```

18.24
When Assumptions Appear To Be Violated

When evidence of violation of assumptions appears, you can pursue one of two strategies. You can either formulate an alternative model, such as weighted least squares, or you can transform the variables so that the current model will be more adequate. For example, taking logs, square roots, or reciprocals can stabilize the variance, achieve normality, or linearize a relationship.

18.25
Coaxing a Nonlinear Relationship to Linearity

To try to achieve linearity, you can transform either the dependent or independent variables, or both. If you alter the scale of independent variables, linearity can be achieved without any effect on the distribution of the dependent variable. Thus, if the dependent variable is normally distributed with constant variance for each value of X, it remains so.

When you transform the dependent variable, its distribution is changed. This new distribution must then satisfy the assumptions of the analysis. For example, if logs of the values of the dependent variable are taken, log Y—not the original Y—must be normally distributed with constant variance.

The choice of transformations depends on several considerations. If the form of the true model governing the relationship is known, it should dictate the choice. For instance, if it is known that $\hat{Y}=AC^X$ is an adequate model, taking logs of both sides of the equation results in

Equation 18.25

$$log\,\hat{Y}_i = (log\,A) + (log\,C)\,X_i$$
$$\quad\quad\quad [B_0] \quad\quad\quad [B_1]$$

Thus log Y is linearly related to X.

Figure 18.25 A transformed relationship

```
REGRESSION
  /DEPENDENT=Y /ENTER=X
  /SCATTERPLOT=(Y,X)
  /DEPENDENT=LOGY /ENTER=X
  /SCATTERPLOT=(LOGY,X).
```

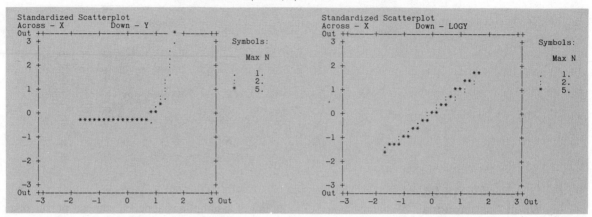

If the true model is not known, you should choose the transformation by examining the plotted data. Frequently, a relationship appears nearly linear for part of the data but is curved for the rest. The first plot in Figure 18.25 is an example. Taking the log of the dependent variable results in the second plot—an improved linear fit.

Other transformations that may diminish curvature are the square root of Y and $-1/Y$. The choice depends, to a certain extent, on the severity of the problem.

18.26
Coping with Skewness

When the distribution of residuals is positively skewed, the log transformation of the dependent variable is often helpful. For negatively skewed distributions, the square transformation is common. It should be noted that the F tests used in regression hypothesis testing are usually quite insensitive to moderate departures from normality.

18.27
Stabilizing the Variance

If the variance of the residuals is not constant, you can try a variety of remedial measures:

• When the variance is proportional to the mean of Y for a given X, use the square root of Y if all Y_i are positive.

• When the standard deviation is proportional to the mean, try the logarithmic transformation.

• When the standard deviation is proportional to the square of the mean, use the reciprocal of Y.

• When Y is a proportion or rate, the arc sine transformation may stabilize the variance.

18.28
Transforming the Salary Data

The assumptions of constant variance and normality appear to be violated with the salary data (see Figures 18.20 and 18.22a). A regression equation using logs of beginning and current salary was developed to obtain a better fit to the assumptions. Figure 18.28a is a scatterplot of Studentized residuals against predicted values when logs of both variables are used in the regression equation.

Figure 18.28a   Scatterplot of transformed salary data

```
COMPUTE LOGBEG=LG10(SALBEG).
COMPUTE LOGNOW=LG10(SALNOW).
REGRESSION
  /DEPENDENT=LOGNOW
  /METHOD=ENTER LOGBEG
  /SCATTERPLOT=(*SRESID,*PRED).
```

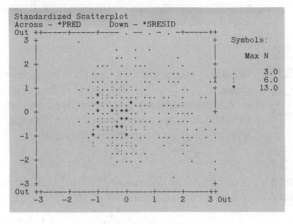

Compare Figures 18.20 and 18.28a and note the improvement in the behavior of the residuals. The spread no longer increases with increasing salary level. Also compare Figures 18.22a and 18.28b and note that the distribution in Figure 18.28b is nearly normal.

Figure 18.28b   Histogram of transformed salary data

```
COMPUTE LOGBEG=LG10(SALBEG).
COMPUTE LOGNOW=LG10(SALNOW).
REGRESSION
  /DEPENDENT=LOGNOW
  /METHOD=ENTER LOGBEG
  /RESIDUALS=HISTOGRAM(SRESID) SIZE(SMALL).
```

```
Histogram - Studentized Residual

  N  Exp N      (* = 1 Cases,    . : = Normal Curve)
  3   .37   Out ***
  1   .73  3.00 :
  3  1.85  2.67 *:*
  4  4.23  2.33 ***:
 10  8.65  2.00 ********:*
 14 15.85  1.67 ************* .
 21 26.01  1.33 ******************** .
 31 38.23  1.00 ***************************** .
 48 50.34   .67 *************************************************** .
 55 59.38   .33 ******************************************************* .
 63 62.74   .00 ****************************************************************:.
 64 59.38  -.33 *****************************************************************:*****
 62 50.34  -.67 *************************************************:************
 44 38.23 -1.00 **************************************:******
 28 26.01 -1.33 ************************:**
 14 15.85 -1.67 ************* .
  7  8.65 -2.00 ******* .
  1  4.23 -2.33 * .
  1  1.85 -2.67 *.
  0   .73 -3.00 .
  0   .37   Out
```

For the transformed data, the multiple R increases slightly to 0.8864, and the outlier plot contains only four cases (compare with Figures 18.10 and 18.23). Thus, the transformation appears to have resulted in a better model.

18.29
A Final Comment on Assumptions

Rarely are assumptions not violated one way or another in regression analysis and other statistical procedures. However, this is not a justification for ignoring the assumptions. Cranking out regressions with little thought to possible departures from the necessary assumptions can lead to problems in interpreting and applying results. Significance levels, confidence intervals, and other results are sensitive to certain types of violations and cannot be interpreted in the usual fashion if serious departures exist.

By carefully examining residuals and, if need be, using transformations or other methods of analysis, you are in a much better position to pursue analyses that solve the problems you are investigating. Even if everything isn't perfect, you can at least knowledgeably gauge the possible extent of difficulties.

18.30
MULTIPLE REGRESSION MODELS

Beginning salary seems to be a good predictor of current salary, given the evidence shown above. Nearly 80% ($R^2 = 0.77$ from Figure 18.10) of the observed variability in current salaries can be explained by beginning salary levels. But how do variables such as education level, years of experience, race, and sex affect the salary level at which one enters the company?

18.31
Predictors of Beginning Salary

Multiple linear regression extends bivariate regression by incorporating multiple independent variables. The model can be expressed as:

$$Y_i = \beta_0 + \beta_1 X_{1i} + \beta_2 X_{2i} + \ldots + \beta_p X_{pi} + e_i \qquad \text{Equation 18.31}$$

The notation X_{pi} indicates the value of the pth independent variable for case i. Again, the β terms are unknown parameters and the e_i terms are independent random variables that are normally distributed with mean 0 and constant variance σ^2. The model assumes that there is a normal distribution of the dependent variable for every combination of the values of the independent variables in the model. For example, if child's height is the dependent variable and age and maternal height are the independent variables, it is assumed that for every combination of age and maternal height there is a normal distribution of children's heights and, though the means of these distributions may differ, all have the same variance.

18.32
The Correlation Matrix

One of the first steps in calculating an equation with several independent variables is to calculate a correlation matrix for all variables, as shown in Figure 18.32. The variables are the log of beginning salary, years of education, sex, years of work experience, race, and age in years. Variables sex and race are represented by *indicator variables,* that is, variables coded as 0 or 1. SEX is coded 1 for female and 0 for male, and MINORITY is coded 1 for nonwhite and 0 for white.

Figure 18.32   The correlation matrix

```
COMPUTE LOGBEG=LG10(SALBEG).
REGRESSION
  /DESCRIPTIVES=CORR
  /VARIABLES=LOGBEG,EDLEVEL,SEX,WORK,MINORITY,AGE
  /DEPENDENT=LOGBEG
  /METHOD=ENTER EDLEVEL TO AGE.
```

	LOGBEG	EDLEVEL	SEX	WORK	MINORITY	AGE
LOGBEG	1.000	.686	-.548	.040	-.173	-.048
EDLEVEL	.686	1.000	-.356	-.252	-.133	-.281
SEX	-.548	-.356	1.000	-.165	-.076	.052
WORK	.040	-.252	-.165	1.000	.145	.804
MINORITY	-.173	-.133	-.076	.145	1.000	.111
AGE	-.048	-.281	.052	.804	.111	1.000

The matrix shows the correlations between the dependent variable (LOGBEG) and each independent variable, as well as the correlations between the independent variables. Particularly note any large intercorrelations between the independent variables, since such correlations can substantially affect the results of multiple regression analysis.

18.33
Correlation Matrices and Missing Data

For a variety of reasons, data files frequently contain incomplete observations. Respondents in surveys scrawl illegible responses or refuse to answer certain questions. Laboratory animals die before experiments are completed. Patients fail to keep scheduled clinic appointments. Thus, before computing the correlation matrix, you must usually decide what to do with cases that have missing values for some of the variables.

Before even considering possible strategies, you should determine whether there is evidence that the missing-value pattern is not random. That is, are there reasons to believe that missing values for a variable are related to the values of that variable or other variables? For example, people with low incomes may be less willing to report their financial status than more affluent people. This may be even more pronounced for people who are poor but highly educated.

One simple method of exploring such possibilities is to subdivide the data into two groups—those observations with missing data on a variable and those with complete data—and examine the distributions of the other variables in the file across these two groups. The SPSS procedures CROSSTABS and T-TEST are particularly useful for this. For a discussion of more sophisticated methods for detecting nonrandomness, see Frane (1976).

If it appears that the data are not missing randomly, use great caution in attempting to analyze the data. It may be that no satisfactory analysis is possible, especially if there are only a few cases.

If you are satisfied that the missing data are random, several strategies are available. First, if the same few variables are missing for most cases, consider excluding those variables from the analysis. Since this luxury is not usually available, you can alternatively keep all variables but eliminate the cases with missing values on any of them. This is termed *listwise* missing-value treatment since a case is eliminated if it has a missing value on any variable in the list.

If many cases have missing data for some variables, listwise missing-value treatment may eliminate too many cases and leave you with a very small sample. One common technique is to calculate the correlation coefficient between a pair of variables based on all cases with complete information for the two variables, regardless of whether the cases have missing data on any other variable. For example, if a case has values only for variables 1, 3, and 5, it is used only in computations involving variable pairs 1 and 3, 1 and 5, and 3 and 5. This is *pairwise* missing-value treatment.

Several problems can arise with pairwise matrices, one of which is inconsistency. There are some relationships between coefficients that are impossible but may occur when different cases are used to estimate different coefficients. For example, if age and weight and age and height have a high positive correlation, it is impossible in the same sample for height and weight to have a high negative correlation. However, if the same cases are not used to estimate all three coefficients, such an anomaly can occur.

Another problem with pairwise matrices is that no single sample size can be obtained since each coefficient may be based on a different number of cases. In addition, significance levels obtained from analyses based on pairwise matrices must be viewed with caution, since little is known about hypothesis testing in such situations.

Missing-value problems should not be treated lightly. You should always select a missing-value treatment based on careful examination of the data and not leave the choices up to system defaults. In this example, complete information is available for all cases, so missing values are not a problem.

18.34
Partial Regression
Coefficients

The summary output when all independent variables are included in the multiple regression equation is shown in Figure 18.34a. The *F* test associated with the analysis of variance table is a test of the null hypothesis that

$$\beta_1 = \beta_2 = \beta_3 = \beta_4 = \beta_5 = 0 \qquad \text{Equation 18.34a}$$

In other words, it is a test of whether there is a linear relationship between the dependent variable and the entire set of independent variables.

Figure 18.34a   Statistics for the equation and analysis of variance table

```
COMPUTE LOGBEG=LG10(SALBEG).
REGRESSION VARIABLES=LOGBEG EDLEVEL SEX WORK MINORITY AGE
    /DEPENDENT=LOGBEG
    /METHOD=ENTER EDLEVEL TO AGE.
```

Multiple R	.78420	Analysis of Variance			
R Square	.61498		DF	Sum of Squares	Mean Square
Adjusted R Square	.61086	Regression	5	6.83039	1.36608
Standard Error	.09559	Residual	468	4.27638	.00914
		F = 149.50125	Signif F = .0000		

The statistics for the independent variables in Figure 18.34b are parallel to those obtained in regression with a single independent variable (see Figure 18.3b). In multiple regression, the coefficients labeled **B** are called *partial regression coefficients* since the coefficient for a particular variable is adjusted for other independent variables in the equation. The equation that relates the predicted log of beginning salary to the independent variables is

$$\begin{aligned}
\text{LOGBEG} = {} & 3.3853 + 0.00102(\text{AGE}) - 0.10358(\text{SEX}) \qquad \text{Equation 18.34b} \\
& - 0.05237(\text{MINORITY}) + 0.03144(\text{EDLEVEL}) \\
& + 0.00161(\text{WORK})
\end{aligned}$$

Since the dependent variable is in log units, the coefficients can be approximately interpreted in percentage terms. For example, the coefficient of -0.104 for the SEX variable when females are coded as 1 indicates that female salaries are estimated to be about 10% less than male salaries, after statistical adjustment for age, education, work history, and minority status.

Figure 18.34b   Statistics for variables in the equation

```
COMPUTE LOGBEG=LG10(SALBEG).
REGRESSION VARIABLES=LOGBEG EDLEVEL SEX WORK MINORITY AGE
    /DEPENDENT=LOGBEG
    /METHOD=ENTER EDLEVEL TO AGE.
```

		------ Variables in the Equation ------			
Variable	B	SE B	Beta	T	Sig T
AGE	.001015	6.6132E-04	.078106	1.535	.1254
SEX	-.103576	.010318	-.336987	-10.038	.0000
MINORITY	-.052366	.010837	-.141573	-4.832	.0000
EDLEVEL	.031443	.001748	.591951	17.988	.0000
WORK	.001608	9.2407E-04	.091428	1.740	.0826
(Constant)	3.385300	.033233		101.866	.0000

18.35
Determining Important
Variables

In multiple regression, you sometimes want to assign relative importance to each independent variable. For example, you might want to know whether education is more important than previous work experience in predicting beginning salary. There are two possible answers, depending on which of the following questions is asked:

- How important are education and work experience when each one is used alone to predict beginning salary?
- How important are education and work experience when they are used to predict beginning salary along with other independent variables in the regression equation?

The first question is answered by looking at the correlation coefficients between salary and the independent variables. The larger the absolute value of the correlation coefficient, the stronger the linear association. Figure 18.32 shows that education correlates more highly with the log of salary than does previous work experience (0.686 and 0.040, respectively). Thus, you would assign more importance to education as a predictor of salary.

The answer to the second question is considerably more complicated. When the independent variables are correlated among themselves, the unique contribution of each is difficult to assess. Any statement about an independent variable is contingent upon the other variables in the equation. For example, the regression coefficient *(B)* for work experience is 0.0007 when it is the sole independent variable in the equation, compared to 0.00161 when the other four independent variables are also in the equation. The second coefficient is more than twice the size of the first.

18.36
Beta Coefficients

It is also inappropriate to interpret the *B*'s as indicators of the relative importance of variables. The actual magnitude of the coefficients depends on the units in which the variables are measured. Only if all independent variables are measured in the same units—years, for example—are their coefficients directly comparable. When variables differ substantially in units of measurement, the sheer magnitude of their coefficients does not reveal anything about relative importance.

One way to make regression coefficients somewhat more comparable is to calculate *beta* weights, which are the coefficients of the independent variables when all variables are expressed in standardized (*Z*-score) form (see Figure 18.34b). The beta coefficients can be calculated directly from the regression coefficients using

$$BETA_k = B_k\left(\frac{S_k}{S_Y}\right)$$ **Equation 18.36**

where S_k is the standard deviation of the *k*th independent variable.

However, the values of the beta coefficients, like the *B*'s, are contingent on the other independent variables in the equation. They are also affected by the correlations of the independent variables and do not in any absolute sense reflect the importance of the various independent variables.

18.37
Part and Partial Coefficients

Another way of assessing the relative importance of independent variables is to consider the increase in R^2 when a variable is entered into an equation that already contains the other independent variables. This increase is

$$R^2_{change} = R^2 - R^2_{(i)}$$ **Equation 18.37a**

where $R^2_{(i)}$ is the square of the multiple correlation coefficient when all independent variables except the *i*th are in the equation. A large change in R^2 indicates that a variable provides unique information about the dependent variable that is not available from the other independent variables in the equation. The signed square root of the increase is called the *part correlation coefficient*. It is the correlation between Y and X_i when the linear effects of the other independent variables have been removed from X_i. If all independent variables are uncorrelated, the change in R^2 when a variable is entered into the equation is simply the square of the correlation coefficient between that variable and the dependent variable.

The output in Figure 18.37 shows that the addition of years of education to an equation that contains the other four independent variables results in a change in R^2 of 0.266 (0.51593^2). The square of the part coefficient tells only how much R^2 increases when a variable is added to the regression equation. It does not indicate what proportion of the unexplained variation this increase constitutes. If most of the variation had been explained by the other variables, a small part correlation is all that is possible for the remaining variable. It may therefore be difficult to compare part coefficients.

Figure 18.37   Zero-order, part, and partial correlation coefficients

```
COMPUTE LOGBEG=LG10(SALBEG).
REGRESSION VARIABLES=LOGBEG,EDLEVEL,SEX,WORK,MINORITY,AGE
   /STATISTICS=R CHA ZPP F
   /DEPENDENT=LOGBEG
   /METHOD=ENTER AGE /ENTER SEX /ENTER MINORITY /ENTER WORK
   /ENTER EDLEVEL.
```

```
Variable(s) Entered on Step Number  5..    EDLEVEL    EDUCATIONAL LEVEL


Multiple R           .78420
R Square             .61498           R Square Change    .26619
Adjusted R Square    .61086           F Change        323.55404
Standard Error       .09559           Signif F Change    .0000

F =      149.50125       Signif F =   .0000



-------------- Variables in the Equation --------------

Variable      Correl Part Cor  Partial       F  Sig F

AGE          -.047795 .044040  .070796    2.357  .1254
SEX          -.548020 -.287918 -.420903  100.761  .0000
MINORITY     -.172836 -.138596 -.217989   23.349  .0000
WORK          .039940 .049897  .080154    3.026  .0826
EDLEVEL       .685719 .515935  .639342  323.554  .0000
(Constant)                             10376.613  .0000
```

A coefficient that measures the proportional reduction in variation is

$$Pr_i^2 = \frac{R^2 - R_{(i)}^2}{1 - R_{(i)}^2}$$

Equation 18.37b

The numerator is the square of the part coefficient; the denominator is the proportion of unexplained variation when all but the ith variable are in the equation. The signed square root of Pr_i^2 is the *partial correlation coefficient*. It can be interpreted as the correlation between the ith independent variable and the dependent variable when the linear effects of the other independent variables have been removed from both X_i and Y. Since the denominator of Pr_i^2 is always less than or equal to 1, the part correlation coefficient is never larger in absolute value than the partial correlation coefficient.

Plots of the residuals of Y and X_i, when the linear effects of the other independent variables have been removed, are a useful diagnostic aid. They are discussed in Section 18.46.

18.38
Building a Model

Our selection of the five variables to predict beginning salary has been arbitrary to some extent. It is unlikely that all relevant variables have been identified and measured. Instead, some relevant variables have no doubt been excluded, while others that were included may not be very important determinants of salary level. This is not unusual; you must try to build a model from available data, as voluminous or scanty as the data may be. Before considering several formal procedures for model building, we will examine some of the consequences of adding and deleting variables from regression equations. The REGRESSION statistics for variables not in the equation are also described.

18.39
Adding and Deleting
Variables

The first step in Figure 18.39 shows the equation and summary statistics when years of education is the sole independent variable and log of beginning salary is the dependent variable. Consider the second step in the same figure, when another variable, sex, is added. The value displayed as **R Square Change** in the second step is the change in R^2 when sex is added. R^2 for education alone is 0.47021, so R^2_{change} is $0.57598 - 0.47021$, or 0.10577.

Figure 18.39   Adding a variable to the equation

```
COMPUTE LOGBEG=LG10(SALBEG).
REGRESSION VARIABLES=LOGBEG,EDLEVEL,SEX
   /STATISTICS=DEFAULTS CHA
   /DEPENDENT=LOGBEG
   /METHOD=ENTER EDLEVEL /ENTER SEX.
```

```
Beginning Block Number  1.  Method:  Enter      EDLEVEL


Variable(s) Entered on Step Number  1..    EDLEVEL    EDUCATIONAL LEVEL


Multiple R              .68572                                         Analysis of Variance
R Square                .47021       R Square Change    .47021                              DF      Sum of Squares     Mean Square
Adjusted R Square       .46909       F Change         418.92011        Regression           1             5.22252         5.22252
Standard Error          .11165       Signif F Change    .0000          Residual           472             5.88425          .01247

                                                                       F =     418.92011      Signif F =  .0000


----------------- Variables in the Equation ------------------           -------------- Variables not in the Equation --------------

Variable          B          SE B        Beta        T    Sig T         Variable     Beta In  Partial  Min Toler       T   Sig T

EDLEVEL        .036424     .001780      .685719    20.468  .0000         SEX         -.348017 -.446811   .873274  -10.839  .0000
(Constant)    3.310013     .024551                134.821  .0000


End Block Number   1   All requested variables entered.

Beginning Block Number  2.  Method:  Enter      SEX


Variable(s) Entered on Step Number  2..     SEX       SEX OF EMPLOYEE


Multiple R              .75893                                         Analysis of Variance
R Square                .57598       R Square Change    .10577                              DF      Sum of Squares     Mean Square
Adjusted R Square       .57418       F Change         117.48552        Regression           2             6.39725         3.19863
Standard Error          .09999       Signif F Change    .0000          Residual           471             4.70951          .01000

                                                                       F =     319.89574      Signif F =  .0000


----------------- Variables in the Equation ------------------

Variable          B          SE B        Beta        T    Sig T

EDLEVEL        .029843     .001705      .561830    17.498  .0000
SEX           -.106966     .009869     -.348017   -10.839  .0000
(Constant)    3.447542     .025386                135.806  .0000


End Block Number   2   All requested variables entered.
```

The null hypothesis that the true population value for the change in R^2 is 0 can be tested using

$$F_{change} = \frac{R^2_{change}(N - p - 1)}{q(1 - R^2)} = \frac{(0.1058)(474\text{-}2\text{-}1)}{1(1\text{-}0.5760)} = 117.48 \qquad \textbf{Equation 18.39}$$

where N is the number of cases in the equation, p is the total number of independent variables in the equation, and q is the number of variables entered at this step. Sometimes, this is referred to as a *partial F test*. Under the hypothesis that the true change is 0, the significance of the value labeled **F Change** can be obtained from the F distribution with q and $N - p - 1$ degrees of freedom.

The hypothesis that the real change in R^2 is 0 can also be formulated in terms of the β parameters. When only the ith variable is added in a step, the hypothesis that the change in R^2 is 0 is equivalent to the hypothesis that β_i is 0. The F value displayed for the change in R^2 is the square of the t value displayed for the test of the coefficient, as shown in Figure 18.39. For example, the t value for sex from Figure 18.39 is -10.839. This value squared is 117.48, the value displayed for **F Change.**

When q independent variables are entered in a single step, the test that R^2 is 0 is equivalent to the simultaneous test that the coefficients of all q variables are 0. For example, if sex and age were added in the same step to the regression equation that contains education, the F test for R^2 change would be the same as the F test which tests the hypothesis that $\beta_{sex} = \beta_{age} = 0$.

Entering sex into the equation with education has effects in addition to changing R^2. For example, note the decrease in magnitude of the regression coefficient for education from Step 1 to Step 2 (from 0.03642 to 0.02984) in Figure 18.39. This is attributable to the correlation between sex and level of education.

When highly intercorrelated independent variables are included in a regression equation, results may appear anomalous. The overall regression may be significant while none of the individual coefficients are significant. The signs of the regression coefficients may be counterintuitive. High correlations between independent variables inflate the variances of the estimates, making individual coefficients quite unreliable without adding much to the overall fit of the model. The problem of linear relationships between independent variables is discussed further in Section 18.50.

18.40
Statistics for Variables Not in the Equation

When you have independent variables that have not been entered into the equation, you can examine what would happen if they were entered at the next step. Statistics describing these variables are shown in Figure 18.40. The column labeled **Beta In** is the standardized regression coefficient that would result if the variable were entered into the equation at the next step. The F test and level of significance are for the hypothesis that the coefficient is 0. (Remember that the partial F test and the t test for the hypothesis that a coefficient is 0 are equivalent.) The partial correlation coefficient with the dependent variable adjusts for the variables already in the equation.

Figure 18.40   Coefficients for variables not in the equation

```
COMPUTE LOGBEG=LG10(SALBEG).
REGRESSION WIDTH=80
   /VARIABLES=LOGBEG,EDLEVEL,SEX,WORK,MINORITY,AGE
   /STATISTICS=OUTS F
   /DEPENDENT=LOGBEG
   /METHOD=FORWARD.
```

```
-------------- Variables not in the Equation --------------

Variable      Beta In  Partial  Min Toler         F  Sig F

WORK          .144245  .205668   .773818    20.759  .0000
MINORITY     -.129022 -.194642   .847583    18.507  .0000
AGE           .139419  .205193   .804253    20.659  .0000
```

From statistics calculated for variables not in the equation, you can decide what variable should be entered next. This process is detailed in Section 18.42.

18.41
The "Optimal" Number of Independent Variables

Having seen what happens when sex is added to the equation containing education (Figure 18.39), consider now what happens when the remaining three independent variables are entered one at a time in no particular order. Summary output is shown in Figure 18.41. Step 5 shows the statistics for the equation with all independent variables entered. Step 3 describes the model with education, sex, and work experience as the independent variables.

Figure 18.41   All independent variables in the equation

```
COMPUTE LOGBEG=LG10(SALBEG).
REGRESSION VARIABLES=LOGBEG,EDLEVEL,SEX,WORK,AGE,MINORITY
  /STATISTICS=HISTORY F
  /DEPENDENT=LOGBEG
  /METHOD=ENTER EDLEVEL /ENTER SEX /ENTER WORK /ENTER AGE
  /ENTER MINORITY.
```

```
                                        Summary table
                                        -------------

Step  MultR   Rsq  AdjRsq    F(Eqn) SigF  RsqCh      FCh SigCh     Variable BetaIn Correl
  1   .6857  .4702  .4691   418.920 .000  .4702  418.920  .000  In: EDLEVEL   .6857  .6857   EDUCATIONAL LEVEL
  2   .7589  .5760  .5742   319.896 .000  .1058  117.486  .000  In: SEX      -.3480 -.5480   SEX OF EMPLOYEE
  3   .7707  .5939  .5913   229.130 .000  .0179   20.759  .000  In: WORK      .1442  .0399   WORK EXPERIENCE
  4   .7719  .5958  .5923   172.805 .000  .0019    2.149  .143  In: AGE       .0763 -.0478   AGE OF EMPLOYEE
  5   .7842  .6150  .6109   149.501 .000  .0192   23.349  .000  In: MINORITY -.1416 -.1728   MINORITY CLASSIFICATION
```

Examination of Figure 18.41 shows that R^2 never decreases as independent variables are added. This is always true in regression analysis. However, this does not necessarily mean that the equation with more variables better fits the population. As the number of parameters estimated from the sample increases, so does the goodness of fit to the sample as measured by R^2. For example, if a sample contains six cases, a regression equation with six parameters fits the sample exactly, even though there may be no true statistical relationship at all between the dependent variable and the independent variables.

As indicated in Section 18.10, the sample R^2 in general tends to overestimate the population value of R^2. Adjusted R^2 attempts to correct the optimistic bias of the sample R^2. Adjusted R^2 does not necessarily increase as additional variables are added to an equation, and it is the preferred measure of goodness of fit because it is not subject to the inflationary bias of unadjusted R^2. This statistic is shown in the column labeled **AdjRsq** in the output.

Although adding independent variables increases R^2, it does not necessarily decrease the standard error of the estimate. Each time a variable is added to the equation, a degree of freedom is lost from the residual sum of squares and one is gained for the regression sum of squares. The standard error may increase when the decrease in the residual sum of squares is very slight and not sufficient to make up for the loss of a degree of freedom for the residual sum of squares. The F value for the test of the overall regression decreases when the regression sum of squares does not increase as fast as the degrees of freedom for the regression.

Including a large number of independent variables in a regression model is never a good strategy, unless there are strong, previous reasons to suggest that they all should be included. The observed increase in R^2 does not necessarily reflect a better fit of the model in the population. Including irrelevant variables increases the standard errors of all estimates without improving prediction. A model with many variables is often difficult to interpret.

On the other hand, it is important not to exclude potentially relevant independent variables. The following sections describe various procedures for selecting variables to be included in a regression model. The goal is to build a concise model that makes good prediction possible.

18.42
Procedures for Selecting Variables

You can construct a variety of regression models from the same set of variables. For instance, you can build seven different equations from three independent variables: three with only one independent variable, three with two independent variables, and one with all three. As the number of variables increases, so does the number of potential models (ten independent variables yield 1,023 models).

Although there are procedures for computing all possible regression equations, several other methods do not require as much computation and are more frequently used. Among these procedures are forward selection, backward elimination, and stepwise regression. None of these variable selection procedures is best in any absolute sense; they merely identify subsets of variables that, for the sample, are good predictors of the dependent variable.

18.43
Forward Selection

In *forward selection*, the first variable considered for entry into the equation is the one with the largest positive or negative correlation with the dependent variable. The F test for the hypothesis that the coefficient of the entered variable is 0 is then calculated. To determine whether this variable (and each succeeding variable) is entered, the F value is compared to an established criterion. You can specify one of two criteria in SPSS. One criterion is the minimum value of the F statistic that a variable must achieve in order to enter, called *F-to-enter* (keyword FIN), with a default value of 3.84. The other criterion you can specify is the probability associated with the F statistic, called *probability of F-to-enter* (keyword PIN), with a default of 0.05. In this case, a variable enters into the equation only if the probability associated with the F test is less than or equal to the default 0.05 or the value you specify. By default, the probability of F-to-enter is the criterion used.

These two criteria are not necessarily equivalent. As variables are added to the equation, the degrees of freedom associated with the residual sum of squares decrease while the regression degrees of freedom increase. Thus, a fixed F value has different significance levels depending on the number of variables currently in the equation. For large samples, the differences are negligible.

The actual significance level associated with the F-to-enter statistic is not the one usually obtained from the F distribution, since many variables are being examined and the largest F value is selected. Unfortunately, the true significance level is difficult to compute since it depends not only on the number of cases and variables but also on the correlations between independent variables.

If the first variable selected for entry meets the criterion for inclusion, forward selection continues. Otherwise, the procedure terminates with no variables in the equation. Once one variable is entered, the statistics for variables not in the equation are used to select the next one. The partial correlations between the dependent variable and each of the independent variables not in the equation, adjusted for the independent variables in the equation, are examined. The variable with the largest partial correlation is the next candidate. Choosing the variable with the largest partial correlation in absolute value is equivalent to selecting the variable with the largest F value.

If the criterion is met, the variable is entered into the equation and the procedure is repeated. The procedure stops when there are no other variables that meet the entry criterion.

To include a specific number of independent variables in the equation, you can specify the number of steps and REGRESSION will select only the first n variables that meet entry requirements. Another criterion that is always checked before a variable is entered is the tolerance, which is discussed in Section 18.52.

Figure 18.43a shows output generated from a forward-selection procedure using the salary data. The default entry criterion is PIN=0.05. In the first step, education (variable EDLEVEL) is entered since it has the highest correlation with beginning salary. The significance level associated with education is less than 0.0005, so it certainly meets the criterion for entry.

Figure 18.43a   Summary statistics for forward selection

```
COMPUTE LOGBEG=LG10(SALBEG).
REGRESSION VARIABLES=LOGBEG,EDLEVEL,SEX,WORK,MINORITY,AGE
   /STATISTICS=HISTORY F
   /DEPENDENT=LOGBEG
   /METHOD=FORWARD.
```

Step	MultR	Rsq	AdjRsq	F(Eqn)	SigF	RsqCh	FCh	SigCh		Variable	BetaIn	Correl
1	.6857	.4702	.4691	418.920	.000	.4702	418.920	.000	In:	EDLEVEL	.6857	.6857
2	.7589	.5760	.5742	319.896	.000	.1058	117.486	.000	In:	SEX	-.3480	-.5480
3	.7707	.5939	.5913	229.130	.000	.0179	20.759	.000	In:	WORK	.1442	.0399
4	.7830	.6130	.6097	185.750	.000	.0191	23.176	.000	In:	MINORITY	-.1412	-.1728

To see how the next variable, SEX, was selected, look at the statistics shown in Figure 18.43b for variables not in the equation when only EDLEVEL is in the equation. The variable with the largest partial correlation is SEX. If entered at the next step, it would have an F value of approximately 117 for the test that its coefficient is 0. Since the probability associated with the F is less than 0.05, variable SEX is entered in the second step.

Figure 18.43b   Status of the variables at the first step

```
COMPUTE LOGBEG=LG10(SALBEG).
REGRESSION WIDTH=80
   /VARIABLES=LOGBEG,EDLEVEL,SEX,WORK,MINORITY,AGE
   /STATISTICS=F
   /DEPENDENT=LOGBEG
   /METHOD=FORWARD.
```

```
------------------ Variables in the Equation ------------------

Variable              B          SE B        Beta         F     Sig F

EDLEVEL            .036424     .001780     .685719    418.920    .0000
(Constant)        3.310013     .024551               18176.773   .0000


------------ Variables not in the Equation ------------

Variable     Beta In   Partial   Min Toler       F    Sig F

SEX         -.348017  -.446811    .873274    117.486   .0000
WORK         .227473   .302405    .936316     47.408   .0000
MINORITY    -.083181  -.113267    .982341      6.121   .0137
AGE          .157180   .207256    .921128     21.140   .0000
```

Once variable SEX enters at Step 2, the statistics for variables not in the equation must be examined (see Figure 18.40). The variable with the largest absolute value for the partial correlation coefficient is now years of work experience. Its F value is 20.759 with a probability less than 0.05, so variable WORK is entered in the next step. The same process takes place with variable MINORITY and it is entered, leaving AGE as the only variable out of the equation. However, as shown in Figure 18.43c, the significance level associated with the AGE coefficient F value is 0.1254, which is too large for entry. Thus, forward selection yields the summary table for the four steps shown in Figure 18.43a.

Figure 18.43c   The last step

```
COMPUTE LOGBEG=LG10(SALBEG).
REGRESSION WIDTH=80
  /VARIABLES=LOGBEG,EDLEVEL,SEX,WORK,MINORITY,AGE
  /STATISTICS=F
  /DEPENDENT=LOGBEG
  /METHOD=FORWARD.
```

```
------------ Variables not in the Equation ------------

Variable      Beta In  Partial  Min Toler        F  Sig F
AGE           .078106  .070796   .297843     2.357  .1254
```

18.44
Backward Elimination

While forward selection starts with no independent variables in the equation and sequentially enters them, *backward elimination* starts with all variables in the equation and sequentially removes them. Instead of entry criteria, removal criteria are specified.

Two removal criteria are available in SPSS. The first is the minimum F value (FOUT) that a variable must have in order to remain in the equation. Variables with F values less than this *F-to-remove* are eligible for removal. The second criterion available is the maximum probability of F-to-remove (keyword POUT) a variable can have. The default FOUT value is 2.71 and the default POUT value is 0.10. The default criterion is POUT.

Figure 18.44a   Backward elimination at the first step

```
COMPUTE LOGBEG=LG10(SALBEG).
REGRESSION VARIABLES=LOGBEG,EDLEVEL,SEX,WORK,MINORITY,AGE
  /STATISTICS=COEFF ZPP F
  /DEPENDENT=LOGBEG
  /METHOD=BACKWARD.
```

```
----------------------------- Variables in the Equation -----------------------------

Variable           B          SE B       Beta   Correl Part Cor  Partial          F  Sig F

AGE           .001015   6.6132E-04    .078106  -.047795  .044040  .070796      2.357  .1254
SEX          -.103576      .010318   -.336987  -.548020 -.287918 -.420903    100.761  .0000
MINORITY     -.052366      .010837   -.141573  -.172836 -.138596 -.217989     23.349  .0000
EDLEVEL       .031443      .001748    .591951   .685719  .515935  .639342    323.554  .0000
WORK          .001608   9.2407E-04    .091428   .039940  .049897  .080154      3.026  .0826
(Constant)   3.385300      .033233                                         10376.613  .0000
```

Look at the salary example again, this time constructing the model with backward elimination. The output in Figure 18.44a is from the first step, in which all variables are entered into the equation. The variable with the smallest partial correlation coefficient, AGE, is examined first. Since the probability of its F (0.1254) is greater than the default POUT criterion value of 0.10, variable AGE is removed.

Figure 18.44b Backward elimination at the last step

```
COMPUTE LOGBEG=LG10(SALBEG).
REGRESSION VARIABLES=LOGBEG,EDLEVEL,SEX,WORK,MINORITY,AGE
  /STATISTICS=COEFF ZPP F
  /DEPENDENT=LOGBEG
  /METHOD=BACKWARD.
```

------------------------------ Variables in the Equation ------------------------------									---------- not in ----------		
Variable	B	SE B	Beta	Correl	Part Cor	Partial	F	Sig F	Variable	F	Sig F
SEX	-.099042	.009901	-.322234	-.548020	-.287333	-.419331	100.063	.0000	AGE	2.357	.1254
MINORITY	-.052245	.010853	-.141248	-.172836	-.138282	-.216998	23.176	.0000			
EDLEVEL	.031433	.001751	.591755	.685719	.515768	.638270	322.412	.0000			
WORK	.002753	5.4582E-04	.156592	.039940	.144891	.226848	25.444	.0000			
(Constant)	3.411953	.028380					14454.046	.0000			

The equation is then recalculated without AGE, producing the statistics shown in Figure 18.44b. The variable with the smallest partial correlation is MINORITY. However, its significance is less than the 0.10 criterion, so backward elimination stops. The equation resulting from backward elimination is the same as the one from forward selection. This is not always the case, however. Forward- and backward-selection procedures can give different results, even with comparable entry and removal criteria.

18.45
Stepwise Selection

Stepwise selection of independent variables is really a combination of backward and forward procedures and is probably the most commonly used method. The first variable is selected in the same manner as in forward selection. If the variable fails to meet entry requirements (either FIN or PIN), the procedure terminates with no independent variables in the equation. If it passes the criterion, the second variable is selected based on the highest partial correlation. If it passes entry criteria, it also enters the equation.

After the first variable is entered, stepwise selection differs from forward selection: the first variable is examined to see whether it should be removed according to the removal criterion (FOUT or POUT), as in backward elimination. In the next step, variables not in the equation are examined for entry. After each step, variables already in the equation are examined for removal. Variables are removed until none remain that meet the removal criterion. To prevent the same variable from being repeatedly entered and removed, PIN must be less than POUT (or FIN greater than FOUT). Variable selection terminates when no more variables meet entry and removal criteria.

In the salary example, stepwise selection with the default criteria results in the same equation produced by both forward selection and backward elimination (see Figure 18.45).

Figure 18.45 Stepwise output

```
COMPUTE LOGBEG=LG10(SALBEG).
REGRESSION VARIABLES=LOGBEG EDLEVEL SEX WORK MINORITY AGE
    /STATISTICS=R COEFF OUTS F
    /DEPENDENT=LOGBEG
    /METHOD=STEPWISE.
```

```
Listwise Deletion of Missing Data

Equation Number 1    Dependent Variable..   LOGBEG

Beginning Block Number  1.  Method: Stepwise


Variable(s) Entered on Step Number  1..    EDLEVEL    EDUCATIONAL LEVEL


Multiple R            .68572
R Square             .47021
Adjusted R Square    .46909
Standard Error       .11165

F =     418.92011      Signif F =  .0000
```

------------------ Variables in the Equation ------------------						------------- Variables not in the Equation --------------				
Variable	B	SE B	Beta	F	Sig F	Variable	Beta In	Partial	Min Toler	F	Sig F
EDLEVEL	.036424	.001780	.685719	418.920	.0000	SEX	-.348017	-.446811	.873274	117.486	.0000
(Constant)	3.310013	.024551		18176.773	.0000	WORK	.227473	.302405	.936316	47.408	.0000
						MINORITY	-.083181	-.113267	.982341	6.121	.0137

```
Equation Number 1    Dependent Variable..   LOGBEG


Variable(s) Entered on Step Number  2..    SEX     SEX OF EMPLOYEE


Multiple R            .75893
R Square             .57598
Adjusted R Square    .57418
Standard Error       .09999

F =     319.89574      Signif F =  .0000
```

------------------ Variables in the Equation ------------------						------------- Variables not in the Equation --------------				
Variable	B	SE B	Beta	F	Sig F	Variable	Beta In	Partial	Min Toler	F	Sig F
EDLEVEL	.029843	.001705	.561830	306.191	.0000	WORK	.144245	.205668	.773818	20.759	.0000
SEX	-.106966	.009869	-.348017	117.486	.0000	MINORITY	-.129022	-.194642	.847583	18.507	.0000
(Constant)	3.447542	.025386		18443.284	.0000	AGE	.139419	.205193	.804253	20.659	.0000

```
Variable(s) Entered on Step Number  3..    WORK     WORK EXPERIENCE


Multiple R            .77066
R Square             .59391
Adjusted R Square    .59132
Standard Error       .09796

F =     229.13001      Signif F =  .0000
```

------------------ Variables in the Equation ------------------						------------- Variables not in the Equation --------------				
Variable	B	SE B	Beta	F	Sig F	Variable	Beta In	Partial	Min Toler	F	Sig F
EDLEVEL	.032572	.001775	.613209	336.771	.0000	MINORITY	-.141248	-.216998	.759669	23.176	.0000
SEX	-.094035	.010076	-.305945	87.099	.0000	AGE	.076331	.067540	.298392	2.149	.1433
WORK	.002536	5.5664E-04	.144245	20.759	.0000						
(Constant)	3.384569	.028452		14150.645	.0000						

```
Equation Number 1    Dependent Variable..   LOGBEG


Variable(s) Entered on Step Number  4..    MINORITY  MINORITY CLASSIFICATION


Multiple R            .78297
R Square             .61304
Adjusted R Square    .60974
Standard Error       .09573

F =     185.74958      Signif F =  .0000
```

------------------ Variables in the Equation ------------------						------------- Variables not in the Equation --------------				
Variable	B	SE B	Beta	F	Sig F	Variable	Beta In	Partial	Min Toler	F	Sig F
EDLEVEL	.031433	.001751	.591755	322.412	.0000	AGE	.078106	.070796	.297843	2.357	.1254
SEX	-.099042	.009901	-.322234	100.063	.0000						
WORK	.002753	5.4582E-04	.156592	25.444	.0000						
MINORITY	-.052245	.010853	-.141248	23.176	.0000						
(Constant)	3.411953	.028380		14454.046	.0000						

```
End Block Number  1   PIN =     .050 Limits reached.
```

The three procedures do not always result in the same equation, though you should be encouraged when they do. The model selected by any method should be carefully studied for violations of the assumptions. It is often a good idea to develop several acceptable models and then choose among them based on interpretability, ease of variable acquisition, parsimony, and so forth.

18.46
Checking for Violation of Assumptions

The procedures discussed in Sections 18.17 through 18.22 for checking for violations of assumptions in bivariate regression apply in the multivariate case as well. Residuals should be plotted against predicted values as well as against each independent variable. The distribution of residuals should be examined for normality.

Several additional residual plots may be useful for multivariate models. One of these is the partial regression plot. For the jth independent variable, it is obtained by calculating the residuals for the dependent variable when it is predicted from all the independent variables excluding the jth and by calculating the residuals for the jth independent variable when it is predicted from all of the other independent variables. This removes the linear effect of the other independent variables from both variables. For each case, these two residuals are plotted against each other.

A partial regression plot for educational level for the regression equation that contains work experience, minority, sex, and educational level as the independent variables is shown in Figure 18.46a. (Summary statistics for the regression equation with all independent variables are displayed in the last step of Figure 18.45.)

Figure 18.46a   Partial regression plot from PLOT

```
COMPUTE LOGBEG=LG10(SALBEG).
REGRESSION VARIABLES=LOGBEG SEX MINORITY EDLEVEL WORK
  /DEPENDENT=LOGBEG
  /METHOD=ENTER MINORITY SEX WORK
  /SAVE=RESID(RES1)
  /DEPENDENT=EDLEVEL
  /METHOD=ENTER MINORITY SEX WORK
  /SAVE=RESID(RES2).
PLOT FORMAT=REGRESSION /VSIZE=30 /HSIZE=70
  /PLOT=RES1 WITH RES2.
```

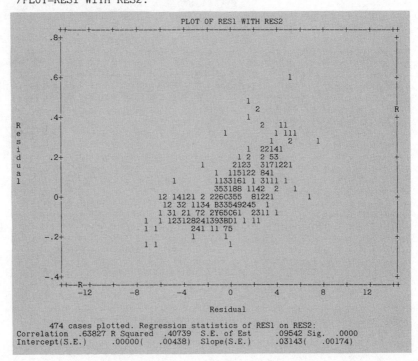

Several characteristics of the partial regression plot make it a particularly valuable diagnostic tool. The slope of the regression line for the two residual variables (0.03143) is equal to the coefficient for the EDLEVEL variable in the multiple regression equation after the last step (Step 4 in Figure 18.45). Thus, by examining the bivariate plot, you can conveniently identify points that are influential in the determination of the particular regression coefficient (see Section 18.23). The correlation coefficient between the two residuals, 0.638, is the partial correlation coefficient discussed in Section 18.37. The residuals from the least-squares line in Figure 18.46a are equal to the residuals from the final multiple regression equation, which includes all the independent variables.

The partial regression plot also helps you assess inadequacies of the selected model and violations of the underlying assumptions. For example, the partial regression plot of educational level does not appear to be linear, suggesting that an additional term, such as years of education squared, might also be included in the model. This violation is much easier to spot using the partial regression plot than the plot of the independent variable against the residual from the equation with all independent variables. Figures 18.46b and 18.46c show the residual scatterplot and partial regression plot produced by the REGRESSION procedure. Note that the nonlinearity is much more apparent in the partial regression plot.

Figure 18.46b   Residual scatterplot from REGRESSION

```
COMPUTE LOGBEG=LG10(SALBEG).
REGRESSION VARIABLES=LOGBEG SEX MINORITY EDLEVEL WORK
  /DEPENDENT=LOGBEG
  /METHOD=STEPWISE
  /SCATTERPLOT=(*RESID,EDLEVEL).
```

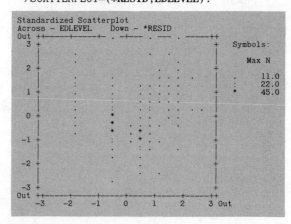

Figure 18.46c   Partial regression plot from REGRESSION

```
COMPUTE LOGBEG=LG10(SALBEG).
REGRESSION VARIABLES=LOGBEG SEX MINORITY EDLEVEL WORK
   /DEPENDENT=LOGBEG
   /METHOD=STEPWISE
   /PARTIALPLOT=EDLEVEL.
```

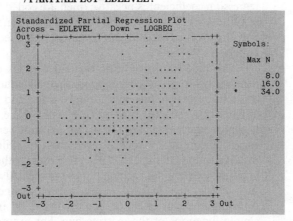

Figure 18.46d contains the summary statistics when the number of years of education squared is included in the multiple regression equation. The multiple R^2 increases from 0.61 (Step 4 in Figure 18.45) to 0.71, a significant improvement.

Figure 18.46d   The regression equation with education squared

```
COMPUTE LOGBEG=LG10(SALBEG).
COMPUTE ED2=EDLEVEL*EDLEVEL.
REGRESSION VARIABLES=LOGBEG SEX MINORITY EDLEVEL ED2 WORK
   /DEPENDENT=LOGBEG
   /METHOD=ENTER.
```

```
Variable(s) Entered on Step Number  1..  WORK      WORK EXPERIENCE
                                    2..  MINORITY  MINORITY CLASSIFICATION
                                    3..  SEX       SEX OF EMPLOYEE
                                    4..  EDLEVEL   EDUCATIONAL LEVEL
                                    5..  ED2


Multiple R          .84302     Analysis of Variance
R Square            .71068                       DF     Sum of Squares   Mean Square
Adjusted R Square   .70759     Regression         5           7.89331       1.57866
Standard Error      .08286     Residual         468           3.21345        .00687

                               F =    229.91286     Signif F =  .0000
```

18.47
Interpreting the Equation

The multiple regression equation estimated above suggests several findings. Education appears to be the best predictor of beginning salary, at least among the variables included in this study (Figure 18.44a). The sex of the employee also appears to be important. Women are paid less than men since the sign of the regression coefficient is negative (men are coded 0 and women are coded 1). Years of prior work experience and race are also related to salary, but when education and sex are included in the equation, the effect of experience and race is less striking.

Do these results indicate that there is sex discrimination at the bank? Not necessarily. It is well recognized that all education is not equally profitable. Master's degrees in business administration and political science are treated quite differently in the marketplace. Thus, a possible explanation of the observed results is that women enter areas that are just not very well paid. Although this may suggest inequities in societal evaluation of skills, it does not necessarily imply discrimination at the bank. Further, many other potential job-related skills or qualifications are not included in the model. Also, some of the existing variables, such as age, may make nonlinear as well as linear contributions to the fit. Such contributions can often be approximated by including new variables that are simple functions of the existing one. For example, the age values squared may improve the fit.

18.48
Statistics for Unselected Cases

As previously noted, a model usually fits the sample from which it is derived better than it fits the population. A sometimes useful strategy for obtaining an estimate of how well the model fits the population is to split the sample randomly into two parts. One part is then used to estimate the model, while the remaining cases are reserved for testing the goodness of fit.

It is also sometimes interesting to split the data on some characteristics of the sample. For example, you can develop the salary equation for males alone and then apply it to females to see how well it fits. For example, Figure 18.48 shows histograms of residuals for males (denoted as selected cases) and females (unselected cases). Note that the females' salaries are too large when predicted from the male equation since most of the residuals are negative. The multiple R for the females is 0.45596, which is smaller than the 0.73882 for males (stepwise selection was used).

Figure 18.48   Histograms for males (selected) and females (unselected)

```
COMPUTE LOGBEG=LG10(SALBEG).
COMPUTE ED2=EDLEVEL*EDLEVEL.
REGRESSION WIDTH=90
  /SELECT SEX EQ 0
  /VARIABLES=LOGBEG,EDLEVEL,ED2,SEX,WORK,MINORITY,AGE
  /DEPENDENT=LOGBEG
  /METHOD=STEPWISE
  /RESIDUALS=HISTOGRAM.
```

```
Histogram - Standardized Residual
- Selected Cases
  N  Exp N       (* = 1 Cases,     . : = Normal Curve)
  6   .20    Out ******
  0   .40   3.00
  0  1.01   2.67 .
  1  2.30   2.33 *.
  1  4.71   2.00 *   .
  6  8.63   1.67 ******  .
  7 14.16   1.33 *******      .
 14 20.81   1.00 **************    .
 24 27.40    .67 ************************:****
 36 32.32    .33 **********************************:****
 39 34.15    .00 *************************************:*****
 48 32.32   -.33 ********************************:****************
 41 27.40   -.67 ***************************:****************
 17 20.81  -1.00 ****************    .
 12 14.16  -1.33 ************ .
  3  8.63  -1.67 ***     .
  0  4.71  -2.00 .
  2  2.30  -2.33 *:
  1  1.01  -2.67 :
  0   .40  -3.00
  0   .20    Out


Histogram - Standardized Residual
- Unselected Cases
  N  Exp N       (X = 1 Cases,     . : = Normal Curve)
  0   .17    Out
  0   .33   3.00
  0   .84   2.67 .
  0  1.93   2.33 .
  0  3.94   2.00   .
  1  7.22   1.67 X      .
  2 11.85   1.33 XX        .
  2 17.42   1.00 XX           .
  3 22.94    .67 XXX              .
  5 27.06    .33 XXXXX               .
 23 28.59    .00 XXXXXXXXXXXXXXXXXXXXXXX    .
 23 27.06   -.33 XXXXXXXXXXXXXXXXXXXXXXX
 36 22.94   -.67 XXXXXXXXXXXXXXXXXXXXXX:XXXXXXXXXXXXX
 49 17.42  -1.00 XXXXXXXXXXXXXXX:XXXXXXXXXXXXXXXXXXXXXXXXXXXXXXXXXXX
 20 11.85  -1.33 XXXXXXXXXX:XXXXXXXX
 14  7.22  -1.67 XXXXX:XXXXXXX
 15  3.94  -2.00 XXX:XXXXXXXXXX
 15  1.93  -2.33 X:XXXXXXXXXXXX
  4   .84  -2.67  :XXX
  0   .33  -3.00
  4   .17    Out XXXX
```

18.49
Problems of Multicollinearity

Preceding sections deal with the consequences of correlated independent variables in regression analysis. The estimates of the β and the sum of squares attributable to each variable are dependent on the other variables in the equation. Variances of the estimators also increase when independent variables are interrelated. This may result in a regression equation with a significant R^2, although virtually none of the coefficients is significantly different from 0. If any independent variable is a perfect linear combination of other independent variables, the correlation matrix is *singular* and a unique, unbiased least-squares solution does not exist.

Although situations involving singularities do occur, they are not as common as those involving near-singularities—variables that are almost linear combinations of other independent variables. These variables are often called *multicollinear*.

18.50
Methods of Detection

Multicollinearities can be detected in several ways. Large coefficients in the correlation matrix always signal the presence of multicollinearity. However, multicollinearity can exist without any of the correlation coefficients being very large.

One of the most frequently used indicators of interdependency between variables is the tolerance (see Section 18.51). If the variable has a large R^2—or equivalently a small tolerance—when it is predicted from the other independent variables, a potentially troublesome situation exists. Not only are the variances of the estimators inflated, but computational problems can occur.

18.51
SPSS and Multicollinearity

In the SPSS REGRESSION procedure, various steps are taken to warn you of multicollinearity. Before an independent variable is entered into the equation, its tolerance with other independent variables already in the equation is calculated. The tolerance is the proportion of variability in an independent variable not explained by the other independent variables. It is calculated as $1 - R_i^2$, where R_i^2 is the squared multiple correlation when the ith independent variable is considered the dependent variable and the regression equation between it and the other independent variables is calculated. SPSS prints the tolerances as shown in Figure 18.51.

Figure 18.51   Tolerances

```
VARIABLE    TOLERANCE

AGE          0.31792
SEX          0.72998
MINORITY     0.95839
EDLEVEL      0.75966
WORK         0.29784
```

It is possible for a variable not in the equation to have an acceptable tolerance level but when entered to cause the tolerance of other variables already in the equation to become unacceptably small (Berk, 1977; Frane, 1977). Thus, the tolerances of all the variables in the equation are recomputed at each step. If either the tolerance of the variable or the tolerance of any variable already in the equation is less than 0.0001, a warning is issued and the variable is not entered unless the default TOLERANCE criterion has been altered (see Section 18.58).

In SPSS, you can print both the tolerance of a variable and the minimum tolerance of all independent variables in the equation if the variable were entered.

18.52
RUNNING PROCEDURE REGRESSION

The REGRESSION procedure provides five equation-building methods: forward selection, backward elimination, stepwise selection, forced entry, and forced removal. The subcommands for residual analysis help detect influential data points, outliers, and violations of the regression model assumptions.

18.53
Building the Equation

To build a simple regression model, you must specify two required subcommands: a DEPENDENT subcommand that indicates the dependent variable and a METHOD subcommand that names the method to be used. For example, to build the simple bivariate model of beginning salary and current salary discussed earlier in the chapter, specify

```
REGRESSION DEPENDENT=SALNOW
   /METHOD=ENTER SALBEG.
```

The beginning (SALBEG) and current (SALNOW) salaries are named, with the latter specified as the dependent variable. The ENTER keyword enters beginning salary into the equation. The output produced by this command is shown in Figures 18.3b, 18.10, and 18.11a.

18.54
VARIABLES Subcommand

The optional VARIABLES subcommand lists all variables to be used in the regression analysis. The order of variables on the VARIABLES subcommand determines the order of variables in the correlation matrix. The keyword TO can be used on the VARIABLES subcommand to imply consecutive variables on the active system file. On subsequent DEPENDENT and METHOD subcommands, the keyword TO refers to the order of variables on the VARIABLES subcommand.

The VARIABLES subcommand is followed by a variable list or either one of the following keywords:

ALL *Include all user-defined variables in the active system file.*

(COLLECT) *Include all variables named on the DEPENDENT and METHOD subcommands.* This is the default if the VARIABLES subcommand is not included.

If you do not include a VARIABLES subcommand or you specify the keyword (COLLECT), the METHOD subcommand(s) must include a variable list. If used, the VARIABLES subcommand must precede the first DEPENDENT and METHOD subcommands, as in:

```
REGRESSION VARIABLES=SALBEG SALNOW LOGBEG
  EDLEVEL SEX WORK MINORITY AGE
   /DEPENDENT=LOGBEG
   /METHOD=ENTER EDLEVEL TO AGE.
```

18.55
DEPENDENT Subcommand

The DEPENDENT subcommand indicates the dependent variable for the regression analysis. The DEPENDENT subcommand is followed by a variable name or variable list. If you specify more than one variable on the DEPENDENT subcommand, SPSS produces a separate equation for each dependent variable specified.

You can specify more than one analysis with multiple DEPENDENT and METHOD subcommands. For example, to run both a bivariate and multivariate analysis in the same REGRESSION procedure, specify

```
REGRESSION VARIABLES=SALBEG SALNOW LOGBEG
  EDLEVEL SEX WORK MINORITY AGE
   /DEPENDENT=SALNOW
   /METHOD=ENTER SALBEG
   /DEPENDENT=LOGBEG
   /METHOD=ENTER EDLEVEL TO AGE.
```

The first DEPENDENT subcommand defines a single equation with SALNOW as the dependent variable, and the METHOD subcommand enters SALBEG into the equation. The second DEPENDENT subcommand defines another equation, with LOGBEG as the dependent variable. The associated METHOD subcommand enters variables EDLEVEL to AGE into the equation. The TO convention for naming consecutive variables used in the second METHOD subcommand refers to the order in which the variables are named on the VARIABLES subcommand, not their order on the active system file. See Figures 18.34a and 18.34b for the output from the second equation.

If you specify more than one variable on the DEPENDENT subcommand, SPSS produces a separate equation for each dependent variable specified.

18.56
METHOD Subcommand

At least one METHOD subcommand must immediately follow each DEPENDENT subcommand, specifying the method to be used in developing the regression equation. The available methods are:

FORWARD (varlist)	*Forward variable selection.* The variables named are entered one at a time based on entry criteria (Section 18.43).
BACKWARD (varlist)	*Backward variable elimination.* All variables named are entered and then removed one at a time based on removal criteria (Section 18.44).
STEPWISE (varlist)	*Stepwise variable entry and removal.* The variables named are examined at each step for entry or removal (Section 18.45).
ENTER (varlist)	*Forced entry.* All variables named are entered in a single step.
REMOVE (varlist)	*Forced removal.* The variables named are removed in a single step. REMOVE must have an accompanying variable list.
TEST (varlist)	*Test indicated subsets of independent variables.* TEST offers an easy way to test a variety of models using R^2 change and its test of significance as the criterion for the "best" model. TEST must have an accompanying variable list.

A variable list is required with the REMOVE and TEST keywords and is optional for the other METHOD keywords, provided you include a VARIABLES subcommand. The default variable list for methods FORWARD, BACKWARD, STEP-WISE, and ENTER includes all variables named on the VARIABLES subcommand that are not named on the preceding DEPENDENT subcommand. For example, to request the backward-elimination method discussed in Section 18.44, specify:

```
REGRESSION VARIABLES=LOGBEG EDLEVEL SEX WORK MINORITY AGE
    /DEPENDENT=LOGBEG
    /METHOD=BACKWARD.
```

The keyword METHOD is optional and may be omitted. For example, the command

```
REGRESSION VARIABLES=LOGBEG EDLEVEL SEX WORK MINORITY AGE
    /DEPENDENT=LOGBEG
    /BACKWARD.
```

produces the same results as the previous example.

You can specify multiple METHOD subcommands. For example, you might want to force one variable into the equation first and then enter the remaining variables in a forward-selection fashion, as in:

```
REGRESSION VARIABLES=LOGBEG EDLEVEL SEX WORK MINORITY AGE
    /DEPENDENT=LOGBEG
    /METHOD=ENTER EDLEVEL
    /METHOD=FORWARD SEX TO AGE.
```

18.57
STATISTICS Subcommand

By default, REGRESSION displays the four sets of statistics described for keywords R, ANOVA, COEFF, and OUTS below. These statistics are shown in Figures 18.3b, 18.10, and 18.11a for the bivariate equation, and in Figures 18.34a and 18.34b for the multivariate equation. You can specify exactly which statistics you want displayed by any of the following keywords on the STATISTICS subcommand.

DEFAULTS	*R, ANOVA, COEFF, and OUTS.* These statistics are displayed when the STATISTICS subcommand is omitted or if no keywords are specified on the subcommand. If you specify statistics keywords on a STATISTICS subcommand, the default statistics will not appear unless you specify them explicitly, either individually or with the DEFAULTS keyword.
ALL	*All statistics except F, LINE, and END.*
R	*Multiple R.* Displays multiple R, R^2, adjusted R^2, and the standard error. (See Figure 18.10.)
ANOVA	*Analysis of variance table.* Displays degrees of freedom, sums of squares, mean squares, F value for multiple R, and the observed significance level of F. (See Figure 18.11a.)

CHA	*Change in* R^2 *between steps,* F *value for change in* R^2*, and significance of* F. (See Figure 18.39.)
BCOV	*Variance-covariance matrix.* Displays a matrix with covariances above the diagonal, correlations below the diagonal, and variances on the diagonal.
XTX	*Swept correlation matrix.*
COLLIN	*Collinearity diagnostics.* Includes the variance inflation factor (VIF), the eigenvalues of the scaled and uncentered cross-products matrix, condition indices, and variance-decomposition proportions (Belsley et al., 1980).
SELECTION	*Aids to selecting set of regressors.* Includes Akaike information criterion (AIK), Amemiya's prediction criterion (PC), Mallow's conditional mean squared error of prediction criterion (Cp), and Schwarz Bayesian criterion (SBC) (Judge et al., 1985).
COEFF	*Statistics for variables in the equation.* Displays regression coefficient *B*, standard error of *B*, standardized coefficient beta, *t* value for *B*, and two-tailed significance level of *t*. (See Figure 18.44a.)
OUTS	*Statistics for variables not in the equation that have been named on the VARIABLES subcommand.* Statistics are beta if the variable were entered, *t* value for beta, significance level of *t*, partial correlation with the dependent variable controlling for variables in the equation, and minimum tolerance. (See Figure 18.40.)
ZPP	*Zero-order, part, and partial correlation.* (See Figure 18.37.)
CI	*Confidence intervals.* Displays the 95% confidence interval for the unstandardized regression coefficient. (See Figure 18.8.)
SES	*Approximate standard error of the standardized regression coefficients.* (See Meyer and Younger, 1976.)
TOL	*Tolerance.* Displays tolerance and VIF for variables in the equation and, for variables not in the equation, the tolerance a variable would have if it were the only variable entered next.
F	F *value for* B *and significance of* F. Displayed instead of *t* for COEFF and OUTS. (See, for example, Figures 18.43b, 18.43c, 18.44a, and 18.44b.)
LINE	*Summary line for each step in step methods.* Displays a single summary line for each step in BACKWARD, FORWARD, or STEPWISE methods and the default or requested statistics at the end of each method block (BACKWARD, FORWARD, STEPWISE, ENTER, REMOVE, or TEST).
HISTORY	*Step history.* Displays a summary report with a summary line for each method (ENTER, REMOVE, or TEST, if the equation changes) or step if the method entails steps (FORWARD, BACKWARD, or STEPWISE). If history is the only statistic requested, COEFF is displayed for the final equation. (See Figures 18.41 and 18.43a.)
END	*One summary line per step or method block.* Displays a summary line per step for BACKWARD, FORWARD, or STEPWISE, and one summary line per block for ENTER, REMOVE, or TEST, if the equation changes.

The STATISTICS subcommand must appear before the DEPENDENT subcommand that initiates the equation and remains in effect until overridden by another STATISTICS subcommand. For example, to produce the output in Figure 18.8, specify

```
REGRESSION VARIABLES=SALBEG SALNOW
  /STATISTICS=CI
  /DEPENDENT=SALNOW
  /METHOD=ENTER SALBEG.
```

18.58
CRITERIA Subcommand

You can control the statistical criteria by which REGRESSION chooses variables for entry into or removal from an equation with the CRITERIA subcommand. Place the CRITERIA subcommand after the VARIABLES subcommand and before the DEPENDENT subcommand. A CRITERIA subcommand affects any subsequent DEPENDENT and METHOD subcommands and remains in effect until overridden with another CRITERIA subcommand.

The CRITERIA keywords are

DEFAULTS	*PIN(0.05), POUT(0.10), and TOLERANCE(0.0001).* These are the defaults if no CRITERIA subcommand is specified. If criteria have been changed, DEFAULTS restores the default values.
PIN(value)	*Probability of* F-*to-enter.* The default value is 0.05.
POUT(value)	*Probability of* F-*to-remove.* The default value is 0.10.
FIN(value)	F-*to-enter.* The default value is 3.84. FIN overrides the default PIN criteria. If both FIN and PIN are specified on the same CRITERIA subcommand, only the last one specified will be in effect.
FOUT(value)	F-*to-remove.* The default value is 2.71. FOUT overrides the default POUT criteria. If both FOUT and POUT are specified on the same CRITERIA subcommand, only the last one specified will be in effect.
TOLERANCE(value)	*Tolerance.* The default value is 0.0001. All variables must pass both tolerance and minimum tolerance tests before entering the equation. The minimum tolerance is the smallest tolerance for that variable or any other variable in the equation if the variable is entered.
MAXSTEPS(n)	*Maximum number of steps.* For the STEPWISE method, the default is twice the number of independent variables. For the FORWARD and BACKWARD methods, the default maximum is the number of variables meeting the PIN and POUT or FIN and FOUT criteria. The MAXSTEPS value applies to the total model. The default value for the total model is the sum of the maximum number of steps over each method in the model.
CIN (value)	*Reset the value of the percent for confidence intervals.* The default is 95%. This sets the percent interval used in the computation of the temporary variables MCIN and ICIN.

For example, to change stepwise entry and removal criteria to FIN and FOUT and use their default values of 3.84 and 2.71, respectively, specify

```
REGRESSION VARIABLES=LOGBEG EDLEVEL SEX WORK MINORITY AGE
  /CRITERIA=FIN,FOUT
  /DEPENDENT=LOGBEG
  /METHOD=STEPWISE.
```

18.59
ORIGIN Subcommand

The regression model contains a constant term. You can use the ORIGIN subcommand to suppress this term and obtain regression through the origin. The NOORIGIN subcommand, which is the default, requests that equations include a constant term.

Place the ORIGIN or NOORIGIN subcommand between the VARIABLES subcommand and the DEPENDENT subcommand for the equation. For example,

```
REGRESSION VARIABLES=SALBEG SALNOW,EDLEVEL
  /DEPENDENT=SALNOW
  /METHOD=ENTER SALBEG
  /ORIGIN
  /DEPENDENT=SALBEG
  /METHOD=ENTER EDLEVEL.
```

requests two equations, the first with a constant term (the default) and the second with regression through the origin.

There are no specifications for the ORIGIN and NOORIGIN subcommands. Once specified, the ORIGIN subcommand remains in effect until NOORIGIN is requested.

18.60
SELECT Subcommand

Use the SELECT subcommand to select a subset of cases for computing the regression equation. Only selected cases contribute to the correlation coefficients and to the regression equation. Residuals and predicted values are calculated and reported separately for both selected and unselected cases. The SELECT subcommand can precede or immediately follow the VARIABLES subcommand and is in effect for the entire REGRESSION procedure. The form of the SELECT subcommand is:

/SELECT= varname relation value

The *relation* can be EQ, NE, LT, LE, GT, or GE.

For example, to generate separate residuals histograms for males and females based on the equation developed for males alone (SEX=0), as shown in Figure 18.49, specify:

```
REGRESSION SELECT SEX EQ 0
    /VARIABLES=LOGBEG EDLEVEL SEX WORK MINORITY AGE
    /DEPENDENT=LOGBEG
    /METHOD=STEPWISE
    /RESIDUALS=HISTOGRAM.
```

18.61
MISSING Subcommand

Use the MISSING subcommand to specify the treatment of cases with missing values. If the MISSING subcommand is omitted, a case with user- or system-missing values for any variable named on the VARIABLES subcommand is excluded from the computation of the correlation matrix on which all analyses are based. The MISSING subcommand can precede or immediately follow the VARIABLES subcommand and is in effect for the entire REGRESSION procedure.

The available keywords are:

LISTWISE	*Delete cases with missing values listwise.* Only cases with valid values for all variables listed on the VARIABLES subcommand are included in analyses. If INCLUDE is also specified, only cases with system-missing values are deleted listwise. LISTWISE is the default.
PAIRWISE	*Delete cases with missing values pairwise.* Cases with complete data on the pair of variables being correlated are used to compute the correlation coefficient. If INCLUDE is also specified, only cases with system-missing values are deleted pairwise.
MEANSUBSTITUTION	*Replace missing values with the variable mean.* All cases are used for computations, with the mean of a variable substituted for missing observations. If INCLUDE is also specified, user-missing values are included in the computation of the means and only system-missing values are substituted.
INCLUDE	*Include all cases with user-missing values.* Only cases with system-missing values are excluded.

If you specify any combination of LISTWISE, PAIRWISE, and MEANSUBSTITUTION on the same MISSING subcommand, only the last one specified will be in effect. If INCLUDE is also specified, it will also be in effect.

18.62
DESCRIPTIVES Subcommand

You can request a variety of descriptive statistics with the DESCRIPTIVES subcommand. These statistics are displayed for all variables specified on the VARIABLES subcommand, regardless of which variables you specify for computations. Descriptive statistics are based on all valid cases for each variable if you have specified PAIRWISE or MEANSUB on the MISSING subcommand. Otherwise, only cases that are included in the computation of the correlation matrix are used. If you specify the DESCRIPTIVES subcommand without any keywords, the statistics listed for keyword DEFAULTS are displayed. If you name any statistics on DESCRIPTIVES, only those explicitly requested are displayed.

The following descriptive statistics are available:

DEFAULTS *MEAN, STDDEV, and CORR.* This is the default if DESCRIPTIVES is specified without any keywords.

MEAN *Variable means.*

STDDEV *Variable standard deviations.*

VARIANCE *Variable variances.*

CORR *Correlation matrix.*

SIG *One-tailed significance levels for the correlation coefficients.*

BADCORR *Correlation matrix only if some coefficients cannot be computed.*

COV *Covariance matrix.*

XPROD *Cross-product deviations from the mean.*

N *Number of cases used to compute the correlation coefficients.*

ALL *All descriptive statistics.*

For example, to produce the correlation matrix shown in Figure 18.32, specify:

```
REGRESSION DESCRIPTIVES=CORR
  /VARIABLES=LOGBEG EDLEVEL SEX WORK MINORITY AGE
  /DEPENDENT=LOGBEG
  /METHOD=ENTER EDLEVEL TO AGE.
```

18.63
Analyzing Residuals

Once you have built an equation, REGRESSION can calculate 21 temporary variables containing several types of residuals, predicted values, and related measures. You can use these variables to detect outliers and influential data points and to examine the regression assumptions described in Sections 18.17 through 18.22.

The following temporary variables are available for the analysis of residuals:

PRED *Unstandardized predicted values.*

RESID *Unstandardized residuals.*

DRESID *Deleted residuals.*

ADJPRED *Adjusted predicted values.*

ZPRED *Standardized predicted values.*

ZRESID *Standardized residuals.*

SRESID *Studentized residuals.*

SDRESID *Studentized deleted residuals.* (See Hoaglin & Welsch, 1978.)

SEPRED *Standard errors of the predicted values.*

MAHAL *Mahalanobis' distances.*

COOK *Cook's distances.* (See Cook, 1977.)

LEVER *Centered leverage values.* (See Velleman & Welsch, 1981.)

DFBETA *The change in the regression coefficient that results from the deletion of the ith case. A DFBETA value is computed for each case for each regression coefficient generated in a model.*

SDBETA *Standardized DFBETA. An SDBETA value is computed for each case for each regression coefficient generated in a model.* (See Belsley et al., 1980.)

DFFIT	*DFFIT is the change in the predicted value when the ith case is deleted.* (See Belsley et al., 1980.)
SDFIT	*Standardized DFFIT.* (See Belsley et al., 1980.)
COVRATIO	*Ratio of the determinant of the covariance matrix with the ith case deleted to the determinant of the covariance matrix with all cases included.* (See Belsley et al., 1980.)
MCIN	*Lower and upper bounds for the prediction interval of the mean predicted response.* A lowerbound LMCIN and an upperbound UMCIN are generated. The default confidence interval is 95%. The interval may be reset with the CIN subcommand. (See Dillon & Goldstein, 1984.)
ICIN	*Lower and upper bounds for the prediction interval for a single observation.* (See Dillon & Goldstein, 1978.) A lowerbound LICIN and an upperbound UICIN are generated. The default confidence interval is 95%. The interval may be reset with the CIN subcommand.

Residuals analysis is specified with four subcommands: RESIDUALS, CASEWISE, PARTIALPLOT, and SCATTERPLOT. You can specify these subcommands in any order, but you cannot specify more than one of each per equation, and they must immediately follow the last METHOD subcommand that completes an equation. The residuals subcommands affect only the equation they follow. Requesting any residuals analysis always produces descriptive statistics on at least four of the temporary variables (PRED, ZPRED, RESID, and ZRESID).

All variables are standardized before plotting. If an unstandardized version of a variable is requested, the standardized version is plotted.

18.64
RESIDUALS Subcommand

Use the RESIDUALS subcommand to obtain the statistics and plots listed below. Specifying the RESIDUALS subcommand without any specifications produces the display described for keyword DEFAULTS. If any keywords are specified on RESIDUALS, *only* the displays for those keywords are produced.

DEFAULTS	*HISTOGRAM(ZRESID), NORMPROB(ZRESID) and OUTLIERS(ZRESID) plots, SIZE(LARGE), and DURBIN.* These are produced if RESIDUALS is specified without any specifications.
HISTOGRAM(tempvars)	*Histogram of standardized temporary variables named.* The default temporary variable is ZRESID. Other variables that can be plotted are PRED, RESID, ZPRED, DRESID, ADJPRED, SRESID, and SDRESID. (See Figure 18.22a.)
NORMPROB(tempvars)	*Normal probability (P-P) plot of standardized values.* The default variable is ZRESID. Other variables that can be plotted are PRED, RESID, ZPRED, DRESID, ADJPRED, SRESID, and SDRESID. (See Figure 18.22b.)
SIZE(plotsize)	*Plot sizes.* The plot size can be specified as SMALL or LARGE. The default is LARGE if the display width is at least 120 and the page length is at least 55.
OUTLIERS(tempvars)	*The ten most extreme values for the temporary variables named.* The default temporary variable is ZRESID. Other variables can be RESID, DRESID, SRESID, SDRESID MAHAL, and COOK.
DURBIN	*Durbin-Watson test statistic.* (See Section 18.21.)
ID(varname)	*Identification labels for casewise and outlier plots.* Cases are labeled with values of the variable named after the ID keyword. By default, the plots are labeled with the sequential case number. ID also labels the CASEWISE list of cases. (See Figure 18.23.)
POOLED	*Pooled plots and statistics when the SELECT subcommand is in effect.* All cases in the active system file are used. The default is separate reporting of residuals statistics and plots for selected and unselected cases.

For example, to produce the output shown in Figures 18.22a and 18.22b, specify:

```
REGRESSION VARIABLES=SALBEG SALNOW
  /DEPENDENT=SALNOW
  /METHOD=ENTER SALBEG
  /RESIDUALS=HISTOGRAM(SRESID) NORMPROB
   OUTLIERS(MAHAL) ID(SEXRACE) SIZE(SMALL).
```

18.65
CASEWISE Subcommand

You can display a casewise plot of one of the temporary variables accompanied by a listing of the values of the dependent and the temporary variables. The plot can be requested for all cases or limited to outliers. Specifying the CASEWISE subcommand without keywords produces the output listed for DEFAULTS.

The following can be specified on the CASEWISE subcommand:

DEFAULTS   *OUTLIERS(3), PLOT(ZRESID), DEPENDENT, PRED, and RESID.* This is the default if CASEWISE is specified without any keywords.

OUTLIERS(value)   *Limit plot to cases with a standardized absolute value of the plotted variable greater than the specified value.* The default value is 3. (See Figure 18.23.)

ALL   *Include all cases in the casewise plot.* The plot includes all cases, including outliers. The keyword OUTLIERS is ignored when ALL is specified.

PLOT(tempvar)   *Plot the standardized values of the temporary variable named.* The default variable is ZRESID. The other variables that can be plotted are RESID, DRESID, SRESID, and SDRESID. (See Figure 18.23.)

varlist   *List values of the DEPENDENT and temporary variables named.* Any temporary variable can be listed. The defaults are DEPENDENT (the dependent variable), PRED, and RESID. (See Figures 18.16 and 18.23.)

For example, to produce the casewise plot shown in Figure 18.16, specify:

```
REGRESSION VARIABLES=SALBEG SALNOW
  /DEPENDENT=SALNOW
  /METHOD=ENTER SALBEG
  /RESIDUALS=ID(SEXRACE)
  /CASEWISE=ALL DEPENDENT PRED RESID SEPRED.
```

To plot outliers whose absolute values are equal to or greater than 3 based on ZRESID, you need only specify the CASEWISE subcommand. To base the plot on Studentized residuals and label it with an ID variable, as shown in Figure 18.23, specify:

```
REGRESSION VARIABLES=SALBEG SALNOW
  /DEPENDENT=SALNOW
  /METHOD=ENTER SALBEG
  /RESIDUALS=ID(SEXRACE)
  /CASEWISE=PLOT(SRESID).
```

If you request more variables than will fit on the page width set either with the SET WIDTH command or the WIDTH subcommand in REGRESSION, your output will be truncated (see Section 18.69).

18.66
SCATTERPLOT Subcommand

Use the SCATTERPLOT subcommand to generate scatterplots for the variables in the equation. You must name at least one pair of variables on the SCATTERPLOT subcommand, and you must precede temporary variable names with an asterisk. You can also specify the SIZE keyword to control the size of the plots. All scatterplots are standardized.

The specifications for SCATTERPLOT are:

(varname,varname) *The pair of variables to be plotted.* Available variables are PRED, RESID, ZPRED, ZRESID, DRESID, ADJPRED, SRESID, SDRESID, and any variable named on the VARIABLES subcommand. Temporary variables should be preceded by an asterisk on this subcommand.

SIZE(plotsize) *Plot sizes.* The plot size can be SMALL or LARGE. The default is SMALL.

The first variable named inside the parentheses is plotted on the vertical (Y) axis, and the second is plotted on the horizontal (X) axis. For example, to generate the scatterplot shown in Figure 18.20, specify:

```
REGRESSION VARIABLES=SALBEG SALNOW
   /DEPENDENT=SALNOW
   /METHOD=ENTER SALBEG
   /SCATTERPLOT=(*SRESID,*PRED).
```

To produce a scatterplot for SRESID and PRED based on the logarithmic transformation of both the dependent and independent variables, as shown in Figure 18.28a, use the SCATTERPLOT subcommand above along with the following transformation commands:

```
COMPUTE LOGBEG=LG10(SALBEG).
COMPUTE LOGNOW=LG10(SALNOW).
REGRESSION VARIABLES=LOGBEG,LOGNOW
   /DEPENDENT=LOGNOW
   /METHOD=ENTER LOGBEG
   /SCATTERPLOT=(*SRESID,*PRED).
```

To produce more than one scatterplot, simply add pairs of variable names in parentheses, as in

```
/SCATTERPLOT=(*SRESID,*PRED) (SALBEG,*PRED)
```

18.67
PARTIALPLOT Subcommand

Use the PARTIALPLOT subcommand to generate partial residual plots. Partial residual plots are scatterplots of the residuals of the dependent variable and an independent variable when both variables are regressed on the rest of the independent variables.

If no variable list is given on the PARTIALPLOT subcommand, a partial residual plot is produced for every independent variable in the equation. Plots are displayed in descending order of the standard errors of the regression coefficients. All plots are standardized.

The specifications on the PARTIALPLOT subcommand are:

varlist *Independent variables for partial residual plot.* At least two independent variables must be in the equation (determined by the METHOD subcommand) for a partial residual plot to be produced. You can specify the keyword ALL to obtain the default plots for every independent variable in the equation.

SIZE(plotsize) *Plot sizes.* The plot size can be specified as SMALL or LARGE. The default plot size is SMALL.

For example, the following commands produced Figure 18.46a:

```
COMPUTE LOGBEG=LG10(SALBEG).
REGRESSION VARIABLES=LOGBEG SEX MINORITY EDLEVEL WORK
  /DEPENDENT=LOGBEG /METHOD=STEPWISE
  /PARTIALPLOT=EDLEVEL.
```

18.68
SAVE Subcommand

Use the SAVE subcommand to save any or all of the 12 temporary variables described in Section 18.63. The format is the name of the temporary variable followed by an optional new variable name in parentheses, as in:

```
GET FILE=BANK.
REGRESSION VARIABLES=SALBEG, SALNOW
  /DEPENDENT=SALNOW
  /METHOD=ENTER SALBEG
  /SAVE=SEPRED(SE).
PLOT CUTPOINTS=EVERY(20) /SYMBOLS='*'
  /PLOT=SE WITH SALBEG.
```

This example saves the standard errors of the predicted values with variable name SE. Then the PLOT procedure is used to plot the standard errors against the values of the independent variable SALBEG. Figure 18.14a shows the plot.

If you don't specify a new variable name, SPSS generates a new variable name by default.

If you specify DFBETA or SDBETA, the number of new variables saved is equal to the total number of variables in the equation, including the constant. For example, the command

```
REGRESSION DEPENDENT=SALBEG
 /METHOD=ENTER AGE SEX
 /SAVE=DFBETA(DFBVAR).
```

will create and save three new variables with the names DFBVAR0, DFBVAR1, and DFBVAR2.

You can use the keyword FITS to automatically save the temporary variables DFFIT, SDFIT, DFBETA, SDBETA, and COVRATIO, as in:

```
/SAVE=FITS.
```

If you specify FITS, you cannot specify new variable names. SPSS automatically generates new variable names.

18.69
WIDTH Subcommand

You can use the WIDTH subcommand to control the width of the display produced by the REGRESSION procedure. The default is the width specified on the SET command. The WIDTH subcommand in REGRESSION overrides the width specified on SET.

You can use the WIDTH subcommand to change the appearance of your output. For example, in Figure 18.39 statistics for variables in the equation and variables not in the equation are displayed side by side. In Figure 18.43b, the command

```
REGRESSION WIDTH=80
  /VARIABLES=LOGBEG EDLEVEL SEX WORK MINORITY AGE
  /STATISTICS=F /DEPENDENT=LOGBEG /METHOD=FORWARD.
```

displays the statistics for variables not in the equation below the statistics for variables in the equation.

A smaller page width limits the number of statistics that can be displayed in a summary line and may also cause casewise output to be truncated (see Section 18.65). Specifying a smaller page width may also reduce the size of scatterplots and normal-probability plots in the residuals output.

18.70
EXERCISES   **Syntax**

1. Find the syntax errors in the following REGRESSION commands.

   a. `REGRESSION VARIABLES=IQ TO ACHIEVE`
      `/METHOD=STEPWISE /DEPENDENT=ACHIEVE.`

   b. `REGRESSION VARIABLES=IQ TO ACHIEVE /METHOD=ENTER.`

   c. `REGRESSION VARIABLESS=IQ TO ACHIEVE /DEPENDENT=ACHIEVE`
      `/SCATTERPLOT(*RESID, *PRED)/METHOD=STEPWISE.`

2. Write an SPSS command that requests a multiple regression equation, stepwise variable selection, and means and standard deviations. Y is the dependent variable and X1 and X2 are the independent variables.

3. What are the dependent and independent variables in each analysis in the following specification:

   ```
   REGRESSION VARIABLES=X Y A B C
   /DEPENDENT=X /METHOD=ENTER
   /DEPENDENT=Y /METHOD=ENTER
   /DEPENDENT=X Y /METHOD=ENTER.
   ```

4. What is wrong with the following command?

   ```
   REGRESSION VARIABLES=Y X1 TO X10
   /DEPENDENT=Y /METHOD=STEPWISE /METHOD=REMOVE.
   ```

5. What is wrong with the following command?

   ```
   REGRESSION VARIABLES SAVINGS TO GROWTH
   /DEPENDENT=SAVINGS /METHOD=ENTER
   /SCATTERPLOT (RESID, PRED).
   ```

6. Write the REGRESSION subcommands to obtain the following analyses:

   a. A scatterplot of the residual and variable X1.

   b. A histogram of the residuals.

   c. A listing of the cases with the 10 largest residuals labeled with the variable ID.

   d. A listing for all cases of the predicted and observed values of the dependent variable Y.

Statistical Concepts

1. Why is the hypothesis $\beta_1=\beta_2=\ldots=\beta_k=0$ of interest?

2. What assumptions are you checking when you examine a casewise serial plot (a plot of residuals in time sequence)?

3. What null hypothesis is tested by the following statistics:

   a.
   $$F = \frac{\text{MEAN SQUARE REGRESSION}}{\text{MEAN SQUARE RESIDUAL}}$$

   b.
   $$F_{change} = \frac{R^2_{change}(N-p-1)}{q(1-R^2)}$$

4. Is the following regression output possible if a variable is added at each step and none are dropped from the equation?

STEP	MULTR	RSQ
1	0.5821	0.3388
2	0.6164	0.3799
3	0.6025	0.3630
4	0.6399	0.4095

5. A researcher writes his own regression analysis program. The program produces the following regression line and confidence band. Do you think the new computer program is working properly?

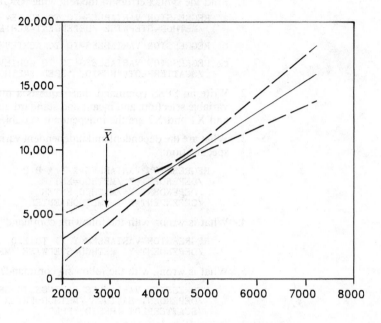

6. For what values of X can you make the best (least variable) predictions of the mean of Y at X? For what values of X can you make the best predictions of new values of Y?

7. What violations of assumptions, if any, are suggested by the following plots:

a.
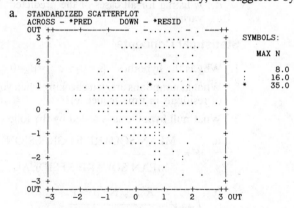

b.
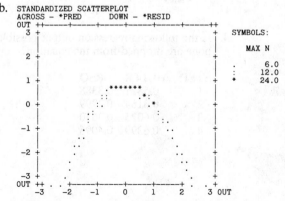

c. CASEWISE PLOT OF STANDARDIZED RESIDUAL

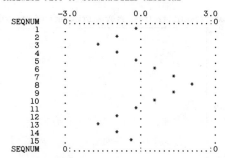

```
                    -3.0          0.0          3.0
         SEQNUM     0:................:................:0
             1      .              .    *      .
             2      .            *  .           .
             3      .        *      .           .
             4      .            *  .           .
             5      .              .*           .
             6      .              .   *        .
             7      .              .      *     .
             8      .              .        *   .
             9      .              .      *     .
            10      .              .   *        .
            11      .              . *          .
            12      .          *   .            .
            13      .        *     .            .
            14      .            *  .            .
            15      .              *.            .
         SEQNUM     0:................:................:0
```

d. HISTOGRAM - STANDARDIZED RESIDUAL
```
     N   EXP N        (* = 1 CASES,   . : = NORMAL CURVE)
     0    .33   OUT
     0    .17   3.00
     0    .24   2.88
     0    .34   2.75
     0    .48   2.63
     0    .66   2.50 .
     0    .89   2.38 .
     0   1.19   2.25 .
     0   1.57   2.13  .
     0   2.03   2.00  .
     0   2.58   1.88   .
     0   3.24   1.75    .
     2   4.00   1.63 **   .
    16   4.86   1.50 ****.**********
    18   5.82   1.38 *****:***************
     9   6.85   1.25 ******:**
    12   7.95   1.13 *******:****
    12   9.07   1.00 ********:***
     8  10.20    .88 ********  .
    16  11.29    .75 *********:*****
    21  12.30    .63 **********:*********
     6  13.20    .50 ******    .
     6  13.94    .38 ******      .
     8  14.49    .25 ********     .
     6  14.83    .13 ******        .
    17  14.95    .00 **************:**
     9  14.83   -.13 ********:*
    15  14.49   -.25 *************:*
    10  13.94   -.38 **********   .
    11  13.20   -.50 **********  .
     7  12.30   -.63 *******   .
     8  11.29   -.75 ********  .
    13  10.20   -.88 *********:***
    10   9.07  -1.00 ********:*
     8   7.95  -1.13 *******:
    11   6.85  -1.25 ******:****
    15   5.82  -1.38 *****:*********
    10   4.86  -1.50 ***:*****
    12   4.00  -1.63 ***:********
     4   3.24  -1.75 **:*
     0   2.58  -1.88    .
     0   2.03  -2.00  .
     0   1.57  -2.13  .
     0   1.19  -2.25 .
     0    .89  -2.38 .
     0    .66  -2.50 .
     0    .48  -2.63
     0    .34  -2.75
     0    .24  -2.88
     0    .17  -3.00
     0    .33   OUT
```

e.

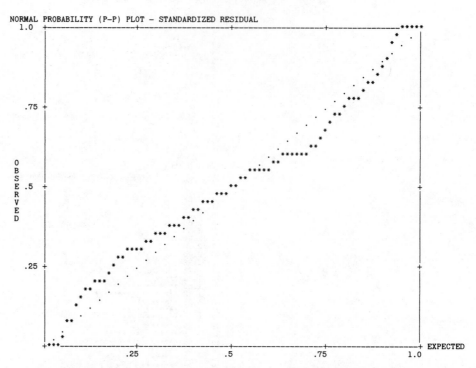

```
NORMAL PROBABILITY (P-P) PLOT - STANDARDIZED RESIDUAL
```

8. From the following statistics for variables not in the equation, which variable is entered next if forward variable selection with *F*-to-enter of 3.84 is used?

```
------------ VARIABLES NOT IN THE EQUATION -------------

VARIABLE     BETA IN   PARTIAL  MIN TOLER        F    SIG F

AGE          .18107    .22453    .92113     25.005   .0000
SEX         -.26483   -.31974    .87327     53.637   .0000
MINORITY    -.07477   -.09575    .98234      4.358   .0374
WORK         .21888    .27364    .93632     38.122   .0000
```

9. From the following statistics for variables in the equation, which variable is removed next if backward elimination with FOUT of 3 is used?

```
----------- IN ------------

VARIABLE         F   SIG F

WORK           1.217   .2705
MINORITY      13.822   .0002
SEX           45.159   .0000
EDLEVEL      238.736   .0000
AGE            4.696   .0307
(CONSTANT)     7.935   .0051
```

10. Suppose you obtain the following correlation matrix:

```
- - - - - - - - - - - - P E A R S O N   C O R R E L A T I O N   C O E F F I C I E N T S - - - - - - - - - - - -

            X1          X2          X3          X5          X4          Y

X1        1.0000     -0.0003      0.0206     -0.1384      0.9999      0.3595
         (    0)     (  300)     (  300)     (  300)     (  300)     (  300)
         P=*****     P=0.498     P=0.361     P=0.008     P=0.000     P=0.000

X2       -0.0003      1.0000     -0.0262     -0.0741     -0.0003     -0.0025
         (  300)     (    0)     (  300)     (  300)     (  300)     (  300)
         P=0.498     P=*****     P=0.325     P=0.100     P=0.498     P=0.483

X3        0.0206     -0.0262      1.0000      0.0364      0.0206      0.0322
         (  300)     (  300)     (    0)     (  300)     (  300)     (  300)
         P=0.361     P=0.325     P=*****     P=0.265     P=0.361     P=0.289

X5       -0.1384     -0.0741      0.0364      1.0000     -0.1384     -0.0083
         (  300)     (  300)     (  300)     (    0)     (  300)     (  300)
         P=0.008     P=0.100     P=0.265     P=*****     P=0.008     P=0.443

X4        0.9999     -0.0003      0.0206     -0.1384      1.0000      0.3595
         (  300)     (  300)     (  300)     (  300)     (    0)     (  300)
         P=0.000     P=0.498     P=0.361     P=0.008     P=*****     P=0.000

Y         0.3595     -0.0025      0.0322     -0.0083      0.3595      1.0000
         (  300)     (  300)     (  300)     (  300)     (  300)     (    0)
         P=0.000     P=0.483     P=0.289     P=0.443     P=0.000     P=*****
```

(COEFFICIENT / (CASES) / SIGNIFICANCE)   (A VALUE OF 99.0000 IS PRINTED IF A COEFFICIENT CANNOT BE COMPUTED)

When running procedure REGRESSION, you try to enter variable X4 into an equation that already contains variables X1 to X3. The following message is obtained:

```
FOR BLOCK NUMBER  2    TOLERANCE = 0.0001 LIMITS REACHED.
NO VARIABLES ENTERED FOR THIS BLOCK.
```

What does this message mean? Why does it occur?

11. Fill in the missing information in the following table and calculate R^2:

```
ANALYSIS OF VARIANCE
                        DF       SUM OF SQUARES      MEAN SQUARE
        REGRESSION       1                           28.90000
        RESIDUAL                   20.30000           6.76667

        F =                     SIGNIF F =  .1307
```

12. Below are regression statistics and values of the independent and dependent variables for five cases. Fill in the missing information in the casewise plot.

```
-------------------- VARIABLES IN THE EQUATION --------------------

VARIABLE           B          SE B        BETA        T   SIG T

X              1.70000       .82260      .76642     2.067   .1307
(CONSTANT)     4.30000      2.72825                 1.576   .2131
```

```
CASEWISE PLOT OF STANDARDIZED RESIDUAL

*: SELECTED   M: MISSING

                  -3.0          0.0          3.0
        CASE # X   0:.............:.............:0     Y      *PRED      *RESID
*RESID
           1 1     .             . *           .      7      6.0000      1.0000
1.0000
           2 2     .             . *           .      9        ?           ?
           3 3     .        *    .             .      6
           4 4     .           * .             .               ?           ?
-1.1000
           5 5     .             .  *          .     15     11.1000     -1.1000
2.2000
        CASE # X   0:.............:.............:0     Y        ?        2.2000
*RESID
                  -3.0          0.0          3.0              *PRED      *RESID
```

13. Fill in the missing information in the following table:

```
------------------- VARIABLES IN THE EQUATION -------------------
```

VARIABLE	B	SE B	T	SIG T
WORK	23.77950	21.55603		.2705
MINORITY	-939.85580		-3.718	.0002
SEX	-1617.52918	240.70102	-6.720	.0000
EDLEVEL		40.77734	15.451	.0000
AGE	33.43079	15.42695		.0307
(CONSTANT)	-2183.78652		-2.817	.0051

Data Analysis

Use the BANK system file for Question 1–2.

1. a. For one of the job categories (or sex-race groups), develop a regression equation relating beginning salary to some of the other variables. Check your assumptions.

    b. Prepare a brief report summarizing your findings.

2. Repeat the analysis in Question 1 looking at current salary instead of beginning salary.

3. Formulate a multiple regression model using one of the data files in Appendix B. (Do not use the PRODUCTS system file.)

    a. Use procedure REGRESSION to obtain least squares estimates of the parameters and summary statistics. What proportion of the variability in the dependent variable is explained by the regression model? Is this a statistically significant fit?

    b. Use the diagnostic plots available in REGRESSION to look for possible violations of the assumptions. Do you have reason to suspect that assumptions have been violated?

    c. Use one of the variable selection methods in REGRESSION to develop a model using the same variables as above. Do any of the coefficients change markedly? Why can this occur?

4. Use the Western Electric data for the following exercises.

    a. Use multiple linear regression analysis to study the relationship between cholesterol level (dependent variable) and age, weight, and number of cigarettes smoked as the independent variables.

    b. Does there appear to be a relationship between the independent variables and the dependent variables? Write a paragraph explaining your results.

    c. Develop a linear regression model between diastolic blood pressure (dependent variable) and whatever independent variables you may think would be related to it. Write a short paper describing your results.

Partial Correlation

In this chapter:

Goals:

- To study the linear association between two variables when the linear effects of one or more additional variables are removed from both variables.

- To test the hypothesis that there is no linear relationship between two variables when the linear effects of additional variables are removed.

Examples:

- Examine the relationship between education and salary when the effects of age and work experience are controlled for.

- Look at the relationship between cigarette consumption and alcohol consumption controlling for the effect of body weight.

- Study the relationship between husbands' and wives' purchasing behaviors when controlling for income and consumer debt.

How it's done:

To find the correlation coefficient between variables X and Y when controlling for the effects of a set of independent variables, the residuals of the regression of X on the independent variables, and the residuals of the regression of Y on the independent variables are calculated. The partial correlation coefficient is then the Pearson product moment correlation coefficient between the two sets of residuals.

Data considerations:

None of the variables involved in the analysis can be nominal. To test the hypothesis that the partial correlation coefficient is zero, the residuals must come from a bivariate normal population. The relationships between the independent variables and the two variables whose correlation is of interest must be linear.

19 Partial Correlation Analysis: Procedure PARTIAL CORR

Whenever you examine the relationship between two variables, you must be concerned with the effects of other variables on the relationship of interest. For example, if you are studying the relationship between education and income, you must worry about controlling for the effects of age and work experience. It may be that a small observed relationship between education and income is due to younger people being more highly educated but less experienced in the work force. If you control for job experience and age, the relationship between education and income may appear stronger.

The partial correlation coefficient, a technique closely related to multiple linear regression, provides us with a single measure of linear association between two variables, while adjusting for the linear effects of one or more additional variables. Properly used, partial correlation is a useful technique for uncovering spurious relationships, identifying intervening variables, and detecting hidden relationships.

19.1 COMPUTING A PARTIAL CORRELATION COEFFICIENT

Consider the steps involved in computing a partial correlation coefficient between salary and education, controlling for age. First, two regression equations must be estimated. The first equation predicts salary from age, and the second predicts education from age. For each of the regression equations, we compute the residuals for each case. The partial correlation coefficient between salary and education, controlling for age, is simply the usual Pearson correlation coefficient between the two sets of residuals.

In our example, the first regression equation removes the linear effects of age from salary. The residuals represent salary after the adjustment for age. The second regression equation removes the linear effects of age from education. The residuals represent education after the adjustment for age. The partial correlation coefficient estimates the linear association between the two variables, after the effects of age are removed.

Since we used linear regression analysis to control for the age variable, we had to make the assumption that the relationships of interest are linear. If there is reason to suspect that the variables are related in a nonlinear way, the partial correlation coefficient is not an appropriate statistical technique to use.

19.2 The Order of the Coefficient

In the previous example, we controlled for the effect of only one variable, age. However, partial correlation analysis is not limited to a single control variable. The same procedure can be applied to several control variables.

The number of control variables determines the order of the partial correlation coefficient. If there is one control variable, the partial correlation coefficient is a first-order partial. If there are five control variables, it is a fifth-order partial.

Sometimes the ordinary correlation coefficient is called a zero-order correlation since there are no control variables. (In fact it is not necessary to keep computing regression equations, since partial correlation coefficients of a particular order can be computed recursively from coefficients of a lower order.)

19.3
Tests of Statistical Significance

The assumption of multivariate normality is required to test the null hypothesis that the population partial coefficient is 0. The test statistic is

$$t = r \sqrt{\frac{N - \theta - 2}{1 - r^2}}$$

Equation 19.3

where θ is the order of the coefficient and r is the partial correlation coefficient. The degrees of freedom for t are $N-\theta-2$.

19.4
DETECTING SPURIOUS RELATIONSHIPS

Partial correlation analysis can be used to detect spurious correlations between two variables. A spurious correlation is one in which the correlation between two variables results solely from the fact that one of the variables is correlated with a third variable that is the true predictor.

Consider the following example described by Kendall and Stuart (1973). Figure 19.4a is the correlation matrix between four variables measured in 16 large cities: crime rate, percentage of foreign-born males, number of children under age 5 per 1000 women between ages 15 and 44, and percentage of church membership.

Figure 19.4a   Zero-order correlation matrix

```
PARTIAL CORR VARIABLES=CRIME CHURCH BY PCTFRNM UNDER5 (1)
    /STATISTICS=CORR.
```

```
- - - - - - - - - - - - - - -  P A R T I A L   C O R R E L A T I O N   C O E F F I C I E N T S  - - - - - - - - - - - - -

ZERO ORDER PARTIALS

                  CRIME      CHURCH     PCTFRNM     UNDER5

CRIME            1.0000      -.1400      -.3400      -.3100
                (    0)     (   14)     (   14)     (   14)
                P= .       P= .303     P= .099     P= .121

CHURCH           -.1400     1.0000       .3300       .8500
                (   14)     (    0)     (   14)     (   14)
                P= .303    P= .        P= .106     P= .000

PCTFRNM          -.3400      .3300      1.0000       .4400
                (   14)     (   14)     (    0)     (   14)
                P= .099    P= .106     P= .        P= .044

UNDER5           -.3100      .8500       .4400      1.0000
                (   14)     (   14)     (   14)     (    0)
                P= .121    P= .000     P= .044     P= .

(COEFFICIENT / (D.F.) / SIGNIFICANCE)      (" . " IS PRINTED IF A COEFFICIENT CANNOT BE COMPUTED)
```

You can see that the correlation coefficient between crime rate (CRIME) and church membership (CHURCH) is negative (-.14). The simplest conclusion is that church membership is a deterrent to crime. Although such a conclusion is no doubt comforting to theologians, let's examine the observed relationship further.

From Figure 19.4a you see that the crime rate is negatively correlated with the percentage of foreign-born males (PCTFRNM) and with the number of children per women (UNDER5). Both of these variables are positively correlated with church membership. That is, both foreigners and women with many children tend to be church members.

Let's see what happens to the relationship between crime and church membership when we control for the linear effects of being foreign born and having many children. Figure 19.4b shows the partial correlation coefficient between crime and church membership when the percentage of foreign-born males is held constant. Note that the correlation coefficient, -0.03, is now close to 0.

Figure 19.4b   First-order partials, controlling for percentage of foreign born males

```
PARTIAL CORR VARIABLES=CRIME CHURCH BY PCTFRNM (1).
```

```
- - - - - - - - - - - P A R T I A L   C O R R E L A T I O N   C O E F F I C I E N T S - - - - - - - - - - - - -
CONTROLLING FOR..    PCTFRNM

              CRIME      CHURCH
CRIME        1.0000      -.0313
            (    0)      (   13)
            P= .        P= .456

CHURCH       -.0313      1.0000
            (   13)      (    0)
            P= .456     P= .

  (COEFFICIENT / (D.F.) / SIGNIFICANCE)      (" . " IS PRINTED IF A COEFFICIENT CANNOT BE COMPUTED)
```

Figure 19.4c   First-order partials, controlling for number of children

```
PARTIAL CORR VARIABLES=CRIME CHURCH BY UNDER5 (1).
```

```
- - - - - - - - - - - P A R T I A L   C O R R E L A T I O N   C O E F F I C I E N T S - - - - - - - - - - - - -
CONTROLLING FOR..    UNDER5

              CRIME      CHURCH
CRIME        1.0000       .2466
            (    0)      (   13)
            P= .        P= .188

CHURCH        .2466      1.0000
            (   13)      (    0)
            P= .188     P= .

  (COEFFICIENT / (D.F.) / SIGNIFICANCE)      (" . " IS PRINTED IF A COEFFICIENT CANNOT BE COMPUTED)
```

Similarly, Figure 19.4c is the partial correlation coefficient between crime and church membership when the number of young children per woman is held constant. The partial correlation coefficient is now positive, 0.25. The second-order partial correlation coefficient controlling for both foreign-born males and number of children is shown in Figure 19.4d. Again, the relationship between church membership and crime is positive, 0.23.

Figure 19.4d   Second-order partial correlations

```
PARTIAL CORR VARIABLES=CRIME CHURCH BY PCTFRNM UNDER5 (2).
```

```
- - - - - - - - - - - P A R T I A L   C O R R E L A T I O N   C O E F F I C I E N T S - - - - - - - - - - - - -
CONTROLLING FOR..    PCTFRNM    UNDER5

              CRIME      CHURCH
CRIME        1.0000       .2321
            (    0)      (   12)
            P= .        P= .212

CHURCH        .2321      1.0000
            (   12)      (    0)
            P= .212     P= .

  (COEFFICIENT / (D.F.) / SIGNIFICANCE)      (" . " IS PRINTED IF A COEFFICIENT CANNOT BE COMPUTED)
```

From examination of the partial coefficients it appears that the original negative relationship between church membership and crime may be due to the presence of law-abiding foreigners with large families. In 1935, when the study was done, foreigners were less likely to commit crimes and more likely to be church members. These relationships cause the overall coefficient between the two variables to be negative. However, when these two variables are controlled for, the relationship between church membership and crime changes drastically.

19.5 DETECTING HIDDEN RELATIONSHIPS

Theory or intuition sometimes suggest that there should be a relationship between two variables even though the data indicate no correlation. In this situation it is possible that one or more additional variables are suppressing the expected relationship. For example, it may be that A is not correlated with B because A is negatively related to C, which is positively related to B.

For example, assume that a marketing research company wants to examine the relationship between the need for transmission rebuilding kits and the intent to purchase such a kit. Initial examination of the data finds almost no correlation (0.01) between the need for such a kit and the intent to buy. However, the data show a *negative* relationship (−0.5) between income and the need to buy, and a *positive* relationship (0.6) between income and intent to buy. If we control for the effect of income using a partial correlation coefficient, the first-order partial between need and intent, controlling for income, is 0.45. Thus, income hid the relationship between need and intent to buy.

19.6 INTERPRETING THE RESULTS OF PARTIAL CORRELATION ANALYSIS

Proper interpretation of partial correlation analysis requires knowledge about the way the variables may be related. You must know, for example, the nature of the relationship between need for a transmission and family income; that is, does income influence need, or need influence income? If you assume that need for a transmission influences family income, then need is specified as the control variable. One way of codifying the requisite assumptions in using partials in multivariate analysis is known as "path analysis" (see Wright, 1960, and Duncan, 1966).

19.7 RUNNING PROCEDURE PARTIAL CORR

Procedure PARTIAL CORR produces partial correlation coefficients that describe the relationship between two variables while adjusting for the effects of one or more additional variables. PARTIAL CORR first calculates a matrix of Pearson product-moment (zero-order) correlations and bases the partial correlations on this matrix. Alternatively, it can read the zero-order correlation matrix as input. Other procedures that produce zero-order correlation matrices that can be read by PARTIAL CORR include CORRELATIONS (Chapter 14), REGRESSION (Chapter 18), FACTOR (Chapter 21), and DISCRIMINANT (see the *SPSS Advanced Statistics User's Guide*). For more information on matrices, see the *SPSS Reference Guide*.

19.8 VARIABLES Subcommand

The VARIABLES subcommand is the only required subcommand for the PARTIAL CORR procedure. There are three required specifications on the VARIABLES subcommand:

• A *correlation list* of one or more pairs of variables for which partial correlations are computed. This list does *not* include the control variables.

• A *control list* of one or more variables that will be used as controls for the variables in the correlation list. Use the keyword BY to separate the control list from the correlation list.

• One or more *order values*, enclosed in parentheses, indicating the order of partials desired from the correlation and control list. The value(s) specified in parentheses should not exceed the number of variables on the control list.

For example, the command

```
PARTIAL CORR VARIABLES=CRIME CHURCH BY PCTFRNM (1).
```

produces a first-order partial correlation between CRIME and CHURCH, controlling for the effects of PCTFRNM. This command produces Figure 19.4b.

You can use the TO keyword on the correlation or control list to imply consecutive variables on the active system file.

19.9
Correlation List

The correlation list specifies pairs of variables to be correlated while controlling for the variable(s) in the control list. If you provide a simple list of variables, PARTIAL CORR computes the partial correlation of each variable with every other variable in the list, producing a square, symmetric matrix. Since the partial correlation coefficient is a symmetrical measure, the upper and lower triangles of the matrix are mirror images of each other.

You can request specific variable pairs by using the keyword WITH. Each variable specified before the keyword WITH is correlated with each variable specified after the keyword, and there are no redundant coefficients. The first variable list defines the rows of the matrix, and the second list defines the columns. For example,

```
PARTIAL CORR VARIABLES=VAR1 VAR2 VAR3 WITH VAR4 VAR5 BY VAR6(1).
```

produces a 3 × 2 rectangular partial correlation matrix with no redundant coefficients.

19.10
Control List and Order Values

The control list names the variables to be used as controls for each pair of variables specified on the correlation list. You can specify up to 100 control variables. The control list is followed by the order values, enclosed in parentheses, that specify the orders of partials to be computed. You can specify up to 5 order values. The order values must be integers between 1 and the number of control variables.

The correlation between a pair of variables is referred to as a zero-order correlation; controlling for one variable produces a first-order partial correlation; controlling for two variables produces a second-order partial; and so on. The number of control variables determines the orders that can be requested, while the order value or values indicate the partial correlation matrix or matrices to be produced.

One partial will be produced for every unique combination of control variables that add up to the order value. For example, the command

```
PARTIAL CORR VARIABLES=CRIME CHURCH BY PCTFRNM UNDER5 (1).
```

produces two first-order correlation matrices: the partial correlation between CRIME and CHURCH, controlling for PCTFRNM, and the partial correlation between CRIME and CHURCH, controlling for UNDER5. The command

```
PARTIAL CORR VARIABLES=CRIME CHURCH BY PCTFRNM UNDER5 (2).
```

produces one second-order partial correlation between CRIME and CHURCH, controlling for both PCTFRNM and UNDER5. This command produces Figure 19.4d. The command

```
PARTIAL CORR VARIABLES=CRIME CHURCH BY PCTFRNM UNDER5 (1 2).
```

produces three partial correlation matrices: two first-order partials and one second-order partial.

19.11
Specifying Multiple Analyses

You can specify up to 25 partial correlation analyses on one PARTIAL CORR command using multiple VARIABLES subcommands, separated by slashes, as in:

```
PARTIAL CORR VARIABLES=CRIME CHURCH BY PCTFRNM UNDER5 (1 2)
 /VARIABLES=CRIME PCTMALE BY PCTFRNM CHURCH UNDER5 (3).
```

You can name or imply up to 400 variables.

19.12
SIGNIFICANCE Subcommand

The optional SIGNIFICANCE subcommand determines whether the significance level is based on a one-tailed or two-tailed test. The available keywords are:

ONETAIL   *One-tailed test of significance.* This is the default if you omit the SIGNIFI-CANCE subcommand.

TWOTAIL   *Two-tailed test of significance.*

19.13
STATISTICS Subcommand

By default, PARTIAL CORR displays the matrix of partial correlation coefficients, degrees of freedom, and significance levels. You can obtain additional statistics with the STATISTICS subcommand.

The available keywords are:

CORR   *Zero-order correlations with degrees of freedom and significance level.*

DESCRIPTIVES   *Mean, standard deviation, and number of nonmissing cases.* Descriptive statistics are not available with matrix input.

BADCORR   *Zero-order correlation coefficients if, and only if, any of the zero-order correlations cannot be computed.* Coefficients that cannot be computed are printed as a period (.).

ALL   *All additional statistics available with PARTIAL CORR.*

NONE   *No additional statistics.* This is the default if you omit the STATIS-TICS subcommand.

If you specify both CORR and BADCORR, CORR will be in effect, and the zero-order correlation matrix will be displayed. For example, the command

```
PARTIAL CORR VARIABLES=CRIME CHURCH BY PCTFRNM UNDER5 (1)
 /STATISTICS=CORR.
```

produces the zero-order correlation matrix in Figure 19.4a.

19.14
MISSING Subcommand

By default, cases are excluded from the analysis on a listwise basis. If a case has a missing value for any of the specified variables, it is not used in the computation of any of the partial correlation coefficients. If you specify multiple analysis lists with multiple VARIABLES subcommands, missing values are handled separately for each analysis list.

Use the keyword ANALYSIS on the MISSING subcommand to exclude cases with missing values on a pair-by-pair basis when the zero-order correlation matrix is computed. A case missing on one or both of a pair of variables is not used. Pairwise deletion has the advantage of using as much of the data as possible. However, there are two problems in using pairwise deletion. First, the number of cases differs across coefficients; second, the coefficients represent different populations since they are based on different cases (with some overlap). When pairwise deletion is in effect, the degrees of freedom for a particular partial coefficient are based on the smallest number of cases used in the calculation of any of the zero-order correlations.

You can specify one of the following two keywords:

LISTWISE *Exclude missing values listwise.* Cases missing on any of the variables listed, including the set of control variables, are not used in the calculation of zero-order correlation coefficients. This is the default.

ANALYSIS *Exclude cases with missing values on a pair-by-pair basis.* Cases missing on one or both of a pair of variables are not used in the calculation of zero-order correlation coefficients.

Additionally, you can also specify one of the following two keywords:

EXCLUDE *Exclude cases with user-missing values.* Cases with user-missing values are excluded from the analysis. This is the default.

INCLUDE *Include cases with user-missing values.* Cases with user-missing values are included in the analysis.

By default, SPSS assumes MISSING=LISTWISE EXCLUDE.

19.15
FORMAT Subcommand

By default, the partial correlation matrix produced by PARTIAL CORR requires four lines per coefficient, one line for each of the following: the partial correlation coefficient, the degrees of freedom, the significance level, and a blank line between coefficients. Use the FORMAT subcommand to change the matrix to a condensed format or to display coefficients in serial form instead of matrix form.

Specify one of the following keywords after the FORMAT subcommand:

MATRIX *Display the coefficients, degrees of freedom, and significance level in matrix format.* This is the default.

CONDENSED *Suppress the display of the degrees of freedom and significance level.* A single asterisk after the coefficient indicates significance at the 0.01 level, and two asterisks indicate significance at the 0.001 level.

SERIAL *Display only the nonredundant coefficients in serial string format.* Degrees of freedom and significance levels are also displayed.

19.16
MATRIX Subcommand

Procedure PARTIAL CORR can read and write matrix materials, which can be processed more quickly than individual cases. Use the following keywords to specify matrix input and output:

OUT *Write matrix materials.* After the keyword OUT, specify in parentheses either a name for the matrix system file or an asterisk (*) to replace the active system file. The matrix file contains the correlation coefficients, as well as the mean, standard deviation, and number of cases used to compute each coefficient.

IN *Read matrix materials.* After IN, specify in parentheses either the name of the matrix system file to read or an asterisk (*) to read matrix materials from the active system file.

For example, the command

```
PARTIAL CORR MATRIX=IN(CORMTRX)
 /VARIABLES=CRIME CHURCH BY PCTFRNM UNDER5 (1 2).
```

uses the matrix system file CORMTRX to produce the partial correlation analysis.

The matrix system file used for the analysis must contain at least a correlation matrix and the number of cases used to compute the coefficients. For more information about matrix data files, see Chapter 2 or the *SPSS Reference Guide*.

19.17
EXERCISES

Syntax

1. Find the syntax errors in the following commands.

   a. PARTIAL CORR VARIABLES=FIREMEN DAMAGE BY FIRE.

   b. PARTIAL CORR VARIABLES=SHOESIZE IQ BY AGE SEX(3).

   c. PARTIAL CORR VARIABLES=SALARY EDUC EMPTIME(1)
      /STATISTICS=CORR BADCORR.

2. Write the SPSS command to compute the zero-order correlation matrix for the variables VAR1, VAR2, VAR3, and VAR4 and the first and secord-order partial correlations between VAR1 and VAR2, controlling for VAR3 and VAR4.

Statistical Concepts

1. In a study of the 25 largest cities in the United States, a researcher discovers a high correlation between the number of churches and the number of television sets. Given the following correlation matrix, how would you explain this apparent relationship?

	TVS	CHURCHES	TAXRATE	POPSIZE
TVS	1.0000	.7465**	−.0298	.9004**
CHURCHES	.7465**	1.0000	−.0543	.8068**
TAXRATE	−.0298	−.0543	1.0000	.0846
POPSIZE	.9004**	.8068**	.0846	1.0000

* – Signif. LE .05   ** – Signif. LE .01   (2–tailed)   " . " is printed if a coefficient cannot be computed

2. In a study of factors affecting death rates, a researcher discovers that the death rate (DEATHS) by county is positively related to both the number of doctors (DOCTORS) and hospitals (HOSPITAL) per 100,000 population. Intrepret this finding based on the following zero-order correlation matrix and first-order partial correlations.

```
- - - - - - - - - -  P A R T I A L   C O R R E L A T I O N   C O E F I C I E N T S  - - - - - - - - - -

ZERO ORDER PARTIALS


                DOCTORS   HOSPITAL    DEATHS       AGE

DOCTORS         1.0000      .9100      .6470      .7910
              (     0)    (    98)    (    98)    (    98)
              P= .       P= .000    P= .000    P= .000

HOSPITAL         .9100     1.0000      .5540      .5890
              (    98)    (     0)    (    98)    (    98)
              P= .000    P= .       P= .000    P= .000

DEATHS           .6470      .5540     1.0000      .8650
              (    98)    (    98)    (     0)    (    98)
              P= .000    P= .000    P= .       P= .000

AGE              .7910      .5890      .8650     1.0000
              (    98)    (    98)    (    98)    (     0)
              P= .000    P= .000    P= .000    P= .


(COEFFICIENT / (D.F.) / SIGNIFICANCE)      (" . " IS PRINTED IF A COEFICIENT CANNOT BE COMPUTED)

CONTROLLING FOR..     AGE


                DEATHS

DOCTORS         -.1212
              (    97)
              P= .116

HOSPITAL         .1098
              (    97)
              P= .140


(COEFFICIENT / (D.F.) / SIGNIFICANCE)      (" . " IS PRINTED IF A COEFICIENT CANNOT BE COMPUTED)
```

3. Based on the theory, "You get what you pay for," you expect to find negative relationhip between the price of a house (PRICE) and the amount of money spent on repairs in the first year of ownership (REPAIRS). But instead, you find virtually no relationship, as revealed in the following zero-order correlation matrix:

```
ZERO ORDER PARTIALS

                 PRICE      REPAIRS      INCOME
PRICE          1.0000        .0100       .7000
               (    0)      (   98)     (   98)
               P= .         P= .461     P= .000

REPAIRS         .0100      1.0000        .4000
               (   98)      (    0)     (   98)
               P= .461     P= .         P= .000

INCOME          .7000        .4000     1.0000
               (   98)      (   98)     (    0)
               P= .000     P= .000     P= .
```

But controlling for income reveals the following first-order partial correlation:

```
CONTROLLING FOR..    INCOME

                 PRICE      REPAIRS
PRICE          1.0000       -.4125
               (    0)      (   97)
               P= .         P= .000

REPAIRS        -.4125      1.0000
               (   97)      (    0)
               P= .000     P= .
```

a. Do these results support your theory?
b. Give a possible explanation for these results.

Discriminant Analysis

In this chapter:

Goals:

- To classify cases into one of several mutually exclusive groups on the basis of various characteristics.
- To establish which characteristics are important for distinguishing among the groups.
- To evaluate the accuracy of the classification.

Examples:

- Predict which offenders are going to jump bail on the basis of severity of crime, age, number of previous offenses, and family income.
- Predict success or failure of a business on the basis of number of employees, earnings-to-profits ratio, net assets, and years in existence.
- Predict which people are likely to buy a product on the basis of income, place of residence, number of children, and education of head of household.
- Predict which people should be admitted to a coronary care unit on the basis of duration and location of chest pain, lab results, and family history of heart disease.

How it's done:

Based on a set of cases for which group membership is known, linear combinations of the characteristics are formed and serve as the basis for assigning cases to groups. The coefficients for the linear combinations are so chosen that they result in the "best" separation among the groups. The accuracy of the classification can be estimated by applying the model to cases for whom group membership is known and comparing predicted group membership to actual.

Data considerations:

Each case must have a value for the group variable (which may be unknown for some of the cases) and values for the characteristics used for classification. For cases used in developing the equation, group membership must be known. Additional cases for whom group membership is not known can also be included, and these will be classified using the model. The grouping variable can be nominal or ordinal. The classification variables are assumed to be from a multivariate normal distribution.

General references:

Kleinbaum & Kupper (1978)
Tatsuoka (1971)
Lachenbruch (1975)

20 To Grant or Not to Grant: Discriminant Analysis

The ability to correctly predict outcomes is a skill valued in many professions. A good stockbroker can predict the future value of a stock; a good marketing professional, the type of people who will purchase a particular product; a good surgeon, which patients will benefit from a surgical intervention. If you ask any of these professionals how they arrive at a prediction, they will most likely mention experience. They've seen a lot of stocks decrease and increase in value. They know what distinguishes a profitable corporation from an unprofitable one. They compare companies, products, and treatments, and determine which ones are successes and which ones are failures. How the different pieces of information are used to arrive at a prediction cannot easily be described. It's a process that varies from person to person and from problem to problem.

There is a class of statistical techniques that attempts to quantify the prediction process. It is based on the same principles as human decision making. Information is obtained for a set of cases for which the outcome is known. This is the equivalent of experience. The subjective "synthesis" of the information is replaced by equations that are derived from the data and used to classify the cases into groups. Unlike human decision making, the process is objective and reproducible.

20.1 DISCRIMINANT ANALYSIS

In this chapter, we will consider one of these techniques: discriminant analysis. The goal of discriminant analysis, as outlined above, is to classify cases into one of several mutually exclusive groups on the basis of a set of observed characteristics. (Mutually exclusive means that a case can belong to only one group. For example, a patient may be either a good surgical risk, a poor surgical risk, or an uncertain surgical risk. The same patient can fall into only one of the categories. You can't be both a good risk and a bad risk.)

The actual characteristics (independent variables) used to establish the decision rule depend on the problem. You must select independent variables that you think are potentially good predictors of the outcome. For example, if you're trying to predict surgical success, you might want to include characteristics such as the severity and duration of the disease and the age of the patient. If you're trying to predict corporate success, you would include variables such as profits, sales, and expenditures. During the course of the analysis, you can determine whether all of the variables you've selected help in distinguishing among the groups, or whether some of them provide little information. If you fail to include variables that are good predictors, you will arrive at a prediction rule that does not work well. For a more detailed discussion of discriminant analysis, see Kleinbaum & Kupper (1978), Tasuoka (1971), and Lachenbruch (1975).

20.2
Basic Discriminant Analysis

To illustrate the basics of discriminant analysis, let's consider a credit-worthiness example described by Churchill (1979). (Determining who should be granted credit was one of the early applications of discriminant analysis to business.) The Consumer Finance Company, which screens credit applicants, wants to be able to classify cases into one of two groups: good credit risks and poor or equivocal risks. It has available for analysis 30 cases for which the credit rating is known. That is, these cases have been observed for a certain period of time, and the company knows whether each of the cases has turned out to be a good risk or a poor risk. The characteristics available to be used for arriving at a prediction are the annual income (in thousands of dollars), the number of credit cards, the number of children, and the age of the head of the household. On the basis of this sample, we will try to determine the relationship between the independent variables and the group to which a case belongs. Once we know what the relationship is, we can use this information to predict to whom credit should be granted, based on income, credit cards, children, and age of the head of the household.

20.3
Necessary Assumptions

You can use discriminant analysis whenever you want to predict group membership. However, you have no guarantee that the results you obtain will be the best you can do. In order for linear discriminant analysis to be optimal, that is, result in the smallest number of cases being incorrectly classified, certain conditions must be met. Each of your groups must be a sample from a multivariate normal population, and all of the populations must have the same covariance matrix.

In discriminant analysis, your grouping variable can be any measure on any type of scale. For example, it can be nominal, such as religion, or ordinal, such as satisfaction with a product. The independent variables, however, cannot be nominal. If you have nominal independent variables, they must be coded into a set of dummy variables. For example, if one of your variables is the color of a car, you must create a set of dichotomous variables to represent it. That is, you have one two-category variable that tells you whether a car is yellow or not, another two-category variable which tells you whether a car is blue or not, and so on.

20.4
Describing the Sample

The first step of any analysis should be to examine the data. This will give you some idea of how much or how little the groups differ on individual characteristics. Figure 20.4 contains means and standard deviations for each of the variables for the two groups. From this you can see that the average income for people in the second group (good credit risks) is $19,660, while for poor or equivocal risks it is $11,865. The average income for both of the groups combined is $14,463. There also appear to be differences in the number of credit cards and the age of the household for the two groups. The number of children, however, appears to be fairly similar in both.

Figure 20.4 Group means and standard deviations

```
DISCRIMINANT GROUPS=RISK(1,2)
 /VARIABLES=INCOME CREDIT AGEHEAD CHILDREN
 /STATISTICS=MEAN STDDEV.
```

```
GROUP MEANS

     GROUP          INCOME          CREDIT         AGEHEAD        CHILDREN
          1        11.86500         3.40000        32.20000         2.45000
          2        19.66000         6.40000        43.60000         2.40000

     TOTAL         14.46333         4.40000        36.00000         2.43333

GROUP STANDARD DEVIATIONS

     GROUP          INCOME          CREDIT         AGEHEAD        CHILDREN
          1         2.47371         2.08756         4.58372         1.50350
          2         4.26854         2.98887         4.32563         1.50555

     TOTAL          4.86128         2.77427         7.03195         1.47819
```

Descriptive statistics provide basic information about the distributions of the variables in the groups and help identify differences among the groups. In discriminant analysis and other multivariate statistical techniques, however, the emphasis is on analyzing the variables together, not one at a time. This allows you to incorporate information about the relationships of variables into the analysis.

In discriminant analysis, like multiple linear regression analysis, a linear combination of the independent variables is formed. This linear combination is used to assign cases to the groups. For example, consider the following equation:

Score= $-8.38 + .21 \times$ Income $+ .08 \times$ Credit $+ .13 \times$ Age of the head $+ .07$ x Children

For each case, we can compute a score based on the values of the independent variables and the constant. Based on this score, we can determine to which group a case belongs. Cases with scores above a certain cutoff are assigned to the good-risk group, and cases with scores below the cutoff are assigned to the poor-risk group.

20.5
Estimating the Coefficients

Where do the coefficients for the equation come from? In regression analysis, we compute the coefficients so that the sum of the squared differences between the observed and predicted values is as small as possible. In discriminant analysis, we select the coefficients so that the scores are similar within a group but differ as much as possible among the groups. Specifically, for our example, we want all of the good risks to have large scores, while the poor risks have small scores. Unless the scores differ across groups, we won't be able to distinguish among them. The actual computation of the coefficients is complicated, so we'll leave their calculation to the computer. Figure 20.5a contains the discriminant function coefficients for this example. (In the output, the letter E followed by a number indicates that the result is expressed in scientific notation. The number after the E, if it is positive, tells you how many places to move the decimal point to the right. If the number after the E is negative, it tells you how many places to move the decimal point to the left.)

Figure 20.5a Discriminant function coefficients

```
DISCRIMINANT GROUPS=RISK(1,2)
 /VARIABLES=INCOME CREDIT AGEHEAD CHILDREN
 /STATISTICS=RAW.
```

```
                FUNC  1
INCOME          0.2126181
CREDIT          0.8034637E-01
AGEHEAD         0.1326113
CHILDREN        0.7396355E-01
(CONSTANT)     -8.382677
```

Using these coefficients, we can calculate the score for a 42-year-old head of household with an income of $20,000, 10 credit cards, and 2 children as

Score= −8.38 + .21 × 20 + .08 × 10 + .07 × 2 +.13 × 42 = 2.2

Figure 20.5b   Average scores

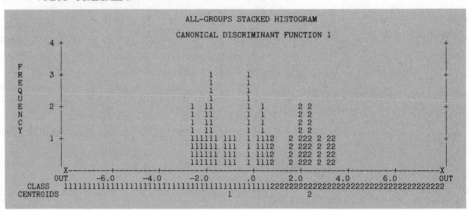

```
  GROUP      FUNC   1

       1    -1.13549
       2     2.27098
```

Figure 20.5c   Distribution of discriminant scores

```
DISCRIMINANT GROUPS=RISK(1,2)
 /VARIABLES=INCOME CREDIT AGEHEAD CHILDREN
 /PLOT=COMBINED.
```

```
                                ALL-GROUPS STACKED HISTOGRAM

                              CANONICAL DISCRIMINANT FUNCTION 1

          4 +                                                                    +
        F
        R
        E   3 +                         1      1                                  +
        Q                               1      1
        U                               1      1
        E                               1      1
        N   2 +           1  11         1  1        2 2                           +
        C                 1  11         1  1        2 2
        Y                 1  11         1  1        2 2
                          1  11         1  1        2 2
            1 +          111111 111   1 1112   2 222 2 22                         +
                        111111 111   1 1112   2 222 2 22
                        111111 111   1 1112   2 222 2 22
                        111111 111   1 1112   2 222 2 22
            X------------+---------+---------+---------+---------+---------+------X
           OUT    -6.0      -4.0      -2.0       .0       2.0       4.0       6.0    OUT
        CLASS   11111111111111111111111111111111111111111111122222222222222222222222222222222222222
     CENTROIDS                                    1              2
```

Figure 20.5b shows the average scores for cases in the two groups. Poor credit risks have an average score of −1.13, while good credit risks have an average score of 2.27. Since the coefficients for all of the variables are positive, this means that higher incomes, numbers of credit cards, ages of head of households, and children are associated with good credit card risks. Not an unexpected finding, is it? Figure 20.5c shows the distributions of the discriminant score for cases in each of the two groups. The number 1 represents the poor credit risks; the number 2, good credit risks. Since there is little or no overlap in the two sets of discriminant scores, we will be able to classify the cases well. If there is a lot of overlap in the discriminant scores for the two groups, we can't accurately predict group membership.

**20.6
Testing for Equality of the
Discriminant Function Means**

Since we want to use the discriminant scores to classify the cases into one of two groups, it is of interest to know whether the average scores in the two groups differ significantly. That is, we want to test the null hypothesis that, in the population, there is no difference in the means of the discriminant scores for the two groups. The *Wilks' lambda statistic* is often used for this. Wilks' lambda, together with its observed significance level, is shown in Figure 20.6. The observed significance level is very small, less than 0.0005, so we can reject the null hypothesis that the two groups have the same mean. If we could not reject the null hypothesis that the groups have the same means, there would be little point in trying to classify cases into groups based on their discriminant scores. On the other hand, the fact that two groups have significantly different means doesn't indicate that we will be able to separate the cases well. There may be s much overlap in their distributions that good classification is not possible, even though the means are significantly different.

Figure 20.6   Lambda and the significance level

```
DISCRIMINANT GROUPS=RISK(1,2)
  /VARIABLES=INCOME CREDIT AGEHEAD CHILDREN.
```

```
                              CANONICAL DISCRIMINANT FUNCTIONS


                   PERCENT OF   CUMULATIVE    CANONICAL  :  AFTER
 FUNCTION  EIGENVALUE  VARIANCE    PERCENT    CORRELATION : FUNCTION  WILKS' LAMBDA  CHI-SQUARED  D.F.  SIGNIFICANCE
                                                         :    0        0.2657550      34.455       4     0.0000
    1*      2.76286    100.00     100.00       0.8568810  :

     * MARKS THE   1 CANONICAL DISCRIMINANT FUNCTIONS REMAINING IN THE ANALYSIS.
```

20.7
Assigning Cases to Groups

Although it's possible to classify the cases into groups based on the actual discriminant scores, it's convenient to convert the discriminant scores into probabilities and then to use these probabilities for assigning the cases to groups. What we must calculate is the probability that a case with a score D is a member of a particular group. For example, we need to know the probability that someone with a score of −.2 is a good credit risk and the probability that someone with that score is a poor credit risk. (Since we only have two groups in this example, these two probabilities must sum to one; that is, a case is either a good risk, or a poor risk.) A case is assigned to that group for which, based on the available information, it has the largest probability of membership. If the case has a probability of 0.3 of being a good credit risk, and a probability of 0.7 of being a poor credit risk, we would assign it to the poor risk group. Again we can use SPSS to calculate these probabilities for us.

Figure 20.7 contains discriminant scores and probabilities of group membership for a subset of cases used in our analysis. The group to which a case actually belongs is listed in the column labeled "Actual Group." The group to which a case is assigned based on the discriminant analysis is shown in the column labeled "Highest Group." If the actual group to which a case belongs and the group to which a case is assigned based on the discriminant analysis are not the same, asterisks are printed after the the actual group number.

Figure 20.7   Discriminant scores and probabilities

```
DISCRIMINANT GROUPS=RISK(1,2)
  /VARIABLES=INCOME CREDIT AGEHEAD CHILDREN
  /PLOT=CASES.
```

CASE SEQNUM	MIS VAL	SEL	ACTUAL GROUP	HIGHEST GROUP	PROBABILITY P(D/G) P(G/D)	2ND HIGHEST GROUP P(G/D)	DISCRIMINANT SCORES...
16			1	1	0.1005 0.5516	2 0.4484	0.5069
17			1	1	0.1053 0.5705	2 0.4295	0.4844
18			1	1	0.8744 0.9948	2 0.0052	−0.9774
19			1	1	0.3190 0.9174	2 0.0826	−0.1390
20			1	1	0.7942 0.9927	2 0.0073	−0.8746
21			2	2	0.7301 0.9903	1 0.0097	1.9260
22			2	2	0.8961 0.9981	1 0.0019	2.4015
23			2	2	0.9872 0.9968	1 0.0032	2.2549
24			2	2	0.9310 0.9978	1 0.0022	2.3575
25			2	2	0.5496 0.9773	1 0.0227	1.6727
26			2	2	0.7276 0.9902	1 0.0098	1.9227
27			2	2	0.1484 0.7067	1 0.2933	0.8259
28			2	2	0.3103 0.9999	1 0.0001	3.2856
29			2	2	0.6243 0.9994	1 0.0006	2.7607
30			2	2	0.3024 0.9999	1 0.0001	3.3024

The probabilities involved in the the classification of cases into groups are displayed in the next set of columns. The number of interest here is the probability that a case is a member of a particular group based on its discriminant score. This probability is labeled "P(G/D)." (Those of you familiar with probability will recognize this notation as symbolizing the probability of group membership given a particular score. The entry P(D/G) is the probability of a particular score given membership in a group. Bayes' rule is used to arrive at the posterior probability, P(G/D), from the conditional probability P(D/G) and the prior probability.) For a particular case we can calculate the probability that it is a member of each of the groups.

Let's consider the values shown for case 27 in Figure 20.7. The column labeled "Highest Probability Group" contains the number of the group to which the case is assigned based on the discriminant score. This is the group with the highest probability, P(G/D). The probability that case 27 is a member of group 2 is estimated to be 0.7067, so case 27 is assigned to group 2. (The probability that the case is a member of group 1 is shown in the column entitled "2nd Highest." For case 27 the probability that it is a member of group 1 is 0.2933. Since a case must be a member of one or the other group, these two probabilities must sum to 1.) The actual group number for case 27 is also 2, so the case is correctly classified on the basis of the discriminant analysis. If the case was incorrectly classified, the output would contain asterisks after the actual group number. The values of the discriminant scores from which the probabilities are estimated are shown in the column labeled **Discriminant Scores....**

20.8
How Well Are the Cases Classified?

Although we can figure out the number of cases correctly and incorrectly classified by comparing the actual groups and predicted groups from Figure 20.7, it is easier to just look at Figure 20.8, which is a summary of the classification results. From the table you can see how cases in each of the groups are classified by the discriminant analysis. Each row and column corresponds to one of the groups. The numbers on the diagonal are cases that are correctly classified. That is, they have the same actual and predicted group numbers. For example, there are 20 cases in the poor-risk group. All of these are correctly predicted to be members of the poor risk group by the discriminant analysis; that's why there's a 20 in the cells labeled **Actual Group 1** and **Predicted Group 1**. There are no poor-risk cases who were predicted to be members of group 2, the good-risk group; that's why there's a 0 in that cell of the table. The percentages shown in the cells of Figure 20.8 tell you what percent of the members of each group falls into each of the predicted groups. Since all poor risks are correctly predicted to be poor risks, 100% of poor risks fall into the first cell of the table, and 0% of poor risks fall into predicted group 2, the good risks. At the bottom of the table, you see the percent of cases in all groups that is correctly classified by the discriminant analysis. In this example, all cases are correctly classified. Such perfect classification is unusual and should not be expected for analyses of this nature.

Figure 20.8 Summary of classification results

```
DISCRIMINANT GROUPS=RISK(1,2)
  /VARIABLES=INCOME CREDIT AGEHEAD CHILDREN
  /STATISTICS=TABLE.
```

ACTUAL GROUP	NO. OF CASES	PREDICTED GROUP MEMBERSHIP 1	2
GROUP 1 poor risk	20	20 100.0%	0 0.0%
GROUP 2 good risk	10	0 0.0%	10 100.0%

PERCENT OF "GROUPED" CASES CORRECTLY CLASSIFIED: 100.00%

20.9
From a Sample to the Population

A model usually fits the sample from which it is derived better than it will fit another sample from the same population. For example, in regression analysis, the sample R^2 is an overly optimistic estimate of how the model would fit another set of data. The percentage of cases classified correctly by the discriminant function is also an inflated estimate of how well the rule would work when applied to other cases. There are several ways to obtain a better estimate of the true misclassification rate. If the sample is large enough to be randomly split into two parts, you can use one part to estimate the coefficients and the other part to see how well they work. If you do this you're not using the same cases to both build a model and to see how well it works. Another technique for obtaining misclassification rates is called the "jackknifing" or "leaving-one-out" method. In this method, each case is left out in turn from the estimation of the function. The function is then used to classify the "left-out" case.

20.10
Comparing the Results to Chance

The percentage of cases classified correctly is often taken as an index of the effectiveness of the discriminant model. When evaluating this measure, it is important to compare the observed misclassification rate to that expected by chance alone. For example, if you have two groups of equal size, assigning cases to groups based on whether a coin comes up heads or tails results in an expected misclassification rate of 50%. In this situation, a discriminant analysis that results in an observed misclassification rate of 50% is no better than chance. As the number of equal-sized groups increases, the percentage of cases that can be classified correctly by chance alone decreases. If there are 10 groups, you would expect only 10% of the cases to be correctly classified by chance.

20.11
More about Discriminant Analysis

The credit risk example involves only two groups. Discriminant analysis, however, is not restricted to the two-group situation. You can use it to predict group membership for any number of groups. When you have more than two groups, the number of discriminant functions computed is one less than the number of groups. For each case, scores are obtained for each discriminant function, and all of these scores are used in assigning the cases to groups.

20.12
Selecting Variables for Inclusion in the Model

In the example, we had four variables we could use for classifying the cases, and we built a model that included all of them. We made no attempt to determine whether all of the variables contributed to our ability to classify the cases. It's possible that some of the variables did not contribute any new information to the problem. Eliminating such variables from the model may be desirable. As in linear regression analysis, stepwise variable selection procedures may be used in discriminant analysis to identify variables that appear to be important in distinguishing the groups.

20.13
Relationship to Multiple Regression Analysis

In the two-group situation only, there is a close relationship between regression analysis and discriminant analysis. If you code the two groups as 0 and 1, for example, and use this as the dependent variable in a regression analysis, the regression coefficients you obtain for the independent variables will be proportional to the discriminant coefficients for the same variables. (*Proportional* means that you can multiply all of the discriminant coefficients by the same number and arrive at the regression coefficients.) When you have a dependent variable with only two categories, however, you are obviously violating the regression assumption that there is a normal distribution of the values of the dependent variable for all combinations of the independent variables, and the usual hypothesis tests for regression analysis are not appropriate.

20.14
RUNNING PROCEDURE DISCRIMINANT

To run the DISCRIMINANT procedure you need only two subcommands. The GROUPS subcommand specifies the variable to be used in establishing the groups. The VARIABLES subcommand indicates which variables are to be used in predicting group membership. See the *SPSS Reference Guide* for a complete list of the subcommands available with procedure DISCRIMINANT.

20.15
Specifying the Groups

Use the GROUPS subcommand to specify the variable used to establish the group and its range of values. You can have only one GROUPS subcommand.

For example, the subcommand,

```
GROUPS = RISK(1,2)
```

indicates that RISK is the variable that identifies the group, and it can have integer values of 1 and 2. The subcommand

```
GROUPS = PATHOLGY(1,4)
```

indicates the variable PATHOLGY is to be used for forming groups, and it can have the four integer values between 1 and 4.

Cases with values outside the range are not used in obtaining the discriminant functions. However, such cases are classified into one of the existing groups if classification is requested.

20.16
Specifying the Variables

List all variables to be used in predicting group membership on the VARIABLES subcommand. You can specify only numeric variables, and you can have only one VARIABLES subcommand. For example,

```
DISCRIMINANT GROUPS=RISK(1,2)
/VARIABLES=INCOME CREDIT AGEHEAD CHILDREN.
```

requests a two-group discriminant analysis based on the values of the variable RISK. The variables named INCOME, CREDIT, AGEHEAD, and CHILDREN are to be used as predictors.

20.17
Selecting Variables

By default, DISCRIMINANT enters all variables specified on the variable list. This method is termed the *direct-entry method*. Optionally, you can specify any one of five different stepwise methods on the METHOD subcommand. These methods enter and remove variables one at a time, selecting them on the basis of specific criteria. Different criteria are used for different stepwise methods.

The METHOD subcommand has one of the following specifications:

DIRECT   *All variables are entered simultaneously, provided they satisfy the tolerance criterion. For a discussion of controlling the tolerance criterion, see the SPSS Reference Guide. DIRECT is the default method.*

WILKS   *The variable that minimizes the overall Wilks' lambda is selected.*

MAHAL   *The variable that maximizes the Mahalanobis' distance between the two closest groups is selected.*

MAXMINF   *The variable that maximizes the smallest F ratio between pairs of groups is selected.*

MINRESID   *The variable that minimizes the sum of unexplained variation between groups is selected.*

RAO   *The variable that produces the largest increase in Rao's V is selected. Rao's V is a generalized measure of the overall separation between groups.*

With all methods, all variables must satisfy the tolerance criterion before they can be entered. With the stepwise methods, all variables must also satisfy the partial F ratio criterion before they can be entered. If you wish to change the default F value

(1) for entering variables, specify /FIN=value. To change the F value for removing variables, specify /FOUT=value.

20.18
Requesting Additional Statistics

The STATISTICS subcommand requests additional statistics for DISCRIMINANT. You can specify the STATISTICS subcommand by itself or with one or more keywords.

If you specify the STATISTICS subcommand with no keywords, DISCRIMINANT calculates MEAN, STDDEV, and UNIVF (each defined below). If you include a keyword or keywords on the STATISTICS subcommand, DISCRIMINANT calculates only the statistics you request. The following keywords can be specified on the STATISTICS subcommand:

MEAN *Means.* Prints total and group means for all independent variables in the analysis. This (along with STDDEV and UNIVF) is the default if you specify the STATISTICS subcommand by itself, with no keywords.

STDDEV *Standard deviations.* Prints total and group standard deviations for all independent variables in the analysis. This (along with MEAN and UNIVF) is the default if you specify the STATISTICS subcommand by itself, with no keywords.

UNIVF *Univariate* F *ratios.* Prints F for each variable. This is a one-way analysis of variance test for equality of group means on a single discriminating variable. This (along with MEAN and STDDEV) is the default if you specify the STATISTICS subcommand by itself, with no keywords.

COV *Pooled within-groups covariance matrix.*

CORR *Pooled within-groups correlation matrix.*

BOXM *Box's* M *test.* This is a test for equality of group covariance matrices.

GCOV *Group covariance matrices.*

TCOV *Total covariance matrix.*

RAW *Unstandardized canonical discriminant functions.*

TABLE *Classification results table.*

FPAIR *Matrix of pairwise* F *ratios for each pair of groups.* The F's are for significance tests for the Mahalanobis' distances between groups. This statistic is available only with stepwise methods.

COEFF *Classification function coefficients.* Although DISCRIMINANT does not directly use these coefficients to classify cases, you can use them to classify other samples.

ALL *All optional statistics available for DISCRIMINANT.*

20.19
Requesting Classification Plots

Classification plots are useful for examining the relationship of groups to each other and graphically depicting misclassification. The PLOT subcommand requests classification plots. You can specify the PLOT subcommand by itself or with one or more keywords.

COMBINED *All-groups plot.* The first two functions define the axes. This statistic produces histograms for one-function analyses. This (along with CASES) is the default if you specify the PLOT subcommand by itself, with no keywords.

CASES *Discriminant scores and classification information.* This (along with COMBINED) is the default if you specify the PLOT subcommand by itself, with no keywords.

SEPARATE *Separate-groups plots.* These are the same types of plots produced by keyword COMBINED. However, each plot contains cases for one group only. If your model has three groups, three scatterplots are produced, unless you restrict the analysis to compute only one function. For one-function analyses, histograms are produced.

ALL *All plots available for DISCRIMINANT.*

20.20
A DISCRIMINANT Example

The SPSS commands used to produce the figures in this chapter are

```
DATA LIST /CASEID 1-2 RISK 3 INCOME 5-7(1) CREDIT 8-9
  AGEHEAD 10-11 CHILDREN 12.
VALUE LABELS RISK 1 'POOR RISK' 2 'GOOD RISK'.
BEGIN DATA
...
END DATA.
DISCRIMINANT GROUPS=RISK(1,2)
  /VARIABLES=INCOME CREDIT AGEHEAD CHILDREN
  /STATISTICS=MEAN STDDEV RAW TABLE /PLOT=CASES COMBINED.
```

- The DATA LIST command defines the variables and their location in the file. The VALUE LABELS command assigns value labels to variable RISK.
- The GROUPS subcommand on DISCRIMINANT specifies RISK as the variable that forms the groups. GROUP also defines a range of values for variable RISK (see Section 20.15).
- The VARIABLES subcommand on DISCRIMINANT specifies the variables used in group membership (see Section 20.16).
- The STATISTICS and PLOT subcommands request optional statistics and plots for the analysis (see Sections 20.18 and 20.19).

20.21
EXERCISES

Syntax

1. A department store manager wants a discriminant analysis to distinguish between good, poor, and equivocal credit risks (RISK) based on the following variables:

   `INCOME CREDIT AGEHEAD CHILDREN JOBTIME RESTIME HOMEOWNR`

   The risk variable is coded as 1=poor or equivocal risk and 2=good risk. Write the DISCRIMINANT command necessary to obtain a discriminant analysis.

2. A sociologist wants to discriminate between emotionally expressive (EMOTION =1) and emotionally reserved (EMOTION=0) people, using the following variables:

   `ETHNIC SEX IQ SES EMOTINDX INCOME EDUCATN`

   Write the DISCRIMINANT command needed to produce a discriminant analysis.

3. Find the syntax errors in the following DISCRIMINANT commands.

   a. `DISCRIMINANT GROUPS=GRADUATE`
      `/VARIABLES=GPA INCOME YEARS.`

   b. `DISCRIMINANT VARIABLES=V1 V2 V3 /METHOD=WILKS`
      `/STATISTICS=COV.`

Statistical Concepts

1. Consider the discriminant-function coefficients and variable values shown below. For the cases shown, calculate the discriminant scores. (The constant is −10.34.)

```
UNSTANDARDIZED CANONICAL DISCRIMINANT FUNCTION COEFFICIENTS

              FUNC 1

IQ              .22
EDUC            .95
SAT             .10
TESTSCOR        .35
GRA            1.52
```

CASE SEQ	IQ	EDUC	SAT	TESTSCORE	GPA	DISCRIMINANT SCORE
1	115	12	580	59	3.2	??
2	121	14	780	45	3.9	??
3	127	12	720	52	2.0	??

2. Two discriminant functions, each with four variables, are being considered in a two-group analysis. Histograms of their discriminant scores are shown below. Which function, if either, do you prefer? Why?

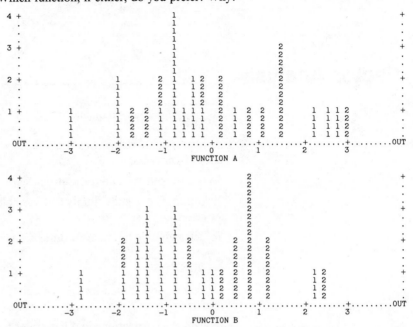

3. Two discriminant functions, one with five variables (Function A), and one with two variables (Function B), have been developed for a data set. Fill in the missing entries in the classification tables and indicate which function you would prefer for classifying new cases. Why do you prefer this function?

FUNCTION A		NO. OF CASES	PREDICTED GROUP MEMBERSHIP 1	2
GROUP EUROPEAN ORIGIN	1	17	16	??
			??%	5.88%
GROUP ASIAN ORIGIN	2	??	0	42
			0.0%	100.0%

PERCENT OF GROUPED CASES CORRECTLY CLASSIFIED: ??%

FUNCTION B		NO. OF CASES	PREDICTED GROUP MEMBERSHIP 1	2
GROUP EUROPEAN ORIGIN	1	17	15	2
			??%	??%
GROUP ASIAN ORIGIN	2	42	2	??
			??%	??%

PERCENT OF GROUPED CASES CORRECTLY CLASSIFIED: ??%

Factor Analysis

In this chapter:

Goals:

- To identify underlying constructs or "factors" that explain the correlations among a set of variables.
- To test hypotheses about the structure of variables.
- To summarize a large number of variables with a smaller number of "derived" variables.
- To determine the number of dimensions required to represent a set of variables.

Examples:

- Determine the dimensions on which consumers rate coffees. These might be heartiness, genuineness, and freshness.
- Explain the correlations in a battery of tests on the basis of factors that measure overall intelligence and mathematical and verbal skills.
- Determine the characteristics of leaders. These might be efficiency, likeability, and respect.

How it's done:

Each variable is expressed as a linear combination of a small number of common factors which are shared by all variables, and a unique factor that is specific to that variable. The correlations between the variables arise from the sharing of the common factors. The common factors in turn are estimated as linear combinations of the original variables. To improve the interpretability of the factors, solutions can be rotated. A good factor solution is both simple and meaningful.

Data considerations:

Since the correlation matrix between all pairs of variables serves as the starting point for factor analysis, the level of measurement of the variables must be such that the correlation coefficient is an acceptable summary statistic. If there are many cases with missing values for a subset of variables, eliminating cases with missing values for any variables in the analysis may leave few remaining cases. A correlation matrix with each coefficient computed from all cases with nonmissing values for that pair of variables may be used. However, this may produce a correlation matrix with inconsistencies.

General references:

Kim & Mueller (1978)
Harman (1967)
Afifi & Clark (1984)

21

Factor Analysis: Procedure FACTOR

What are creativity, love, and altruism? Unlike variables such as weight, blood pressure, and temperature, they cannot be measured on a scale, sphygmomanometer, or thermometer, in units of pounds, millimeters of mercury, or degrees Fahrenheit. Instead they can be thought of as unifying constructs or labels that characterize responses to related groups of variables. For example, answers of "strongly agree" to items such as he (or she) sends me flowers, listens to my problems, reads my manuscripts, laughs at my jokes, and gazes deeply into my soul, may lead you to conclude that the love "factor" is present. Thus, love is not a single measurable entity but a construct which is derived from measurement of other, directly observable variables. Identification of such underlying dimensions or factors greatly simplifies the description and understanding of complex phenomena, such as social interaction. For example, postulating the existence of something called "love" explains the observed correlations between the responses to numerous and varied situations.

Factor analysis is a statistical technique used to identify a relatively small number of factors that can be used to represent relationships among sets of many interrelated variables. For example, variables such as scores on a battery of aptitude tests may be expressed as a linear combination of factors that represent verbal skills, mathematical aptitude, and perceptual speed. Variables such as consumer ratings of products in a survey can be expressed as a function of factors such as product quality and utility. Factor analysis helps identify these underlying, not directly observable, constructs.

A huge number of variables can be used to describe a community—degree of industrialization, commercial activity, population, mobility, average family income, extent of home ownership, birth rate, and so forth. However, descriptions of what is meant by the term "community" might be greatly simplified if it were possible to identify underlying dimensions, or factors, of communities. This was attempted by Jonassen and Peres (1960), who examined 82 community variables from 88 counties in Ohio. This chapter uses a subset of their variables (shown in Table 21.0) to illustrate the basics of factor analysis.

Table 21.0 Community variables

POPSTABL	population stability
NEWSCIRC	weekly per capita local newspaper circulation
FEMEMPLD	percentage of females 14 years or older in labor force
FARMERS	percentage of farmers and farm managers in labor force
RETAILNG	per capita dollar retail sales
COMMERCL	total per capita commercial activity in dollars .
INDUSTZN	industrialization index
HEALTH	health index
CHLDNEGL	total per capita expenditures on county aid to dependent children
COMMEFFC	index of the extent to which a community fosters a high standard of living
DWELGNEW	percentage of dwelling units built recently
MIGRNPOP	index measuring the extent of in- and out-migration
UNEMPLOY	unemployment index
MENTALIL	extent of mental illness

21.1
THE FACTOR
ANALYSIS MODEL

The basic assumption of factor analysis is that underlying dimensions, or factors, can be used to explain complex phenomena. Observed correlations between variables result from their sharing these factors. For example, correlations between test scores might be attributable to such shared factors as general intelligence, abstract reasoning skill, and reading comprehension. The correlations between the community variables might be due to factors like amount of urbanization, the socioeconomic level or welfare of the community, and the population stability. The goal of factor analysis is to identify the not-directly-observable factors based on a set of observable variables.

The mathematical model for factor analysis appears somewhat similar to a multiple regression equation. Each variable is expressed as a linear combination of factors which are not actually observed. For example, the industrialization index might be expressed as

$$INDUSTZN = a(URBANISM) + b(WELFARE) + c(INFLUX) \qquad \textbf{Equation 21.1a}$$
$$+ U_{INDUSTZN}$$

This equation differs from the usual multiple regression equation in that URBANISM, WELFARE, and INFLUX are not single independent variables. Instead, they are labels for groups of variables that characterize these concepts. These groups of variables constitute the factors. Usually, the factors useful for characterizing a set of variables are not known in advance but are determined by factor analysis.

URBANISM, WELFARE, and INFLUX are called *common factors,* since all variables are expressed as functions of them. The U in Equation 21.1a is called a *unique factor,* since it represents that part of the industrialization index that cannot be explained by the common factors. It is unique to the industrialization index variable.

In general, the model for the ith standardized variable is written as

$$X_i = A_{i1}F_1 + A_{i2}F_2 + \ldots + A_{ik}F_k + U_i \qquad \textbf{Equation 21.1b}$$

where the F's are the common factors, the U is the unique factor, and the A's are the constants used to combine the k factors. The unique factors are assumed to be uncorrelated with each other and with the common factors.

The factors are inferred from the observed variables and can be estimated as linear combinations of them. For example, the estimated urbanism factor is expressed as

$$URBANISM = C_1\ POPSTABL + C_2\ NEWSCIRC \qquad \textbf{Equation 21.1c}$$
$$+ \ldots + C_{14}\ MENTALIL$$

While it is possible that all of the variables contribute to the urbanism factor, we hope that only a subset of variables characterizes urbanism, as indicated by their large coefficients. The general expression for the estimate of the jth factor F_j is

$$F_j = \sum_{i=1}^{p} W_{ji}X_i = W_{j1}X_1 + W_{j2}X_2 + \ldots + W_{jp}X_p \qquad \textbf{Equation 21.1d}$$

The W_i's are known as factor score coefficients, and p is the number of variables.

21.2
Ingredients of a Good Factor Analysis Solution

Before examining the mechanics of a factor analysis solution, let's consider the characteristics of a successful factor analysis. One goal is to represent relationships among sets of variables parsimoniously. That is, we would like to explain the observed correlations using as few factors as possible. If many factors are needed, little simplification or summarization occurs. We would also like the factors to be meaningful. A good factor solution is both simple and interpretable. When factors can be interpreted, new insights are possible. For example, if liquor preferences can be explained by such factors as sweetness and regional tastes (Stoetzel, 1960), marketing strategies can reflect this.

21.3
STEPS IN A FACTOR ANALYSIS

Factor analysis usually proceeds in four steps.

- First, the correlation matrix for all variables is computed, as in Figure 21.4. Variables that do not appear to be related to other variables can be identified from the matrix and associated statistics. The appropriateness of the factor model can also be evaluated. At this step you should also decide what to do with cases that have missing values for some of the variables.

- In the second step, factor extraction—the number of factors necessary to represent the data and the method of calculating them—must be determined. At this step, you also ascertain how well the chosen model fits the data.

- The third step, rotation, focuses on transforming the factors to make them more interpretable.

- At the fourth step, scores for each factor can be computed for each case. These scores can then be used in a variety of other analyses.

21.4
Examining the Correlation Matrix

The correlation matrix for the 14 community variables is shown in Figure 21.4. Since one of the goals of factor analysis is to obtain "factors" that help explain these correlations, the variables must be related to each other for the factor model to be appropriate. If the correlations between variables are small, it is unlikely that they share common factors. Figure 21.4 shows that almost half the coefficients are greater than 0.3 in absolute value. All variables, except the extent of mental illness, have large correlations with at least one of the other variables in the set.

Figure 21.4   Correlation matrix of 14 community variables

```
FACTOR VARIABLES=
  POPSTABL NEWSCIRC FEMEMPLD FARMERS RETAILNG COMMERCL INDUSTZN
  HEALTH CHLDNEGL COMMEFFC DWELGNEW MIGRNPOP UNEMPLOY MENTALIL
  /PRINT=CORRELATION.
```

CORRELATION MATRIX:

	POPSTABL	NEWSCIRC	FEMEMPLD	FARMERS	RETAILNG	COMMERCL	INDUSTZN	HEALTH	CHLDNEGL	COMMEFFC	DWELGNEW	MIGRNPOP
POPSTABL	1.00000											
NEWSCIRC	-.17500	1.00000										
FEMEMPLD	-.27600	.61600	1.00000									
FARMERS	.36900	-.62500	-.63700	1.00000								
RETAILNG	-.12700	.62400	.73600	-.51900	1.00000							
COMMERCL	-.06900	.65200	.58900	-.30600	.72700	1.00000						
INDUSTZN	-.10600	.71200	.74200	-.54500	.78500	.91100	1.00000					
HEALTH	-.14900	-.03000	.24100	-.06800	.10000	.12300	.12900	1.00000				
CHLDNEGL	-.03900	-.17100	-.58900	.25700	-.55700	-.35700	-.42400	-.40700	1.00000			
COMMEFFC	-.00500	.10000	.47100	-.21300	.45200	.28700	.35700	.73200	-.66000	1.00000		
DWELGNEW	-.67000	.18800	.41300	-.57900	.16500	.03000	.20300	.29000	-.13800	.31100	1.00000	
MIGRNPOP	-.47600	-.08600	.06400	-.19800	.00700	-.06800	-.02400	.08300	.14800	.06700	.50500	1.00000
UNEMPLOY	.13700	-.37300	-.68900	.45000	-.65000	-.42400	-.52800	-.34800	.73300	-.60100	-.26600	.18100
MENTALIL	.23700	.04600	-.23700	.12100	-.19000	-.05500	-.09500	-.27900	.24700	-.32400	-.26600	-.30700

	UNEMPLOY	MENTALIL
UNEMPLOY	1.00000	
MENTALIL	.21700	1.00000

21.5
Factor Extraction

The goal of the factor extraction step is to determine the factors. In this example, we will obtain estimates of the initial factors from principal components analysis. Other methods for factor extraction are described in Section 21.8. In principal components analysis, linear combinations of the observed variables are formed. The first principal component is the combination that accounts for the largest amount of variance in the sample. The second principal component accounts for the next largest amount of variance and is uncorrelated with the first. Successive components explain progressively smaller portions of the total sample variance, and all are uncorrelated with each other.

It is possible to compute as many principal components as there are variables. If all principal components are used, each variable can be exactly represented by them, but nothing has been gained since there are as many factors (principal components) as variables. When all factors are included in the solution, all of the variance of each variable is accounted for, and there is no need for a unique factor in the model. The proportion of variance accounted for by the common factors, or the *communality* of a variable, is 1 for all the variables, as shown in Figure 21.5a. In general, principal components analysis is a separate technique from factor analysis. That is, it can be used whenever uncorrelated linear combinations of the observed variables are desired. All it does is transform a set of correlated variables to a set of uncorrelated variables (principal components).

To help us decide how many factors we need to represent the data, it is helpful to examine the percentage of total variance explained by each. The total variance is the sum of the variance of each variable. For simplicity, all variables and factors are expressed in standardized form, with a mean of 0 and a standard deviation of 1. Since there are 14 variables and each is standardized to have a variance of 1, the total variance is 14 in this example.

Figure 21.5a contains the initial statistics for each factor. The total variance explained by each factor is listed in the column labeled **EIGENVALUE.** The next column contains the percentage of the total variance attributable to each factor. For example, the linear combination formed by Factor 2 has a variance of 2.35, which is 16.8% of the total variance of 14. The last column, the cumulative percentage, indicates the percentage of variance attributable to that factor and those that precede it in the table. Note that the factors are arranged in descending order of variance explained. Note also that although variable names and factors are displayed on the same line, there is no correspondence between the lines in the two halves of the table. The first two columns provide information about the individual variables, while the last four columns describe the factors.

Figure 21.5a   Initial statistics

```
FACTOR VARIABLES=POPSTABL TO MENTALIL.
```

```
EXTRACTION  1  FOR ANALYSIS  1, PRINCIPAL-COMPONENTS ANALYSIS (PC)


INITIAL STATISTICS:


VARIABLE      COMMUNALITY      FACTOR    EIGENVALUE    PCT OF VAR    CUM PCT

POPSTABL       1.00000            1        5.70658        40.8         40.8
NEWSCIRC       1.00000            2        2.35543        16.8         57.6
FEMEMPLD       1.00000            3        2.00926        14.4         71.9
FARMERS        1.00000            4         .89745         6.4         78.3
RETAILNG       1.00000            5         .75847         5.4         83.8
COMMERCL       1.00000            6         .53520         3.8         87.6
INDUSTZN       1.00000            7         .50886         3.6         91.2
HEALTH         1.00000            8         .27607         2.0         93.2
CHLDNEGL       1.00000            9         .24511         1.8         94.9
COMMEFFC       1.00000           10         .20505         1.5         96.4
DWELGNEW       1.00000           11         .19123         1.4         97.8
MIGRNPOP       1.00000           12         .16982         1.2         99.0
UNEMPLOY       1.00000           13         .10202          .7         99.7
MENTALIL       1.00000           14         .03946          .3        100.0
```

Figure 21.5a shows that almost 72% of the total variance is attributable to the first three factors. The remaining eleven factors together account for only 28.1% of the variance. Thus, a model with three factors may be adequate to represent the data.

Several procedures have been proposed for determining the number of factors to use in a model. One criterion suggests that only factors that account for variances greater than 1 (the eigenvalue is greater than 1) should be included. Factors with a variance less than 1 are no better than a single variable, since each variable has a variance of 1. Although this is the default criterion in FACTOR, it is not always a good solution (see Tucker, Koopman, & Linn, 1969).

Figure 21.5b is a plot of the total variance associated with each factor. Typically, the plot shows a distinct break between the steep slope of the large factors and the gradual trailing off of the rest of the factors. This gradual trailing off is called the *scree* (Cattell, 1966) because it resembles the rubble that forms at the foot of a mountain. Experimental evidence indicates that the scree begins at the kth factor, where k is the true number of factors. From the scree plot, it again appears that a three-factor model should be sufficient for the community example.

Figure 21.5b   Scree plot

```
FACTOR VARIABLES=POPSTABL TO MENTALIL
  /PLOT=EIGEN.
```

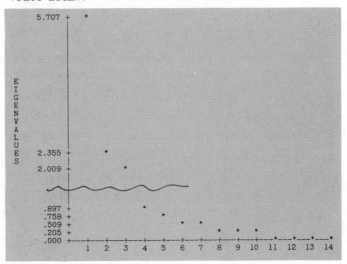

21.6
The Three Factors   Figure 21.6 contains the coefficients that relate the variables to the three factors. The figure shows that the industrialization index can be expressed as

$$\text{INDUSTZN} = 0.844F_1 + 0.300F_2 + 0.238F_3 \qquad \text{Equation 21.6a}$$

Similarly, the health index is

$$\text{HEALTH} = 0.383F_1 - 0.327F_2 - 0.635F_3 \qquad \text{Equation 21.6b}$$

Figure 21.6   Factor matrix

```
FACTOR VARIABLES=POPSTABL TO MENTALIL.

  FACTOR MATRIX:

                   FACTOR  1        FACTOR  2        FACTOR  3

  POPSTABL         -.30247          .68597          -.36451
  NEWSCIRC          .67238          .28096           .49779
  FEMEMPLD          .89461          .01131           .08063
  FARMERS          -.68659          .20002          -.40450
  RETAILNG          .85141          .24264           .09351
  COMMERCL          .72503          .39394           .19896
  INDUSTZN          .84436 •        .29956 •         .23775 •
  HEALTH            .38347         -.32718          -.63474
  CHLDNEGL         -.67430         -.12139           .52896
  COMMEFFC          .63205         -.15540          -.64221
  DWELGNEW          .45886         -.73940           .18706
  MIGRNPOP          .07894         -.74371           .24335
  UNEMPLOY         -.78714         -.09777           .30110
  MENTALIL         -.30025          .45463           .27134
```

Each row of Figure 21.6 contains the coefficients used to express a standardized variable in terms of the factors. These coefficients are called *factor loadings*, since they indicate how much weight is assigned to each factor. Factors with large coefficients (in absolute value) for a variable are closely related to the variable. For example, Factor 1 is the factor with the largest loading for the INDUSTZN variable. The matrix of factor loadings is called the *factor pattern* matrix.

When the estimated factors are uncorrelated with each other (orthogonal), the factor loadings are also the correlations between the factors and the variables. Thus, the correlation between the health index and Factor 1 is 0.383. Similarly, there is a slightly smaller correlation (−0.327) between the health index and Factor 2. The matrix of correlations between variables and factors is called the *factor structure* matrix. When the factors are orthogonal, the factor structure matrix and the factor pattern matrix are equivalent. As shown in Figure 21.6, such a matrix is labeled the factor matrix in SPSS output.

21.7
More on the Factor Matrix

There is yet another interpretation of the factor matrix in Figure 21.6. Whether the factors are orthogonal or not, the factor loadings are the standardized regression coefficients in the multiple regression equation with the original variable as the dependent variable and the factors as the independent variables. If the factors are uncorrelated, the values of the coefficients are not dependent on each other. They represent the unique contribution of each factor, and are the correlations between the factors and the variable.

To judge how well the three-factor model describes the original variables, we can compute the proportion of the variance of each variable explained by the three-factor model. Since the factors are uncorrelated, the total proportion of variance explained is just the sum of the variance proportions explained by each factor.

Consider, for example, the health index. Factor 1 accounts for 14.7% of the variance for this variable. This is obtained by squaring the correlation coefficient for Factor 1 and HEALTH (0.383). Similarly, Factor 3 explains 40.3% (-0.635^2) of the variance. The total percentage of variance in the health index accounted for by this three-factor model is therefore 65.7% (14.7 + 10.7 + 40.3). The proportion of variance explained by the common factors is called the *communality* of the variable.

The communalities for the variables are shown in Figure 21.7, together with the percentage of variance accounted for by each of the retained factors. This table is labeled **FINAL STATISTICS,** since it shows the communalities and factor statistics after the desired number of factors has been extracted. When factors are estimated using the method of principal components, the factor statistics are the same in the tables labeled as initial and final. However, the communalities are different since all of the variances of the variables are not explained when only a subset of factors is retained.

Figure 21.7 Communality of variables

FACTOR VARIABLES=POPSTABL TO MENTALIL.

```
FINAL STATISTICS:

VARIABLE     COMMUNALITY  *  FACTOR   EIGENVALUE   PCT OF VAR   CUM PCT
                          *
POPSTABL       .69491     *    1       5.70658        40.8        40.8
NEWSCIRC       .77882     *    2       2.35543        16.8        57.6
FEMEMPLD       .80696     *    3       2.00926        14.4        71.9
FARMERS        .67503     *
RETAILNG       .79253     *
COMMERCL       .72044     *
INDUSTZN       .85921     *
HEALTH         .65699     *
CHLDNEGL       .74921     *
COMMEFFC       .83607     *
DWELGNEW       .79226     *
MIGRNPOP       .61855     *
UNEMPLOY       .71981     *
MENTALIL       .37047     *
```

Communalities can range from 0 to 1, with 0 indicating that the common factors explain none of the variance, and 1 indicating that all the variance is explained by the common factors. The variance that is not explained by the common factors is attributed to the unique factor and is called the *uniqueness* of the variable.

21.8
Methods for Factor Extraction

Several different methods can be used to obtain estimates of the common factors. These methods differ in the criterion used to define "good fit." Principal axis factoring proceeds much as principal components analysis, except that the diagonals of the correlation matrix are replaced by estimates of the communalities. At the first step, squared multiple correlation coefficients can be used as initial estimates of the communalities. Based on these, the requisite number of factors is extracted. The communalities are reestimated from the factor loadings, and factors are again extracted with the new communality estimates replacing the old. This continues until negligible change occurs in the communality estimates.

The method of unweighted least squares produces, for a fixed number of factors, a factor pattern matrix that minimizes the sum of the squared differences between the observed and reproduced correlation matrices (ignoring the diagonals). The generalized least-squares method minimizes the same criterion; however, correlations are weighted inversely by the uniqueness of the variables. That is, correlations involving variables with high uniqueness are given less weight than correlations involving variables with low uniqueness.

The maximum-likelihood method produces parameter estimates that are the most likely to have produced the observed correlation matrix if the sample is from a multivariate normal distribution. Again, the correlations are weighted by the inverse of the uniqueness of the variables, and an iterative algorithm is employed.

21.9
Summary of the Extraction Phase

In the factor extraction phase, the number of common factors needed to adequately describe the data is determined. This decision is based on eigenvalues and percentage of the total variance accounted for by different numbers of factors. A plot of the eigenvalues (the scree plot) is also helpful in determining the number of factors.

21.10
The Rotation Phase

Although the factor matrix obtained in the extraction phase indicates the relationship between the factors and the individual variables, it is usually difficult to identify meaningful factors based on this matrix. Often the variables and factors do not appear correlated in any interpretable pattern. Most factors are correlated with many variables. Since one of the goals of factor analysis is to identify factors that are substantively meaningful (in the sense that they summarize sets of closely related variables), the *rotation* phase of factor analysis attempts to transform the initial matrix into one that is easier to interpret.

Consider Figure 21.10a, which is a factor matrix for four hypothetical variables. From the factor loadings, it is difficult to interpret any of the factors, since the variables and factors are intertwined. That is, all factor loadings are quite high, and both factors explain all of the variables.

Figure 21.10a   Hypothetical factor matrix

```
FACTOR MATRIX:


                  FACTOR   1        FACTOR   2
V1                  .50000            .50000
V2                  .50000           -.40000
V3                  .70000            .70000
V4                 -.60000            .60000
```

Figure 21.10b   Rotated hypothetical factor matrix

```
ROTATED FACTOR MATRIX:

                  FACTOR   1        FACTOR   2
V1                  .70684           -.01938
V2                  .05324           -.63809
V3                  .98958           -.02713
V4                  .02325            .84821
```

In the factor matrix in Figure 21.10b, variables V1 and V3 are highly related to Factor 1, while V2 and V4 load highly on Factor 2. By looking at what variables V2 and V4 have in common (such as a measurement of job satisfaction, or a characterization of an anxious personality), we may be able to identify Factor 2. Similar steps can be taken to identify Factor 1. The goal of rotation is to transform complicated matrices like that in Figure 21.10a into simpler ones like that in Figure 21.10b.

Consider Figure 21.10c, which is a plot of variables V1 to V4 using the factor loadings in Figure 21.10a as the coordinates, and Figure 21.10d, which is the corresponding plot for Figure 21.10b. Note that Figure 21.10c would look exactly like Figure 21.10d if the dotted lines were rotated to be the reference axes. When the axes are maintained at right angles, the rotation is called orthogonal. If the axes are not maintained at right angles, the rotation is called oblique. Oblique rotation is not discussed in this introductory guide.

The purpose of rotation is to achieve a simple structure. This means that we would like each factor to have nonzero loadings for only some of the variables. This helps us interpret the factors. We would also like each variable to have nonzero loadings for only a few factors, preferably one. This permits the factors to be differentiated from each other. If several factors have high loadings on the same variables, it is difficult to ascertain how the factors differ.

Rotation does not affect the goodness of fit of a factor solution. That is, although the factor matrix changes, the communalities and the percentage of total variance explained do not change. The percentage of variance accounted for by each of the factors does, however, change. Rotation redistributes the explained variance for the individual factors. Different rotation methods may actually result in the identification of somewhat different factors.

A variety of algorithms are used for orthogonal rotation to a simple structure. The most commonly used method is the *varimax* method, which attempts to minimize the number of variables that have high loadings on a factor. This should enhance the interpretability of the factors.

Consider Figure 21.10e, which shows the factor matrices for the community data before rotation and again after a varimax (and quartimax and equamax) orthogonal rotation procedure.

Figure 21.10c   Prior to rotation

```
FACTOR VARIABLES=V1 V2 V3 V4
 /ROTATION=NOROTATE
 /PLOT=ROTATION(1,2).
```

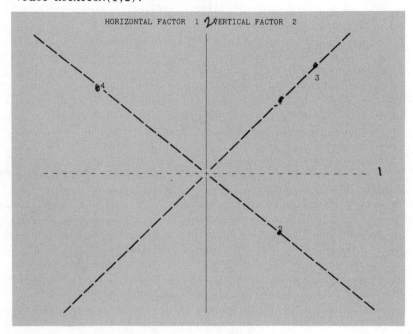

Figure 21.10d   Orthogonal rotation

```
FACTOR VARIABLES=V1 V2 V3 V4
 /ROTATION=VARIMAX
 /PLOT=ROTATION(1,2).
```

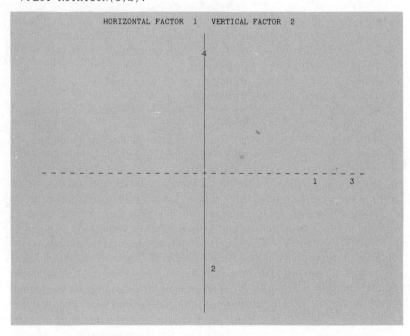

Figure 21.10e   Factor matrices for community data

```
FACTOR VARIABLES=POPSTABL TO MENTALIL
 /EXTRACTION=PC
 /ROTATION=VARIMAX
 /ROTATION=QUARTIMAX
 /ROTATION=EQUAMAX.
```

```
FACTOR MATRIX (unrotated):

              FACTOR  1      FACTOR  2      FACTOR  3

POPSTABL      -.30247        .68597         -.36451
NEWSCIRC       .67238        .28096          .49779
FEMEMPLD       .89461        .01131          .08063
FARMERS       -.68659        .20002         -.40450
RETAILNG       .85141        .24264          .09351
COMMERCL       .72503        .39394          .19896
INDUSTZN       .84436        .29956          .23775
HEALTH         .38347       -.32718         -.63474
CHLDNEGL      -.67430       -.12139          .52896
COMMEFFC       .63205       -.15540         -.64221
DWELGNEW       .45886       -.73940          .18706
MIGRNPOP       .07894       -.74371          .24335
UNEMPLOY      -.78714       -.09777          .30110
MENTALIL      -.30025        .45463          .27134

ROTATED FACTOR MATRIX (varimax):

              FACTOR  1      FACTOR  2      FACTOR  3

POPSTABL      -.13553        .00916         -.82247
NEWSCIRC       .86634       -.14256          .08920
FEMEMPLD       .78248        .37620          .23055
FARMERS       -.65736       -.04537         -.49077
RETAILNG       .83993        .29454          .01705
COMMERCL       .83432        .11068         -.11000
INDUSTZN       .91325        .15773          .01730
HEALTH        -.05806        .79424          .15101
CHLDNEGL      -.39791       -.75492          .14486
COMMEFFC       .21186        .88794          .05241
DWELGNEW       .17484        .22931          .84208
MIGRNPOP      -.12119       -.00660          .77706
UNEMPLOY      -.57378       -.62483          .01311
MENTALIL       .03133       -.47460         -.37979

ROTATED FACTOR MATRIX (quartimax):

              FACTOR  1      FACTOR  2      FACTOR  3

POPSTABL      -.14884        .00769         -.82018
NEWSCIRC       .85549       -.20254          .07706
FEMEMPLD       .81105        .32272          .21214
FARMERS       -.66736       -.00515         -.47920
RETAILNG       .85885        .23432         -.00105
COMMERCL       .83802        .04963         -.12529
INDUSTZN       .92229        .09267          .00000
HEALTH         .00097        .79832          .14028
CHLDNEGL      -.44778       -.72272          .16242
COMMEFFC       .27508        .87127          .03590
DWELGNEW       .20527        .22763          .83565
MIGRNPOP      -.10781        .01249          .77896
UNEMPLOY      -.61627       -.58226          .03168
MENTALIL      -.00897       -.48069         -.37326

ROTATED FACTOR MATRIX (equamax):

              FACTOR  1      FACTOR  2      FACTOR  3

POPSTABL      -.12961        .01218         -.82338
NEWSCIRC       .86917       -.12003          .09470
FEMEMPLD       .77037        .39514          .23949
FARMERS       -.65223       -.05898         -.49613
RETAILNG       .83157        .31678          .02580
COMMERCL       .83185        .13387         -.10273
INDUSTZN       .90854        .18199          .02554
HEALTH        -.08047        .79116          .15682
CHLDNEGL      -.37857       -.76645          .13585
COMMEFFC       .18756        .89284          .06103
DWELGNEW       .16236        .22710          .84518
MIGRNPOP      -.12675       -.01613          .77603
UNEMPLOY      -.55688       -.64006          .00379
MENTALIL       .04688       -.47050         -.38327
```

The unrotated factor matrix is difficult to interpret. Many variables have moderate-size correlations with several factors. After rotation, the number of large and small factor loadings increases. Variables are more highly correlated with single factors. Interpretation of the factors also appears possible. For example, the first factor shows string positive correlation with newspaper circulation, percentage of females in the labor force, sales, commercial activity, and the industrialization index. It also shows a strong negative correlation with the number of farmers. Thus Factor 1 might be interpreted as measuring something like "urbanism." The second factor is positively correlated with health and a high standard of living and negatively correlated with aid to dependent children, unemployment, and mental illness. This factor describes the affluence or welfare of a community. The last factor is associated with the instability or influx of a community. Thus, communities may be fairly well characterized by three factors—urbanism, welfare, and influx.

21.11
Factor Loading Plots

A convenient means of examining the success of an orthogonal rotation is to plot the variables using the factor loadings as coordinates. In Figure 21.11a, the variables are plotted using Factors 1 and 2 after varimax rotation of the two factors. The plotted numbers represent the number of the variable; e.g., 7 represents the seventh variable (INDUSTZN). The coordinates correspond to the factor loadings in Figure 21.10e for the varimax-rotated solution. The coordinates are also listed under each plot (these have been omitted in Figure 21.11b). In Figure 21.11b, the variables are plotted using Factors 1 and 2 before rotation.

Figure 21.11a Varimax-rotated solution

```
FACTOR VARIABLES=POPSTABL TO MENTALIL
 /WIDTH=80
 /ROTATION=VARIMAX
 /PLOT=ROTATION(1,2).
```

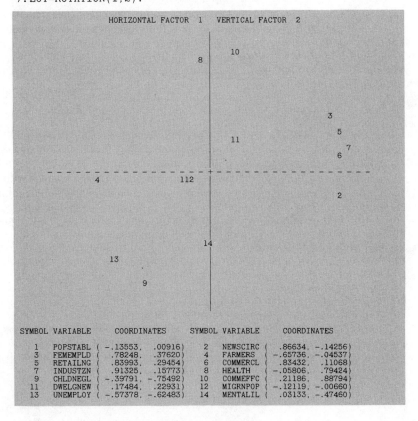

Figure 21.11b   Unrotated solution

```
FACTOR VARIABLES=POPSTABL TO MENTALIL
 /WIDTH=80
 /ROTATION=NOROTATE
 /PLOT=ROTATION(1,2).
```

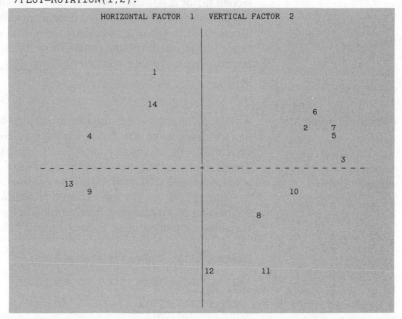

If a rotation has achieved a simple structure, clusters of variables should occur near the ends of the axes and at their intersection. Variables at the end of an axis are those that have high loadings on only that factor. Variables near the origin of the plot have small loadings on both factors. Variables that are not near the axes are explained by both factors. If a simple structure has been achieved, there should be few, if any, variables with large loadings on more than one factor.

21.12
Interpreting the Factors

To identify the factors, it is necessary to group the variables that have large loadings for the same factors. Plots of the loadings, as discussed in Section 21.11, are one way of determining the clusters of variables. Another convenient strategy is to sort the factor pattern matrix so that variables with high loadings on the same factor appear together, as shown in Figure 21.12a. Small factor loadings can be omitted from such a table. In Figure 21.12b, no loadings less than 0.5 in absolute value are displayed. Note that the mental illness variable, as expected, does not correlate highly with any of the factors.

Figure 21.12a   Sorted loadings

```
FACTOR VARIABLES=POPSTABL TO MENTALIL
 /FORMAT=SORT
 /ROTATION=VARIMAX.
```

ROTATED FACTOR MATRIX:

	FACTOR 1	FACTOR 2	FACTOR 3
INDUSTZN	.91325	.15773	.01730
NEWSCIRC	.86634	-.14256	.08920
RETAILNG	.83993	.29454	.01705
COMMERCL	.83432	.11068	-.11000
FEMEMPLD	.78248	.37620	.23055
FARMERS	-.65736	-.04537	-.49077
COMMEFFC	.21186	.88794	.05241
HEALTH	-.05806	.79424	.15101
CHLDNEGL	-.39791	-.75492	.14486
UNEMPLOY	-.57378	-.62483	.01311
MENTALIL	.03133	-.47460	-.37979
DWELGNEW	.17484	.22931	.84208
POPSTABL	-.13553	.00916	-.82247
MIGRNPOP	-.12119	-.00660	.77706

Figure 21.12b Sorted and blanked loadings

```
FACTOR VARIABLES=POPSTABL TO MENTALIL
 /FORMAT=SORT BLANK(.5)
 /ROTATION=VARIMAX.
```

ROTATED FACTOR MATRIX:

	FACTOR 1	FACTOR 2	FACTOR 3
INDUSTZN	.91325		
NEWSCIRC	.86634		
RETAILNG	.83993		
COMMERCL	.83432		
FEMEMPLD	.78248		
FARMERS	-.65736		
COMMEFFC		.88794	
HEALTH		.79424	
CHLDNEGL		-.75492	
UNEMPLOY	-.57378	-.62483	
MENTALIL			
DWELGNEW			.84208
POPSTABL			-.82247
MIGRNPOP			.77706

21.13
Factor Scores

Since one of the goals of factor analysis is to reduce a large number of variables to a smaller number of factors, it is often desirable to estimate factor scores for each case. The factor scores can be used in subsequent analyses to represent the values of the factors. Plots of factor scores for pairs of factors are useful for detecting unusual observations.

Recall from Section 21.1 that a factor can be estimated as a linear combination of the original variables. That is, for case k, the score for the jth factor is estimated as

$$\hat{F}_{jk} = \sum_{i=1}^{p} W_{ji} X_{ik}$$

Equation 21.13a

where X_{ik} is the standardized value of the ith variable for case k and W_{ji} is the factor score coefficient for the jth factor and the ith variable. Except for principal components analysis, exact factor scores cannot be obtained. Estimates are obtained instead.

There are several methods for estimating factor score coefficients. Each has different properties and results in different scores (see Tucker, 1971; Harman, 1967). The three methods available in SPSS FACTOR (Anderson-Rubin, regression, and Bartlett) all result in scores with a mean of 0. The Anderson-Rubin method always produces uncorrelated scores with a standard deviation of 1, even when the original factors are estimated to be correlated. The regression factor scores (the default) have a variance equal to the squared multiple correlation between the estimated factor scores and the true factor values. (These are shown on the diagonal in Figure 21.13b.) Regression method factor scores can be correlated even when factors are assumed to be orthogonal. If principal components extraction is used, all three methods result in the same factor scores, which are no longer estimated but are exact.

Figure 21.13a contains the factor score coefficients used to calculate regression method factor scores for the community data. The correlation matrix for the estimated scores is shown in Figure 21.13b.

Figure 21.13a   Factor coefficient matrix

```
FACTOR VARIABLES=POPSTABL TO MENTALIL
 /PRINT=FSCORES
 /EXTRACTION=ML /ROTATION=VARIMAX.
```

```
FACTOR SCORE COEFFICIENT MATRIX:

               FACTOR  1      FACTOR  2      FACTOR  3

POPSTABL       -.00150         .03191        -.15843
NEWSCIRC        .05487        -.06095         .03524
FEMEMPLD        .01729         .14014         .05328
FARMERS        -.01797         .00113        -.11462
RETAILNG        .03728         .09460        -.03577
COMMERCL        .20579        -.11667        -.10723
INDUSTZN        .77285        -.27024         .00882
HEALTH         -.02786         .09971        -.00161
CHLDNEGL        .08404        -.44657         .16521
COMMEFFC       -.05030         .23211        -.03623
DWELGNEW       -.05117         .07034         .68792
MIGRNPOP        .00029        -.03198         .09778
UNEMPLOY        .03856        -.26435         .05378
MENTALIL        .01264        -.04224        -.01691
```

Figure 21.13b   Covariance matrix for estimated regression factor scores

```
FACTOR VARIABLES=POPSTABL TO MENTALIL
 /PRINT=FSCORES
 /EXTRACTION=ML /ROTATION=VARIMAX.
```

```
COVARIANCE MATRIX FOR ESTIMATED REGRESSION FACTOR SCORES:

               FACTOR  1      FACTOR  2      FACTOR  3

FACTOR  1       .96763
FACTOR  2       .03294         .87641
FACTOR  3       .00042         .02544         .89452
```

To see how factor scores are calculated, consider Table 21.13, which contains standardized values for the original 14 variables for 5 counties, and factor score values for the three factors. For each factor, the factor scores are obtained by multiplying the standardized values by the corresponding factor score coefficients. Thus, for Adams county the value for Factor 1 is -1.328.

$-.00150 \times -.36 + .05487 \times -.93 + .01729 \times -1.06 + ...$ **Equation 21.13b**
$+ .01264 \times -.76 = -1.328$

Table 21.13   Standardized values and factor scores

	County				
Variable	Adams	Butler	Crawford	Cuyahoga	Hamilton
POPSTABL	−0.36	−1.49	2.44	−0.13	−0.30
NEWSCIRC	−0.93	0.39	−0.26	2.04	1.17
FEMEMPLD	−1.06	0.41	0.24	1.30	1.03
FARMERS	2.20	−0.67	0.01	−0.93	−0.90
RETAILNG	−1.41	0.49	0.58	1.15	1.07
COMMERCL	−0.89	−0.30	−0.07	1.58	2.02
INDUSTZN	−1.14	−0.11	0.03	1.53	1.85
HEALTH	−0.25	−0.56	−1.32	−0.36	−1.17
CHLDNEGL	−1.26	0.79	−0.61	0.63	0.99
COMMEFFC	−0.20	0.78	−0.87	−0.78	−1.66
DWELGNEW	−0.52	0.52	−1.09	−0.01	−0.22
MIGRNPOP	−0.98	0.16	−0.60	0.63	1.13
UNEMPLOY	−0.75	−0.36	−0.44	1.56	0.76
MENTALIL	−0.76	−0.77	−0.46	−0.14	0.61
Factor	**Scores**				
Factor 1	−1.328	−0.089	0.083	1.862	2.233
Factor 2	0.897	0.027	0.197	−1.362	−1.79
Factor 3	−0.830	0.831	−1.290	0.342	0.226

21.14
RUNNING
PROCEDURE FACTOR

A variety of extraction and rotation techniques are available in the SPSS FACTOR procedure. The extraction methods available include principal components analysis (Section 21.5) and the maximum-likelihood factor method. The factor rotation methods are varimax, equamax, quartimax, and oblimin.

You can also request scree plots and factor loading plots to help in selecting and interpreting factors. FACTOR will accept a correlation matrix or a factor loading matrix as input, as well as actual data values.

21.15
Global and Analysis Block
Subcommands

There are two basic types of FACTOR subcommands: global and analysis block. Global subcommands are specified once and are in effect for the entire FACTOR procedure. Analysis block subcommands apply only to the ANALYSIS subcommand that precedes them.

The global subcommands are VARIABLES, MISSING, WIDTH, and MATRIX. The VARIABLES subcommand identifies the variables from the active system file available for analysis by FACTOR. The MISSING subcommand provides several alternative missing-value treatments. WIDTH controls the width of the display. The MATRIX subcommand enables you to perform factor analysis from a matrix of correlations or factors.

An analysis block begins with an ANALYSIS subcommand, which names a subset of variables from the list specified on the VARIABLES subcommand. If you omit the ANALYSIS subcommand, all variables named on the VARIABLES subcommand are used. The analysis block subcommands are ANALYSIS, EXTRACTION, ROTATION, DIAGONAL, PLOT, PRINT, and SAVE.

The EXTRACTION subcommand initiates the extraction phase. (A principal components analysis is performed if there is no EXTRACTION subcommand.) The ROTATION subcommand, which specifies the rotation method to use, initiates the rotation phase. The default varimax rotation is obtained if you omit both EXTRACTION and ROTATION. No rotation occurs if EXTRACTION is specified without ROTATION.

The CRITERIA and FORMAT subcommands may be specified for each analysis block, but once specified they remain in effect for subsequent analysis blocks unless explicitly overridden.

21.16
Subcommand Order

The global subcommands VARIABLES and MISSING must be the first specifications. If the MATRIX subcommand is used, it must appear before the analysis block. WIDTH can appear anywhere.

The placement of CRITERIA is important, since it affects any extractions and rotations that follow, until a new CRITERIA subcommand is specified. More than one CRITERIA subcommand may be specified within an analysis block.

21.17
VARIABLES Subcommand

The VARIABLES subcommand lists the variables to analyze. If you do not specify a subsequent EXTRACTION or ROTATION subcommand, the default principal components analysis with varimax rotation is produced. For example, the command

```
FACTOR VARIABLES= POPSTABL NEWSCIRC FEMEMPLD FARMERS RETAILNG
 COMMERCL INDUSTZN  HEALTH CHLDNEGL COMMEFFC DWELGNEW MIGRNPOP
 UNEMPLOY MENTALIL.
```

produces a principal components analysis with varimax rotation for the specified variables. If the variables exist in that order on the active system file, the command

```
FACTOR VARIABLES=POPSTABL TO MENTALIL.
```

produces the same results. The output is shown in Figures 21.5a, 21.6, and 21.7.

VARIABLES is the only required subcommand and must be placed before all other subcommands except MISSING, WIDTH, and MATRIX. Only variables named on the VARIABLES subcommand can be referred to in subsequent subcommands. You can specify only one VARIABLES subcommand on a FACTOR command.

21.18
MISSING Subcommand

FACTOR results are based on the correlation matrix for the variables listed on the VARIABLES subcommand. Use the MISSING subcommand to specify the missing-value treatment for this matrix. If you omit the MISSING subcommand, or include it with no specifications, missing values are deleted listwise.

LISTWISE *Delete missing values listwise.* Only cases with valid values on all variables on the VARIABLES subcommand are used. This is the default.

PAIRWISE *Delete missing values pairwise.* Cases with complete data on each pair of variables correlated are used.

MEANSUB *Replace missing values with the variable mean.* This includes both user-missing and system-missing values.

INCLUDE *Include missing values.* Cases with user-missing values are treated as valid observations. System-missing values are excluded from analysis.

For example, the command

```
FACTOR VARIABLES=IQ GPA TESTSCOR STRESS SAT PSYCHTST
 /MISSING=PAIRWISE.
```

requests a default analysis that uses pairwise missing-value treatment in calculating the correlation matrix.

You can specify only one MISSING subcommand per FACTOR command. The MISSING subcommand must be placed before all other subcommands except VARIABLES and WIDTH. MISSING is ignored with matrix input.

21.19
WIDTH Subcommand

The WIDTH subcommand controls the display width for factor output. For example, the subcommand

```
 /WIDTH=80
```

requests output that is 80 characters wide. The value on WIDTH must be an integer. This value overrides the one specified on the SET command. You can specify only one WIDTH subcommand per FACTOR command. The WIDTH subcommand can be placed anywhere.

21.20
ANALYSIS Subcommand

The ANALYSIS subcommand allows you to perform analyses on subsets of variables named on the VARIABLES subcommand. For example, the command

```
FACTOR VARIABLES=POPSTABL TO MENTALIL
 /ANALYSIS=FEMEMPLD FARMERS INDUSTZN HEALTH CHILDNEGL DWELGNEW
 /ANALYSIS=POPSTABL NEWSCIRC FEMEMPLD COMMERCL UNEMPLOY MENTALIL.
```

requests two default principal components analyses. The first uses variables FEMEMPLD, FARMERS, INDUSTZN, HEALTH, CHLDNEGL, and DWELGNEW, and the second uses variables POPSTABL, NEWSCIRC, FEMEMPLD, COMMERCL, UNEMPLOY, and MENTALIL.

If you do not include the ANALYSIS subcommand, FACTOR uses all of the variables listed on the VARIABLES subcommand for the analysis and produces the following message:

```
>NOTE    11284
>Since the ANALYSIS subcommand is not used, all variables on the VARIABLES
>subcommand will be used for the first analysis.
```

The TO keyword in a variable list on the ANALYSIS subcommand refers to the order of variables on the VARIABLES subcommand, not to their order in the file. Otherwise, the usual SPSS conventions for variable lists are followed. You can use the keyword ALL to refer to all of the variables listed on the VARIABLES subcommand.

If you follow the VARIABLES subcommand with another analysis block subcommand prior to the ANALYSIS subcommand, you implicitly initiate an analysis block. For example, the command

```
FACTOR VARIABLES=POPSTABL TO MENTALIL
 /PRINT=DEFAULT CORRELATION
 /ANALYSIS=FEMEMPLD FARMERS INDUSTZN HEALTH CHILDNEGL DWELGNEW
 /ANALYSIS=POPSTABL NEWSCIRC FEMEMPLD COMMERCL UNEMPLOY MENTALIL.
```

requests three analyses. The first uses all variables and displays the correlation matrix along with the defaults, and the second and third use different subsets of the variable list and display only the defaults.

21.21 EXTRACTION Subcommand

To specify the extraction method, use the EXTRACTION subcommand with one of the following keywords:

PC *Principal components analysis.* This is the default.
PAF *Principal axis factoring.*
ML *Maximum likelihood.*
ALPHA *Alpha factoring.*
IMAGE *Image factoring.*
ULS *Unweighted least squares.*
GLS *Generalized least squares.*

You can specify more than one EXTRACTION subcommand. For example, the command

```
FACTOR VARIABLES=IQ GPA TESTSCOR STRESS SAT PSYCHTST
 /EXTRACTION=ML
 /EXTRACTION=PC.
```

produces output based on two extraction methods—maximum likelihood and principal components. You can specify multiple EXTRACTION subcommands in each analysis block to produce output for different extraction methods.

If you use the EXTRACTION subcommand without a subsequent ROTATION subcommand, the factor pattern matrix is not rotated (see Section 21.24).

21.22 DIAGONAL Subcommand

Use the DIAGONAL subcommand to specify initial diagonal values in conjunction with principal axis factoring (EXTRACTION=PAF). You can specify any one of the following:

value list *Diagonal values.* User-supplied diagonal values are used only for principal axis factoring.
DEFAULT *1's on the diagonal for principal components or initial communality estimates on the diagonal for factor methods.*

You must supply the same number of diagonal values as there are variables in the analysis. For example, the command

```
FACTOR VARIABLES=IQ GPA TESTSCOR SAT EDYEARS
 /DIAGONAL=.55 .45 .35 .40 .50
 /EXTRACTION=PAF.
```

assigns five diagonal values for the specified principal axis factoring. You can use the prefix *n* and an asterisk to indicate replicated values. For example, 5*0.80 is the same as specifying 0.80 five times.

21.23
CRITERIA Subcommand

Use CRITERIA to control criteria for extractions and rotations that follow the subcommand. The following keywords are available:

FACTORS(nf)   *Number of factors extracted.* The default is the number of eigenvalues greater than MINEIGEN (see MINEIGEN).

MINEIGEN(eg)   *Minimum eigenvalue used to control the number of factors.* The default value is 1.

ITERATE(ni)   *Number of iterations for the factor solution.* The default value is 25.

ECONVERGE(e1)   *Convergence criterion for extraction.* The default value is 0.001.

RCONVERGE(e2)   *Convergence criterion for rotation.* The default value is 0.0001.

KAISER   *Kaiser normalization in rotation.* This is the default.

NOKAISER   *No Kaiser normalization.*

DELTA(d)   *Value of delta for direct oblimin rotation.* The default value is 0.

DEFAULT   *Use default values for all criteria.*

More than one CRITERIA subcommand may be specified within an analysis block. Each CRITERIA subcommand affects the subsequent extractions and rotations. Once specified, criteria stay in effect for subsequent analysis blocks unless explicitly overridden by new CRITERIA subcommands. For example, the command

```
FACTOR VARIABLES=IQ GPA TESTSCOR STRESS SAT PSYCHTST
 /CRITERIA=FACTORS(2)
 /EXTRACTION=ML
 /ANALYSIS=ALL
 /EXTRACTION=ULS
 /CRITERIA=DEFAULT
 /EXTRACTION=ML.
```

produces three factor analyses for the same set of variables. The first analysis limits the number of factors extracted to 2, using the maximum-likelihood extraction method. The second analysis also limits the number of factors to 2 but uses the unweighted least squares extraction method. The third analysis extracts all factors whose eigenvalue is greater than 1, using the maximum-likelihood extraction method.

21.24
Rotating Factors

Four rotation methods are available in FACTOR: varimax, equamax, quartimax, and oblimin (see Section 21.10). When both the EXTRACTION and ROTATION subcommands are omitted, the factors are rotated using the varimax method. However, if EXTRACTION is specified but ROTATION is not, the factors are not rotated. To specify a rotation method other than these defaults, use the ROTATION subcommand.

VARIMAX   *Varimax rotation.* This is the default if both EXTRACTION and ROTATION are omitted.

EQUAMAX   *Equamax rotation.*

QUARTIMAX   *Quartimax rotation.*

OBLIMIN   *Direct oblimin rotation.* OBLIMIN uses a default delta value of 0. Use the CRITERIA subcommand to change this default (see Section 21.23).

NOROTATE   *No rotation.* This is the default if EXTRACTION is specified but ROTATION is not.

To obtain a factor loading plot based on unrotated factors, use the PLOT subcommand (see Section 21.27) and specify NOROTATE in the ROTATION subcommand. For example, the following command produced Figure 21.11b:

```
FACTOR VARIABLES=POPSTABL TO MENTALIL
 /WIDTH=80
 /ROTATION=NOROTATE
 /PLOT=ROTATION(1,2).
```

You can specify more than one rotation for a given extraction by using multiple ROTATION subcommands. See Section 21.23 for information on controlling rotation criteria.

21.25
PRINT Subcommand

By default, the statistics listed below under INITIAL, EXTRACTION, and ROTATION are displayed. Use the PRINT subcommand to request additional statistics. If you specify PRINT, only those statistics explicitly named are displayed. You can use only one PRINT subcommand for each analysis block.

UNIVARIATE	*Numbers of valid observations, means, and standard deviations for the variables named on the ANALYSIS subcommand.*
INITIAL	*Initial communalities, eigenvalues, and percentage of variance explained.* (See Sections 21.5 and 21.7.)
CORRELATION	*Correlation matrix for the variables named on the ANALYSIS subcommand.*
SIG	*Significance levels of correlations.* These are one-tailed probabilities.
DET	*The determinant of the correlation matrix.*
INV	*The inverse of the correlation matrix.*
AIC	*The anti-image covariance and correlation matrices.*
KMO	*The Kaiser-Meyer-Olkin measure of sampling adequacy and Bartlett's test of sphericity.* (See Section 21.4.)
EXTRACTION	*Communalities, eigenvalues, and rotated factor loadings.* (See Sections 21.5 through 21.8.)
REPR	*Reproduced correlations and their residuals.*
ROTATION	*Rotated factor pattern and structure matrices, factor transformation matrix, and factor correlation matrix.* (See Sections 21.10.)
FSCORE	*The factor score coefficient matrix.* By default, this is based on a regression solution.
DEFAULT	*INITIAL, EXTRACTION, and ROTATION statistics.* If you use the EXTRACTION subcommand without a subsequent ROTATION subcommand, only the statistics specified by INITIAL and EXTRACTION are displayed by default.
ALL	*All available statistics.*

21.26
FORMAT Subcommand

Use the FORMAT subcommand to reformat the display of the factor loading and structure matrices to help you interpret the factors (see Section 21.12). You can use only one FORMAT subcommand per analysis block. The following keywords may be specified on FORMAT:

SORT   *Order the factor loadings by magnitude.*
BLANK(n) *Suppress coefficients lower in absolute value than* n.
DEFAULT *Turn off blanking and sorting.*

For example, the command

```
FACTOR VARIABLES=POPSTABL TO MENTALIL
 /FORMAT=SORT BLANK(.5).
```

produces the output in Figure 21.12b.

The FORMAT subcommand should only be specified once within each analysis block. Once specified, the FORMAT subcommand remains in effect for subsequent analysis blocks, unless it is explicitly overridden with a new FORMAT subcommand.

21.27
PLOT Subcommand

To obtain a scree plot (Section 21.5) or a factor loading plot (Section 21.11), use the PLOT subcommand with the following keywords:

EIGEN   *Scree plot.* Plots the eigenvalues in descending order.
ROTATION(n1 n2)   *Factor loading plot.* The specifications $n1$ and $n2$ refer to the factor numbers used as the axes. Several pairs of factors in parentheses can be specified on one ROTATION specification. A plot is displayed for each pair of factors enclosed in parentheses.

You can specify only one PLOT subcommand per analysis block. Plots are based on rotated factors. To get an unrotated factor plot, you must explicitly specify NOROTATE on the ROTATION subcommand (see Section 21.24).

The plots in Figures 21.5b and 21.11a as well as two additional factor plots can be produced by specifying

```
FACTOR VARIABLES=POPSTABL TO MENTALIL
 /PLOT=EIGEN ROTATION(1 2)(1 3)(2 3).
```

21.28
SAVE Subcommand

Use the SAVE subcommand to compute and save factor scores on the active system file. (Factor scores cannot be produced from matrix input.) The specifications on the SAVE subcommand include the method for calculating factor scores, how many factor scores to calculate, and a *rootname* to be used in naming the factor scores.

First, choose one of the following method keywords (see Section 21.13):

REG   *The regression method.* This is the default.
BART   *The Bartlett method.*
AR   *The Anderson-Rubin method.*

Next, specify within parentheses the number of desired factor scores and a rootname up to seven characters long to be used in naming the scores. The maximum number of scores equals the order of the factor solution. You can use keyword ALL to calculate factor scores for all extracted factors.

FACTOR uses the rootname to name the factor scores sequentially, as in root1, root2, root3, etc. If you are calculating factor scores for a many-factor solution, make sure that the rootname is short enough to accommodate the number of the highest-order factor score variable. When FACTOR saves the variables on the active system file, it automatically supplies a variable label indicating the method used to calculate it, its positional order, and the analysis number.

For example, the following FACTOR command saves factor scores for a study of abortion items:

```
FACTOR VARIABLES=ABDEFECT TO ABSINGLE
 /MISSING=MEANSUB
 /CRITERIA=FACTORS(2)
 /EXTRACTION=ULS
 /ROTATION=VARIMAX
 /SAVE AR (ALL FSULS).
```

FACTOR calculates two factor scores named FSULS1 and FSULS2 using the Anderson-Rubin method and saves them on the active system file.

You can use multiple SAVE subcommands for an extraction. For example,

```
FACTOR VARIABLES=ABDEFECT TO ABSINGLE
 /MISSING=MEANSUB
 /EXTRACTION=ULS
 /ROTATION=VARIMAX
 /SAVE AR (ALL FSULS)
 /SAVE BART (ALL BFAC).
```

saves two sets of factor scores. The first set is computed using the Anderson-Rubin method and the second is computed using the Bartlett method.

21.29 EXERCISES

Syntax

1. Consider these variables:

   ```
   PCTHOMES PASTSALE DSTRCTYP AVGINCOM PCTBUSNS BUSNSTYP PCTFAMLY
   AVGAGE AVGEDUC PRICE
   ```

   Write the FACTOR command needed to obtain a factor analysis with default output.

2. Modify the FACTOR command from the previous question to perform a factor analysis using maximum likelihood extraction and produce a factor-loading plot for the first two factors.

3. What is wrong with the FACTOR command shown below?

   ```
   FACTOR EXTRACTION=ML
      /VARIABLES=IQ GPA TESTSCOR SAT EDUCATN SES NBRHOOD.
   ```

Statistical Concepts

1. A factor analysis done by a marketing firm produced the factor loadings shown below. Interpret each factor—that is, describe what each factor represents.

	FACTOR 1	FACTOR 2	
MAGAZINE	−.7347	.0398	Type of magazines read
IQ	.0146	.1128	IQ score
OCCSTAT	.0852	.8521	Status of occupation
NBRHOOD	−.0513	−.7952	Type of neighborhood living in
RECREATN	.8707	−.0667	Main recreation interest
EDUCATN	−.0283	.8901	Level of education
INCOME	.1002	.6724	Level of income
POLITACT	.1964	−.0783	Degree of political activity
SPORT	.7095	.0332	Interest in professional sports
CULTURE	−.8948	−.0427	Interest in plays, concerts, etc.

2. Consider the factor pattern matrix shown below:

	FACTOR 1	FACTOR 2	FACTOR 3	
VERBAL	.64453	−.03421	−.03381	Verbal score
MATH	.89116	.07376	.06516	Math score
LOGIC	.91583	−.05229	.08890	Logic score
GPA	.14429	.12238	−.05362	Grade point average
SAT	.18742	.32156	−.12154	Standard aptitude test
SES	.08321	.91842	.14885	Socio-economic status
EDUCATN	.09312	.96593	−.10436	Education level
TESTSCOR	.41127	.34432	−.14892	Test score
STRESS	.08552	.06648	.95422	Stress level
PSYCHTST	.11383	.11524	.89989	Psychology test
IQ	.69877	−.08321	.24661	IQ score

   a. Write the factor models for TESTSCOR and PSYCHTST.

   b. Interpret each factor—that is, describe what each factor represents.

3. Consider the following table:

VARIABLE	COMMUNALITY	FACTOR	EIGENVALUE	PCT OF VAR	CUM PCT
AGE	1.00000	1	2.27	32.4	32.4
MEDHIST	1.00000	2	2.05	29.3	61.7
BLOODPRS	1.00000	3	1.73	24.7	86.4
WEIGHT	1.00000	4	.64	9.1	95.5
IQ	1.00000	5	.15	2.1	97.6
PSYCHTST	1.00000	6	.10	1.4	99.0
STRESS	1.00000	7	.07	1.0	100.0

   a. Sketch a scree plot based on the table.

   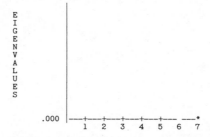

   b. Which factors would you use, and why?

4. Using the table shown below, rank the variables in terms of the amount of variance explained by the common factors.

VARIABLE	COMMUNALITY	FACTOR	EIGENVALUE	PCT OF VAR	CUM PCT
INCOME	.75204	1	3.10020	38.7	38.7
AGE	.69423	2	2.06981	25.9	64.6
URBAN	.84189	3	2.00548	25.1	89.7
OCCUPATN	.90143				
EDUCATN	.72054				
PASTSALE	.93876				
SEX	.52210				
RECREATN	.64771				

Cluster Analysis

In this chapter:

Goals:

- To identify relatively homogeneous groups of cases based on selected attributes.
- To classify variables into homogeneous groups.

Examples:

- Group cities into homogeneous clusters so that comparable cities can be selected to test various marketing strategies.
- Cluster skulls excavated from various archeological digs into the civilizations from which they originated.
- Group television shows into homogeneous categories based on viewer characteristics. This can be used to identify segments for marketing.
- Identify subgroups of patients with similar disease profiles based on a variety of signs and symptoms.

How it's done:

Measures that compute the similarity or distance between all pairs of objects are computed. Based on these, similar objects are grouped into clusters using one of several criteria for cluster formation. The clustering algorithm terminates when all objects are merged into a single cluster.

Data considerations:

Variables must be measured on at least an ordinal scale so that distance or similarity criteria can be computed. Special similarity measures can be computed for binary variables. If the variables to be used for the cluster analysis are measured in different units, such as pounds, numbers of children, and income in dollars, some type of standardization of the variables prior to analysis should be considered.

General references:

Romesburg (1984)
Everitt (1977)
Anderberg (1973)

22 Cluster Analysis: Procedure CLUSTER

Despite the old adage that opposites attract, it appears instead that likes cluster together. Birds of a feather, yuppies, and many other animate and inanimate objects that share similar characteristics are found together. By studying such clusters, you can determine the characteristics the objects share, as well as those in which they differ. In statistics, the search for relatively homogeneous groups of objects is called *cluster analysis.*

In biology, cluster analysis is used to classify animals and plants. This is called numerical taxonomy. In medicine, cluster analysis is used to identify diseases and their stages. For example, by examining patients who are diagnosed as depressed, you might find that there are several distinct subgroups of patients with different types of depression. In marketing, cluster analysis is used to identify persons with similar buying habits. By examining their characteristics, you may be able to target future marketing strategies more efficiently. See Romesburg (1984) for more examples of the use of cluster analysis.

Although both cluster analysis and discriminant analysis classify objects or cases into categories, discriminant analysis requires you to know group membership for the cases used to derive the classification rule. For example, if you are interested in distinguishing among several disease groups, cases with known diagnoses must be available. Then, based on cases whose group membership is known, discriminant analysis derives a rule for allocating undiagnosed patients. In cluster analysis, group membership for all cases is unknown. In fact, even the number of groups is often unknown. The goal of cluster analysis is to identify homogeneous groups or clusters.

In this chapter the fundamentals of cluster analysis are illustrated using a subset of data presented in a Consumer Reports (1983) survey of beer. Each of 20 beers is characterized in terms of cost per 12 ounces, alcohol content, sodium content, and the number of calories per 12-ounce serving. The question we pose is: From these variables is it possible to identify several distinct subgroups of beer?

22.1 BASIC STEPS

As in other statistical procedures, a number of decisions must be made before you embark on the actual analysis. Which variables will serve as the basis for cluster formation? How will the distance between cases be measured? What criteria will be used for combining cases into clusters?

Selecting the variables to include in an analysis is always crucial. If important variables are excluded, poor or misleading findings may result. For example, in a regression analysis of salary, if variables such as education and experience are not included, the results may be questionable. In cluster analysis, the initial choice of variables determines the characteristics that can be used to identify subgroups. If you are interested in clustering schools within a city and do not include variables like the number of students or the number of teachers, size is automatically excluded as a criterion for establishing clusters. By excluding all measures of taste or quality from the beer data, only physical characteristics and price will determine which beers are deemed similar.

22.2
How Alike are the Cases?

The concepts of distance and similarity are basic to many statistical techniques. Distance is a measure of how far apart two objects are, and similarity measures closeness. Distance measures are small and similarity measures are large for cases that are similar. In cluster analysis, these concepts are especially important, since cases are grouped on the basis of their "nearness." There are many different definitions of distance and similarity. Selection of a distance measure should be based both on the properties of the measure and on the algorithm for cluster formation. See Section 22.10 for further discussion of distance measures.

To see how a simple distance measure is computed, consider Table 22.2a, which shows the values of calories and cost for two of the beers. There is a 13-calorie and 5-cent difference between the two beers. This information can be combined into a single index or distance measure in many different ways. A commonly used index is the *squared Euclidean distance,* which is the sum of the squared differences over all of the variables. In this example, the squared Euclidean distance is $13^2 + 5^2$, or 194.

Table 22.2a   Values of calories and cost for two beers

	Calories	Cost
Budweiser	144	43
Lowenbrau	157	48

The squared Euclidean distance has the disadvantage that it depends on the units of measurement for the variables. For example, if the cost were given as pennies per ounce instead of per twelve ounces, the distance measure would change. Another disadvantage is that when variables are measured on different scales, as in this example, variables that are measured in larger numbers will contribute more to the distance than variables that are recorded in smaller numbers. For example, the 13-calorie difference contributes much more to the distance score than does the 5-cent difference in cost.

One means of circumventing this problem is to express all variables in standardized form. That is, all variables have a mean of 0 and a standard deviation of 1. This is not always the best strategy, however, since the variability of a particular measure can provide useful information (see Sneath & Sokal, 1973).

Table 22.2b shows the Z scores for calories and cost for Budweiser and Lowenbrau based on the means and standard deviations for all twenty beers. The squared Euclidean distance based on the standardized variables is $(0.38 - 0.81)^2 + (-0.46 - (-0.11))^2$, or 0.307. The differences in calories and cost are now weighted equally.

Table 22.2b   *Z* scores for the calories and cost variables

	Calories	Cost
Budweiser	0.38	-0.46
Lowenbrau	0.81	-0.11

22.3
Forming Clusters

Just as there are many methods for calculating distances between objects, there are many methods for combining objects into clusters. A commonly used method for forming clusters is hierarchical cluster analysis, using one of two methods: agglomerative, or divisive. In *agglomerative* hierarchical clustering, clusters are formed by grouping cases into bigger and bigger clusters until all cases are members of a single cluster. *Divisive* hierarchical clustering starts out with all cases grouped into a single cluster and splits clusters until there are as many clusters as there are cases. For a discussion of nonhierarchical clustering methods, see Everitt (1980).

22.4
Agglomerative Clustering

Before discussing the rules for forming clusters, consider what happens during the steps of agglomerative hierarchical cluster analysis. At the first step all cases are considered separate clusters: there are as many clusters as there are cases. At the second step, two of the cases are combined into a single cluster. At the third step, either a third case is added to the cluster already containing two cases, or two additional cases are merged into a new cluster. At every step, either individual cases are added to clusters or already existing clusters are combined. Once a cluster is formed, it cannot be split; it can only be combined with other clusters. Thus, hierarchical clustering methods do not allow cases to separate from clusters to which they have been allocated. For example, if two beers are deemed members of the same cluster at the first step, they will always be members of the same cluster, although they may be combined with additional cases at a later step.

22.5
Criteria for Combining Clusters

There are many criteria for deciding which cases or clusters should be combined at each step. All of these criteria are based on a matrix of either distances or similarities between pairs of cases. One of the simplest methods is *single linkage*, sometimes called "nearest neighbor." The first two cases combined are those that have the smallest distance (or largest similarity) between them. The distance between the new cluster and individual cases is then computed as the minimum distance between an individual case and a case in the cluster. The distances between cases that have not been joined do not change. At every step, the distance between two clusters is the distance between their two closest points.

Another commonly used method is called *complete linkage*, or the "furthest neighbor" technique. In this method, the distance between two clusters is calculated as the distance between their two furthest points. Other methods for combining clusters are described in Section 22.10.

22.6
PERFORMING A CLUSTER ANALYSIS

Before considering other distance measures and methods of combining clusters, consider Figure 22.6a, which shows the original and standardized values for calories, sodium, alcohol, and cost for the 20 beers, and Figure 22.6b, which displays the squared Euclidean distance coefficients for all possible pairs of the 20 beers, based on the standardized values.

Figure 22.6a   Original and standardized values for the 20 beers from procedure LIST

```
DESCRIPTIVES CALORIES SODIUM ALCOHOL COST
   /SAVE.
LIST VARIABLES=ID BEER CALORIES SODIUM ALCOHOL COST
   ZCALORIE TO ZCOST.
```

ID	BEER	CALORIES	SODIUM	ALCOHOL	COST	ZCALORIE	ZSODIUM	ZALCOHOL	ZCOST
1	BUDWEISER	144	15	4.7	.43	.38	.01	.34	-.46
2	SCHLITZ	151	19	4.9	.43	.61	.62	.61	-.46
3	LOWENBRAU	157	15	4.9	.48	.81	.01	.61	-.11
4	KRONENBOURG	170	7	5.2	.73	1.24	-1.2	1.00	1.62
5	HEINEKEN	152	11	5.0	.77	.65	-.60	.74	1.90
6	OLD MILWAUKEE	145	23	4.6	.28	.42	1.22	.21	-1.5
7	AUGSBERGER	175	24	5.5	.40	1.41	1.38	1.40	-.67
8	STROHS BOHEMIAN STYLE	149	27	4.7	.42	.55	1.83	.34	-.53
9	MILLER LITE	99	10	4.3	.43	-1.1	-.75	-.18	-.46
10	BUDWEISER LIGHT	113	8	3.7	.44	-.64	-1.1	-.97	-.39
11	COORS	140	18	4.6	.44	.25	.46	.21	-.39
12	COORS LIGHT	102	15	4.1	.46	-1.0	.01	-.45	-.25
13	MICHELOB LIGHT	135	11	4.2	.50	.09	-.60	-.32	.02
14	BECKS	150	19	4.7	.76	.58	.62	.34	1.83
15	KIRIN	149	6	5.0	.79	.55	-1.4	.74	2.04
16	PABST EXTRA LIGHT	68	15	2.3	.38	-2.1	.01	-2.8	-.81
17	HAMMS	136	19	4.4	.43	.12	.62	-.05	-.46
18	HEILEMANS OLD STYLE	144	24	4.9	.43	.38	1.38	.61	-.46
19	OLYMPIA GOLD LIGHT	72	6	2.9	.46	-2.0	-1.4	-2.0	-.25
20	SCHLITZ LIGHT	97	7	4.2	.47	-1.2	-1.2	-.32	-.18

```
Number of cases read:  20    Number of cases listed:  20
```

Figure 22.6b   The squared Euclidean distance coefficient matrix

```
CLUSTER ZCALORIE ZSODIUM ZALCOHOL ZCOST
   /PRINT=DISTANCE.
```

Squared Euclidean Dissimilarity Coefficient Matrix

Case	1	2	3	4	5	6	7	8
2	.4922							
3	.3749	.5297						
4	7.0040	8.2298	4.8424					
5	6.1889	7.0897	4.4835	.8700				
6	2.5848	1.6534	3.7263	17.0154	15.2734			
7	4.0720	1.8735	3.1573	12.1251	11.5371	3.1061		
8	3.3568	1.5561	3.6380	14.8000	12.0038	1.3526	2.0742	
9	3.0662	5.4473	4.9962	11.4721	9.5339	7.4577	13.3723	9.6850
10	3.9181	6.8702	5.8179	11.5391	10.0663	8.9551	15.7993	11.5019
11	.2474	.3160	.7568	8.4698	6.8353	1.8432	3.6498	1.9953
12	2.5940	4.1442	4.4322	12.1519	9.1534	5.4981	11.2604	6.4385
13	1.1281	2.8432	1.7663	5.9995	4.9519	6.0530	9.0610	6.8673
14	5.6782	5.3399	4.2859	4.2382	1.6427	11.5628	8.6397	7.0724
15	8.3245	10.1947	6.6075	.7483	.6064	19.5528	16.0117	16.9620
16	16.4081	19.7255	20.8463	33.3380	28.0650	17.6015	32.1339	20.5466
17	.5952	.6788	1.4051	10.0509	7.9746	1.6159	4.3782	1.8230
18	1.9394	.6307	2.1757	11.9216	9.5828	1.2688	1.7169	.3092
19	13.1887	17.6915	16.7104	23.2048	19.8574	19.0673	30.9530	22.3479
20	4.4010	7.4360	6.2635	10.8241	9.1372	10.4511	16.4825	12.7426

Case	9	10	11	12	13	14	15	16
10	.9349							
11	3.4745	4.5082						
12	.6999	1.5600	2.2375					
13	1.6931	1.3437	1.6100	1.6536				
14	10.2578	10.9762	5.1046	7.8646	5.4275			
15	10.2201	10.3631	9.6179	10.9556	5.9694	4.1024		
16	8.6771	6.9127	15.2083	7.1851	12.2231	24.6793	29.7992	
17	3.3828	4.2251	.1147	1.8315	1.7851	5.6395	10.9812	13.1806
18	7.3607	9.4595	1.0094	4.9491	5.0762	5.9553	13.7962	20.0105
19	4.6046	3.0565	13.4011	5.3477	7.9175	20.5149	19.3851	2.8209
20	.3069	.7793	5.1340	1.5271	1.9902	10.8954	9.0403	9.0418

Case	17	18	19
18	1.0802		
19	12.3170	20.1156	
20	5.1327	10.0114	3.6382

The first entry in Figure 22.6b is the distance between Case 1 and Case 2, Budweiser and Schlitz. This can be calculated from the standardized values in Figure 22.6a as

$$D^2 = (0.38 - 0.61)^2 + (0.01 - 0.62)^2 + (0.34 - 0.61)^2 + (-0.46 - (-0.46))^2 \qquad \text{Equation 22.6}$$
$$= 0.49$$

Since the distance between pairs of cases is symmetric (that is, the distance between Case 3 and Case 4 is the same as the distance between Case 4 and Case 3), only the lower half of the distance matrix is displayed.

22.7
Icicle Plots

Once the distance matrix has been calculated, the actual formation of clusters can commence. Figure 22.7a summarizes a cluster analysis that uses the complete linkage method. This type of figure is sometimes called a vertical icicle plot because it resembles a row of icicles hanging from eaves.

Figure 22.7a   Vertical icicle plot for the 20 beers

```
CLUSTER ZCALORIE ZSODIUM ZALCOHOL ZCOST
 /ID=BEER /METHOD=COMPLETE
 /PLOT=VICICLE.
```

```
Vertical Icicle Plot using Complete Linkage

(Down) Number of Clusters   (Across) Case Label and number

    O   P   M   C   B   S   M   B   K   H   K   A   H   S   O   H   C   S   L   B
    L   A   I   O   U   C   I   E   I   E   R   U   E   T   L   A   O   O   U   U
    Y   B   C   O   D   H   E   I   R   I   O   G   I   R   D   M   O   H   E   D
    M   S   H   O   H   L   L   L   K   I   N   N   S   L   O   M   R   L   N   W
    P   T   E   R   W   I   E   E   S   N   E   E   B   E   H   S   S   I   B   E
    I       L   S   E   T       R       N   N   B   E   H   S       T   N   I
    A   E   O       I   Z   L   E   L   E       R   M   I   I   M   S   Z   B   S
    G   X   B   L           I   T   I   N   B   A   A   R   L   I       E   R   E
    O   T       I   L   L   G       T   R   O   N   S   O       L       R   A   R
    L   R   L   G   I   I   H   L   E   R   U   G       H   M   W   A   U
    D   A   I   H   G   G       I       R   D   E   O   E   I   A   U       K
        G   T   T   H   H   L   G   L   G   R       L   M   L   O   K       E
        L   E       T   T   I   H   I       R   O   D   I   W   E   E
        I           S   S   G   T   G   R   G   L       A   A   E
        G               T   H       H       R   D   S   N   R
        H                   T       T           G       T       O
        T                                           Y   Y   S   L
                                                    L   T   T   D
                                                    E   Y   Y
                                                        L   L
                                                        E   E

      1   1   1   1   1   2       1   1           1           1   1
      9   6   3   2   0   0   9   4   5   5   4   7   8   8   6   7   1   2   3   1
   1 +XXXXXXXXXXXXXXXXXXXXXXXXXXXXXXXXXXXXXXXXXXXXXXXXXXXXXXXXXXXXXXXXXXX
   2 +XXXX XXXXXXXXXXXXXXXXXXXXXXXXXXXXXXXXXXXXXXXXXXXXXXXXXXXXXXXXXXXXX
   3 +XXXX XXXXXXXXXXXXXXXXXXXXXXXXX  XXXXXXXXXXXXXXXXXXXXXXXXXXX
   4 +XXXX XXXXXXXXXXXXXX  XXXXXXXXX  XXXXXXXXXXXXXXXXXXXXXXXXXXX
   5 +XXXX XXXXXXXXXXXXXX  XXXXXXXXX  XXXXXXXXXX  XXXXXXXXXXXXXXX
   6 +XXXX XXXXXXXXXXXXXX  X XXXXXXX  XXXXXXXXXX  XXXXXXXXXXXXXXX
   7 +XXXX XXXXXXXXXXXXXX  X XXXXXXX  X XXXXXXX   XXXXXXXXXXXXXXX
   8 +X X  XXXXXXXXXXXXXX  X XXXXXXX  X XXXXXXX   XXXXXXXXXXXXXXX
   9 +X  X  X XXXXXXXXXXX  X XXXXXXX  X XXXXXXX   XXXXXXXXXXXXXXX
  10 +X  X  X  X XXXXXXX   X XXXXXXX  X XXXXXXX   XXXXXXXXXXXXXXX
  11 +X  X  X  X XXXXXXX   X XXXXXXX  X XXXXXXX   XXXX   XXXXXXX
  12 +X  X  X  X XXXXXXX   X XXXXXXX  X XXXX  X   XXXX   XXXXXXX
  13 +X  X  X  X  XXXX  X  X XXXX  X  X XXXX  X   XXXX   XXXXXXX
  14 +X  X  X  X  XXXX  X  X XXXX  X  X XXXX  X   XXXX   XXXXXXX
  15 +X  X  X  X  XXXX  X  X  X  X  X  X XXXX  X   XXXX   XXXXXXX
  16 +X  X  X  X  XXXX  X  X  X  X  X  X XXXX  X   XXXX  X  XXXX
  17 +X  X  X  X  XXXX  X  X  X  X  X  X  XXXX  X   XXXX  X  X  X
  18 +X  X  X  X  XXXX  X  X  X  X  X  X  X  X  X   XXXX  X  X  X
  19 +X  X  X  X  X  X  X  X  X  X  X  X  X  X  X   XXXX  X  X  X
```

The columns of Figure 22.7a correspond to the objects being clustered. They are identified both by a sequential number ranging from 1 to the number of cases and, when possible, by the labels of the objects. Thus, the first column corresponds to beer number 19, Olympia Gold Light, while the last column corresponds to the first beer in the file, Budweiser. In order to follow the sequence of steps in the cluster analysis, the figure is read from bottom to top.

As previously described, all cases are considered initially as individual clusters. Since there are twenty beers in this example, there are 20 clusters. At the first step the two closest cases are combined into a single cluster, resulting in 19 clusters. The bottom line of Figure 22.7a shows these 19 clusters. Each case is represented by a single X separated by blanks. The two cases that have been merged into a single cluster, Coors and Hamms, do not have blanks separating them. Instead they are represented by consecutive X's. The row labeled **18** in Figure 22.7a corresponds to the solution at the next step, when 18 clusters are present. At this step Miller Lite and Schlitz Light are merged into a single cluster. Thus, at this point there are 18 clusters, 16 consisting of individual beers and 2 consisting of pairs of beers. At each subsequent step an additional cluster is formed by joining either a case to an already existing multicase cluster, two separate cases into a single cluster, or two multicase clusters.

For example, the row labeled **5** in Figure 22.7a corresponds to a solution that has five clusters. Beers 19 and 16, the very light beers, form one cluster; beers 13, 12, 10, 20, and 9 form the next. These beers, Michelob Light, Coors Light, Budweiser Light, Schlitz Light, and Miller Light, are all light beers, but not as light as the two in the first cluster. The third cluster consists of Becks, Kirin, Heineken, and Kronenbourg. These are all imported beers. Although no variable in this example explicitly indicates whether beers are domestic or imported, the cost variable (see Figure 22.6b) causes the imported beers to cluster together since they are quite a bit more expensive than the domestic ones. A fourth cluster consists of Augsberger, Heilemans Old Style, Strohs Bohemian Style, and Old Milwaukee. Inspection of Figure 22.7b shows that all of these beers are distinguished by high sodium content. The last cluster consists of five beers, Hamms, Coors, Schlitz, Lowenbrau, and Budweiser. These beers share the distinction of being average. That is, they are neither particulary high nor particularly low on the variables measured. Note from Figure 22.7b that, based on the standard deviations, beers in the same cluster, when compared to all beers, are more homogeneous on the variables measured.

Figure 22.7b   Cluster characteristics

```
CLUSTER ZCALORIE ZSODIUM ZALCOHOL ZCOST
 /ID=BEER
 /SAVE CLUSTER(5)
 /METHOD=COMPLETE(CLUSMEM).
VALUE LABELS CLUSMEM5 1 'AVERAGE' 2 'EXPENSIVE'
 3 'HIGH NA' 4 'LIGHT' 5 'VERY LIGHT'.
TABLES OBSERVATION= COST CALORIES ALCOHOL SODIUM
 /FTOTAL=TOTAL
 /FORMAT:CWIDTH(10,9)
 /TABLE= CLUSMEM5+TOTAL BY CALORIES +COST+ALCOHOL+SODIUM
 /STATISTICS=MEAN STDDEV.
```

	CALORIES PER 12 FLUID OUNCES		COST PER 12 FLUID OUNCES		ALCOHOL BY VOLUME (IN %)		SODIUM PER 12 FLUID OUNCES IN MG	
	Mean	Standard Deviation	Mean	Standard Deviation	Mean	Standard Deviation	Mean	Standard Deviation
CLUSMEM5								
AVERAGE	146	8	.44	.02	4.7	.2	17	2
EXPENSIVE	155	10	.76	.03	5.0	.2	11	6
HIGH NA	153	15	.38	.07	4.9	.4	25	2
LIGHT	109	16	.46	.03	4.1	.2	10	3
VERY LIGHT	70	3	.42	.06	2.6	.4	11	6
TOTAL	132	30	.50	.14	4.4	.8	15	7

Cluster formation continues in Figure 22.7a until all cases are merged into a single cluster, as shown in the first row. Thus, all steps of the cluster analysis are displayed in Figure 22.7a. If we were clustering people instead of beers, the last row would be individual persons, higher up they would perhaps merge into families, these into neighborhoods, and so forth. Often there is not one single, meaningful cluster solution, but many, depending on what is of interest.

22.8
The Agglomeration Schedule

The results of the cluster analysis are summarized in the *agglomeration schedule* in Figure 22.8, which contains the number of cases or clusters being combined at each stage. The first line is Stage 1, the 19-cluster solution. Beers 11 and 17 are combined at this stage, as shown in the columns labeled **Clusters Combined.** The squared Euclidean distance between these two beers is displayed in the column labeled **Coefficient.** Since this is the first step, this coefficient is identical to the distance measure in Figure 22.6b for Cases 11 and 17. The last column indicates at which stage another case or cluster is combined with this one. For example, at the tenth stage, Case 1 is merged with Cases 11 and 17 into a single cluster. The column entitled **Stage Cluster 1st Appears** indicates at which stage a cluster is first formed. For example, the entry of 4 at Stage 5 indicates that Case 1 was first involved in a merge in the previous step (Stage 4). From the line for Stage 4, you can see that, at this point, Case 1 was involved in a merge with Case 3. From the last column of Stage 5 we see that the new cluster (Cases 1, 2, and 3) is next involved in a merge at Stage 10, where the cases combine with Cases 11 and 17.

Figure 22.8 Agglomeration schedule using complete linkage

```
CLUSTER ZCALORIE ZSODIUM ZALCOHOL ZCOST
 /ID=BEER
 /PRINT=SCHEDULE
 /METHOD=COMPLETE.
```

Agglomeration Schedule using Complete Linkage

Stage	Clusters Cluster 1	Combined Cluster 2	Coefficient	Stage Cluster 1st Appears Cluster 1	Cluster 2	Next Stage
1	11	17	.114695	0	0	10
2	9	20	.306903	0	0	8
3	8	18	.309227	0	0	9
4	1	3	.374859	0	0	5
5	1	2	.529696	4	0	10
6	5	15	.606378	0	0	7
7	4	5	.870016	0	6	15
8	9	10	.934909	2	0	11
9	6	8	1.352617	0	3	14
10	1	11	1.405148	5	1	16
11	9	12	1.559987	8	0	12
12	9	13	1.990205	11	0	17
13	16	19	2.820896	0	0	19
14	6	7	3.106108	9	0	16
15	4	14	4.238164	7	0	17
16	1	6	4.378198	10	14	18
17	4	9	12.151937	15	12	18
18	1	4	19.552841	16	17	19
19	1	16	33.338028	18	13	0

The information in Figure 22.8 that is not available in the icicle plot is the value of the distance between the two most dissimilar points of the clusters being combined at each stage (the column labeled **Coefficient**). By examining these values, you can get an idea of how unlike the clusters being combined are. Small coefficients indicate that fairly homogeneous clusters are being merged. Large coefficients indicate that clusters containing quite dissimilar members are being combined. The actual value depends on the clustering method and the distance measure used.

These coefficients can also be used for guidance in deciding how many clusters are needed to represent the data. You usually want to stop agglomeration as soon as the increase between two adjacent steps becomes large. For example, in Figure 22.8 there is a fairly large increase in the value of the distance measure from a four-cluster to a three-cluster solution (Stages 16 and 17).

22.9
Some Additional Displays and Modifications

The agglomeration schedule and icicle plot illustrate the results produced by a hierarchical clustering solution. Several variations of these plots may also be useful. For example, when there are many cases, the initial steps of the cluster analysis may not be of particular interest. You might want to display solutions for only certain numbers of clusters. Or you might want to see the results at every kth step. Figure 22.9a contains the icicle plot of results at every fifth step.

Figure 22.9a   Icicle plot with results at every fifth step

```
CLUSTER ZCALORIE ZSODIUM ZALCOHOL ZCOST
 /ID=BEER
 /METHOD=COMPLETE
 /PLOT=VICICLE(1,19,5).
```

```
Vertical Icicle Plot using Complete Linkage

 (Down) Number of Clusters  (Across) Case Label and number

        O   P   M   C   B   S   M   B   K   H   K   A   H   S   O   H   C   S   L   B
        L   A   I   O   U   C   I   E   I   E   R   U   E   T   L   A   O   C   O   U
        Y   B   C   O   D   H   L   C   R   I   O   G   I   R   D   M   O   H   W   D
        M   S   H   S   E   I   E   S   N   E   E   B   E   H   M   S   S   I   E   W
        P   T   E   S   I   T   R       N   K   N   E   M   S   I           T   N   E
        I       L   I   T   R               E   N   M   S   L       W       Z   B   I
        A       X   B   I   E           L   B   O   G   N   B   O           T   R   S
        G       T   R   G   R   L   L   I   R   U   E   S   O   H   A       Z   A   E
        O       R   L   H   L   I   I   T   R   E   S       O   H   A       U   U   R
        L       A   I   T   L   G   I   E   G   R   R       L   E   K
        D       L   G   H   I   G   H   T           G       M   K   E
                I   H       G   H   T                       I   E
                G   T       H   T                           A
                H           T                               N
                T                                           S
                                                            T
                                                            Y
                                                            L
                                                            E

        1   1   1   1   1   2           1       1           1       8   8   6   1   1
        9   6   3   2   0   0   9   4   5   5   4   7   8   8       7   1   2   3   1
    1 +XXXXXXXXXXXXXXXXXXXXXXXXXXXXXXXXXXXXXXXXXXXXXXXXXXXXXXXXXXXXX
    6 +XXXX XXXXXXXXXXXXX X XXXXXXX XXXXXXXXX XXXXXXXXXXXX
   11 +X  X  X  X  XXXXXXX X  XXXXXXX X  XXXXXXX XXXX  XXXXXXX
   16 +X  X  X  X  X  XXXX X  X  X  X  X  XXXX X  XXXX X  XXXX
```

When there are many cases, all of them may not fit across the top of a single page. In this situation it may be useful to turn the icicle plot on its side. This is called a horizontal icicle plot. Figure 22.9b contains the horizontal icicle plot corresponding to Figure 22.7a.

Figure 22.9b Horizontal icicle plot

```
CLUSTER ZCALORIE ZSODIUM ZALCOHOL ZCOST
 /ID=BEER
 /METHOD=COMPLETE
 /PLOT=HICICLE.
```

```
Horizontal Icicle Plot Using Complete Linkage

                            Number of Clusters

                                     1111111111
        C A S E             1234567890123456789
 Label                 Seq  +++++++++++++++++++

 OLYMPIA GOLD LIGHT     19  XXXXXXXXXXXXXXXXXXX
                            XXXXXXX
                            XXXXXXX
 PABST EXTRA LIGHT      16  XXXXXXXXXXXXXXXXXXX
                            X
                            X
 MICHELOB LIGHT         13  XXXXXXXXXXXXXXXXXXX
                            XXXXXXXX
                            XXXXXXXX
 COORS LIGHT            12  XXXXXXXXXXXXXXXXXXX
                            XXXXXXXXX
                            XXXXXXXXX
 BUDWEISER LIGHT        10  XXXXXXXXXXXXXXXXXXX
                            XXXXXXXXXXXX
                            XXXXXXXXXXXX
 SCHLITZ LIGHT          20  XXXXXXXXXXXXXXXXXXX
                            XXXXXXXXXXXXXXXXXX
                            XXXXXXXXXXXXXXXXXX
 MILLER LITE             9  XXXXXXXXXXXXXXXXXXX
                            XXX
                            XXX
 BECKS                  14  XXXXXXXXXXXXXXXXXXX
                            XXXXX
                            XXXXX
 KIRIN                  15  XXXXXXXXXXXXXXXXXXX
                            XXXXXXXXXXXXXX
                            XXXXXXXXXXXXXX
 HEINEKEN                5  XXXXXXXXXXXXXXXXXXX
                            XXXXXXXXXXXXX
                            XXXXXXXXXXXXX
 KRONENBOURG             4  XXXXXXXXXXXXXXXXXXX
                            XX
                            XX
 AUGSBERGER              7  XXXXXXXXXXXXXXXXXXX
                            XXXXXX
                            XXXXXX
 HEILEMANS OLD STYLE    18  XXXXXXXXXXXXXXXXXXX
                            XXXXXXXXXXXXXXXXX
                            XXXXXXXXXXXXXXXXX
 STROHS BOHEMIAN STYL    8  XXXXXXXXXXXXXXXXXXX
                            XXXXXXXXXXX
                            XXXXXXXXXXX
 OLD MILWAUKEE           6  XXXXXXXXXXXXXXXXXXX
                            XXXX
                            XXXX
 HAMMS                  17  XXXXXXXXXXXXXXXXXXX
                            XXXXXXXXXXXXXXXXXXX
                            XXXXXXXXXXXXXXXXXXX
 COORS                  11  XXXXXXXXXXXXXXXXXXX
                            XXXXXXXXXX
                            XXXXXXXXXX
 SCHLITZ                 2  XXXXXXXXXXXXXXXXXXX
                            XXXXXXXXXXXXXXX
                            XXXXXXXXXXXXXXX
 LOWENBRAU               3  XXXXXXXXXXXXXXXXXXX
                            XXXXXXXXXXXXXXXX
                            XXXXXXXXXXXXXXXX
 BUDWEISER               1  XXXXXXXXXXXXXXXXXXX
```

Although the composition of clusters at any stage can be discerned from the icicle plots, it is often helpful to display the information in tabular form. Figure 22.9c contains the cluster memberships for the cases at different stages of the solution. From Figure 22.9c, you can easily tell which clusters cases belong to in the two- to five-cluster solutions.

Figure 22.9c Cluster membership at different stages

```
CLUSTER ZCALORIE ZSODIUM ZALCOHOL ZCOST
 /ID=BEER
 /PRINT=CLUSTER(2,5)
 /METHOD=COMPLETE.
```

Cluster Membership of Cases using Complete Linkage

		Number of Clusters			
Label	Case	5	4	3	2
BUDWEISER	1	1	1	1	1
SCHLITZ	2	1	1	1	1
LOWENBRAU	3	1	1	1	1
KRONENBOURG	4	2	2	2	1
HEINEKEN	5	2	2	2	1
OLD MILWAUKEE	6	3	1	1	1
AUGSBERGER	7	3	1	1	1
STROHS BOHEMIAN STYL	8	3	1	1	1
MILLER LITE	9	4	3	2	1
BUDWEISER LIGHT	10	4	3	2	1
COORS	11	1	1	1	1
COORS LIGHT	12	4	3	2	1
MICHELOB LIGHT	13	4	3	2	1
BECKS	14	2	2	2	1
KIRIN	15	2	2	2	1
PABST EXTRA LIGHT	16	5	4	3	2
HAMMS	17	1	1	1	1
HEILEMANS OLD STYLE	18	3	1	1	1
OLYMPIA GOLD LIGHT	19	5	4	3	2
SCHLITZ LIGHT	20	4	3	2	1

22.10 MORE ON CALCULATING DISTANCES AND SIMILARITIES

There are many methods for estimating the distance or similarity between two cases. But even before these measures are computed, you must decide whether the variables need to be rescaled. When the variables have different scales, such as cents and calories, and they are not standardized, any distance measure will reflect primarily the contributions of variables measured in the large units. For example, the beer data variables were standardized prior to cluster analysis to have a mean of 0 and a standard deviation of 1. Besides standardization to Z scores, variables can be standardized by dividing by just the standard deviation, the range, the mean, or the maximum. See Romesburg (1984) or Anderberg (1973) for further discussion.

Based on the transformed data it is possible to calculate many different types of distance and similarity measures. Different distance and similarity measures weight data characteristics differently. The choice among the measures should be based on which differences or similarities in the data are important for a particular application. For example, if one is clustering animal bones, what may matter is not the actual differences in bone size but relationships among the dimensions, since we know that even animals of the same species differ in size. Bones with the same relationship between length and diameter should be judged as similar, regardless of their absolute magnitudes. See Romesburg (1984) for further discussion.

The most commonly used distance measure, the squared Euclidean distance, has been discussed previously. Sometimes its square root, the Euclidean distance, is also used. A distance measure that is based on the absolute values of differences is the *city-block* or *Manhattan* distance. For two cases it is just the sum of the absolute differences of the values for all variables. Since the differences are not squared, large differences are not weighted as heavily as in the squared Euclidean distances. The *Chebychev* distance defines the distance between two cases as the maximum absolute difference in the values over all variables. Thus, it ignores much of the available information.

When variables are binary, special distance and similarity measures are required. Many are based on the familiar measures of association for contingency tables. See the *SPSS Reference Guide* or the *SPSS Base System User's Guide* for further description of the numerous measures computed by the PROXIMITIES procedure.

22.11
METHODS FOR
COMBINING
CLUSTERS

Many methods can be used to decide which cases or clusters should be combined at each step. In general, clustering methods fall into three groups: linkage methods, error sums of squares or variance methods, and centroid methods. All are based on either a matrix of distances or a matrix of similarities between pairs of cases. The methods differ in how they estimate distances between clusters at successive steps. Since the merging of clusters at each step depends on the distance measure, different distance measures can result in different cluster solutions for the same clustering method. See Milligan (1980) for comparisons of the performance of some of the different clustering methods.

One of the simplest methods for joining clusters is *single linkage*, sometimes called "nearest neighbor." The first two cases combined are those with the smallest distance, or greatest similarity, between them. The distance between the new cluster and individual cases is then computed as the minimum distance between an individual case and a case in the cluster. The distances between cases that have not been joined do not change. At every step the distance between two clusters is taken to be the distance between their two closest points.

Another commonly used method is called *complete linkage,* or the "furthest neighbor" technique. In this method the distance between two clusters is calculated as the distance between their two furthest points.

The *average linkage between groups method,* often called UPGMA (unweighted pair-group method using arithmetic averages), defines the distance between two clusters as the average of the distances between all pairs of cases in which one member of the pair is from each of the clusters. For example, if Cases 1 and 2 form cluster A and Cases 3, 4, and 5 form cluster B, the distance between clusters A and B is taken to be the average of the distances between the following pairs of cases: (1,3) (1,4) (1,5) (2,3) (2,4) (2,5). This differs from the linkage methods in that it uses information about all pairs of distances, not just the nearest or the furthest. For this reason it is usually preferred to the single and complete linkage methods for cluster analysis.

The UPGMA method considers only distances between pairs of cases in different clusters. A variant of it, *the average linkage within groups,* combines clusters so that the average distance between all cases in the resulting cluster is as small as possible. Thus, the distance between two clusters is taken to be the average of the distances between all possible pairs of cases in the resulting cluster.

Another frequently used method for cluster formation is *Ward's method.* For each cluster the means for all variables are calculated. Then for each case the squared Euclidean distance to the cluster means is calculated. These distances are summed for all of the cases. At each step, the two clusters that merge are those that result in the smallest increase in the overall sum of the squared within-cluster distances.

The *centroid method* calculates the distance between two clusters as the distance between their means for all of the variables. One disadvantage of the centroid method is that the distance at which clusters are combined can actually decrease from one step to the next. Since clusters merged at later stages are more dissimilar than those merged at early stages, this is an undesirable property.

In the centroid method, the centroid of a merged cluster is a weighted combination of the centroids of the two individual clusters, where the weights are proportional to the sizes of the clusters. In the *median method,* the two clusters being combined are weighted equally in the computation of the centroid, regardless of the number of cases in each. This allows small groups to have equal effect on the characterization of larger clusters into which they are merged. Squared Euclidean distances should be used with both centroid and median methods.

Some of the above methods, such as single and complete linkage and the average distances between and within clusters, can be used with similarity or distance measures. Other methods require particular types of distance measures. In particular, the median, centroid, and Ward's methods should use squared Euclidean distances. When similarity measures are used, the criteria for combining is reversed. That is, clusters with large similarity-based measures are merged.

22.12 RUNNING PROCEDURE CLUSTER

Use the CLUSTER procedure to obtain hierarchical clusters for cases when the number of cases is not too large. (If the number of cases exceeds several hundred, use the QUICK CLUSTER procedure described in the *SPSS Reference Guide*.) Variables can also be clustered if the data are in the appropriate format (for example, if you have a correlation matrix or some other measure of distance). CLUSTER provides several measures of dissimilarity and allows you to specify missing-value treatment. A matrix of similarity or dissimilarity coefficients can be entered and used to cluster cases or variables.

Procedure PROXIMITIES (see the *SPSS Reference Guide* or the *SPSS Base System User's Guide*) is useful for computing a wide variety of distance and similarity coefficients for either cases or variables. Options for standardizing matrix data are also available. (The CLUSTER procedure does not allow for data standardizations. Examples in this chapter were first standardized with the DESCRIPTIVES procedure; see the *SPSS Reference Guide* or the *SPSS Base System User's Guide*.) Proximity matrices from procedure PROXIMITIES can be used in the CLUSTER procedure, as well as in other procedures that permit matrix input.

By default, CLUSTER performs cluster analysis using the average linkage between groups and squared Euclidean distances and displays the agglomeration schedule and a vertical icicle plot (see Sections 22.14 through 22.17).

22.13 Specifying the Variables

The first specification on CLUSTER is a list of variables to use in computing similarities or distances between cases, as in

```
CLUSTER ZCALORIE ZSODIUM ZALCOHOL ZCOST.
```

The variable list is the only required specification and must precede any optional subcommands. If you are using matrix data specified with the MATRIX subcommand (see the *SPSS Reference Guide* or the *SPSS Base System User's Guide*), the variable list should be omitted.

22.14 METHOD Subcommand

The METHOD subcommand specifies the clustering method. If you do not specify a method, CLUSTER uses the average linkage between groups method (see Section 22.11). You can specify more than one method on a single METHOD subcommand.

BAVERAGE *Average linkage between groups (UPGMA). This is the default.*
WAVERAGE *Average linkage within groups.*
SINGLE *Single linkage or nearest neighbor.*

COMPLETE   *Complete linkage or furthest neighbor.*

CENTROID   *Centroid clustering (UPGMC).* Squared Euclidean distances should be used with this method.

MEDIAN   *Median clustering (WPGMC).* Squared Euclidean distances should be used with this method.

WARD   *Ward's method.* Squared Euclidean distances should be used with this method.

For example, the command

```
CLUSTER ZCALORIE ZSODIUM ZALCOHOL ZCOST
 /METHOD=SINGLE COMPLETE.
```

requests clustering with both the single and complete methods.

22.15
MEASURE Subcommand

Use the MEASURE subcommand to specify the distance measure to use for clustering cases (see Section 22.2 and 22.10). If you omit MEASURE, CLUSTER uses squared Euclidean distances. You can specify only one distance measure.

MEASURE has the following keywords:

SEUCLID   *Squared Euclidean distances.* This is the default. This measure should be used with the centroid, median, and Ward's methods of clustering. The distance between two cases is the sum of the squared differences in values for each variable:

$$\text{Distance}(X, Y) = \sum_i (X_i - Y_i)^2$$

EUCLID   *Euclidean distances.* The distance between two cases is the square root of the sum of the squared differences in values for each variable:

$$\text{Distance}(X, Y) = \sqrt{\sum_i (X_i - Y_i)^2}$$

COSINE   *Cosine of vectors of variables.* This is a pattern similarity measure:

$$\text{Similarity}(X, Y) = \frac{\sum_i (X_i Y_i)}{\sqrt{\sum_i (X_i^2) \sum_i (Y_i^2)}}$$

BLOCK   *City-block or Manhattan distances.* The distance between two cases is the sum of the absolute differences in values for each variable:

$$\text{Distance}(X, Y) = \sum_i |X_i - Y_i|$$

CHEBYCHEV   *Chebychev distance metric.* The distance between two cases is the maximum absolute difference in values for any variable:

$$\text{Distance}(X, Y) = MAX_i |X_i - Y_i|$$

POWER(p,r)   *Distances in an absolute power metric.* The distance between two cases is the *r*th root of the sum of the absolute differences to the *p*th power in values on each variable:

$$\text{Distance}(X, Y) = \left(\sum_i (X_i - Y_i)^p \right)^{\frac{1}{r}}$$

Appropriate selection of integer parameters *p* and *r* yields Euclidean, squared Euclidean, Minkowski, city-block, minimum, maximum, and many other distance metrics.

DEFAULT   *Same as SEUCLID.*

22.16
PRINT Subcommand

CLUSTER automatically displays the clustering method, the similarity or distance measure used for clustering, and the number of cases. Use the PRINT subcommand to obtain additional output.

SCHEDULE | *Agglomeration schedule.* Display the order in which and distances at which clusters combine to form new clusters as well as the last cluster level at which a case (or variable) joined the cluster (see Figure 22.8). The agglomeration schedule is displayed by default if you do not specify PRINT. If you specify PRINT, you must request SCHEDULE explicitly.

CLUSTER(min,max) | *Cluster membership. Min* and *max* specify the minimum and maximum numbers of clusters in the cluster solutions. For each case, CLUSTER displays an identifying label and values indicating which cluster the case belongs to in a given cluster solution. Cases are identified by case number plus the value of any string variable specified on the ID subcommand (see Section 22.18).

DISTANCE | *Matrix of distances or similarities between items.* The type of matrix produced (similarities or dissimilarities) depends upon the measure selected. With a large number of clustered cases, DISTANCE uses considerable computer processing time.

NONE | *No display output.* Use PRINT=NONE when you want to suppress all display output, such as when you are using SAVE.

For example, the command

```
CLUSTER ZCALORIE ZSODIUM ZALCOHOL ZCOST
 /ID=BEER
 /PRINT=CLUSTER(2,5)
 /METHOD=COMPLETE.
```

produces Figure 22.9c.

22.17
PLOT Subcommand

CLUSTER produces the vertical icicle plot by default. Use the PLOT subcommand to obtain a horizontal icicle plot or a dendrogram. When you specify PLOT, only the requested plots are produced.

VICICLE(min,max,inc) | *Vertical icicle plot.* The optional *min, max,* and *inc* specifications indicate the minimum and maximum numbers of cluster solutions to plot and the increment to use between cluster levels. Min, max, and inc must be integers. By default, the increment is 1 and all cluster solutions are plotted. VICICLE is the default if the PLOT subcommand is omitted.

HICICLE(min,max,inc) | *Horizontal icicle plot.* Has the same specifications as VICICLE. (See Figure 22.9b.)

DENDROGRAM | *Dendrogram.* The dendrogram is scaled by joining the distances of the clusters.

NONE | *No display output.* Use PLOT=NONE to suppress all plots.

For example, Figure 22.9a was produced by the following command:

```
CLUSTER ZCALORIE ZSODIUM ZALCOHOL ZCOST
 /ID=BEER
 /METHOD=COMPLETE
 /PLOT=VICICLE(1,19,5).
```

If there is insufficient memory to plot a dendrogram or icicle plot, CLUSTER performs the cluster analysis, skips the plot, and displays an error message. To obtain a plot when this occurs, request more memory or specify an increment for VICICLE or HICICLE.

22.18
ID Subcommand

By default, CLUSTER identifies cases by case number. Name a string variable on the ID subcommand to identify cases with string values. For example, the subcommand

```
/ID=BEER
```

produces the beer-name labels in Figures 22.7a, 22.9a, 22.9b, and 22.9c.

22.19
MISSING Subcommand

CLUSTER uses listwise deletion as the default missing-value treatment. A case with missing values for any clustering variable is excluded from the analysis. Use the MISSING subcommand to treat user-defined missing values as valid.

INCLUDE   *Include user-missing values.*
LISTWISE   *Delete cases with missing values listwise.* This is the default.

Cases with system-missing values for clustering variables are never included in the analysis.

22.20
SAVE Subcommand

Use the SAVE subcommand to save cluster memberships at specified cluster levels as new variables on the active system file. You must specify a rootname for each cluster method for which you want to save cluster membership, as in:

```
CLUSTER A B C
 /METHOD=BAVERAGE(CLUSMEM)
 /SAVE=CLUSTERS(3,5).
```

This command saves each case's cluster memberships for the three-, four-, and five-cluster solutions. The new variables derive their names from the rootname CLUSMEM and appear on the active system file in the order CLUSMEM5, CLUSMEM4, and CLUSMEM3. CLUSTER prints the names of variables it adds to the active system file.

22.21
EXERCISES

Syntax

1. Find the error in the following CLUSTER command:

```
CLUSTER V1(1,3) V2 V3 /METHOD=MEDIAN /MEASURE=COSINE.
```

2. An ornithologist wants a cluster analysis using the following variables for a sample of 85 birds:

```
 WINGSPAN BEAKCURV BEAKWDTH MIGRLNTH MATELNTH FSHDIET INSDIET
GRNDIET
```

Write the simplest CLUSTER command for this study.

3. A sociologist studying popular culture wants to see if 60 automobiles can be clustered according to the following variables.

```
 WEIGHT LENGTH WIDTH HGHTLEN WINDOWS CHROME DOODADS
```

Write the commands to perform a cluster analysis using the Euclidean distance and nearest neighbor method.

Statistical Concepts

1. Consider the following four cases:

CASE	OBEDENCE	GUARDING	HUNTING	ONEPERSN
1	1.4	-0.6	-0.9	-0.2
2	-3.1	0.8	2.4	1.9
3	1.5	1.8	-0.3	2.2
4	2.1	2.6	-0.6	2.0

    a. Compute the matrix of squared Euclidean distance coefficients:

```
Squared Euclidean Dissimilarity Coefficient Matrix

Case          1              2              3

  2          ??

  3          ??             ??

  4          ??             ??             ??
```

    b. Which of these four cases would be combined first into a cluster?

2. Using the vertical icicle plot below and assuming agglomerative clustering, describe the clusters at

    a. Step 7

    b. Step 5

    c. Step 3

```
Vertical Icicle Plot using Complete Linkage

(Down) Number of Clusters   (Across) Case Label and number

       S  B  F  C  C  M  C  E  G  M
       W  L  A  O  O  O  H  D  O  O
       I  U  R  T  L  N  E  D  U  Z
       S  E  M  T  B  T  D  A  D  Z
       S     E  A  Y  E  D  M  A  A
             R  G     R  D        R
             S  E     E  A        E
                      Y  R        L
                                  L
                      J           A
                      A
                      C
                      K

      1
      0  9  5  4  7  8  6  3  2  1
   1 +XXXXXXXXXXXXXXXXXXXXXXXXXXXX
   2 +XXXX  XXXXXXXXXXXXXXXXXXXXXX
   3 +XXXX  XXXX  XXXXXXXXXXXXXXXX
   4 +XXXX  XXXX  X  XXXXXXXXXXXXX
   5 +XXXX  XXXX  X  XXXX  XXXXXXX
   6 +X  X  XXXX  X  XXXX  XXXXXXX
   7 +X  X  XXXX  X  X  X  XXXXXXX
   8 +X  X  X  X  X  X  X  XXXXXXX
   9 +X  X  X  X  X  X  X  XXXX  X
```

3. If a program designed to do agglomerative hierarchical clustering produced the following icicle plot, would you trust it?

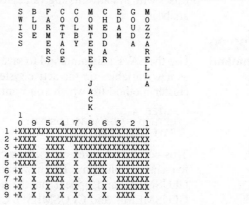

```
       1  1  1     1     1        1     1
       5  2  6  7  1  4  4  6  5  0  9  3  8  2  3  1
    1 +XXXXXXXXXXXXXXXXXXXXXXXXXXXXXXXXXXXXXXXXXXX
    2 +XXXXXXXXX  XXXXXXXXXXXXXXXXXXXXXXXXXXXXXXXX
    3 +XXXXXXXXX  XXXX  XXXXXXXXXXXXXXXXXXXXXXXXXX
    4 +XXXX  XXXX  XXXX  XXXXXXXXXXXXXXXXXXXXXXXXX
    5 +X  X  XXXX  XXXX  XXXXXXXXXXXXXXXXXXXXXXXXX
    6 +X  X  XXXX  XXXX  XXXXXXX  XXXXXXXXXXXXXXXX
    7 +X  X  X  X  XXXX  XXXXXXX  XXXXXXXXXXX  XXXX
    8 +X  X  X  X  XXXX  XXXXXXX  XXXX  XXXXXXX  XXXX
    9 +X  X  X  X  X  X  XXXXXXX  XXXX  XXXXXXXXXX
   10 +X  X  X  X  X  X  XXXX  X  XXXX  XXXXXXXXXXXX
   11 +X  X  X  X  X  X  XXXX  X  XXXX  XXXXXXX  XXXX
   12 +X  X  X  X  X  X  XXXX  X  XXXX  X  XXXXXXX  XXXX
   13 +X  X  X  X  X  X  XXXX  X  X  X  XXXXXXX  X  X
   14 +X  X  X  X  X  X  XXXX  X  X  X  XXXX  X  X  X
   15 +X  X  X  X  X  X  X  X  X  X  X  XXXX  X  X  X
```

4. Consider the following icicle plot:

```
Horizontal Icicle Plot Using Complete Linkage

                                  Number of Clusters
           C A S E                123456789
        Label            Seq      +++++++++
        MOBY DICK          9      XXXXXXXXX
                                    XXX
                                    XXX
        ODYSSEY            4      XXXXXXXXX
                                    X
                                    X
        GREAT EXPECTATIONS 10     XXXXXXXXX
                                    XXXX
                                    XXXX
        OLIVER TWIST       6      XXXXXXXXX
                                    XX
                                    XX
        TOM JONES          5      XXXXXXXXX
                                    XXXX
                                    XXXX
        MADAM BOVARY       7      XXXXXXXXX
                                    XXXXXXX
                                    XXXXXXX
        PORTRAIT OF A LADY 8      XXXXXXXXX
                                    XXXXXXXXX
                                    XXXXXXXXX
        ANNA KARENINA      3      XXXXXXXXX
                                    XXXXXXX
                                    XXXXXXX
        BLEAK HOUSE        2      XXXXXXXXX
                                    XXXXX
                                    XXXXX
        CANDIDE            1      XXXXXXXXX
```

Describe the books in the clusters when you have a three-cluster solution and a five-cluster solution.

Multivariate
Analysis of Variance

In this chapter:

Goals:

- To test hypotheses about the relationship between a set of interrelated dependent variables and one or more classification or grouping variables.

- To identify the subset of dependent variables contributing to differences among groups.

Examples:

- Compare four instructional methods based on student achievement levels, satisfaction, anxiety, and long-term retention of material.

- Evaluate the effectiveness of three types of chemotherapy and two dosages of radiation based on length of patient survival, length of time the patient is disease-free, and quality of life.

- Compare five new ice-cream flavors on the basis of amount consumed, preference rating, and estimate of price.

How it's done:

The variability in the dependent variables is subdivided into two components: that attributable to differences between groups (the hypothesis sums of squares matrix), and that attributable to variability within groups (the error sums of squares matrix). Various test statistics that compare the magnitudes of these two matrices are computed.

Data considerations:

Each case has a set of dependent variables and one or more discrete grouping variables. The dependent variables are measured only once for each case. The multivariate analysis of variance model requires that for each group the dependent variables are from a multivariate normal distribution and that the variance-covariance matrices are equal for all groups.

General references:

Finn (1974)
Bock (1975)
Morrison (1967)

23 Grades and Sports: Multivariate Analysis of Variance

Educators and parents alike often ponder why some students are successful in high school and college and others are not. Among the variables that might influence scholastic achievement is participation in varsity sports. In this chapter, we will use data from the 1970 Explorations in Equality of Opportunity survey, which queried over 2,000 people who were originally surveyed in 1955 as high school sophomores, to examine the relationships between academic achievement and participation in varsity sports. (The data were originally collected by Bruce Eckland and were made available by the Inter-University Consortium for Political and Social Research at the University of Michigan. Neither the original source or collectors of the data nor the Consortium bears any responsibility for the analyses or interpretations presented here.)

There are many variables that can be used to characterize a student's academic achievement. Grade point average and performance on achievement tests quickly come to mind. Since these variables are not independent, we will need special statistical procedures for analyzing them together. Before embarking on new techniques, let's review some of the procedures we have already considered for testing hypotheses about means.

23.1 UNIVARIATE TESTS

When we have two groups and wish to test the hypothesis that the two group means are equal, we can use the t test. For example, we can test the null hypothesis that boys and girls do not differ in spelling ability using the T-TEST procedure. When there are more than two groups, we can use the ONEWAY procedure to test the hypothesis that several group means are equal. For example, we can test the null hypothesis that there is no difference in spelling ability for students in the North, South, West, and East.

When cases are classified on the basis of several factors, the ANOVA procedure can be used. For example, if we want to examine spelling abilities in male and female students who live in the four regions of the country, we can use the ANOVA procedure. We can test three hypotheses: that there is no difference between males and females, that there is no difference among the regions of the country, and that there is no interaction between region and sex.

23.2 SEVERAL DEPENDENT VARIABLES

In all of the previous examples, we are concerned with a single dependent variable, such as spelling ability. What if we are interested in more than just spelling ability? We want to know whether students differ in a variety of academic areas: mathematical achievement, reading comprehension, problem solving, as well as spelling. One strategy is to perform a series of univariate analyses of variance for each of the dependent variables. However, there are several drawbacks to this approach. Multiple univariate analyses ignore the interdependencies among the dependent variables. Information about the correlation structure of the variables is lost. It is possible that groups may not differ significantly on the individual variables, but when considered simultaneously the overall difference is significant. Multiple univariate analyses also do not control for Type I error. That is, the probability of finding significant differences by chance alone greatly increases as the number of comparisons made increases. What we really need in this situation is an analysis of variance procedure for analyzing several dependent variables simultaneously.

23.3 MULTIVARIATE ANALYSIS OF VARIANCE

The extension of analysis of variance to the case of multiple dependent variables is called *multivariate analysis of variance,* or MANOVA. Univariate analysis of variance is just a special case of MANOVA—the case with a single dependent variable. The hypotheses tested with MANOVA are similar to those tested with ANOVA. The difference is that instead of dealing with a single mean, we deal with a set of means. For example, we can test whether average scores on a battery of three tests differ among students in the four regions of the country. For more detailed discussions of multivariate analyses of variance, see Finn (1974), Bock (1975), and Morrison (1967).

23.4 Assumptions

When we have a single dependent variable, two assumptions are needed for the proper application of the ANOVA test: the groups must be random samples from normal populations, and the dependent variable must have the same variance in each of those populations. Similar assumptions are needed for MANOVA. Since we are dealing with several dependent variables, however, we must make assumptions about the joint distribution of the variables—that is, the distribution of the variables considered together. For MANOVA, the dependent variables must come from a multivariate normal population with the same variance-covariance matrix in each group. (A *variance-covariance matrix,* as its name indicates, is a square arrangement of elements, with the variances of the variables on the diagonal, and the covariances of pairs of variables off the diagonal. A variance-covariance matrix can be transformed into a correlation matrix by dividing each covariance by the standard deviations of the two variables.) Later sections of the chapter will present tests for these assumptions.

23.5 Comparing Three Groups

Before we consider more complex generalizations of ANOVA techniques, let's consider a simple one-way analysis of variance and its extension to the case of multiple dependent variables. As you will recall, a one-way analysis of variance is used to test the hypothesis that, in the population, several groups have the same mean. For example, you might want to test the hypothesis that men who do not exercise, men who exercise occasionally, and men who exercise regularly have the same average heart rate. If additional related variables such as blood pressure and respiratory rate are also to be considered, a test that allows comparison of several means is required.

To illustrate this simple MANOVA test and introduce some of the SPSS MANOVA output, we will use the previously described high school data set to test hypotheses about grade point averages and composite verbal and math scores for students who do not participate in varsity sports, participate somewhat, and participate a lot.

23.6
Descriptive Statistics

One of the first steps in any statistical analysis, regardless of how simple or complex it may be, is examination of the individual variables. This preliminary screening provides information about a variable's distribution and permits identification of unusual or outlying values.

When multivariate analyses are undertaken, however, it is not sufficient to just look at the characteristics of the variables individually. Information about their joint distribution must also be obtained. Identification of outliers must also be based on the joint distribution of variables. For example, a height of six feet is not very unusual, and neither is a weight of 100 pounds, nor is being a man. A six-foot-tall male who weighs 100 pounds, however, is fairly atypical and needs to be identified, not for just humanitarian reasons, but to ascertain that the values have been correctly recorded, and if so, to gauge the effect of such a lean physique on subsequent analyses.

Figure 23.6a contains descriptive statistics for each of the two variables for students who did not participate in varsity sports, participated somewhat, and participated a lot. From the figure, you can see that the grade point average is 5.169 for the 260 students who did not participate and 5.06 for the 100 students who participated a lot. For the entire sample of 493 students, the grade point average is 5.073.

Figure 23.6a   Cell means and standard deviations

```
MANOVA GPA SCORE BY VARSITY(1,3)
  /PRINT=CELLINFO(MEANS).
```

```
Cell Means and Standard Deviations
Variable .. GPA            H.S. Grade Average
      FACTOR          CODE              Mean   Std. Dev.        N   95 percent Conf. Interval

   VARSITY           NONE             5.169     2.095         260    4.913       5.425
   VARSITY           SOME             4.845     1.924         103    4.469       5.221
   VARSITY           A LOT            5.060     1.852         100    4.692       5.428
For entire sample                    5.073     2.007         463    4.890       5.257

 - - - - - - - - - - - - - - - - - - - - - - - - - - - - - - - - - - - - - - - -
Variable .. SCORE        Composite Verbal and Math Scores
      FACTOR          CODE              Mean   Std. Dev.        N   95 percent Conf. Interval

   VARSITY           NONE             7.581     4.196         260    7.068       8.093
   VARSITY           SOME             7.204     4.250         103    6.373       8.035
   VARSITY           A LOT            7.730     3.760         100    6.984       8.476
For entire sample                    7.529     4.113         463    7.153       7.905
```

Another way to visualize the distribution of grade point averages in each of the groups is with box-and-whisker plots, as shown in Figure 23.6b The upper and lower boundaries of the boxes are the 25th and 75th percentile values. Each box contains the middle 50% of the values for each group. The asterisk (*) inside the box identifies the group median. The larger the box, the greater the spread of the observations. The lines emanating from each box (the whiskers) extend to the smallest and largest observations in a group that are less than one interquartile range from the end of the box. These are marked with an X. Any points outside of this range but less than one-and-a-half interquartile ranges from the end of the box are marked with O's (for *outlying*). Points more than 1.5 interquartile distances away are marked with E's (for *extreme*). If there are multiple points at a single position, the number of points is also displayed.

Figure 23.6b   Box plots of grade point averages

```
MANOVA GPA SCORE BY VARSITY(1,3)
  /PLOT=BOXPLOT.
```

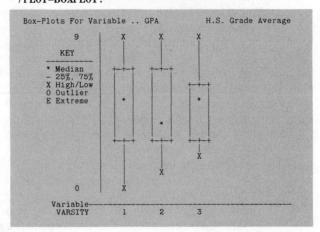

23.7
Tests of Normality

Although the summary statistics presented in Figures 23.6a and 23.6b provide some information about the distributions of the dependent variables, more detailed information about the distributions is often desirable, especially since one of the necessary assumptions for testing hypotheses in MANOVA is that the dependent variables have a multivariate normal distribution. Testing for multivariate normality is not straightforward. If variables have a multivariate normal distribution, however, each one taken individually must be normally distributed. (The opposite is not necessarily true. It is possible that variables that individually have normal distributions when considered together will not necessarily have a multivariate normal distribution.)

Examination of normal probability plots helps us to assess whether individually the variables are normally distributed. Figure 23.7 is a normal plot of the composite verbal and math scores. If the variable has a normal distribution, you would expect the points to cluster around a straight line. In this case, we see some curvature indicating that the distribution is not quite normal. Transformations of the dependent variables can be considered when deviations from normality are substantial.

Figure 23.7 Normal probability plot of composite verbal and math scores

```
MANOVA GPA SCORE BY VARSITY(1,3)
 /PLOT=NORMAL.
```

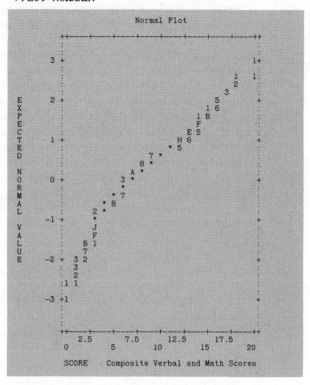

23.8 Tests of Homogeneity of Variance

One of the assumptions needed for the two-sample multivariate *t* test is that the variance-covariance matrices of the dependent variables are equal in the two groups. Box's *M* test, which is based on the determinants of the variance-covariance matrices, provides a test that several covariance matrices are equal. The test is very sensitive to departures from normality, however, and its results should be interpreted with caution. Figure 23.8 shows Box's *M* test for the varsity data. The significance level for the statistic can be based on either the *F* or chi-square distribution, and both approximations are given in the output. Given the result of Box's *M* test, there appears to be no reason to suspect the homogeneity-of-dispersion-matrices assumption.

Figure 23.8 Homogeneity of variance for the varsity data

```
MANOVA GPA SCORE BY VARSITY(1,3)
 /PRINT=HOMOGENEITY(BOXM).
```

```
Multivariate test for Homogeneity of Dispersion matrices

Boxs M =                          6.32069
F WITH (6,925086) DF =            1.04523, P =   .393 (Approx.)
Chi-Square with 6 DF =            6.27141, P =   .393 (Approx.)
```

23.9
Testing the Hypothesis

When we use analysis of variance to test hypotheses about a single dependent variable, all tests are based on the F-ratio. When we have several dependent variables, a variety of multivariate tests of significance are available. They are all based on the eigenvalues of the hypotheses and error matrices. (The hypothesis matrix contains distances between group means for the dependent variables, while the error matrix is an indicator of how much variability there is in the responses within groups.) Four commonly used criteria are *Pillai's trace, Wilks' lambda, Hotelling's trace,* and *Roy's largest root.*

When deciding which multivariate test to use, you must consider the power and robustness of the test. The test should detect differences when they exist and not be affected much by departures from the assumptions. For most practical situations, when differences among the groups are spread along several dimensions, the ordering of the test criteria in terms of decreasing power is Pillai's, Wilks', Hotelling's and Roy's. Pillai's trace is also the most robust. That is, the significance level based on it is reasonably correct even when the assumptions are not exactly met. This is important since all of the necessary assumptions are seldom met exactly, and a test that is overly sensitive to the assumptions is of limited use (Olson, 1976).

Figure 23.9 contains the values for the previously described statistics for the varsity example. The first three statistics are all transformed into statistics that have approximately an F-distribution. There is no straightforward transformation for Roy's largest root criterion to a statistic with a known distribution, so only the value of the largest root is displayed. From the column labeled "Sig. of F," you see that the observed significance level is large, about 0.66, for the first three tests. Thus we have no reason to reject the null hypothesis that grade point averages and college aptitude scores differ for the three groups.

Figure 23.9   Statistical values for the varsity data

```
MANOVA GPA SCORE BY VARSITY(1,3).
```

```
EFFECT .. VARSITY
Multivariate Tests of Significance (S = 2, M = -1/2, N = 228 1/2)

Test Name              Value      Approx. F     Hypoth. DF       Error DF       Sig. of F

Pillais               .00520        .59995          4.00           920.00           .663
Hotellings            .00522        .59794          4.00           916.00           .664
Wilks                 .99480        .59895          4.00           918.00           .663
Roys                  .00421
Note.. F statistic for WILK'S Lambda is exact.
```

23.10
Examining Univariate Differences

If we had found a significant multivariate difference among the three groups, we could examine each of the dependent variables individually to see which variables contribute to the observed overall difference. Even though we didn't find a difference, let's look at the univariate results to see how this output is arranged. Figure 23.10 shows the results of univariate analyses of variance for each of the dependent variables. Each row of the figure corresponds to a one-way analysis of variance for a dependent variable. As expected, there are no significant differences for either of the variables. The significance levels for the univariate tests have not been adjusted for comparison of several variables, and they should be interpreted with this in mind.

Figure 23.10   Univariate analysis of variance for each dependent variable

```
EFFECT .. VARSITY (CONT.)
Univariate F-tests with (2,460) D. F.

Variable      Hypoth. SS      Error SS      Hypoth. MS      Error MS            F      Sig. of F
GPA              7.79483    1853.70841        3.89742        4.02980      .96715        .381
SCORE           15.62408    7801.73229        7.81204       16.96029      .46061        .631
```

23.11
A Factorial Design

So far we have considered a very simple multivariate design: a one-way analysis of variance. We are now ready to examine a somewhat more complex factorial design. The students represented in our data set are subdivided not only by their participation in varsity sports, but also by whether they are male or female. Since students are classified by varsity participation categories and sex, we have a two-way factorial design with three categories for varsity participation and two categories for sex.

23.12
Examining the Data

The previously described tables and plots are a good first step in examining the data. There are some additional displays that are useful for summarizing the data and looking for violations of the assumptions. Figure 23.12a is a plot of the six cell means for the two variables. From this plot, you can get an idea of the spread of the means. The top row of numbers indicates how many cell means there are in each interval. You can see that, for the grade point average, there are two means close to 5.22 and one mean close to 5.46.

Figure 23.12a   Plots of cell means

```
MANOVA GPA SCORE BY VARSITY(1,3) SEX(1,2)
  /PLOT=CELLPLOTS.
```

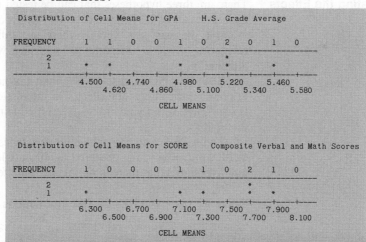

Both univariate and multivariate analyses of variance require equal variances in all of the cells. However, there are many situations in which there is a relationship between the cell means and the variances. Plotting means against standard deviations and variances is useful for uncovering such relationships.

Figure 23.12b is a plot of the means versus standard deviations for the grade point variable. There does not appear to be a readily discernible relationship between the two variables in this plot. If patterns were evident, transformations of the dependent variables might be used to stabilize the variances.

Figure 23.12b   Plot of mean vs. standard deviation for the grade point variable

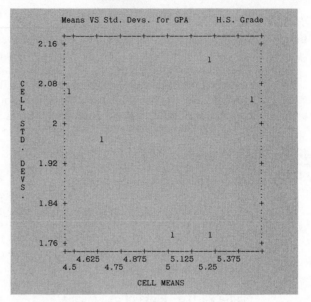

23.13
Testing the Effects

There are three hypotheses that can be tested for a two-way factorial design: two hypotheses about the main effects and one hypothesis about the interaction. In our example, we can test whether there are differences among the three varsity categories, the two categories of sex, and whether there is a varsity by sex interaction.

SPSS MANOVA displays separate output for each effect. The first effect displayed is the interaction effect. The interaction effect is examined first since, if it is significant, it is not advisable to test the main effects (see Chapter 16 for further discussion).

Figure 23.13a contains the multivariate tests of significance for the VARSITY by SEX interaction. The observed significance level is 0.15, so we will not reject the null hypothesis that there is no interaction effect.

Figure 23.13a   VARSITY by SEX interactions

```
MANOVA GPA SCORE BY VARSITY(1,3) SEX(1,2).

EFFECT .. VARSITY BY SEX
Multivariate Tests of Significance (S = 2, M = -1/2, N = 227 )

Test Name         Value        Approx. F      Hypoth. DF      Error DF      Sig. of F

Pillais           .01471       1.69270           4.00          914.00         .150
Hotellings        .01486       1.68982           4.00          910.00         .150
Wilks             .98533       1.69126           4.00          912.00         .150
Roys              .01177
Note.. F statistic for WILK'S Lambda is exact.
```

Multivariate tests for the SEX main effect are shown in Figure 23.13b. The observed significance level is small, 0.002, so we will reject the null hypothesis that there is no difference between males and females. Examination of Figure 23.13c, the univariate results, suggests that the differences between the two sexes are primarily due to the differences in grade point averages. The observed significance level for the composite college tests is large.

Figure 23.13b   Multivariate tests for SEX effect

```
EFFECT .. SEX
Multivariate Tests of Significance (S = 1, M = 0, N = 227 )

Test Name          Value          Exact F       Hypoth. DF        Error DF       Sig. of F

Pillais            .02801         6.57021           2.00           456.00          .002
Hotellings         .02882         6.57021           2.00           456.00          .002
Wilks              .97199         6.57021           2.00           456.00          .002
Roys               .02801
Note.. F statistics are exact.
```

Figure 23.13c   Univariate results for SEX effect

```
EFFECT .. SEX (CONT.)
Univariate F-tests with (1,457) D. F.

Variable       Hypoth. SS        Error SS       Hypoth. MS       Error MS              F       Sig. of F

GPA            25.88464       1795.14752        25.88464        3.92811        6.58959         .011
SCORE          15.86965       7709.85412        15.86965       16.87058         .94067         .333
```

Tests for the VARSITY effect are shown in Figure 23.13d. As before, there are no significant differences among the three categories of varsity participation. You will notice that the statistics for the VARSITY effect are different in Figure 23.13d when compared to Figure 23.9. This is because the number of cases in the various combinations of factor levels is not equal and the analysis of variance results for "unbalanced" designs depends on the other factors in the analysis.

Figure 23.13d   Multivariate tests for VARSITY effect

```
EFFECT .. VARSITY
Multivariate Tests of Significance (S = 2, M = -1/2, N = 227 )

Test Name          Value         Approx. F       Hypoth. DF        Error DF       Sig. of F

Pillais            .00314          .35945           4.00           914.00          .838
Hotellings         .00315          .35811           4.00           910.00          .838
Wilks              .99686          .35878           4.00           912.00          .838
Roys               .00257
Note.. F statistic for WILK'S Lambda is exact.
```

23.14
RUNNING PROCEDURE MANOVA

The SPSS MANOVA procedure can be used to analyze a large variety of multivariate and univariate designs. It can also generate a large assortment of optional output. That's why the procedure has quite a few subcommands and keywords. However, to run simple designs like the ones discussed in this chapter, you need only a small number of specifications.

23.15
Specifying the Variables

To run the MANOVA procedure, you must indicate which variables are dependent variables, which variables are factors, and which variables (if any) are covariates.

An example of a simple MANOVA command is

```
MANOVA GPA SCORE BY VARSITY(1,3).
```

The first variables listed are the dependent variables. In this example, they are called GPA and SCORE. The keyword BY separates the dependent variables from the factor variables. There is one factor variable, VARSITY, which follows the keyword BY. Each factor name must be followed by two integer values enclosed in parentheses and separated by a comma. These are the lowest and highest values for the factor. The VARSITY factor has three levels coded as 1, 2, and 3. Cases with factor values outside the designated range are excluded from the analysis. For example, the command

```
MANOVA GPA SCORE BY VARSITY(1,2).
```

would include in the analysis only cases which have values of 1 or 2 for the VARSITY variable. MANOVA requires the factor levels to be integers. If you have noninteger factor values, they must be recoded to integers. Factors with empty categories must also be recoded, since MANOVA expects cases in all of the groups which fall between the minimum and the maximum factor values.

If you have more than one factor variable, list all of them after the BY keyword. For example,

```
MANOVA GPA SCORE BY VARSITY(1,3) SEX(1,2).
```

specifies that there are two factors: VARSITY and SEX.

If several factors have the same range, you can specify a list of factors followed by a single value range, in parentheses, as in the command

```
MANOVA SALES REVENUE BY TVAD RADIOAD MAGAD NEWSPAD(1,4).
```

If you have covariates in your analysis, they are listed after the factors and after the keyword WITH. For example,

```
MANOVA GPA SCORE BY VARSITY(1,3) SEX(1,2) WITH IQ.
```

indicates that the IQ variable is to be used as a covariate.

23.16
Requesting Optional Output

The PRINT subcommand is used to request optional output. For example,

```
MANOVA GPA SCORE BY VARSITY(1,3)
 /PRINT=CELLINFO(MEANS).
```

requests the display of cell means for GPA and SCORE for all values of VARSITY, and produced Figure 23.6a.

23.17
Requesting Cell Information

You can obtain information about the individual cells (combinations of factors) in the analysis using the CELLINFO keyword on the PRINT subcommand. Following the keyword, in parentheses, you must list the information desired. For example,

```
/PRINT=CELLINFO(MEANS)
```

requests means, standard deviations, and counts for each of the cells. Similarly,

```
/PRINT=CELLINFO(COV)
```

prints variance-covariance matrices for each group. To obtain correlations for each group, specify

```
PRINT=CELLINFO(COR)
```

You can request more than one set of statistics by specifying more than one keyword within the parentheses. For example,

```
/PRINT=CELLINFO(MEANS,COR)
```

requests both descriptive statistics and correlation matrices for each cell.

23.18
Requesting Homogeneity Tests

The HOMOGENEITY keyword on the PRINT subcommand is used to request tests for homogeneity of variance. As with CELLINFO, you must list the desired tests in parentheses after the keyword. For example, the following PRINT specification was used to generate all the cell information and tests discussed in this chapter:

```
/PRINT=CELLINFO(MEANS) HOMOGENEITY(BARTLETT,COCHRAN,BOXM)
```

23.19
Specifying Plots

Plots are requested with the PLOT subcommand. For example,

```
MANOVA GPA SCORE BY VARSITY(1,3)
 /PLOT=BOXPLOT.
```

requests boxplots for each dependent variable, and produced Figure 23.6b. The following keywords may be used for the PLOT subcommand:

CELLPLOTS *Plot cell statistics, including plots of cell means versus cell variances and cell standard deviations, and a histogram of cell means.*

BOXPLOT *Plot a boxplot for each dependent variable.*

NORMAL *Plot a normal plot and a detrended normal plot for each dependent variable.*

STEMLEAF *Plot a stem-and-leaf display for each dependent variable.*

23.20
Specifying the Model

If you wish to analyze your data as a complete factorial, you don't need additional specifications. A complete factorial is the default. (A complete factorial is a design in which all main effects and all orders of interactions are included.)

If you wish to analyze a model other than a complete factorial, the last subcommand must be a DESIGN specification. For example, if you want to analyze a model which has only main effects, you must specify

```
/DESIGN=VARSITY SEX.
```

The keyword BY is used on the DESIGN subcommand to indicate interactions. For example,

```
/DESIGN=A B C, A BY B, B BY C.
```

specifies a model with three main effects and two two-way interactions.

23.21
A MANOVA Example

The following MANOVA command was used to generate some of the figures in this chapter:

```
MANOVA GPA SCORE BY VARSITY(1,3)
 /PRINT=CELLINFO(MEANS) HOMOGENEITY(BOXM)
 /PLOT=CELLPLOTS BOXPLOT NORMAL.
```

- MANOVA specifies two dependent variables (GPA and SCORE) and one factor variable (VARSITY). A value range from 1 to 3 is specified for the factor variable (see Section 23.15).
- The PRINT subcommand requests descriptive statistics: the cell means, standard deviations, and counts. PRINT also requests Box's *M* test (see Sections 23.16 through 23.18).
- The PLOT subcommand requests plots for cell statistics, boxplots for each interval variable, and normal plots for each continuous variable (see Section 23.19).

23.22 EXERCISES

Syntax

1. Find the errors in the MANOVA commands below:

    a. `MANOVA ESTEEM SEX(1,2) ATTRACT(1,5) IQ(1,3).`

    b. `MANOVA INCOME PRESTIGE BY AGE(1,4) SEX(1,2) EDUC.`

    c. `MANOVA ETHNOCNT POLITICS BY INTEGRTN(1,2) BY RACE(1,2) BY`
       `   SEX(1,2)`
       `      /PRINT=CELLINFO(MEANS).`

2. A researcher wants to obtain a univariate analysis of variance using a full-factorial model and writes the following MANOVA command. Will this produce the analysis she wants?

    ```
    MANOVA ENDURNCE BY SEX(1,2) PROGRAM(1,2) PASTSCOR(1,5)
       /DESIGN=SEX PROGRAM PASTSCOR SEX BY PROGRAM SEX BY PASTSCOR
       PROGRAM BY PASTSCOR.
    ```

Statistical Concepts

1. a. Plot the means and variances shown below against each other. Is any relationship evident? If so, how are they related?

Mean	Variance
−2.13	0.28
−0.56	0.02
−11.10	6.51
−1.21	0.09
−6.99	2.65
−3.14	0.65
−18.83	27.12
−9.40	5.02
−5.63	2.08
−4.74	1.47
−15.58	15.8

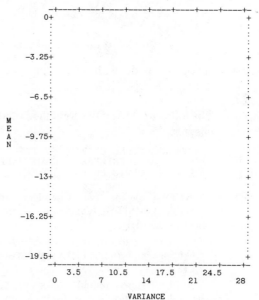

PLOT OF MEAN WITH VARIANCE

b. Obtain the standard deviations from the variances given in (a) and plot the means shown in (a) against these standard deviations. Is any relationship evident? If so, how are they related?

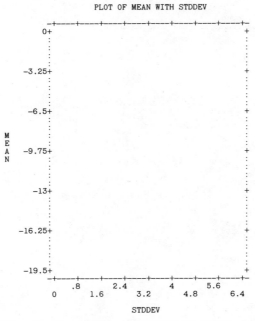

PLOT OF MEAN WITH STDDEV

c. Why are plots like the ones done for (a) and (b) an important part of a MANOVA analysis?

2. A two-sample Hotelling's T^2 test resulted in the output below:

Multivariate Tests of Significance (S = 1, M = 1 , N = 48)

Test Name	Value	Approx. F	Hypoth. DF	Error DF	Sig. of F
Hotellings	21.945	6.997	1.00	46.00	.011

Would you reject the null hypothesis that there is no difference between the two groups?

3. Use the box-and-whisker plots shown below to answer the following questions:

Box-Plots For variable .. EDVALUE

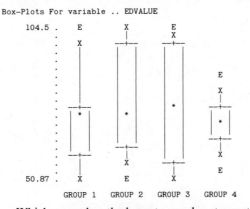

a. Which group has the largest spread, not counting outliers?
b. Which group has the largest median?
c. Does the assumption of equal group variances seem reasonable for these data? Why or why not?

4. a. Which of the normal probability plots shown below are inconsistent with the assumption of normality?

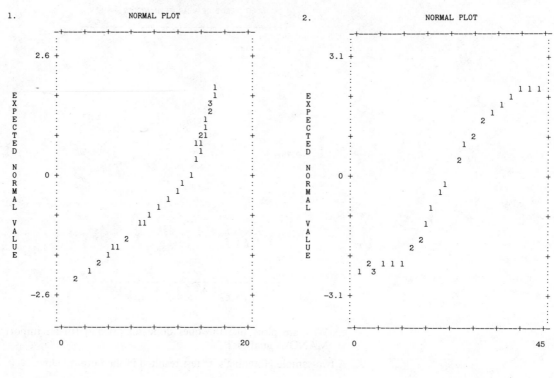

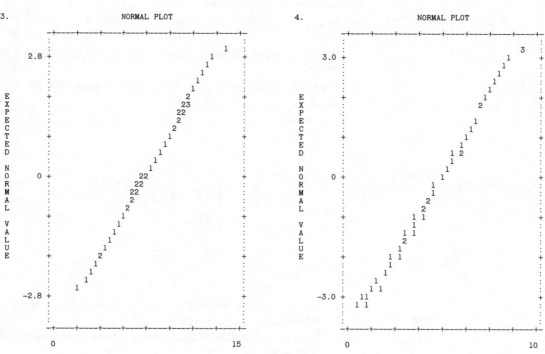

Appendix
A
Answers to Selected Exercises

Chapter 1

1. a. LASTNAME is a valid SPSS variable name.
    b. FIRSTNAME is not a valid SPSS variable name. It is more than eight characters long.
    c. SS_NO is a valid SPSS variable name.
    d. PHONE# is a valid SPSS variable name.
    e. S&L is not a valid SPSS variable name. The ampersand (&) is a special character that cannot be used in a variable name.
    f. $INCOME is not a valid SPSS variable name. Variable names must start with a letter. The dollar sign ($) can be used in a variable name—but it cannot be the first character of the name.

2. a. 5
    b. VAR1, VAR2, VAR3, VAR4, VAR5

3. No. There are no data definition commands defining the data or specifying the name of the external SPSS system file that contains the data.

Chapter 2

1. In fixed-field format, if you have more than one record per case, you must specify the number of records on the RECORDS subcommand, as in:

```
DATA LIST FIXED RECORDS=2
  /1 ID 1-3 AGE 5-7 SEX 8
  /2 EDUC 1-2 JOBCAT 4.
```

2. If you specify a single column range for a variable list, the number of columns must be divisible by the number of variables, since SPSS divides the columns equally between the variables. In this example, any multiple of 3 could be a correct specification, such as:

```
DATA LIST FIXED
  /VAR1 TO VAR3 1-9.
```

3. You can specify a maximum of three values per variable on the MISSING VALUES command—but two of the values can define a range, as in:

```
MISSING VALUES JOBCAT (96 THRU 99).
```

4. Variable labels must be enclosed in apostrophes or quotation marks, as in:

```
VARIABLE LABELS
  DAYOFWK 'DAY OF DEATH'
  VITAL10 'STATUS AT TEN YEARS'
  FAMHX 'FAMILY HISTORY'.
```

5. A slash is required to separate value labels for one variable or variable list from the next variable or variable list, as in:

```
VALUE LABELS
  ITEM1 TO ITEM3 1 'YES' 2 'NO'
  /SALARY 1 'LESS THAN $20,000'
          2 '$20,000 TO $49,000'
          3 '$50,000 OR MORE'.
```

6. With freefield format, all variables preceding a format in parentheses must have a format explicity specified unless they are separated by an asterisk. If WT58, HT58, and DBP58 are numeric variables (the default format), simply specify:

```
DATA LIST FILE=CORONARY FREE
  /WT58 HT58 DBP58 * NAME  (A20).
```

Chapter 3

1. a. The RECODE command does not account for values between 5 and 6, values between 9 and 10, and values between 14 and 15.

    b. To make sure all values of a continuous variable are recoded, use overlapping endpoints, and specify the new values in descending order, as in:

```
RECODE HOURWAGE
  (15 THRU HI=4) (10 THRU 15=3) (5 THRU 10=2) (LO THRU 5=1).
```

2. a. 13
    b. 19
    c. 15
    d. 11
    e. 13

3. a. 2
    b. 9
    c. 3
    d. 4

4. No. The treatment of missing values is different. The first COMPUTE command will only return a missing value if a case has missing values for all three variables: X1, X2, and X3. The second COMPUTE command will return a missing value if a case has a missing value for any of the three variables.

5. a. IF (JOBCAT EQ 2) OR (JOBCAT EQ 4) OR (JOBCAT=6) TRAINEE=1.

    or

    IF ANY(JOBCAT,2,4,6) TRAINEE=1.

    b. IF EDLEVEL LE 12 AND SALNOW LE 10000 LOW=1.

    c. IF (AGE LE 20 OR OR AGE GE 55) OLDYOUNG=1.

    (With the exception of the specifications for the ANY function, the parentheses in the above IF commands are optional.)

6. | JOBCAT | AGE | SALNOW | EDLEVEL | TRAINEE | ACHIEVER | LOW |
    |--------|-----|--------|---------|---------|----------|-----|
    | 6 | 29 | 16080 | 16 | 1 | 1 | 0 |
    | 5 | 40 | 41400 | 16 | 0 | 1 | 0 |
    | 1 | 54 | 8880 | 12 | 0 | 0 | 1 |
    | 2 | 32 | 22000 | 17 | 1 | 0 | 0 |
    | 3 | 31 | 19020 | 19 | 0 | 0 | 0 |

7. a. Since the first SELECT IF command remains in effect for the remainder of the SPSS session, the second SELECT IF command will result in no cases being selected.

    b. There are two ways to produce separate frequency tables for males and females in this example. You can use the TEMPORARY command, as in:

```
TEMPORARY.
SELECT IF (SEX EQ 'M').
FREQUENCIES VARIABLES=SALARY.
TEMPORARY.
SELECT IF (SEX EQ 'F').
FREQUENCIES VARIABLES=SALARY.
```

    Or you can use the SPLIT FILE command, as in:

```
SORT CASES BY SEX.
SPLIT FILE BY SEX.
FREQUENCIES VARIABLES=SALARY.
```

Chapter 4

1. a. On the RENAME subcommand, the number of variables on both sides of the equals sign must be the same, as in:

```
GET FILE=CARDIAC
  /RENAME (HT58 WT58 AGE58=HEIGHT WEIGHT AGE).
```

    b. SAVE OUTFILE=NEWFILE.

    c. The INTO subcommand is missing, as in:

```
AUTORECODE VARIABLES=AGE SEX
  /INTO NEWAGE NEWSEX.
```

2. No new variables based on aggregate functions have been specified.

3. By default, AUTORECODE assigns consecutive integer values in ascending alphabetical order to string variables. So the values for NEWSCALE would be:

```
NAME    SCALE    NEWSCALE
Moe     High        1
Larry   Medium      3
Curly   Low         2
```

4.
```
GET FILE=PRETEST.
SORT CASES BY CASENO.
SAVE OUTFILE=PRETEST.
GET FILE=POSTTEST.
SORT CASES BY CASENO.
SAVE OUTFILE=POSTTEST.
MATCH FILES FILE=PRETEST /FILE=POSTTEST
 /BY CASENO.
```

Chapter 5

1. Titles cannot exceed 60 characters. Titles can be continued on more than one line if each line is enclosed in apostrophes or quotation marks and continuation lines are preceded by a plus (+) sign.

2. Comments that follow commands on the same line cannot be continued on the next line.

3. The SET WIDTH value must be between 80 and 132.

4. The FINISH command is always unconditional. If you place it within a DO IF—END IF structure, the session is terminated when the FINISH command is encountered, regardless of the DO IF specifications. No commands beyond FINISH are executed.

Chapter 6

1. a. Either the keyword TO or FROM should be used instead of the equals sign, as in:

   `LIST CASES TO 10 BY 2.`

   b. System variables (variables that begin with a dollar sign, such as $CASENUM) cannot be specified on the LIST command).

   c. The FROM value cannot be larger than the TO value.

2.
```
LIST CASES TO 100 BY 3
 /FORMAT=SINGLE.
```

Chapter 7

Syntax

1. a. False. Slashes can go anywhere between the subcommands.

   b. False. Frequently, commands can be made more readable with blanks around equals signs.

   c. True. The keyword is NOTABLE with no intervening blank.

   d. False. As long as the second and any subsequent continuation lines of a command in batch mode begins with at least one blank, the command is free format.

   e. False. Commas and blanks are interchangeable when separating variable names in a list.

   f. False. The order you enter the variable names is up to you and affects only the order in which the output is displayed.

   g. False. Keyword NOTABLE (when spelled correctly) eliminates the frequency tables.

   h. True. Bar charts are requested for variables FIRSTCHD and DAYOFWK.

2. a. Incorrect. The BARCHART subcommand is missing and MISSING=INCLUDE would have generated a bar for the missing value.

   b. Incorrect. MISSING=INCLUDE would have generated a bar for the missing value.

   c. Correct. This command creates the bar chart plus a frequency table also displayed in descending order of frequency.

3. a. False. The FREQUENCIES syntax is fine.

   b. False. The three lines of information following the GET command indicate that the file was located and read correctly.

   c. False. The message following the GET command shows that the file was recognized as an SPSS system file.

   d. True. The error message points directly to the variable name as having caused the problem. The DISPLAY command gives you all dictionary information on a system file including the variable names (see Chapter 4).

Statistical Concepts

1. a. Bar chart.
   b. Bar chart.
   c. Histogram.
   d. Histogram.
   e. Bar chart.
   f. Histogram.
   g. Histogram.

2. a. True.
   b. True.
   c. False.
   d. False.
   e. False.
   f. True.

3.

VALUE LABEL	VALUE	FREQUENCY	PERCENT	VALID PERCENT	CUM PERCENT
	1	23	46.0	47.9	47.9
	2	12	24.0	25.0	72.9
	3	10	20.0	20.8	93.8
	4	3	6.0	6.3	100.0
MISSING	9	2	4.0	MISSING	
	TOTAL	50	100.0	100.0	

4. Histogram A provides the best summary of the data. B has too many intervals and C has too few.

5. HT58   STATURE, 1958 -- TO NEAREST 0.1 INCH

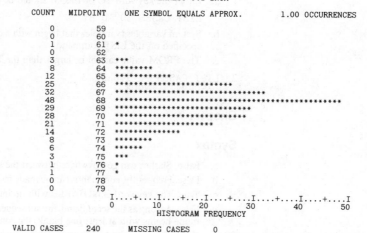

```
      COUNT   MIDPOINT   ONE SYMBOL EQUALS APPROX.         1.00 OCCURRENCES

         0      59
         0      60
         1      61  *
         0      62
         3      63  ***
         8      64  ********
        12      65  ************
        25      66  *************************
        32      67  ********************************
        48      68  ************************************************
        29      69  *****************************
        28      70  ****************************
        21      71  *********************
        14      72  **************
         8      73  ********
         6      74  ******
         3      75  ***
         1      76  *
         1      77  *
         0      78
         0      79
                    I....+....I....+....I....+....I....+....I....+....I
                    0        10       20       30       40       50
                               HISTOGRAM FREQUENCY

VALID CASES     240      MISSING CASES     0
```

6. a.

VALUE LABEL	VALUE	FREQUENCY	PERCENT	VALID PERCENT	CUM PERCENT
	1.00	6	24.0	24.0	24.0
	2.00	3	12.0	12.0	36.0
	3.00	6	24.0	24.0	60.0
	4.00	2	8.0	8.0	68.0
	5.00	4	16.0	16.0	84.0
	8.00	1	4.0	4.0	88.0
	9.00	2	8.0	8.0	96.0
	10.00	1	4.0	4.0	100.0
	TOTAL	25	100.0	100.0	

   b.

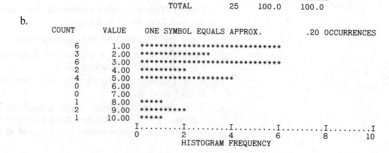

```
     COUNT   VALUE    ONE SYMBOL EQUALS APPROX.          .20 OCCURRENCES

        6    1.00   *****************************
        3    2.00   ***************
        6    3.00   *****************************
        2    4.00   **********
        4    5.00   ********************
        0    6.00
        0    7.00
        1    8.00   *****
        2    9.00   **********
        1   10.00   *****
                    I........I........I........I........I........I
                    0        2        4        6        8       10
                               HISTOGRAM FREQUENCY
```

c.

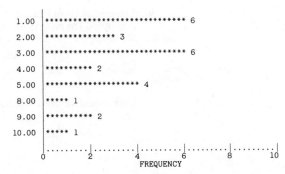

d. The histogram is preferable since codes of 6 and 7 are included, even if they do not occur in the data.

7. a. False.
   b. False.
   c. False.
   d. True.

Chapter 8

Syntax

1. ```
   DATA LIST /BOAST 1-2 ACTUAL 4-5
   COMPUTE BLUFF=BOAST - ACTUAL.
   BEGIN DATA
   90 79
   93 81
   87 77
   96 89
   89 72
   END DATA.
   FREQUENCIES VARIABLES=BLUFF /STATISTICS=ALL
   ```

2. ```
   FREQUENCIES VARIABLES=BLUFF /STATISTICS=ALL
        /HISTOGRAM /FORMAT=NOTABLE.
   ```

3. ```
   DESCRIPTIVES VARIABLES=BOAST ACTUAL BLUFF.
   ```

Statistical Concepts

1. a. Mild case is the mode.
   b. Moderately severe is the median.
   c. Doesn't make sense since scale is not interval.

2. a. Black is the mode.
   b. No ordering so median does not make sense.
   c. No ordering so mean does not make sense.

3. a. Nominal.
   b. Ratio.
   c. Ordinal.
   d. Ratio.
   e. Interval.
   f. Nominal.

4. The 78th observation.

5. a. 0.267
   b. 0.267 since the mean, median, and mode are identical for a normal distribution.
   c. 0.012
   d. 0

6. The average of the standardized scores must be zero, so a mistake must have occurred.

7. 72% of the sample are females.

8. a. False.
   b. False.
   c. True.
   ```

9. The median is not influenced by extreme values, so it would reflect the low pay levels of the employees. The mean is affected by extremes, so a single salary with seven digits would inflate the mean.

10.
```
MEAN          1.700     MEDIAN      2.000     MODE     2.000
STD DEV       1.059     VARIANCE    1.122     RANGE    4.000
MINIMUM        .000     MAXIMUM     4.000
```

11.

Case	Standard score	Original score
1	1	12
2	0	10
3	−2	6

12.

Student	Score	Standardized score
1	70	0
2	58	−1.00
3	94	2.00

13. a.
```
VARIABLE      STD DEV      VARIANCE VALID N

VARA           6.529        42.622      10
```
b.
```
VARIABLE      RANGE      MINIMUM     MAXIMUM VALID N

VARB          19.000       .000      19.000     10
```
c.
```
VARIABLE       MEAN           SUM VALID N

VARC          8.500        85.000      10
```

14. All statistics except the total sample size stay the same.

Chapter 9

Syntax

1. You can only specify the PLOT subcommand once on the EXAMINE command. You can, however, specify more than one type of plot on the same PLOT subcommand, as in:

```
EXAMINE VARIABLES=INCOME IQ
  /PLOT=HISTOGRAM STEMLEAF.
```

2. MEAN is not a valid keyword for the STATISTICS subcommand. You can obtain the mean (and other descriptive statistics) with the DESCRIPTIVE keyword, as in:

```
EXAMINE VARIABLES=ATTNSPAN BY TVHOURS
  /STATISTICS=DESCRIPTIVE
  /PLOT=SPREADLEVEL.
```

3. Percentile values must be enclosed in parentheses, as in:

```
EXAMINE VARIABLES=GPA BY MAJOR BY SEX
  /PLOT=NONE /STATISTICS=EXTREME(3)
  /PERCENTILES(25, 50, 75).
```

4.
```
EXAMINE VARIABLES=INCOME BY RELIGION RELIGION BY POSTLIFE
  /PLOT=BOXPLOT
  /STATISTICS=NONE.
```

5. The Levene test for homogeneity of variance is calculated when you specify SPREADLEVEL on the PLOT subcommand, as in:

```
EXAMINE VARIABLES=INCOME BY RELIGION RELIGION BY POSTLIFE
  /PLOT=BOXPLOT SPREADLEVEL
  /STATISTICS=NONE.
```

Statistical Concepts

1. a.
```
Frequency     Stem &  Leaf

     6.00        2  .  122258
    10.00        3  .  0124555589
     3.00        4  .  001
     1.00 Extremes    (80)
```

b.
```
    Frequency    Stem &  Leaf
        4.00        2  *  1222
        2.00        2  .  58
        4.00        3  *  0124
        6.00        3  .  555589
        3.00        4  *  001
        1.00 Extremes   (80)
```

c.
```
    Frequency    Stem &  Leaf
        1.00        2  *  1
        3.00        2  t  222
        1.00        2  f  5
        0.00        2  s
        1.00        2  .  8
        2.00        3  *  01
        1.00        3  t  2
        5.00        3  f  45555
        0.00        3  s
        2.00        3  .  89
        3.00        4  *  001
        1.00 Extremes   (80)
```

2.
```
    Frequency    Bin Center
        6.00        25.00   ******
       10.00        35.00   **********
        3.00        45.00   ***
        1.00 Extremes       *

    Bin width :    10.00
    Each star:     1 case(s)
```

3. The stem-and-leaf plot provides more information about the actual data values than the histogram does.

4. a. The median for warehouse 1 is approximately 8.

    b. The interquartile range for warehouse 2 is approximately 10.

    c. Approximately 22.

    d. Warehouse 2.

    e. Warehouse 2. It has the lowest median delivery. However, if consistency and "worst case" delivery times are important factors, warehouse 1 would be a better choice.

5.
```
                Frequency Table

     Bin                          Cum
    Center    Freq      Pct       Pct

    <150.0     .00       .00       .00
    162.5    17.00     68.00     68.00
    187.5     3.00     12.00     80.00
    212.5     4.00     16.00     96.00
    237.5     1.00      4.00    100.00
```

6. a. No—you can only determine salary in $100 increments, with the exception of the extreme value of $35,150.

    b.
```
        $21,500
        $21,600
        $22,300
        $22,400
        $22,400
        $23,000
        $23,100
        $23,600
        $23,800
        $24,200
        $24,300
        $24,500
        $24,500
        $25,000
        $25,400
        $25,700
        $25,800
        $25,900
        $26,700
        $27,000
        $27,700
        $28,500
        $30,000
        $30,500
        $35,150
```

7. The null hypothesis of the Levene test is that all groups come from populations with equal variances. It is useful for two-sample t-tests and analysis of variance.

8. The null hypothesis is not rejected. Therefore, you can assume that all groups come from populations with equal variances.

9. E is the normal probability plot for A; F is the normal probability plot for B; D is the normal probability plot for C.

10.

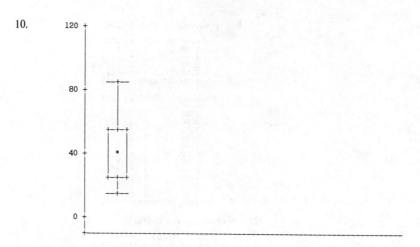

Chapter 10

Syntax

1. a. False. The CROSSTABS command produces one 2 × 2 table for ADDRESS by LOCATION.
    b. True. The variable specified before the first BY keyword becomes the row variable.
    c. False. The variable LOCATION is the column variable.
    d. False. The VARIABLES subcommand is not required.
    e. False. Keyword ROW requests row percentages only. Use keyword TOTAL to request total percentages.
    f. True. Keyword ROW requests row percentages only.
    g. False. No statistics are requested. Use the STATISTICS subcommand to request statistics.

2. a. Incorrect. When you use integer mode, you must specify a range for each variable named with the VARIABLES subcommand. Keyword TOTAL requests total percentages, but these are not shown in the output.
    b. Correct. To use integer mode, use the VARIABLES subcommand followed by the variables and the ranges you want to use in the tables. Separate the VARIABLES subcommand and the TABLES subcommand with a slash.
    c. Incorrect. The VARIABLES subcommand is specified correctly but needs a slash following the range. The TABLES subcommand requests a table with the variables reversed.
    d. Incorrect. The ranges should be specified with the VARIABLES subcommand.

3. VARA is the frequency count for each cell. VARB is the row variable and VARC is the column variable.

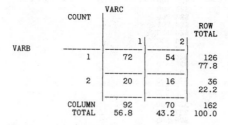

Statistical Concepts

1. a. False.
    b. True.
    c. False.
    d. False.

2. a. No.
    b. Yes.
    c. Yes (no for symmetric).
    d. Yes.

3. None.

4. They are easier to interpret, and values from different tables can be compared.

5. This is not a good strategy since calculating many statistics and reporting only the ones with large values distorts significance levels.

6. GPA is the independent variable. PERFORM is the dependent variable. Look at row percentages.

7.

COUNT ROW PCT COL PCT	DEPTH			ROW TOTAL
	SMALL 1	MEDIUM 2	LARGE 3	
CURE NO 1	29 42.0 65.9	10 14.5 50.0	30 43.5 60.0	69 60.5
YES 2	15 33.3 34.1	10 22.2 50.0	20 44.4 40.0	45 39.5
COLUMN TOTAL	44 38.6	20 17.5	50 43.9	114 100.0

8.

COUNT EXP VAL RESIDUAL	VARB		ROW TOTAL
	1	2	
VARA 1	13 30.0 -17.0	47 30.0 17.0	60 60.0%
2	37 20.0 17.0	3 20.0 -17.0	40 40.0%
COLUMN TOTAL	50 50.0%	50 50.0%	100 100.0%

CHI-SQUARE	D.F.	SIGNIFICANCE	MIN E.F.	CELLS WITH E.F.< 5
45.37500	1	0.0000	20.000	NONE
48.16667	1	0.0000	(BEFORE YATES CORRECTION)	

NUMBER OF MISSING OBSERVATIONS =   0

9. a.

COUNT	VARB		ROW TOTAL
	COUGH 1	NO COUGH 2	
VARA SMOKER 1	30	20	50 50.0
NONSMOKER 2	15	35	50 50.0
COLUMN TOTAL	45 45.0	55 55.0	100 100.0

CHI-SQUARE	D.F.	SIGNIFICANCE	MIN E.F.	CELLS WITH E.F.< 5
7.91919	1	0.0049	22.500	NONE
9.09091	1	0.0026	(BEFORE YATES CORRECTION)	

NUMBER OF MISSING OBSERVATIONS =   0

b.

COUNT	VARB		ROW TOTAL
	COUGH 1	NO COUGH 2	
VARA SMOKER 1	300	200	500 50.0
NONSMOKER 2	150	350	500 50.0
COLUMN TOTAL	450 45.0	550 55.0	1000 100.0

CHI-SQUARE	D.F.	SIGNIFICANCE	MIN E.F.	CELLS WITH E.F.< 5
89.70101	1	0.0000	225.000	NONE
90.90909	1	0.0000	(BEFORE YATES CORRECTION)	

NUMBER OF MISSING OBSERVATIONS =   0

10. a. The expected values are in the table below:

```
                        VARB
             COUNT  |
             EXP VAL| SMOKER  NONSMOKE  ROW
                    |              R    TOTAL
                    |      1|      2|
    SEX      --------+-------+-------+
              1 |      45 |     55 |   100
    MALE        |    37.5 |   62.5 |  50.0%
             --------+-------+-------+
              2 |      30 |     70 |   100
    FEMALE      |    37.5 |   62.5 |  50.0%
             --------+-------+-------+
             COLUMN      75     125     200
             TOTAL     37.5%   62.5%  100.0%
```

```
CHI-SQUARE     D.F.       SIGNIFICANCE       MIN E.F.     CELLS WITH E.F.< 5
----------     ----       ------------       --------     ------------------

  4.18133       1           0.0409            37.500            NONE
  4.80000       1           0.0285          ( BEFORE YATES CORRECTION )
```

NUMBER OF MISSING OBSERVATIONS =   0

b. There is one degree of freedom for this table.

c. The chi-square value without Yates' correction is 4.80.

Chapter 11

Syntax

1. The correct syntax for the MEANS is

   ```
   MEANS TABLES=SALNOW BY SEX BY JOBCAT
     /MISSING=DEPENDENT.
   ```

2. The CROSSBREAK subcommand on MEANS requires the VARIABLES subcommand. The correct syntax is

   ```
   MEANS VARIABLES=EDLEVEL(LO,HI) SEX MINORITY (0,1)
     /CROSSBREAK=EDLEVEL BY SEX BY MINORITY.
   ```

3. a. This MEANS command produces two tables: SALNOW BY SEX and SALNOW BY MINORITY.

   b. This is the correct MEANS command to produce the output shown.

   c. This MEANS command specifies MINORITY as the dependent variable on which to calculate means.

Statistical Concepts

1. a. MEANS
   b. CROSSTABS
   c. FREQUENCIES
   d. MEANS
   e. CROSSTABS

2. CROSSTABS prints numbers (and percentages) of cases that fall in each cell of the table, while MEANS prints statistics for a dependent variable for combinations of values of the independent variables.

3. a. False.
   b. False.

4. a.
```
          D E S C R I P T I O N   O F   S U B P O P U L A T I O N S

    Criterion Variable    DBP58      AVERAGE DIAST BLOOD PRESSURE 58
        Broken Down by    FAMHXCVR   FAMILY HISTORY OF CHD
                  by      VITAL10    STATUS AT TEN YEARS


    Variable      Value  Label                    Mean    Std Dev   Cases

    For Entire Population                        88.7908   13.0499    239


    FAMHXCVR      Y      YES                      91.6935   13.0039     62
       VITAL10    0      ALIVE                    90.4000   12.0593     45
       VITAL10    1      DEAD                     95.1176   15.0868     17

    FAMHXCVR      N      NO                       87.7740   12.9490    177
       VITAL10    0      ALIVE                    86.6015   11.1137    133
       VITAL10    1      DEAD                     91.3182   17.0304     44

    Total Cases = 240
    Missing Cases =    1 OR   0.4 PCT.
```

   b. Yes.
   c. No.

5. The table is not interpretable since the mean makes no sense for a nominal variable.

Chapter 12

Syntax

1. a. Group 1 has cases where the value for SHOESIZE is less than 8. Group 2 has cases where the value for SHOESIZE is equal to or greater than 8.
    b. Group 1 has cases where the value for SHOESIZE equals 1. Group 2 has cases where the value for SHOESIZE equals 9.
    c. Group 1 has cases where the value for SHOESIZE equals 1. Group 2 has cases where the value for SHOESIZE equals 2.

2. a. Correct.
    b. Incorrect. You must specify the independent-samples test before the paired-samples test, as in:

    ```
    T-TEST  GROUPS=SEX/VARIABLES=WEIGHT/PAIRS=TEST1 TEST2.
    ```

    c. Incorrect. A paired-samples test requires at least two variables.
    d. Correct.
    e. Incorrect. Use one, two, or no values to specify the groups.

3.  ```
    T-TEST  GROUPS=TYPE(1,2) /VARIABLES=RECALL.

    T-TEST  PAIRS=SELF ACTUAL.
    ```

Statistical Concepts

1. a. False.
    b. False.
    c. True.
    d. False.
    e. True.
    f. False.
    g. False.
    h. True.

2. a. Since the researcher is interested in detecting only levels which are too high, a one-tailed test is appropriate.
    b. The company would prefer a two-tailed test since larger differences are required to attain statistically significant results.
    c. 0.041

3. It is possible, but unlikely.

4. a. FREQUENCIES.
    b. Histograms, skewness, and kurtosis.

5. a. That the means of the two populations are equal.
    b. That the means of the two populations are equal.

6. a. Paired.
    b. Paired.
    c. Independent.
    d. Paired.
    e. Paired.

7. a. When the two populations have different variances.
    b. When the two populations have similar variances.
    ```

8. a. $\quad$ ------------------------------- T - T E S T ---------------------------------------

| GROUP 1 - TYPE | EQ | 1. |
| GROUP 2 - TYPE | EQ | 2. |

VARIABLE	NUMBER OF CASES	MEAN	STANDARD DEVIATION	STANDARD ERROR	* *	F VALUE	2-TAIL PROB.	* POOLED VARIANCE ESTIMATE *			SEPARATE VARIANCE ESTIMATE		
								T VALUE	DEGREES OF FREEDOM	2-TAIL PROB.	T VALUE	DEGREES OF FREEDOM	2-TAIL PROB.
RECALL COMMERCIAL RECALL SCORE					*			*			*		
GROUP 1	66	17.1087	2.804	0.345	*			*			*		
					*	2.57	0.000	* 2.12	146	0.036	* 2.02	103.96	0.046
GROUP 2	82	16.3093	1.750	0.193	*			*			*		

b. $\quad$ ------------------------------- T - T E S T ---------------------------------------

VARIABLE	NUMBER OF CASES	MEAN	STANDARD DEVIATION	STANDARD ERROR	* *	(DIFFERENCE) MEAN	STANDARD DEVIATION	STANDARD ERROR	* *	CORR.	2-TAIL PROB.	* *	T VALUE	DEGREES OF FREEDOM	2-TAIL PROB.
SELF SELF-REPORTED ARRESTS		8.9620	6.458	0.727	*				*			*			
	79				*	-0.2912	5.216	0.587	*	0.654	0.000	*	-0.50	78	0.621
ACTUAL ACTUAL ARRESTS		9.2532	6.248	0.703	*				*			*			

Chapter 13

Syntax

1. PLOT PLOT = INCOME WITH AGE.

3. PLOT PLOT = INCOME WITH AGE BY SEX.

5. The PLOT subcommand was omitted.

Statistical Concepts

1. a. MEANS
   b. CROSSTABS
   c. PLOT
   d. CROSSTABS
   e. MEANS
   f. PLOT

2. a. Unrelated; d. Nonlinear (curvilinear) relationship.

Chapter 14

Syntax

1. CORRELATION MONEY INVEST SALARY WEALTH
     /PRINT=ONETAIL.

3. a. CORRELATION VARIABLES= A B C D /FORMAT=SERIAL.

   b. CORRELATION VARIABLES=ONE TWO THREE MANY /STATISTICS=XPROD.

   c. You need to specify more than one variable, as in:

   CORRELATION VARIABLES=AGE INCOME EDUC.

4. a. PLOT must be the last subcommand.

   b. The keyword PLOT is omitted from the specifications.

   c. Keyword WITH should be used instead of BY.

Statistical Concepts

1. a. Positive c. Negative e. Negative g. Positive

3. The correlation coefficient is meaningless, since product code does not measure anything at the interval level.

5. The correlation coefficient is appropriate only when variables are measured at the interval or ratio level and when the relationship between them is linear. When he computes a large number of correlation coefficients, some of them will be large enough to be statistically significant because of sampling variation alone.

9. The intercept is 10,000 and the slope is 500. The predicted income for a 40-year-old is $30,000.

12. You can't tell which correlation is larger.

Chapter 15

Syntax

1. a. ONEWAY INCOME BY EDUCATION(1,6)
   /RANGES=LSD /RANGES=SCHEFFE.

   b. ONEWAY INCOME BY EDUCATION(1,6).

   c. ONEWAY INCOME BY EDUCATION(1,6) /RANGES=SCHEFFE.
   or
   ONEWAY INCOME BY SEX(1,2) /RANGES=SCHEFFE.

2. ONEWAY WELL BY EDUC6 (1,6).

Statistical Concepts

1. a. This is not true since the interval 4.89 to 13.23 either does or does not include the population mean. Ninety-five percent of the intervals obtained by repeated sampling would be expected to include the population mean.

   b. True.

2.
ANALYSIS OF VARIANCE

SOURCE	D.F.	SUM OF SQUARES	MEAN SQUARES	F RATIO
BETWEEN GROUPS	3	184.00	61.33	2.83
WITHIN GROUPS	36	780.84	21.69	
TOTAL	39	964.84		

3. No. The total sum of squares must be the sum of the between and within-groups sums of squares. The mean square must be the sum of squares divided by the degrees of freedom.

4. Group 1 is different from Groups 3, 4, and 5.

5. Group 1 is different from Groups 3, 4, 5, and 6. Group 2 is different from Groups 4, 5, and 6. Group 3 is different from Group 6.

6. Group 1 cannot be significantly different from itself.

7. No. Multiple comparison procedures are more stringent (require larger differences for significant differences) than t tests.

Chapter 16

Syntax

1. ANOVA VARIABLES=DIAS BY RACE (1,4) CHD (0,1).

2. a. ANOVA VARIABLES=SCORE BY REGION (1,4) SEX (1,2).

   b. ANOVA VARIABLES=SCORE BY REGION (1,4) SEX (1,2).

   c. ANOVA VARIABLES=SCORE BY RACE (1,3) SEX (1,2).

   d. ANOVA VARIABLES=SCORE1 SCORE2 BY RACE (1,3) SEX (1,2).

3. a. 12 cells.

   b. 9 cells.

   c. 6 cells.

Statistical Concepts

1. Neither statement is true.

2.
* * * A N A L Y S I S   O F   V A R I A N C E * * *

```
        VAR A
   BY   FACTOR1
        FACTOR2
```

SOURCE OF VARIATION	SUM OF SQUARES	DF	MEAN SQUARE	F
MAIN EFFECTS	524.61	5	104.92	1.03
FACTOR1	310.11	3	103.37	1.02
FACTOR2	214.50	2	107.25	1.05
2-WAY INTERACTIONS	104.17	6	17.36	0.17
FACTOR1 FACTOR2	104.17	6	17.36	0.17
EXPLAINED	628.78	11	57.17	0.56
RESIDUAL	4988.02	49	101.80	
TOTAL	5616.80	60		

3. Yes.

Chapter 17

Syntax

1. a. Expected values cannot be zero.
   b. `NPAR TESTS  K-W TUMOR BY DIET (0,1).`
   c. `NPAR TESTS  M-W TUMOR BY DIET (0,1).`

2. `NPAR TESTS  M-W TUMOR BY DIET (0,1).`

3. a. `RECODE MEDS (2=3) (3=2).`
      `NPAR TESTS M-W=RECOVER BY MEDS(1,2).`
   b. `NPAR TESTS K-W=RECOVER BY MEDS(1,3).`

Statistical Concepts

1. a. Ordinal.
   b. Ordinal.
   c. Ordinal.
   d. Nominal.
   e. Ordinal.

2. a. Rank correlation coefficient.
   b. Mann-Whitney test.
   c. Kruskal-Wallis one-way ANOVA
   d. Sign test and Wilcoxon test.

3. a. Two independent samples come from populations having the same distribution.
   b. The distribution of two paired variables is the same.
   c. The probability of observations falling into the categories are equal to those specified by the researcher.

4. The parametric test is more powerful. It will find true differences more often than the nonparametric test.

Chapter 18

Syntax

1. a. The DEPENDENT subcommand must come before the METHOD subcommand.
   b. A DEPENDENT subcommand is required.
   c. The METHOD subcommand should come immediately after the DEPENDENT subcommand and before the SCATTERPLOT subcommand.

2. `REGRESSION DESCRIPTIVES=MEAN STDDEV`
   `/VARIABLES=X1 X2 Y /DEPENDENT=Y /METHOD=STEPWISE.`

3. a. Analysis 1: X dependent; Y, A, B, and C independent.
   b. Analysis 2: Y dependent; X, A, B, and C independent.
   c. Analysis 3: X dependent; A, B, and C independent.
   d. Analysis 4: Y dependent; A, B, and C independent.

4. The REMOVE method must explicitly name the variables to be removed.

5. Temporary residual variables must be preceded by an asterisk on the SCATTERPLOT subcommand.

6. a. `REGRESSION  . . ./SCATTERPLOT (*RESID,X1)`
   b. `REGRESSION  . . ./RESIDUALS=HIST`
   c. `REGRESSION  . . ./RESIDUALS=OUTLIERS ID(ID)`
   d. `REGRESSION  . . ./CASEWISE=DEPENDENT PRED ALL`

Statistical Concepts

1. This hypothesis is of interest because it specifies that there is no linear relationship between the dependent variable and the independent variables.

2. You are checking the assumption of independence of errors when you examine a casewise serial plot.

3. a. $\beta_1 = \beta_2 = \ldots \beta_k = 0$

    b. The coefficients for the variables entered at this step are zero, or the increase in R^2 for the population is zero.

4. Multiple R^2 cannot decrease as additional variables are entered into an equation.

5. No. The band must be narrowest at the mean, $\overline{X}$.

6. You can make the best predictions of the mean of Y at the mean of the X's. The best predictions of values of Y are at $\overline{X}$.

7. a. The assumption of equality of variance appears violated. As the predicted values increase in magnitude, so does the spread of the residuals.

    b. Since there is a definite pattern to the residuals, the assumption of linearity appears to be violated.

    c. There appears to be a pattern to the residuals. Groups of negative residuals are followed by groups of positive residuals, suggesting that the observations are not independent.

    d. The assumption of normality appears to be violated since the histogram of residuals is definitely not normal.

    e. The normal probability plot suggests that the normality assumption is violated.

8. The variable SEX would be the next to enter since it has the largest F value and the value exceeds 3.84.

9. The variable WORK would be removed next since it has the smallest F value and the F value is less than 3.

10. When several variables are very highly correlated, inclusion of all of them in a regression model can lead to computational difficulties and unstable coefficients. In this case, X4 is very highly correlated with X1, and the squared multiple correlation between X4 and the other independent variables, X1, X2, and X3, is greater than 0.9999.

11. ```
ANALYSIS OF VARIANCE
                    DF   SUM OF SQUARES   MEAN SQUARE
REGRESSION   1   28.90000   28.90000
RESIDUAL   3   20.30000   6.76667

F =   4.27094   SIGNIF F = .1307
```

12. ```
CASEWISE PLOT OF STANDARDIZED RESIDUAL

*: SELECTED   M: MISSING

              -3.0           0.0           3.0
   CASE # X    0:.............:.............:0    Y        *PRED      *RESID
        1 1    .                 . *        .     7        6.0000     1.0000
        2 2    .                 . *        .     9        7.7000     1.3000
        3 3    .           *     .          .     6        9.4000    -3.4000
        4 4    .              *  .          .    10       11.1000    -1.1000
        5 5    .                 .   *      .    15       12.8000     2.2000
   CASE # X    0:.............:.............:0    Y        *PRED      *RESID
              -3.0           0.0           3.0
```

13. ```
------------------ VARIABLES IN THE EQUATION ------------------

VARIABLE   B   SE B   BETA   T   SIG T

WORK   23.77950   21.55603   .06583   1.103   .2705
MINORITY   -939.85580   252.80301   -.12368   -3.718   .0002
SEX   -1617.52918   240.70102   -.25615   -6.720   .0000
EDLEVEL   630.05377   40.77734   .57734   15.451   .0000
AGE   33.43079   15.42695   .12517   2.167   .0307
(CONSTANT) -2183.78652   775.23833   -2.817   .0051
```

# Chapter 19

## Syntax

1.  a.  There should be an order value in parentheses following the control variable, as in:

        PARTIAL CORR VARIABLES=FIREMEN DAMAGE BY FIRE(1).

    b.  The order value in parentheses cannot exceed the number of control variables. Since there are only two control variables, you cannot specify an order value of 3.

    c.  The keyword BY is required before the control variable. Additionally, If you specify both CORR and BADCORR on the STATISTICS subcommand, the keyword BADCORR is ignored.

2.  PARTIAL CORR VARIABLES=VAR1 VAR2 BY VAR3 VAR4 (1 2)
    /STATISTICS=CORR.

3.  The number of churches and the number of televisions are both highly correlated with population (POPSIZE). Controlling for population might reveal that there is little or no relationship between number of churches and number of televisions.
```

4. The three variables—DEATHS, DOCTORS, and HOSPITAL—are all positively correlated with AGE. Controlling for AGE eliminates the apparent positive relationship between DEATHS and DOCTORS and between DEATHS and HOSPITAL. Although the partial correlation between DOCTORS and DEATHS is negative, it is small and not statistically significant.

5. a.   Yes—the partial correlation reveals a statistically significant negative correlation between the price of a house and the repair costs in the first year.

   b.   One possible explanation is that those who can afford more expensive homes can also afford needed repairs. Less expensive homes may need more repair work, but those who buy them may not have the disposable income to spend on repairs.

Chapter 20

Syntax

1. DISCRIMINANT GROUPS=RISK(1,2)
     /VARIABLES=INCOME CREDIT AGEHEAD CHILDREN
     JOBTIME RESTIME HOMEOWNR.

2. DISCRIMINANT GROUPS=EMOTION(0,1)
     /VARIABLES=ETHNIC SEX IQ SES EMOTINDX INCOME EDUCATN.

3. a.   The value range in parentheses after the grouping variable is missing.
   b.   The GROUPS subcommand is missing.

Statistical Concepts

1.
CASE SEQ	DISCRIMINANT SCORE
1	109.87
2	129.26
3	122.24

2. Function B is preferrable because there is less overlap in the discriminant scores than in Function A. If there is a lot of overlap in the scores for the two groups, group membership cannot be accurately predicted.

3.

FUNCTION A		NO. OF CASES	PREDICTED GROUP MEMBERSHIP 1	2
GROUP EUROPEAN ORIGIN	1	17	16 94.12%	1 5.88%
GROUP ASIAN ORIGIN	2	42	0 0.0%	42 100.0%

PERCENT OF GROUPED CASES CORRECTLY CLASSIFIED: 98.31%

FUNCTION B		NO. OF CASES	PREDICTED GROUP MEMBERSHIP 1	2
GROUP EUROPEAN ORIGIN	1	17	15 88.24%	2 11.76%
GROUP ASIAN ORIGIN	2	42	2 4.76%	40 95.24%

PERCENT OF GROUPED CASES CORRECTLY CLASSIFIED: 93.22%

Function B is preferrable because it correctly classifies 93% of the cases with only two variables. Although Function B correctly classifies a higher percentage, the additional three variables do not substantially improve classification.

Chapter 21

Syntax

1. FACTOR VARIABLES=PCTHOMES PASTSALE DSTRCTYP AVGINCOM PCTBUSNS
     PCTFAMLY AVGAGE AVGEDUC PRICE.

2. FACTOR VARIABLES=PCTHOMES PASTSALE DSTRCTYP AVGINCOM PCTBUSNS
     PCTFAMLY AVGAGE AVGEDUC PRICE
     /EXTRACTION=ML /PLOT=ROTATION(1,2).

3. The VARIABLES subcommand must appear before all other subcommands.

Statistical Concepts

1. Factor 1 appears to represent recreational interests, while Factor 2 seems to represent status. Political activity and IQ seem to have nothing to do with either factor.

2. a. $TESTSCOR = 0.41127F_1 + 0.34432F_2 - 0.14892F_3$
      $PSYCHTST = 0.11383F_1 + 0.11524F_2 + 0.89989F_3$

   b. Factor 1 appears to represent mental capabilities, Factor 2 represents status, and Factor 3 represents psychological state. Variables GPA, SAT, and TESTSCORE, which are achievement scores, don't seem to relate to any of the factors.

3. a.

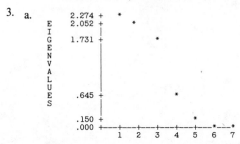

   b. Factors 1, 2, and 3, since each accounts for a substantial portion of the variance and the other four factors account for only 13.6% of the variance.

4. PASTSALE, OCCUPATN, URBAN, INCOME, EDUCATN, AGE, RECREATN, SEX.

Chapter 22

Syntax

1. The variable list should not include any specifications other than variable names.

2. ```
CLUSTER WINGSPAN BEAKCURV BEAKWDTH MIGRLNTH MATELNTH
   FSHDIET INSDIET GRNDIET.
```

3. ```
CLUSTER WEIGHT LENGTH WIDTH HGHTLEN WINDOWS CHROME DOODADS
   /METHOD=SINGLE /MEASURE=EUCLID.
```

Statistical Concepts

1. a.
```
   Squared Euclidean Dissimilarity Coefficient Matrix

   Case              1              2              3

     2            37.5100
     3            11.8900        29.5400
     4            15.6600        39.2900         1.1300
```

   b. Cases 3 and 4.

2. a. Cluster 1: SWISS, BLUE. Cluster 2: FARMERS, COTTAGE. Cluster 3: All other cheeses.

   b. Cluster 1: SWISS, BLUE. Cluster 2: FARMERS, COTTAGE. Cluster 3: COLBY. Cluster 4: MONTEREY JACK, CHEDDAR. Cluster 5: EDAM, GOUDA, MOZZARELLA.

   c. Cluster 1: FARMERS, COTTAGE. Cluster 2: MOZZARELLA, GOUDA, EDAM. Each remaining case constitutes a single cluster.

3. No. At stages 8 and 9, an existing cluster was split into two clusters.

4. In a three-cluster solution, the clusters are 1: Moby Dick and Odyssey; 2: Great Expectations and Oliver Twist; and 3: all others. In a five cluster solution, the clusters are 1: Moby Dick; 2: Odyssey; 3: Great Expectations and Oliver Twist; 4: Tom Jones; and 5: everything else.

Chapter 23

Syntax

1. a. The BY keyword is needed between ESTEEM and SEX.

   b. Either there should be a value range in parentheses after the variable EDUC or it should be preceded by the keyword WITH to indicate that EDUC is a covariate.

   c. Only one BY keyword can be used.

2. No. Only the main effects and two-way effects have been specified on the DESIGN subcommand.

Statistical Concepts

1. a. There appears to be a curvilinear relationship, with the means decreasing as the variances increase.

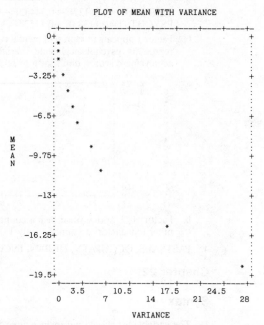

PLOT OF MEAN WITH VARIANCE

b. The means are proportional to the standard deviations, with MEAN=−4*STTDEV (approximately).

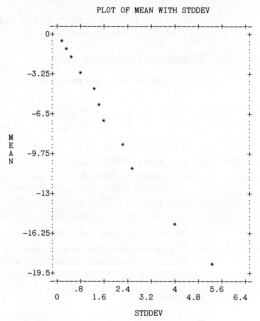

PLOT OF MEAN WITH STDDEV

   c. MANOVA requires equality of variances.

2. Yes.

3. a. Group 3.
    b. Group 3.
    c. No. The lengths of the "boxes" and the spread of values for the four groups differ greatly, indicating different variances.

4. 1 and 2.

Appendix B Codebooks

B.1
THE WESTERN
ELECTRIC STUDY

The Western Electric study was undertaken in 1957 to prospectively study factors related to the incidence of coronary heart disease in men who were initially disease-free. Participants were selected through random sampling of 5397 men who were 40 to 55 years of age and employed for at least two years at the Western Electric Company's Hawthorne Works in the Chicago area. The procedures according to which participants were selected, examined, and followed are described in Paul, et al. (1963). A sample of 240 men from the Western Electric study is included on the tape. Chapters 2 and 7 describe the data.

```
                LIST OF VARIABLES ON THE ACTIVE FILE

     NAME                                            POSITION

     CASEID    CASE IDENTIFICATION NUMBER               1
                  PRINT FORMAT: F4
                  WRITE FORMAT: F4

     FIRSTCHD  FIRST CHD EVENT                           2
                  PRINT FORMAT: F1
                  WRITE FORMAT: F1

               VALUE     LABEL

                  1      NO CHD
                  2      SUDDEN  DEATH
                  3      NONFATALMI
                  5      FATAL    MI
                  6      OTHER   CHD

     AGE       AGE AT ENTRY                              3
                  PRINT FORMAT: F2
                  WRITE FORMAT: F2

     DBP58     AVERAGE DIAST BLOOD PRESSURE 58           4
                  PRINT FORMAT: F3
                  WRITE FORMAT: F3

     EDUYR     YEARS OF EDUCATION                        5
                  PRINT FORMAT: F2
                  WRITE FORMAT: F2

     CHOL58    SERUM CHOLESTEROL 58 -- MG PER DL         6
                  PRINT FORMAT: F3
                  WRITE FORMAT: F3

     CGT58     NO OF CIGARETTES PER DAY IN 1958          7
                  PRINT FORMAT: F2
                  WRITE FORMAT: F2

     HT58      STATURE, 1958 -- TO NEAREST 0.1 INCH      8
                  PRINT FORMAT: F5.1
                  WRITE FORMAT: F5.1

     WT58      BODY WEIGHT, 1958 -- LBS                  9
                  PRINT FORMAT: F3
                  WRITE FORMAT: F3

     DAYOFWK   DAY OF DEATH                             10
                  PRINT FORMAT: F1
                  WRITE FORMAT: F1
                  MISSING VALUES:  9

               VALUE     LABEL

                  1      SUNDAY
                  2      MONDAY
                  3      TUESDAY
                  4      WEDNSDAY
                  5      THURSDAY
                  6      FRIDAY
                  7      SATURDAY
                  9 M    MISSING
```

```
            VITAL10    STATUS AT TEN YEARS                              11
                          PRINT FORMAT: F1
                          WRITE FORMAT: F1

                       VALUE     LABEL

                          0       ALIVE
                          1       DEAD

            FAMHXCVR   FAMILY HISTORY OF CHD                            12
                          PRINT FORMAT: A1
                          WRITE FORMAT: A1

                       VALUE     LABEL

                          N       NO
                          Y       YES

            CHD        INCIDENCE OF CORONARY HEART DISEASE              13
                          PRINT FORMAT: F1
                          WRITE FORMAT: F1
```

B.2
THE BANK DATA FILE

The bank data file (Roberts, 1979) contains information about 474 employees hired by a midwestern bank between 1969 and 1971. The study is described in Chapters 11 and 18.

```
                   LIST OF VARIABLES ON THE ACTIVE FILE

            NAME                                               POSITION

            ID         EMPLOYEE CODE                              1
                          PRINT FORMAT: F4
                          WRITE FORMAT: F4

            SALBEG     BEGINNING SALARY                           2
                          PRINT FORMAT: F5
                          WRITE FORMAT: F5
                          MISSING VALUES:  0

            SEX        SEX OF EMPLOYEE                            3
                          PRINT FORMAT: F1
                          WRITE FORMAT: F1
                          MISSING VALUES:  9

                       VALUE     LABEL

                          0       MALES
                          1       FEMALES

            TIME       JOB SENIORITY                              4
                          PRINT FORMAT: F2
                          WRITE FORMAT: F2
                          MISSING VALUES:  0

            AGE        AGE OF EMPLOYEE                            5
                          PRINT FORMAT: F6.2
                          WRITE FORMAT: F6.2
                          MISSING VALUES:   .00

            SALNOW     CURRENT SALARY                             6
                          PRINT FORMAT: F5
                          WRITE FORMAT: F5
                          MISSING VALUES:  0

            EDLEVEL    EDUCATIONAL LEVEL                          7
                          PRINT FORMAT: F2
                          WRITE FORMAT: F2
                          MISSING VALUES:  0

            WORK       WORK EXPERIENCE                            8
                          PRINT FORMAT: F6.2
                          WRITE FORMAT: F6.2

            JOBCAT     EMPLOYMENT CATEGORY                        9
                          PRINT FORMAT: F1
                          WRITE FORMAT: F1
                          MISSING VALUES:  0

                       VALUE     LABEL

                          1       CLERICAL
                          2       OFFICE TRAINEE
                          3       SECURITY OFFICER
                          4       COLLEGE TRAINEE
                          5       EXEMPT EMPLOYEE
                          6       MBA TRAINEE
                          7       TECHNICAL
```

```
        MINORITY  MINORITY CLASSIFICATION                         10
                      PRINT FORMAT: F1
                      WRITE FORMAT: F1
                      MISSING VALUES:  9

                  VALUE    LABEL

                     0     WHITE
                     1     NONWHITE

        SEXRACE   SEX & RACE CLASSIFICATION                        11
                      PRINT FORMAT: F8.2
                      WRITE FORMAT: F8.2

                  VALUE    LABEL

                   1.00    WHITE MALES
                   2.00    MINORITY MALES
                   3.00    WHITE FEMALES
                   4.00    MINORITY FEMALES
```

B.3
THE PRODUCTS DATA FILE

The products data file contains information on ratings of 19 products by a convenience sample of 100 couples enrolled in an evening MBA program (Davis & Ragsdale, 1983). The goals of the study were to study husband and wife agreement in product purchases. The study is described further in Chapter 12.

For each of the 19 products, the following information is available: husband's rating of the product; husband's prediction of the wife's rating; wife's rating of the product; wife's prediction of the husband's rating; husband's assessment of his relative influence on the decision to buy; and wife's assessment of her relative influence.

```
               LIST OF VARIABLES ON THE PRODUCTS SYSTEM FILE

        NAME                                              POSITION

        H1S      VTR HUSB SELF                               1

                 How likely are you to buy a video-tape unit
                 for in-home education, languages, and so
                 forth?

                     PRINT FORMAT: F1
                     WRITE FORMAT: F1

                 VALUE    LABEL

                    1     DEFINITELY
                    2     VERY LIKELY
                    3     SOMEWHAT LIKELY
                    4     INDIFFERENT
                    5     SOMEWHAT UNLIKELY
                    6     VERY UNLIKELY
                    7     DEFINITELY NOT

        H2S      POP-TOP CANS HUSB SELF                      2
                 Pop-top cans for canned vegetables, soups,
                 or hash.
                     PRINT FORMAT: F1
                     WRITE FORMAT: F1

        H3S      ALARM HUSB SELF                             3
                 A home burglar alarm system that operates
                 via your telephone.
                     PRINT FORMAT: F1
                     WRITE FORMAT: F1

        H4S      TELLER HUSB SELF                            4
                 Automatic tellers in supermarkets that
                 enable deposits or withdrawals from your
                 checking and savings accounts.
                     PRINT FORMAT: F1
                     WRITE FORMAT: F1

        H5S      BIG TV HUSB SELF                            5
                 A big TV that projects a picture on a
                 large screen.
                     PRINT FORMAT: F1
                     WRITE FORMAT: F1

        H6S      PLUMB HUSBAND SELF                          6
                 Do-it-yourself plumbing fixtures.
                     PRINT FORMAT: F1
                     WRITE FORMAT: F1
```

```
H7S        WASHDRY HUSB SELF                                    7
           A combination washer and dryer.
                PRINT FORMAT: F1
                WRITE FORMAT: F1

H8S        AIR HUSB SELF                                        8
           An energy-saving window air-conditioner.
                PRINT FORMAT: F1
                WRITE FORMAT: F1

H9S        COUNS HUSB SELF                                      9
           Investment counseling via closed-circuit TV.
                PRINT FORMAT: F1
                WRITE FORMAT: F1

H10S       CANDY HUSB SELF                                     10
           A natural candy bar with no sugar or
           preservatives.
                PRINT FORMAT: F1
                WRITE FORMAT: F1

H11S       PHONE HUSB SELF                                     11
           A hands-free telephone--talk and listen up
           to 20 feet.
                PRINT FORMAT: F1
                WRITE FORMAT: F1

H12S       PAINT HUSB SELF                                     12
           A rental service for paintings and lithographs.
                PRINT FORMAT: F1
                WRITE FORMAT: F1

H13S       AIRFARE HUSB SELF                                   13
           Economy airfare (no food or liquor served)
           between Chicago and New York.
                PRINT FORMAT: F1
                WRITE FORMAT: F1

H14S       SHOP SERV HUSB SELF                                 14
           A shop-at-home service using closed-circuit
           TV and your telephone.
                PRINT FORMAT: F1
                WRITE FORMAT: F1

H15S       ELECT AUTO HUSB SELF                                15
           An electric-powered automobile--250 miles
           without a recharge.
                PRINT FORMAT: F1
                WRITE FORMAT: F1

H16S       SAUNA HUSB SELF                                     16
           An easy-to-install sauna.
                PRINT FORMAT: F1
                WRITE FORMAT: F1

H17S       AUTO-TRAIN HUSB SELF                                17
           An auto-train service between Chicago and
           Denver.
                PRINT FORMAT: F1
                WRITE FORMAT: F1

H18S       CHEESE BOARD HUSB SELF                              18
           A disposable cheese board containing an
           assortment of French dinner cheeses.
                PRINT FORMAT: F1
                WRITE FORMAT: F1

H19S       RAINCOAT HUSB SELF                                  19
           A disposable fashion raincoat.
                PRINT FORMAT: F1
                WRITE FORMAT: F1

H20S       VACUUM HUSB SELF                                    20
           A vacuum system with outlets in every
           room of the house.
                PRINT FORMAT: F1
                WRITE FORMAT: F1

W1S        VTR WIFE SELF                                       21
                PRINT FORMAT: F1
                WRITE FORMAT: F1

W2S        POP-TOP CANS WIFE SELF                              22
                PRINT FORMAT: F1
                WRITE FORMAT: F1

W3S        ALARM WIFE SELF                                     23
                PRINT FORMAT: F1
                WRITE FORMAT: F1

W4S        TELLER WIFE SELF                                    24
                PRINT FORMAT: F1
                WRITE FORMAT: F1

W5S        BIG TV WIFE SELF                                    25
                PRINT FORMAT: F1
                WRITE FORMAT: F1

W6S        PLUMB WIFE SELF                                     26
                PRINT FORMAT: F1
                WRITE FORMAT: F1

W7S        WASHDRY WIFE SELF                                   27
                PRINT FORMAT: F1
                WRITE FORMAT: F1
```

```
W8S       AIR WIFE SELF                                    28
              PRINT FORMAT: F1
              WRITE FORMAT: F1

W9S       COUNS WIFE SELF                                  29
              PRINT FORMAT: F1
              WRITE FORMAT: F1

W10S      CANDY WIFE SELF                                  30
              PRINT FORMAT: F1
              WRITE FORMAT: F1

W11S      PHONE WIFE SELF                                  31
              PRINT FORMAT: F1
              WRITE FORMAT: F1

W12S      PAINT WIFE SELF                                  32
              PRINT FORMAT: F1
              WRITE FORMAT: F1

W13S      AIRFARE WIFE SELF                                33
              PRINT FORMAT: F1
              WRITE FORMAT: F1

W14S      SHOP SERV WIFE SELF                              34
              PRINT FORMAT: F1
              WRITE FORMAT: F1

W15S      ELECT AUTO WIFE SELF                             35
              PRINT FORMAT: F1
              WRITE FORMAT: F1

W16S      SAUNA WIFE SELF                                  36
              PRINT FORMAT: F1
              WRITE FORMAT: F1

W17S      AUTO-TRAIN WIFE SELF                             37
              PRINT FORMAT: F1
              WRITE FORMAT: F1

W18S      CHEESE BOARD WIFE SELF                           38
              PRINT FORMAT: F1
              WRITE FORMAT: F1

W19S      RAINCOAT WIFE SELF                               39
              PRINT FORMAT: F1
              WRITE FORMAT: F1

W20S      VACUUM WIFE SELF                                 40
              PRINT FORMAT: F1
              WRITE FORMAT: F1

H10       VTR HUSB SPOUSE                                  41

          How likely is your spouse to buy a video-tape
          unit for in-home education, languages, and
          so forth?

              PRINT FORMAT: F1
              WRITE FORMAT: F1

          VALUE     LABEL

              1       DEFINITELY
              2       VERY LIKELY
              3       SOMEWHAT LIKELY
              4       INDIFFERENT
              5       SOMEWHAT UNLIKELY
              6       VERY UNLIKELY
              7       DEFINITELY NOT

H20       POP-TOP CANS HUSB SPOUSE                         42
              PRINT FORMAT: F1
              WRITE FORMAT: F1

H30       ALARM HUSB SPOUSE                                43
              PRINT FORMAT: F1
              WRITE FORMAT: F1

H40       TELLER HUSB SPOUSE                               44
              PRINT FORMAT: F1
              WRITE FORMAT: F1

H50       BIG TV HUSB SPOUSE                               45
              PRINT FORMAT: F1
              WRITE FORMAT: F1

H60       PLUMB HUSB SPOUSE                                46
              PRINT FORMAT: F1
              WRITE FORMAT: F1

H70       WASHDRY HUSB SPOUSE                              47
              PRINT FORMAT: F1
              WRITE FORMAT: F1

H80       AIR HUSB SPOUSE                                  48
              PRINT FORMAT: F1
              WRITE FORMAT: F1

H90       COUNS HUSB SPOUSE                                49
              PRINT FORMAT: F1
              WRITE FORMAT: F1

H100      CANDY HUSB SPOUSE                                50
              PRINT FORMAT: F1
              WRITE FORMAT: F1
```

H110	PHONE HUSB SPOUSE PRINT FORMAT: Fl WRITE FORMAT: Fl	51
H120	PAINT HUSB SPOUSE PRINT FORMAT: Fl WRITE FORMAT: Fl	52
H130	AIRFARE HUSB SPOUSE PRINT FORMAT: Fl WRITE FORMAT: Fl	53
H140	SHOP SERV HUSB SPOUSE PRINT FORMAT: Fl WRITE FORMAT: Fl	54
H150	ELECT AUTO HUSB SPOUSE PRINT FORMAT: Fl WRITE FORMAT: Fl	55
H160	SAUNA HUSB SPOUSE PRINT FORMAT: Fl WRITE FORMAT: Fl	56
H170	AUTO-TRAIN HUSB SPOUSE PRINT FORMAT: Fl WRITE FORMAT: Fl	57
H180	CHEESE BOARD HUSB SPOUSE PRINT FORMAT: Fl WRITE FORMAT: Fl	58
H190	RAINCOAT HUSB SPOUSE PRINT FORMAT: Fl WRITE FORMAT: Fl	59
H200	VACUUM HUSB SPOUSE PRINT FORMAT: Fl WRITE FORMAT: Fl	60
W10	VTR WIFE SPOUSE PRINT FORMAT: Fl WRITE FORMAT: Fl	61
W20	POP-TOP CANS WIFE SPOUSE PRINT FORMAT: Fl WRITE FORMAT: Fl	62
W30	ALARM WIFE SPOUSE PRINT FORMAT: Fl WRITE FORMAT: Fl	63
W40	TELLER WIFE SPOUSE PRINT FORMAT: Fl WRITE FORMAT: Fl	64
W50	BIG TV WIFE SPOUSE PRINT FORMAT: Fl WRITE FORMAT: Fl	65
W60	PLUMB WIFE SPOUSE PRINT FORMAT: Fl WRITE FORMAT: Fl	66
W70	WASHDRY WIFE SPOUSE PRINT FORMAT: Fl WRITE FORMAT: Fl	67
W80	AIR WIFE SPOUSE PRINT FORMAT: Fl WRITE FORMAT: Fl	68
W90	COUNS WIFE SPOUSE PRINT FORMAT: Fl WRITE FORMAT: Fl	69
W100	CANDY WIFE SPOUSE PRINT FORMAT: Fl WRITE FORMAT: Fl	70
W110	PHONE WIFE SPOUSE PRINT FORMAT: Fl WRITE FORMAT: Fl	71
W120	PAINT WIFE SPOUSE PRINT FORMAT: Fl WRITE FORMAT: Fl	72
W130	AIRFARE WIFE SPOUSE PRINT FORMAT: Fl WRITE FORMAT: Fl	73
W140	SHOP SERV WIFE SPOUSE PRINT FORMAT: Fl WRITE FORMAT: Fl	74
W150	ELECT AUTO WIFE SPOUSE PRINT FORMAT: Fl WRITE FORMAT: Fl	75
W160	SAUNA WIFE SPOUSE PRINT FORMAT: Fl WRITE FORMAT: Fl	76

| W170 | AUTO-TRAIN WIFE SPOUSE PRINT FORMAT: F1 WRITE FORMAT: F1 | 77 |

| W180 | CHEESE BOARD WIFE SPOUSE PRINT FORMAT: F1 WRITE FORMAT: F1 | 78 |

| W190 | RAINCOAT WIFE SPOUSE PRINT FORMAT: F1 WRITE FORMAT: F1 | 79 |

| W200 | VACUUM WIFE SPOUSE PRINT FORMAT: F1 WRITE FORMAT: F1 | 80 |

| H1R | VTR HUSB INFLUENCE | 81 |

Who would have more influence in deciding to buy this product?

PRINT FORMAT: F1
WRITE FORMAT: F1

VALUE   LABEL

    1   HUSB DECIDE
    2   HUSB MORE INFLUENCE
    3   HUSB/WIFE EQUAL
    4   WIFE MORE INLUENCE
    5   WIFE DECIDE

| H2R | POP-TOP CANS INFLUENCE PRINT FORMAT: F1 WRITE FORMAT: F1 | 82 |

| H3R | ALARM HUSB INFLUENCE PRINT FORMAT: F1 WRITE FORMAT: F1 | 83 |

| H4R | TELLER HUSB INFLUENCE PRINT FORMAT: F1 WRITE FORMAT: F1 | 84 |

| H5R | BIG TV HUSB INFLUENCE PRINT FORMAT: F1 WRITE FORMAT: F1 | 85 |

| H6R | PLUMB HUSB INFLUENCE PRINT FORMAT: F1 WRITE FORMAT: F1 | 86 |

| H7R | WASHDRY HUSB INFLUENCE PRINT FORMAT: F1 WRITE FORMAT: F1 | 87 |

| H8R | AIR HUSB INFLUENCE PRINT FORMAT: F1 WRITE FORMAT: F1 | 88 |

| H9R | COUNS HUSB INFLUENCE PRINT FORMAT: F1 WRITE FORMAT: F1 | 89 |

| H10R | CANDY HUSB INFLUENCE PRINT FORMAT: F1 WRITE FORMAT: F1 | 90 |

| H11R | PHONE HUSB INFLUENCE PRINT FORMAT: F1 WRITE FORMAT: F1 | 91 |

| H12R | PAINT HUSB INFLUENCE PRINT FORMAT: F1 WRITE FORMAT: F1 | 92 |

| H13R | AIRFARE HUSB INFLUENCE PRINT FORMAT: F1 WRITE FORMAT: F1 | 93 |

| H14R | SHOP SERV HUSB INFLUENCE PRINT FORMAT: F1 WRITE FORMAT: F1 | 94 |

| H15R | ELECT AUTO HUSB INFLUENCE PRINT FORMAT: F1 WRITE FORMAT: F1 | 95 |

| H16R | SAUNA HUSB INFLUENCE PRINT FORMAT: F1 WRITE FORMAT: F1 | 96 |

| H17R | AUTO-TRAIN HUSB INFLUENCE PRINT FORMAT: F1 WRITE FORMAT: F1 | 97 |

| H18R | CHEESE BOARD HUSB INFLUENCE PRINT FORMAT: F1 WRITE FORMAT: F1 | 98 |

| H19R | RAINCOAT HUSB INFLUENCE PRINT FORMAT: F1 WRITE FORMAT: F1 | 99 |

| H20R | VACUUM HUSB INFLUENCE PRINT FORMAT: F1 WRITE FORMAT: F1 | 100 |

```
W1R        VTR WIFE INFLUENCE                                 101
               PRINT FORMAT: F1
               WRITE FORMAT: F1

W2R        POP-TOP CANS INFLUENCE                             102
               PRINT FORMAT: F1
               WRITE FORMAT: F1

W3R        ALARM WIFE INFLUENCE                               103
               PRINT FORMAT: F1
               WRITE FORMAT: F1

W4R        TELLER WIFE INFLUENCE                              104
               PRINT FORMAT: F1
               WRITE FORMAT: F1

W5R        BIG TV WIFE INFLUENCE                              105
               PRINT FORMAT: F1
               WRITE FORMAT: F1

W6R        PLUMB WIFE  INFLUENCE                              106
               PRINT FORMAT: F1
               WRITE FORMAT: F1

W7R        WASHDRY WIFE INFLUENCE                             107
               PRINT FORMAT: F1
               WRITE FORMAT: F1

W8R        AIR WIFE INFLUENCE                                 108
               PRINT FORMAT: F1
               WRITE FORMAT: F1

W9R        COUNS WIFE INFLUENCE                               109
               PRINT FORMAT: F1
               WRITE FORMAT: F1

W10R       CANDY WIFE INFLUENCE                               110
               PRINT FORMAT: F1
               WRITE FORMAT: F1

W11R       PHONE WIFE INFLUENCE                               111
               PRINT FORMAT: F1
               WRITE FORMAT: F1

W12R       PAINT WIFE INFLUENCE                               112
               PRINT FORMAT: F1
               WRITE FORMAT: F1

W13R       AIRFARE WIFE INFLUENCE                             113
               PRINT FORMAT: F1
               WRITE FORMAT: F1

W14R       SHOP SERV WIFE INFLUENCE                           114
               PRINT FORMAT: F1
               WRITE FORMAT: F1

W15R       ELECT AUTO WIFE INFLUENCE                          115
               PRINT FORMAT: F1
               WRITE FORMAT: F1

W16R       SAUNA WIFE INFLUENCE                               116
               PRINT FORMAT: F1
               WRITE FORMAT: F1

W17R       AUTO-TRAIN WIFE INFLUENCE                          117
               PRINT FORMAT: F1
               WRITE FORMAT: F1

W18R       CHEESE BOARD WIFE INFLUENCE                        118
               PRINT FORMAT: F1
               WRITE FORMAT: F1

W19R       RAINCOAT WIFE INFLUENCE                            119
               PRINT FORMAT: F1
               WRITE FORMAT: F1

W20R       VACUUM WIFE INFLUENCE                              120
               PRINT FORMAT: F1
               WRITE FORMAT: F1

CASEID                                                        121
               PRINT FORMAT: F3
               WRITE FORMAT: F3

VISUAL     PICTURE ACCOMPANIED QUESTION                       122
               PRINT FORMAT: F1
               WRITE FORMAT: F1

           VALUE     LABEL

               0     NO PICTURES
               1     PICTURES

HSSCALE    HUSBAND SELF SCALE                                 123

           The sum of scores for all twenty products.

               PRINT FORMAT: F8.2
               WRITE FORMAT: F8.2

HRSCALE    HUSBAND INFLUENCE SCALE                            124
               PRINT FORMAT: F8.2
               WRITE FORMAT: F8.2

HOSCALE    HUSBAND SPOUSE SCALE                               125
               PRINT FORMAT: F8.2
               WRITE FORMAT: F8.2
```

```
              WSSCALE    WIFE SELF SCALE                                126
                            PRINT FORMAT: F8.2
                            WRITE FORMAT: F8.2

              WOSCALE    WIFE SPOUSE SCALE                              127
                            PRINT FORMAT: F8.2
                            WRITE FORMAT: F8.2

              WRSCALE    WIFE INFLUENCE SCALE                           128
                            PRINT FORMAT: F8.2
                            WRITE FORMAT: F8.2

              FAMSCORE   FAMILY BUYING SCORE                            129
                         The sum of husband's and wife's total
                         scores.
                            PRINT FORMAT: F8.2
                            WRITE FORMAT: F8.2

              SSDIFF     HUSBAND—WIFE DIFFERENCE SCALE                  130
                         Husband's total scores minus wife's total
                         scores.
                            PRINT FORMAT: F8.2
                            WRITE FORMAT: F8.2

              RRDIF      HUSB—WIFE RELATIVE INFLUENCE SCALE             131
                         Husband's influence score minus wife's
                         influence score.
                            PRINT FORMAT: F8.2
                            WRITE FORMAT: F8.2
```

B.4
THE GENERAL
SOCIAL SURVEY FILE

The General Social Surveys have been conducted since 1972 to study social indicators (Davis, 1982). Each survey is an independently drawn sample of English-speaking persons 18 years of age or over, living in non-institutional arrangements within the continental United States. The data described below are a subset of variables from the 1982 survey dealing with patterns of social interaction.

```
DOCUMENTS      ENTERED 07/13/82
               THIS SYSTEM FILE CONTAINS DATA FOR THE 1972–1982
               GENERAL SOCIAL SURVEYS, CONDUCTED BY THE NATIONAL
               OPINION RESEARCH CENTER.
          (Entered 08 FEB 83)

               LIST OF VARIABLES ON THE ACTIVE FILE

          NAME                                               POSITION

          PRESTIGE   RESP'S OCCUPATIONAL PRESTIGE SCORE           1
                        PRINT FORMAT: F2
                        WRITE FORMAT: F2
                        MISSING VALUES:  0

                     VALUE    LABEL

                        0 M  DK,NA,NAP

          AGE                                                      2
                        PRINT FORMAT: F2
                        WRITE FORMAT: F2
                        MISSING VALUES:  0, 98, 99

                     VALUE    LABEL

                        0 M  NAP
                       98 M  DK
                       99 M  NA

          EDUC       HIGHEST YEAR SCHOOL COMPLETED                3
                        PRINT FORMAT: F2
                        WRITE FORMAT: F2
                        MISSING VALUES:  97, 98, 99

                     VALUE    LABEL

                       97 M  NAP
                       98 M  DK
                       99 M  NA

          SEX                                                      4
                        PRINT FORMAT: F2
                        WRITE FORMAT: F2

                     VALUE    LABEL

                        1    MALE
                        2    FEMALE

          SOCREL     SPEND EVE WITH RELATIVES                     5
                     How often do you spend a social evening
                     with relatives?
                        PRINT FORMAT: F2
                        WRITE FORMAT: F2
                        MISSING VALUES:  -1, 8, 9
```

```
                          VALUE   LABEL

                           -1  M  NAP
                            1     ALMOST   DAILY
                            2     SEV TIMES A WEEK
                            3     SEV TIMES A MNTH
                            4     ONCE A MONTH
                            5     SEV TIMES A YEAR
                            6     ONCE A YEAR
                            7     NEVER
                            8  M  DK
                            9  M  NA
```

SOCOMMUN   SPEND EVE WITH NEIGHBOR   6
           How often do you spend a social evening
           with someone who lives in your neighborhood?
                PRINT FORMAT: F2
                WRITE FORMAT: F2
                MISSING VALUES: -1, 8, 9

           See SOCREL for value labels.

SOCFREND   SPEND EVE WITH FRIENDS   7
           How often do you spend a social evening
           with friends who live outside the
           neighborhood?
                PRINT FORMAT: F2
                WRITE FORMAT: F2
                MISSING VALUES: -1, 8, 9

           See SOCREL for value labels.

SOCBAR   SPEND EVE AT BAR   8
           How often do you go to a bar or tavern?
                PRINT FORMAT: F2
                WRITE FORMAT: F2
                MISSING VALUES: -1, 8, 9

           See SOCREL for value labels.

SOCPARS   SPEND EVENING WITH PARENTS   9
           How often do you spend a social evening
           with your parents?
                PRINT FORMAT: F2
                WRITE FORMAT: F2
                MISSING VALUES: -1, 8, 9

```
                          VALUE   LABEL

                           -1  M  NOT APPROPRIATE (no such relatives)
                            1     ALMOST   DAILY
                            2     SEV TIMES A WEEK
                            3     SEV TIMES A MNTH
                            4     ONCE A MONTH
                            5     SEV TIMES A YEAR
                            6     ONCE A YEAR
                            7     NEVER
                            8  M  DK
                            9  M  NA
```

SOCSIBS   SPEND EVENING WITH SIBLINGS   10
           How often do you spend a social evening
           with a brother or sister?
                PRINT FORMAT: F2
                WRITE FORMAT: F2
                MISSING VALUES: -1, 8, 9

           See SOCPARS for value labels.

ANOMIA5   LOT OF AVERAGE MAN GETTING WORSE   11
           In spite of what some people say, the
           lot (situation/condition) of the average
           man is getting worse, not better.
                PRINT FORMAT: F2
                WRITE FORMAT: F2
                MISSING VALUES: 0, 8, 9

```
                          VALUE   LABEL

                            1     AGREE
                            2     DISAGREE
                            8  M  DK
                            9  M  NA
```

ANOMIA6   NOT FAIR TO BRING CHILD INTO WORLD   12
           It's hardly fair to bring a child into
           the world with the way things look for
           the future.
                PRINT FORMAT: F2
                WRITE FORMAT: F2
                MISSING VALUES: 0, 8, 9

                                    See ANOMIA5 for value labels.

        ANOMIA7   OFFICIALS NOT INTERESTED IN AVERAGE MAN   13
                   Most public officials (people in public
                   office) are not really interested in the
                   problems of the average man.
                        PRINT FORMAT: F2
                        WRITE FORMAT: F2
                        MISSING VALUES: 0, 8, 9

                                    See ANOMIA5 for value labels.

        TVHOURS   HOURS PER DAY WATCHING TV   14
                   On the average day, about how may hours
                   do you personally watch television?
                        PRINT FORMAT: F2
                        WRITE FORMAT: F2
                        MISSING VALUES: -1, 98, 99

                   VALUE   LABEL

                    -1 M   NAP
                    98 M   DK
                    99 M   NA

Bibliography

Anderberg, M. R. 1973. *Cluster analysis for applications.* New York: Academic Press.

Anderson, R., and S. Nida. 1978. Effect of physical attractiveness on opposite and same-sex evaluations. *Journal of Personality* 46 (3): 401–413.

Beard, C. M., V. Fuster, and L. R. Elveback. 1982. Daily and seasonal variation in sudden cardiac death, Rochester, Minnesota, 1950–1975. *Mayo Clinic Proceedings* 57: 704–706.

Belsley, D. A., E. Kuh, and R. E. Welsch. 1980. *Regression Diagnostics: Identifying influential data and sources of collinearity.* New York: John Wiley & Sons.

Berk, K. N. 1978. Comparing subset regression procedures. *Technometrics* 20: 1–6.

———. 1977. Tolerance and condition in regression computation. *Journal of the American Statistical Association* 72: 863–866.

Black and Sherba. 1983. Contracting to problem solve to lose weight. *Behavior Therapy* 14: 105–109.

Blalock, H. M. 1979. *Social statistics.* New York: McGraw-Hill.

Bock, R. D. 1975. *Multivariate statistical methods in behavioral research.* New York: McGraw-Hill.

Borgatta, E. F., and G. W. Bohrnstedt. 1980. Level of measurement once over again. *Sociological methods and research* 9 (2): 147–160.

Cattell, R. B. 1966. The meaning and strategic use of factor analysis. In R. B. Cattell, ed., *Handbook of Multivariate Experimental Psychology.* Chicago: Rand McNally.

Cedercreutz, C. 1978. Hypnotic treatment of 100 cases of migraine. In F. H. Frankel and H. S. Zamansky, eds., *Hypnosis at Its Bicentennial.* New York: Plenum.

Churchill, G. A., Jr. 1979. *Marketing research: methodological foundations.* Hinsdale, Illinois: Dryden Press.

Conover, W. J. 1974. Some reasons for not using the Yates continuity correction on 2 × 2 contingency tables. *Journal of the American Statistical Association* 69: 374–376.

Consumer Reports. 1983. Beer. *Consumer Reports* (July): 342–348.

Cook, R. D. 1977. Detection of influential observations in linear regression. *Technometrics* 19: 15–18.

Daugirdas, J. T. *Unpublished data.*

Davis, J. A. 1982. *General Social Surveys, 1972–1982: Cumulative Codebook.* Chicago: National Opinion Research Center.

Davis, H., and E. Ragsdale. 1983. Unpublished working paper. Chicago: University of Chicago, Graduate School of Business.

Dillon, W. R., and M. Goldstein. 1978. *Discrete discriminant analysis.* New York: John Wiley & Sons.

——. 1984. *Multivariate analysis: Methods and applications.* New York: John Wiley & Sons.

Dineen, L. C., and B. C. Blakesley. 1973. Algorithm AS 62: A generator for the sampling distribution of the Mann-Whitney *U* statistic. *Applied Statistics* 22: 269–273.

Draper, N. R., and H. Smith. 1981. *Applied Regression Analysis,* 2nd ed. New York: John Wiley & Sons.

Everitt, B. S. 1980. *Cluster analysis.* 2nd ed. London: Heineman Educational Books Ltd.

Everitt, B. S. 1977. *The analysis of contingency tables.* London: Chapman and Hall.

Feinberg, S. E. 1977. *The analysis of cross-classified categorical data.* Cambridge: MIT Press.

Finn, J. D. 1974. *A general model for multivariate analysis.* New York: Holt, Rinehart & Winston.

Frane, J. W. 1976. Some simple procedures for handling missing data in multivariate analysis. *Psychometrika* 41: 409–415.

———. 1977. A note on checking tolerance in matrix inversion and regression. *Technometrics* 19: 513–514.

Goodman, L. A., and W. H. Kruskal. 1954. Measures of association for cross-classification. *Journal of the American Statistical Association* 49: 732–764.

Greeley, A. M., W. C. McCready and G. Theisen. 1980. *Ethnic drinking subcultures.* New York: Praeger Publishers.

Gunst, R. F., and R. L. Mason. 1980. *Regression analysis and its application: A data-oriented approach.* New York: Marcel Dekker.

Haberman, S. J. 1978. *Analysis of qualitative data,* Vol. 1. London: Academic Press. .

Hansson, R. O., and K. M. Slade. Altruism toward a deviant in city and small town.

Harman, H. H. 1967. *Modern factor analysis.* 2nd ed. Chicago: University of Chicago Press.

Hoaglin, D. C., and R. E. Welsch. 1978. The hat matrix in regression and ANOVA. *American Statistician* 32: 17–22.

Hocking, R. R. 1976. The analysis and selection of variables in linear regression. *Biometrics* 32: 1–49.

Jonassen, C. T., and S. H. Peres. 1960. *Interrelationships of dimensions of community systems.* Columbus: Ohio State University Press.

Kim, J. O., and C. W. Mueller. 1978. *Introduction to factor analysis.* Beverly Hills: Sage Press.

King, M. M., et al. 1979. Incidence and growth of mammary tumors induced by 7,12-dimethylbenz(a) anthracene as related to the dietary content of fat and antioxident. *Journal of the National Cancer Institute* 63 (3): 657–663.

Kleinbaum, D. G., and L. L. Kupper. 1978. *Applied regression analysis and other multivariable methods.* North Scituate, Massachusetts: Duxbury Press.

Lachenbruch, P. A. 1975. *Discriminant analysis.* New York: Hafner Press.

Lee, E. T. 1980. *Statistical methods for survival data analysis.* Belmont, California: Lifetime Learning Publications.

Loether, H. J., and D. G. McTavish. 1976. *Descriptive and inferential statistics: an introduction.* Boston: Allyn and Bacon.

Mantel, N. 1974. Comment and a suggestion on the Yates continuity correction. *Journal of the American Statistical Association* 69: 378–380.

Meyer, L. S., and M. S. Younger. 1976. Estimation of standardized coefficients. *Journal of the American Statistical Association* 71: 154–157.

Milligan, G. W., and P. D. Isaac. 1980. The validation of four ultrametric clustering algorithms. *Pattern Recognition* 12: 41–50.

Morrison, D. F. 1967. *Multivariate statistical methods.* New York: McGraw-Hill.

Neter, J., and W. Wasserman. 1974. *Applied linear statistical models.* Homewood, Illinois: Richard D. Irwin Inc.

Olson, C. L. 1976. On choosing a test statistic in multivariate analysis of variance. *Psychological Bulletin* 83: 579-586.

Overall, J. E., and C. Klett. 1972. *Applied multivariate analysis.* New York: McGraw-Hill.

Paul, O., et al. 1963. A longitudinal study of coronary heart disease. *Circulation* 28: 20–31.

Rabkin, S. W., F. A. Mathewson and R. B. Tate. 1980. Chronobiology of cardiac sudden death in men. *Journal of the American Medical Association* 244 (12): 1357–1358.

Roberts, H. V. 1979. *An analysis of employee compensation.* Rpt. 7946, Center for Mathematical Studies in Business and Economics, University of Chicago: October.

———. 1980. Statistical bases in the measurement of employment discrimination. In E. Robert Livernash, ed., *Comparable worth: issues and alternatives.* Washington, D.C.: Equal Employment Advisory Council: 173–195.

Romesburg, H. C. 1984. *Cluster analysis for researchers.* Belmont, California: Lifetime Learning Publications.

Siegel, S. 1956. *Nonparametric statistics for the behavioral sciences.* New York: McGraw-Hill.

Sigall, H., and N. Ostrove. 1975. Beautiful but dangerous: effects of offender attractiveness and nature of the crime on juridic judgment. *Journal of Personality and Social Psychology* 31: 410–414.

Smirnov, N. V. 1948. Table for estimating the goodness of fit of empirical distributions. *Annals of mathematical statistics* 19: 279–281.

Sneath, P. H. A., and R. R. Sokal. 1973. *Numerical taxonomy.* San Francisco: W.H. Freeman and Co.

Snedecor, G. W., and W. G. Cochran. 1967. *Statistical methods.* Ames, Iowa: Iowa State University Press.

Somers, R. H. 1962. A new symmetric measure of association for ordinal variables. *American Sociological Review* 27: 799–811.

Speed, M. F. 1976. Response curves in the one-way classification with unequal numbers of observations per cell. *Proceedings of the Statistical Computing Section,* American Statistical Association.

SPSS Inc. 1983. *SPSS-X statistical algorithms.* Chicago: SPSS Inc.

___. 1987. *SPSS-X user's guide.* Chicago: SPSS Inc.

Stevens, S. S. 1946. On the theory of scales of measurement. *Science* 103: 677–680.

Stoetzel, J. 1960. A factor analysis of liquor preference of French consumers. *Journal of Advertising Research* 1 (1): 7-11.

Tatsuoka, M. M. 1971. *Multivariate analysis.* New York: John Wiley & Sons.

Theil, H. 1967. *Economics and information theory.* Chicago: Rand McNally.

Tucker, L. R. 1971. Relations of factor score estimates to their use. *Psychometrika* 36: 427–436.

Tucker, R. F., R. F. Koopman, and R. L. Linn. 1969. Evaluation of factor analytic research procedures by means of simulated correlation matrices. *Psychometrika* 34: 421–459.

Velleman, P. F., and R. E. Welsch. 1981. Efficient computing of regression diagnostics. *American Statistician* 35: 234–242.

Winer, B. J. 1971. *Statistical principles in experimental design.* New York: McGraw-Hill.

Wynder, E. L. 1976. Nutrition and cancer. *Federal Proceedings* 35: 1309–1315.

Wyner, G. A. 1980. Response errors in self-reported number of arrests. *Sociological Methods and Research* 9 (2): 161–177.

Index _____